D0161356

DISCARD

Milestones in Archaeology

Milestones in Archaeology

A Chronological Encyclopedia

Tim Murray

Santa Barbara, California   Denver, Colorado   Oxford, England

Library of Congress Cataloging-in-Publication Data
Murray, Tim, 1955–
Milestones in archaeology : a chronological encyclopedia / Timothy Murray.
p. cm.
Includes bibliographical references and index.
ISBN-13: 978-1-57607-186-1 (hard copy : alk. paper)
ISBN-10: 1-57607-186-3 (hard copy : alk. paper)
ISBN-13: 978-1-85109-645-9 (ebook)
ISBN-10: 1-85109-645-0 (ebook)
1. Archaeology–History–Encyclopedias. 2. Archaeologists–Biography–Encyclopedias. 3. Antiquities–Encyclopedias. 4. Excavations (Archaeology)–Encyclopedias. I. Title.

CC100.M87 2007
930.103–dc22

2006103177

11 10 09 08 07 1 2 3 4 5 6 7 8 9 10

Production Editor: Alisha Martinez
Editorial Assistant: Sara Springer
Production Manager: Don Schmidt
Media Editor: Caroline Price
Media Resources Coordinator: Ellen Brenna Dougherty
Media Resources Manager: Caroline Price
File Manager: Paula Gerard

ABC-CLIO, Inc.
130 Cremona Drive, P.O. Box 1911
Santa Barbara, California 93116–1911

This book is also available on the World Wide Web as an ebook.
Visit http://www.abc-clio.com for details.

This book is printed on acid-free paper ♾
Manufactured in the United States of America

To Susan.
Not quite 25 years, and not nearly so interesting.

Contents

List of Maps

Acknowledgments

This book was originally commissioned by Kristi Ward, and I thank her and successive editors at ABC-CLIO for their patience and support, particularly Simon Mason, Peter Westwick, and Alex Mikaberidze, as we battled delays brought about by the effects of chronic illness.

It is no understatement that this book would not have been completed without the crucial input of Susan Bridekirk, my editorial assistant. Thanks are due to the vice-chancellor of La Trobe University for allowing me to retain Susan's vital services and to complete the work we began in the early 1990s with *The Encyclopedia of Archaeology*. I thank Wei Ming of the Archaeology Program at La Trobe University for drawing the maps.

Introduction

This book presents a new approach to writing the history of archaeology and, as such, it is very much a product of an earlier project, *Encyclopedia of Archaeology* (1999–2001), which was also published by ABC-CLIO. Having said this, I have to admit (not without some irony) that *Milestones* was commissioned before the five-volume encyclopedia that precedes it. This reversal of sequence has had a significant impact on the shape and content of *Milestones,* which is now considerably changed from my original conception. There are several obvious reasons for this, the most important being that my own knowledge and understanding of the history of archaeology was transformed by the contributions to the *Encyclopedia* and from the rapid growth of research in this field that has occurred over the past few years. The opportunity to contemplate the history of archaeology on a global scale has, as I observed in the introduction to volumes 3, 4, and 5 (*History and Discoveries)* brought home the commonalities as well as the differences in the practice of archaeology around the world.

Another important reason why *Milestones* has changed from what was originally envisaged has more to do with a desire to explore different ways of writing the history of archaeology. In the *Encyclopedia* project I was able to develop a mix of longer biographical essays and shorter pieces dealing with specific countries, sites, or discoveries. Although some synthetic and general survey entries were included (not least some methodological reflections about writing the history of archaeology), the thrust of the volumes was very much directed toward documenting the origins and growth of archaeology on a global scale. In *Milestones* my goal has changed to one of sharpening this contrast between documentation and reflection through the inclusion of three long essays that act as general surveys of matters not specifically covered in individual milestones and form the framework of a developing interpretation of the history of archaeology. Thus, in *Milestones* I move beyond an editorial role where the editorial board and I selected entries and commissioned authors to write them, to one where I have selected and written the milestones and the longer interpretative essays. Taken together these represent a partial statement of how I currently see the history of archaeology, including many of the significant passages in its history, the overarching themes about the significance of archaeological knowledge, and the great challenges that have motivated (and continue to motivate) its practitioners. As I will shortly discuss, there are several excellent single-volume histories of archaeology that cover the general area of *Milestones,* but in this work I have defined and occupied a middle ground between a straightforward work of reference (as was the case in *Encyclopedia of Archaeology*) and an extended narrative of the history of archaeology. By means of this mix I have sought to explore different ways of communicating with both specialist and nonspecialist audiences.

The growth in the scale and sophistication of interest in the history of archaeology has been a strong motivation here. Archaeology has long been a complex social institution, but until recently its practitioners have not been particularly interested in exploring these aspects of the "everyday" life of their discipline. However this attitude has begun to change, and it is the transformation in the historiography of archaeology that has also wrought significant changes to the original vision for this book. At its core *Milestones,* as you see it now, is in part a reaction to developments that have occurred within archaeology over the past decade, but in larger part a consequence of my own interest in the field. Of course the history of archaeology is not the sole preserve of archaeologists, and it is one of the most encouraging signs that historians of science and especially historians writing essentially popular works (usually biographies) have paid growing attention to archaeology and its practitioners (see, for example, Adkins 2003; Walker 1995).

Notwithstanding the importance of these changes, I have two reasons for wanting to shift the focus away from a detailed discussion of historiography per se in this introduction. First, (to put it bluntly) many of the methodological issues raised by exploring a history of archaeology are not unique to that discipline. Other disciplines, such as anthropology, geology, and of course biology and physics, have far longer (and stronger) traditions in this area. Indeed, such disciplines or fields have been significant contributors (either by way of methodology or examples) to the development of the history, philosophy, and sociology of science, the perspectives of which will necessarily play an important role in the immediate future of the historiography of archaeology. The second reason for shifting focus away from detailed methodological considerations in this context is that it provides an opportunity to consider some of the implications that an upsurge in research into the history of archaeology might have for our cognate disciplines of anthropology and history. Both disciplines have strong historiographic traditions, but I think it is a fair generalization that the historians of neither discipline have paid much specific attention to archaeology. Of course George Stocking and many others have written about Sir John Lubbock when considering the genesis of an evolutionary anthropology (Stocking 1968, 1987), there has been a useful focus on significant passages of the history of British archaeology in the nineteenth century (see especially Morse 2005; van Riper 1993), and some have further considered the work of Gordon Childe within the general context of discussions of the concept of culture. But apart from these, and a North American focus on the anthropology of Franz Boas and the work of theorists such as Julian Steward and Leslie White, interest has been generally slight (see, for example, De Waal Malefijt 1974; Handler 2000; Harris 1968; Service 1985; Voget 1975).

So it might be interesting to consider how (if at all) recent explorations into the genesis of archaeology might affect the current story of the genesis of anthropology and history, primarily in the nineteenth century. This has been the focus of much of my own research in the history of archaeology and, as I have acknowledged many times elsewhere, this is not an innocent task. Although I am perfectly happy to accept (as many others have done) that writing the history of archaeology requires no other justification than inherent interest, my goals have more to do with diagnosing the condition of contemporary archaeology and understanding the nature of its relationships with contemporary anthropology and history.

Surveying the Historiography of Archaeology

These days almost everyone has noticed the sheer *amount* of history of archaeology being written. At a recent Cambridge conference on the historiography of archaeology, Bruce Trigger was moved to remark that the task of revising his influential *History of Archaeological Thought* (1989) had become very much more difficult in recent years. But Trigger was reflecting about the quantity of published work he had to synthesize rather than any inherent difficulty in the content of what was being written. This is because much of this history writing has been devoted to theories, methods, discoveries, and the lives of "great" archaeologists. While such studies are obviously important in establishing some of the aspects of archaeological practice, they alone do not produce satisfying accounts of the process of archaeological knowledge production.

Although historians of archaeology have become much more sensitive to the demands of context, there remain few analyses of the institutional structures of the discipline, the wider intellectual context of archaeology, or other sociological aspects of archaeological knowledge production (though the latter are increasing). The result of these shortcomings has been rightly criticized by some archaeologists and by historians of the human sciences who have taken an interest in archaeology. Much of what has been produced is teleological, with the nature of archaeological knowledge transcending social and historical context. Until recent years, analysis of the taken-for-granteds of the history of archaeological practice, such as institutional structures, relations with governments and the general public, organizing concepts and categories, and archaeology's relationships with its cognate disciplines, have been few and of variable quality.

After the late 1980s things began to change with the publication of two books. First, Trigger's *A History of Archaeological Thought* represented a quantum leap from what was then available in English. Second, Alain Schnapp's *Conquest of the Past* (1996) has done so much to remind prehistoric archaeologists of the riches of "The Great Tradition" as well as the great virtues of antiquarianism as a system of study.

Around the same time archaeologists more versed in the history and philosophy of science, such as Wiktor Stoczkowski and myself, began deploying perspectives from that field, and serious discussion about the historiography of archaeology began to occur in mainstream contexts such as the Society for American Archaeology. Andrew Christenson's *Tracing Archaeology's Past* (1989) was the first collection of essays in English from researchers strongly committed to writing the history of archaeology in North America.

It is significant that at that early stage many of the issues raised by such history writing (for example, justifications for history writing, the respective pluses and minuses of the internalist and externalist perspectives, the perils of presentism, and that old favorite, whether the history of archaeology is better written by historians of science or by archaeologists) were all given a thorough airing. Subsequent discussion, for example Trigger's entry on historiography in the *Encyclopedia of the History of Archaeology* (2001), tended to reinforce these trends, which were also the subject of really intense debate in *Studying Human Origins: Disciplinary History and Epistemology* (2001), edited by Raymond Corbey and Wil Roebroeks. Trigger, Corbey, and Roebroeks sought to classify academic production through a pretty straightforward division between popular, intellectual, and social histories (Trigger) or through an application of Ernst Mayr's taxonomy—lexicographic, chronological, biographical, cultural and sociological, and problematic histories (Corbey and Roebroeks). But the editors of *Studying Human Origins* were after more than classification. Their goal was to seriously explore the why, what, how, and indeed whether of such histories. Difficult questions such as why historians seemed to be ignoring the history of archaeology were asked, and the manifest shortcomings of archaeologists as historians of their own discipline were given thorough discussion. This is a common theme, sometimes taking on the characteristics of a turf war.

Such naïveté on the one hand, and the sometimes casual disparagement of histories being written outside (or indeed sometimes in ignorance of) the canons of the history of science on the other, might be taken as clear testimony that we have a long way to go before the history of archaeology becomes a respectable pursuit. I do not think so. In fact, I think that the contrary is the case, as archaeologists have become more skilled at articulating archives, oral histories and other testimonies in their analysis (Marc-Antoine Kaeser's recent *L'Univers du prehistorien* [2004], and the ancestral archives issue of the British journal *Antiquity* edited by Nathan Schlanger [2002] are excellent examples). Historians of science have also become somewhat more understanding of the wide range of motivations archaeologists are responding to when they work in this area.

The Basis of a Personal Approach: Anthropology and Archaeology

I came to the history of archaeology through undergraduate research in the history of anthropology, specifically the history of nineteenth-century race theory. My first work focused on the monogenist/polygenist debate (over the issue of whether human beings were the result of one creation or origin or of many), as exemplified by the Scottish anatomist Robert Knox and his English disciple, James Hunt—one of the founders of the Anthropological Society of London, a great follower of Paul Broca, and the publisher of much European anthropology. Understanding Knox's most famous work *The Races of Men* (1850) posed significant intellectual challenges, not because so much of what he was saying was repugnant, but because at its core it represented a coherent and marvelous rich intellectual tradition spanning anatomy, philosophy, biology, ethnology, archaeology, and of course philology that was radically at odds with my own training as an anthropologist. Knox's search for a scientific English anthropology that was both polygenist (the argument that human races had different origins) and antievolutionist provides an excellent example of how disciplines lose their histories, as dominant readings of disciplinary approach and purpose reinforce their dominance through the socializing power of disciplinary history.

But a case could be made that although it was distinctly marginal to contemporary philosophical orthodoxies in the mid-nineteenth century, the transcendentalism of *naturphilosophie* played a significant role in the development of ethnology (particularly in the construction of the concept of culture). A close analysis of Knox's *The Races of Men* reveals something of the spirit that drove this alternative anthropology, and the conflict between these alternative anthropologies and archaeologies in mid-nineteenth-century England also provides an opportunity to explore the ways in which the participants sought support from science and society and the conditions under which that support was given.

I continued to explore these ideas in doctoral research focused on an inquiry into the authorities archaeologists appeal to justify their knowledge claims in contemporary archaeology. The existence of such hidden histories in anthropology persuaded me that such were likely to exist unremarked in archaeology too, and that the naturalness of contemporary views of the archaeologist's project was illusory. In my view denaturalizing such views could provide a basis on which to seriously address problems within contemporary archaeological theory. Historical research has helped broaden my approach to this problem from being narrowly epistemological to asking a more encompassing question: what makes archaeological accounts of the past plausible? A consideration of plausibility then led me to more detailed investigations of the links between archaeology and the society that sustains its practice. This, in turn, has greatly increased the significance of the history of archaeology as a primary source of information about related inquiries into disciplinary traditions and the "culture" of archaeology.

What happened as a result of this research into the authority of archaeological knowledge claims, and related reflections on the nature of contemporary theoretical archaeology, is much more than I can deal with here, and I continue to publish on it. What I can do is to very briefly introduce the themes that have underwritten aspects of this inquiry under very broad umbrella raised by Stocking some twenty years ago. My account of the history of archaeology is directed toward the identification of enduring structures of archaeological knowledge—those structures that provide the criteria in terms of which knowledge claims are justified as being both rational and reliable and that also provide practitioners with the ability to distinguish meaningful knowledge and the relevance of models, theories, and approaches drawn from archaeology's cognate disciplines. Stocking's cogent summary of the "ethos" of anthropology, as we have come to know it, has been a great help here:

> Another way of looking at the matter is to suggest that the general tradition we call retrospectively "anthropological" embodies a number of antinomies logically inherent or historically embedded in the Western intellectual tradition: an ontological opposition between materialism and idealism, an epistemological opposition between empiricism and apriorism, a substantive opposition between the biological and the cultural, a methodological opposition between the nomothetic and the idiographic, an attitudinal opposition between the racialist and the egalitarian, an evaluational opposition between the progressivist and the primitivist—among others. (1984, 4)

Archaeology, through its close connections to anthropology and history, has inherited these long-standing epistemological and ontological antinomies, which have at various times in the history of the discipline sanctioned historicist or universalist, materialist or idealist, empiricist or rationalist emphases within the practice of archaeology, precisely as they have done in our cognate disciplines.

In this view, by the end of the nineteenth century the connections and distinctions between archaeology and anthropology and between archaeology and history had essentially been established. Archaeology, its conceptual field defined and secure within various traditions of anthropological and historical research and its methodology developed to a stage where the discussion of temporal and cultural classifications could appeal to a widening store of empirical phenomena, was free to pursue problems of largely internal moment. Although in the United States the predominance of cultural rather than social anthropology meant that the boundaries between archaeology and "historical" anthropology were somewhat blurred, the same emphasis on the writing of prehistory, and on technical matters of classification and data retrieval, was still present.

I have described the long and intense association between archaeology and anthropology, as well as between archaeology and history, as being one of enrollment and symbiosis, beginning in the nineteenth century when all three disciplines began to take on their modern forms, and concluding around the end of that century. This association, although differing in particulars over the course of the twentieth century, continues to provide substantial aspects of the archaeological agenda and by far the most important body of theory used by archaeologists in their day-to-day practice.

But it is also the case that the process of translating archaeological data into anthropological or historical information (or indeed of applying the perspectives of those disciplines to archaeological data) did not (and does not) always go smoothly, and archaeologists might have had to take seriously the idea that such simple translations might be problematic. But has this really affected the way archaeologists seek to make the past meaningful? Are practitioners able to abandon science in favor of intelligibility in conventional human science terms?

I have sought to understand whether the plausibility of archaeological knowledge claims has been gauged primarily in terms of determinate rules of scientific method or whether the real determinants of plausibility were "cognitive" or "cultural." It was something of a surprise to find that even at the high point of empiricism in the mid-nineteenth century, where the methodological rhetoric held that archaeology contributed to the development of an approach to understanding human prehistory that explicitly shunned myth and the a priori in favor of the objectivity of science, the performance of practitioners fell way short of the mark. This difference between rhetoric and performance (especially as it applies to claims for the scientific status of archaeology) continues to this day, mostly unremarked.

The Idea of *Milestones*

I began this introduction with a statement that *Milestones* represented a different approach to writing the history of archaeology. At one level this difference derives from its structure. *Milestones* adapts a conventional chronological approach (i.e., from oldest to most recent) to the detailed analysis of the origins and development of archaeology. This analysis occurs in two contexts. The first comprises three long narratives dealing with overarching themes and issues, and the second is made up of individual entries (some quite short, others several thousands of words) that deal with specific discoveries, techniques, books, events, issues, or personalities.

I have already stressed that no history of archaeology is innocent of perspective or purpose, and I have sought to make my own perspectives and purposes as clear as I can. Every history has different emphases. Some, such as

Trigger's *A History of Archaeological Thought,* focus on the genesis and development of archaeological ideas within the Anglo-Saxon world (although Trigger above all other historians well recognizes the riches of other traditions and this is reflected in the second edition of this major work). Others, such as Alain Schnapp's *Discovery of the Past,* tell the story of the extraordinarily intense world of antiquarianism and its practitioners between the sixteenth and nineteenth centuries in Europe. Schnapp's concern was to explain why antiquarianism was of such great importance during the time of humanism and to chart the process whereby that importance was transformed in the nineteenth century into a support or warrant for nationalism and positivism. More specialized and particular histories, such as Rosemary Sweet's excellent history of English antiquarianism in the eighteenth century (2004) or Patricia Levine's discussion of the creation of a discipline of archaeology in the next century (1986), have less sweeping but nonetheless clearly defined goals.

Given the demands of context or space, all histories of archaeology involve selection. It has been a difficult task to sift through five hundred years of antiquarian and archaeological activity all around the globe, to isolate the milestones you see before you, and to develop a narrative history that places this selection in context while supporting the ideas and perspectives I advance in this book. It is important to note that in this sense *Milestones* is more than a straightforward work of reference. I have already mentioned that it draws heavily on the vast store of information contained in the *Encyclopedia of Archaeology,* but excellent works of reference have also been a great help (particularly those by the doyen of this particular field Brian Fagan—see especially the *Oxford Companion to Archaeology* [1996] and *Eyewitness to Discovery* [1996], but for example see also Bahn [1996], de Grummond [1996], Ellis [2000], Gibbon [1998], and Orser [2002]). These and the vast literature of the history of archaeology have provided the specific data on which this book is based.

Having said that every history of archaeology involves differences of emphasis and hence selection, I should also observe that notwithstanding all these differences there is a high degree of commonality about what are significant or exemplary sites, concepts, practitioners, institutions, and events in the history of the discipline. Of course historians of antiquarianism will focus on the sixteenth to eighteenth centuries, historians of human evolution will do the same for the nineteenth and twentieth centuries, or indeed historians of specific nations or areas such as China or southwest Asia, will be able to spend much more time on teasing out details that are lost when a global perspective is taken. In the introductions to the first two volumes (*The Great Archaeologists*) and the following three volumes (*History and Discoveries*) of the *Encyclopedia of Archaeology*, I wondered whether the notion of there being a discipline of archaeology with overarching perspectives, approaches, methodologies, and techniques was a viable one. Quite rightly archaeologists (and others) are worried by the implications of colonialism or that the perspectives of a single class or gender will marginalize those of others. In a sense, histories of archaeology can also create the sense of there being a "canon" of archaeological practice, and the fact there is widespread agreement that many disciplinary landmarks or milestones are widely understood and accepted might be seen as proof that it exists. This is especially true in the case of major discoveries or the development of significant methodologies or techniques. But it is also understood that this is not necessarily the case when it comes to theoretical and methodological issues where distinct national and regional traditions come into play. My own view is that it is possible for us to conceive of archaeology as a discipline taking distinct shape by the end of the nineteenth century and then being dramatically transformed throughout the twentieth century by differing contexts of discovery and practice. In this sense understanding diversity is to also conceive of unity.

The Structure of *Milestones*

Milestones is broken up into three parts: pre-nineteenth century, nineteenth century, and twentieth century. Of course this chronological division is simplistic in that nothing in life, not even archaeology, is so readily compartmentalized. In *Milestones* I deal with this by locating the entries within various themes that are used to build the bigger, overarching picture in the long essays.

Thus, in Section One, which deals with the pre-nineteenth-century origins of the discipline, I consider antiquarianism and natural history within a context of understanding ancient objects and landscapes and track the emerging relationships between archaeology, history, and anthropology that have proved to be so enduring. These themes (and the milestones that exemplify them) are knitted together in a long essay—"The Birth of Archaeology"—that traces the development of the archaeological perspective across more than three hundred years of social and cultural history.

The same format is used in Section Two—the nineteenth century—where a long essay, "The Archaeology of Origins, Nations, and Empires," explores themes as various as the link between the classification of archaeology of high human antiquity, the revelation of ancient empires, the decipherment of ancient scripts, the origins of archaeology in the New World, and the development of theories to understand the meaning of human prehistory.

Section Three—the twentieth century—continues this approach through a long essay, "World Archaeology," that links milestones and themes such as the growth of archaeological science, the search for human ancestors, debates about archaeological theory and the role of archaeology in society, and the nature of relationships between archaeology and anthropology and between archaeology and history.

This structure played a significant role in the selection of the milestones and the differing ways they are presented. I have already discussed the fact that all histories of archaeology are selective and have made the obvious point that in a global history such as *Milestones* the work of many significant archaeologists or the histories of various methodologies, theories, and techniques can only be considered in the most fleeting way (if at all). Readers will note that some milestones are quite short and highly specific—the publication of a major book, an exhibition, the foundation of a museum—while others are quite long and detailed, drawing the reader beyond the specifics of a discovery into broader or deeper matters.

The milestones you see in this book were selected on a number of grounds: first, because of priority—this is the first application of a technique or analytical process; second, because of the influence a particular person, book, idea, institution, or discovery had on subsequent practice; and third, because the field or area of archaeological practice was particularly influential. The type of treatment thus depended on the relationship between a particular milestone and the longer essay or the reason(s) for its selection. A final consideration was the extent of secondary information about the particular milestone. If the event, person, or technique, for example, was widely understood and there was a substantial literature to refer readers to, I judged that the space I saved through offering a more cursory treatment could better be used elsewhere.

One final observation about balance needs to be made. There is a dramatic difference in the number of milestones listed for Section Three as distinct from Sections One and Two. This disparity has much to do with the massive growth in archaeology as a global enterprise in the twentieth century. Not only was there much more archaeology done during that time than at any other, it was also more highly varied and more complex and its public impact (if possible) was even greater. During the twentieth century we saw the age of our hominin ancestors pushed back into the millions of years and a very great variety of forms discovered. At the same time the archaeology of much more recent periods (historical or postmedieval archaeology) assumed real importance. The number and range of milestones in Part Three is a reflection of this activity.

References

Adkins, L. 2003. *Empires of the plain. Henry Rawlinson and the lost languages of Babylon.* London: Harper Collins.

Bahn, P., ed. 1996. *Cambridge illustrated history of archaeology.* Cambridge: Cambridge University Press.

de Grummond, N., ed. 1996. *An encyclopedia of the history of classical archaeology.* Westport, CT: Greenwood.

De Waal Malefijt, A. 1974. *Images of man: a history of anthropological thought.* New York: Knopf.

Ellis, L., ed. 2000. *Archaeological method and theory: an encyclopedia.* New York: Garland.

Gibbon, G., ed. 1998. *Archaeology of prehistoric native America: an encyclopedia.* New York: Garland.

Handler, R., ed. 2000. *Excluded ancestors, inventible traditions: essays toward a more inclusive history of anthropology.* Madison: University of Wisconsin Press.

Harris, M. 1968. *The rise of anthropological theory.* New York: Crowell.

Kaeser, Marc-Antoine. 2004. *L'Univers du prehistorien. Science, foi et politique dans l'oeuvre et la vie d'Edouard Desor (1811–1882).* Paris: L'Harmattan.

Levine, P. 1986. *The amateur and the professional. Antiquarians, historians and archaeologists in Victorian England 1838–1886.* Cambridge: Cambridge University Press.

Morse, M. 2005. *How the Celts came to Britain. Druids, ancient skulls and the birth of archaeology.* Stroud, UK: Tempus.

Orser, C., Jr., ed. 2002. *Encyclopedia of historical archaeology.* New York: Routledge.

Schlanger, N., ed. 2002. Ancestral Archives. Explorations in the History of Archaeology. *Antiquity* 76 (291).

Service, E. 1985. *A century of controversy: ethnological issues from 1860–1960.* Orlando, FL: Academic Press.

Stocking, G. W., Jr. 1968. *Race, culture and evolution: essays in the history of anthropology.* New York: Free Press.

Stocking, G. W., ed. 1984. *Functionalism historicized: essays on British social anthropology.* Madison: University of Wisconsin Press.

Stocking, G. W., Jr., 1987. *Victorian anthropology.* New York: Free Press.

Sweet, R. 2004. *Antiquaries. The discovery of the past in eighteenth-century Britain.* London: Hambledon.

Van Riper, A. B. 1993. *Men among the mammoths: Victorian science and the discovery of human prehistory.* Chicago: University of Chicago Press.

Voget, F. 1975. *A history of ethnology.* New York: Holt, Rinehart and Winston.

Walker, A. 1995. *Aurel Stein. Pioneer of the Silk Road.* London: John Murray.

Chronological List of Milestones

Section One: Archaeology before 1800

1138	*Historia Regum Britanniae*
1412–1449	Voyages of Cyriac of Ancona
1471	Foundation of the Palazzo dei Conservatori
1512	Publication of the *Anglica Historia*
1519	Raphael's Survey of Rome
1533	Creation of the King's Antiquary
1586	Publication of *Britannia*
1586–1770	English Antiquaries and Antiquarian Societies
1603	Foundation of the Accademia dei Lincei
1613	Duke of Arundel Brings His Collection of Classical Antiquities to London
1616–1637	Collections and Correspondence of de Peiresc
1626	Worm Issues His Circular
1630	Sweden Passes Law to Protect National Antiquities
1652–1655	Publication of *Oedipus Aegypticus*
1656	Publication of *The Antiquities of Warwickshire*
1658	Publication of *Annals of the World Deduced from the Origin of Time*
1666	Swedish Archaeological Service Founded
1666	Foundation of the French Academy in Rome
1669	Publication of *De Solido Intra Olidum Naturaliter Contento Dissertationis Prodromus*
1670–1780	Grand Tour and the Society of Dilettanti
1683	Foundation of the Ashmolean Museum
1709–1800	Rediscovery of Herculaneum and Pompeii
1715	First Archaeological Collections in Russia
1717	Publication of *Metallotheca Vaticana, Opus Posthumum*
1719–1724	Publication of *L'antiquité expliquée et représentée en figures*
1723	Publication of *De l'origine et des usages de la pierre de foudre*

1723–1726	Publication of *De Etruria Regali Libri Septem*
1724	Publication of *Itinerarium Curiosum*
1752–1767	Publication of *Recueil d'antiquités égyptiennes, étrusques, romaines, et gauloises*
1753	Foundation of the British Museum
1756	Publication of *Antichita Romane*
1764–1798	Sir William Hamilton's Collections
1764	Publication of *Geschichte de Kunst der Altertums*
1768	Foundation of the Hermitage
1779–1793	Foundation of the Louvre
1782	Russia Gets a Slice of Classical Antiquity
1784	Foundation of the Asiatic Society of Bengal
1787	Excavation of a Burial Mound in Virginia
1787	Investigation of Palenque Begins
1793	Publication of *Nenia Britannica*
1797	John Frere Writes to the Society of Antiquaries of London
1797	Napoleon Loots Rome

Section Two: Archaeology in the Nineteenth Century

1807	Establishment of the National Museum of Denmark
1808–1814	Napoleon I Funds the Excavation of Roman Sites and Antiquities
1812	Publication of *The Ancient History of North and South Wiltshire*
1815–1835	Foundation of Great Egyptian Collections in England and France
1816	British Museum Purchases the Parthenon Marbles
1820	Publication of *Descriptions of the Antiquities Discovered in the State of Ohio and Other Western States*
1823	Publication of *Reliquiae diluvianae*
1824	Decipherment of Egyptian Hieroglyphics
1826	Publication of *Description de l'Egypte*
1829–1831	French Expédition Scientifique de Morée
1833–1900	Discovery of the Neanderthals
1836–1857	Decipherment of Cuneiform
1839–1843	Rediscovering Maya Civilization
1841–1864	High Human Antiquity in the Somme Valley

1843–1845	Paul Botta Excavates "Nineveh"
1846–1866	Establishment of Major U.S. Archaeological Institutions
1847	Publication of *Ancient Monuments of the Mississippi Valley*
1847	Publication of *The Manners and Customs of the Ancient Egyptians*
1848	*Guide to Northern Archaeology* Published in English
1849	Publication of *Nineveh and Its Remains*
1849	Publication of *Primeval Antiquities of Denmark* in English
1850–1900	Typology Makes History
1851	Publication of Wilson's *Archaeology and Prehistoric Annals of Scotland*
1852	Romano-Germanic Central Museum Established in Mainz by Ludwig Lindenschmidt
1857	Iron Age Site of La Tène discovered
1858–1859	Excavation at Brixham Cave
1858	Mariette, Antiquities Law, and the Egyptian Museum
1859	Publication of *Denkmaler aus Aegypten und Aethiopien*
1860	Discovery of Angkor Wat and Khmer Civilization
1861	Foundation of the Archaeological Survey of India
1862–1875	Research into Prehistoric Aquitaine
1865	International Congress of Prehistory Established
1865	Publication of *Pre-historic Times*
1869–1872	De Mortillet Classifies the Stone Age
1870–1891	Schliemann Excavates Troy, Mycenae, Ilios, Orchomenos, and Tiryns
1875–1881	Excavation of Olympia
1877	Publication of *A Thousand Miles up the Nile*
1877	Greenwell Publishes *British Barrows*
1877	William H. Jackson Visits Chaco Canyon
1879–1902	Recognition of Palaeolithic Cave Art at Altamira
1887	Discovery of the Amarna Tablets
1887–1896	Publication of *Excavations in Cranborne Chase*
1888–1895	First *Homo Erectus*
1888–1900	American Excavations in Mesopotamia at the Site of Nippur
1891–1904	Seriation and History in the Archaeology of Predynastic Egypt
1895–1940	Uhle Begins Scientific Archaeology in Peru

Section Three: Archaeology in the Twentieth Century and Beyond

1900–1935	Discovery of Minoan Civilization
1901–1908	Excavation of Gournia
1903	Publication of *Die typologische Methode*
1904	Publication of *Les vases céramiques ornés de la Gaule romaine*
1906–1930	Discovering the Riches of Central Asia–The Journeys of Sir Aurel Stein
1906–1931	Discovery of the Hittites
1907	Publication of *Die Methode der Ethnologie*
1907–1932	The World's First Archaeological Salvage Project?
1909–1911	Paleopathology in Nubia
1911	Publication of *Die Herkunft der Germanen*
1911	Machu Picchu Found
1911–1913	Stratigraphic Excavation in the Americas
1920–Present	Discovery of the Indus Civilization
1921	Publication of *Les hommes fossiles, eléments de paléontologie humaine*
1921–Present	Discoveries at Zhoukoudian Cave
1922	Publication of *The Population of the Valley of Teotihuacán*
1922–1932	Discovering Tutankhamen's Tomb
1922–1934	Excavation of Ur
1923	National Museum of Iraq Established
1924	Publication of *Air Survey and Archaeology*
1924	Discovery of *Australopithecus africanus*
1924	Publication of *Introduction to Southwestern Archaeology*
1925	Publication of *The Dawn of European Civilization*
1926–1942	Discovery of Olmec Civilization
1927	The Pecos Conference
1927–Present	Excavation of the Athenian Agora
1928	Publication of *Formation of the Chinese People*
1928–1930	Excavation of Skara Brae
1928–Present	Historical Archaeology at Colonial Williamsburg
1929	Establishing Dendrochronology
1929–1932	Foundation of the Indo-Pacific Prehistory Association
1931	Publication of *The Zimbabwe Culture*
1932	Publication of *Greek Sculpture and Painting to the End of the Hellenistic Period*

1932 and 1936	Publication of *The Mesolithic Age in Britain* and *The Mesolithic Settlement of Northern Europe*
1932–1948	Godwin and the Fenland Research Committee
1934	Publication of *The Desert Fayum*
1934–1957	Excavation of Jamestown
1934–1937	Excavation of Maiden Castle
1934	Foundation of the Society for American Archaeology
1934–Present	Trials of the *Royal Savage*
1936	Publication of *Man Makes Himself*
1936–1937	Excavation of Fell's Cave
1940	Lascaux Discovered
1941–1951	Excavation of Sainte-Marie among the Hurons
1942	Publication of *Origin and Development of Andean Civilization*
1946–1970	Discovery of Dead Sea Scrolls
1947	First Meeting of the Pan-African Congress on Prehistory and Quaternary Studies
1948	Publication of *A Study of Archaeology*
1948–1954	Excavation of Jarmo
1948–Present	Excavations at Sterkfontein and Swartkrans
1949–1953	Excavation of Star Carr
1950	Discovery of Radiocarbon Dating
1952–Present	Archaeology and Television
1952–1958	Excavation of Jericho
1953	Publication of *Prehistoric Settlement Patterns in the Viru Valley, Peru*
1953	Linear B Deciphered
1953–1965	Understanding the Mousterian
1955	Rebirth of Industrial Archaeology
1955	Piltdown Unmasked
1955–1961	Excavation of Verulamium
1957	Publication of *Prehistoric Technology*
1957–1961	Excavation of Shanidar Cave
1958	Archaeometry Defined
1958	Publication of *Method and Theory in American Archaeology*
1959	Excavation of Igbo-Ukwu
1959	Discovery of *Zinjanthropus boisei*
1959–1980	Saving Abu Simbel

1960	Historical Archaeology First Taught at University
1960	Excavation of a Bronze Age Ship at Cape Gelidonya
1960	Deiphering the Dynastic Sequence at Piedras Negras
1960–1970	Excavation of Fishbourne Palace
1960–1980	Southeastern and Southern Africa during the Iron Age: the Chifumbaze Complex
1960–Present	Thermoluminescence in Archaeology
1961	Jorge R. Acosta Finishes Work at Tula
1961	Raising the *Vasa*
1961	Publication of *World Prehistory: An Outline*
1961–1965	First Excavation of Catal Hüyük
1961–1983	Excavations at Olorgesailie and Koobi Fora
1962	Discovering the Pleistocene in Australia
1962–1964	Field Archaeology in Epirus
1963	Publication of *The Archaeology of Ancient China*
1963	Controversial Interpretation of Banpo Published
1964–1980	Discovery of *Homo Habilis*
1966	Publication of *The Evolution of Urban Society*
1966–1977	Discovery of Early Humans in Ethiopia
1966–1980	Excavation of Chavin de Huantar
1967	Publication of *Britannia: A History of Roman Britain*
1967	Publication of *Ceramics of Monte Alban*
1967–1981	Excavation of Ozette
1967–1982	Raising the *Mary Rose*
1968	Publication of *Analytical Archaeology*
1968	Publication of *New Perspectives in Archaeology*
1969	Excavation of Port Essington
1970	Publication of *A Guide to Artifacts of Colonial America*
1970–Present	Early Agriculture at Kuk Swamp, New Guinea
1972–1976	Excavation of the *Batavia*
1973–1978	Excavation of Meadowcroft
1973–1994	Excavation of Vindolanda
1973–Present	Excavations in the City of York
1973–Present	The Garbage Project
1974	Discovery of the Terracotta Warriors
1974–1981	Discovery of Footprints of Our Earliest Ancestors
1974–1998	Excavation of Jenne-Jeno
1975	Discovery of "Lucy"

1975	Excavation of Ban Chiang
1977	Publication of *In Small Things Forgotten*
1977	Discovery of King Philip's Tomb
1978–1979	Excavation of the Hochdorf Tomb
1980–Present	Application of GIS Technology to Archaeology
1981	Lake Mungo Inscribed on the World Heritage List
1981	Ice Age Tasmania Clashes with the Political Present
1983–1990	The Lapita Homeland Project
1984	Discovery of Lindow Man
1985–Present	Finding the *Titanic*
1986	Chan Chan Inscribed on the World Heritage List
1986	Ironbridge Gorge Inscribed on the World Heritage List
1987	Discovering the "Lord of Sipan"
1989–1990	The Vermillion Accord and NAGPRA
1989–1991	Publication of *Columbian Consequences*
1990	Publication of *A Forest of Kings*
1991	Discovery of the African Burial Ground
1991	Discovery of "Otzi the Iceman"
1991	Excavation of New York City's "Five Points"
1991	Dating the Settlement of New Zealand
1994	Discovery of Chauvet Cave
1996	Publication of *Novgorod in Focus*
1996–Present	Fate of "Kennewick Man"
2000	Meeting of the Eighth International Congress of Egyptologists
2002	Announcement of Toumai Fossil
2003	Earliest Stone Tools Found at Gona
2004	Discovery of the "Hobbit"

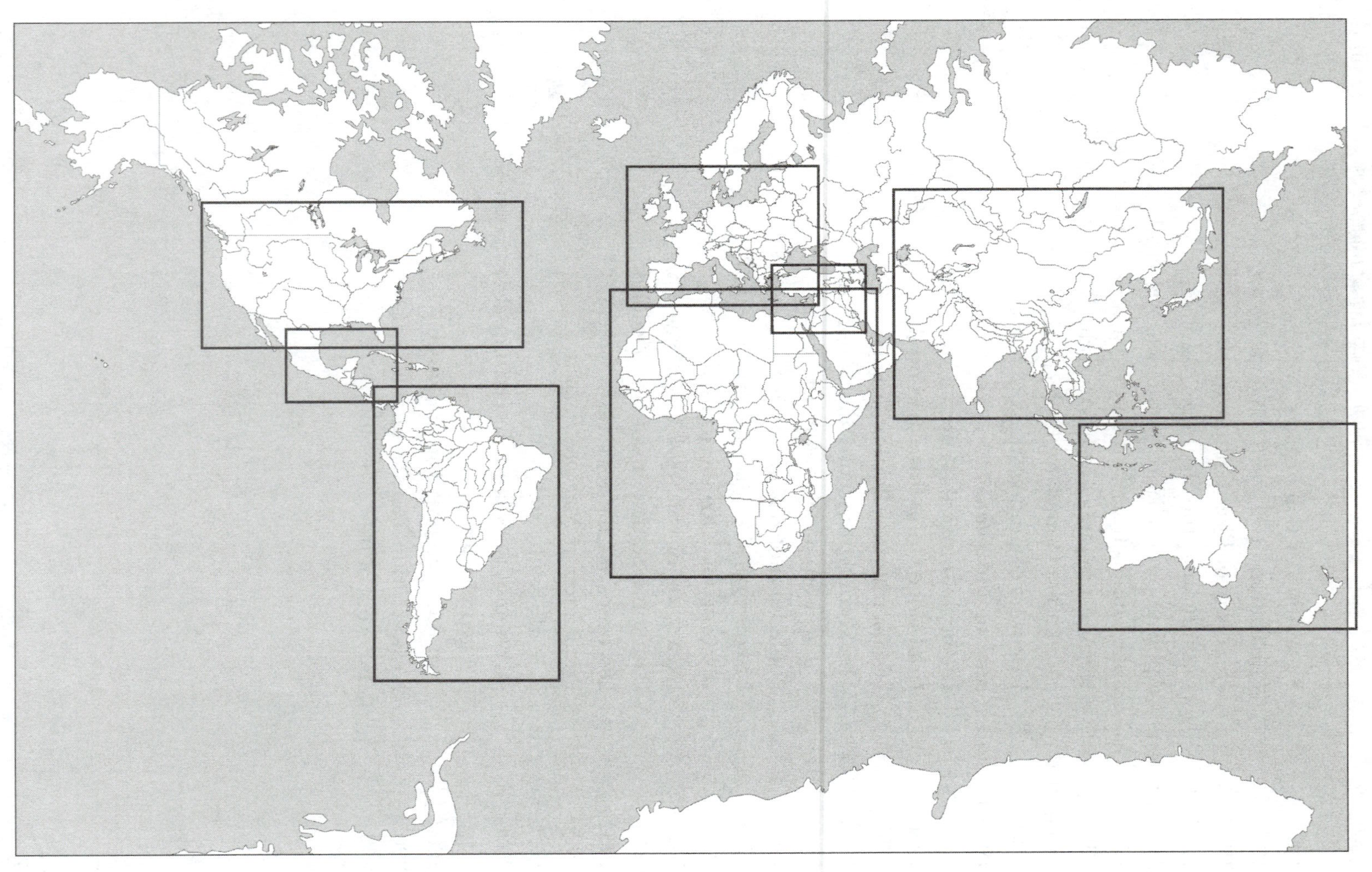

World map

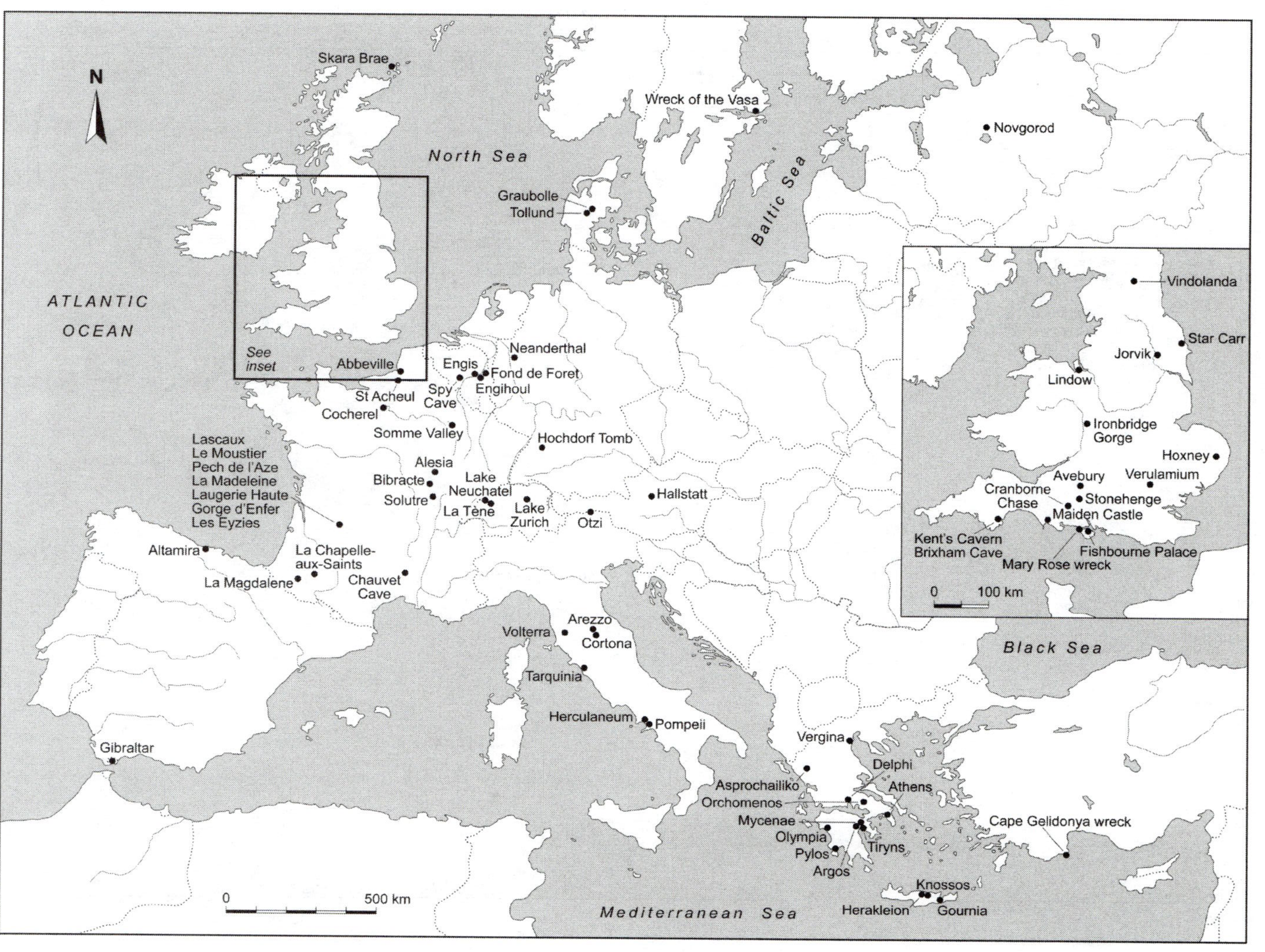
N
ATLANTIC
OCEAN
North Sea
Baltic Sea
Black Sea
Mediterranean Sea
Skara Brae
Wreck of the Vasa
Novgorod
Graubolle
Tollund
See inset
Abbeville
St Acheul
Cocherel
Somme Valley
Spy Cave
Engis
Fond de Foret
Engihoul
Neanderthal
Hochdorf Tomb
Lascaux
Le Moustier
Pech de l'Aze
La Madeleine
Laugerie Haute
Gorge d'Enfer
Les Eyzies
Alesia
Bibracte
Solutre
Lake Neuchatel
La Tène
Lake Zurich
Otzi
Hallstatt
Altamira
La Chapelle-aux-Saints
La Magdalene
Chauvet Cave
Arezzo
Volterra
Cortona
Tarquinia
Herculaneum
Pompeii
Gibraltar
Vergina
Delphi
Asprochailiko
Athens
Orchomenos
Mycenae
Olympia
Tiryns
Pylos
Argos
Knossos
Herakleion
Gournia
Cape Gelidonya wreck
0
500 km
Vindolanda
Star Carr
Jorvik
Lindow
Ironbridge Gorge
Hoxney
Avebury
Verulamium
Cranborne Chase
Stonehenge
Maiden Castle
Kent's Cavern
Brixham Cave
Fishbourne Palace
Mary Rose wreck
0
100 km

Europe

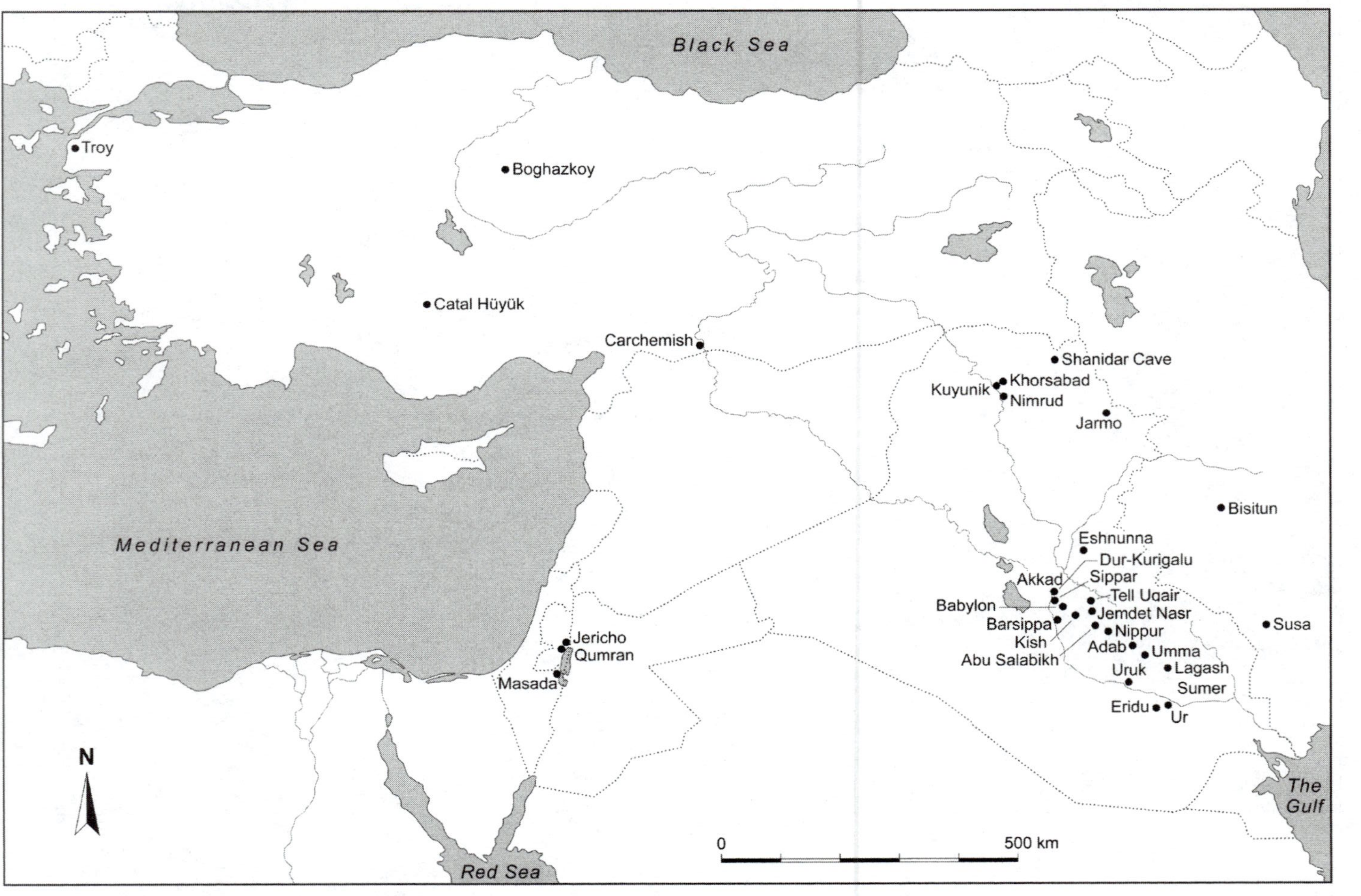
Black Sea
Troy
Boghazkoy
Catal Hüyük
Carchemish
Shanidar Cave
Kuyunik
Khorsabad
Nimrud
Jarmo
Mediterranean Sea
Bisitun
Eshnunna
Dur-Kurigalu
Akkad
Sippar
Tell Uqair
Babylon
Jemdet Nasr
Barsippa
Susa
Nippur
Kish
Adab
Umma
Abu Salabikh
Lagash
Uruk
Sumer
Eridu
Ur
Jericho
Qumran
Masada
N
The Gulf
0
500 km
Red Sea

Near East

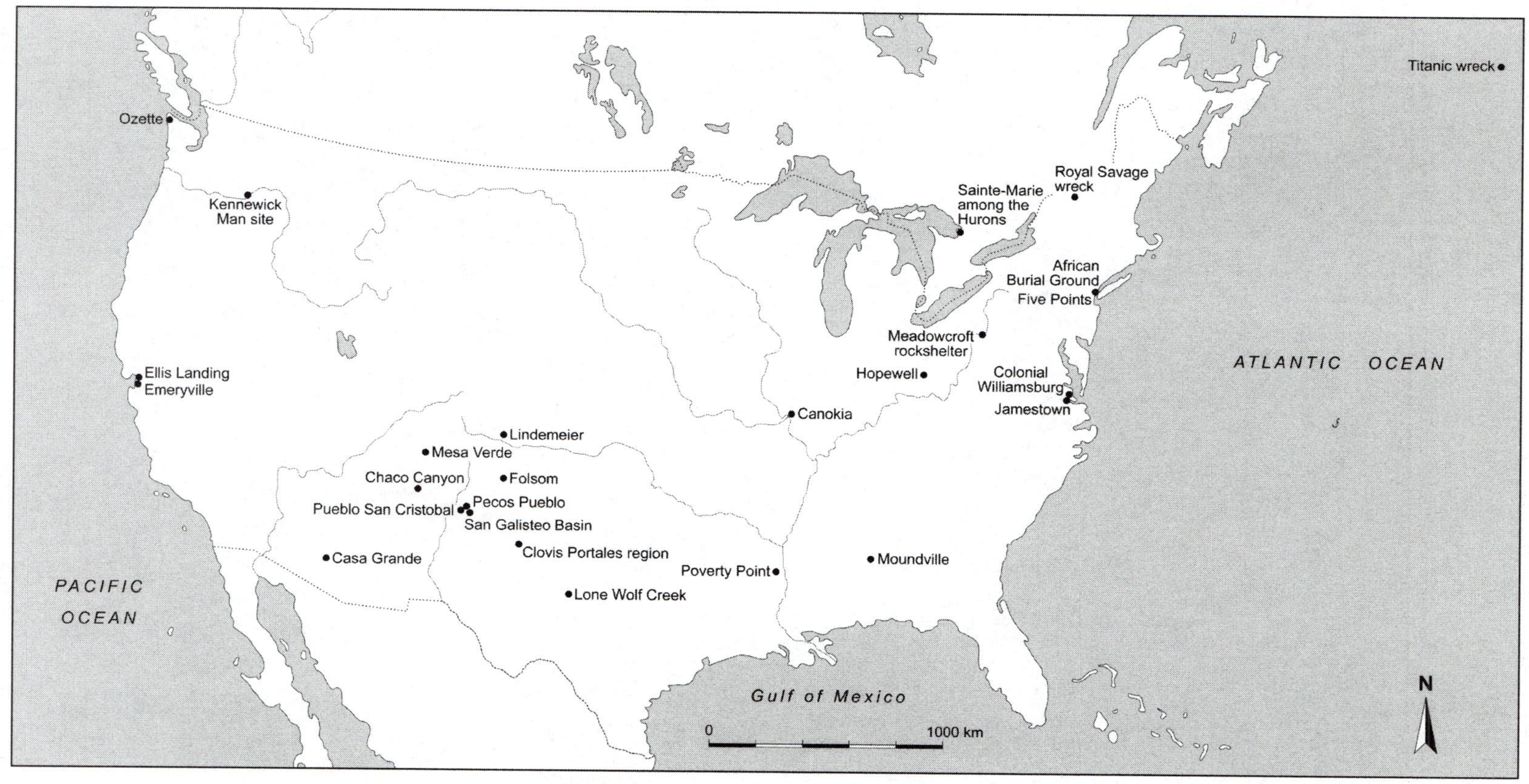

North America

Mesoamerica

South America

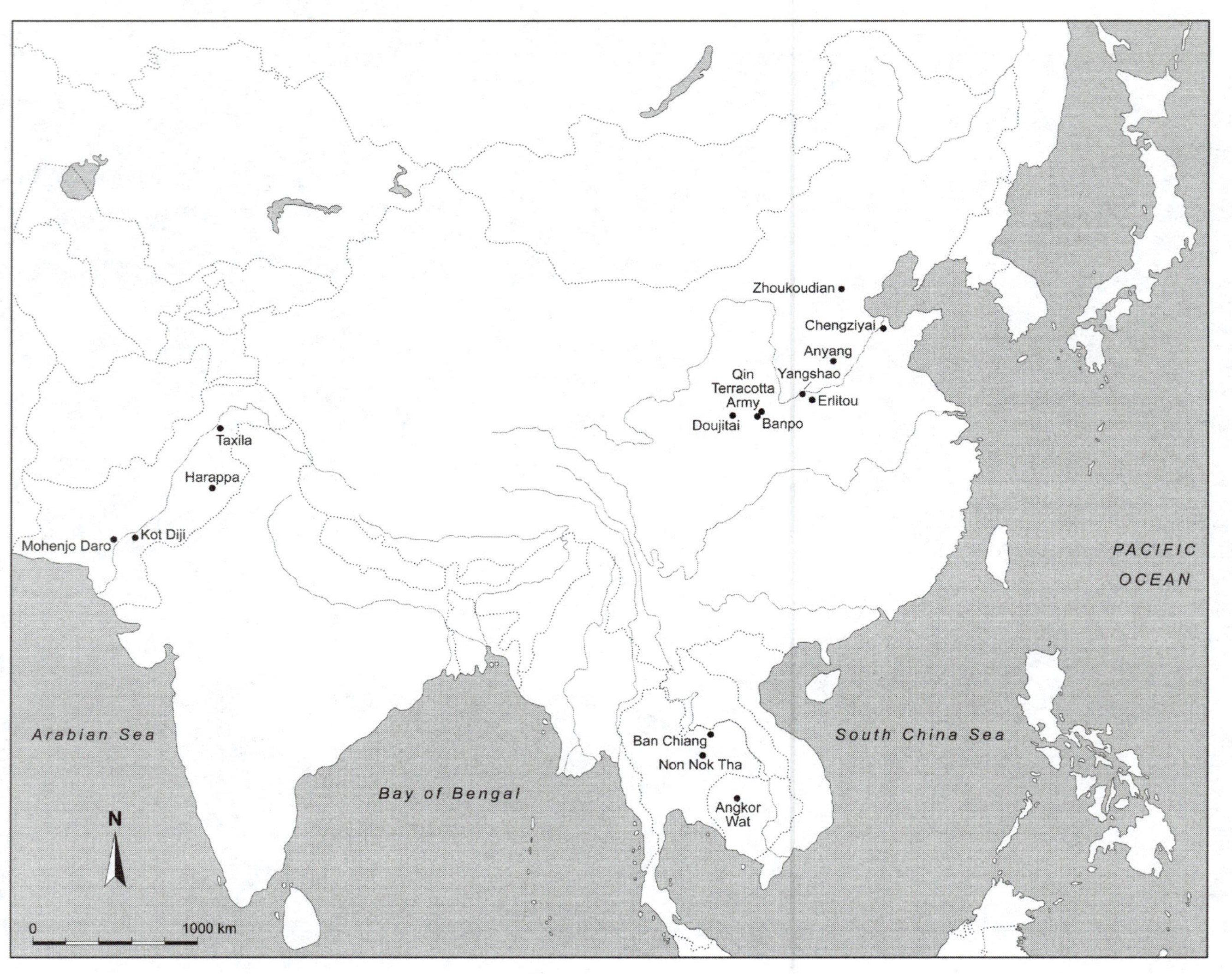
Zhoukoudian
Chengziyai
Anyang
Qin Terracotta Army
Yangshao
Erlitou
Doujitai
Banpo
Taxila
Harappa
Kot Diji
Mohenjo Daro
PACIFIC OCEAN
Arabian Sea
South China Sea
Ban Chiang
Non Nok Tha
Bay of Bengal
Angkor Wat
N
0
1000 km

Asia

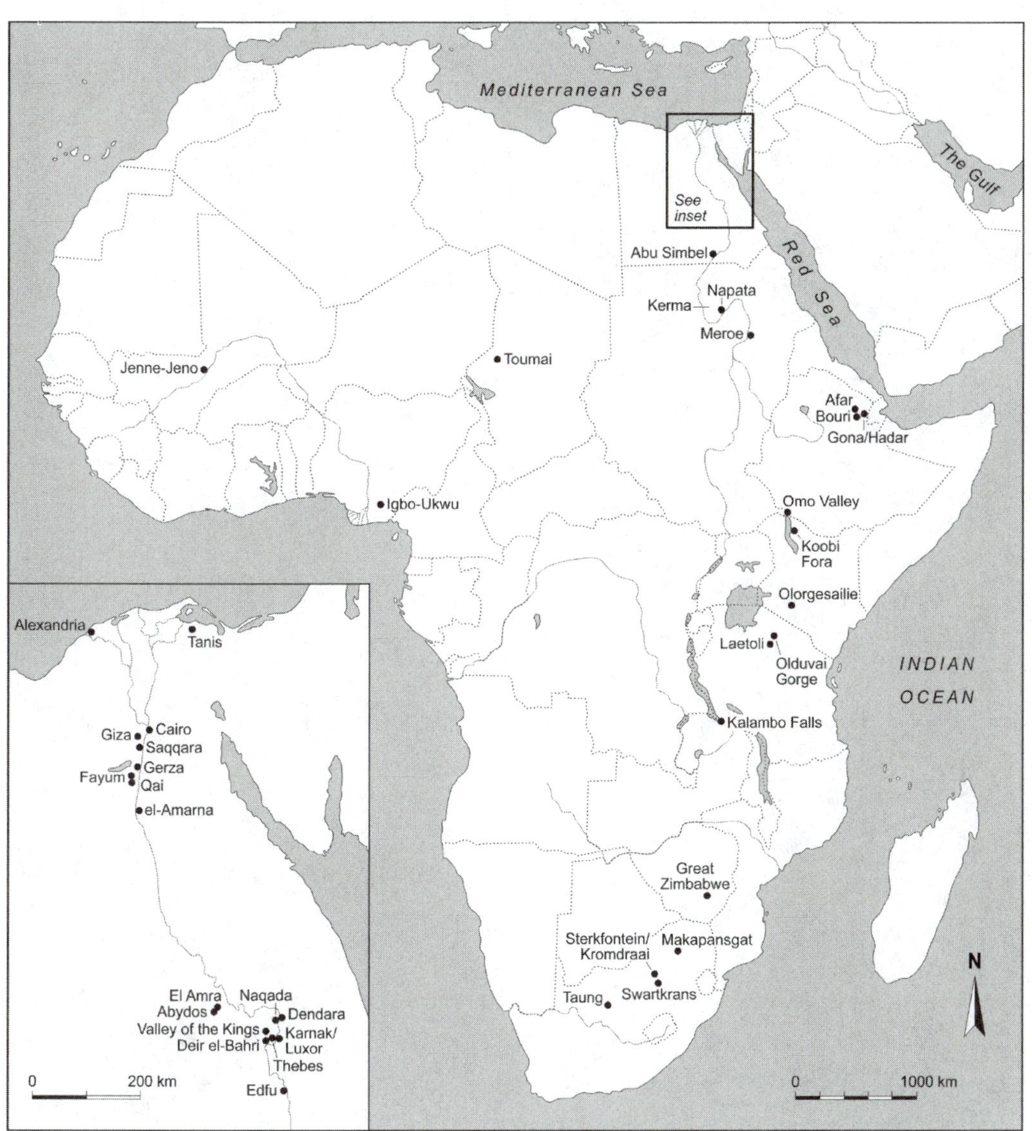
Mediterranean Sea
See inset
The Gulf
Red Sea
Abu Simbel
Napata
Kerma
Meroe
Toumai
Jenne-Jeno
Afar
Bouri
Gona/Hadar
Igbo-Ukwu
Omo Valley
Koobi Fora
Olorgesailie
Laetoli
Olduvai Gorge
INDIAN OCEAN
Kalambo Falls
Great Zimbabwe
Sterkfontein/ Kromdraai
Makapansgat
Taung
Swartkrans
N
0
1000 km
Alexandria
Tanis
Giza
Cairo
Saqqara
Gerza
Fayum
Qai
el-Amarna
El Amra
Naqada
Abydos
Dendara
Valley of the Kings
Karnak/ Luxor
Deir el-Bahri
Thebes
Edfu
0
200 km

Africa

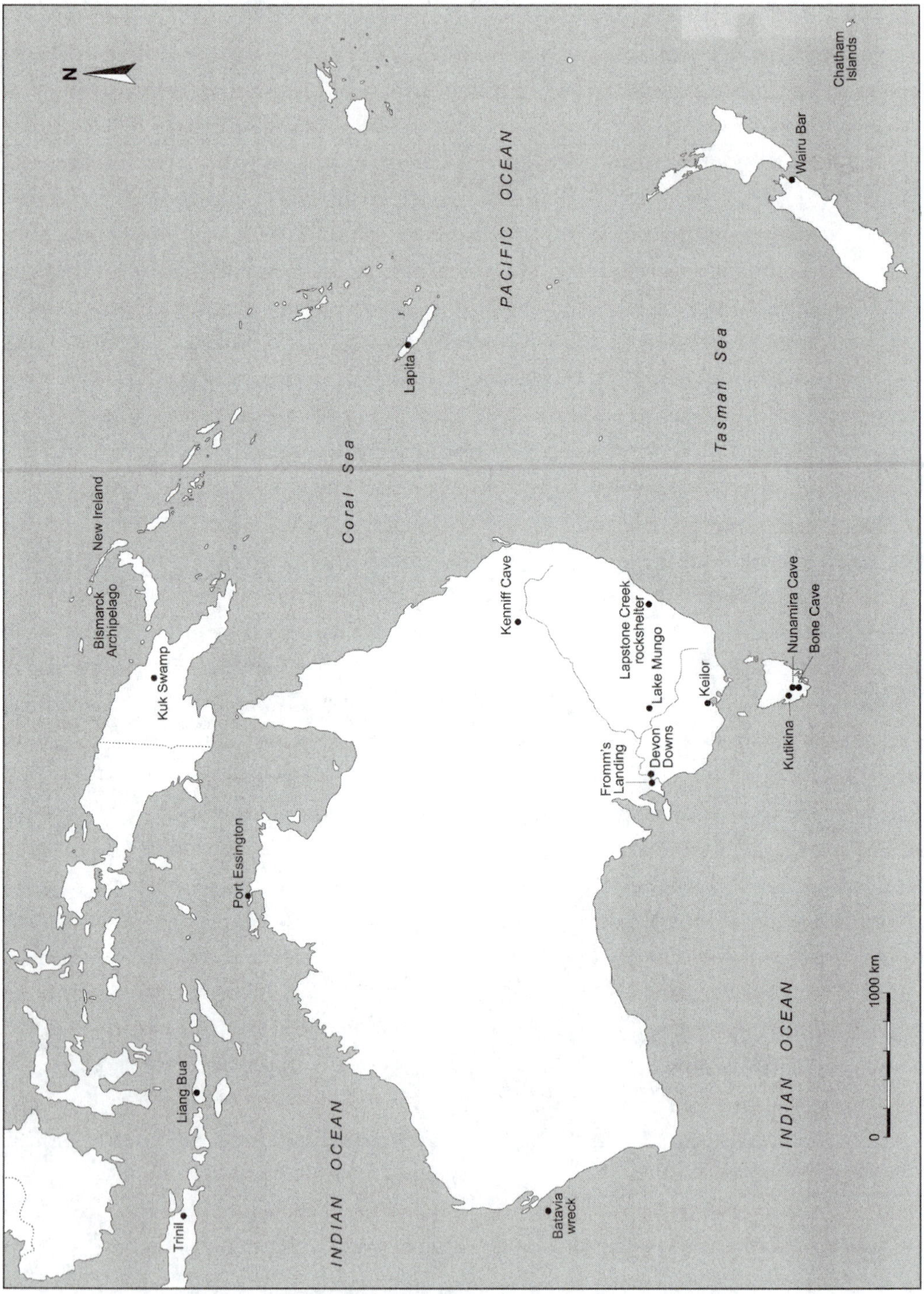

Australia and New Zealand

Section One

Archaeology before 1800

THE BIRTH OF ARCHAEOLOGY

This essay surveys the origins and development of archaeology over the roughly seven hundred years from the publication of Geoffrey of Monmouth's *Historia Regum Britanniae* (1138) to the end of the eighteenth century. Although archaeology as a discipline distinct from, say, history or anthropology cannot be convincingly demonstrated to exist before the beginning of the nineteenth century, the areas of inquiry that gave rise to it, such as natural history or the study of antiquities, grew and flourished during this period. The long gestation of archaeology (and of history and anthropology as well) is testimony to the importance of its core questions to human societies—questions that go to the heart of identity and the meaning and purpose of human lives.

Alain Schnapp has stressed the importance of antiquarianism as a coherent field of inquiry in itself. In *The Discovery of the Past* (1996), Schnapp argued that archaeology did not replace antiquarianism and that the traditions of antiquarianism lived on to create a parallel framework for analyzing antiquity (see also Schnapp 2002). Others before (see especially Piggott 1950, 1975, 1976a, 1976b) and since (Sweet 2004) have argued for the richness and variety of the antiquarian tradition in archaeology and have defended it against attack as a kind of wrong turning on the road to the disciplines of archaeology, anthropology, or history. In the present context, apart from freely acknowledging the strength of Schnapp's advocacy, my focus is on the genesis of archaeology. Thus, my discussion of many of the core elements of antiquarianism will be partial in the sense that I will consider only those aspects that came to play an important part in the development of archaeological method and theory and the place of archaeological knowledge on the cognitive map of the human sciences. For many, particularly those interested in human prehistory, archaeology did indeed consume antiquarianism.

The forty-two milestones that are discussed in Section One of this book range from Europe to Africa and the Americas, from classical antiquity to great power politics in the late eighteenth century, and from the origins of civilizations to the origins of human beings. They mark the publication of famous histories, both national and "universal"; the development of studies of landscape, field monuments, and material culture; the enhancement of methods of decipherment and classification; and the foundation of the institutions that fostered the birth of archaeology.

Of course, many significant histories and antiquarian studies are not included in these milestones, but it has not been my intention to be encyclopedic. Rather, my goal has been to deploy the milestones as guides or exemplars to help create a comprehensive picture of the forces that were to create archaeology in the nineteenth century. But we need to be clear that this is far from being the only picture possible, and my selection (and the synthetic narrative of this essay and those that follow) is very much the product of the way I see the origins and growth of archaeology as a distinct discipline. Consequently, it would be very unwise (and wholly unwarranted) for readers to conclude that the conception of the discipline of archaeology (and the milestones that have been selected to exemplify its origins and growth) that underpin this book will remain unchanged or undisputed. Other historians of archaeology (notably those collected in Bahn 1996 and Trigger 1989) have chosen differently. Given the importance of this context as a basis for selection and discussion, it is necessary to say a few words about the approach that has guided me.

Writing *This* History of Archaeology

The history of archaeology should be written in terms of the two distinct meanings of the term "discipline" proposed by the contributors to Lemaine et al. (1976). These are, respectively, disciplines as bodies of specialized knowledge and/or skills and disciplines as social and political institutions. I have also argued that if the history of archaeology were written in such a way then valid objections to much current disciplinary history (see, for example, Fahenstock 1984; Kristiansen 1981; Leone 1973; McVicar 1984a; Piggott 1981; Rowe 1975) would be met and overcome.

This different framework of archaeological historiography should provide a firmer basis for investigating the conceptual and sociological aspects of archaeological practice, thereby helping us toward a better understanding of the origins of archaeological goals, theories, questions, and perspectives. Thinking about the nature of archaeology as a discipline also gives access to criteria spanning both the context of justification (how archaeologists justify claims to knowledge of the past) and the context of discovery (the circumstances under which archaeologists create knowledge of the past), which are used by archaeologists and others to warrant that their knowledge claims are both rational and reliable.

I have also made the point that the pursuit of these investigations and assessments and the production of core data for the history, philosophy, and sociology of archaeological knowledge are complex and difficult exercises. The most important factor militating against a simple, straightforward accounting of the nature of the archaeological database, archaeological methods and goals, and the position of archaeology on the cognitive map of the human sciences is the fact that archaeology did not spring unbidden from material things. Instead, it arose to expand the empirical basis for our understanding of peoples who left no written record of their activities and to increase our knowledge of those for whom we had only sketchy or incomplete written testaments.

The history of archaeology is therefore intimately linked with the histories of the human, earth, and life sciences. Furthermore, categories such as "database," "method," and "goals" are unstable by virtue of their historical contextuality, and the characterization of them at any point is dependent on a wide range of similarly unstable factors spanning the experience of cognate disciplines, views of scientific method, and broadly sociopolitical factors.

An inevitable circularity is built into the search for what "caused" archaeology. Was it the problem, the database, the method, or a combination of the three? The search for the origins of archaeology, just like the search for the origins of any discipline or "idea" (see, for example, Daniel 1964) is a search without end, in the sense that most investigators begin with a fairly clear understanding of what is being sought, and only subsequently find that what were first thought to be stable categories vanish into a morass of interrelatedness. Worse still, the bulk of such searches, even after following the thread of the Great Chain of Being (Lovejoy 1964), come to a halt with the classical Greeks.

Not surprisingly, histories of the "origins and rise" of archaeology (see, for example, Daniel 1959, 1964, 1967) have generally stressed that the "cause" of archaeology was clearly multivariate—a problem to be solved, a database waiting patiently through the eons to have its significance "discovered," and a method that linked perennial problem and newfound significance. Those same types of disciplinary histories (see also Grayson 1983) have also, rightly, argued that changes in the conceptualization of problem and database, and developments in methodology, had all been occurring well before claims for the foundation of a discipline of archaeology were made and accepted during the nineteenth century.

More importantly, each element, problem, database, and method was itself the product of multivariate causality. Developments in those fields of natural history that were to coalesce into disciplines such as geology, biology, paleontology, ethnology, and anthropology during the nineteenth century directly affected each element. It is significant to note that changes in interpretative fashion and orientation within established fields such as history and philosophy had a similar effect. Added to this, the sociopolitical context of inquiries within nascent or established disciplines acted as a further variable.

Discovery-oriented disciplinary histories, no matter whether they emphasize the discovery of critically disturbing data (such as the establishment of a high human antiquity) or the discovery of methods or models (such as the interactionist methodology of the sixteenth and seventeenth century English antiquaries, or the Three-Age System), all stress an interactive process between historical chance and some notion of "the time being right."

There is much of value in such histories, especially the characterization of emergent disciplines and the precise analysis of vital moments where conjunctions occur among problem, database, and method. Indeed, such information is a vital resource for historians who may wish to consider the origins and rise of a less than hermetically sealed and teleological archaeology. However, to pursue the symmetrical analysis of the histories of disciplines, where "failures" and "wrong turnings" are as important as what we now perceive as being successful steps along the path of a discipline in the making, additional data are necessary. Characteristically, these additional data are also the sources of additional causal variables.

Here broadly "sociological" issues such as the community identity of practitioners, the formation of areas of specialization, differential perceptions of the importance of discoveries or the viability of methodologies, and the cognitive plausibility of interpretations and explanations come firmly into play. Revolutionary discoveries or changes of approach that are the meat and drink of discovery-oriented disciplinary histories also provide an opportunity for other historians of archaeology to pursue such sociological investigations. The slow acceptance of the Three-Age System in the German states and among some sectors of the British archaeological community, widely differing attitudes about the role of evolutionary theory in human paleontology present among European practitioners during the late nineteenth century, and divergent views of the meaning and extent of human antiquity are obvious candidates for further research within the methodology of the sociology of scientific knowledge.

An emphasis on disciplinary history that also considers the interaction of knowledge, skills, and institutions of socialization helps to focus our attention on the mechanics of conviction and justification. Why (and how) were practitioners and other consumers convinced that claims to knowledge of the prehistoric and protohistoric past were rational and reliable? Similarly, how and in what ways did sociopolitical context influence the activities of practitioners? With the benefit of hindsight and the need to use history to justify disparate readings of the nature of archaeology as a discipline, we may sometimes be led to the false belief that the mechanics of conviction must always either be objective or subjective, rational or irrational.

Yet this need not be so. A view that stresses the historically contingent nature of rationality need make no claims whatsoever about the "subjectivity" or "objectivity" of disciplinary practice at any point in time. A sociological approach to understanding the production of archaeological knowledge therefore demands a historicist rather than a teleologist approach to disciplinary history, even though what disciplines have become clearly plays an important part in the selection of historical problems and the plausibility of the solutions offered to them.

For these reasons, the case studies I discuss later in this essay stress the link between the mechanics of conviction and the methodological and conceptual parameters of archaeology. The same reasons explain the fact that I focus the vast bulk of this essay on the eighteenth-century foundations of archaeology and a consideration of notions of progress, the meaning of human mental and physical variety, and the conflict between conjectural history and historicism as vital elements of that history. To be fair, however, I also need to point out that I have used this focus to support a view that antinomies that arose from the investigation of these issues were, in conjunction with the fact that the development of archaeology succeeded the development of ethnology and changes in the goals of history writing, to play a critical role in the development of what were considered to be viable and significant archaeological problems and the establishment of accepted criteria of plausible and reliable archaeological knowledge.

This is not to say that the approach I have taken to writing the history of the eighteenth century is irremediably presentist, or that by omitting other features of a complex historical process I have sought only the information that supports my goals in this book. The milestones combine to offer a description of the power and impact of these issues and lend further support to the claim that they formed the critical arena for establishing the meaning and value of archaeological data and the discipline of archaeology itself.

How (and why) was it possible for antiquaries and natural historians (archaeologists in the making) to convince others, especially historians and ethnologists in the making, of the potential of the archaeological record as a source of information about the nature of human beings and the meaning of human history? This essay sketches a partial answer to that question and goes on to suggest that the grounds of conviction and justification established in the years between the discovery of the Americas in the late fifteenth century and the formulation of the Three-Age System in the nineteenth century were to shape the cognitive landscape of archaeology well into the twentieth century.

I have been working toward what may well seem to be a "natural" position on the historiography of archaeology. The form of disciplinary history—the significant events, critical discoveries, influential practitioners, and characterizations of the relationships between archaeology and other disciplines—clearly depends, as McVicar (1984b) has noted, on the view of historical causality held by the historian. Critically, it also depends on the view of archaeology held by the historian.

For example, historians of anthropology, such as Harris (1968), Langham (1981), Leaf (1979), Voget (1975), and Stocking (1968, 1983a, 1984), account for the origins and rise of archaeology within the origin and rise of anthropology and ethnology. Even though these authors and others (for example, Lowie 1937; Service 1985) recognize that during the course of the nineteenth century archaeology had an impact on the development of anthropology and ethnology, and further developed its problematic under the influence of its own practical momentum, they argue that much of this action was constrained by a more general problematic, making sense of the "ethnographic other" and the causes of cultural differences among metropolitan European populations.

Similarly, historians of geology, paleontology, and biology (for example, Bowler 1976; Burchfield 1974, 1975; Mayr 1982; Porter 1977; Rudwick 1963, 1971, 1972), when they mention archaeology at all, stress the importance of stratigraphic theory, comparative zoological anatomy, or systems of classification to the development of archaeology. Archaeology in these disciplinary histories is portrayed either as the subject of influence or "loans," or as a discipline that drew its higher-level theoretical functions from more abstract disciplinary formulations such as anthropology, biology, or historiography.

My search for the primary determinants of archaeology's position on the cognitive map of the "human" sciences has injected selectivity into the overall account I provide in Section One. Furthermore, bearing in mind the fact that the disciplines of archaeology and anthropology are both nineteenth-century formulations, my search for archaeological authorities will take the reader past the murky depths of eighteenth-century historiography and natural history, which other commentators have taken to be the seedbed of the nineteenth-century human sciences (Barnes and Shapin 1979; Bottomore and Nisbett 1978; Bowen 1981; Burrow 1966; Harris 1968; Leopold 1980; Mandrou 1978; Rousseau and Porter 1981; Stocking 1973, 1983a, 1984; Weber 1974). My discussion of the important process whereby the human or social sciences coalesced from such generalized and still barely understood apprehensions is, by necessity, a cursory one. Although I will emphasize the conflict between universal history and historicism, and between rationalism and empiricism, there is much of importance by way of context that has to be sacrificed to clearly establish the background to Stocking's cogent summary of the "ethos" of anthropology as we have come to know it:

> Another way of looking at the matter is to suggest that the general tradition we call retrospectively "anthropological" embodies a number of antinomies logically inherent or historically embedded in the Western intellectual tradition: an ontological opposition between materialism and idealism, an epistemological opposition between empiricism and apriorism, a substantive opposition between the biological and the cultural, a methodological opposition between the nomothetic and the idiographic, an attitudinal opposition between the racialist and the egalitarian, an evaluational opposition between the progressivist and the primitivist—among others. (1984, 4)

In the remainder of this essay I concentrate discussion on the eighteenth-century seedbed of archaeology, but in doing so I stress that the attitudes and concerns of that period owe a great deal to the work of earlier antiquaries and travelers. The milestones from the fifteenth, sixteenth, and seventeenth centuries are testimony to the foundational work of antiquaries and natural historians all over Europe whose investigations spanned from earliest prehistory to the classical world. Indeed, it is the geographical and temporal breadth of this inheritance that has allowed me to concentrate discussion on the history of antiquarianism in Britain, particularly the antiquarian researches into and speculations about prehistoric Britain.

The milestones in Section One underscore the fact that during this period vibrant antiquarian traditions were also created in Italy, France, and Sweden (as well as in other parts of Europe). Thus, the focus on Britain should not be seen as an argument that all great developments in antiquarianism or natural history flowed from there. This was most certainly not the case, as the milestones concerning savants as influential as the Comte de Caylus and Athanasius Kircher clearly demonstrate.

We should also not assume that antiquarians in different European countries were essentially out of contact with one another or working alone. In fact, the exact opposite was true. Antiquarians and natural historians across Europe founded a community of scholars sharing information, perspectives, and, of course, disagreements.

Notwithstanding the strength of these connections, which were reinforced by the creation of societies, academies, and museums, local social, cultural, and political forces created variety. This can be seen in the different histories of heritage-preservation legislation in the different European jurisdictions—very early in Sweden because of the agitations of Johan Bure and others, and very late in Britain. It is also evident in the particular circumstances surrounding the relationships among the papacy, the great families of Florence and elsewhere, and the surviving treasures of ancient Rome that led to the foundation of museums and the incorporation of the ideals of classical art into the heart of the Renaissance. In an important sense the ideals of the "local" and the "universal" linked most obviously in connections that were established (either real or imagined) between the various European countries and the classical and Biblical pasts. Among the milestones are expressions of such ideals in the Grand Tour and the work of the Society of Dilettanti, the collection of classical antiquities, the creation of great synthetic works such as those by Johann Winckelmann, and of course, the all-important "universal" histories of the great French thinkers of the seventeenth and eighteenth centuries.

I have used the situation in Britain as a case study in the development of methodologies in the antiquarian study of prehistoric Europe because it allows us to observe the process whereby diverse sources of evidence—material culture, written documents, landscape studies, oral histories, ethnographic observations, and good old-fashioned ratiocination—were used to create plausible images of a time before written history. But this is a partial history in other senses, too. Apart from the milestone recording Nicolaus Steno's great discovery of the principles of stratigraphy, I do not discuss in any detail the great advances made in the classification of natural phenomena, be they plants, animals, fossils, or rocks, which were such a fundamental feature in the development of natural history during this period. Similarly, the focus of the essay on explicating the origins of prehistoric archaeology is at the expense of a similarly detailed consideration of the development of studies of classical antiquity (and their subsequent transformation into the principles of classical archaeology). Nonetheless, the milestones included in Section One of this book explore many of the most significant passages in that disciplinary history, which is also fully discussed in other secondary works (see, for example, Schnapp 1996). But enough of caveats and explanations!

History Writing, Sociocultural Theory, and the Problem of Prehistoric Humans

Some years ago Marvin Harris thought it controversial to locate the origins of anthropology in the Enlightenment:

> Yet the importance of this epoch in the formation of the science of culture has gone unrecognized, principally because of the prolonged influence of anthropologists who were uninterested in such a science or who denied that it was possible . . . Those who believe that it is man's unique destination to live outside the determinate order of nature will not concede the importance of the eighteenth century. (1968, 8)

Although Harris was engaged in dispute with Hodgen (1964), even in 1968 the significance of the eighteenth century was already widely recognized. It is also not the case that there is any necessary link between such a recognition and an acceptance of Harris's argument that human beings do not lie outside the determinate order of nature. Landmark studies such as Burrow's indispensable analysis of Victorian social theory (1966) and the essays collected as *Race, Culture, and Evolution* (1968), which were written by Stocking after 1962, firmly established the importance of the eighteenth century to the development of anthropology and the human sciences generally. Similarly, histories of archaeology, such as those by Daniel (1943, 1950, 1957, 1959, 1964, 1967) and Heizer (1962), sought in the eighteenth century the first attempts to integrate the apprehension of the ethnographic other with the already recognized (by Mercati and others) human origin of ceraunia (see also Trigger 1989; Goodrum 2002).

Notwithstanding the now widespread agreement about the significance of the eighteenth century, there is still some dispute about the relative significance of the various types of inquiries that were to coalesce in the nineteenth century, first as ethnology, and later as anthropology. Burrow, for example, in his account of the activities of the Ethnological and Anthropologicial Societies of London, explained the nature of Victorian social theory in terms of a close link with the conjectural (or universal) histories of the Scottish primitivists (see, for example, A. Ferguson [1767] *An Essay on the History of Civil Society;* J. Millar [1771] *Observations Concerning the Distinction of Ranks in Society;* W. Robertson [1777] *A History of America*). In doing this he relegated the biological/physical anthropological inquiries of the period to a peripheral, losing role in the history of anthropology.

This aspect of Burrow's analysis has been explicitly resisted by Weber (1974) and Stocking (1968, 1971, 1973, 1987), both of whom find an important place for the development of physical anthropology from Johann Blumenbach (1795) within the general context of the eighteenth-century universal histories. Harris (1968) also stresses the significance of investigations into human physical variety. Weber (1974) seeks to critique histories of anthropology that emphasize the development of sociocultural theory at the expense of an image of anthropology investigating (and attempting to interrelate) all areas of evidence pertinent to an understanding of human beings. She and Stocking have mentioned that the first history of anthropology (Bendyshe 1865) devoted far more attention to the physical than the sociocultural. Indeed, representatives of the continental tradition of anthropology, such as Topinard, Quatrefages, Pouchet, Vogt, and Waitz, followed a similar path during the nineteenth century. There has been less dispute about the importance of the rise of philology for the development of anthropology (see especially Stocking 1973). Disputation over the relative significance of the constituent elements of anthropology (i.e., over which aspect of anthropological inquiry lies at the core of the anthropological program) serves to illustrate three important points.

First, histories of anthropology or archaeology written within a teleological framework tend to obscure the importance of those aspects of disciplines that appear to the contemporary practitioner to be peripheral. Given the current domination of a sociocultural reading of anthropology, and the racist evils of much of eighteenth- and nineteenth-century physical anthropology, observers such as Burrow have emphasized the sociocultural and the philological at the expense of the physical (and indeed of the archaeological). Such histories may convince practitioners of sociocultural anthropology and, in the past, have convinced archaeologists and physical anthropologists. However, during times when the relationship between archaeology and anthropology is in dispute, different histories are required that seek meaning in those areas previously considered peripheral to the development of disciplinary identity and practice.

Second, the origins of anthropology are complex and multivariate, and the development of contrasting views of the role of the discipline and the relative significance of its almost impossibly broad database are an important aspect of any explanation of the existence of differing anthropological traditions.

Third, the complexity of the sources of anthropology does not end with the establishment of its sociocultural, physical, linguistic, and archaeological elements. The history of anthropology (and by extension the history of archaeology) reveals a complex interaction of changing trends in historiography, moral philosophy, and epistemology. When the very real contemporary sociopolitical implications of these changing trends and the terms of their interactions with the database of anthropology are understood, Stocking's view of anthropology as a discipline wherein long-standing antinomies have been developed and played out gains great analytic force.

My particular reading of the eighteenth-century and early nineteenth-century history of the human sciences hinges on a view of the differences between ethnographies, written documents, and those material phenomena that were to become archaeological data in the nineteenth century. It also advances the argument that the broad objectives of an inquiry into the nature of the prehistoric past, and the nature of meaningful knowledge of that past, were established long before the foundation of archaeology in the nineteenth century. In this view the "rise" of archaeology was conditioned by the development of a methodology that could plausibly translate mute material phenomena into data, which were then applied to those objectives and acquired meaning through such application. The antinomies logically inherent in anthropology were also logically inherent in archaeology.

In the following case study I outline the development of an interactionist antiquarian methodology that, although first developed in the sixteenth century (and therefore prior to the eighteenth-century debates and issues that were to stimulate and condition the development of ethnology and anthropology in the nineteenth century), was to become the basis for nineteenth-century archaeological methodology. Significantly, during the eighteenth and early nineteenth centuries, English antiquarian studies were directly affected by the perceived need to establish the meaning of the ethnographic other in terms of the prehistory of Europe and vice versa.

The important point here is that during the eighteenth century widespread attempts were made to find a means of plausibly and reliably apprehending human prehistory. Although there were differences of opinion about whether such a program entailed a methodological distinction between the human and natural sciences (see especially Vico 1948; Moravia 1980), or whether empiricist or rationalist epistemologies were most appropriate to the job at hand, it was widely recognized that the apprehension of a "past before writing" entailed the development of models of human nature (see especially Helvetius 1777; Locke 1692). The interpenetration of essentially epistemological and conceptual issues was to directly influence the presence of different interpretations of the significance of the ethnographic other as a guide to an understanding of both human nature and the specifics of human prehistory. This gained additional importance as a spur to a historiographic conflict between the claims of universal (conjectural) history and historicism (see Berlin 1980; Meinecke 1972).

Did history demonstrate universal human progress, or was progress confined to certain races? Was it possible to consider human material progress as antithetical to moral decline? Could one generalize about the historical experience of human beings, or was it more meaningful to consider the spiritual and moral differences between human groups? (See also M. Abrams 1953; P. Abrams 1968, 1982; Bock 1978; Bowen 1981; Bury 1955; Foucault 1970; R. Laudan 1985; Pagden 1982; Prawer 1970; Schenk 1966; Sorabji 1983; Teggart 1949; Trompf 1979; Walzel 1965.)

Significantly, such debates, conducted through the work of Turgot (1750), Rousseau (1755, 1762), Monboddo (1774), Montesquieu (1748), Voltaire (1745), von Holbach (1770), Condorcet (1795), and Herder (1794), and the works of the Scottish Enlightenment philosophers drew the bulk of their empirical inspiration from a contemplation of the ethnographic other. Given the importance of finding a plausible image of human beings during prehistory, it is significant to note that apart from establishing the similarities between the technologies of prehistoric Europe and those of contemporary "savages," antiquarian studies were the consumers rather than the producers of approaches and perspectives.

This was not the case for the developing fields of physical anthropology and philology, which were, during the course of the eighteenth century, to make an increasing contribution to the empirical reservoir of human studies and to directly influence the terms of extant debates. Indeed, by the close of the eighteenth century, philology and physical anthropology had become central to debates about human nature and the meaning of human history (see Burrow 1966; Stocking 1973; Weber 1974).

The increasing importance of ethnographic studies of social and cultural forms, physical anthropology, and philology, relative to the static contribution and subordinate position of antiquarian studies during the eighteenth century, requires more detailed discussion. However, before turning to that issue it is important to briefly discuss the terms of a debate that encompassed the entire suite of antinomies that Stocking has argued are logically inherent in anthropology.

Here I speak of the conflict between the doctrines of monogenesis and polygenesis (monogenism and polygenism). The bare bones of both doctrines are quite straightforward. For the monogenist, variability in human physical, cultural, and social forms was the product of history—of human beings acting in diverse and changing environments. Consequently, monogenists claimed that there had been only a single creation and that human nature was plastic.

Polygenists, on the other hand, considered that the exigencies of human history, and the modifying influence of the environment, were simply insufficient to explain what they considered to be high levels of human physical, social, and cultural variability. Accordingly, for the polygenist the only rational explanation for such variability, even if it flew in the face of revealed religion, was that there were separate creations.

These are simplistic descriptions. Some monogenists accepted aspects of the polygenist program and vice versa, not all polygenists were racial determinists, and not all monogenists adopted an egalitarian viewpoint on the mental and moral condition of contemporary "savages." The debate between monogenism and polygenism was to consume human studies during the latter part of the eighteenth century, and to go on to become the "question of questions" that would provide the disciplinary problematic of anthropology in the nineteenth century. In so doing it was also to shape the disciplinary problematic of archaeology, and to make an important contribution to the cognitive plausibility of rival evolutionist and diffusionist explanations of culture change and the concept of the archaeological culture itself.

A critical feature of the debate was its significance to contemporary social and political issues ranging from the causes of criminality, the pros and cons of Irish Home Rule, the abolition of slavery, the proper treatment of aboriginal peoples within the boundaries of European empires, and the causes of national and racial conflict within Europe itself (see Stocking 1971, 1973, 1987; Weber 1974).

During the eighteenth century, antiquarian studies were rarely used in such debates, although as we shall see in the case of the British antiquaries, there were important examples of the application of monogenist and polygenist perspectives to the reconstruction of remote British history (see especially Horsman 1976). Both monogenists and polygenists garnered the bulk of their evidence from the ethnographic present and historical past, primarily because of a uniformitarian assumption by monogenists that the causes of variability were still operating. Polygenists attempted to resist such claims by pointing to historical and ethnographic cases of the "permanence of type," and to examples of variability that appeared to have no clear environmental cause. This concentration on the present and the recent past was further supported by the fact that antiquaries themselves, faced with increasing confusion within their database, sought interpretation and explanation from the same sources.

Significantly, it was widely recognized by both monogenists and polygenists that the prehistoric past probably held an important part of the answer to that question of questions. However, it was also widely understood that access to that past was constrained by the very fact that no reliable guide to establishing the historical relationship between prehistoric European materials and the contemporary ethnographic other existed. The fog that had descended on European antiquarian studies also blanketed the history of the ethnographic other.

During the eighteenth century this problem with antiquarian methodology was one of a number of others that allowed the debate to flourish. Despite the great advances in the methodology of physical anthropology promoted by Blumenbach, Peter Camper (1722–1789), and others, and the multiplication of putatively objective studies of head size and shape (see Gould 1984), no widely accepted explanation for the causes of variation in the human physique had been established. Furthermore, there was no agreement about whether the physical character of human beings could be causally related to other sources of variability.

Similarly, there was no sense of widespread agreement about the causes of sociocultural variability between contemporary and historically known groups. Indeed, the quality of the ethnographies (generally travelers' tales) was indifferent to say the least. In the nineteenth century this was to become a major focus of research among the disputant parties and would lead to the construction of a wide variety of questionnaires and eventually to the practice of professional ethnographic fieldwork (see Fowler 1975; Stocking 1983b; Urry 1984).

Antiquarian studies were to undergo similar changes during the nineteenth century, eventually leading to the establishment of archaeology as a discipline. The dispersal of the "fog" by the Three-Age System was critically important to that foundation, but it was not the only force. For example, an increasingly important role in answering that question of questions was assumed by studies of the material remnants of prehistoric human action. In doing this the new information also more forcefully contributed to the historiographic debate between universal history and historicism, as the search for the determinants of human cultural variability within Europe began to drift away from a sole concentration on the linguistic, the physical, and the theories of society that had been formulated during the eighteenth century.

But the increasing significance of what were to become archaeology and archaeological data was the product of debates around the antinomies discussed by Stocking, and the fact that a methodology had been found that at last allowed mute material to be translated into historically and ethnologically relevant information about people in the prehistoric past.

In 1862, Daniel Wilson summarized the foundations of the new discipline in a way that made quite clear the close association of archaeology and other sources of information about human action in the search for a solution to that question of questions:

> The object aimed at in the following work is to view Man, as far as possible, unaffected by those modifying influences which accompany the development of nations and the maturity of a true historic period, in order thereby to ascertain the sources from whence such development and maturity proceeded. These researches into the origin of civilization have accordingly been pursued under the belief . . . that the investigations of the archaeologist, when carried on in an enlightened spirit, are replete with interest in relation to some of the most important problems of modern science. To confine our studies to mere antiquities is like reading by candle-light at noonday; but to

> reject the aid of archaeology in the progress of science, and especially of ethnological science, is to extinguish the lamp of the student when most dependent on its borrowed rays . . . We are no longer permitted to discuss merely the diversities of existing races. It seems as if the whole comprehensive question of man's origin must be reopened, and determined afresh in its relations to modern science. (1862, vii)

The Construction of Remote British History

This discussion of Camden's and Speed's demolition of Geoffrey of Monmouth's account of remote British history (written in 1138) and their replacement of it by an account broadly indicative of sixteenth- and seventeenth-century English antiquarian practice illustrates the means by which material things could acquire significance as historical documents within a broader sociopolitical and historiographic context. It also illustrates how the inductive philosophy of science of the period could readily articulate with sociopolitical context to dispatch Geoffrey's account as being essentially mythopoeic. There is a neat contrast here between the fate of the *Historia* and that of Hesiod's *Works and Days,* or Lucretius' *On the Nature of the Universe,* two mythopoeic discourses that fared rather better when the Three-Age System was formulated by Thomsen and subsequently accepted by many continental and English antiquaries.

My primary interest here is not to present a detailed account of English antiquarianism during these centuries, the outlines of which have already been sketched by Kendrick (1950) and Piggott (1976b, 1976c, 1976d, 1978). My concentration on the antiquaries of the sixteenth and seventeenth centuries, primarily because of their development of the "interactionist" methodology, recognizes that there were traditions in antiquarian study stretching back to the medieval period. These have been discussed by Southern (1973), who is critical of Kendrick's position that the sixteenth century was dominated by a struggle between Monmouth's account and the tenets of Renaissance humanism. Notwithstanding Southern's views, and accepting that there were other traditions in sixteenth-century English antiquarian practice, Kendrick's argument that the conflict between the two sources is really a conflict between styles of historiography is accepted here. Again, while the background sociopolitical context of antiquarianism is an important factor in the following discussion, I do not offer a more complete, nor sophisticated analysis than may be found in a combination of G. Chambers (1984),

Fergusson (1979), Hunter (1975), Levy (1964, 1967), McVicar (1984b), and Styles (1956).

Instead, I concentrate on outlining the rise of, and the causes of changes to, a new antiquarian methodology, and then go on to discuss some of the links between it and the wider social context of antiquarian knowledge.

This new methodology, which I call "interactionist," allowed antiquaries to plausibly relate new (the ethnographic other, field monuments, coins and inscriptions) and old (the Bible and the classical ethnographies) sources of evidence and interpretation. This interactionist methodology came to be the hallmark of English antiquarian practice during the sixteenth and seventeenth centuries. In discussing the causes of changes to this new methodology I will emphasize three important shifts in the context of antiquarian practice.

First, material phenomena increased in historical importance as empirical information about the British prehistoric past and material culture associated with the ethnographic other.

Second, which links to the first, the picture of the pre-Roman British past grew increasingly complex, and the historical relationships of items of material culture could not be plausibly established through the interactionist methodology alone.

Third, there was a shift away from empiricist to rationalist (romantic) frameworks of interpretation and justification during the eighteenth century—typified by the later work of William Stukeley (see for example, Berman 1972; Brown 1977, 1980; Chippindale 1985; Hunter 1975, 1981; Jacob 1975; Jacob and Jacob 1980; Michell 1982; David Miller 1981; Mulligan and Mulligan 1981; Piggott 1950, 1975, 1976e, 1976f, 1976g, 1976h, 1981, 1985a, 1986; Wood 1980).

Notwithstanding the "excesses" of practitioners such as Stukeley, and the confusion of others, such as Colt Hoare, which led many observers to doubt whether the "true" history of the remote British past could ever be established, the rude stone monuments, barrows, and other items of remnant material culture were still recognized as the products of historical human action, although precisely *whose* action remained a matter for conjecture and debate between rival interpretations of the meaning of those phenomena.

I argue that the forces that led to the recognition of the historical and "ethnological" importance of material things also conditioned the methodological status of material things as supplements to other more culturally familiar data sets, perspectives, methodologies, and problems.

The interactionist methodology of English antiquarianism had to allow practitioners to do two things: first, to marshal all available ethnographic, material cultural, and textual evidence to counteract what were considered to be irrational or mythological histories; and second, to grade (implicitly or explicitly) the historical reliability of all the sources of evidence as testaments to the human past.

Significantly, the history that antiquarians either sought to write or contribute to was the history of Britain in its mental, moral, and political particulars. Ethnographic generalization was, therefore, practically mediated by textual and material cultural analysis. As McVicar (1984b) and others have shown, new sociopolitical contexts and new relationships to the past (see McVicar's discussion of Anachronism, p. 55, drawn largely from McLean 1972) demanded new histories. The *Historia*, which had served old contexts and old attitudes to the past, was one of the first major victims of the new methodology.

Although Geoffrey's work was never again considered to be a benchmark history after the seventeenth century, aspects of the work (particularly the Arthurian myth) were to survive the onslaught of Baconianism to inspire Malory, Tennyson, and, of course, a legion of musical theater and Hollywood directors.

Geoffrey's purpose was to chronicle the history of the Britons through 1900 years, stretching from Brutus, the son of Aeneas, who seized the island from the Giants and settled it with Trojan refugees, down to Cadwallader, who cravenly surrendered Britain to the Saxons in the seventh century AD. There was also another and deeper purpose than to provide a rattling yarn. The *Historia* sought to restore to the remnant Britons a sense of pride in their history, and to remind them of the prophesies of Merlin—that they had triumphs yet to come. On the same political level Geoffrey also wished to provide "a precedent for the dominions and ambitions of the Norman kings" (Tatlock 1950, 426).

The standard sources on the *Historia* (Chambers 1918; Giles 1842; Hammer 1942; Jones 1964; Kendrick 1950; Lloyd 1942; Piggott 1941; Tatlock 1950) debate many issues concerning the sources of the work and its reception by scholars, even those of Geoffrey's own time. Its influence, however, is unquestioned. Kendrick's superb study is in fact a chronicle of that influence, charting the objections to the work from antiquarians such as Polydore Vergil, Leland, Camden, and Speed. It is the antiquarian objections to the work that most concern us here, because the sixteenth- and seventeenth-century antiquaries marshaled the product of a different historical methodology against it.

Principal among these antiquaries were William Camden and John Speed. Camden became the archetypical English antiquary, as much because of his education and political connections as because of the enormous influence of his great work *Britannia* (1586). Camden's connections with the power structure of Tudor England were considerable. For example, Sir Fulke Greville gained him the position of Clarenceaux King at Arms (within the College of Arms) in 1597.

It was a congenial post for Camden because the primary business of the College was granting coats of arms to families recently entitled to them and confirming the existing rights of others. Previous members of the College, such as Robert Talbot, had used the position to cultivate antiquarian researches, in his case an attempt to identify the places mentioned in a Roman geography of Britain, the *Antonine Itinerary*. There were others who carried on this tradition (see Piggott 1976b, 18). The working out of the genealogies of titled families was to form the basis of much antiquarian activity well into the eighteenth century, and many antiquarian surveys devoted considerable attention to local titled families.

A concern with the past thus had direct political, social, and economic consequences for many who were in the Tudor (and later Stuart and Georgian) power structures or who sought entry to them. The best example of the use of the past, apart from Parliament's obsession with precedent and the functioning of common law, is provided by Henry VIII when he sought justification for the split with Rome and the foundation of a Church of England. The appointment of John Leland as the first King's Antiquary is significant testimony to seriousness of Henry's appeal to the traditions of British history (see Kendrick 1950).

Previous accounts of Camden by historians of archaeology (the best being Kendrick 1950; Parry 1995; Piggott 1976c—there is still no full-scale study) have naturally emphasized the importance of *Britannia,* in its many editions, as a model for the emerging style of antiquarian discourse. Piggott (1976b, 1976c especially, but note also the other papers that make up 1976a) has contributed a great deal to our understanding of the intellectual and sociopolitical context of antiquarianism. In addition, the authors listed have produced good general accounts of Tudor historiography. Camden's own educational background of Renaissance humanism is equally significant.

MacCaffrey (1970) has emphasized the importance of classical learning to the scholars of Camden's time:

> Their interests in classical learning were not in its historical, but in its contemporary relevance. It was not curiosity about the past but concern for the present and future moral well-being of men which led them to their studies. They saw the works of the classical authors as authoritative and inspiring guides to the moral development of contemporary men, which was for them the raison d'etre of all their labours. (xv–xvi)

This is in contrast to another style of antiquarian research, that of knowing the past for its own sake. MacCaffrey (1970, xvi) sharpens this contrast by establishing that antiquaries who pursued an understanding of the past from this standpoint were more interested in the classical topographers and geographers such as Strabo and Ptolemy, the authors of early reports of the British landscape. He may well have been describing Talbot's program: "These antiquaries had begun with the task of reconciling the ancient descriptions of Europe with the political geography of the sixteenth century" (MacCaffrey 1970, xvi).

This task implied that collection and analysis would also include the need to provide the fullest possible description of the entire basis of ancient social and cultural life. Such detailed descriptions subsequently provided clear evidence of differences and similarities in customs and laws, both within Britain and between Britain and Europe as a whole, that could broaden the understanding of history itself. The development of county histories such as Lambarde's *Perambulation of Kent* (1576) and John Stow's survey of London (1598) are cases in point. Significantly, the actual visitation of places mentioned in the histories was not regarded as being essential, the authority of previous authors was enough to justify their inclusion.

Camden adopted a different course, and in so doing raised the possibility that the analysis of material remains could play a greater role in sifting mythopoeic historical "re-creations" from "objective" histories. What caused the change in methodology to include an accent on actual observation and an increased emphasis on incorporating material objects as authorities potentially on a par with the written documents? What also changed antiquarian studies from being set apart from the concerns of the age to becoming a source of national interest?

Clearly the spirit of Baconian empiricism had much to do with the skepticism of other than direct observation or eyewitness accounts. Yet this skepticism most certainly was not applied to the Bible, nor to the more general and derivative classical ethnographies. In fact these and the new ethnographies from the Americas were to become the standards, the givens, the bedrock assumptions of English antiquarianism of the sixteenth, seventeenth, and eighteenth centuries.

The prescription that evidence of the senses was more powerful than the authority of ancient authors had a role to play in the new emphasis on visiting sites and cataloguing coins and inscriptions, but equally clearly, there were practical difficulties encountered by an empiricist epistemology when it came to "filling the gaps" in the material cultural record. It transpired that material culture, after it had been subjected to proper scrutiny and classification, would be used along with the ethnographic data to fill the gaps in the historical record. What was rational, what was plausible, would be determined by the degree of fit between the classical and Biblical authorities on the one hand, and the material culture and ethnographies on the other. Yet this interactionist methodology was closely constrained by "cultural" and political determinants of what was plausible to believe. In the event, the weight of plausibility was to rest with literary sources.

The discussion of British origins was central to the intellectual and political background of *Britannia.* Geoffrey's Brutus story had held sway, despite continuous criticism, since the twelfth century. The first major attack in the sixteenth century, most closely associated with Polydore Vergil, Robert Fabyan, and John Rastell (see Kendrick 1950, 38–44), argued that Geoffrey's *Historia* completely lacked verification from any ancient source. Kendrick has argued that Tudor nationalists did not react favorably to the attack or to Vergil's attempts to justify it. In the debate that followed, the traditional basis for understanding the earliest periods of British history was itself questioned, and the construction of British history itself became problematic. The issue became one of methodology and epistemology: how were accounts of the remote past to be justified? Any solution would have political ramifications.

Ortelius may have encouraged Camden to "acquaint the world with Britain" (Camden's preface to *Britannia*), but Camden's real goal was to "restore Britain to its antiquities and its antiquities to Britain." The glory of Britain would be best served by establishing a clear and rationally defensible history that linked it to Rome. It would also be effectively served by justifying the Anglo-Saxon dominance of British (read English) power structures (see Horsman 1976). Camden's attack on Geoffrey's British history was as much an attack on its racial elements as it was on its fabulous nature. There was a great deal at stake.

Camden dismissed the Brutus story as a myth, one of those myths that have nationalist justification by disguising "the truth with a mixture of fable and bring[ing] in the gods themselves to act a part . . . thereby to render the beginnings either of a city or of a nation, more noble and majestical" (1586, ix). However, Camden did not mention another vital aspect of using such myths—to explain a past that was beyond direct observation or written documents—although he does hint at the importance of such explanations given the investment of national or ethnic pride in their particular constitution.

Despite Geoffrey's own appeals to authority, for example the use of Biblical chronology to provide a time frame for the action in Britain, it is unlikely that he wrote a history of Britain that was historical in the same sense as a traditional medieval chronicle or a Tudor history.

By Camden's time, classical, particularly Roman, accounts had become the foundation of an understanding of the pre-Roman British past. However, Camden added an extra dimension through his discussion of monuments and artifacts (particularly coins) as well as the customs and languages of France and Britain. Clearly, if any new account was to convince the lawyers and the English educated public of the sixteenth and seventeenth centuries, it had to be broadly based and allow rational assessment by the lights of Baconian empiricism.

The supply of written documents (including the depth of their textual exegesis), Roman and post-Roman inscriptions, and descriptions of field monuments had greatly increased since the Middle Ages, providing a broad base from which to begin writing the history of a past that had left no contemporary written documents. The analysis of material remains thus became a way of establishing the reliability of claims based on written documents that sometimes gave divergent testimony. An important issue here is that Geoffrey's history had assumed a kind of authority itself, based in part on the fact that for many people it was not only an agreeable reconstruction, but also because it was a *written* one. An attack on Geoffrey's work implied an equally critical attitude to the Bible and the classical authorities. In practice these core areas of antiquarian "culture" were not examined with anything approaching the vigor reserved for Geoffrey and other "fabulists."

What Geoffrey had constructed out of chronicles, king lists, folk tales, and his own imagination, Camden made from the Biblical and classical sources and the surviving monuments and artifacts. A final issue remains here, concerning whether the goals of Geoffrey's history were the same as Camden's. Both had national and political goals, both sought to glorify the nation through its past, and both had racial interests. Geoffrey sought to attain his goals by way of myth couched in terms of a Biblical and folkloric background to give it a measure of plausibility. Camden stressed the fact that he had chosen another path.

Camden's stated authorities were his senses and the exercise of logic, but in practice these were constrained by the a priori conceptual power of the Bible and the classical authorities. Thus, for Camden it was not just a matter that these authorities impregnated his supposedly hypothesis-free observation statements; it was far more than this. Camden's *Britannia* above all represents an extension of the Roman histories by means of using the monuments, coins, and inscriptions to supplement classical documentary sources.

By virtue of the success of *Britannia* and through his contacts with other antiquaries and historians, such as Sir Robert Bruce Cotton (Mirrlees 1962) and John Speed, Camden influenced much of the style of sixteenth- and seventeenth-century English antiquarian debate. Indeed, succeeding editions of *Britannia* (note especially the 1695 and 1722 editions) acted as a kind of barometer of antiquarian methodology, or at least as a point of departure for other antiquaries, through to the end of the eighteenth century. Camden was also instrumental in the first foundation of the Society of Antiquaries of London, until the nineteenth century the premier antiquarian and "archaeological" society in England (see Evans 1956), despite its regular brushes with monarchs suspicious of the political implications of "backward-looking curiosity" (see Daniel 1976). In sum, Camden's methodology, based as it was on the squaring of classical and Biblical authorities with the material cultural evidence, became the cornerstone of the interactionist methodology to be developed by John Speed and used by generations of English antiquaries who were to follow him.

John Speed's (1552–1629) *The Historie of Great Britaine under the conquests of the Romans, Saxons, Danes and Normans. Their Originals, Manners, Habits, Warres, Coins, and Seals: with the Successions, Lives, Acts, and Issues of the English Monarchs from Julius Caesar, unto the Raigne of King James, of famous memorie* (1632), to give the work its full title, exemplifies the development of the interactionist methodology that was also applied to the interpretation of pre-Roman material culture by natural historians such as Edward Lhwyd (1660–1709).

Speed was fully aware that there had been considerable loss of information since that remote past, the data being "eaten up with Time's teeth, as Ovid speaks" (1632, A4, in the Proeme), and advised that its reconstruction was going to be a difficult task:

> Varro (that learned Roman writer; who lived an hundred years before the birth of our Saviour Christ), called the first world to the Flood uncertain; and thense to the first Olympias fabulous: Because in that time (sayth he) there is nothing related (for the most part) but Fables amongst the Greeks, Latins and other learned nations. And therefore Plutarch beginneth the lives of his worthy men no higher than Theseus: because (sayth he) what hath been written before, was but of strange things, and sayings full of monstrous fables imagined and devised by Poets, which are altogether uncertain and most untrue. (1632, A4, in the Proeme)

He continued the point by linking the unreliability of these fabulous reconstructions with what is close to a paraphrase of Camden's warnings about the corruption of antiquity by the concerns of the present. Antiquity for Speed (as for Camden) could really serve the needs of the present only if it had a separate objective existence. Thus, the constant emphasis on the independence of the past and the need for the defense of that independence, given the great power ascribed to any plausible reconstruction of the past.

> These things thus standing, let us give leave to Antiquity, who sometimes mingleth falsehoods with truth, to make the beginnings of Policies seem more honourable: and whose power is so far screwed into the world's conceit, that with Hierome we may say, Antiquity is allowed with such general applause, that known untruths many times are pleasing unto many. Yet with better regard to reverend Antiquity, whom Jobs opposer will us inquire after and to our own relations in delivering their censures, let this be considered; That more things are let slip, than are comprehended in any man's writings, and yet more therein written, than any man's life (though it be long) will admit him to read. Neither let us be forestalled with any prejudiced opinions of the reporters, that in some things may justly be suspected, or in affection, which by nature we owe to our natural country; nor consent (as Livy speaketh) to stand with the ancientness of reports, when it seems to take away the certainty

> of truth. To keep a man betwixt both, myself with Bildad do confess, that I am but yesterday, and know nothing. (Speed 1632, A5, left and right)

Notwithstanding these methodological prescriptions, Speed (like Camden and the other antiquaries of their era) had to accept the priority of the Bible and the classical sources. The Moderns might seek to displace the Ancients in the sciences, but how was it to be possible that the Ancients could be similarly displaced in antiquarian studies and in ancient history? More important, how was it possible for their plausibility to be assessed when the values of all other sources of evidence were gauged in the terms of their degree of fit with the classical and Biblical authorities?

Speed's own reconstruction had Britain settled during the time of the patriarchs, approximately 1,650 years before the flood (1632, 11, Chapter 3 of Book 5). After the flood Japhet came to Europe, a fact "on which all authorities agree." Citing Polydore Vergil and Sebastian Munster in support, Speed considered that all stories of this early history were conjectural (1632, 12) and went on to derive the Gauls and the Welsh from Gomer (the eldest son of Japhet) on the corruption of Gomer to Combri and then to Cimbri, the Welsh calling their country Cumbri. Having sought authority in the Bible and in the work of Cicero and Appian Alexandrinus, Speed found room to appeal to Camden for the grounds needed to reject the Brutus story:

> Now that Britain had here first inhabitants from Gaul, sufficient is proved by the name, site, religion, manners and languages, by all which the most ancient Gauls and Britons have been as linked together in some mutual society; as is at large proved by our arch-Antiquary in his famous work. (1632, 12)

Following the developed tradition that the search for origins also implied a reconstruction of manners and customs, Speed disposed of the Brutus story between pages 12 and 20 (in a virtual repetition of the grounds offered by Camden) and proposed a reconstruction of the earliest Britons based on the classical ethnographies:

> It remaineth that somewhat be mentioned of the *Manners* and *Customs* of the people and times, though not so pleasing or acceptable as were to be wished, for the clouds of ignorance and barbarous incivility did then shadow and overspread almost all the Nations of the earth: wherein I desire to lay imputation

> no further than is sufficiently warranted by the most authentic writers: and first from Caesar, who foremost of all the Romans discovered and described our ancient Britons. (1632, 20; original emphasis)

It is important to realize that Speed considered himself to be completely objective in this reconstruction. Maintaining that much of what can be ascertained about the manners and customs of these ancient Britons did not sit well with contemporary models, Speed insisted that their brute reality had to be presented unvarnished if the English were to escape the fabulous histories of the poets. The authorities that Speed used to reconstruct the broad picture of manners and customs were almost exclusively literary.

For the fact that the Britons painted their bodies, Speed used Herodian, Pliny, Dio Nicaeus, Solinus, Tertullian, Martial, and Camden as sources; for hairstyles, Caesar, Mamertinus, Tacitus, Strabo, Xiphilinus, and Entropius; for longevity, Plutarch, Diodorus Siculus, Strabo, Caesar, and Pomponius Mela; for domestic matters, Caesar, Strabo, Diodorus Siculus, and Dion; for wives, Eusebius; for food taboos and diet, Caesar, Diodorus Siculus, Pliny, and Strabo; for religion, Lucan. The same pattern of classical authority applied to wars, as well as to trade, commerce, and shipping, although these last three were supplemented by the studies of coins and seals in Sir Robert Bruce Cotton's collection published by Camden, Cotton, and Speed. Stone artifacts were not mentioned.

Kendrick (1950, 121–125) has written convincingly about the influence of the accounts of sixteenth-century explorers of Amerindians on the forms of the reconstructions developed to illustrate ancient British life. Both he and Piggott (1975, 1976b, 1976d, 1978) have stressed their importance alongside the highly influential drawings of Virginians made by John White (see also Hulton and Quinn 1964) as providing another source of authority for the reconstructions of sixteenth- and seventeenth-century English antiquaries.

In Speed's *Historie,* for example, the four illustrations of ancient Britons (two pairs of men and women), the earlier pair appear unclothed and the later pair appear close to fully clothed, mirror White's illustrations of Virginians (see Kendrick 1950, 124). Speed also did not fail to make the connection between the "wilder Irish" and the Virginians on the basis that both groups wore no clothes (1632, 39).

What was in fact happening in Speed's work was the grafting of the Amerindian ethnographies (an important new source of information about the remote past after the link made by Montaigne) onto the Biblical and classical authorities—with a dash of coins and seals to complete the material contingent. Speed summarized the value of the new methodology with his usual perspicacity, but notice that light was to be gained primarily from the "collision" of literary sources:

> Touching all which, the reports of Authors are very discrepant: and therefore as light is gotten at by a collision of flints, we will assay, whether out of those writers contradictions (brought to the stroke and confronted together) we may strike some glimmering light, to direct us how to paint them forth, who so delighted in painting themselves. (1632, 40)

Although Camden and Speed focused the bulk of their attention on coins, seals, and other items of material culture bearing inscriptions, the methodology of comparison, rational reconstruction, and close observation of the empirical phenomena (be they field monuments or church brasses) was matched by those antiquaries who concentrated on ceraunia (see, for example, Dugdale 1656). Full discussions of these appear in Grayson 1983; Laming-Emperaire 1964; Oakley 1976; Peake 1940; Piggott 1976b, 1976f; Daniel 1975. Lhwyd and Plot, to name only two antiquaries more inclined to natural history, without qualm linked empirical observation of these fossils and their modern representatives with close textual and folkloric studies in a way that anticipated important elements of the new interactionist methodology that was to become associated with the Three-Age System.

Significantly, both Camden and Speed, having located a source for the British, and therefore a description of them drawn from the classical and Biblical sources, paid scant attention to the need to ascertain whether those earliest Britons changed before the time of the Romans. For them, it was enough to connect Japhet and Caesar (to paraphrase Stocking's famous dictum about Edward Burnett Tylor and Brixham Cave; see 1968, 105–106) without employing what they considered to be the kind of myth that had caused the downfall of Geoffrey's *Historia.* Here the perceptions of "everyday savage life" drawn primarily from the Amerindian ethnographies added color and texture to an account that rated literary sources as far more authoritative than either ethnography or material culture.

By the mid- to late seventeenth century, such an implicit account was not enough. The cause of this appears to be the slow recognition (drawn largely from studies by topographers, antiquaries, and others) that there was considerable variability in pre-Roman "British" material culture (and in the societies and cultures of the ethnographic other)—a variability about which the classical authors had been silent.

Here the interactionist methodology began to change in terms of the relative utility of its authorities. Now its object was more aligned toward classifying material culture and establishing meaning through comparison with the material culture of the ethnographic other, *before* applying classical and Biblical texts. An excellent and underappreciated example of this attempt to reveal a reality of the past not confined by the tastes and interests of the present is supplied by the remarkable character of John Aubrey (1626–1697) (see Hunter 1975; Fowles 1981). Although Lhwyd (Gunter 1945) and Dugdale (Hamper 1827) both emphasized the importance of empiricism to antiquarian studies, Aubrey's own statement in the only recently published *Monumenta Britannica* enhances the liberating effect of the revised interactionist methodology for the antiquaries of the seventeenth and early eighteenth centuries:

> I do here endeavour (for want of written record) to work out and restore after a kind of algebraical method, by comparing them that I have seen with one another and reducing them to a kind of equation: to (being but an ill orator myself) make the stones give evidence for themselves. (cited in Fowles 1981, xviii)

This was easier said than done. For although Aubrey could query the utility of the classical accounts, and perhaps even be wary of the application of ethnographic generalizations, nevertheless without them his "algebraical method" could rarely achieve more than description and classification. The historical meanings of the various classes of field monuments and portable artifacts still had to be established.

However, change in the interactionist methodology did not stop there. Additional tensions arose that were to occasion further doubts about the ability of antiquarian studies to banish the a priori.

Hunter (1971, 1975, 1981), Piggott (1937, 1975, 1976f, 1981, 1985a, 1985b), and Sweet (2004) have effectively demonstrated that antiquarian methodology, so much a part of Baconian empiricism, was in the course of the eighteenth century to become increasingly difficult to adhere to, as a result of the upswing in Romantic historicism and rationalism that had struck the sciences generally (see also David Miller 1981 for a broader perspective from the Royal Society during this period). Nonetheless, critical elements of the interactionist methodology remained, in the form of the authorities appealed to by William Stukeley (1687–1765) for what are now taken to be his wilder excesses of interpretation (see Chambers 1984; Piggott 1985a, 1986). In an important sense there were trends to a return of the primacy of the written text over the ethnographic other and the evidence derived from the material remains of the past.

This is not to say that Stukeley was a Camden or Speed with a rather credulous attitude to classical ethnography, oak groves, and standing stones. Instead he, like Colt-Hoare, was responding to a different set of sociopolitical forces. He was also responding to an increasing need to establish the historical meaning of the, by then, extremely confused state of inquiries into pre-Roman British antiquities. In such a circumstance the classical and Biblical authorities that had formed the essentially literary cornerstone of the interactionist methodology could only be used at the price of reduced empirical assessment. Although many found Stukeley's accounts of "barbarous Druidic rituals" among the henge monuments to be plausible, the fact remained that many were far from convinced as they contemplated the wide variability that now seemed to characterize pre-Roman British antiquities. Whereas Camden, Speed, and others could readily establish the historical value of the coins, seals, and inscriptions they used (precisely because of the presence of writing), the task of later antiquaries, such as Aubrey and Stukeley, was made the more difficult when writing no longer came to their rescue.

Consequently, the traditional reading (based on the greater authority of literary sources ably supplemented by lashings of the ethnographic other and material culture) of the interactionist methodology began to break down. How could such authorities assist in the understanding of events that they may not have witnessed? In the absence of a reliable ordering of pre-Roman antiquities, the interactionist method as practiced by Stukeley could only produce a frozen history. Meaning and, more importantly, the basis of conviction could no longer be considered to flow unproblematically from reason and the senses. The nature of British prehistory once again became shrouded in conjecture and the two goals of the interactionist methodology—an attack on mythopoeic histories and the grading of the reliability of sources of historical evidence—could not be convincingly attained.

What was urgently required was a means of sorting out the nightmare of pre-Roman British antiquities, so that the interactionist methodology could function once again. In the event the Danish scholar Christian Thomsen (1786–1865) was to provide the solution, but in so doing the new emphasis on material culture established by the Three-Age System was to effectively realign the authorities that had been the backbone of interactionism. No longer were Caesar or Strabo (or for that matter the Bible) to hold pride of place over the material remains of the past and the ethnographic other as the framework in terms of which the meaning of the material phenomena of the prehistoric British past was to be made manifest. This at least was the methodological rhetoric used by its promoters.

Concluding Remarks

In this essay I have sketched two important aspects of the context of antiquarian studies during the eighteenth century, the wider framework of thought and dispute about human nature and the meaning of human history and developments in the interactionist methodology during the sixteenth and seventeenth centuries. I have done this to establish background aspects of the "rise" of archaeology in the nineteenth century and its relationship to ethnology and anthropology. Although I have not discussed other aspects such as the "rise" of the earth sciences and the growth of antiquarian studies related to the classical world, I have broadly sketched the position of antiquarian studies on the cognitive map of human studies during the eighteenth century.

In this essay I briefly described some of the antinomies inherent in the study of human beings that began to surface between the sixteenth and eighteenth centuries. I also claimed that these antinomies greatly influenced the positions taken by disputant parties on that question of questions—the meaning of human physical, cultural, and linguistic difference. Here notions of progress and decline, arguments about the possibility of meaningfully generalizing about the experience of human history, the ontological dualism of materialism and idealism, and the epistemological conflict between empiricism and rationalism are focused in a conflict about the significance of a priori assumptions about human beings, about whether it was possible to free the study of human beings from the "tyranny of hypothesis."

Apart from demonstrating the similarity between aspects of prehistoric European technology and those of contemporary "savages," antiquarian studies were considered by the bulk of the disputant parties to be peripheral to the prosecution of this great conflict. Although all disputants considered that an understanding of human prehistory was essential to the workable solution to that question of questions, the material residues of prehistoric human action had less of a role to play than the contemplation of the ethnographic other, the evidence from physical anthropology, and the discoveries of philology.

I have explained this situation by stressing two related tensions in antiquarian studies. First, although the interactionist methodology gave meaning and texture to prehistoric material culture, it did so by assuming the interpretative and explanatory primacy of literary and ethnographic sources. If those sources were primary, what possible value was there for the disputant parties to devote their attention to the study of prehistoric material culture? Second, during the eighteenth century, the history of pre-Roman Britain became even more confusing than before. To paraphrase Nyerup, a dense fog hid the historical meaning of those antiquities (Daniel 1975, 38). The fact that the interactionist methodology, as it was constituted during that period, could do nothing to lift it, did not mean that the historical value of ethnography was denied. In fact, the reverse was true. Depending on the participant's viewpoint the only sure guides to human prehistory were the contemplation of the ethnographic other and intellectual reconstructions based on how it would have been "rational" for human beings to act. This reconstruction of the interactionist antiquarian methodology has a contemporary ring.

Therefore, although antiquarian studies had little, of themselves, to offer the student of human nature, the character of the disputes surrounding the meaning of human history directly influenced the "culture" of the antiquarians. Here were the great questions; here were the issues of moment. If the study of human antiquities, particularly those of prehistoric periods, was to attain meaning beyond the contemplation of the aesthetic or the shuffling of spearpoints in cabinets of curiosities, then practitioners needed to apply their data to answer questions of moment. Equally important was the recognition, derived from eighteenth-century human studies, that the investigation of pre-Roman British history could be conducted in terms of that question of questions.

The discovery of the ethnographic other, the recognition that ceraunia had a human origin, and the gradual formalization of human studies around the issue of the meaning of human diversity created a framework wherein material phenomena could be plausibly regarded as testimonies to prehistoric human action. This same framework also allowed the meanings of those material testimonies to be made manifest through the application of theories of human history that articulated other classes of evidence—the human physique, changes and developments in human languages, and the cultures and societies of the ethnographic other. Although there was considerable conflict over which of these theories was correct, there was general agreement about the interpretative primacy of these other classes of evidence and the critical importance of the issues that developed through the debates that had taken place during the eighteenth century.

To summarize, in my view the meaning and value of archaeological data were established primarily through their application to arguments springing from the various antinomies listed above. Thus archaeology came into existence precisely because all parties involved in such arguments were convinced that archaeological data could meaningfully contribute to their discussion and possible solution. Significantly, such a conviction was possible because a methodology had been established that could plausibly translate mute material phenomena into historical and ethnological evidence.

References

Abramowicz, A. 1981. Sponte nascitur ollae. . . . In *Towards a history of archaeology,* ed. G. Daniel, 146–149. London: Thames and Hudson.

Abrams, M. H. 1953. *The mirror and the lamp: Romantic theory and the cultural tradition.* Oxford: Oxford University Press.

Abrams, P. 1968. *The origins of British sociology 1834–1914.* Chicago: University of Chicago Press.

Abrams, P. 1982. *Historical sociology.* Ithaca, NY: Cornell University Press.

Bahn, P., ed. 1996. *The Cambridge illustrated history of archaeology.* Cambridge: Cambridge University Press.

Barnes, B., and S. Shapin, eds. 1979. *Natural order: Historical studies of scientific culture.* London: Sage.

Bendyshe, T. 1865. The history of anthropology. *Anthropological Society of London Memoirs* 1: 335–458.

Berlin, I. 1980. The concept of scientific history. *Concepts and Categories,* ed. H. Hardy, 103–142. Oxford: Oxford University Press. Originally published in *History And Theory* 1 (1960).

Berman, M. 1972. The early years of the Royal Institution 1799–1810: A re-evaluation. *Science Studies* 2: 205–240.

Blumenbach, J. F. 1795. *The anthropological treatises of Johann Friedrich Blumenbach.* Trans. and ed. T. Bendyshe. London: Longman, Roberts and Green, 1865.

Bock, K. 1978. Theories of progress, development, evolution. In *A history of sociological analysis,* ed. T. Bottomore and R. Nisbet, 39–79. New York: Basic Books.

Bottomore, T., and R. Nisbet, eds. 1978. *A history of sociological analysis.* New York: Basic Books.

Bowen, M. 1981. *Empiricism and geographical thought from Francis Bacon to Alexander Von Humboldt.* Cambridge: Cambridge University Press.

Bowler, P. J. 1976. *Fossils and progress. Palaeontology and the idea of progressive evolution in the nineteenth century.* New York: Science History Publications.

Brown, I. G. 1977. Critick in antiquity: Sir John Clerk of Penicuik. *Antiquity* 51: 201–210.

Brown, I. G. 1980. *The hobby-horsical antiquary: A Scottish character 1640–1830.* Edinburgh: National Library of Scotland.

Burchfield, J. D. 1974. Darwin and the Dilemma of geological time. *Isis* 65: 301–321.

Burchfield, J. D. 1975. *Lord Kelvin and the age of the earth.* Macmillan: London.

Burrow, J. W. 1966. *Evolution and society.* Cambridge: Cambridge University Press.

Bury, J. B. 1955. *The idea of progress.* New York: Dover.

Camden, W. 1586. *Britannia,* ed. E. Gibson. Newton Abbo, UK: David and Charles, 1971.

Cassirer, E. 1951. *The philosophy of the Enlightenment,* trans. F. C. A. Koelln and J. P. Pettegrove. Princeton, NJ: Princeton University Press.

Chambers, G. R. 1984. Archaeology, antiquities, and taste. *Archaeological Review from Cambridge* 3: 19–28.

Chambers, R. W. 1918. Geoffrey of Monmouth and the Brut as sources of early British history. *History* 3: 225–228.

Chippindale, C. 1985. *Stonehenge complete.* London: Thames and Hudson.

Condorcet, Marquis De. 1795. *Esquisse D'un Tableau Historique Des Progres De l'Esprit Humain.* Paris: Masson, 1822.

Daniel, G. E. 1943. *The Three Ages: An essay on archaeological method.* Cambridge: Cambridge University Press.

Daniel, G. E. 1950. *A hundred years of archaeology.* London: Duckworth.

Daniel, G. E. 1957. The 150th anniversary of the Danish National Museum. *Antiquity* 32: 169–171.

Daniel, G. E. 1959. The idea of man's antiquity. *Scientific American* 201: 167–176.

Daniel, G. E. 1964. *The idea of prehistory.* Harmondsworth, UK: Pelican Books.

Daniel, G. E. 1967. *The origins and growth of archaeology.* Harmondsworth, UK: Pelican Books.

Daniel, G. E. 1975. *One hundred and fifty years of archaeology.* 2nd ed. London: Duckworth.

Daniel, G. E. 1976. Cambridge and the backward looking curiosity: an inaugural lecture. Cambridge: Cambridge University Press.

Dugdale, W. 1656. *The Antiquities Of Warwickshire Illustrated; From Records, Leiger Books, Manuscripts, Charters, Evidences, Tombes, And Armes: Beautified With Maps, Prospects, And Portraitures.* London.

Evans, J. 1956. *A history of the Society of Antiquaries of London.* Oxford: Oxford University Press.

Fahenstock, P. J. 1984. History and theoretical development: The importance of a critical historiography of archaeology. *Archaeological Review from Cambridge* 3: 7–18.

Fergusson, A. B. 1979. *Clio unbound—Perception of the social and cultural past in Renaissance England.* Durham, NC: Duke University Press.

Foucault, M. 1970. *The order of things.* London: Tavistock.

Fowler, D. 1975. Notes on inquiries in anthropology: A bibliographic essay. In *Toward a science of man: Essays in the history of anthropology,* ed. T. H. H. Thoresen, 15–32. The Hague: Mouton.

Fowles, J. 1981. Foreword. In *Monumenta Britannica or a miscellany of British antiquities, Parts One and Two,* ed. J. Fowles, ix–xxii. Boston: Little, Brown.

Gay, P. 1966. *The Enlightenment.* 2 vols. New Haven, CT: Yale University Press.

Giles, J. A. 1842. *The British history of Geoffrey of Monmouth.* London: Bohn.

Goodrum, M. R. 2002. The meaning of ceraunia: archaeology, natural history and the interpretation of prehistoric stone artefacts in the eighteenth century. *British Journal of the History of Science* 2002: 255–269.

Gould, S. J. 1984. *The mismeasure of man.* Harmondsworth, UK: Penguin Books.

Gräslund, B. 1981.The background to C. J. Thomsen's Three Age System. In *Towards a history of archaeology,* ed. G. Daniel, 45–50. London: Thames and Hudson.

Grayson, D. 1983. *The establishment of human antiquity.* New York: Academic Press.

Gunter, R. T. ed. 1945. Life and letters of Edward Lhwyd. In *Early Science in Oxford,* vol. 14. London: Dawsons of Pall Mall.

Hammer, J. 1942. Some additional manuscripts of Geoffrey of Monmouth's *Historia Regnum Britanniae. Modern Language Quarterly* 3: 235–242.

Hamper, W. 1827. *Life, Diary and Correspondence of Sir William Dugdale.* London: T. Davison, printed for Harding, Lepard & Co.

Hampson, N. 1968. *The Enlightenment.* Harmondsworth, UK: Penguin Books.

Harris, M. 1968. *The rise of anthropological theory.* New York: Crowell.

Hazard, P. 1973. *The European mind 1680–1715.* Harmondsworth, UK: Penguin Books.

Heizer, R. F., ed. 1962. *Man's discovery of his past: Literary landmarks in archaeology.* Englewood Cliffs, NJ: Prentice-Hall.

Helvetius, C. A. 1777. *A treatise on man,* trans. W. Hooper. London.

Herder, J. G. Von. 1794. *Outline of a philosophy of the history of man,* trans. T. Churchill. London: Luke Hansard, 1805.

Hodgen, M. T. 1936. *The doctrine of survivals: a chapter in the history of scientific method in the study of man.* London: Allenson.

Hodgen, M. T. 1964. *Early anthropology in the sixteenth and seventeenth centuries.* Philadelphia: University of Pennsylvania Press.

Holbach, P. von. 1770. *Systeme De La Nature.* London: Amsterdam: M. M. Rey.

Horsman, R. 1976. Origins of racial Anglo-Saxonism in Great Britain before 1850. *Journal of the History of Ideas* 37: 387–410.

Hulton, P., and D. B. Quinn. 1964. *The American drawings of John White.* London: British Museum Press.

Hunter, M. 1971. The Royal Society and the origins of British archaeology. *Antiquity* 45: 113–121; 187–192.

Hunter, M. 1975. *John Aubrey and the realm of learning.* London: Duckworth.

Hunter, M. 1981. *Science and society in Restoration England.* Cambridge: Cambridge University Press.

Jacob, J. R. 1975. Restoration, reformation and the origins of the Royal Society. *History of Science* 13: 155–176.

Jacob, J. R., and M. C. Jacob. 1980. The Anglican origins of modern science: The metaphysical foundations of the Whig constitution. *Isis* 71: 251–267.

Jones, T. 1964. The early evolution of the legend of Arthur. *Nottingham Mediaeval Studies* 8: 3–21.

Kendrick, T. D. 1950. *British antiquity.* London: Methuen.

Klindt-Jensen, O. 1975. *A history of Scandinavian archaeology.* London: Thames and Hudson.

Kristiansen, K. 1981. A social history of Danish archaeology (1805–1975). In *Towards a history of archaeology,* ed. G. Daniel, 20–44. London: Thames and Hudson.

Laming-Emperaire, A. 1964. *Origines de l'archeologie prehistorique en France.* Paris: A. and J. Picard.

Langham, I. 1981. *The building of British social anthropology: W.H.R. Rivers and his Cambridge disciples in the development of kinship studies, 1898–1931.* Dordrecht, The Netherlands: Reidel.

Laudan, L. 1969. Theories of scientific method from Plato to Mach: A bibliographical review. *History of Science* 7: 1–63.

Laudan, R. 1985. Review of Paolo Rossi the Dark Abyss of Time: the history of the earth and the history of nations from Hooke to Vico. *Philosophy of Science* 52: 644–645.

Leaf, M. 1979. *Man, mind and science.* New York: Columbia University Press.

Lemaine, G., R. Macleod, M. Mulkay, and P. Weingart, eds. 1976. *Perspectives on the emergence of scientific disciplines.* The Hague: Mouton.

Leone, M. P. 1973. Archaeology as the science of technology: Mormon town plans and fences. In *Research and Theory in Current Archaeology,* ed. C. Redmond, 125–150. New York: Wiley.

Leopold, J. 1980. *Culture in comparative and evolutionary perspective: E.B. Tylor and the making of primitive culture.* Berlin: Dietrich Reimer Verlag.

Levy, F. J. 1964. The making of Camden's *Britannia. Bibliotheque d'Humanisme Et Renaissance* 37: 70–98.

Levy, F. J. 1967. *Tudor historical thought.* San Marino, CA: The Huntington Library.

Lloyd, J. E. 1942. Geoffrey of Monmouth. *English Historical Review* 57: 460–468.

Locke, J. 1692. *An essay concerning human understanding.* Oxford: Clarendon, 1894.

Lovejoy, A. O. 1964. *The Great Chain of Being.* Cambridge, MA: Harvard University Press.

Lowie, R. H. 1937. *The history of ethnological theory.* New York: Random House.

MacCaffrey, W. T. 1970. Introduction. In *The History of the Most Renowned and Victorious Princess Elizabeth Late Queen of England,* by W. Camden, xi–xxxix. Chicago: University of Chicago Press.

McLean, A. 1972. *Humanism and the rise of science.* London: Heinemann.

McVicar, J. B. 1984a. Theme editorial. *Archaeological Review from Cambridge* 3: 2–6.

McVicar, J. B. 1984b. Social change and the growth of antiquarian studies in Tudor and Stuart England. *Archaeological Review from Cambridge* 3: 48–67.

Mandrou, R. 1978. *From humanism to science 1480–1700.* Harmondsworth, UK: Penguin Books.

Mayr, E. 1982. *The growth of biological thought. Diversity, evolution, inheritance.* Cambridge, MA: Belknap Press.

Mays, M. 1981. Strabo IV 4.1: A reference to Hengistbury Head? *Antiquity* 55: 55–57.

Meinecke, F. 1972. Historism: The rise of the new historical outlook. London: Routledge and Kegan Paul.

Michell, J. 1982. *Megalithomania: Artists, antiquarians and archaeologists at the old stone monuments.* London: Thames and Hudson.

Miller, D. 1981. The Royal Society of London, 1800–1835: A study in the cultural politics of scientific organization. Ph.D. diss., University of Pennsylvania.

Mirrlees, H. 1962. *A fly in amber . . . an extravagant biography of the romantic antiquary Sir Robert Bruce Cotton.* London: Faber.

Monboddo, J. B. 1774. *Of the origin and process of language,* vol. 1. Edinburgh: J. Balfour and T. Cadell.

Montesquieu, de. 1748. *The Spirit of the Laws.* New York: Hafner, 1949.

Moravia, S. 1980. The Enlightenment and the sciences of man. *History of Science* 18: 247–268.

Mulligan, L., and G. Mulligan. 1981. Reconstructing restoration science: Styles of leadership and social composition of the early Royal Society. *Social Studies of Science* 11: 327–364.

Murray, T. 1976. Aspects of polygenism in the works of Robert Knox and James Hunt. B.A. (Hons) thesis, University Of Sydney.

Oakley, K. P. 1976. The Piltdown problem reconsidered. *Antiquity* 50: 9–13.

Pagden, A. 1982. *The fall of natural man: The American Indian and the origins of comparative ethnology.* Cambridge: Cambridge University Press.

Parry, G. 1995. *Trophies of time.* Oxford: Oxford University Press.

Peake, H. J. E. 1940. The study of prehistoric times. *Journal of the Royal Anthropological Institute* 70: 103–146.

Piggott, S. 1937. Prehistory and the Romantic Movement. *Antiquity* 11: 31–38.

Piggott, S. 1941. The Sources of Geoffrey of Monmouth. *Antiquity* 15: 269–286.

Piggott, S. 1950. *William Stukeley: An eighteenth century antiquary.* Oxford: Oxford University Press.

Piggott, S. 1975. *The druids.* London: Thames and Hudson.

Piggott, S. 1976a. *Ruins in a landscape: Essays in antiquarianism.* Edinburgh: Edinburgh University Press.

Piggott, S. 1976b. Antiquarian thought in the sixteenth and seventeenth centuries. In *Ruins in a landscape: Essays in antiquarianism,* ed. S. Piggott, 1–24. Edinburgh: Edinburgh University Press.

Piggott, S. 1976c. William Camden and *the Britannia.* In *Ruins in a landscape: Essays in antiquarianism,* ed. S. Piggott, 33–54. Edinburgh: Edinburgh University Press.

Piggott, S. 1976d. Brazilian Indians on an Elizabethan monument. In *Ruins in a landscape: Essays in antiquarianism,* ed. S. Pigott, 25–32. Edinburgh: Edinburgh University Press.

Piggott, S. 1976e. Celts, Saxons and the early Antiquaries. In *Ruins in a landscape: Essays in antiquarianism,* ed. S. Pigott, 55–76. Edinburgh: Edinburgh University Press.

Piggott, S. 1976f. Ruins in a landscape. Aspects of seventeenth and eighteenth century antiquarianism. In *Ruins In A Landscape: Essays In Antiquarianism,* ed. S. Pigott, 101–132. Edinburgh: Edinburgh University Press.

Piggott, S. 1976g. The ancestors of Jonathan Oldbuck. In *Ruins in a landscape: Essays in antiquarianism,* ed. S. Pigott, 133–160. Edinburgh: Edinburgh University Press.

Piggott, S. 1976h. The origins of the English county archaeological societies. In *Ruins in a landscape: Essays in antiquarianism,* ed. S. Pigott, 171–195. Edinburgh: Edinburgh University Press.

Piggott, S. 1978. *Antiquity depicted: Aspects of archaeological illustration.* London: Thames and Hudson.

Piggott, S. 1981. "Vast perennial memorials": The first antiquaries look at megaliths. In *Antiquity and man,* ed. J. D. Evans, B. Cunliffe, and C. Renfrew, 19–25. London: Thames and Hudson.

Piggott, S. 1985a. *William Stukeley: An eighteenth century antiquary.* 2nd rev. ed. London: Thames and Hudson.

Piggott, S. 1985b. Dr Plot, ring ditches and the fairies. *Antiquity* 59: 206–209.

Piggott, S. 1986. William Stukeley: New facts and an old forgery. *Antiquity* 60: 115–122.

Porter, R. S. 1977. *The making of geology. Earth science in Britain 1660–1815.* Cambridge: Cambridge University Press.

Prawer, S. S., ed. 1970. *The Romantic Period in Germany.* London: Weidenfeld and Nicholson.

Rodden, J. 1981. The development of the Three Age System: Archaeology's first paradigm. In *Towards a History of Archaeology,* ed. G. Daniel, 51–68. London: Thames and Hudson.

Rousseau, G. S., and R. S. Porter, eds. 1981. *The ferment of knowledge: Studies in the historiography of the eighteenth century.* Cambridge: Cambridge University Press.

Rousseau, J. 1755. *First and second discourses.* New York: St. Martin's, 1964.

Rousseau, J. 1762. *The social contract.* Dutton: New York, 1938.

Rowe, J. H. 1975. Review of "A History of American Archaeology," by G. R. Willey and J. A. Sabloff. *Antiquity* 49: 156–158.

Rudwick, M. J. 1963. The foundation of the Geological Society of London: Its scheme for co-operative research and its struggle for independence. *British Journal for the History of Science* 1: 326–355.

Rudwick, M. J. 1971. Uniformity and progress, reflections on the structure of geological theory in the age of Lyell. In *Perspectives in the History of Science and Technology,* ed. D. Roller, 209–227. Norman: University of Oklahoma Press.

Rudwick, M. J. 1972. *The meaning of fossils: Episodes in the history of palaeontology.* London: Macdonald and Co.

Schenk, H. G. 1966. *The mind of the European romantics.* London: Constable.

Schnapp, A. 1996. *The discovery of the past.* London: British Museum Press.

Schnapp, A. 2002. Between antiquarians and archaeologists—continuities and ruptures. *Antiquity* 76: 134–140.

Service, E. R. 1985. *A century of controversy: Ethnological issues from 1860–1960.* Orlando, FL: Academic Press.

Sklenar, K. 1983. *Archaeology in Central Europe: the first 500 Years.* Leicester, UK: Leicester University Press.

Sorabji, R. 1983. *Time, creation, and the continuum: Theories in antiquity and the early Middle Ages.* Ithaca, NY: Cornell University Press.

Southern, R. W. 1973. Aspects of the European tradition of historical writing: The sense of the past. *Transactions of the Royal Historical Society* 5th Series, xxxiii: 246–256.

Speed, J. 1632. *The historie of Great Britaine.* London: John Dawson for George Humble.

Stocking, G. W., Jr. 1968. *Race, culture, and evolution.* New York: Free Press.

Stocking, G. W., Jr. 1971.What's in a name? The origins of the Royal Anthropological Institute (1837–71). *Man* (Ns) 6: 369–390.

Stocking, G. W., Jr. 1973. From chronology to ethnology: James Cowles Prichard and British Anthropology, 1800–1850. In The Reprint Edition of J. C. Prichard *Researches into the Physical History of Man* (1831), ix–cx. Chicago: University of Chicago Press.

Stocking, G. W., Jr. 1983a. History of anthropology. Whence/whither. In *Observers observed. Essays on ethnographic fieldwork,* ed. G. W. Stocking, 3–12. Madison: University of Wisconsin Press.

Stocking, G. W., Jr. 1983b. The ethnographer's magic. Fieldwork in British anthropology from Tylor to Malinowski. In *Observers observed. Essays on ethnographic fieldwork,* ed. G. W. Stocking, 70–120. Madison: University of Wisconsin Press.

Stocking, G. W., Jr. 1984. Functionalism historicized. In *Observers observed. Essays on ethnographic fieldwork,* ed. G. W. Stocking, 3–9. Madison: University of Wisconsin Press.

Stocking, G. W., Jr. 1987. *Victorian anthropology*. New York: Free Press.

Styles, P. 1956. Politics and historical research in the early seventeenth century. In *English historical scholarship in the sixteenth and seventeenth centuries,* ed. L. Fox, 44–72. London: Oxford University Press.

Sweet, R. 2004. *Antiquaries. The discovery of the past in eighteenth century Britain.* London: Hambledon and London.

Tatlock, J. S. P. 1950. *The legendary history of Britain. Geoffrey of Monmouth's Historia Regnum Britanniae and its early vernacular versions.* Berkeley: University of California Press.

Teggart, F. J., ed. 1949. *The idea of progress.* Rev. ed. Berkeley: University of California Press.

Trigger, B. G. 1989. *A history of archaeological thought.* Cambridge: Cambridge University Press.

Trompf, G. 1979. *The idea of historical recurrence in Western thought, from antiquity to the Reformation.* Berkeley: University of California Press.

Turgot, A. R. J. 1750. *Plan de deux discours sur l'histoire universelle.* Paris: Guillaumin, 1844.

Urry, J. 1984. Englishmen, Celts and Iberians: The ethnographic survey of the United Kingdom 1892–1899. In *Functionalism historicized,* ed. G. W. Stocking, Jr., 83–105. Madison: University of Wisconsin Press.

Vico, G. 1948. *The new science.* Ithaca, NY: Cornell University Press.

Voget, F. W. 1975. *A history of ethnology.* New York: Holt, Rinehart and Winston.

Voltaire. 1745. Essai sur les moeurs et l'esprit des nations. Paris: Chez Werdet Et Lequien Fils, 1829.

Walzel, O. 1965. *German romanticism.* New York: Frederick Unger.

Weber, G. 1974. Science and society in nineteenth century anthropology. *History of Science* 15: 260–283.

Wilson, D. 1862. *Prehistoric man,* 2 vols. London: Macmillan.

Wood, P. 1980. Methodology and apologetics: Thomas Sprat's history of the Royal Society. *British Journal for the History of Science* 13: 1–26.

MILESTONES BEFORE 1800

Historia Regum Britanniae *(1138)*

Written by the medieval scholar and historian Geoffrey of Monmouth (ca. 1100–1154) the *Historia* was widely available in Benedictine monastic libraries in Britain and Normandy in some form by 1139. The surviving edition of the *Historia* is believed to date from 1147. It comprises Geoffrey's medieval Latin translations and retellings of ancient British legends from written Latin, Cymric (Welsh), and Breton sources of the eighth, ninth, and tenth centuries.

Some of these sources detailed the settling of Britain by the Trojan Brutus, who defeated two giants, founded the city of New Troy (London), and went on to conquer the whole island, which was called Brutayne after him. After his death, the kingdom was divided among his three sons into England, Scotland, and Wales. While this legend was based on the extant work of the chronicler Nennius, another, which details a long list of pre-Roman British kings, seems to be invented. Many of Geoffrey's sources have been lost.

Trojan antecedents firmly established Britain as a country of ancient and epic origins, clearly an appropriate historical pedigree to underpin its burgeoning political greatness. At the same time that Geoffrey was turning myth into history, historians working in other European kingdoms were involved in the same process, recording stories that established the antiquity of their national foundations and their descent from classical heroes. The Trojan foundation myth of Britain remained popular and unchallenged until the sixteenth century, when Tudor historian Polydore Vergil questioned its authenticity.

But writing a history for the whole of the twelfth century British kingdom—the island of Britain and a large part of northern France—required that other more recent and widespread myths and legends had to be recorded. In the retelling of the stories about the pre-Saxon King Arthur and his knights, Geoffrey of Monmouth drew on a shared Celtic or Gaulish mythology, which belonged to the Breton speakers of the English kingdom—in Wales, Normandy, Brittany, and other parts of Britain and France. Indeed, the Breton languages spoken in Wales and in Brittany were almost identical at the time that Geoffrey was working on his book and remained so until the reign of Henry I, when they developed substantial differences.

Geoffrey of Monmouth was a Benedictine scholar, raised by an uncle who was an archbishop. Geoffrey became a priest at the age of 50 and died a bishop. It was not coincidental that the Benedictine order was well established within the Breton-speaking areas of Britain and France, nor that they were Geoffrey's patrons and promulgators of copies of his book. It was also to their advantage to have a way of uniting disparate groups within their parishes. The first mention of Geoffrey's book was by Henry of Huntingdon in 1139, who records that he read it in the company of Theobald, the archbishop of Canterbury, in a Benedictine monastery in Normandy on their way to Rome.

The publication of *Historia Regum Britanniae* marks a milestone in the literary history of Europe. Within fifty years of its completion, stories about the Holy Grail, Lancelot, Tristan, Perceval, and the Round Table had appeared, and Merlin and Arthur had become as popular in Germany and Italy as they were in England and France. The book was later translated into Anglo-Norman, and then translated into English in 1240.

As important as its long-term impact on European civilization was, the *Historia's* short-term influence on the people of greater Britain, which included a large part of France at the time, was even greater. The popularity of the legends and stories published there helped to defuse racial animosities among Welsh, Breton, British, French, and Teuton, and these various groups became more politically unified through their mutual belief in a shared origin and history.

See also Publication of the *Anglica Historia* (1512); Publication of *Britannia* (1586).

Further Reading

Curley, M. J. 1994. *Geoffrey of Monmouth.* New York: Twayne.
Kendrick, T. D. 1950. *British antiquity.* New York: Barnes and Noble.

Voyages of Cyriac of Ancona (1412–1449)

An indefatigable traveler whose diaries and letters received wide circulation among those (particularly in Italy) who were interested in the classical past, Cyriac—or Ciriaco de' Pizzecolli (1391–1452)—played a foundational role in raising the awareness among early Renaissance scholars of the material remains of (especially) classical Greece. Cyriac, as a merchant and diplomatic agent working for the Vatican, was extremely well connected, and his observations of sites and their contents (particularly inscriptions and statues) were acute. He was also quite aware of the fact that so much of what he was seeing was in the process of disappearing through destruction, neglect, or simple decay over time.

In the course of his travels (1412–1449) Cyriac copied nearly a thousand inscriptions in Greek and Latin from as far afield as Italy, Greece, the Aegean, and Asia Minor. His diaries also contain detailed drawings of carvings, statues, and buildings, many of which have long since vanished.

See also Raphael's Survey of Rome (1519); Publication of *Britannia* (1586).

Further Reading

Ashmole, B. 1956. Cyriacus of Ancona and the Temple of Hadrian at Cyzicus. *Journal of the Warburg and Courtauld Institute* xix: 179–191.

Bodnar, E. W., and C. Foss. 2003. *Cyriac of Ancona: Later Travels.* The I Tatti Renaissance Library. Cambridge MA: Harvard University Press.

Momigliano, A. 1950. Ancient history and the antiquarian. *Journal of the Warburg and Courtauld Institute* xiii: 285–315.

Weiss, R. 1969. *The Renaissance discovery of classical antiquity.* Oxford: Blackwell.

Foundation of the Palazzo dei Conservatori (1471)

Three thousand years of continuous occupation has made the city of Rome a massive archaeological site. Since its fall in the fifth century AD, Romans could readily observe their city's past, and the construction of any new building there usually entailed the unearthing of still more. Unfortunately the remnants of buildings were so numerous that they were also an excellent source of building material. Rome of the Middle Ages and Renaissance not only stood on its past, it was literally constructed from pieces of it.

During the Middle Ages, the Lateran church built by the emperor Constantine housed a collection of ancient Roman bronze statuary unearthed from the site. The acquisition of classical works of art by the Roman Catholic Church was testimony to its inheritance of the power and glory of ancient Rome. In 1471, Pope Sixtus IV passed an edict forbidding the exploitation and export of antiquities, which were being excavated and sold and were leaving the city of Rome at a rapid rate. At the same time, in an effort to raise the level of appreciation of Roman art and antiquities, to proclaim them part of the glories of present-day Rome, and to try to stop the best pieces from leaving Rome itself, Sixtus IV founded the world's first public museum in the Palazzo dei Conservatori on the Capitoline Hill.

The first statues to be taken to the Palazzo for public exhibition were those in the Lateran: *Lo Spinario* (boy removing a thorn); the *Capitoline Wolf* (which was in fact Etruscan); the *Capitoline Camillus;* and a colossal marble head, hand, and globe from a figure believed to be Constantius II. To these Sixtus IV added the recently excavated gilded bronze statue of Hercules and two marble works of art—the ossuary of Agrippina the Elder and a fragment of a larger group of a lion and a horse. Together they became the best display of antiquities in Rome at that time, better than any contemporary private collection, and they attracted great numbers of local and international visitors to the city.

As part of the rebuilding of the city of Rome, Michelangelo was contracted to redesign and remodel the Capitoline, which included building the twin of the Palazzo dei Conservatori, the Palazzo Nuovo, which was finished in 1655. The collections housed in these palazzi grew throughout the sixteenth, seventeenth, and eighteenth centuries through the generosity of popes, who not only donated parts of their own collections but also purchased other private collections to prevent their being lost to Rome. These included the collection of Cardinal Albani, comprising 408 sculptures, both Roman Imperial portraits and images of philosophers, and some of the great statues excavated at Hadrian's villa, such as the *Dying Trumpeter or Gladiator,* and the *Capitoline Venus and Faun.* Both palazzi were amalgamated, renamed, and reestablished as the Musei Capitolini in 1816, after significant parts of their collections, which had been pillaged by Napoleon I in 1797, were repatriated.

In 1503 Pope Julius II, the Medici patron of Raphael and Michelangelo, founded another museum in the Belvedere Palazzetto in the Vatican. He donated the *Belvedere Apollo* to be the center of the new collection on display, and it was joined by other famous pieces such as *Laocoön.* This was the beginning of what was later to become the Vatican Museum. From the start it attracted a different audience than that of the Palazzo dei Conservatori, that of artists, scholars, and students. Through these visitors the collections of the Belvedere Palazzetto had a significant impact of the tastes and artistic ideals of the aristocrats and royal families of Europe. King Francis I of France selected this collection for casts to be made to take back to Paris to influence the artists of France, which he saw as the new Rome.

See also Raphael's Survey of Rome (1519); Duke of Arundel Brings His Collection of Classical Antiquities to London (1613); Foundation of the French Academy in Rome (1666); Grand Tour and the Society of Dilettanti (1670–1780); Napoleon Loots Rome (1797).

Further Reading

Jones, H. S., ed. 1926. *The sculptures of the Palazzo dei Conservatori by members of the British School at Rome.* Oxford: Clarendon Press.

Schnapp, A. 1996. *The discovery of the past.* London: British Museum Press.

Publication of the Anglica Historia *(1512)*

Sent by the pope to England in 1501 to collect Vatican taxes, the Italian Polydore Vergil (ca. 1470–1555) stayed on, at the invitation of Henry VII, to write a new Tudor history of England. He became an English subject, and eventually an archdeacon in the church, finishing the first manuscript version of his history in 1512. However, two more editions were printed and published in Basel (in what became modern Switzerland). The first, published in 1534, covered British history up until 1513, and the second, published in 1555, covered events until 1538. Vergil returned to Italy in 1553 after surviving the reign of Henry VIII, eyewitness to a politically turbulent time in England.

Vergil's history of England claimed to be more objective than all others that had gone before. This was partly attributable to the fact that he was a foreigner and less attached to popular national myths and partly because he was a secular Renaissance scholar and a humanist. The latter fact meant that Vergil valued evidence and argument and investigated and compared records and sources. However, notwithstanding his commitment to the tenets of humanism, he was not above attributing events to evil spirits and turning history into propaganda. The book was dedicated to Henry VIII, the Tudor king who was most determined to enhance his dynasty's grip on power by using the past to support its right to rule. There are even rumors (unconfirmed) that Vergil destroyed documents that did not support his interpretation of the Tudor ascendancy.

The *Anglica Historia* was organized chronologically; it began with an introductory description of English geography and demography and then lists of kings' reigns and events up until the beginning of the sixteenth century (in later editions until the mid-sixteenth century). Where it differed from other histories was in its investigations of details, its examination of the facts and evidence of previous inferences, and its new interpretations of the latter, only some of which were obvious propaganda for the Tudors. It also differed in that Vergil not only wrote about the early history of Britain but also wrote about more recent history. He recorded the memories of his contemporaries, the differences between current and older languages and oral traditions, and his observations of current English customs.

However, Vergil's history became most contentious when he examined the Brutus foundation myth as recorded by Geoffrey of Monmouth. He looked hard at the evidence and sources and found no reliable records to support Geoffrey's account, judging it to lack credibility. He proposed that the first settlement of Britain was probably by Gaulish tribes from across the English Channel in France. This new barbaric past, so different from Geoffrey's glamorous classical one, made Vergil's whole history unpopular in England. It was republished and circulated in Europe as the definitive account of English history, but reviled in England as a Roman Catholic attack on national traditions.

Researching and writing history in Tudor times could be very dangerous. In 1513 Vergil fell out with the powerful Cardinal Wolsey and was imprisoned in the Tower of London. It was only the personal intervention of the pope that freed him. Consequently, his descriptions of Wolsey and his part in events during the English Reformation were hardly objective. By 1533, Henry VIII was citing Vergil's *Anglica Historia* accounts of King Henry I and his power struggles with the church as historical precedents that helped support the validity of his usurpation of the Roman Catholic Church's powers and the establishment of the Church of England with Henry as its head.

See also *Historia Regum Britanniae* (1138); Creation of the King's Antiquary (1533); Publication of *Britannia* (1586).

Further Reading

Kendrick, T. 1950. *British antiquity.* London: Methuen.

Parry, G. 1995. *Trophies of time.* Oxford: Oxford University Press.

Vergil, P. *The Anglica Historia of Polydore Vergil, A.D. 1485–1537,* D. Hay (ed. and trans.) Camden Series, 1950. London: Office of the Royal Historical Society.

Raphael's Survey of Rome (1519)

Raphael Sanzio (1483–1520), the great Florentine Renaissance painter who created his most famous work in Rome, was also an architect and one of the first archaeological draftsmen. Raphael was commissioned by Pope Julius II to

Portrait of Raphael Sanzio. (Corbis)

paint frescoes in the Vatican, and the images he used in these alone would testify to his close observation and knowledge of the ruins of the classical world and to his ability to reconstruct them. However, one of his greatest achievements was associated with his appointment in 1514, by the Medici pope Leo X, to design the basilica of Saint Peter in the Vatican. As part of his preparation Raphael studied the architectural ruins of Rome in an effort to create a new style melding Rome's glorious past with its powerful Christian present.

As a consequence of these detailed studies Raphael wrote to Leo X requesting that the pope halt the destruction of significant ancient ruins. He noted that in the twelve years of his living in Rome so much had been lost that "it has been the shame of our age to have permitted it" (Schnapp 1996, 341). In response, Leo X commissioned Raphael to survey and record ruins so that they might be reconstructed. This task was apparently finished in 1519, but few drawings survive, and the study was never published. Raphael also recommended that the buildings, statues, and architectural material not be used as sources for contemporary buildings, but it was to be fourteen years before Leo X established the Offices of the Papal Commissioner of Treasures and other for Antiquities and Mines to control the exploitation of Rome's heritage.

It is the letter itself that had the greatest and most immediate impact. In it Raphael recommended that the study of art and archaeology be taken seriously, and he introduced two concepts on which the study would be founded: period style and classical orders. Raphael's proposed survey and reconstruction of ancient Rome, and his descriptions and analysis of classical architecture and classical style with which he argues in support of conservation and reconstruction, had a major impact on other artists, scholars, and architects. The survey and recording methodologies Raphael and his staff developed clearly demonstrated that the material evidence of the past could be valued as a source of knowledge and not just as building material. So too the interest of historians in classical texts, and the interest of antiquarians in coins, gems, and pottery, spread to other cities in Italy, creating a broader interest in and respect for remnants of the past.

Raphael died prematurely in 1520, and Michelangelo finished the design of St. Peter's in his stead. Raphael did, however, finish the superb frescoes in the Logge Vaticane commissioned by Leo X, which not only reflect his extensive knowledge of the classical world, but also his investigations into, and reproduction of, ancient stucco and fresco painting techniques. They stand as one of the most remarkable artistic achievements of the Italian Renaissance.

See also Foundation of the Palazzo dei Conservatori (1471): Foundation of the Accademia dei Lincei (1603).

Further Reading

Schnapp, A. 1996. *The discovery of the past.* London: British Museum Press.

Creation of the King's Antiquary (1533)

John Leland (1506–1552) was educated at St. Paul's School, Christ's College Cambridge, and All Soul's College Oxford and in Paris. He became a priest and in 1530 became Henry VIII's chaplain and librarian. In 1533 the special position of King's Antiquary was created for Leland, and he was authorized to search for manuscripts of historical interest. From 1536 until 1542 he undertook an antiquarian tour of England and Wales, inspecting monuments, buildings, and libraries of manuscripts, documents, and records. As a result of this he presented to Henry a volume later edited as *The Laboryouse Journey and the Serche of J. Leylande for Englandes Antiquities, given of Hym as a Newe Yeares Gyfte to Kinge Henry the VIII* in 1549. Consequently, Leland has been acknowledged as England's first true antiquary.

A recorder of details and a collector of information, Leland tried to convince Henry to found a national library to collect and preserve the many records he had located that were put at risk during the Reformation of the church in England. He was a more conventional historian than Polydore Vergil; he did not query the Brutus foundation myth or the interpretations of previous historians.

Leland subsequently planned to write a book of "the history and antiquities of the nation" that would provide an encyclopedic topographical account of Britain with descriptions of great families and royal palaces and updated chronicles of kings and aristocrats, but the huge task of sorting and compiling vast collections of records seems to have overwhelmed him. He became ill and died before its completion. Leland's manuscripts, including his five-volume *Collectanea,* which was the basis of his unfinished work, his notes on antiquities, catalogs of manuscripts in monastic libraries, and account of British writers were deposited in 1632 in the Bodleian Library at Oxford, where other antiquarians, especially William Camden and William Dugdale, used them. His work remains one of the few accounts of England and its antiquities recorded during the first few years of the Reformation, while the medieval church still had some power and many of its treasures were intact, and before its dissolution and the resulting social upheavals.

See also *Historia Regum Britanniae* (1138); Publication of the *Anglica Historia* (1512); English Antiquaries and Antiquarian Societies (1586–1770); Publication of *The Antiquities of Warwickshire* (1656).

Further Reading

Burton, E. 1896. *The life of John Leland (the first English antiquary) with extensive notes and a bibliography of his works, including those in ms / printed from a hitherto unpublished work by the learned Edward Burton.* London: A. Cooper.

Leland, J. 1710–12. *The itinerary: of John Leland the Antiquary, in nine volumes.* Published by Mr. Thomas Hearne. Oxford: Printed at the Theater.

Leland, J. 1907. *The itinerary of John Leland in or about the years 1535–1543,* ed. L. Toulmin Smith. London: G. Bell.

Parry, G. 1995. *The trophies of time: English antiquarians of the seventeenth century.* Oxford: Oxford University Press.

Publication of Britannia *(1586)*

At the tender age of 31, William Camden (1551–1623) took his prodigious learning in the classics, numismatics, geography, topography, and history and created *Britannia,* one of the truly enduring works of the English Renaissance. Written in Latin and translated into English by Philemon Holland in 1610, *Britannia* (through successive editions and revisions—1587, 1590, 1594, 1600, and 1607) set the benchmark for English antiquarian studies for years to come.

Camden was eminently suited to his task. Educated at Oxford, he became a schoolmaster, which afforded him considerable time to undertake antiquarian journeys during holidays. In 1592 he was made headmaster of Westminster School, and in 1597 formal government recognition of his erudition followed when he was first appointed Richmond Herald, then promoted to Clarenceux King of Arms within the College of Arms. For Camden, a Renaissance humanist, the notion of making the classical sources relevant to understanding the contemporary world was deeply ingrained. But Camden was

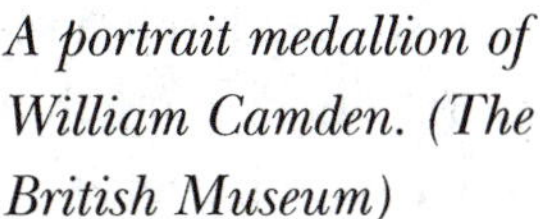
A portrait medallion of William Camden. (The British Museum)

also an Englishman of his time—proud of the singular history of the country and enormously proud of its potential. Antiquarian pursuits were hardly apolitical.

In 1577 the Flemish geographer Abraham Ortelius urged him to compile his antiquarian research (really peregrinations through the English countryside) into a book where the Roman geography of the *Antonine Itinerary* and other similar texts would be brought into the modern world. This would have the dual effect of enhancing classical scholarship and creating new knowledge about Roman antiquities in England. But the *Britannia* achieved far more than this. Indeed, while paying due attention to Roman remains, Camden's most serious focus was on British antiquities that had presumably been created before the arrival of the Romans. It seems that the many journeys into the countryside had helped him fall under the spell of British history and make a serious and rational attempt to write the history of the country before the coming of the Romans (and therefore of history itself).

What Camden was able to do was to articulate numerous lines of evidence (and the power of his own thought) to create a history that referenced the Romans (and later the Saxons) as crucial points of knowledge that could be taken back into the deeper past. Camden used the Roman ethnographies and geographies and his own comprehensive knowledge of numismatics, geography, linguistics, and field monuments to create a new methodology for antiquarianism that was to provide a model for his successors, such as John Speed.

The *Britannia* is firmly rooted in place and landscape. Camden's method was to provide clear and detailed descriptions of places, regions, and counties that directly connected people to the landscape—both ruined and living. What shines through hundreds of years later is this sense of connection and Camden's evolving capacity to make history where previously there was none. By working with *all* the information—textual, geographical, artifactual—and the results of personal observation he had at hand, Camden succeeded in creating something entirely new and setting a challenge to his successors that they were rarely able to meet. *Britannia* is a sure testimony to the benefits of fieldwork, but it is a surer testimony of the power of Camden's intellect.

See also *Historia Regum Britanniae* (1138); Publication of the *Anglica Historia* (1512); Creation of the King's Antiquary (1533); English Antiquaries and Antiquarian Societies (1586–1770); Publication of *The Antiquities of Warwickshire* (1656).

Further Reading

Boon, G. C. 1987. Camden and the *Britannia*. *Archaeologia Cambrensis* 136: 1–19.

Camden, W. 1722. *Britannia : or a chorographical description of Great Britain and Ireland, together with the adjacent islands. Written in Latin by William Camden, . . . and translated into English, with additions and improvements by Edmund Gibson.* London: printed by Mary Matthews, for Awnsham Churchill, and sold by William Taylor.

Camden, W. 1971. *Camden's Britannia, 1695 a facsimile of the 1695 edition published by Edmund Gibson [translated from the Latin], with an introduction by Stuart Piggott and a bibliographical note by Gwyn Walters.* Newton Abbott, UK: David and Charles.

Herendeen, W. H. 1988. William Camden: Historian, herald, and antiquary. *Studies in Philology* 85: 192–210.

Houts, E. M. C. van. 1992. Camden, Cotton and the Chronicles of the Norman Conquest of England. *British Library Journal* 18: 148–162.

Kendrick, T. D. 1950. *British antiquity.* London: Methuen.

Nurse, B. 1993. The 1610 edition of Camden's *Britannia. Antiquaries Journal* 73: 158–160.

Parry, G. 1995. *Trophies of time.* Oxford: Oxford University Press.

Piggott, S. 1951. William Camden and the *Britannia. Proceedings of the British Academy* 37: 199–217.

English Antiquaries and Antiquarian Societies (1586–1770)

The research and publication of William Camden's *Britannia* in 1586 inspired the foundation of the Elizabethan Society of Antiquaries. This organization was made up of Camden's gentlemen friends and fellow scholars, Robert Cotton, John Stow, and Henry Spelman; colleagues and fellow heralds William Dethick and Francis Thynne; and keepers of state archives Arthur Agarde and Thomas Talbot, all of whom had assisted Camden with their expertise while he was compiling *Britannia.* All were antiquarians and were fascinated by antiquity or by antique sources, monuments, and artifacts.

Camden had been inspired to compile *Britannia* by the Flemish geographer Abraham Ortelius, who contacted him to compare notes on former Roman provinces. Through him, Camden and his fellow English antiquarians corresponded with a network of antiquarian scholars all over Europe, such as Nicholas Fabri de Peiresc in France and Ole Worm in Denmark.

Camden and *Britannia* established the credentials of British antiquarians and distinguished them from historians. Antiquarians recorded antiquities and did not write history or rely on the work of other historians. They also organized their knowledge differently; historians of the time worked chronologically, while antiquarians organized their material according to landscape,

John Aubrey. (From John Britton's Memoir of Aubrey, *published in 1841)*

regions or rivers, and parishes; through customs, institutions, and laws; by types of objects, such as coins and inscriptions; or by types of monuments, such as standing stones or graves.

From 1586 and for the next twenty years the Elizabethan Antiquarian Society held regular meetings to discuss the research of its members at various locations all over London—Robert Cotton's library, the Inns of Court, the Herald's Office, or the Record Office in the Tower of London. And once the Roman provinces had been explored it became necessary to look at monuments and artifacts and customs that originated before or after Rome. There was much to do, and the society thrived. Later members included Archbishop Ussher, Elias Ashmole, John Aubrey, and the Earl of Arundel.

Meetings of the Elizabethan Antiquarian Society continued until 1607 when King James I expressed his displeasure with their activities. It has been suggested that perhaps this was because of the society's recent examinations of the history of Parliament and its relationship with the king and the origins of his privileges. Or because the Stuart hold on power was so tenuous that history of any kind (but more recent history in particular) was seen as a threat, and there was a real fear of secret societies and their possible political activities. Antiquarian studies continued nonetheless, but in 1630 King Charles I imprisoned Cotton and other antiquarians because the original sources of an anti-Stuart political pamphlet were found in Cotton's library. Although they were eventually released, Cotton's library was closed, even to him, and almost a century later the British Museum acquired the greater part of it.

The Civil War completely disrupted antiquarian studies but with the Restoration they gradually returned to royal favor. King Charles II was an enlightened monarch who established the Royal Society in 1660 to encourage the development of science and knowledge in Britain, and it soon became the center of the intellectual life of the country. While he remained wisely disinterested in political and religious subjects and in recent history, Charles became fascinated by the pre-Roman ancient stone monuments of Avebury, which had been brought to his attention by the antiquarian Sir John Aubrey (1626–1697).

Aubrey was elected a member of the Royal Society in 1663 in recognition of his fieldwork investigating and detailing British prehistoric and Roman remains. The paper Aubrey presented to the Royal Society on Avebury caught King Charles' attention. This was the first time the Royal Society had discussed an antiquarian subject, and this was the first formal recognition of antiquarianism as a contributor to knowledge in Britain. Aubrey spent the rest of his life recording monuments and collecting information about antiquities, and his collection was deposited in the Bodleian Library in Oxford after his death. It was not until 1980 that Aubrey's work, which he called *Monumenta Britannica,* was published for the first time.

In 1707, the Society of Antiquaries of London was officially founded. Three friends—Humfrey Wanly, John Talman, and John Bagford—had been meeting in London taverns since 1701 to discuss their interests, and the group formed the basis of the new society. It is the oldest learned society in Great Britain and Ireland that is concerned with archaeology and history. The society became a formal association in 1717; its purpose was to make knowledge of British antiquities more universal. The great antiquarian and early field archaeologist William Stukeley was its first secretary.

The Society of Antiquaries of London had a membership of about 150 when it was granted a royal charter by King George II in 1751, and it began to collect manuscripts, books, prints, and drawings. The society's first fellows included the architectural draftsman James Stuart, pottery magnate Josiah

Wedgewood, and Rome-based collectors and Grand Tour guides Charles Townley and Richard Payne Knight. Foreign honorary members included Johann Winckelmann and Giovanni Piranesi.

In 1753 the society rented rooms in Chancery Lane to house its growing collections, and by 1781 it joined the Royal Society and the Royal Academy at Somerset House. In 1770 the society began to publish the observations of its fellows in *Archaeologia,* the world's longest-running archaeological journal.

See also Publication of *Britannia* (1586); Collections and Correspondence of de Peiresc (1616–1637); Worm Issues His circular (1626); Publication of *Antichita Romane* (1756); Publication of *Geschichte de Kunst des Alterthums* (1764).

Further Reading

Nurse, B. 2001. Society of Antiquaries of London. In *Encyclopedia of Archaeology: History and Discoveries,* ed. T. Murray, vol. 3, 1178–1181. Santa Barbara, CA: ABC-CLIO.

Sweet, R. 2004. *Antiquaries: The discovery of the past in eighteenth-century Britain.* London: Hambledon and London.

Foundation of the Accademia dei Lincei (1603)

The oldest learned academy in Europe that is still in operation, the Accademia was founded in Rome on 17 August 1603 by Italian aristocrats Prince Federico Cesi, Count Anastasio de Filis, and Francesco Stelluti and Dutch doctor Jan Heck to study nature, letters, and philosophy and to "celebrate God's wondrous creations." Antiquarian and archaeological studies were a long-standing interest of its founders. The use of lincei, or lynxes, is an allusion to the sharp eyes of the cats (and, by extension, those of the academicians).

Galileo Galilei joined the Accademia in 1611, and it is no coincidence that its first publication in 1613 was by him (on the phenomenon of sunspots). Galileo's defense of Copernicus's heliocentric doctrine was fully supported by the Accademia, despite the anger of the Catholic church. However, the group's influence waned after Cesi's death.

The Accademia was revived in 1795 with a donation by Napoleon I, suppressed by the pope during the 1830s, revived again in 1838, and suppressed again in 1840. Finally, it was reestablished by the liberal pope Pius IX, who excluded the study of letters and philosophy from its charter. In 1875 the prime minister of the new Italian state founded the Accademia Nazionale dei Lincei, and the Vatican founded its own Accademia Pontificia dei Nuovi Lincei.

In 1939 it became the Accademia d'Italia and then returned to its old name Accademia Nazionale dei Lincei after 1944. In this last incarnation the membership of the Accademia comprises many well-known archeologists; it publishes papers on classical archaeology such as *Notizie degli Scavi* (Excavation News) and organizes lectures and conferences.

See also English Antiquaries and Antiquarian Societies (1586–1770); Publication of *Oedipus Aegypticus* (1652–1655); Foundation of the French Academy in Rome (1666); Grand Tour and the Society of Dilettanti (1670–1780).

Further Reading

The Web site of the Accademia (http://www.lincei.it/informazioni/index.php) has a useful general history in English.

Duke of Arundel Brings His Collection of Classical Antiquities to London (1613)

Thomas Howard, Earl of Arundel (1585–1646), was one of the earliest of the English to take "The Grand Tour" and one of the first collectors of larger classical sculpture. Educated at Westminster School and Trinity College, Cambridge, his great passion was classical antiquity. A keen antiquary, he joined the Society of Antiquaries and was close to several fellow members such as Cotton, Spelman, Camden, and Seldon.

In 1609 Howard traveled to Holland, France, and Italy for the first time. Between 1612 and 1615 he was again in Europe, this time traveling to Italy with his wife, Lady Alathea, and the young architect Inigo Jones. Rome was experiencing extensive renovation and rebuilding and consequently there were many discoveries of pieces of Roman art, which became fashionable to display in private houses. Aristocrats from all over Europe began to compete for these artifacts as essential components in fashionable interior decor. While the first public collection and display of Roman art and artifacts had been held in Rome in 1471, and the Vatican government was intent on policing the city's ruins and keeping the best finds in Rome itself, it was still possible to sell and to export some pieces regarded as being "second rate."

The earl's host in Rome was Vincenzo Guistiniani, art patron and collector of classical antiquities, who helped him to obtain permission to excavate some ruined houses in 1613. Arundel and Inigo Jones unearthed a number of portrait busts, which they were allowed to send back to England. It has been suggested that the earl was granted the privilege to excavate because at this stage he was still a Roman Catholic (he converted to Protestantism in 1615) and therefore a sympathetic friend at the English court. It has even been argued that the busts were planted in the site for the Englishmen to find. Nevertheless, the earl and Jones were the first British nationals to be given permission to excavate abroad, marking the beginning of a long tradition of British archaeological research in Italy.

The sojourn in Rome with all its classical treasures and this latter personal archaeological experience reinforced Arundel's passion for collecting and displaying antiquities. While the earl never got his hands dirty again, he did begin to use agents in Venice to acquire antiquities from the eastern Mediterranean. Later he would employ his own agent, William Petty, to locate, and Sir Thomas Roe, British ambassador in Constantinople to facilitate the purchase and transport of works of art and inscriptions from the Greek Islands and Asia Minor back to London.

After his return to England in 1615, the earl collected widely and voraciously across Europe via dealers and agents—libraries, statues, paintings and drawings, collections of intaglios and medals, and curiosities were all sent to him in England. He built sculpture and picture galleries at Arundel House on the Strand in London to house and display his collections; pieces of sculpture were placed in the garden and ancient inscriptions were incorporated into the garden walls.

In 1628 Howard displayed some 200 marbles, which were published by John Selden in a catalog entitled *Marmora Arundeliana.* In 1637 the earl wrote and published *De Pictura Veterum,* a treatise on links between aesthetic and social and political values. The earl encouraged access to his collection and the study and discussion of it, thus founding classical scholarship in England. His collections also inspired an interest in collecting among the English upper classes who visited them. They began to plan their own trips to Italy and to change the interiors and architecture of their mansions. Collecting became an aristocratic craze in England during the 1640s and 1650s. Arundel left England for France in 1641 and died in Padua, Italy, five years later. After his death his collections were dispersed among his family and later sold off to other aristocratic collectors. His collection of marble statues, which included the *Parian Chronicle* or *Marmor Chronicon,* was given to Oxford University in 1667 and became known as the *Arundel Marbles.* These are housed in the Ashmolean Museum.

See also Foundation of the Palazzo dei Conservatori (1471); Publication of *Britannia* (1586); Establishment of the Ashmolean Museum (1683).

Further Reading

Howarth, David. 1985. *Lord Arundel and his circle.* London: Yale University Press.

Collections and Correspondence of de Peiresc (1616–1637)

From the fifteenth century, scholars across Europe were keen to explore what we would now call the links between history and identity. Antiquarian studies became a highly significant element in political discourse. By the sixteenth century the consensus among French antiquaries was that modern France was the result of the interaction between Gauls and Romans and between the descendents of these people and the Germanic Franks. However, antiquaries tended to regard the Gauls as the most important participants in French prehistory before the Roman conquest because they were seen as the original inhabitants of France—the most truly French of all of their ancestors. To more fully understand these mysterious people, who were described by the Romans, but who left no written records of their own and almost no visible monuments, the investigation of a broader range of material culture was considered necessary. Up to this point the study of material culture had been a low priority among antiquaries (in France and elsewhere). Nicolas Fabri de Peiresc (1580–1637) changed attitudes toward this kind of study among his peers and successors.

De Peiresc was a typical Renaissance scholar and antiquarian. After attending a Jesuit college in Avignon and studying philosophy in Aix-en-Provence, in 1599 he toured Italy, visiting Padua, Venice, Florence, and Rome; meeting Italian scholars such as Galileo, Aldrovandi, and Barberini; and becoming familiar with the intellectual milieu of the Italian Renaissance. Between 1602 and 1604 he studied law at Montpellier and then became a senator in the Aix parliament. In 1606 he traveled to England and Holland, once again visiting antiquarians, such as William Camden and the artist Peter Paul Rubens, and inspecting collections of books and antiquities. Between 1616 and 1623 he lived in Paris, pursuing his antiquarian research, after which he moved back to Aix. However, de Peiresc was never limited by his provincial existence and maintained communications with a very large network of contemporary French and other European scholars. Literally thousands of his letters (many to the greatest scholars of his time) have survived.

De Peiresc was an extraordinary polymath—lawyer, botanist, philologist, mathematician, naturalist, astronomer (he discovered the Orion nebula in

1610)—but his real passion was to "unravel the secrets of antiquity." To this end he owned a library of some 5,000 volumes and 200 manuscripts. He kept extensive dossiers of notes on his travels and the collections he had seen. At the time of his death he had 18,000 antique coins; more than a thousand engraved gems and cameos; and many vases, inscriptions, fibulae, fossils, seals, paintings, bronze statues, and miscellaneous antiquities. He also bred pedigree cats (he introduced the Angora breed into Europe) and kept a garden of rare and imported plants, from where he introduced ginger, jasmine, tulips, and the rhododendron into France.

De Peiresc was not a fieldworker or an excavator of monuments; his passion was artifacts. He did not want to use his collections to create a library or a museum—what he wanted from material culture was the knowledge that was bound up in them. In this way he turned antiquarianism into a respected intellectual specialty. Using description, analysis, and comparison, he created knowledge from the artifact and its provenance—and this could be shared with other antiquarians and reused by them to further their own studies. De Peiresc took antiquarianism and collecting from the realms of dilettantism, status symbol, fashion, and taste to scholarly expertise. He could interpret evidence of the past and write history from it, rather than relying on written sources for its elucidation.

Alain Schnapp describes de Peiresc as a paradox: he was internationally famous and recognized as the greatest French antiquarian of his time, yet he never published anything. His fame was the result of his international reputation and the impact of his work on other scholars. His biography, which was written by Petrus Gassendi in 1641, went through five Latin editions between 1641 and 1656, when it was translated into English as *The Mirrour of True Nobility and Gentility*. De Peiresc's intention, according to Schnapp, was "to create an invisible, Europe-wide college of savants of which he was administrator and patron" (p. 134). His collections were broken up after his death. Some of his artifacts eventually found their way, via other owners, into the great European collections in the Louvre and the British Museum, and some of his notes were deposited in the Bibliotheque Nationale in Paris, where they were read by, and had enormous influence on, the next generation of French antiquarians, such as Jacob Spon, Bernard de Montfaucon, and the Comte de Caylus.

See also Publication of *Britannia* (1586); Publication of *L'antiquité expliquée et représentée en figures* (1719–1724); Publication of the *Recueil d'antiquités égyptiennes, étrusques, romaines, et gauloises* (1752–1767).

Further Reading

De Grummond, N., ed. 1996. *An encyclopedia of the history of classical archaeology.* Westport, CT: Greenwood Press.

Miller, P. N. 2000. *Peiresc's Europe: Learning and virtue in the seventeenth century.* New Haven and London: Yale University Press.

Schnapp, A. 1996. *The discovery of the past.* London: British Museum Press.

Worm Issues His Circular (1626)

Ole Worm (1588–1654) was educated at the University of Copenhagen, where he successively became professor of pedagogy, Greek, physics, and medicine before becoming personal physician to King Christian IV of Denmark. He was a contemporary and colleague of the Swedish antiquarian Johan Bure and shared his interests in rune stones and collecting archaeological and ethnographic artifacts and other antiquities. Worm corresponded widely with other antiquarians across Europe, learned Old Norse from Icelanders in order to translate runes, and speculated about tumuli with the English antiquarian Sir Henry Spelman.

In 1626, probably inspired by Bure's work in Sweden, Worm contacted every member of the clergy in Denmark through a royal circular, requesting they report any rune stones, burial sites, or other historic remains. Draftsmen were then sent to record and map the results of the replies. This mass of information was the basis of Worm's six volumes on Danish monuments published in 1644, which comprised a record of Danish antiquities, with illustrations and maps.

Worm also established the Museum Wormianum, a kind of extended cabinet of curiosities, to display his collections and the donations of others. This collection was passed on to King Frederick III after Worm's death. It was installed in the old castle in Copenhagen and then moved in 1680 to a new building in Christiansborg, where it was opened to the public as the Kunstkammer (Royal Collection), which in time became a part of the National Museum of Denmark.

See also Sweden Passes Law to Protect National Antiquities (1630); Swedish Archaeological Service Founded (1666).

Further Reading

Klindt-Jensen, O. 1975. *A history of Scandinavian archaeology.* London: Thames and Hudson.

Murray, T. 2001. Ole Worm. In *Encyclopedia of archaeology: History and discoveries,* ed. T. Murray, vol. 3, 1330–1331. Santa Barbara, CA: ABC-CLIO.

Schnapp, A. 1996. *The discovery of the past.* London: British Museum Press.

Sweden Passes Law to Protect National Antiquities (1630)

In 1630 Sweden became the first European country to pass a law protecting its antiquities. This was directly attributable to the work of the Swedish antiquarian Johan Bure (1568–1652), who deciphered Nordic runic inscriptions and spent decades locating and recording monuments, archaeological sites, and memorial stones, one of the first systematic archaeological surveys of a nation's heritage.

The son of a pastor in Uppsala, Sweden, Bure received a strict classical education, learning Greek and Latin, and teaching himself Hebrew. In 1602 he became tutor to Crown Prince Gustavus Adolphus, the future king of Sweden, who was to become one of the great politicians and military leaders of seventeenth-century Europe.

Interest in the antiquities of Rome and Greece that was so strong throughout the southern parts of Europe and England was matched by an interest in Nordic monuments and antiquities in countries farther to the north. In these countries the histories of antiquarianism and the growth of nationalism are especially close. During the seventeenth century, the dual kingdoms of Sweden/Finland and Denmark/Norway were political rivals, determined to justify their ambitions in Europe by recalling the triumphs of their past. While many antiquarians throughout Europe had begun to record the monuments and antiquities of their countries and regions, it was in Scandinavia that prehistoric antiquarian collections and surveys became the most advanced or comprehensive of their time.

The decipherment of runes allowed antiquarians to read the earliest records of the northern kingdoms, and extensive field surveys revealed monuments that were quickly regarded as objects of national pride. Bure was one of the first antiquarians to begin to decipher Nordic runes, a script used on monuments, memorial stones, and artifacts throughout northern Europe, and he was also one of the first to collect and systematically analyze and assemble these ancient inscriptions. He established a runic alphabet and transcription rules, proposed a dating system, and began a collection of Swedish inscriptions.

From 1599 until 1637 Bure and two assistants undertook topographic and archaeological surveys all over Sweden, carefully recording and drawing monuments and copying ancient examples of runic epigraphy. In this way Bure transformed the antiquarian tour into a systematic study. He is regarded as one of the founders of landscape archaeology.

Bure's travels and collections were strongly supported by his former pupil, now King Gustavus Adolphus of Sweden, and in 1630 the king published a statute protecting Swedish antiquities. With its proclamation, Sweden became the first modern state in the world to legislate to protect its heritage. Just as important, Sweden was protecting a heritage that was neither Greek nor Roman, recognizing that the evidence of its unique past was worthy of protection and study in its own right.

See also Worm Issues His Circular (1626); Swedish Archaeological Service Founded (1666).

Further Reading

Klindt-Jensen, Ole. 1975. *A history of Scandinavian archaeology.* London: Thames and Hudson.

Murray, T. 2001. Johan Bure. In *Encyclopedia of archaeology: History and discoveries,* ed. T. Murray, vol. 1, 236–237. Santa Barbara, CA: ABC-CLIO.

Schnapp, A. 1996. *The discovery of the past.* London: British Museum Press.

Publication of Oedipus Aegypticus *(1652–1655)*

The first European antiquarian to study and try to decipher Egyptian hieroglyphics, Athanasius Kircher (1601–1680) published the four-volume *Oedipus Aegypticus* and a number of influential books about ancient Egypt. He also established the Musaeum Celeberimum (literally the Celebrated Museum), one of Rome's "grand tourist" attractions during the seventeenth century.

Kircher was a German Jesuit priest who was appointed professor of mathematics, physics, and oriental languages at the Jesuit college in Rome in 1635. On his way to Rome he visited and impressed the great French antiquarian Nicolas Fabri de Peiresc, who encouraged his interest in ancient Egypt and gave him a letter of introduction to the powerful Roman Barberini family, whose members included the current pope, Urban VII, and his nephew, Cardinal Barberini, who became Kircher's mentor.

Two years before Kircher's arrival in Rome, the pope and the Roman inquisition had condemned and imprisoned the astronomer Galileo on charges of heresy for stating that the earth revolved around the sun. Kircher's three predecessors in his chair at the Jesuit college, who were compelled to teach Aristotle's account of the universe, had dutifully disputed with Galileo, despite the fact that they thought he might be right. Kircher, with his interest in ancient Egypt, ancient languages, and scientific instruments, much less controversial subjects than astronomy and science, was probably regarded by both the Jesuits and the pope as a safe appointment who would provide a respite from scientific conflict.

The Jesuit order had been founded in the sixteenth century, and its college was erected on the ruins of the ancient Roman temple for the Egyptian goddess Isis. By the seventeenth century the order had become a powerful worldwide missionary organization; two of its members were already in Beijing, as court astronomers to the Chinese emperors. Indeed, Kircher's ultimate ambition had been to go to China as a missionary, but he was to live in Rome for the rest of his life, where he proved very useful as papal propagandist. After eight years of teaching at the college he was allowed to pursue his research, collecting, and publications full time.

Kircher's first book, *Prodromus Coptus* (the Coptic Forerunner), appeared in 1636. It was dedicated to Cardinal Barberini and published by the papacy's official press known literally as "the propaganda of the faith." The book was Kircher's solution to the Vatican library's dilemma of possessing many Coptic manuscripts but having no one who could read them. Italian contacts with Egypt had been minimal because of its domination by the Ottoman Empire, so no Coptic dictionaries or grammars were available. Kircher acquired a medieval manuscript that included a Coptic-Arabic grammar, and he translated it into Latin.

Kircher's interest in Coptic was the consequence of his interest in ancient Egypt. He believed that Coptic, as the liturgical language of the Egyptian Christians and written in an alphabet adapted from Greek during the late Roman Empire, was probably originally derived from ancient Egyptian and could be the key to deciphering Egyptian hieroglyphics. While Kircher's instinct about the relationship between Coptic and hieroglyphics was fundamentally right, he did not succeed in deciphering hieroglyphics, although he believed that he could. Decipherment occurred two centuries later with the aid of the Rosetta stone and the brilliance of Jean-François Champollion, who kept his own annotated copy of Kircher's *Prodromos Coptus* for reference in his library.

In 1643 Kircher's second book, *Lingua Aegyptiaca Restituta* (the Egyptian Language Restored), revised the first, the Coptic forerunner, and completely translated the Coptic-Arabic manuscript that contained it. In 1648 Kircher helped the Italian sculptor Bernini design a fountain around an Egyptian obelisk reerected in the Piazza Navonna, the new pope's family piazza. The obelisk itself had been brought to Rome for the Isis sanctuary by the emperor Domitian (82–96 AD) and had since been torn down and moved twice. Kircher supplied the Latin translations of the inscriptions on the obelisk that inspired Bernini's design and were then engraved onto plaques beneath it. The form of the fountain reflected Kircher's concepts of geology, which were developed in his book *The Subterranean World* (1665). He also published the *Pamphili Obelisk* in 1650, a pamphlet about the obelisk itself and a foretaste of his next and greatest work.

Kircher's four volumes of *Oedipus Aegypticus* (Egyptian Oedipus), published between 1652 and 1655, were the culmination of twenty years of Egyptian studies. Taking three years to print, the book comprised hundreds of illustrations, descriptions, and interpretations of the various Egyptian antiquities that could be found in Rome. While it was a book that spread interest in Egyptian antiquities among European scholars and made Egyptian antiquities accessible to an antiquarian audience, few were convinced Kircher could actually read hieroglyphics.

Kircher's last Egyptian work, *Sphinx Mystagoga* (the Initiatory Sphinx), published in 1676 in both Rome and Amsterdam, not only proved how international his work had become but also how the interest in ancient Egypt had grown. Inspired by the Egyptian mummy cases of a French collector, the book details the cases, their illustrations of mummification and scenes from ancient Egypt, and their hieroglyphics.

In spite of his friendship with the Barberini family, Kircher maintained the patronage of the next two popes, impressing them with his vast knowledge. He continued to collect material for the museum and to write and publish on a variety of subjects (for example, magnetism, cosmology, geology [focusing on volcanoes and Atlantis], the Jesuits in China, magic lanterns, microscopes, universal music making, symbolic logic, the Tower of Babel, and Noah's Ark), as befitting the contemporary description of him as "a living encyclopedia." Kircher was also one of the first to visit the recently unearthed Etruscan tomb near Viterbo and left an account of how a local guide told him that the stone-carved chambers and beds were actually made for underground cave dwellers.

In 1678, the engraving of the Musaeum Celeberimum on the front cover of its first published catalog depicts elegantly vaulted rooms stuffed full of Roman statues, Egyptian obelisks, Greek vases, a preserved crocodile, musical instruments, a human skeleton, shells, fossils, and stalactites. As it continued to expand over 50 years Kircher's museum moved out of the Jesuit college to bigger premises. Its collections were eventually dispersed between the Villa Guilia (protohistoric material), the Museo Nazionale delle Terme (classical and Christian material), the Palazzo Venezia (medieval material), and the Museo Pigorini (prehistoric and ethnographic material).

See also Collections and Correspondence of de Peiresc (1616); Decipherment of Egyptian Hieroglyphics (1824); Publication of *De Etruria Regali Libri Septem* (1723–1726).

Further Reading

Findlen, P., ed. 2004. *Athanasius Kircher: The last man who knew everything.* London: Routledge.

Rowland, I. 2000. *The ecstatic journey: Athanasius Kircher in Baroque Rome.* Chicago: University of Chicago Library.

Publication of The Antiquities of Warwickshire *(1656)*

Sir William Dugdale (1605–1686), one of England's best-known antiquaries, was born in Warwickshire, a gentleman of modest means and little formal education. His interest in local antiquarian matters brought him into contact with others interested in compiling a history of Warwickshire, particularly Sir Symon Archer (1581–1662). Archer introduced Dugdale to the London-based antiquaries who were part of the court of King Charles I, in particular Thomas, Earl of Arundel. In 1639 Dugdale was appointed to a junior post in the College of Arms, which provided sufficient funds to allow him to pursue his studies in London. The outbreak of the Civil War in 1642 caused him to escape to Oxford with the rest of the court and allowed him access to the great antiquarian riches of the university's Bodleian Library.

Dugdale's first task was to collaborate with Richard Dodsworth in compiling a history of English religious houses, the *Monasticon Anglicanum* (1655–1673). The fact that Dodsworth died before the publication of the first volume meant that Dugdale was primarily responsible for the following two volumes. This in itself would probably have been Dugdale's crowning achievement if it had not been for his other project, *The Antiquities of Warwickshire* (1656), which became an exemplar of all a detailed, serious, and scholarly seventeenth century antiquarian tract could be. Dugdale was thorough in his documentary research and created archives and genealogies that provided the resources for his description and analysis of the monuments of the county and the great collections of coins, seals, and other items of ancient material culture.

See also Publication of *Britannia* (1586); English Antiquaries and Antiquarian Societies (1586–1770).

Further Reading

Broadway, J. 1999. *William Dugdale and the significance of county history in early Stuart England.* Stratford-upon-Avon, UK: Dugdale Society in association with the Shakespeare Birthplace Trust.

Dugdale, W. 1765. *The antiquities of Warwickshire: illustrated. From records, leiger-books, manuscripts, charters, evidences, tombes and armes. Beautified with maps, prospects, and portraictures. This edition is carefully copied, . . . from the old one, published in the year 1656.* London: John Jones.

Schnapp, A. 1996. *The discovery of the past.* London: British Museum Press.

Trigger, B. 1989. *A history of archaeological thought.* Cambridge: Cambridge University Press.

Publication of Annals of the World Deduced from the Origin of Time *(1658)*

James Ussher (1581–1665) was a successful churchman and academic in Dublin, Ireland, where his family had helped to found Trinity College. He came to the notice of King James I of England, who was impressed by his scholarly arguments in defense of the Protestant Church against ongoing Roman Catholic attacks. He was made archbishop of Armagh, the primate of Ireland, in 1625.

Ussher had met the antiquarians William Camden and Sir Robert Bruce Cotton when he first traveled to London to acquire books for Christ Church College. He got to know them even better when he lived there researching his books on the antiquity of the British church, *A Discourse of the Religion Anciently Professed by the Irish and British* (1623 and 1631), and the spread of Christianity in Britain before the arrival of St. Augustine in the seventh century, *Britannicarum Ecclesiarum Antiquitates* (1639).

But it was his interest in establishing a chronology for the whole of human history that was to ensure his reputation and importance for the next two hundred years. Ussher examined every chronology available, from those written by the ancient Greeks and in the Old Testament to those created by contemporary Dutch and French scholars. He recalibrated political years with astronomical ones, counted all the equinoxes since the creation; read relevant documents in Hebrew, Persian, Arabic, and Ethiopian; and laid out his findings in *Annales Veteris et Novi Tesamenti* (or *Annals of the World Deduced from the Origin of Time*) published in 1658. In this book he conclusively proved that the world was created at 6 p.m. Saturday, 22 October 4004 BC.

His arguments were such that *Annals* became the acknowledged universal chronology until the middle of the nineteenth century. His dates were so incontestable that they were printed in the margins of Bibles for the next few centuries. Ussher was given a state funeral in Westminster Abbey by Oliver Cromwell, and his collections of Anglo-Saxon and Oriental manuscripts and notes on church history and antiquarian research were donated to Trinity College Library.

See also Publication of *Britannia* (1586); English Antiquaries and Antiquarian Societies (1586–1770).

Further Reading

Barr, J. 1984–1985. Why the world was created in 4004 BC: Archbishop Ussher and Biblical chronology. *Bulletin of the John Rylands University Library of Manchester* 67: 575–608.

Parry, G. 1995. *The trophies of time.* Oxford: Oxford University Press.

Swedish Archaeological Service Founded (1666)

During the seventeenth century, the kingdom of Sweden became a great power in northern Europe through its victories during the Thirty Years' War. In that context, and without any Greek or Roman pedigrees to justify and substantiate its position of power, antiquarian research and knowledge about its own unique past became an important part of defining its national identity. Sweden appointed its first director of national antiquities, Johan Bure (1568–1652), in 1599.

Bure's contact with the kings of Sweden guaranteed their involvement in antiquarian research, and as a result, ensured national and provincial government support. On Bure's advice King Gustavus Adolphus II (1594–1632) issued his famous "antiquarian instruction" in 1630 to protect and record the nation's monuments and antiquities.

Johan Hadorph (1630–1693) succeeded Bure as director of national antiquities. Hadorph not only shared Bure's passion for antiquities, but also had influential connections. He had studied history at Uppsala University and then, in 1660, become the university's secretary, working closely with its enlightened chancellor, Magnus Gabriel de la Gardie, who was also the political chancellor of Sweden. In 1662 the university founded a chair of antiquities and appointed Olof Verelius (1618–1682) as its first professor of antiquarian studies.

In 1666, with the support of Hadorph, la Gardie, and the powerful science professor Olof Rudbeck (1630–1702), Verelius was appointed royal antiquary, and, with royal, national, and provincial government approvals, and a legislative proclamation, a College of Antiquities was founded, affiliated to Uppsala University. As Klindt-Jensen (1975) describes:

> The preamble to this proclamation deplored the prevailing apathy toward ancient monuments: nothing was being done to prevent their decay and destruction—even such ruins as were left were being dispersed—and there was no recognition of their true worth as testimony to posterity of the 'heroic achievements of the kings of Sweden and Gotland, their subjects, and other great men—the imposing castles, fortresses, and dolmens, the stones bearing runic inscriptions, the tombs and ancestral barrows.' Henceforth it was forbidden to break up or interfere with these monuments whether situated on crown land or private property. Officials were to ensure that this prohibition was respected; priests and their assistants had the special duty of inspecting all field-monuments and sending drawings of them to the king. (p. 27)

At the same time Hadorph left the university to become director of national antiquities and secretary of an antiquities committee that was established to administer the legislation. The committee was supported by paid research, conservation, and publication staff and was provided with an office and storage facilities in the Gustavianum (now the Museum of Nordic Antiquities). Its specific tasks were to:

> preserve the country's ancient monuments; publish Icelandic sagas and ancient Swedish laws; create a Swedish dictionary; document rune stones and coins and seals; and carry out archaeological excavations. Priests and public officials were ordered to participate in field surveys and to send the results of any pillaging of monuments to the Antiquities Committee. (Hegardt 2001, 1225)

Hadorph went on annual antiquarian expeditions with draftsmen and writers to find and record the reported monuments and any folk traditions. One of his draftsmen, Elias Brenner (1647–1717), was a student of both Olof Verelius (1618–1682) and Johannes Schefferus (1621–1679), the latter providing Brenner with his first insights into numismatics (coins) which Brenner was to elevate to the status of a science in the 1690s. The study of numismatics in Scandinavia would have a crucial impact on the development of prehistoric chronology during the nineteenth century. Hadorph wrote and published illustrated reports of monuments and finds and collected archaeological material and artifacts. He also undertook his own fieldwork, uncovering an ancient paved road marked by runic-inscribed standing stones near Taby in Uppland and excavating the Viking town of Birka.

Hadorph, Verelius, the college, and the committee ensured that the laws to protect ancient Swedish monuments were renewed in 1669 and 1676. In 1670 a bronze sword unearthed in Skane became the first prehistoric artifact to be handed to the committee, and in 1675 three bracteates from the same area were also acquired. At this stage the study of artifacts and material culture was not a recognized area of research in itself, but the use of such material to elucidate historic literary sources was recognized as being worthwhile. Here was another area that required protection—the material culture and artifacts associated with ancient monuments, and so in 1684 the antiquities laws were extended to protect archaeological material: "found piecemeal in the ground, ancient coins of all varieties and finds of gold, silver and copper, metal vessels and other rarities many of which are at present being discovered and secretly hoarded" (Klindt-Jensen 1975, 27).

Of equal importance was the fact that all of these archaeological finds had to be sent directly to the king, who would pay their finders a reward. The Antiquities College argued that these finds should be preserved "both for the glory of the nation and for the scientific interest" and that they were not to be looted and sold off (Klindt-Jensen 1975, 29).

With artifacts accumulating in the Gustavianum, Hadorph began to lobby for the creation of a museum similar to the Danish Royal Kunstkammer, set up as a result of the collections made by Ole Worm and the Danish crown. Despite deteriorating political relations with Denmark, he visited Copenhagen and examined its antiquities collections, and maintained a prolific correspondence with Danish antiquarians.

The antiquities committee was initially based in Uppsala, but in 1690 it was moved to the capital, Stockholm. Gradually its activities decreased, and in 1692 it was renamed the Antiquities Archive, reflecting its now passive role. Hadorph died in 1693.

Sweden's period as a great power finished by 1718, partly because of a disastrous war with Russia, which was emerging as the great power of northeastern Europe. The last secretary of the Antiquities Archive completed his term of office in 1777, and no one was appointed in his place. In 1780 the archive was dissolved. After the reorganization of the Literary Academy in 1786, the Academy of Literature, History, and Antiquities took over the duties of the archive and its secretary became the director of national antiquities (Hegardt 2001, 1225).

See also Worm Issues His Circular (1626); Sweden Passes Law to Protect National Antiquities (1630).

Further Reading

Klindt-Jensen, Ole. 1975. *A history of Scandinavian archaeology*. London: Thames and Hudson.

Hegardt, J., ed. 2001. Sweden. In *Encyclopedia of Archaeology, History and Discoveries*, ed. T. Murray, vol. 3, 1224–1228. Santa Barbara, CA: ABC-CLIO.

Foundation of the French Academy in Rome (1666)

As absolute monarch of the most powerful and wealthy kingdom in Europe during the seventeenth century, Louis XIV, "le roi soleil" (the sun king), identified with, and regarded himself as the successor of, the Roman emperor Augustus. He compared the political dominance of his kingdom to that of imperial Rome.

The French classical painter Nicholas Poussin spent much of his life in Rome (from 1624 until his death in 1665), where he introduced fellow artist Charles Le Brun (1619–1690) to its inspiring monuments and collections. Back in Paris Le Brun belonged to an artistic intelligentsia who admired the Academia di Santa Luca in Rome for its teaching methods and for the traditions of great art based on the examples of ancient Greece and Rome, which it wanted to transmit to Italian artists.

Le Brun first came to the attention of King Louis XIV (1638–1715) for his decoration of the superb chateau of Vaux-le-Vicomte, built for the king's finance minister Nicolas Fouquet. Louis placed Le Brun in charge of the decorations of the new palace of Versailles, where he supervised the large team of artists and craftsmen who made the tapestries, paintings, sculptures, ornaments, and furniture—all the decorative ensembles for the palace. Le Brun executed many of the paintings at Versailles, including the ceiling painting with its massed classical allusions in the Hall of Mirrors—*The King Governs Alone.* He also accompanied Louis on his military campaigns and royal perambulations so that he could make studies of the king and the events in his life for paintings.

Through Le Brun's growing contact and influence with the king, Cardinal Mazarin (principal minister to King Louis XIV), and the king's consort, Queen Anne of Austria, the proposal to establish an academy in Paris, modeled on that of the Academia di Santa Luca in Rome, won royal support. The Academie Royale was founded in 1648 with the aim of raising the status of fine arts to the same level as that of epic poetry and ancient rhetoric. It deliberately moved painting and sculpture away from its guilds of craftspeople and into the realm of intellectuals and scholars. To create the best and most relevant contemporary art, artists were required not only to familiarize themselves with the great art of the Italian Renaissance, but also with the art that had inspired it—that of classical Rome and Greece. As well artists needed to be familiar with classical history, mythology, and literature. If they were to continue to receive commissions from their major patron, the royal court, they had to do justice to the representation of their king's role in contemporary history.

Louis XIV, addressing the Academie, expressed it best: "I entrust to you the most precious thing on earth—my fame" (Walsh 1999, 89). In 1664, in recognition of the importance of the king's iconography, Colbert, Louis XIV's secretary of state, was made minister of fine arts, responsible for the Academie. Together he and Le Brun controlled the art of the French nation through their advice to the king and their control of the Academie. They dictated subjects, styles, and universal standards and rules for art and artistic taste. Le Brun became one of the most powerful men in France as King Louis XIV's "First Painter"—advising the king on artistic matters and attending to important royal commissions (from 1661). In 1665 he became the king's "Rector," during which time he helped to found the French Academy in Rome, and then in 1683 he became director of France's Academie Royale.

The French Academy in Rome was founded in 1666 by Colbert, on Le Brun's advice, to improve the fine arts of France by providing a base for French artists to study in Rome and to make copies of manuscripts, illustrations of antiquities, and casts of the originals of the great art of ancient Rome and Greece (that which could not be acquired) to send back to France. It became a center for studying ancient monuments and the latest finds—and so it also became involved in archaeology. This permanent base in Rome also provided opportunities to increase the royal collections through the purchase of works of art that came onto the market from private collectors and collections (such as the Germanicus and Cincinnatus sculptures now in the Louvre) and to inspect and negotiate for others that had been recently unearthed or looted from classical sites. Its directors were "cultural spies" who kept the royal court and the Academie Royale informed of the latest and the greatest art in Rome.

Within the first twenty years of its founding the French Academy in Rome had sent numerous casts, copies, and originals back to France, where they adorned the palaces and gardens of the king. However, the loss of so many original antiquities to France and other European countries resulted in Pope Innocent XI's passing a law curtailing the export of antiquities in 1686. By this time the academy itself was the home of more than a hundred plaster casts of some of the finest pieces of classical art in private collections or in the Vatican and Capitoline museums, and it had to move to larger premises to display them. It became an important destination in Rome in its own right, for both local and foreign visitors, because it was the only place where all of the best pieces were displayed and could be viewed together.

See also Foundation of the Palazzo dei Conservatori (1471); Foundation of the Louvre (1779–1793); Napoleon Loots Rome (1797).

Further Reading

De Grummond, N., ed. 1996. *An encyclopedia of the history of classical archaeology.* Westport, CT: Greenwood Press.

Walsh, L. 1999. Charles Le Brun, "art dictator of France." In *Academies, museums and canons of art,* eds. G. Perry and C. Cunningham. New Haven, CT: Yale University Press in Association with the Open University Press.

Publication of De Solido Intra Olidum Naturaliter Contento Dissertationis Prodromus *(1669)*

Danish medical graduate Nicolaus Steno (1638–1686), or Niels Stensen as he was known in Denmark, studied at Copenhagen, Leiden, and Paris universities before becoming physician to the Medici duke Ferdinand II in Florence in 1665. His study of fossil and recent sharks' teeth inspired an interest in geology. Steno traveled through Tuscany studying strata and collecting fossils, visiting private collections, quarries, and caves, and then on to the island of Elba to see its famous crystal mines. In 1667 Steno converted to Catholicism and was ordered home by the king of Denmark. He gave up science and became a priest and later a bishop in Germany. But he summarized the results of this geological work in *De Solido Intra Olidum Naturaliter Contento Dissertationis Prodromus* (Forerunner of a dissertation of a solid naturally contained within a solid) before giving up his scientific interests forever. Steno's book examined the nature of crystal formation in rocks, which he argued had to be solid before the enclosing rock solidified around it, and outlined the process of sedimentation and the formation of geological strata, by arguing for a process of superposition. In the same work he demonstrated the organic origins of fossils and described the characteristic forms of crystals and their growth and geometry.

Prodromus was published in 1669. It is surprising it was not censored, given the questions it raised about the age of the earth's crust and the processes involved in shaping it, which, if taken to their logical conclusion, challenged Genesis. It was translated into English in 1673 under the auspices of the Royal Society, and was probably read by Robert Hooke, Martin Lister, and John Ray, and fossil collector Robert Plot, who were also questioning the chronology of the earth based on geological evidence. The link between geology and prehistory and archaeology was established. Despite a relatively brief scientific career, Nicolaus Steno's work on the formation of rock layers and the fossils they contain was crucial to the development of modern geology. The principles he stated continue to be used today.

See also Publication of *Oedipus Aegypticus* (1652–1655); Publication of *Annals of the World Deduced from the Origin of Time* (1658); Publication of *Metallotheca Vaticana, Opus Posthumum* (1717).

Further Reading

Cioni, R. 1962. *Niels Stensen: scientist–bishop.* New York: P. J. Kenedy and Sons.

Poulsen, J., and E. Snorrason, eds. 1986. *Nicolaus Steno 1638–1686: a reconsideration by Danish scientists.* Gentofte, Denmark: Nordisk Insulinlaboratorium.

Rudwick, M. J. S. 1976. *The meaning of fossils: Episodes in the history of paleontology.* Chicago: University of Chicago Press.

Grand Tour and the Society of Dilettanti (1670–1780)

For hundreds of years Rome and Italy, as the center of European Christianity, had been a place of pilgrimage for many visitors. During the seventeenth century they also became the favorite secular destination of the aristocracy and gentry of France and England, who after experiencing a classical education sought to visit classical sites, believing that in so doing they became closer to the past they were learning about.

The term "Grand Tour" was first used in the French translation of *A Voyage or a Compleat Journey Through Italy* by Richard Lassels, published in 1670. The English were the pioneers of the Grand Tour, and most of the early accounts of similar journeys (for which there was a large market) were written by them in the late seventeenth century. Armchair travel was safer than the real thing; in those early days of European tourism, travel was indeed a risky business and included perilous ocean and mountain crossings, bandits, wars, disease, and death. However, by the end of the seventeenth century the paths were so well worn that there was enough infrastructure to support greater numbers of travelers: better and safer roads, regular coaches, accommodation, food, and protection.

In 1615 the great English scientist Francis Bacon wrote in his essay "Of Travel" that an educational trip abroad was a necessity for every young gentleman. But there were additional reasons alongside that of education. Aristocratic young men had to be kept busy until they inherited, so many traveled to get them out of the country to where they could gamble and "sow their wild oats" far enough away so as not to be troublesome. Others traveled for reasons of health and "social finishing," their numbers swelling to include scholars and wealthy sons of the middle classes. The English remained the most numerous grand tourers, and they established the itinerary. The "Grand Tour" had to take in Paris and then Italy via the Mediterranean or the Alps. When in Italy tourers visited Florence, Venice, and Rome, and by the mid-eighteenth century they ventured farther south to Naples to view the newly discovered cities of Herculaneum and Pompeii. A Grand Tour could take years, and it could involve a whole entourage, but at the very least it required a tutor or tour leader.

By the beginning of the eighteenth century there were even more reasons to travel. Italy itself was undergoing a period of great cultural development that was strongly supported by the impact of the classical world on its artists and intellectuals. As a result, the works of many great contemporary Italian artists in the areas of music, painting, sculpture, and architecture were becoming attractions in themselves.

The history of the Society of Dilettanti, founded in London in 1732, illustrates the significance of, and the changes to, the "Grand Tour" over time.

The Society was initially a dining and drinking club, and its members were young male graduate grand tourers from the upper and middle classes of England who had enjoyed Italy—and its wine, classical sites, and culture—and retained a passion for the place. There was also a hint of political radicalism in that many members disliked the conservatism and parochialism of English cultural and political life under the Whig government of Sir Robert Walpole. By 1736 there were forty-six members and thereafter membership was limited to just fifty-four, some of whom were also members of the Society of Antiquaries of London, and eventually trustees of the British Museum.

Sir Thomas Coke, first Earl of Leicester and one of the founders of the Society had taken six years to complete his Grand Tour and had returned to build the neo-Palladian Holkham Hall in Norfolk to house his collection of classical sculpture. Another founder, Lord Burlington, toured twice in 1715 and 1727 and pursued his interests in Roman central heating and gardens. Other members included the great collectors of sculpture Charles Townley and William Weddell and the art scholar Richard Payne Knight.

The Society gradually transformed itself into a serious participant in the Greek revival and into a respected learned group who sponsored both the research and the publication of knowledge of the classical world in England. Between 1751 and 1754 the Society funded an expedition by English architects James Stuart and Nicholas Revett to record the monuments of Athens (published between 1762 and 1816). In 1765 the Society funded Richard Chandler to survey the monuments of Ionia (or coastal Turkey), which they published between 1769–1779. These were monumental contributions to scholarship.

The Society also funded students from the Royal Academy to travel to Italy and paint. In England their interests and resulting publications and paintings influenced fashions in architecture, the decorative arts, clothing, and jewelry. On his return to London in 1759, Stuart designed the first neoclassical interior in Europe at Spencer House; it comprised wall decorations copied from Herculaneum and copies of Greek and Roman furniture.

The golden age of the Grand Tour was from the mid- to late eighteenth century. This corresponded with the most politically peaceful period in Europe for centuries. From 1713 and the Treaty of Utrecht until 1793 and the French Revolution, Europe experienced forty years without war. The character of the Grand Tour changed during this period. Eventually just touring was not enough—acquiring antiquities and souvenirs became another substantial reason for traveling to Europe—and the Society of Dilettanti began to fund archaeological expeditions and publish the results.

While many antiquities did make it back to England, this avaricious touring caused authorities throughout Italy to tighten access to classical antiquities and to pass laws to ensure that the best pieces stayed in Italy. The Vatican acquired many private collections, and a number of museums (among them the great Capitoline and Vatican museums) were created to house and display them. This led to a highly profitable trade in copies and fakes, and in Italy a whole school of artists, such as Batoni, Canaletto, and Piranesi, developed that catered to English tastes and was funded by English visitors. As time passed the Grand Tour itinerary was enlarged to include sites farther south in the Mediterranean. After Naples and the archaeological sites of Herculaneum and Pompeii, grand tourers moved on to Sicily, and then later into Greece.

In 1766 Sir Joshua Reynolds was elected a member of the Society of Dilettanti. Between 1777 and 1779 he painted two portraits of his fellow members that seem to mark both the Society's heyday and predict its passing. The first

Joshua Reynolds. (Library of Congress)

portrait was painted to mark the reception into the Society of Sir William Hamilton, the great eighteenth-century patron, aristocrat, diplomat, collector. The second shows a group of members, including Sir Joseph Banks, one of the great patrons of nineteenth century British science, who undertook a scientific expedition to the Pacific with Captain James Cook. Banks was the representative of a new age for, and a new kind of, collecting and collectors, that of institutionalized collecting by museums and the creation of disciplines within universities to educate those who studied the past. This kind of collecting and new breed of collectors would contribute to the establishment of scientific archaeology during the nineteenth century.

The French Revolution and the Napoleonic wars finished the golden age of the Grand Tour, as once again Europe became unsafe for travelers. However, it was Napoleon's own grand tour to Egypt, with an entourage of soldiers, scientific experts, and scholars, that turned the eyes of Europe toward the east and deeper into the past. It would be Egypt and the Near East that would absorb the antiquarian energies of Europe during the nineteenth century and contribute to the rise of archaeology.

See also Duke of Arundel Brings His Collection of Classical Antiquities to London (1613); Rediscovery of Herculaneum and Pompeii (1709–1800); Sir William Hamilton's Collections (1764–1798).

Further Reading

Black, J. 1992. *The British abroad: the grand tour in the 18th century.* Stroud, UK: A. Sutton.
Ford, B. 1981. The grand tour. *Apollo* CXIV/235: 390–400.

Foundation of the Ashmolean Museum (1683)

Opening on 24 May 1683 the Ashmolean Museum was based around the private collection of the antiquarian Elias Ashmole (1617–1692), who donated it after his death to the University of Oxford. At the core of Ashmole's gift to Oxford was a collection originally assembled by antiquarians John Tradescant the elder (died 1638) and his son John (1608–1662). The first curator of the museum was Robert Plot, an antiquary of distinction. Unusually, from its beginning the Ashmolean Museum was open to the public and had clear research and teaching, as well as display, functions. The fortunes of the museum waxed and waned over the next one hundred and fifty years, and the natural history side of the collections eventually assumed greater importance than the human antiquities.

However, from the mid-nineteenth century onward the character of the museum changed to the form we know today, featuring significant collections of antiquities derived from archaeological excavation and collection. Many famous collections have been presented to the Ashmolean Musuem, an example being Sir Richard Colt Hoare's donation of the Douglas collection of Anglo-Saxon antiquities in 1827. The museum has also benefited from the activities of its keepers, the most famous of whom was Sir Arthur Evans. Under Evans's keepership the Ashmolean once again rationalized its exhibits, expanded, and moved into new premises in Beaumont Street. These changes have ensured that the Ashmolean Museum remains one of the most significant archaeological museums in the world, and the research of its staff allows it to remain at the cutting edge of world archaeology.

See also Publication of *The Ancient History of North and South Wiltshire* (1812); Discovery of Minoan Civilization (1900–1935).

Further Reading

MacGregor, A. 1983. *Ark to Ashmolean: the story of the Tradescants, Ashmole and the Ashmolean Museum.* Oxford: Ashmolean Museum.

Ovenell, R. F. 1986. *The Ashmolean Museum 1683–1894.* Oxford: Clarendon Press.

Rediscovery of Herculaneum and Pompeii (1709–1800)

The site of the Roman town of Herculaneum, covered by twenty meters of lava during the eruption of Vesuvius in AD 79, was rediscovered during the digging of a well in 1709. The landowner to whom the well-digging farmer reported his location of some pieces of architectural marble in turn extracted two statues from what turned out to be the original Roman theater.

In 1738, King Charles III of Naples employed the Spanish military engineer Alcubierre to survey and map land around the town of Portici where he wanted to build a new summer palace. Local informants told Alcubierre of the well site and the finds, and the king granted him permission to investigate further. The first day down the well he unearthed a marble statue—which guaranteed that the king would be interested in greater exploration. Alcubierre then tunneled through the lava using convict chain gangs, gradually unearthing the theater, and then in 1739 the basilica with its marble equestrian statues and wall paintings. The king was briefed every evening on finds and was delighted to decorate his new palace with them. Alcubierre's progress was monitored by scholars from Naples, and from the beginning of his excavations, locations and inventories of artifacts and plans of buildings were made to keep the king and court informed. In the latter task Alcubierre was greatly assisted by the young Swiss engineer Karl Weber. However the narrow tunnels proved to be dangerous as they filled with volcanic dust and gases, and the hard work of tunneling all took its toll on workers and supervisors and slowed the whole process down.

By 1740 there were five sites of supervised digging. Artifacts were displayed at the royal palace and were as jealously guarded as the ruins themselves. A royal edict prohibited visitors taking notes of either sites or finds. By 1741 Alcubierre was too ill to continue his supervision and was replaced by the French engineer Bardet who began to tunnel along the original streets, rather than chopping through walls at random. Huge numbers of small finds—as well as wall paintings, mosaics, and statues—were uncovered, some requiring the development of new excavation techniques if they were to be recovered intact. Ventilation shafts were cut into the lava, fresh air was pumped in using bellows, and ramps had to be installed to lever out larger pieces intact.

In 1745 Alcubierre returned to the site, but by 1750 he had left again because of ill health, and he began to work on the open site of Pompeii, which had been found in 1748. That same year workmen unearthed the Villa of the Papyri at Herculaneum, named for the library of rolls of papyrus discovered in it, and a large suburban villa at Portici across from Herculaneum. Other small finds and numerous bronze and marble sculptures were unearthed.

By this time visitors to Herculaneum and to Pompeii were so numerous, and the demand for information so great, that in 1755 King Charles III founded the Academia Herculanensis to publish the finds. This decision to "go public" may have been in response to the inadequate catalog of the royal collection published in Naples in 1752 by Otavio Bayardi, a former site supervisor, entitled *Promdorom della antichita d'Ercolano.* The Academia Herculanensis comprised scholars who met every two weeks to view and discuss the latest finds and write reports on them. These were collated by a secretary to produce definitive descriptions, which were then illustrated and published in eight volumes between 1757 and 1792 as *Le Antichita di Erccolano.* They caused a sensation, and the neoclassical movement across Europe and in North America took a huge interest in them, copying classical motifs from the volumes and using them in contemporary architecture, painting, furniture, and clothing. Work in the tunnels at Herculaneum was suspended in 1780 and resumed again in 1828 and then continued throughout the nineteenth century.

The truncated cone of Mt. Vesuvius, still an active volcano, looms over the town of Herculaneum, Italy. At the bottom is the old town of Herculaneum that was recently excavated after having been buried in the eruption of AD 79; above it is the modern town of Herculaneum that was built over the ruins of its predecessor. (http://www.istockphoto.com)

The site of the Roman resort city of Pompeii was rediscovered in 1748 during the building of the highway from Naples to Reggio Calabria. Buried at the same time as Herculaneum but by softer volcanic ash and pumice rather than by solidified lava and mud, Pompeii was a larger and richer city and could be excavated via open pits, and was a safer site to work on. Alcubierre kept the chained convicts in the tunnels at Herculaneum and, instead, could employ local people to excavate at Pompeii. Work proceeded slowly at first, but by 1755 the finds began to increase in number and consequence, and wonderful wall paintings and whole architectural precincts were unearthed. Unlike the small town of Herculaneum, Pompeii had magnificent public buildings and temples and many wealthy villas, all of which remained intact under the ash. Part of the fascination with these two Roman cities was not just because of the nature of their fate—fast and terrible—but with the fact that they were not only ruins but also contained evidence of everyday life. They were fixed entities, entire landscapes of what life was like in a Roman town. As with Herculaneum the Pompeii site was also seen as a source of antiquities for the interior decor of the residences of the Bourbon kings of Naples.

The Academia Herculanensis was placed in charge of cataloging and publishing finds from Pompeii as well. Between 1758 and 1766 Johann Winckelmann, the great historian of classical art, visited both sites. He wrote two reports on the excavations at Herculaneum (1762 and 1767) in which he criticized the excavations and the loss of information, but praised Karl Weber's attempts at a systematic approach to excavation and his meticulous mapping of details and in situ observations. Winckelmann was made commissioner of antiquities to the pope in 1763, was a member of the Society of Antiquaries of London and other learned European societies, and was recognized as the expert on the history of classical art. His reports were widely read and translated and popularized the excavations, placing them on the itinerary of the "Grand Tour" and increasing the acquisitive interests of European collectors.

The publication in 1766–1767 of the *Collection of Etruscan, Greek and Roman Antiquities from the Cabinet of the Hon. W. Hamilton* also drew attention to the sites and their artifacts. Architectural draftsmen, such as Robert Adam, and artists, such as Piranesi, visited the sites and published about them. Members of European royalty and the aristocracy regularly visited. European scholars such as Goethe visited and wrote about the sites, while Edward Gibbon's great history, *The Decline and Fall of the Roman Empire,* was published in 1776—the result of the increased interest in Roman history. A "Pompeiian style" of the late eighteenth century in architecture, furnishings, costume, and decorative arts became popular across Europe. Pompeii remains the oldest archaeological site to be continuously excavated since it was first found.

Eventually, the collections of artifacts from the two sites outgrew the Bourbon royal palaces. In the late 1770s, under the order of Charles III's son Ferdinand IV, the Palazzo dei Vecchi Studi, a grand university building in Naples (originally built as a barracks for the royal cavalry in 1585) was transformed into a museum to house the archaeological collections of Herculaneum and Pompeii and the Farnese family collections from Rome. In the early nineteenth century the Palazzo dei Vecchi Studi was renamed the Real Museo Borbonico and is now part of the Museo Nazionale di Napoli.

See also Publication of *Antichita Romane* (1756); Sir William Hamilton's Collections (1764–1798); Publication of *Geschichte de Kunst der Altertums* (1764).

Further Reading

Parslow, C. C. 1995. *Rediscovering antiquity: Karl Weber and the excavation of Herculaneum, Pompeii, and Stabiae.* Cambridge: Cambridge University Press.

Schnapp, A. 1996. *The discovery of the past.* London: British Museum Press.

Trigger, B. 1989. *A history of archaeological thought.* Cambridge: Cambridge University Press.

First Archaeological Collections in Russia (1715)

Russian archaeological collections began under Czar Peter the Great (1696–1725). Ironically, the first items were evidence of Russia's close links to the eastern Mediterranean, rather than to western Europe, which was Russia's cultural and political focus during the early seventeenth century. Under the influence of the European Enlightenment, Czar Peter was attempting to modernize Russia and reduce its isolation from western Europe.

Until Peter the Great, antiquities other than those of the Byzantine period owned by the Russian Orthodox Church had been the lucrative province of grave robbers and looters. Antiquarian studies in Russia first began after Czar Peter returned from his European Grand Tour in 1698 and were part of his ambitions for a more Westernized Russian state. While this antiquarian interest began in Russia almost two hundred years after it had started in Italy, and one hundred years after Britain, Germany, and France had taken it up, it was used to serve the same ends. A past connected to the classical world either directly through history or via knowledge of it had the right bona fides for a politically powerful present and future.

The czar's interest in developing antiquarian studies was further encouraged by his reception of golden artifacts from grave mounds in Siberia. These artifacts, identified as Scythian in provenance, included magnificent gold belt buckles and plaques, some adorned with precious stones or enamels and some that used animal forms. The artifacts were sent to him from the Urals by the rich industrialist Nikita Demidov in 1715; others were sent in 1716 by Matvei Gargarin, the governor of Tobolsk. This Scythian material constituted the first archaeological collections of Russia.

In 1718, Peter the Great outlawed grave robbing and proclaimed that anything old or curious from anywhere in Russia had to be sent to him in his

Peter I. (Library of Congress)

new European-style capital city, St Petersburg. Here he established Russia's first kunstkammer (curiosities room) to display not only archaeological treasures but also anything of interest from natural history.

To some extent the discovery of Russia's eastern cultural history while it was busy trying to integrate culturally into western Europe is the story of Russian history and society as a whole. With its vast territories and different ethnic groups its problem was deciding just which part of its history would become "national." The Russian Orthodox Church had long preserved the history and traditions of the Greek Byzantine world and maintained its connections with the Orthodox Slavic states of eastern Europe. From the eighth century until the fourteenth century, medieval Russia had developed close connections with Scandinavia and the Hanseatic ports around the Baltic Sea and had survived the Mongol invasions. With the fall of Novgorod in 1478 and the establishment of the Muscovite state, the eastern Greek Orthodox world predominated over contacts with western Europe.

In fact, the seventeenth-century Russian state had very little information about its vast eastern territories, which stretched from the Caucasus across central Asia to Siberia and to northern China and as far as Japan—it did not even have a reliable and detailed map of these areas. Despite Czar Peter's concentration on relations with western Europe, he was eventually compelled to do something about Russia's eastern territories, if only in response to the threat of the Spanish and British explorations of the northwest Pacific coast of North America. He was also embarrassed into doing something about eastern Russia by the French, who offered to send a French team of explorers and naturalists to Siberia.

During the 1720s Czar Peter dispatched the naturalist Messerschmidt to study Siberian natural resources and folk art and to buy and collect antiquities. But he died in 1724 before he could finish commissioning the First Kamchatka Expedition under Vitus Bering to explore and map the Pacific coast of Siberia and establish its relationship to northern America. This was eventually completed between 1724 and 1730 (and then was followed by a second expedition 1732–1741), becoming the greatest geographic expedition to be undertaken between those of Columbus in 1492 and that of the English naval captain James Cook in the Pacific in the 1770s.

In 1763, a General Melgunov, on military duty in southern Russia, opened a number of burial barrows on the Black Sea coast. In the first mound, located near Yelizavetgrad (now Kirovgrad) in the Ukraine, Melgunov found many gold and silver artifacts dating to the early Scythian period (the late seventh and sixth centuries BC), which were dispatched to the imperial kunstkammer, where they were united with the more eastern Scythian material that had been previously donated.

Through the Scythians, regarded by some as the ancestors of the Slavic peoples, Russia not only had a direct connection to the Biblical, classical, Hellenistic, and Byzantine periods of the eastern Mediterranean, but also to central Asia and China, although it would take another two centuries of Scythian archaeology to map this out.

See also Foundation of the Hermitage (1768); Russia Gets a Slice of Classical Antiquity (1782).

Further Reading

Artamonov, M. I. 1969. *Treasures from Scythian tombs in the Hermitage Museum.* trans. V. Kupriyanova. London: Thames and Hudson.

Talbot Rice, T. 1958. *The Scythians.* London: Thames and Hudson.

Publication of Metallotheca Vaticana, Opus Posthumum *(1717)*

Michele Mercati (1541–1593), physician to Pope Clement VII in Rome and supervisor of the Vatican botanic gardens, was also interested in geography, geology, and chorology (the distribution of sites and artifacts). He was a contemporary of, and shared the same interests as, the antiquarians William Camden in England, Johan Bure in Sweden, and Ole Worm in Denmark.

The treasuries of the medieval Catholic church, filled with religious relics and pagan objects donated by their followers, also contained donations of natural curiosities, such as fossils, minerals, shells, crystals, animal remains, feathers, and stone artifacts. When aristocrats began their collections, the art was displayed as part of the interior decor and natural science objects were placed in cabinets of curiosities or "Kunstkammers," as they were known in northern Europe. As private collections these cabinets were studied by scientists and scholars only with the permission of their owners. By the sixteenth century many of the collections had become institutionalized, and knowledge of their contents was made more widely available through their publication in catalog form. The cabinets were the forerunners of the great natural history museums set up in the nineteenth century for educational and scientific purposes, and the catalogs were evidence of the beginning of the biological, geological, botanical, and paleontological collections that were to have enormous impact on the development of all of these sciences. They were also the first geological literature.

Mercati created one of the first mineralogical collections in Europe from the Vatican's collection of natural curiosities. In 1570 he wrote *Metallotheca Vaticana, Opus Posthumum*—a catalog of the collection, which also contained new ideas about some of the artifacts. While Mercati believed fossils were the organic remains of past creatures, he also believed they were one-offs created by God, like everything else. More remarkably he argued that the ceraunites, glossopetri, or thunderstones in the collection, the names given to stone tools and weapons, were not the result of natural forces such as lightning, but were made by human beings and used "in the folly of war." Mercati, being a Renaissance scientist, based this hypothesis on Biblical and classical sources for the use of stone tools. He would also have been familiar with ethnographic specimens sent back from the new world of the Americas to the Vatican. By 1570 Spain had been in Central America for seventy years, and France had been in Canada for almost forty years. No doubt these new examples of stone tools and weapons and descriptions of their manufacture and use caused him to note similarities with the older ones in the cabinet of curiosities.

Mercati's ideas were hardly noticed by the learned world during his lifetime. His manuscript was finally published more than one hundred years after his death in 1717 in Rome, after which it gained notoriety. In 1723 the great French scholar Antoine de Jussieu wrote about Mercati's ideas in a paper for the Academie des Sciences in Paris on the possible human origins of stone tools using ethnographic comparisons. English antiquarians William Dugdale in the seventeenth century and John Frere in the late eighteenth century echoed Mercati's hypothesis in their work, and scholars in the nineteenth century would prove him right.

See also Publication of *De l'origine et des usages de la pierre de foudre* (1723); John Frere Writes to the Society of Antiquaries of London (1797).

Further Reading

Goodrum, M. R. 2002. The meaning of ceraunia: archaeology, natural history and the interpretation of prehistoric stone artefacts in the eighteenth century. *British Journal of the History of Science* 2002: 255–269.

Lancisi, G.M. 1719. *Vatican City. Metallotheca.* Rome: J. M. Salvioni.

Mercati, M. *Michaelis Mercati Samminiatensis Metallotheca. Opus posthumum, auctoritate, & muificentiâ Clementis undecimi pontificis maximi e tenebris in lucem eductum; opera autem, & studio Joannis Mariae Lancisii archiatri pontificii illustratum. Cui accessit appendix cum XIX. recens inventis iconibus.*

Schnapp, A. 1996. *The discovery of the past.* London: British Museum Press.

Publication of L'antiquité expliquée et représentée en figures *(1719–1724)*

French Benedictine priest Bernard de Montfaucon (1655–1741) was primarily a Greek paleographer and philologist who published *Palaeogaphia Graeca* in 1708 and contributed to the recognition of his area of expertise as a new science. His next project was the publication of *L'antiquité expliquée et représentée en figures* in ten folio volumes with five supplement volumes between 1719 and 1724.

L'antiquité comprises 1,200 illustrated plates of approximately 40,000 illustrations of statues, reliefs, pottery, monuments, coins, jewelry, architecture, tools, small bronze sculptures, armor, and other antiquities, the result of twenty-six years of research by Montfaucon in private collections and cabinets of curiosities across France and Italy. Many of these images were new and unpublished, and others were from unpublished manuscripts such as that by seventeenth-century French antiquarian Nicolas Fabri de Peiresc.

The primary purpose of *L'antiquité* was to provide cultural, historical, and artistic background for the study of work of ancient authors—particularly for Montfaucon's own passion, Greek authors—to illustrate the antiquities so as to better explain them, and to provide some access to them via illustration so as to better educate those who were interested in them. The volumes were popular with the scholarly audience of their day and were translated into English between 1721 and 1722.

L'antiquité was primarily a philological study and focused on relating ancient texts to artifacts, but it has been argued that in this it was establishing the difference between two disciplines, not just enhancing one. Montfaucon was among the first to define history as text and archaeology as artifact and image.

See also Collections and Correspondence of de Peiresc (1616–1637).

Further Reading

Montfaucon, B. de. 1721–1722. *Antiquity explained, and represented in sculptures, by the learned Father Montfaucon, translated into English by David Humphreys.* London: J. Tonson and J. Watts.

Schnapp, A. 1996. *Discovery of the past.* London: British Museum Press.

Publication of De l'origine et des usages de la pierre de foudre *(1723)*

Although Greek and Roman writers had been aware that some people made and used stone tools, this knowledge was lost after the fall of Rome, only to be rediscovered during the Renaissance, as scholars began to have access to ancient documents and to question medieval oral and written knowledge.

As early as 1570, Michele Mercati (1541–1593) wrote that before the use of iron, stone tools might have been made out of flint to be used "in the madness of war" (*Metallotheca Vaticana*). Mercati believed that while fossils were organic in origin, many of the flints kept as curiosities in cabinets and collections and called ceraunia, or "thunderstones," were actually of human manufacture, and not created by natural forces such as lightning. Mercati had cited Biblical and classical sources such as Lucretius for the use of stone tools. But he also noted that iron working appeared early in Biblical chronology and that the art of metallurgy must have been lost by some nations who had spread out from the Holy Land, forcing them to use stone. His ideas caused few ripples among the scholarly world, and his book remained unpublished until 1717, more than a century after his death.

In 1685 the French Benedictine monk Dom Bernard de Montfaucon (1655–1741), antiquary and polymath, wrote an account of the excavation of a megalithic stone tomb at Cocherel, France, that contained polished stone axes. He ascribed the tomb to people who had no knowledge of iron making, and in passing referred to the possibility of a three-age sequence—stone, copper, and iron—of human development. In reaching this conclusion he was undoubtedly influenced by contemporary research in England and Scandinavia, where similar ideas about stone tools and three-age sequences had been suggested as the result of excavations of tombs.

By the late seventeenth century the colonization and exploration of the Americas had been underway for more than two hundred years, and the wide variety of stone tools (and the way of life of indigenous Native Americans) were well known to Europeans. So it is hardly surprising that by this time many European scholars not only believed that stone tools were made by humans, but also that they were made a very long time ago before metal tools were manufactured.

It was these shared conclusions and the recent publication of Mercati's work that prompted the medical doctor, botanist, and scientist Antoine de Jussieu (1886–1758) to write a paper for the French Académie des Sciences on the possible human origins of stone tools. In the paper de Jussieu compared the thunderstones or worked flints in every European cabinet of curiosities to the stone axes and tools that had recently arrived in Europe from North America and the Caribbean. Like Mercati he attributed the worked flints in the cabinets to a past people who had no knowledge of iron working. Unlike Mercati he could gain additional evidence for his hypothesis of a European stone age by comparing its artifacts to those made in the seventeenth century by Native Americans:

> The populations of France and Germany and of other northern countries, but for the discovery of iron, are quite similar to all the savages of today, and had no less need than them, to cut wood, strip bark, cleave branches and kill wild animals, to hunt for their food and to defend themselves against their enemies. They could hardly have done these things without such tools, which unlike iron, being not subject to rust, are found today in their entirety in the earth, almost with their first polish. (Schnapp 1996, 267)

In this way de Jussieu used Native Americans as sources of information, with behavior and artifacts analogous to the behavior and consequent material culture of stone-age Europeans. Not only was this the first use of comparative ethnology (which eventually came into its own in archaeology in the nineteenth and twentieth centuries), but it was also one of the first uses of archaeological evidence as part of a scientific theory.

What de Jussieu argued was that raw material, form, technology of manufacture, and function were linked in the past as well as in the present, and that the present provided a strong basis for inferring past human behavior. Thus, analogical inference allowed antiquaries to begin the difficult process of creating plausible accounts of the deep European past. De Jussieu had thus shown that archaeological evidence could be used in the same way and had the same validity as other scientific evidence. For the next hundred years or more the disciplines of natural history and geology would help to elucidate prehistoric archaeology and begin to provide it with a scientific methodology and eventually a chronology.

See also Publication of *Metallotheca Vaticana, Opus Posthumum* (1717); Publication of *L'antiquité expliquée et représentée en figures* (1719–1724); John Frere Writes to the Society of Antiquaries of London (1797).

Further Reading

De Jussieu, A.1723. De l'origine et des usages de la pierre de foudre. *M ém. Acad Sci* 6-9.

Goodrum, M. R. 2002. The meaning of ceraunia: archaeology, natural history and the interpretation of prehistoric stone artefacts in the eighteenth century. *British Journal of the History of Science* 2002: 255–269.

Schnapp, A. 1996. *The discovery of the past.* London: British Museum Press.

Publication of De Etruria Regali Libri Septem *(1723–1726)*

Greek and Roman writers recorded details about Etruscan history, architecture, tombs, and fine arts, and Etruscan tombs were known of, and entered, from the early Middle Ages. As early as 1466 an account of the opening of a newly discovered Etruscan tomb at Volterra was published, and an Etruscan vocabulary list had been compiled by 1502. In 1553 Renaissance artist and writer Georgio Vasari discovered an Etruscan bronze chimaera at Arezzo, while other Renaissance artists, such as Michelangelo, Donatello, Brunelleschi, and

Cellini, were all familiar with, and used images from, Etruscan art. During the fifteenth century the great Medici family of the city-state of Florence claimed the Etruscans as their direct ancestors, and by the sixteenth century Cosimo I de'Medici was known as Grand Duke of Etruria.

However, in 1551 German archaeologist Athanasius Kircher visited an Etruscan tomb and was told by local informants that it was the home of recent underground cave dwellers, rather than a rock-cut Etruscan tomb more than 2,000 years old. While the educated upper classes of northern Italy had some idea of a local ancient civilization predating Roman times, there was little general or broader knowledge of it.

In 1616 Sir Thomas Dempster, an expatriate Scottish scholar, wrote the manuscript *De Etruria Regali Libri Septem* (Seven Books on Etruria of the Kings) and dedicated it to Cosimo II de'Medici. Dempster came to Italy as professor of law at Pisa, where he began to investigate the Etruscans. He examined all known information about them—from ancient authors to more modern encounters with architecture, language, origins and history, religion, and art. In his attempts to create a multidisciplinary description of Etruscan culture he examined private collections of antiquities and studied the inscriptions on them—at this time there were few known archaeological sites, even though during the sixteenth and seventeenth centuries material from Etruscan tombs was being unearthed and sold. Dempster was the first scholar to recognize that some customs and institutions attributed to the Romans had in fact been created and used by the Etruscans. He located and named the major Etruscan cities, and he thought their language was probably a form of Hebrew. His manuscript was given to the duke on its completion and absorbed into his library. Dempster stayed on in Italy as professor of humanities at the University of Bologna and died in 1625.

A century later, while on a tour of Italy, Sir Thomas Coke, first Earl of Leicester and one of the founding members of the Society of Dilettanti, purchased Dempster's manuscript in Florence and took it back to England. Coke commissioned illustrations and additional notes on recent archaeological finds to be written by Florentine scholar Buonarroti and published *De Etruria Regali Libri Septem* between 1723 and 1726. Dempster's book created a new interest in the Etruscans, and its publication coincided with the discovery of several new and excavated Etruscan tombs. Both of these events were symptoms and causes of a European-wide mania for the Etruscans or for *Etruscheria,* which in England created an Etruscan style of interior decoration of English country houses and the ceramics made by Josiah Wedgewood called

"Etruria." More significantly, it led to Etruscan sites becoming part of the itinerary of "The Grand Tour."

In northern Italy itself the discovery of new Etruscan sites at Volterra, Arezzo, Siena, and Cortona propelled the study of this older civilization into the limelight of the Italian Enlightenment. In 1726 the Accademia Etrusca Delle Antichita eg Inscrizioni (The Etruscan Academy of Antiquities and Inscriptions) was founded to sponsor meetings, lectures, discussions, and publications on the Etruscans by scholars, politicians, and members of the ancient families of the central Tuscan city of Cortona. The academy leader was called a "lucumo," an Etruscan word for leader. These discussions were published in nine volumes between 1735 and 1791 as the *Saggi di Dissertazine.*

The most notable member of the new academy was the priest Antonio Gori, a professor of history, antiquities scholar, and Etruscan expert. Gori had excavated at Volterra for information about the Etruscans rather than for salable Etruscan antiquities—recording the provenance of artifacts and their place on plans and maps as well as their decorative details. Gori was a prolific promoter of *Etruscheria* and the study of antiquities in general, publishing in 1727 *Inscritiones Graecae et Latinae in Etruria Urbibus Extants* on local classical inscriptions; between 1731 and 1762 ten volumes of *Museum Florentinum,* a comprehensive treatment of collections in Florence and other early Tuscan cities; and between 1736 and 1743 three volumes of *Museum Etruscum.* The latter was an encyclopedia of the current collections of *Etruscheria* held by the academy in Cortona—the result of the donation of a library and collection by one of its members, which remains, along with Dempster's book, an invaluable record of Etruscan culture. Local interest was so great that Tuscan cities began to compete for sites and collections, and Gori set up a rival academy to Cortona's in Florence—the *Societa Colombaria.*

In 1761 Etruscan tombs at Corneto or Tarquinia were excavated, and their painted decorations were opened to the public. Thomas Jenkins was the first Englishman to visit and report on them. Jenkins was an expatriate English artist who lived in Italy, and one of the most powerful antiquarian art dealers and financiers in Rome. Although he was a respected antiquarian expert and a participant in learned societies, he was also in the business of forgeries and fakes. Jenkins underwrote excavations and supplied classical antiquities, paintings, and drawings to many of the major collections in England. He also spied and reported on the exiled Stuart royal family for the new Hanoverian dynasty.

Jenkins reported on his visit to the Tarquinia tomb to the Society of Antiquaries of London, of which he was a member, and in 1763 he also provided illustrations of the site, which were published with his account in *Philosophical Transactions of the Royal Society.* Jenkins's chief competitor and compatriot in Rome was Jacobite exile, Scottish architect, and antiquarian James Byres, who was also swept along by the interest in *Etruscheria.* He began to take tours of Etruscan sites and to provide copies of frescoes. Byres was well known as one of the best guides to Rome, and as a participant in the Grand Tour industry he helped to inform and educate the collectors of Europe. It was Byres who escorted Sir William and Lady Emma Hamilton around the ruins when they visited Rome, and it was Byres who managed to exhaust Edward Gibbon with his knowledge of sites and their history. Byres was also a dealer in antiquities—he sold the Portland vase to Hamilton. In 1766 Byres decided to publish an account of the Etruscan antiquities at Corneto and commissioned engravings to be made. Unfortunately, he was unable to raise enough subscribers to finance the project, and he never finished his proposed accompanying narrative about the details of the tombs and the plates themselves. The plates were published in 1842, long after Byres's death, by the next generation of lovers of *Etruscheria,* and they remain a significant source of information about Etruscan painting.

In the late eighteenth century scholars began to contemplate the possibility of civilizations predating those of Greek and Roman for the very first time. While remains in northern Europe were known to be older than those of the Romans, they were not yet thought to be the products of real or respectable civilizations—only of barbarians. It was not possible to estimate the age of such ruins without a written chronology, which was available and easily accessible for classical civilizations. Initially, Greek and Etruscan material cultures were lumped together, and their cultures were thought to be the same. Sir William Hamilton first outlined the differences between their pottery and suggested that they were in fact quite different cultures. This was a quantum leap in the use and benefits of typology in pottery and was used to great chronological effect during the next century.

The great age of Etruscan archaeology occurred in the nineteenth century, between the 1820s and 1860s, when the best preserved tombs at Cerveteri, Veii, Perugia, Marzabotta, and Vulci were discovered. An exhibition of the Etruscan collection of the Campanari family at the British Museum in London between 1836 and 1837 once again created huge interest in *Etruscheria.*

In 1839 Mrs. Hamilton Gray perpetuated this interest by publishing her popular armchair traveler and best seller *Tour of the Sepulchres of Etruria.* In 1842 the plates of James Byres's *Hypogaie, or the Sepulchral Caverns of Tarquinia, the Capital of Antient Etruria* were finally published, the same year that George Dennis traveled to Tuscany, Italy, with his artist friend Samuel Ainsley to take a good look at the newly discovered Etruscan tombs. The result of this and two other visits was published as *Cities and Cemeteries of Etruria* in 1848 and reprinted twice before the end of the century. The second edition of 1878, updated by Dennis with new finds and maps, was dedicated to Sir Austen Henry Layard, who by then had discovered another ancient civilization dating before the Greeks and Romans.

See also Publication of *Oedipus Aegypticus* (1652–1655); Grand Tour and the Society of Dilettanti (1670–1780); Sir William Hamilton's Collections. (1764–1798)

Further Reading

Pallottino, M. 1975. *The Etruscans,* trans. J. Cremona, ed. David Ridgway. Enlarged ed. Bloomington: Indiana University Press.

Ridgway, D. 1988. *The Etruscans.* 2nd ed. vol. 4. *The Cambridge Ancient History.* Cambridge: Cambridge University Press, 634–675.

Publication of Itinerarium Curiosum *(1724)*

Although the great antiquary John Aubrey (1626–1697) was the first to recognize the nature, size, and complexity of the site of Avebury and was similarly engaged in observing the nearby site of Stonehenge, it was another antiquary, William Stukeley (1687–1765), who published descriptions of both sites and brought them into public prominence. There is no doubt that Stukeley profited greatly from the careful observations of Avebury and Stonehenge that were recorded in Aubrey's unpublished *Monumenta Britannica,* but Stukeley's own observations about British field monuments first published in the *Itinerarium Curiosum* (1724) and later expanded in his two great works on Avebury and Stonehenge, *Abury* (1743) and *Stonehenge* (1740), were a major addition to what was then known.

Aubrey had been inspired by Dugdale's *Antiquities of Warwickshire* (1656) and had thought about doing much the same thing for Wiltshire. Never one to keep his thirst for knowledge within bounds, Aubrey expanded his gaze to all of Britain when he began work on *Monumenta Britannica* in 1663. The purpose of the *Monumenta* was to create a history of pre-Roman Britain through a

The megalithic site of Stonehenge was discussed in significant detail in Itinerarium Curiosum. *(Corel)*

careful analysis of field monuments, because he was convinced they had been fashioned much earlier than was currently thought. Aubrey first visited Avebury in 1649 while out hunting, but his detailed recording of the *Templa Druidum* (as he referred to it) was done more than twenty years later. Two plans of Avebury were produced, one a survey of the area enclosed by the bank and ditch and the other showing its relationship to other landscape features, such as the avenue, sanctuary, and Silbury Hill. While mapping the site Aubrey discovered a secondary circle of stones within the greater circle, the approach roads, and the relationship of Avebury to Silbury Hill and adjacent barrows.

Stukeley first visited Stonehenge in 1716 and was lent a transcription of Aubrey's *Monumenta.* From 1719 to 1724 Stukeley mapped Avebury, and it is fortunate that it survived, as the vast bulk of the site was destroyed in the mid-eighteenth century. During these years he was also in Stonehenge making fundamental discoveries about the site and its landscape. However, Stukeley and his friend the Earl of Pembroke also excavated at Stonehenge. These limited exposures allowed Stukeley to determine how the great stones had been erected. Attention was also paid to nearby barrows, which were sectioned, and the stratigraphy and artifacts carefully recorded.

Reading Stukeley's later works, where flights of interpretative fancy well and truly outweigh the results of careful observation, it is easy to forget just how great a field archaeologist he was. Unlike Aubrey, who could not finish and never got to publish his great *Monumenta*, Stukeley's patient and careful work was read and widely admired. Indeed, Stukeley was much more than a careful recorder of what he saw, but his desire to put flesh on prehistoric bones and to bring the pre-Roman history of Britain to life meant moving outside the bounds of objectivity and rationality. But with regard to his fieldwork and records Stukeley still has much to teach us.

See also Publication of *Britannia* (1586); English Antiquaries and Antiquarian Societies (1586–1770); Publication of *The Antiquities of Warwickshire* (1656).

Further Reading

Haycock, D. B. 2002. *William Stukeley: science, religion and archaeology in 18th century England.* Woodbridge, UK: Boydell.

Piggott, S. 1985. *William Stukeley: An eighteenth century antiquary.* 2nd ed. London: Thames and Hudson.

Stukeley, W. 1724. *Itinerarium curiosum: or, an account of the antiquities, and remarkable curiosities in nature or art, observed in travels through Great Britain.* London: printed for Messrs. Baker and Leigh.

Stukeley, W. 1740. *Stonehenge: a temple restor'd to the British Druids.* London: printed for W. Innys and R. Manby.

Stukeley, W. 1743. *Abury: a temple of the British Druids, with some others, described.* London: printed for the Author; sold by W. Innys.

Sweet, R. 2004. *Antiquaries: The discovery of the past in eighteenth-century Britain.* London: Hambledon and London.

Ucko, P., ed. 1991. *Avebury reconsidered.* London: Unwin Hyman.

Publication of Recueil d'antiquités égyptiennes, étrusques, romaines, et gauloises *(1752–1767)*

Anne Claude Philippe de Tubières-Grimoard de Pestels de Lévis, Comte de Caylus (1692–1765), nobleman, patron of the arts, antiquarian, and artist, did not collect antiquities just to possess and display them—he saw them as sources of information. He was admitted to the Royal Academy of Painting and Sculpture for his ability as an engraver and to the Academie des Inscriptions et Belles Lettres for his documentation and knowledge of ancient monuments and artifacts.

Between 1752 and 1767, Caylus published seven volumes of *Recueil d'antiquités,* an encyclopedic account, with detailed illustrations of different kinds of antiquities. The *Recueil d'antiquités* is now regarded as a remarkable contribution to the development of archaeology. Caylus believed that the detailed recording of objects was fundamental to antiquarian study and that close examination of an artifact would reveal information about how a particular culture at a particular time resolved fundamental issues. Caylus believed artifacts contained their own history if you only knew how to read it.

In the *Recueil d'antiquités* Caylus also argued for the value of using typology—that is, if every artifact were unique it could be used, through the process of comparison, to describe and differentiate between other similar artifacts—as part of a series or set of comparable criteria with which to study the material world. In his analysis of the differences between artifacts from different cultures Caylus anticipated art historian Johann Winckelmann's work later in the eighteenth century.

In its day the *Receuil d'antiquités* was regarded as a strong argument against the reliance of antiquarians on philology and history to interpret and understand ancient monuments and artifacts. It was a declaration of the possibility of their independence from these conservative disciplines, and it asked some critical questions: What would be the value of an artifact if you had neither history, language, nor known chronology to help to explain it, place it, or date it? What could be used instead? In this Caylus anticipated the problems of the study of prehistory in the next century. His insistence on the proper recording of the artifact—on firsthand knowledge of it and detailed illustration—to best understand it, remains one of the fundamentals of archaeology.

With publication of the *Receuil d'antiquités* Caylus also sought to make knowledge of antiquities more broadly available to other scholars. He realized that not everyone who was interested in studying artifacts had his privileged access to private collections or the ability to start their own. In this endeavor, as in all of his others, Caylus made substantial contributions to the Enlightenment.

See also Publication of *Oedipus Aegypticus* (1652–1655); Publication of *L'antiquité expliquée et représentée en figures* (1719–1724); Publication of *Geschichte de Kunst der Altertums* (1764).

Further Reading

Grummond, N. de. 1996. Caylus, Anne Claude Philippe, Comte de. In *Encyclopedia of the history of classical archaeology*, ed. N. de Grummond. vol. 1, 261–262. Westport, CT: Greenwood Press.

Ridley, R. T. 1992. A pioneer art-historian and archaeologist of the eighteenth century: the Comte de Caylus and his *Receuil. Storia dell'arte* 76: 362–375.

Schnapp, A. 1996. *The discovery of the past.* London: British Museum Press.

Foundation of the British Museum (1753)

Founded by act of the British parliament in 1753, the British Museum is widely regarded as having one of the greatest collections of antiquities anywhere in the world. As with many great museums, such as the Ashmolean and the Louvre, the British Museum was founded on the private collections of individuals, in this case the collections of antiquarians Sir Hans Sloane and Sir Robert Bruce Cotton. In its early years the British Museum was favored by monarchy. In 1757 King George II presented the Royal Library to the museum, and the library of George III was transferred there in 1828.

Notwithstanding the very great importance of the British Museum as a library, the fortunes of its collections of antiquities are of perhaps greater importance. These were also supplemented by royal patronage. For example, George III presented the Rosetta stone to the museum after its capture from the French in Egypt. Parliament was also a benefactor, especially in the celebrated case of the Parthenon marbles purchased from Lord Elgin for 35,000 pounds in 1816. Since that time the British Museum has acquired antiquities from all parts of the world, but it is especially strong in British antiquities, and in those derived from Egypt, western Asia, Greece, and Rome. Major pieces, such as the material from Nimrud, Nineveh, and Khorsabad (building on the collections and excavations of Sir Austen Henry Layard); the magnificent artifacts excavated by Sir Leonard Woolley at Ur; and elements of the mausoleum of Halicarnassus and the temple of Artemis at Ephesus, were acquired through the efforts of its trustees and private collectors. The Egypt Exploration Society was also a major source of Egyptian antiquities from the late nineteenth century until the beginning of the World War II. Notwithstanding the mechanics of assembling such great collections, the British Museum has also played a major role in pure archaeological research. Throughout the twentieth century, research by British Museum staff has added considerably to our knowledge of archaeology on the global scale.

See also British Museum Purchases the Parthenon Marbles (1816); Foundation of Great Egyptian Collections in England and France (1815–1835); Publication of *Nineveh and Its Remains* (1849); Publication of *A Thousand Miles up the Nile* (1877); Excavation of Ur (1922–1934).

Further Reading

The British Museum has a brief but very useful history on its Web site at http://www.thebritishmuseum.ac.uk/visit/history.html.

Boulton, W. H. 1931. *The romance of the British Museum; the story of its origins, growth, purpose and some of its contents.* London: S. Low, Marston and Co.

Caygill, M. 2003. *The British Museum: 250 years.* London: British Museum.

James, T. G. H. 1981. *The British Museum and ancient Egypt.* London: British Museum.

Wilson, D. 2001. *The collections of the British Musuem.* London: British Museum.

Publication of Antichita Romane *(1756)*

Giovanni Piranesi (1720–1778) was born near Venice. The son of a master builder, he was apprenticed to architects and engineers working in Venice. He arrived in Rome in 1740 to work as a draftsman, and then earned a living engraving views of the city to sell to its many Grand Tour tourists.

From the very beginning Piranesi was interested in, and inspired by, the unique remains of ancient Rome. He wanted to record them for posterity and for scholarly interest, and he was aware that many were at risk of disappearing as the modern city of Rome rebuilt itself. He also believed they could be a source of inspiration and knowledge for contemporary modern architects, engineers, and designers. After a decade of studying and illustrating Piranesi began to work on a comprehensive survey and record of Roman monuments, which was eventually published in 1756 as the four volumes of the *Antichita Romane.* Its audience was not only specialist antiquaries, but also a wider audience of architects, designers, and scholars. It was a path-breaking book because of its scope but also because Piranesi's methods of recording the monuments were revolutionary.

Piranesi outlined these in the preface. The simple illustration of the external features of a monument, he argued, was no longer enough. To do the monument and its illustration justice, all information about it had to be studied and recorded, including the inscriptions, historic sources, plan details, cross sections, internal views, descriptions of materials and techniques used to build it, and information about how it had decayed and why. If only some of the monument was left, either above or below the ground, then it could be reconstructed visually using all of the information available from sources and from the remains of its structure and materials at its site. And finally, all of this researching of antique sources and recording and surveying had enabled him to differentiate the original structures of ancient Rome from the medieval and modern accretions. Having done this, his next task was to complete and publish a complete reconstruction of ancient Rome, so that it could be glimpsed in all of its glory.

The four volumes comprised 250 illustrated plates of 315 monuments. The first volume, along with preface and general and cross-indexes, also contained citations of ancient sources, transcribed inscriptions, modern interpretations, history, and details and illustration of the structure of each monument (such as temples, arches, stadia, and thermae). It also laid out the urban plan of the classical city of ancient Rome, with the walls, defenses, aqueducts, and principal civil and religious monuments within its seven hills and the Tiber River.

The second and third volumes were devoted to the funerary architecture of ancient Rome, much of which had survived, and were based on research for a prior publication by Piranesi, *Camere Sepolcrali* (1750). These volumes detail numerous complex decorative forms, motifs, and inventions for the elucidation of designers and architects. However, Piranesi also used cross sections to demonstrate masonry techniques or underground structures used. Volume 4 detailed Rome's great engineering feats, such as its bridges, theaters, and porticoes.

Antichita Romane was widely acclaimed and collected by antiquarians, scholars, designers, and architects, and it was collected by many of the era's artistic patrons such as Catherine the Great of Russia and the Marquis de Marigny, Louis XIV's director of royal buildings. In the *Antichita Romane* Piranesi had moved illustration from the merely informative to the interpretative, from the souvenir to the detailed recreation of the monument in its historic landscape. His "unique achievement . . . rests on the application of a fresh mind to a hitherto restricted world of study, a mind which unusually combined a specialist understanding of engineering and architectural design with imaginative facilities of the highest order" (Wilton-Ely 1978, 47).

After the 1750s Piranesi's reasoned commitment to recording and celebrating the achievements of ancient Roman civilization turned into the impassioned defense of it. He published a number of polemical books arguing against the growing trend to regard classical Greek civilization as superior to that of classical Rome. The most famous of these was *Campo Marzio* (1762), published as a response to Winckelmann's attack on the decadence of the late Roman Empire.

During the 1760s Piranesi received and executed several decorative and architectural commissions in his own right from Pope Clement XIII and the Rezzonico family of Rome. After the pope's death he set up a successful business dealing in and restoring classical antiquities. His son Francesco (1758–1810) worked with him, and then completed and published more of his father's archaeological publications after his death. These included detailed maps of Hadrian's villa at Tivoli (1781), the emisarium of Lake Fucina (1791), and the excavations at Pompeii. Francesco reissued his father's work in a twenty-seven-volume edition between 1800 and 1807.

See also Foundation of the Palazzo dei Conservatori (1471); Raphael's Survey of Rome (1519); Grand Tour and the Society of Dilettanti (1670–1780); Rediscovery of Herculaneum and Pompeii (1709–1800).

Further Reading

De Grummond, N., ed. 1996. *An encyclopedia of the history of classical archaeology.* Westport, CT: Greenwood Press.

Wilton-Ely, J. 1978. *Piranesi.* London: Lund Humphries.

Sir William Hamilton's Collections (1764–1798)

His mother was a mistress of the Prince of Wales, and William Hamilton grew up with the future king George III of England. He had been a royal equerry, fought in the army, become a member of Parliament, and married a wealthy young heiress before taking up a diplomatic position representing the British government at the court of the king of Naples in 1764. This move by Hamilton was to alleviate the poor health of his wife, whose lung condition could be improved by living in a warm climate, and it prolonged her life by twenty years. After her death Hamilton stayed on in Naples for another twenty years, only being dislodged by a political revolution in 1798.

Hamilton was a product of the Enlightenment. He was a polymath, keenly interested in everything around him. He was an accomplished musician and sportsman, classically educated, an aristocratic patron of the arts and promoter of good taste, and founding member of the Society of Arts (later the Royal Academy) and of the Society of Dilettanti and the Society of Antiquaries. By the time he left London for Naples he had bought and sold two impressive collections of paintings comprising works by Holbein, Rubens, Titian, Poussin, Watteau, and Velazquez.

Hamilton's diplomatic role at the minor court of Naples initially seemed fairly low key. He was there at his own expense, and his official tasks were to keep his eye on local politics and report on rumors about both pretenders to the English throne and any of their supporters. But the Grand Tour increased the numbers of English travelers to Naples, and Hamilton took on the role of helping English visitors get access to the sites and collections of Herculaneum and Pompeii, which he found fascinating.

The court of Naples proved to be an extraordinary place during the last half of the eighteenth century. Its ruler, Ferdinand IV, son of the king of Spain, had married Maria Carolina, daughter of the Austrian empress Marie Therese and sister of the French queen Marie Antoinette. With its position on the superb bay of Naples and Vesuvius smoking in the background, with antiquities and evidence of classical art being unearthed constantly, and with the presence of many international grand tourers, the court enjoyed a cosmopolitan golden age. Ferdinand was a generous patron of the arts, and he redesigned and rebuilt much of the city, establishing a new opera house that attracted the great musicians of Europe. Local aristocrats and peasants moved to the city to enjoy its social and cultural life. Ferdinand loved hunting, shooting, and gambling and left the decisions of government to his wife, Maria Carolina. She was at one time or another both anti-French and anti-Spanish, and Hamilton was able to persuade her to remain politically neutral to England's advantage on a number of occasions.

Meanwhile, when he was not out shooting and hunting with Ferdinand or designing English gardens with Maria Carolina, Hamilton investigated Mount Vesuvius. He observed its eruption between 1765 and 1767 in great detail, writing two letters to the Royal Society of England that were published in *Philosophical Transactions* and reprinted elsewhere. As a result of these accounts he was made a member of the Royal Society, after which he wrote them a third letter with drawings of the changing shape of the volcanic cone. In 1767 he sent his collection of volcanic rocks and lava from Mount Vesuvius to the British Museum. Two years later he traveled to Mount Etna on Sicily and once again wrote an account of the volcano for the Royal Society. And still later he visited Catania to report to the Society on the effects of an earthquake. In 1772, these letters were published as a book, *Observations on Mount Vesuvius, Mount Etna and Other Volcanoes,* which sold so well it was reprinted twice.

At the same time he was pursuing his interest in geology, Hamilton's passion for collecting the Roman and Greek antiquities of southern Italy grew. Following in the footsteps of his friend Johann Winckelmann, who had recently published *History of Ancient Art* and *Monumenti Inediti,* Hamilton published details of his first collection entitled *Antiquités étruscques, grecques, et romaines, tirées du cabinet de M. Hamilton, envoye extrordinaire et plenipotniaire de S.M. Britanniques en cour de Naples* in 1767. It was both a record of the collection as well as a kind of sales catalog, rather than a sophisticated intellectual tract such as those Winckelmann was writing. Nonetheless it popularized collecting and collections by making them more accessible, and it ensured that the price of antiquities vastly increased.

In 1772 Hamilton sold this first collection to the British Museum so that he could keep collecting in Naples. But in parting with his precious artifacts he believed he was doing the best by them and by the British public. As an aristocratic patron he believed their display would raise public consciousness of the classical world and the decorative arts of the past and would inspire a new generation to greater artistic achievements. The display of Hamilton's first collection was a major attraction for the museum, establishing its Greek and Roman collection and having a significant impact on the development of interior design, architecture, and the fine and decorative arts in London over the next few decades. It was only eclipsed by the acquisition of the Greek vases of the fifth and sixth centuries BC, found at Etruscan sites in the 1830s.

Hamilton's second collection was probably his best. Comprising vases with beautifully painted mythological scenes and details of religious and social life, it was a treasure trove of everyday classical life, a rich source of archaeological detail, and an example of superlative art forms. The catalog of the collection was published through subscription, as was another third volume of Hamilton's collections in 1776. By then Hamilton had recognized the fourth century BC Greek origin of these pieces first thought to be Italian or Etruscan.

Hamilton's relationship with the British Museum became strained by the museum's refusal to purchase the Warwick vase from him. He regarded his second collection as more of a financial than a personal investment and wanted to realize its value. By this time Hamilton had spent much of his fortune on collecting and on maintaining his diplomatic household and lifestyle in Naples. Subsequently, he tried to sell objects to the Prussian and Russian royal families. Eventually, he became determined to remove his collection to England when he was whisked away from Naples and its violent revolution on Admiral Lord Nelson's flagship in 1798. Some of the collection went down with another ship that it was on, while most of it, fortunately the best pieces, was left behind and later recovered in 1801. When Hamilton returned to London, old and ill, ridiculed because of his second wife's affair with Nelson, and in need of funds, he sold the remainder to a private collector, whose family kept it until 1917 when it was auctioned and dispersed.

In his final years Hamilton approached the Society of Dilettanti with a proposal to publish a book on Herculaneum. He had first thought of this project in 1775 after he had written a number of letters with illustrative engravings of the site to the London Society of Antiquaries. He planned to write it based on his observations of the excavations over the past forty years. He died before the Society could support the project, however, and his notes for the book disappeared.

See also Foundation of the British Museum (1753); Rediscovery of Herculaneum and Pompeii (1709–1800); Grand Tour and the Society of Dilettanti (1670–1780); Publication of *Geschichte de Kunst der Altertums* (1764).

Further Reading

Carabelli, G. 1996. *In the image of Priapus.* London: Duckworth.

Constantine, D. 2001. *Fields of fire: a life of Sir William Hamilton.* London: Weidenfeld and Nicholson.

Hancarville, Pierre d'. 2004. *The collection of antiquities from the cabinet of Sir William Hamilton.* London: Taschen.

Morris, R. 1979. *HMS Colossus: The story of the salvage of the Hamilton treasures.* London: Hutchinson.

Schnapp, A. 1996. *The discovery of the past.* London: British Museum Press.

Publication of Geschichte der Kunst des Altertums *(1764)*

Johann Joachim Winckelmann (1717–1768) was born in and attended universities in Germany, studying mathematics, medicine, and ancient Greek and Latin, before becoming interested in classical art. Winckelmann worked as a schoolteacher and then as a librarian in the employ of Count von Bunau, an aristocratic historian of early Germany. It was in the latter position that Winckelmann was able to pursue his interests in classical antiquity and the visual arts and to keep up with all the most recent Enlightenment publications on history, politics, and natural science. When he left the count's service, Winckelmann lived briefly in Dresden, where he wrote essays on the significance and inspiration of ancient Greek painting and sculpture, which he had only ever glimpsed as prints or read about in books.

The opportunity to finally see the real thing came when Winckelmann converted to Catholicism and was awarded a stipend by the Saxon court. Moving to Rome in 1755, he began to study and make an inventory of Roman works of art. He was particularly impressed with the statues on display in the Belvedere in the Vatican, and he became a protégé of the powerful Cardinal Albani, eventually being appointed Vatican librarian in 1757. Between 1758 and 1764 Winckelmann wrote his major work, for which he is best known, *Geschichte der Kunst des Altertums* (History of the Art of Antiquity), in its day the most complete and encyclopedic account of the art of ancient Greece and Rome, with shorter sections on Egyptian, Near Eastern, and Etruscan art. In it Winckelmann proposed a system of chronological classification for ancient art. Winckelmann combined literary and visual evidence with the classifications and stylistic analyses undertaken by the Comte de Caylus. He devised a sequence of styles to describe the development of classical art—archaic, early classic, late classic, imitation, and decline—and matched it to a political and historic chronology. Winckelmann's paradigm is still used to describe the evolution of artistic traditions in archaeology.

Winckelmann's work was considered interesting but had very little impact at the time of its publication. In his next book, *Monumenti antichi inediti* (1767, Unpublished Antique Monuments), dedicated to Albani, Winckelmann attempted to put his theory into practice, but without great success. In the introduction to the book he reiterated his phases of stylistic development in the history of Greek art, but the entries themselves, although thorough and erudite, were conventional iconographic analyses. He did make one significant point—that the subjects depicted in ancient art (with a few Roman exceptions) were usually mythological in content, and not historical, as had been previously believed.

Between 1758 and 1759, Winckelmann spent a year in the city of Florence studying 3,000 engraved gems. In 1760 he published them in a catalog and made another breakthrough in the study of ancient art. He correctly used Greek rather than Roman mythology and history to explain the themes and images represented on the gems. He went on to define the features of Etruscan style and the succession of Etruscan stylistic periods. He argued that Etruscan art was earlier than and originally different from Greek art, and he traced the gradual influence of Greek art on Etruscan art until Greek art finally obscured and dominated it. For this work he was elected to the Etruscan Academy of Cortona, the English Royal Society, and the Academy of San Luca in Rome.

In 1763, Winckelmann's authority and growing fame was recognized by his appointment as commissario delle antichita (commissioner of antiquities) to the pope and membership in the Society of Antiquaries of London and other learned organizations. His descriptions and appreciations of art were quoted in guidebooks on Rome, and his work was cited as standard authorities in learned publications on the classical art of Rome and Greece. His new system of classifying classical art was only really widely appreciated toward the end of the eighteenth century, and his books remained important references for classical scholars until well into the nineteenth century.

Winckelmann published two short papers on ancient architecture in 1757 and 1762, another on the use of allegory in ancient art—in an attempt to get contemporary artists to use more of it—and two reports on the excavations at Herculaneum in 1762 and 1764. His accounts of wall paintings, the theater, streetscapes, and evidence of everyday Roman life found at the archaeological site created enormous interest in and wider knowledge of archaeology.

He was preparing another edition of the *History of the Art of Antiquity* when he was stabbed to death in a bar in Trieste. However, the book was eventually published in 1776 and was translated into French, German, Italian, and eventually English (by Americans) in the late nineteenth century. Winckelmann was the product of the Counter-Enlightenment, the prophet of romanticism with its preoccupation with truth, beauty, and nature and with ancient Greece as the ideal. While the French Catholic kings regarded themselves as the new Romans, Protestant German states looked to ancient Greek civilization as their role model.

See also Publication of *Recueil d'antiquités égyptiennes, étrusques, romaines, et gauloises* (1752–1767); Sir William Hamilton's Collections (1764–1798); Napoleon Loots Rome (1797).

Further Reading

Leppmann, W. 1979. *Winckelmann.* New York: Knopf.

Potts, A. 1994. *Flesh and the ideal: Winckelmann and the origins of art history.* New Haven, CT: Yale University Press.

Schnapp, A. 1996. *The discovery of the past.* London: British Museum Press.

Foundation of the Hermitage (1768)

The Hermitage takes its name from the building erected for the Russian empress Catherine the Great in 1764–1765, adjacent to the imperial winter palace in St. Petersburg. The Hermitage comes from the French 'ermitage' meaning a retreat or isolation—and Catherine used it for this purpose. It became a place where she could escape the affairs of state, and where she could store, display, contemplate, and enjoy her growing collection of art.

The first classical statue in the Russian imperial collection was given to Czar Peter the Great in 1720 by Pope Clement XI. It was a Roman copy of the Hellenistic nude *Taurian Venus,* and while the Scythian artifacts in Peter's kunstkammer (cabinet of curiosities) founded the prehistoric archaeological collections, this statue began the classical archaeological collections of what would become one of the great museums of Europe.

Like the other monarchs of western Europe in the seventeenth century, Czar Peter the Great was not only interested in the art of the Italian Renaissance and that of ancient Greece and Rome, but he was also preoccupied with acquiring examples and/or copies of it to enhance the status and taste of the Russian court. The collection of classical antiquities represented much of what Czar Peter wanted for Russia—for it to be an enlightened, modern, competitive, Westernized, and powerful European nation.

Peter and his successors continued to purchase paintings and sculpture to decorate their palaces. The Russian Academy of Fine Arts was established in 1757 as a department of the St. Petersburg Academy of Sciences by the empress Elizabeth. But it was Catherine the Great, Elizabeth's successor, who not only drastically increased the royal collections but also acquired a slice of classical Greece for the Russians to excavate.

The Russian empress Catherine II (1729–1796), also known as "the Great," began her career as a minor German princess, wife of a possible heir to the Russian throne who eventually became Czar Peter III. In 1762, supported by palace guards, she deposed, imprisoned, and assassinated her husband, seizing the throne for herself. Catherine ruled Russia from 1762 until 1796, the last of eighteenth-century Europe's great art patrons, an enlightened monarch who, like Louis XIV of France, regarded art as inspirational as well as inseparable from national propaganda and politics and the promulgation of fame. Catherine established a royal picture gallery and reestablished the Academy of Fine Arts as a separate institution under Count Ivan Shuvalov (who also founded the first Russian university in Moscow for Catherine), endowing it with enough funds to support Russian artists, architects, and designers and to employ French experts to educate them. She also commissioned artworks for her palaces, pieces of state art, such as the large bronze statue of Peter the Great (engraved "To Peter the first from Catherine the second"), as well as many public and royal buildings.

In 1764 Catherine II bought 225 paintings from the Berlin dealer Johann Gotzkowsky, a collector for the Prussian emperor Frederick II, who was having financial difficulties. This major purchase was followed by a number of acquisitions via intermediaries such as Dmitry Golitsyn, the Russian ambassador to Paris and The Hague, and notable experts such as Dennis Diderot and Frederic Grimm. In 1768 the private collections of the Prince de Ligne and Count Karl Coblenz were bought in Brussels for the Hermitage. In 1769 the collections of the late Count Heinrich von Bruhl, art connoisseur and former chancellor to Augustus II, elector of Saxony and king of Poland, were acquired. In 1772 the Italian Renaissance collection of paintings by Raphael, Titian, Rubens, and others belonging to the French banker Baron Crozat made its way to St. Petersburg from Paris. In 1779 the outstanding collection of Sir Robert Walpole, prime minister to kings George I and George II of England, made the same journey, and so did the collection of the Parisian Count Badouin in 1783. At Catherine's death, she had added 2,400 paintings to the collection.

Catherine II's passion for collecting also encompassed terracotta statuettes, engravings, cameos, coins and medals, gemstones (10,000 of them), minerals, and 38,00 volumes for her library, including the complete libraries of Diderot and Voltaire.

As the collections expanded, so did the buildings around the winter palace on the banks of the River Neva. To the small Hermitage were added the old (or large Hermitage), the Raphael Loggia (its first floor a replica of the one painted by Raphael in the Vatican), and the Hermitage Theatre (a reproduction of the ancient theater in Vincenza). The quiet retreat full of paintings had metamorphosed into a vast palace of halls and galleries, stuffed full of decorative arts, furniture, paintings, sculptures, and other collections of smaller artifacts.

In 1852 Czar Nicholas I added a new museum building to the site called the New Hermitage and opened it to the public.

See also First Archaeological Collections in Russia (1715); Russia Gets a Slice of Classical Antiquity (1782).

Further Reading

Burbank, J., and D. L. Ransel. 1998. *Imperial Russia.* Bloomington: Indiana University Press.

Paolucci, A. 2002. *Great museums of Europe.* Milan, Italy: Skira.

Foundation of the Louvre (1779–1793)

The public display of parts of the collections (paintings and furniture) of the kings of France on the first floor of the Luxembourg Palace in Paris was an initiative similar to that taken by many European monarchs during the second half of the eighteenth century and was the direct result of the Enlightenment. It was also proof of just how much art, politics, and society had changed since the reign of Louis XIV.

By the middle of the eighteenth century, the French royal art collections were regarded as more national than royal. They had become part of the cultural patrimony of the state, to be preserved for posterity, with the king as their protector rather than their sole owner. The king was responsible for maintaining, restoring, and conserving the collections, in the same way that he was responsible for the maintaining the state and its good government. Works of art and antiquities had become symbols and sources of national pride and collective ownership.

Despite remodeling the original Louvre Palace into the baroque style, Louis XIV had built an entirely new palace at Versailles, to which he moved his court and the best of the royal collections after 1682. The Louvre Palace, still the primary royal residence in Paris, and the home of the Academie Royale, became the repository for artworks that did not fit the decor of Versailles. However, for many Parisians, the Louvre remained the most important cultural site in France, the place for the ceremonial display of the French national art and power.

In 1745, Charles-Francois Lenormand de Tournehem, uncle of King Louis XV's mistress, Madame de Pompadour, was appointed director of the *batiments de roi* (the king's buildings). To demonstrate the king's generosity; to revitalize the Academie Royale's schools of painting, sculpture, and architecture; to promote historic painting; and to restore the government's control of the arts, Lenormand took the popular idea of a display in the Tuileries and set it up in the unoccupied Luxembourg Palace, originally built for Queen Marie de'Medici. And so it was that the first public art gallery in France opened.

The Louvre Museum in Paris. (PhotoDisc, Inc.)

Entry to the gallery on the second floor of the Luxembourg was free of charge and was much visited by the enlightened Parisian public, both men and women, bourgeois, educated consumers of high culture and potential patrons of the Academie Royale. From the very beginning the display was arranged to instruct visitors through the comparison and juxtaposition of different art styles. However, the poor state of the collection and its long-term neglect were obvious and were criticized by its visitors. In response to this, a survey and catalog were undertaken, and damaged works of art were properly conserved. The display remained open and popular until 1779 when the Luxembourg Palace was reoccupied as the city residence of the Comte de Paris, the brother of the new king Louis XVI.

Since the 1760s the idea of turning the Louvre into a national museum devoted to multiple fields of knowledge, rather than to just the visual arts, had become popular with the Parisian intelligentsia. This new museum would display its collections according to taxonomic classifications similar to those of a natural history museum, based on the historical evolution of different styles of art.

Plans to compensate Parisians for closing the Luxembourg Gallery with a new and larger display in the Grand Gallery of the Louvre Palace were already underway by the time the former closed. However, the new director of the king's buildings, Joseph Siffred Duplessis, Comte d'Angiviller, was more interested in using the new gallery for political rather than educative ends. He wanted it to demonstrate the king's generosity to his people and promote France's artistic, cultural, and political superiority by making it the very best of its kind in Europe. This new display, comprising the king's collection of old masters, examples of grand French history painting, and statues of great Frenchmen, was envisaged not only as bolstering and confirming France's national identity and pride but also as increasing political support for the regime and the king.

During the 1770s and 1780s the Comte d'Angiviller's plans for the grand gallery of the Louvre were drawn up and discussed. Arguments about the details of the construction of large lanterns to maximize natural light in the Louvre were in full swing when the French Revolution rudely interrupted. With the fall of the monarchy the royal collections at Versailles and Paris were declared national property, and the Louvre was the subject of a National Assembly decree within days after the Paris mob attacked the Tuileries. It was placed under the control of the new minister of the interior, Jean-Marie Roland, and became the depot for storing the newly confiscated property of aristocrats, émigrés, churches, and dissolved royal academies. A commission was established to decide what was worthy enough to be accessioned into what would become the new central museum of arts and sciences.

In 1793, Dominique Garat, philosopher and man of letters, replaced Roland, and began to organize the collections and displays so they could be opened to the public as part of the commemoration of the first anniversary of the birth of the republic. There was also a broader political purpose. It was felt that the calm and order displayed in the museum would be a symbol of the calm and order of the new republican government of France. The borders and provinces of the country might be in turmoil, but in Paris civilization reigned.

No matter what the regime, the Louvre remained an important ideological space. For the republic it manifested the benefits of republican ideology, one based on rational philosophy and the belief in progress. It demonstrated that republicans were not barbarians; they were capable of appreciating and promoting the arts and the sciences of Western civilization, but they were just more democratic about doing it. The Louvre became a symbol of revolutionary achievement, and all of its contents were the collective property of the French people.

During the 1790s there were many debates about what would hang and what would be displayed in the national museum. Obviously, royal portraits; paintings about royalist achievements, events, and history; and religious art would not encourage the right kind of republican sentiments, and so these remained in storage. However, any qualms about subject matter disappeared when war booty was put on display. In 1794, within five days of their arrival in Paris, the 150 paintings confiscated by the French army from collections in what is now modern Belgium were displayed to Parisian crowds.

The need for a museum of antiquities was recognized as early as 1794. Antiquities were thought not to present the same potential ideological problems that had been posed by the subjects of paintings, but their very diversity sparked debates about what qualified as antiquities—there were so many different kinds. The need to systematically display and interpret antiquities was the subject of other debates. Did you put them together as inscriptions, medals, gems, mosaics, or instruments, even if they were for different, that is, religious, military, or civil, uses? Did statues go with bas-reliefs if they were from the same period or the same country? Did you divide them up into art to be placed with the other arts in the Louvre or historical documents to be kept in the national library?

Notwithstanding all this behind-the-scenes wrangling, visiting the Louvre proved to be immensely popular with the French public. There are contemporary descriptions about fashionable women rubbing shoulders with artists, peasants, the elderly, children, and soldiers. While access to the Louvre's collections embodied the republican principles of liberty, equality, and fraternity, there were no education guides to make them more accessible. The display was still all about collective ownership and nationalism. Many visitors to the display of looted art put together in1797 at the Louvre after Napoleon's conquest of Italy may not have appreciated that it was the greatest collection of art ever brought together under one roof—what they did know was that it now belonged to them and to France.

See also Foundation of the French Academy in Rome (1666); Napoleon Loots Rome (1797); Napoleon I Funds the Excavation of Romans Sites and Antiquities (1808–1814).

Further Reading

McClellan, A. 1994. *Inventing the Louvre.* Cambridge: Cambridge University Press.

Russia Gets a Slice of Classical Antiquity (1782)

During the reign of Empress Catherine II the status of Russia's two longest foreign policy problems were resolved. Both had to do with extending Russia's borders in the west and, more importantly, in the southeast, and both became entangled with the policies of the other great powers of Europe. The problems encompassed the status and independence of Poland, the need for a Russian seaport on the Black Sea, the need to increase Russian power in the eastern Mediterranean, and the revival of the idea of a Greek empire led by Russia at the expense of the Ottoman Turks.

In 1762, Russia, prompted by a new and strong nonintervention alliance with Prussia, invaded the Polish province of Courland (modern Latvia) and placed a puppet king on its throne. This kept the rest of Poland weak with Courland acting as a buffer between it and Russia. In 1768, threatened by Russia's alliance with Prussia and thwarted by the same in their abilities to manipulate the Polish situation to their own advantage, France and Austria pushed the Turkish/Ottoman Empire into declaring war on Russia.

At first the Russian army was successful, defeating Turkish troops and invading Moldavia, Bucharest, Georgia, and the Crimea, but as they were overstretched and faced other uprisings against them in Poland and central Asia, they concluded a peace treaty with the Ottomans in 1772. As part of these peace negotiations Poland was further divided: Prussia got the western agricultural region, Austria got Galicia (western Ukraine) and the important commercial center of Lvov, and Russia took the Polish part of Livonia (modern Lithuania and southern Latvia). In 1774, a Russian treaty with the Ottoman Empire guaranteed Russia free passage through the Bosporus and Dardanelles, the fortresses of Kerch and Yenikale, a substantial amount of war indemnity, the autonomy of Moldavia and Wallachia (provinces of modern Romania), an end to the oppression of Orthodox Christians in the Caucasus, and recognition of the independence of the Crimea—which in the long term would guarantee its integration into Russia. In 1776, while England was at war with its American colonies and Prussia and Austria were quarrelling over Bavaria, Russian forces entered the Crimea and installed their own puppet ruler or khan.

At around this time the so-called "Greek project" became popular with the Russian empress Catherine II and her governing elite. This was Russia's intention of reestablishing the Greek empire, with its capital at Constantinople and with Catherine II's second grandson, Konstantin Pavlovich, as he had been especially christened for the role in 1779, as its emperor. To this end, Russia moved to incorporate the Crimea by first negotiating an anti-Ottoman agreement with the Austrian emperor Joseph II.

In 1782 the Crimean puppet khanate fell, and before Turkish troops could intervene, Catherine ordered the Russian army into the Crimea. It was officially annexed in 1783, the same year the Eastern Orthodox states of Georgia and Armenia, sandwiched between Turkey and Russia in the Caucasus, became protectorates of Russia and Russian troops were sent to garrison the city of Tiflis (modern Tbilisi).

In 1787, Catherine, accompanied by her court and French and English diplomats, visited the Crimea, where she met the Austrian emperor and the king of Poland. At the same time the Russian army and the Black Sea fleet staged demonstrations of their numbers and efficiency. Russia's imperial power was on show not only for the benefit of Europe but also as a direct threat to the Ottomans. Crimea was called "New Russia," the gates set up at the entrance to the city of Kherson were named "the road to Byzantium," and the new Russian towns with Russian colonists were given Greek names. The second Russo-Turkish war began the same year. The Austrians joined Russia against the Ottomans and took Belgrade and Bucharest.

By 1789 this eastern-based conflict caused the Swedes to go to war with Russia and the Prussians to do the same against Austria. The Russians eventually defeated the Ottoman army and navy and in 1791 a peace treaty was negotiated in which the Russian annexation of the Crimea was recognized. In 1792 Russia once again declared war on Poland, and peace negotiations in 1795 led to its continued division, the complete integration of Courland into Russia, and more territorial gains by Prussia. After the failure of the Kosciousko rebellion later during that same year, Poland disappeared completely.

The Crimean annexation and the network of alliances that had enabled it to proceed moved Russia another step closer to the "Greek idea," one based on past empires and ancient classical history. However, this was as far as the idea of a Russian-led Greek empire got. France under revolutionary government and Napoleon Bonaparte would change all the old rules and alliances. However, the long-term benefit to archaeology, ancient history, and classical studies was established when Russian historians and archaeologists began to explore classical monuments on the northern Black Sea littoral region and to focus again on Byzantine history.

See also Foundation of the Hermitage (1768).

Further Reading

Kamenskii, A. B. 1997. *The Russian empire in the eighteenth century*, trans. D. Griffiths. Armonk, NY: M. E. Sharpe.

Foundation of the Asiatic Society of Bengal (1784)

The Asiatic Society of Bengal was established in 1784 in the British East India Company's capital of Calcutta. Governor and General Warren Hastings was its patron, and Senior Judge Sir William Jones (1764–1794) was its founding president. Jones was a substantial philological scholar who knew Arabic and Persian when he was appointed to India and knew twenty-eight languages by the end of his career there. He became interested in Sanskrit, translating significant pieces of Hindu literature and Hindu and Arabic/Muslim legal treatises, which contributed to the establishment of a code of civil law in India. The Asiatic Society's aims were to inquire into the history, antiquities, arts, sciences, and literature of Asia, and from the beginning it was envisaged that learned Indians would become members (they did finally in 1829). Between 1788 and 1839, the Society collected and published on oriental manuscripts, coins, and antiquities in *Asiatic Researches*, which set the standard for oriental research of the day. In 1847 the Society began to make a wide variety of oriental literature more broadly available in its *Bibliotheca Indica* series. It was the model for the foundation of the Royal Asiatic Society of Great Britain and Ireland (1823) and other Asiatic societies in Europe and North America.

The founding of the Asiatic Society of Bengal was the result of the European Enlightenment—the belief in the value and benefits of knowledge and science—and in a universal history. Biblical history and chronology was based on the idea that all humans were related—and one of the major tasks of the Society in India was to prove it. Jones believed Indians were descendents of Noah's son Ham and that Sanskrit was related to other ancient languages, such as Egyptian, Phoenician, and Celtic. For 3,500 years Sanskrit was the language of religion, philosophy, medicine, math, astronomy, and literature—of every branch of learning not only in India, but also in every other region influenced by Indian culture until their conquest by Islamic peoples and the use of Arabic by the new ruling class and religion. Through his study of Sanskrit, a mixture of several older Indo-Aryan dialects, and by comparing it with the history and developments of other languages, Jones founded Indo-European linguistics.

Through his work Jones changed public opinion toward India. He proved that the people of India had civilization at a time when Europe did not. Jones and his colleagues at the Asiatic Society were evidence of a kind of intellectual archaeology, of exploring and appreciating south Asia through the history of its culture. Together they were among the first who believed in the great contribution of oriental civilization to world history and made it accessible to Europe and to India itself. Because of the Society's members, oriental studies became a respected discipline.

See also Discovery of Angkor Wat and Khmer Civilization (1860); Foundation of the Archaeological Survey of India (1861).

Further Reading

Cannon, G. H. 1990. *The life and mind of Oriental Jones: Sir William Jones, the father of modern linguistics.* Cambridge: Cambridge University Press.

Franklin, M. J. 1995. *Sir William Jones.* Cardiff: University of Wales Press.

Mukherjee, S. N. 1968. *Sir William Jones: A study in eighteenth-century British attitudes to India.* Cambridge: Cambridge University Press.

Excavation of a Burial Mound in Virginia (1787)

Thomas Jefferson (1743–1826) has many claims to fame as a great American president, patriot, scientist, diplomat, and antiquarian. Jefferson was particularly interested in the human history of North America before its occupation by Europeans. Although he thought the greatest source of information would be in the languages of the indigenous tribes and nations, he was also aware of the capacity of archaeological evidence to contribute to our understanding of indigenous history.

His most explicit discussion of such evidence is found in his *Notes on the State of Virginia* (1787), particularly of an Indian mound near his home at Monticello:

> I know of no such thing existing as an Indian monument; for I would not honour with that name arrow points, stone hatchets, stone pipes, and half-shapen images. Of labour on the large scale . . . it be the barrows of which many are to be found all over this country. They are repositories of the dead, . . . but on what particular occasion constructed, was matter of doubt.

Thomas Jefferson, excavator of a mound on the Rivanna River, Virginia. (National Archives)

Some have thought they covered the bones of those who had fallen in battles fought on the spot of interment. Some ascribed them to the custom, said to prevail among the Indians, of collecting, at certain periods, the bones of all their dead, wheresoever deposited at the time of death. Others again supposed them the general sepulchers for towns, conjectured to have been on these grounds; and this opinion was supported by the quality of the lands in which they are found (those constructed of earth being generally in the softest and most fertile meadow-grounds on river sides) and by a tradition, said to be handed down from the Aboriginal Indians, that, when another died a narrow passage was dug to the first, the second reclined against him, and the cover of earth . . . replaced and so on . . .

> But on whatever occasion they may have been made, they are of considerable notoriety among the Indians; for, a party passing, about thirty years ago, through the part of the country where the barrow is, went through the woods and directly to it without any instructions or inquiry and having staid about it sometime, returned with expressions which were construed to be those of sorrow, they returned to the high road, which they had left about half a dozen miles to pay this visit, and pursued their journey. There is another barrow, much resembling this in the low grounds of the South branch of the Shenandoah. . . . This has been opened and found to contain human bones, as the others do. There are also many others in other parts of the country. (Jefferson 1944, 222–224)

Jefferson excavated a mound on the Rivanna River, which he reported as being forty feet in diameter and about ten feet high. Several test pits were dug, along with a trench through the entire mound, which was excavated to ground level. This trench provided clear evidence of stratigraphy, and the state of the human remains (which included those of children) allowed him to conclude that the mound had been used discontinuously as a place of burial.

See also Publication of *Descriptions of the Antiquities Discovered in the State of Ohio and Other Western States* (1820); Publication of *Ancient Monuments of the Mississippi Valley* (1847).

Further Reading

Jefferson, T. 1944. *The Life and Selected Writings of Thomas Jefferson,* eds. A. Koch and W. Reden. New York: Modern Library.

Silverberg, R. 1968. *Mound Builders of ancient America: the archaeology of a myth.* Athens: Ohio University Press.

Willey, G. R., and J. Sabloff. 1973. *A history of American Archaeology.* San Francisco: W. H. Freeman.

Investigation of Palenque Begins (1787)

During the early eighteenth century, Catholic missionaries had taken up residence in the Yucatan hinterland. It was from them and their families and associates that tales of stone houses in the jungle began to circulate. In 1773 the Mexican scholar Ramon Odonez y Aguiar visited what would later be identified as the great Maya site of Palenque and was so impressed by what he had found that he reported it to the governor of what was then Guatemala, Jose Estacheria. Nevertheless, it was almost a decade before the first government-sanctioned expedition to Palenque was organized by Estacheria, who in 1784 sent Jose Antonio Calderon to the site for three days. Calderon reported finding more than two hundred stone houses and, surprisingly, what he thought had to be a large palace. Calderon reported that these ruins were sophisticated enough to be of Roman origin.

Intrigued by Calderon's report, in 1785 Estacheria sent another expedition, this time led by as much of an expert as he could find in Guatemala at that time. The architect Antonio Bernasconi, who was helping to design the new capital Guatemala City, after the old capital of Antigua had been devastated by an earthquake, was appointed to lead the expedition. In contrast to Calderon, Bernasconi's report was full of architectural details, which he emphasized were not recognizably European in any way. This report was sent to King Charles III of Spain.

Before becoming king of Spain, Charles III had spent a number of years as king of Naples and Sicily, where he had encouraged, and been fascinated by, the excavations of the Roman site of Herculaneum. On moving to the Spanish throne, Charles III became interested in the history of his rich Mesoamerican colonies, whose artifacts and treasures filled his royal cabinet of curiosities. After almost two hundred years of colonization, many of the great monuments and sites of Mexico had been obliterated by Spanish state and church authorities, as part of the political repression of native people and their forced conversion to Catholicism. However, many of the accounts of these processes of colonization, and descriptions of monuments before their destruction, had been sent to the Spanish court. Charles III commissioned the scholar Juan Batista Munoz to write a history of the Mesoamerican Indians, and to do this, Munoz had worked through and reorganized all the relevant documents in the Spanish royal archives. In the process he became an expert on the subject. It was Munoz who, on receiving a copy of Bernasconi's report from Governor Estacheria, recognized the significance of these newly discovered ruins and brought them to the attention of his antiquarian monarch.

Indeed, Charles III was so interested that he ordered a more extensive exploration of Palenque to be undertaken and ordered Munoz to write what it needed to accomplish. From the very beginning Munoz grasped that these ruins might be able to provide information about "the origins and history of the ancient Americans" (Bernal 1980, 90). As important, he also believed they could be evidence of the grand and wonderful buildings in Guatemala and the Yucatan described by the conquistadors that had now disappeared. He also believed that these building were probably much older than the

Spanish conquest and that their builders and occupants had been "more superior in culture and knowledge" than the Indians of the fifteenth century, even if they were not equal to European civilization.

Munoz's lists of instructions for the expedition's participants were precise. They were to record the details of:

> doors, niches and windows, looking carefully at what may be found to be of ashlar, as well as those of what is called rough stone and mortar and to the mortar in these: making careful descriptions and drawings of any figures, the sizes and method of cutting of stones and bricks or adobes with particular attention being paid to what are called arches and vaultings. And bring away pieces of the plaster, mortar, stucco, bricks both fired and unfired; potsherds and any other utensils or tools to be found, making excavations where it seems best. (Bernal 1980, 90)

In response to the king's orders in 1787, the new Marquis of Sonora, José Galvez, sent Captain Antonio Del Rio and the Mexican illustrator Amendares to Palenque, both of whom did justice to their royal instructions. Not content with clearing the site and amassing details about the materials and methods of construction, Del Rio also recorded his ideas about its origins and builders. He thought some Greeks, Phoenicians, or Romans had wandered into Mesoamerica and had stayed long enough to teach the local people building and sculpting techniques, and he believed Palenque was the result of local people adapting these crafts for their own ends, in their own style. However, on comparing Palenque with other Maya sites that had been described, he also believed that the ancestors of the contemporary Maya had built Palenque and that the ruins were very old. Pieces from the site, as requested, were sent back to Spain with the Del Rio report.

In 1788, on receiving and reading Del Rio's report and the artifacts, the new king of Spain, Charles IV, ordered a complete archaeological survey of his Mesoamerican colonies, in which every ancient ruin and monument was to be visited and recorded. He appointed the Austrian scholar, Guillermo Dupaix, as leader. Dupaix, in turn, recruited the draftsman Luciano Castenada for the expedition. In 1805 and 1806 they explored and illustrated monuments in the valleys of Mexico and Oaxaca and in the modern Mexican states of Morelos, Cordoba, Puebla, and Veracruz. They discovered the site of Monte Alban. In 1807 the final expedition finished at Palenque. Dupaix was convinced that the citizens of Atlantis had built Palenque, Monte

Alban, and El Tajin. He took a number of artifacts from the site back to Mexico City where they were eventually deposited in the national museum.

Dupaix's report was eventually published in Europe in the 1830s. Del Rio's had been published in 1822. These reports, along with the accounts of the German naturalist Alexander von Humboldt's visit to Mexico, published in 1811, and of Count Waldeck, inspired and tantalized the next generation of Mesoamerican explorers, especially John Stevens and Frederick Catherwood.

See also Rediscovery of Herculaneum and Pompeii (1709–1800); Rediscovering Maya Civilization (1839–1843).

Further Reading

Bernal, Ignacio. 1980. *A history of Mexican archaeology*. New York: Thames and Hudson.

Publication of Nenia Britannica *(1793)*

James Douglas (1753–1819) after a varied secular life as a museum assistant, businessman, mercenary in the Austrian army, and lieutenant in the Leicester militia, gave up his active life to study divinity at Peterhouse College, Cambridge.

In 1780 he was elected a fellow of the Society of Antiquaries, the same year he took up the first of a variety of positions in the church in southern England.

Nenia Britannica, or a Sepulchral History of Great Britain, from the earliest period to its general conversion to Christianity was published in London between 1786 and 1793 and dedicated to the Prince of Wales. The *Nenia Britannica* had originally been issued in twelve parts. It comprised descriptions of British, Roman, and Saxon sepulchral rites and ceremonies and the contents of hundreds of graves opened by Douglas, which included Celtic, British, and Danish barrows, all of which were illustrated by him as sepia aquatints. His training as an army engineer meant that he had a good understanding of basic geological principles (such as stratigraphy), and he was a fine draftsman and surveyor. Indeed, his archaeological explorations began as he surveyed fortifications in the Chatham Lines in Kent (as part of a preparation against a possible invasion of Britain by Napoleon). During this work Douglas discovered many Anglo-Saxon burials, which he carefully planned and drew sections of. His skill in observation also allowed him to credibly distinguish between the tumuli and barrows of different periods, thereby making it very clear that the pre-Saxon history of England was a great deal more complicated than had been thought.

Notwithstanding the very high quality of the *Nenia Britannica* as an example of field excavation and reporting, Douglas's contemporaries largely ignored the work.

The artifacts Douglas found during the course of his excavations were sold by his widow to Sir Richard Colt Hoare, a great barrow excavator of the nineteenth century, who presented them to the Ashmolean Museum in Oxford.

See also Foundation of the Ashmolean Museum (1683); Publication of *The Ancient History of North and South Wiltshire* (1812).

Further Reading

Jessup, R. 1975. *Man of many talents: an informal biography of James Douglas 1753–1819.* London: Phillimore.

Sweet, R. 2004. *Antiquaries: The discovery of the past in eighteenth-century Britain.* London: Hambledon and London.

John Frere Writes to the Society of Antiquaries of London (1797)

In 1797 John Frere, a gentleman farmer and graduate of Cambridge University, was passing through the Suffolk village of Hoxne. Frere was a person of considerable curiosity and the story goes that he paused to watch workmen digging clay for bricks in a pit just south of the village. This was innocent enough, but he also noticed that the workmen were filling potholes in the adjacent road with flints that looked to him to have been shaped into regular forms by human hands. Frere inquired where they had come from and was shown a layer of gravel about 12 feet below the surface, underneath layers of sand and brick-earth. He was sufficiently intrigued by the discovery to write to the Society of Antiquaries of London.

> Letter To The Rev. John Brand, Secretary, Read June 22, 1797
>
> Sir:
>
> I take the liberty to request you to lay before the Society some flints found in the parish of Hoxne, in the county of Suffolk, which, if not particularly objects of curiosity in themselves, must, I think, be considered in that light from the situation in which they were found.

They are, I think, evident weapons of war, fabricated and used by a people who had not the use of metals. They lay in great numbers at the depth of about twelve feet, in a stratified soil, which was dug into for the purpose of raising clay for bricks.

The strata are as follows:

1. Vegetable earth 1 1/2 feet.
2. Argill 7 1/2 feet.
3. Sand mixed with shells and other marine substances 1 foot.
4. A gravelly soil, in which the flints are found, generally at the rate of five or six in a square yard, 2 feet.

In the same stratum are frequently found small fragments of wood, very perfect when first dug up, but which soon decompose on being exposed to the air; and in the stratum of sand (No. 3), were found some extraordinary bones, particularly a jawbone of enormous size, of some unknown animal, with the teeth remaining in it. I was very eager to obtain a sight of this; and finding it had been carried to a neighboring gentleman, I inquired of him, but learned that he had presented it, together with a huge thighbone, found in the same place, to Sir Ashton Lever, and it therefore is probably now in Parkinson's Museum.

The situation in which these weapons were found may tempt us to refer them to a very remote period indeed; even beyond that of the present world; but, whatever our conjectures on that head may be, it will be difficult to account for the stratum in which they lie being covered with another stratum, which, on that supposition, may be conjectured to have been once the bottom, or at least the shore, of the sea. The manner in which they lie would lead to the persuasion that it was a place of their manufacture and not of their accidental deposit; and the numbers of them were so great that the man who carried on the brickwork told me that before he was aware of their being objects of curiosity, he had emptied baskets full of them into the ruts of the adjoining road. It may be conjectured that the different strata were formed by inundations happening at distant periods, and bringing down in succession the different materials of which they consist; to which I can only say that the ground in question does not lie at the foot of any higher ground, but does itself overhang a track of boggy earth, which extends under the fourth stratum; so that it should rather seem that torrents had washed away the incumbent strata and left the bogearth bare, than that the bogearth was covered by them, especially as the strata appear to be disposed horizontally, and present their edges to the abrupt termination of the high ground.

If you think the above worthy the notice of the Society you will please to lay it before them.

I am, Sir,
with great respect,
Your faithful humble Servant (Frere 1800)

Frere received no comment save the secretary's thanks for his "curious and most interesting communication." But in 1859 when Hugh Falconer, John Evans, and Joseph Prestwich were in the process of proving high human antiquity in Britain (following from their work at Brixham Cave and their visit to the sites excavated by Boucher de Perthes in France), Hoxne (and Frere) finally got their due. In 1997, two hundred years after Frere's letter was read, a memorial was erected in the chancel of St Bartholomew's Church at Finningham, Suffolk. It reads: "John Frere FRS FSA who from his discoveries at Hoxne was the first to realise the immense antiquity of mankind."

See also High Human Antiquity in the Somme Valley (1841–1864); Excavation at Brixham Cave (1858–1859); Publication of *Pre-historic Times* (1865).

Further Reading

Frere, J. 1800. Account of flint weapons discovered at Hoxne in Suffolk. *Archaeologia* 13: 204–205.

Grayson, D. K. 1983. *The establishment of human antiquity.* New York: Academic Press.

Van Riper, A. B. 1995. *Men among the mammoths: Victorian science and the discovery of human prehistory.* Chicago: University of Chicago Press.

Napoleon Loots Rome (1797)

In 1796 General Napoleon Bonaparte (1769–1821) led the army of the French republic into Italy. While the general was the first to admit he didn't know much about art, he certainly understood its political value—and the ideological importance of the Louvre Museum. Experts in art and antiquities often accompanied the French army, to help advise on the location and the quality of collections of war booty to be brought back to Paris. In Italy, in the absence of experts, Napoleon had requested and been sent a list of works of art that he was to bring back to Paris. Works of art and antiquities were often specifically included in the terms of surrender or armistice that Napoleon

Napoleon Bonaparte. (Library of Congress)

negotiated with the rulers of various Italians states that he had defeated, such as Piedmont and Parma.

In 1797 in Bologna Napoleon signed an armistice with delegates of the papal states, whereby 100 paintings and statues, and 500 volumes from the Vatican collections in Rome, chosen by special French republican commissioners, were to be given to France. The commissioners had used published catalogs and travel guides to compile this list of art and antiquities, the criteria of which were celebrity and rarity.

The sculptures the *Belvedere Apollo,* the *Laocoön,* and the *Belvedere Torso,* at the top of the list, were the greatest prizes of all. For centuries they had been universally admired, sources of artistic and literary inspiration and emulation. The rest of the 83 antique marbles taken back to Paris included Hadrian's *Antinous, Juno, the Nile* and *Tiber river gods,* and portraits of members of Roman imperial families, poets, dramatists, and orators. The paintings were among those identified by Poussin almost a century before as the best of the Italian Renaissance—works by Raphael, Cominichino. Caravaggio, Saachi, and

Guericino—and they had been copied and emulated by art students ever since. While many of these were guaranteed to inspire the artists of the republic, others were by minor painters and were chosen to fill in gaps in the extant French collections in the Louvre.

The French government justified their confiscation of art and antiquities on ideological, pedagogical, and military grounds, similar to those of the former royal government. The republican French empire had succeeded the ancient Roman one. The Louvre Museum and Paris were now the center of this new imperial dream. Paris, as the new political capital of a Europe shaped by republican forces should be the capital of art and knowledge as well, and the Louvre would become the museum of this new world order. As the politically and culturally superior nation in Europe, France had the great responsibility to safeguard the world's treasures for the benefit of mankind and posterity.

The art collection from Rome made its way to Paris, along with other war booty from Venice, in what was called the "third convoy." The progress of this convoy was the subject of bulletins in Paris. Its arrival was greatly anticipated, and it was paraded through the city, to the Champs de Mars, its arrival timed to coincide with the first anniversary of the fall of Robespierre and the end of the Reign of Terror, as part of a greater festival of liberty. The convoy was organized into three sections: natural history, books and manuscripts, and fine arts. While the two latter were safely packed into containers, it was the site of the exotic plants and animals belonging to the first category that really stirred the crowd.

Plans for a whole new gallery to display the sculptures from Rome were drawn up in 1797, estimated to be completed in 1799. When Napoleon visited the Louvre after his coup d'etat of 18 Brumaire he discovered the project was behind schedule. He appointed the Italian archaeologist Ennio Quirino Visconti (1751–1818) as the Louvre's keeper of antiquities. In 1800 the first of the new sculpture rooms was opened to the public.

See also Foundation of the Louvre (1779–1793); Napoleon I Funds the excavation of Roman Sites and Antiquities (1808–1814).

Further Reading

McClellan, A. 1994. *Inventing the Louvre.* Cambridge: Cambridge University Press.

Ridley, R. 1992. *The eagle and the spade: Archaeology in Rome during the Napoleonic era.* Cambridge: Cambridge University Press.

Section Two

Archaeology in the Nineteenth Century

THE ARCHAEOLOGY OF ORIGINS, NATIONS, AND EMPIRES

This essay surveys the history of archaeology in the nineteenth century, a period of tremendous growth in our understanding of the archaeology of the prehistoric and historic past. During the nineteenth century a distinct discipline of archaeology came into being, and by the end of the century archaeologists had widened their geographical as well as their temporal foci to cover virtually the entire globe, and they had begun to explore the truly remote time before the evolution of modern human beings. The forty-six milestones discussed in Section Two of this book reflect this extraordinary diversity—from the foundation of the National Museum of Denmark (and the great developments in Scandinavian archaeology that followed) to the discovery of Biblical empires of the Near East and the decipherment of their writings and to the foundation of scientific archaeology in the Americas.

During the nineteenth century the great potential of archaeology to inform us about the history of humankind began to be realized. Although it is tempting to see the nineteenth century as a kind of preparation or test bed for the great developments, both theoretical and methodological, that were to follow in the twentieth century, it is perhaps more useful for us to reflect on how much influence (particularly in terms of theory) the nineteenth century was to have on the development of archaeology.

In the first essay, "The Birth of Archaeology," I focused on the important relationships between the emerging disciplines of archaeology, history, and anthropology and claimed that the crucial development for archaeology was the general acceptance (by the end of the eighteenth century) that highly significant information about the histories of nations and races (not just in Europe, but also elsewhere) lay in the remains of societies that had existed before writing. Learning to "read" this new evidence drawn from material culture, landscape, ethnographic analogy, and a host of other sources was seen as a vital step in the creation of prehistoric archaeology, and it flowed from the work of antiquarians. In that essay I made it clear that while the history of the archaeology of the classical world (specifically ancient Greece and Rome) shared much of this methodological inheritance, its links to antiquarianism were to prove much stronger and more enduring.

Much of the reason for the especially close ties between antiquarianism and classical archaeology could be attributed to the fact that both were involved in writing the histories of societies that had left written materials in Latin and Greek. The contribution of archaeology to the overall task was thus most often primarily technical, in the sense of excavating sites and unearthing material culture that could be interpreted with the help of written documents. In the case of prehistoric sites, archaeologists used written documents (such as the "contact" ethnographies of the Romans) as a source of ideas or inferences, rather than as "direct" testimonies. In this sense, during the nineteenth century prehistoric archaeologists were much more directly challenged to develop theories to understand the nature of past societies and to develop explanations for why human culture had changed over time. Notwithstanding this important difference in context, for all branches of archaeology the act of classifying material culture (what, why, and how), and creating chronology (when), and then integrating both to write history became the bedrock on which the discipline grew in the nineteenth century.

In this essay I continue to focus on the development of archaeological theory during the nineteenth century. I do this to build toward an overall goal of understanding the relationship between archaeology and other disciplines that seek to improve our understanding of what it is to be human. Of course, choosing this focus means I will not consider technical matters, and instead I will concentrate on how histories came to be constructed from archaeological information and how practitioners made sense of past societies and the overall meaning of human history.

Naturally, all of this rests on what are now familiar foundations: creating archaeological institutions such as museums and learned societies; passing legislation, making great discoveries, publishing influential syntheses, undertaking fieldwork, collecting artifacts, deciphering ancient scripts, developing method, but above all classifying material culture and later fossil human remains. Again, this focus requires me to be selective in the coverage of the synthesis I offer. I will concentrate discussion on Europe and its links with the Near East. The importance of the developments that took place in the Americas during this century will be discussed more fully in the final essay. While in archaeology (unlike history) the twentieth century was not strictly the "American century," there is little doubt that the great works of method and theory by archaeologists such as Alfred Kidder, Walter Taylor, Robert Braidwood, and Lewis Binford profoundly affected the practice of archaeology during that time.

Once again I base my synthesis around a series of case studies or vignettes. These consider the consequences of classification, the building of archaeological theory, and the developing relationships between archaeology, history, and anthropology during the nineteenth century.

Classification and History: The Three-Age System

The history of the establishment of the Three-Age System and of its widespread acceptance, first in Scandinavia and subsequently in the rest of Europe, has been by far the most thoroughly researched of any passage in the history of archaeology. Although the authors of the new synthetic prehistories, ethnologies, and anthropologies all included an homage to Christian Thomsen as the "father of prehistoric archaeology," real research into the historical context of the Three-Age System begins with Glyn Daniel's classic essay *The Three Ages: An Essay on Archaeological Method* (1943). Subsequently, Daniel was to refine Thomsen's interpretation, and this in turn has been developed and extended by other researchers such as Rodden (1981). Further expansion of context both inside and outside Scandinavia has resulted from the work of Evans (1981), Klindt-Jensen (1975), Kristiansen (1981), Gräslund (1981), Heizer (1962), Rowe (1962), Rowley-Conwy (in press), Sackett (1981), Schnapp (1996), and Trigger (1989).

In this essay I do not use these works to create a synthesis of our knowledge of the history of the Three-Age System. The broad outlines of Thomsen's *Ledetraad til Nordisk Oldkyndighed* are well-enough known. So is the historical context of the work, as Daniel (1943), Clarke (1968), and a host of others have traced the history of archaeology from Hesiod and Lucretius through Mercati, Aldrovandus, Woodward, Worm, and others, and to Thomsen. Given the fact that few other aspects of the history of archaeology have been so well researched it is not surprising that there are some striking differences of interpretation regarding Thomsen's priority and, indeed, the sources of the Three-Age System itself. The most important of these differences stems from the role of archaeological contexts in the formulation of a new stage theory of human social and cultural evolution.

Daniel (1943, 1975, 1981), along with Gräslund (1981), stressed that Thomsen was responding to "internal" stimuli when he developed his "system." As a museum director confronted with the problem of organizing materials for display and interpretation, Thomsen sought a framework that would allow objects to be classified, but one that would also be *real.* Clarke (1968) has taken the view that the formulation of the system was thoroughly presupposed by "external" factors. In his view, as a participant in the Danish inheritance of French Enlightenment, Thomsen thought about the nature and meaning of human history and adapted the perspectives of universal history to his particular needs at the museum. There is no need to fight these battles again, although Daniel (1971, 1976) was not slow to leap to Thomsen's defense.

Unsurprisingly, it now appears most likely that the interaction of "internal" and "external" forces contributed to the development of the concept. Significantly, the formulation of the Three-Age System is a classic example of the interactionist methodology in action. So it can be understood as being simultaneously "archaeological" in the sense of it being the expression of the relationship between archaeology and its cognate disciplines, and "historical" or "ethnological" in the sense that it is the archaeological expression of ethnological understandings and the perceptions of the universal history project. There is supporting evidence for this view. From Gräslund's work (1981) (and the lengthy discussion of Scandinavian precursors found in Klindt-Jensen [1975]) it is clear that Thomsen did not merely stick to establishing relative chronology during the course of formulating and disseminating the Three-Age System. He also interpreted the ethnological significance of the framework.

What was supremely significant about the Three-Age System was that a link between the present and human prehistory could now be reliably established and history written where none had previously existed. Although the present was never considered to be the *same* as the prehistoric past, that past could be brought into view, or made intelligible, by the present. Moreover, the Three-Age System clearly demonstrated to all observers that ethnological theory (that developed out of the universal history project) was not entirely a priori. Here was independent physical evidence of the value of such general ethnological theories.

There has been a great deal less dispute about the meaning of the Three-Age System and the role it played in the growth and development of archaeology. On one level Thomsen's classification replaced the fragmentation and speculation of previous antiquarian studies. On another it represented a combination of three concepts that were, collectively or separately, to form the methodological foundations of many of the nineteenth-century sciences of the earth and of the life forms found upon it—particularly of ethnology (and later) anthropology:

> First, and perhaps most important, was "essentialism," or typological thinking, "actualism," or in archaeological terms, the use of ethnographic analogy, constitutes a second basic concept; while "directionalism," the application of a reasoned or conjectural "directional" history to the chronological ordering of the past, is the third. (Rodden 1981, 52)

The grouping of essentialism, actualism, and directionalism was also to have an impact on ethnology, anthropology, and biology. Indeed, the use of these concepts owed nothing in particular to archaeology qua archaeology, with the possible exception of Camden's and Winckelmann's demonstration of the fact that archaeological remains could be classified on the basis of form, function, or even style. Further, the discovery of the "ethnographic other" had allowed such formal typological classifications to take on a realist, rather than a purely nominalist, aspect. The three concepts must not be seen as separate entities, as the expressions of independent variables. Further, the historical context of their interdependence should not be forgotten.

While it is clear that Thomsen's classification provided relative chronology, direction in the form of a progressivist teleology, and a general characterization of the state of human society at points in the prehistoric past, on the basis of ethnographic analogy, the elements of that classification had previously coalesced in the work of the eighteenth-century conjectural historians. Thomsen's achievement was to establish clear grounds for the empirical confirmation of this classification through archaeological collection and excavation and the long-standing technique of landscape recording and architectural analysis. The interpretation and explanation of the material thus discovered, described, and classified were to remain very much the province of the social and cultural theorist. Finally, in the first prehistories of Sven Nilsson (1787–1883), Jens Worsaae (1823–1885), and Daniel Wilson (1816–1892), practitioners sought to articulate new sources of information about geology, the environment, and human skeletal remains. These new bodies of information both expanded the empirical repertoire of the archaeologist and forged closer links with the emerging earth and social sciences, thus producing the disciplinary configuration of archaeology that remains with us to this day.

In this Nilsson, Worsaae, and Wilson went well beyond Thomsen, by providing the methodological mechanisms and the problems that would expand the significance of archaeological data beyond the essentially eighteenth-century formulation Thomsen gave it. Archaeological data, whether in the form produced by Nilsson and Worsaae, or that provided by the geologists and natural historians seeking a solution to the problem of human antiquity, would provide an exemplar of empirical practice for ethnology that would ultimately see the development of professionalized field techniques and specialisms that contained the seeds of destruction of the program of generalization established by Prichard and others (see Stocking 1983b).

The Theoretical Foundations of Prehistoric Archaeology: Archaeology and Ethnology

Archaeology was slow to be included within the purview of ethnology. Indeed, for much of the nineteenth century other sources of evidence about human action and human history were deemed to be at least, if not more, significant than archaeological data. These sources were physical anthropology, philology, and the comparative analysis of social, religious, and customary forms. It was not until Nilsson and Worsaae demonstrated the links between archaeological, physical anthropological, and ethnographic/folkloric evidence that the ethnological significance of archaeological data could be appreciated.

One outcome of this time lag, between the development of ethnology and the later inclusion of archaeology, was that archaeologists such as Nilsson sought to demonstrate the meaning and value of archaeological data within the terms established for ethnology. Archaeological interpretation and explanation were expanded beyond classification, and ethnology acquired valuable supportive evidence for its more general developmental schema. The most important aspect was, however, the degree to which archaeological questions were constrained by the new generalizing science of ethnology.

In an important introductory essay to the reprint edition of James Cowles Prichard's 1831 *Researches into the Physical History of Man,* George Stocking highlighted the diverse sources for the writing of the first systematic ethnology (Stocking 1973, xxxiv–xlix). Although these pertain only to Prichard's work, with one important exception (the works of the French and Scottish universal historians, and the information derived from archaeological data) much the same pattern of data sources can be established for any ethnological work published during the nineteenth century. Prichard's bibliography illuminates the boundaries of the new science of ethnology he helped to create. It also illuminates the authorities appealed to in case of dispute and debate over ethnological description, interpretation, and explanation.

Predictably, the bulk of these authorities are from the classical histories, ethnographies, and geographies—in fact, much the same sources recognized as authorities by the antiquarian John Speed in the sixteenth century. It is also unsurprising that the second largest group was composed of travel literature, long a popular source of information about the "ethnographic other." The third group reflects Prichard's interest in the causes of human variation. Stocking has termed these writings in the "biological sciences" (1973, xxxvi). Within this third group there is an important subdivision, which Stocking calls "the works of the newer comparative anatomical tradition" (1973, xxxvi).

Stocking then mentions the last two sources as surprises for historians of anthropology. The citations of Sir William Jones (1746–1794) and the origins of philology, although reduced in importance in the first edition of the *Researches,* were to become critical to Prichard's argument in later editions. The last class of works were historical, primarily race histories and chronologies, and in later editions archaeology was to find its place here.

In this essay I will not analyze Prichard's great contribution to ethnology, nor will I trace the changes in his understanding of human cultural and physical history. Others have already explored these issues in detail (see, for example, Burrow [1966]; Harris [1968]; Leopold [1980]; Stocking [1973]; Weber [1974]). Perhaps the most important change in Prichard's thought was the gradual move away from the significance of physical difference and similarity to the cultural and linguistic bases of difference. This change was to have particular significance after 1860 when ethnologists became increasingly unwilling to grant language much power as a test of race or ethnicity. As Stocking has indicated: "They insisted instead, often in polygenist terms, on the legitimacy of a purely physical study of man and on the primacy of physical characters in the classification of human groups" (1973, ciii). It is a matter of record that this new wave of analysis came to be known as anthropology, in conscious reference to its physical rather than mental roots (see Weber 1974).

Notwithstanding changes in theoretical orientation and the significance of the various sources of information about human nature, the question that motivated Prichard, indeed all ethnologists (and later the anthropologists), was the question of human unity or diversity, as I outlined in the first essay.

This was to remain essentially unchanged until the impact of the Darwinian thesis substantially changed the terms of the debate from either a purely physical or a purely cultural one into the hypothetical connection of the two. As Stocking has said:

> Its salience at this point in time reflected the fact that an accumulation of data on human variability had been bought within a framework of comparative anatomy at a historical moment when the knowledge of the processes underlying biological variability was inadequate for its explanation. (1973, xlix)

Prichard, in an address to the Ethnological Society of London that was also reprinted, in a slightly altered form, in the *British Association Annual Report* (1847), made an early attempt to incorporate analyses of material culture and inductions about European prehistory into the general ethnological program. Before his acceptance of the Three-Age System and his acquaintance with Nilsson's work, Prichard had restricted his use of archaeological evidences primarily to Egyptology. Furthermore, he had sought the terms of a racial reconstruction of European prehistory in philology. Significantly, "On the Various Methods of Research Which Contribute to the Advancement of Ethnology and the Relations of That Science to Other Branches of Knowledge" was reprinted in the same edition of the British Association Reports as Norton Shaw's summary of Nilsson's *The Primitive Inhabitants of Scandinavia* (1847, 31–32).

Drawing a distinction between ethnology and natural philosophy Prichard averred:

> Ethnology is, in fact, more nearly allied to history than to natural science. Ethnology professes to give an account, not of what nature produces in the present day, but of what she has produced in times long since past. It is an attempt to trace the history of tribes and races of men from the remote periods which are within reach of investigation, to discover their mutual relations, and to arrive at conclusions, either certain or probable as to their affinity or diversity of origin. All this belongs to *archaeology* than to the science of nature. (1847, 231; original emphasis)

Here Prichard used archaeology more in the sense of a method, rather than as a distinct discipline, which for him encompassed all ethnology. For instance, because ethnology is archaeological or historical, Prichard then considered whether ethnology could be a science and concluded that it is as much a science as geology, because geology is archaeological, too. More so, because "'*[p]aleontology*,' for which '*physical archaeology*' is a synonym, includes both geology and ethnology. The former is the archaeology of the globe; the latter that of its human inhabitants" (Prichard 1847, 231; original emphasis).

Nonetheless, the archaeological method provides only a part of the historical data sought and synthesized by the ethnologist. Paleontology has aided the geologist in much the same way that the works of the ancient historians and researches into the history of language have aided the ethnologist:

> As geology would have been a barren and uninteresting study, and uncertain in most of its results without the aids which the study of organic remains has unexpectedly afforded, serving to identify geological formations and to connect particular series of rocks with periods in the world's history; so it has been through discoveries in the relations of languages that the ethnologist is enabled to trace alliances between nations scattered over distant regions of the earth, of whose connections with each other he would have no idea without such evidence. (Prichard 1847, 232)

Note that the evidence of material culture is not granted the same powers in Prichard's system. Clearly, for Prichard language really was the truest test of race and of historical relationship. Next in importance was the comparative anatomy of Peter Camper (1722–1789) and Johann Blumenbach (1752–1840), which allowed ethnologists to clearly distinguish between peoples on the basis of physical form, even to the level of nationality as argued by Anders Retzius (1796–1860) (Prichard 1847, 233).

Related to this is the link between ethnology and animal physiology. Prichard believed the physical form of human beings had been correctly classified with the animal kingdom by the Comte de Buffon (1707–1788), Georges Cuvier (1769–1832), and Carl von Linne (1707–1778), although he certainly questioned the "insensible gradations" between apes and humans. Accordingly, what Prichard called physiological issues (what we would consider to be biological), such as the laws of hybridity, would have great importance for the monogenist/polygenist debate among students of humankind:

> One series of inquiries which he must elucidate is, whether the great laws of the animal oeconomy are the same in respect to all human races; whether any particular race differs from others in regard to the duration of life and the

various periodical changes of constitution, and in the system of physical functions generally; and whether such diversities, if found to exist, can be explained by reference to external agencies, or imply original difference, and form, therefore, specific character. (1847, 234)

Connected with this search for the actions of external agencies in causing human variety, Prichard next pointed to geography as a basis for establishing the nature of the environmental context. However important these sciences were in building up ethnological facts, history, archaeology, ethnography, and philology were of crucial importance. Referring to the fact that the ancients provide only part of the answer, Prichard emphasized that:

> We must collect all the different lights that can be brought to bear on the history of nations, whether from the testimony of ancient writers, or from manners, customs, and institutions - from old popular traditions, poetry, mythology—from the remains of ancient art, sculpture, architecture, inscriptions—and from sepulchral relics discovered in many countries, consisting of tombs containing embalmed bodies, or more often the mere skulls and skeletons of the ancient inhabitants, which furnish the most authentic testimony that can be procured as to the physical characters of various races of people. Besides all these, there is another source of information more extensively available than any of them, - I allude to the history of languages and their affinities. (1847, 236)

Prichard's preferences obviously lay with language and philology as the most effective ethnological tools. At one stroke mind and historical (ethnical) relationship could be established. Archaeology could only ever have the role of handmaiden to linguistic history in the production of ethnological knowledge, although it could form part of the class of confirming, independent evidence, which would allow the reliability of such knowledge to be objectively determined. Prichard clearly had little feel for archaeology outside the search for inscriptions and architecture, which was the style of archaeology developed for the reconstruction of Egyptian and Mesopotamian civilizations, and, of course, the production of linguistic history:

> The history of mankind is not destined, like the fundamental facts of geology, to be dug out of the bowels of the earth . . . But the discoveries most interesting in relation to ethnology, are those of sepulchral remains, which in various regions of the world have preserved ancient records of the physical characters and arts of many ancient races. (1847, 236)

Prichard wholeheartedly accepted the work of Nilsson, Retzius, Sir William Wilde (1815–1876) and Marcel de Serres (1783–1862) in associating racial types on the basis of skull shape and associated material culture, yet he regarded the evidence of inscriptions as being more reliable for this purpose. In his system, archaeological data were indeed primarily supporting data, as in this sense so were skeletal remains. Although Prichard never worked with the great time spans shortly to be revealed at Brixham Cave and Abbeville, and therefore never had to really question the propriety of the historical constructions of the philologists either from fact or applicability to the reconstruction of a deeper human prehistory, it is doubtful that he would ever have argued that there was a need for a much expanded role for archaeological information. To him material culture was more epiphenomenal of mind than was language.

In fact ethnologists were almost universally slow to devote much of their attention to archaeology. The various questionnaires prepared by the Ethnological Society of Paris and the British Association for the Advancement of Science (see, for example, Fowler 1975) largely ignored archaeological evidence until Pitt-Rivers added questions relevant to it in 1874. Thus, while ethnologists used archaeological data in a supporting role, archaeologists firmly embraced ethnology so that inferences and deductions could be made from established and plausible theories, or so that archaeological evidence gained significance by acting as further evidence for the propriety of these theories. The gaps in the archaeological record were already being seen as only being filled or supplemented by theory borrowed from the generalizing human sciences. Although the discovery of great time depth was to pose new problems for ethnology, and new possibilities for anthropology, the interpretation of later periods of prehistory was to provide the exemplars of practice that fostered the interpretation of human action in deeper prehistory.

The Consequences of the Discovery of High Human Antiquity

The prehistories of Nilsson, Worsaae, and Wilson provided exemplars of how the historical and ethnological significance of archaeological data could be expanded beyond the earlier formulations of Camden, Speed, Aubrey, and Stukeley. This was the result of two responses to the sense of the new prehistories: first, the use of archaeological data by the proponents of a more general inquiry into the nature of humankind, which at this time was encompassed by ethnology; and second, by the use of ethnological method and underdeveloped ethnological theory by the practitioners of prehistoric archaeology.

These two responses, which collectively exhibit a kind of symbiotic relationship, were justified with ease. The data of prehistoric archaeology took their rightful place alongside ethnography, physical anthropology, and philology, barely causing a ripple in terms of the central preoccupations of ethnology. Indeed, no radical recasting of the terms of preexisting debates was deemed necessary. This incorporation was made even easier by the fact that the archaeologists themselves, through their need to write plausible prehistory, effectively preprocessed archaeological data through the application of ethnological methodology and theory. The ascription of cause, part and parcel of the explanation of change and variation, was made possible and was justified by the use of ethnological databases such as ethnography and physical anthropology. Prehistory could not be written without ethnology, but were the data of prehistoric archaeology capable of influencing ethnological theory?

The best way to answer this question is to closely examine the implications of the discovery of unimpeachable evidence for high human antiquity, and the proposition of evolutionary theory. The bulk of my discussion concentrates on the differences that arose between the stated methodology of prehistoric archaeology and the actual practice of evolutionary archaeology between the mid-1860s and 1880. I explain these differences by demonstrating the critical importance of the relationship between prehistoric archaeology and two other fledgling sciences, ethnology and anthropology. I argue that essentially the same a priori propositions that ensured the plausibility of the earlier "short timescale" prehistories continued to do so, despite the discovery of high human antiquity, which has long been regarded as one of the great milestones in the history of archaeology for three major reasons.

First, since the 1860s, historians of archaeology have maintained that the science of prehistoric archaeology received its greatest impetus from this discovery. Second, the apprehension of near-unimaginable time depth had great impact on the development of anthropology and ethnology. Finally, evolutionary archaeology has been considered to be an important outcome of the establishment of high human antiquity providing, through the work of Lubbock and de Mortillet, exemplars of practice for prehistoric archaeologists during the period (see especially Trigger 1989).

The critical data for this discussion are (1) the history of the establishment of high human antiquity; (2) the universal prehistories of Lubbock

(1865, 1882) and de Mortillet; (3) the general works on ethnology and anthropology produced by Edward Tylor (1832–1917) (1865, 1870), Armand de Quatrefages (1810–1892) (1875, 1879), Georges Pouchet (1833–1894) (1864), Karl Vogt (1817–1895) (1864), and Theodore Waitz (1821–1864) (1863); (4) the difficulties associated with quantifying the age of the earth, hence of determining when human beings first appeared on it, and the proper scale for understanding the changes that had taken place in human culture from savage past to civilized present; and (5) the history of human palaeontology during the nineteenth century and its links with physical anthropology during the period under review.

Collectively these data reflect the sociological context of the discovery of high human antiquity—critical discoveries, interpretative frameworks, responses from practitioners of cognate disciplines affected by the discovery, and the perceived problems raised by those critical discoveries. Space forbids the detailed discussion of all of these sources.

The discovery of a high human antiquity has been considered by historians of archaeology and anthropology to have had a dramatic effect on the structures that guided the terms of the more general inquiry into the nature of human beings (Burrow 1966; Daniel 1959, 1971, 1975, 1976; Grayson 1983; Gruber 1965; Stocking 1987; Trigger 1989; van Riper 1993; Weber 1974). But how great an effect? Were the archaeological data of a deeper prehistoric past to be used in the same way as the "short-span" data provided by such prehistorians as Nilsson, Wilson, and Worsaae? Or were those data of such a different order that the theories that underwrote explanation and gave meaning to the inductions of the early prehistorians would simply fail to convince? Could prehistoric archaeologists continue to maintain a close relationship with ethnology, and later anthropology, and thus gain plausible and justifiable grounds for reconstructing and explaining human action in the deep prehistoric past? How would induction fare in the drive to explain human nature so far (temporally) removed from the present?

In my view, during this period first ethnology, and later anthropology, provided the framework of the bulk of archaeological theory, and also establishing the exemplars of practice, standards of proof, and the objectives of prehistoric archaeology. Yet ethnology was itself changed through the discovery of high human antiquity and by a resurgence of interest in physical anthropology that was, in part, caused by the discovery of fossil human skeletal material from first the Neanderthals and later *Homo erectus* in Java (see Boule and Vallois 1946). Ethnology, and later anthropology, determined the degree to which anomalous archaeological data could influence the ways in which human beings were understood. To this extent the change of emphasis from evolutionary archaeology to cultural historical archaeology later in the nineteenth century reflected changes in the orientations of anthropology and ethnology.

The archaeological evidence of a deeper human prehistory was used by the practitioners of ethnology and anthropology for two reasons. First, the new data were evidence of human action, and if theories of human nature were to have any kind of temporal validity, then they had to account for it. Second, this new class of evidence was more empirically reliable than much of the ethnographic evidence previously incorporated (see Harris 1968; Stocking 1968, 1983b). The development of evolutionary anthropology was the primary result of this use.

Practitioners of prehistoric archaeology, most of them natural historians (read geologists and paleontologists), retained the symbiotic relationship with ethnology and anthropology for the same reasons as before. Although great time depth opened the possibility that human beings could be investigated as part of the animal world, in practice the primary question came to be the grounds of difference between animals and human beings. As these differences were thought to stem largely from language, rationality, and culture, the natural loci for the discussion of these issues were anthropology and ethnology.

The use of archaeological data by ethnologists, and the use of ethnological theory by archaeologists, occurred through an extension of the scope of prehistoric archaeology beyond the bounds of the cultural, ethnic, or racial history established by prehistorians such as Nilsson, Worsaae, and Wilson (which was itself a product of the power of ethnology). High human antiquity and the possibility of a human prehistory that would not be interpretable through the structures of culture history expanded ethnology as well as prehistoric archaeology. More importantly, the paleontological and geological investigation of the superficial strata of western Europe, a research program that had been occurring while the Three-Age System was still in its Scandinavian infancy, spawned a class of data that found its nineteenth-century meanings within ethnology and anthropology.

An important contributing factor to this "acquisition" of the deep past by the more recent past was the great uncertainty surrounding the quantification of the new timescale. Vast it may be, but how vast? The disagreements among geologists, fired by the work of Lord Kelvin (see Burchfield 1975) and by unresolved problems in quaternary geology, only increased uncertainty about the truth (or the probability of truth) of interpretations of that deeper past. In practice, the new "vast" timescale was broken up into subclassifications of the Stone Age by Lartet, Lubbock, and de Mortillet (see Daniel 1975) as practitioners sought a means of gaining relative measurements of chronology. These subclassifications provided an important part of the empirical reality of stage theories of human sociocultural evolution produced by Lubbock (1865, 1882), Tylor (1865, 1870), and Lewis Henry Morgan (1818–1881) (1871, 1877). For both the practitioners of prehistoric archaeology and ethnology or anthropology, observation statements were not free from a priori theory.

Another factor was that the new data were incorporated into theories of sociocultural evolution that had their roots in the eighteenth century and owed much to the structures supporting the universal histories of that time. These theories, despite protests by Lubbock, Morgan, and Herbert Spencer (1820–1903), had a marked teleological flavor. They also assumed the reality of human progress, as noted by opponents such as the Duke of Argyll (George Douglas Campbell [1823–1900]) (1869; see also Gillespie 1977). This teleology dictated that ethnographic analogy (effectively the "savage" or "barbarous" present) should be used as the primary basis for explaining sociocultural change and variation during the course of human history.

The net result was that contemporary "savages" and "barbarians" were effectively denied a history (again despite the protests of Lubbock and Tylor). Instead, their peculiarity was explained as being the product of a complex process that included elements of stasis, regression, and progress. This denial of history to the "savage" and "barbarian" was itself a response to the daunting prospect of human action in the deep prehistoric past being unintelligible. The only way to preserve the universality of those structures was to demonstrate their general applicability to the explanation of other contemporary cultures, and then to argue that these contemporary societies could be ordered as modern representatives of prehistoric human sociocultural types. This, when allied to the problem of quantifying the new timescale, effectively squeezed it into a shorter, almost synchronic one, allowing for an easy relationship with ethnology and anthropology as the suppliers of theory. This "squeezing" of human prehistory and the value of uniformitarian models of human behavior remains a significant issue in contemporary archaeology, which I will touch on again in the last essay.

A final factor, which cannot be developed in this essay, was the time lag between the discovery of material culture in unimpeachably old strata and the general acceptance that there were pre-sapient hominid fossils to go with them. This acted to further squeeze the timescale and support the validity of theories of sociocultural evolution underwritten by ethnographic analogy. Despite the predictions of Charles Darwin and Thomas Huxley that fossils intermediate between apes and humans would be found, it was not until near the end of the nineteenth century that Neanderthal fossils were widely accepted as being the remains of hominids ancestral to human beings (see Hammond 1982). However, it was not until the discovery of *Homo erectus* that a fossil hominid was found that was markedly different from contemporary human beings and closer to the apes. Thus, for much of the nineteenth century hard evidence for human evolution, hence evidence for an evolutionary timescale similar to that of other contemporary animals, was simply lacking. Flowing from this, despite the attempts by philologists such as Max Muller to conceptualize the origins of language and the development of the human mind (a task shared with anthropologists such as Tylor), a lack of pre-sapient fossils meant that such theorizing was generally applied to contemporary "savages" and "barbarians" and to languages reconstructed by philologists (see Stocking 1973, 1983a, 1984).

Four explicit problems stemmed from the structure of the new science. First, the work of archaeologists and natural historians had expanded the temporal and spatial scope of the Three-Age System. By the 1870s it was recognized to apply to much of Europe, and in France at least, the Stone Age was now almost unimaginably old. Variability in the material culture of the Stone Age had also been recognized, and new subclassifications had been proposed (see Daniel 1975). This posed two issues that further stimulated field research: the manner in which environmental, ecological, and cultural change and variation could be plausibly interpreted and explained and the linkage between the deeper prehistory of the Stone Age with the histories of particular nations and peoples. The general stage theories of Lubbock (1865, 1882), Tylor (1865, 1870), and Morgan (1871, 1877) were all very well, but the issues of race and ethnicity being debated in the ethnological and anthropological societies of Europe demanded attention.

Second, the work of paleontologists had provided a firm basis for reconstructing paleofaunas, and the geologists had already advanced the contemporary understanding of environmental and ecological change. How was archaeological and paleoenvironmental evidence to be integrated into an explanation of human cultural change and variation?

Third, the problem of time, stemming from the work of geologists and paleontologists, became paramount. Clearly, the wide variety of explanations for cultural change and variation could not be convincingly disentangled without an understanding of the temporal context for that change and variation.

Fourth, there was the triumph (albeit, never total and occurring at different rates in Europe) of Darwinian biology. This clearly stimulated the search for quaternary and tertiary human fossils—whether forms intermediate between apes and man, or simply human fossils with no evidence of deviance from *Homo sapiens.*

National and Ethnic Archaeologies: The Importance of Culture History

Earlier in this essay I outlined the first phase of the incorporation of archaeological data into ethnology. I indicated that this occurred very slowly because ethnologists saw the significance of archaeological data for the development of ethnological theory as being less valuable than that of philology, the comparative analysis of custom and mythology, and the data derived from physical anthropology. I also mentioned that authors of the earliest prehistories, those of nations or ethnic groups, implicitly recognized that for archaeological data to acquire meaning and value, the antiquary or natural historian had to first demonstrate the ethnological potential of those data.

Throughout the rest of the nineteenth century in Europe (as well as elsewhere) the goal of prehistoric archaeology came to be the creation of racial, ethnic, or national prehistories that were based on what became known as culture history. These culture historical prehistories are considered to be quite different forms of prehistory writing to the general works of prehistoric synthesis represented by the work of Lubbock (1865, 1882) and Tylor (1870) and the work of anthropologists with a more pronounced leaning to the physical rather than the mental, such as Pouchet (1864), Quatrefages (1875, 1879), Vogt (1864), and Waitz (1863). Nonetheless, the need for chronology flowed into all types of prehistories. Indeed, the Three-Age System, which advanced no theory to explain cultural change, variation, or succession, was a relative chronology in and of itself.

While the degree of internal variation noticed in assemblages drawn from European sites was at a minimum (that is, internal to the classes of Stone, Bronze, and Iron), the basic progressivist assumptions allied to the broad outlines of relative chronology were more than satisfactory. However, when substantial variation within the "Ages" became apparent, further subdivisions of the classes had to be made (for example the subdivision of the Stone

Age into the Paleolithic and Neolithic proposed by Lubbock or the Abbevillian or Mousterian proposed by de Mortillet). However, not even Lubbock's or de Mortillet's subdivisions could account for variations of material culture *within* them, that is, variability that could not be explained as a function of time or evolution but was more likely to be the result of the actions of human minds. The perception of high levels of synchronous variation was more pronounced in the Neolithic, Bronze, and Iron Ages. True, the evolutionist explanation of variation as the result of human minds adapting to varying conditions of existence could account for some of it, but how could prehistorians account for cultural variability under similar conditions, such as those in western Europe?

The need to explain variability was only one part of the problem. More important still was the need to place more precise chronological boundaries on change and succession in European prehistory. Given the high methodological standards set by the historians such as Leopold von Ranke (1795–1886), how could archaeologists claim reliability for prehistoric reconstructions when time was so illusory? By the end of the nineteenth century, practitioners of prehistoric archaeology became more concerned with variation than with similarity, mirroring a widespread turn away from the universal histories of evolutionary archaeology and anthropology toward the historicism of culture history.

Trigger (1978, 64–65) has advanced two further explanations for the increasing popularity of particularist prehistoric analysis and the reduced attraction of unilinear evolutionary systems. The first of these was the growing popularity of racial, hence historically continuous, explanations for cultural variation and diversity. The second was the rise of antiprogressivist ideologies in the sociopolitical arena brought about by stress in the European economies and by increasing class conflict. Although the latter change in context did not directly contribute to the development of culture historical theory, it most certainly played an important part in securing the plausibility of the interpretations and explanations that were to flow from the national, ethnic, and racial prehistories of the late nineteenth century.

To these we can add the great strides made in recovering the history of the Egyptian and Mesopotamian civilizations that had been made possible through archaeological excavation. The value of archaeology had never stood higher in the public mind, and the techniques and approaches developed through a connection with history had provided a methodological exemplar for the archaeologists of Europe. Here was real time, not the illusory relative units so characteristic of European prehistoric archaeology. Here was the prospect of using archaeological data to write real racial history and to investigate the historical relationships between the "cradle of Western civilization" and its European periphery. The chronological link that was forged between Egypt and Europe also supported the transference of the exemplar of Near Eastern archaeological practice.

The Process of History in Europe: Race and Culture in the Deep Past

The period between the publication of Lubbock's *Pre-historic Times* (1865) and the turn of the century has many notable landmarks for the historian of archaeology. Daniel (1975, 1981b) has very usefully summarized the major European landmarks as the recognition of paleolithic art, the acceptance of Lubbock's and de Mortillet's classifications of the Stone Age, the development of Montelius's classification of the Bronze Age, Hildebrand and Tischler's work on the classification of the Iron Age, the clash between Montelius and Reinach over the roles of diffusion and independent invention, and the rise of hyperdiffusion as an explanation for culture change in European prehistory.

Clearly, European archaeological methodology was also strongly influenced by archaeological events in Egypt and Mesopotamia. Petrie's great series of excavations in Egypt and Palestine provided the means for linking the relative chronologies of Europe (through Greece) to the absolute chronology of Egypt. The prehistories of Greece, Crete, and Asia Minor were also being better understood as a result of the work of Schliemann, Evans, Curtius, Myres, de Morgan, and others. It was indeed a time of great archaeological discoveries, and the archaeological method developed further as a result. In Europe Pitt-Rivers also made a great contribution to excavation and recording methods at Cranborne Chase (see Thompson 1977).

The archaeology of the last quarter of the nineteenth century was conducted against a background of increasing disputation among practitioners about the classification of the Bronze and Iron ages and the explanation of cultural change and succession. Worsaae and de Mortillet (especially in *Le Préhistorique: Antiquité de L'homme* [1883])contributed to the debates, but these representatives of the "golden age of archaeology" were surpassed in influence by Montelius. Indeed, such was the level of disputation taking place throughout Europe that it seemed likely the drive for further subdivision of the Three-Age System by adding the Eolithic and the Eneolithic

(Copper Age) to the original tripartite classification would go far to reduce its value as a comparative classification.

But what did these classifications mean? Montelius held fast to the notion that the original Three-Age System of classification was only broadly historical and had its greatest value in providing evidence for temporal and spatial variability within Europe at any time. Thus, he fully accepted that southern Europe got bronze before northern Europe, but that it was still sensible to retain the importance of that perception within the original categories. But this provided no explanation for the time lag between north and south, and it gave no indication of just how much time was being represented by changes in material culture (see Bohner 1981). By 1909, Montelius had managed to formulate the chronological relationships between Europe and the Aegean in absolute terms, but we shall see that less definite measurements were also being proposed in the 1880s.

Montelius's adherence to the technological/typological system inherited from Thomsen proved to be only one strategy for classifying and establishing absolute chronological relationships between classes. Chantre provided another. In *L'Age du Bronze* (1873–1874) Chantre argued for a geographical classification of European prehistoric cultures that explicitly recognized that there were three broad geographical areas demonstrated within the classifications of the Stone, Bronze, and Iron ages. Clearly, Chantre's classification owed much to archaeological investigations in the Aegean and the Near East. Here was the first attempt to establish the nature of culture areas within Europe and to follow Near Eastern tradition by naming these culture areas as definable groups of people. The names given them reflected either older racial classifications (such as Iberic, used by Boyd Dawkins) or tribal names derived from classical geographies and ethnographies (such as Belgic, used by Arthur Evans). Nilsson had already made the link between definable groups of people and different material culture complexes, and this link had also been used by Wilson (and by Rhind) in reconstructing Scottish prehistory. Nonetheless, archaeologists of the late nineteenth century were to take this basic idea and expand it into a full-blown culture history for Europe as a whole. An important justification for this expansion of the possibilities of culture history stemmed from the development of theories of culture that had been occurring since the work of Gustav Klemm (1802–1867), particularly *Die Werkzeuge und Waffen: ihre Entstehung und Ausbildung* (1858) (see Harris 1968; Leopold 1980; Stocking 1968, 1973).

It must be stressed that the changes in archaeological methodology that either took place, or were to occur later (made possible by these changes), also stemmed from internal puzzles and problems in archaeological data. The complexities of cultural variation demanded two separate types of solutions, and these were linked in the work of Montelius and Petrie. The first was the explanation of change and variation, and the second was the measurement of chronology. Clearly, prehistoric archaeologists could no longer appeal to generalized forces to account for regional variation, except at the level of environmental or technological factors. They had to look to the characterization and explanation of individual entities. The old culture concept provided the working model of a realist rather than a nominalist classification, a classification that could be examined for its potential to explain both micro and macro changes within and between states.

Sklenář (1983), among others, has argued that this necessity brought archaeology back into the realm of history and away from ethnology, anthropology, and geology. In a very limited sense he is right. Understanding the prehistory of Europe was to become a historical problem, but it was certainly a kind of history that owed much to ethnology and anthropology. This was racial and ethnic history, the history of peoples rather than events. Significantly, it was ethnological theory that allowed the racial prehistory of Europe to be written and that was to pose its most significant research issues until well into the twentieth century.

The rise of the culture history in archaeology in all its varied forms was made possible by Klemm's work. The link between mind and environment, which had long been part of Western thought, became itself linked to a more fundamental association between physical form, the mind, and the culturally distinct products of mind. I have mentioned that soon after the broad outlines of European prehistory had been synthesized by Lubbock and de Mortillet, antiquaries began to consider more deeply the causes of cultural change and variation. Nilsson had explained change in Sweden as being the result of movements of racially distinct peoples, engaged in racial conflicts that were so much a part of the way in which nineteenth-century Europeans construed political conflict in their own day. Worsaae, although never really being explicit about the role of migration and conquest, did allow for it within his scheme of environmental changes. Importantly, Lubbock and Tylor had considered the causes of similarity and variation in material culture with greater care than the causes of culture change itself.

Klemm's clear association of mind with race, a sentiment that would have been applauded by ethnological and anthropological theorists such as Robert Knox and James Hunt (see Burrow 1966; Horsman 1976) focused attention on material culture as being a marker of racial history. In this view technology assumed a significance equal to that of language as an ethnic marker, but, more importantly, the newly acquired significance of material culture was a function of linguistic theory itself. Although Muller, among others, rejected the equation between language and ethnic group, the archaeologists of the nineteenth century were not nearly so fussy. For them the problem remained: Were the changes in material culture, and its multitude of variations, the product of distinct groups of people (as Nilsson had earlier been able to establish on the basis of cranial measurement) with distinct histories, or was the prehistory of Europe really the result of many racial and ethnic prehistories? But if this last was the case, were all changes to be explained by migrations and conquests, or was there to be a mixture of independent/parallel development and diffusion?

I have mentioned that Pitt-Rivers outlined two plausible explanations for cross-cultural technological similarities: diffusion and independent invention. During the late nineteenth century the relative merits of both explanations were vigorously canvassed by the supporters of Montelius and Reinach (see Daniel 1971, 1975). These debates continued well into the twentieth century, perhaps reaching their apogee in the hyperdiffusionist work of Smith and Perry, and the propositions of Gustav Kossinna. I shall deal with these developments in the final essay, but it should be understood that what begins here in the second half of the nineteenth century remained at the conceptual core of archaeology until the 1970s.

The "National" Prehistories of Montelius and Boyd Dawkins

I now consider two late-nineteenth-century national prehistories to demonstrate archaeological problems that provided fertile ground for the developing popularity of the culture historical approach outlined above. The two works are very different in their treatments. Montelius held fast to a notion of civilization and culture that is the common property of all people. Boyd Dawkins advanced a more particularist characterization of individual cultures. Montelius argued for a common European prehistory, a common European experience of the past. Boyd Dawkins presented a view that the variability of European prehistoric material culture was the outward expression of real historical processes.

Montelius's *The Civilization of Sweden in Heathen Times* (1888 [the first English translation]) is a self-conscious contribution to the history of civilization, of culture in the abstract, that which distinguishes human beings from the lower forms of life. Woods, Montelius's translator, had this to say:

> It is true that it deals directly with the progress of one particular people; but all archaeology tends to show that there has been a remarkably similar process of development, not only among European peoples, but among all races of the world. It follows that a clear and succinct account of the progress of any one people helps to give us a clear notion of the successive stages of civilization through which all races have passed. (Montelius 1888, v–vi)

For Montelius, "national" prehistories should, first and foremost, contribute to the elucidation of the general progress of civilization. Yet that elucidation required much greater detail as what was known about European prehistory, in particular, expanded. There are further echoes of older concerns. For example, Montelius still felt it necessary to emphasize the historical significance of archaeological remains and the scientific reliability of the knowledge about the prehistoric past produced by archaeology. In so doing he sharply distinguished his perception of admissible archaeological data from that of Nilsson:

> It is true that we meet with no line of kings, no heroic names dating from these earliest times. But is not the knowledge of the people's life, and of the progress of their culture, of more worth than the names of the saga heroes? And ought we not give more credence to the contemporary, irrefutable witness to which alone archaeology now listens, than to the poetical stories which for centuries were preserved only in the memory of the skalds? (Montelius 1888, 3)

Montelius was also fighting a battle against those who sought to devalue the importance of the Three-Age System (see Böhner 1981). It needs to be understood that even at this stage there was by no means universal acceptance of the system, and the burgeoning variation detected in sites across Europe made its universal applicability even less secure (see also Sklenar 1983). Montelius offered a qualified defense of the Three-Age System:

> It might seem unnecessary at present to give any special proof of the correctness of this threefold division of heathen times in the North, inasmuch as the whole account we shall give may be regarded as proving it. But as the present position of Northern archaeology depends so peculiarly upon this division, we shall now point out some circumstances which show how well grounded the opinion is, at least so far as Scandinavia is concerned. (1888, 3)

Two further cautions in the introduction indicate Montelius's unwillingness to present a truly historical reconstruction of Swedish prehistory. The first deals with the causes of culture change:

> How far the beginning of each period coincides with the appearance of a new race which subdued the earlier settlers in the country, is a further question which we must for the present distinguish from that which concerns only the order in which the several heathen periods followed each other. (Montelius 1888, 4)

Here Montelius at least implied that Nilsson's older argument, that the gross changes in culture experienced in the north were most likely the result of invasion and conquest, has at least some validity. The other caution concerns the fragmentary nature of the archaeological record as a natural limitation on induction:

> Before we now make an attempt to set before our readers a picture of life in Sweden during heathen times, we must observe that if that picture shall prove imperfect and blurred, it is partly perhaps owing to the insufficiency of our sources of information about a period so wanting in historical materials . . . Only a small part of what once existed was buried in the ground; only a part of what was buried has escaped the destroying hand of time; of this part all has not yet come to light again; and we know only too well how little of what has come to light has been of any service for our science. (Montelius 1888, 5)

Cautions aside, Montelius introduces the Stone Age with an absolute date of "*To about* B.C. 1500." Then follows a traditional listing of the artifacts and monuments, along with appropriate comparisons with contemporary ethnographies and to other finds from European prehistoric sites. One major absence is the analysis of skeletal remains. Instead of craniometrical measurements and inferences of race or ethnicity, we find that grave goods are described, the various tomb forms are classified, and even causes of death discussed. This makes Montelius's assertion of a near-continuous racial history for Sweden quite different from the racial conflict model proposed by Nilsson. However, it should be noted that Montelius also rules language out of court, thereby restricting the possibilities of culture historical interpretation even further. In Montelius's estimation, significant data for this inquiry are simply lacking, and the dictates of science require that we should pass from it with no signs of regret:

> At the end of the Stone Age the inhabitants of the North were not only still entirely ignorant of metals even gold, but also of the art of writing. And consequently we have no remains of the language of this age to show us what the people was which then called Sweden its fatherland. An attempt has been made to answer this question by means of the skulls found in the graves of the Stone Age. Some are very like those of the Laps, but most bear a close resemblance to the Swedish skulls of the present day; which seems to show that a mixture of two different races had at this very early time already taken place. (1888, 37)

If the Teutonic ancestors of the Swedes were already living in Scania during the Stone Age, how was the shift to the Bronze Age to be explained? Montelius reviewed the explanations, ranging from Nilsson's Phoenicians to Lindenschmidt's Etruscans, but rejected them in favor of trade (1888, 43). The similarity between late Stone Age and Early Bronze Age graves argued against any "great immigration of a new race." What Montelius called the "Bronze Culture" had spread out of Asia in a north and northwesterly direction across Europe, diffusing bronze technology and artifacts during the period "*From about* 1500 to 500 B.C." (1888, 42). It transpires that diffusion is to be appealed to as the explanation for the shift from the Bronze to the Iron Age as well, but by the Iron Age the historical value of legends, sagas, and customs has been increased.

If Montelius's prehistory of Sweden stressed the value of the direct historical approach in the Iron Age, it also stressed the argument that migrations and invasions should only be argued for by the archaeologist if large-scale changes in the background material culture could be detected. In this sense Montelius was appealing to culture historical theory in its linking between racial and ethnic groups and distinct cultural inventories. Major changes of this kind not having occurred at any time in Swedish prehistory, the most parsimonious explanation was for an early settlement of Sweden by the ancestors of the Teutons, and for change in the material culture to be explained via diffusion and local adaptations of diffused technologies and styles.

Boyd Dawkins opted for a different approach. His *Early Man in Britain and his Place in the Tertiary Period* (1880) has a far wider agenda than Montelius's Swedish prehistory; it offers the framework of a complete prehistory of Britain that reviewed the general European evidence for the antiquity of man and the later periods of prehistory. The fourteen chapters of this massive work of synthesis (over 500 pages long) take the reader from a defense of methodology to Britain in the historic period. Although Boyd Dawkins also wished to contribute to a more general history of civilization, this was to be primarily a work of prehistoric synthesis, stressing both sequence and variation.

Boyd Dawkins was not reluctant to begin his project back in the time of what he called the Cave-men and the River-Drift men. After presenting detailed information on the relative chronological positions of the two classes of evidence from the river drift and from the caves, he queried whether these different artifacts represented two distinct groups of people or whether the changes were evidence of a progress in human culture:

> How are they related to each other? Is the culture of the latter the outcome of the development of that of the former? Or is it to be viewed as having been introduced into Europe by a totally different race? (1880, 229)

Boyd Dawkins considered the problem from the perspective of the material culture, and from paleontology, geology, ethnography, and geology. He was in no doubt that after considering the range of evidence available "they may be referred either to two different races, or to two sections of the same race which found their way into Europe at widely different times" (1880, 233).

Further, while the ethnology of the older River-Drift men was essentially unknowable, being lost to the mists of time (significantly *not* the view of Lubbock or Tylor), the ethnology of the Cave-men was a comparatively easy matter. On the basis of similarity in material culture, the Eskimo should be considered to be the most likely direct descendants (1880, 233–242). Furthermore, Boyd Dawkins saw absolutely no connection between the people of the Paleolithic and those of the Neolithic, neither in cranial shape nor in material culture (1880, 242–243).

Boyd Dawkins was to use this argument of complete population replacement on more than one occasion, and he justified it on the grounds of racial hatred known to exist between contemporary primitive peoples, an argument used by Nilsson as well (1868, 253). For example, Boyd Dawkins posed a similar question concerning the fate of the people of the Neolithic. In a chapter headed "The Neolithic Inhabitants of Britain of Iberian Race," which followed a section where he derived the entirety of Neolithic civilization from southwest Asia, Boyd Dawkins broached the delicate topic:

> We have now to discuss the difficult questions as to the relation of the Neolithic inhabitants of Britain to those of the Continent, as well as to races of men still living in the same area. Are they now banished from Europe in the same manner as the Cave-men, or are they still represented in the present population?

Characteristically, Boyd Dawkins considered the problem to be solvable, as long as evidence from osteology, philology, history, ethnology, and geography were to be used. He considered the Neolithic to be a period of race wars between Celt and Iberian, each with a separate homeland within Europe. Here the attribution of classical tribal names for the races of the European Neolithic emphasized the belief that the remnants of such tribes still inhabited parts of Europe (such as the Pyrenees). It is worth quoting Boyd Dawkins's general conclusions for the Neolithic at length:

> From the facts mentioned in the last two chapters, it will be seen that the continuity between the Neolithic Age and the present day has been unbroken. It is marked not merely by the physique of the present Europeans, by many of the domestic animals and cultivated seeds and fruits, and many of the arts, but by the testimony of language, and it is emphasized by the survival of the Neolithic faith in the shape of widely-spread superstitions. In every respect the Neolithic immigrant into Europe was immeasurably superior to the Paleolithic man of the caverns.
>
> At the beginning of the Prehistoric period the small, dark, non-Aryan farmers and herdsmen passed into Europe from Central Asia, bringing with them the Neolithic civilization, which took deep root. The section of them which spread over Gaul, Spain, and the British Isles, is only known to us as the Iberic aborigines . . . After a lapse of time sufficient to allow the non-Aryan Neolithic civilization to penetrate into every part of the Continent, the

> Celtic Aryans poured in, and made themselves masters of a large part of Gaul and Spain in the Neolithic age. It may be inferred from the geographical position of Germany, as well as from the distribution of human skulls, and the evidence of history, that it was also held by these two races of men. The Iberic peoples were probably driven from the regions east of the Rhine by the Celts, and they in their turn by the Belgae, just as within the Historic period the Belgae were pushed farther to the west by the Germans, who in their turn were compelled to leave their ancient homes to be occupied by Sclaves . . . The progress of civilization in Europe has been continuous from the Neolithic Age down to the present time, and in that remote age the history of the nations of the west finds its proper starting-point. (1880, 341)

Boyd Dawkins's image of race war as the basis for cultural change and succession was specifically rejected by Montelius, who explained change through the presence of trade and other less violent means. Nonetheless, it was a picture of European prehistory that was to introduce the cast of tribes and cultures that formed the basis of the cultural taxonomy of European prehistory. Although he subsequently located the source of both Bronze and Iron technology outside Europe and explained the different rates of progress among the European tribes as being in large measure attributable to distance from source (hence the time lag), Boyd Dawkins never again felt the need to argue that the basic racial structure of Europe had been completely replaced by another. True, the Celts invaded Britain only when they had Bronze, and the Belgae and Germani had been themselves displaced, and as a result, had displaced others, but the Celts (and some remnant non-Aryan peoples) survived, although with reduced territories.

Conclusions

From this witches' brew of race conflict, differential rates of progress, and cultural diffusion, prehistorians of the period between the start of the 1880s and the end of World War II fashioned the stuff of the archaeological culture, a development that was to become so powerful in the archaeology of the twentieth century. It is worth noting, by way of a conclusion, that the explanation of European prehistory in terms of the interactive products of discrete archaeologically definable groupings of people owed much more to ethnological theory than to any inherent cultural properties of the archaeological database.

Indeed, it was precisely during the period following the application of the Three-Age System outside Scandinavia that prehistoric archaeology attained the status of a discipline and all the trappings of scientific societies, international conferences, and venues for publication that went with it. Moreover, at least part of the reason for the resurgence of culture historical archaeology toward the close of the nineteenth century was provided by the developing significance of variability within the archaeological record itself. Nonetheless, there is a real sense of archaeology's disciplinary status being achieved as a subdepartment of anthropology or ethnology, a sense reinforced by the fact that during this phase of the discipline's history there were still few professional archaeologists who were not practicing ethnologists or anthropologists. In the next century the numbers of professionals increased dramatically, following such exemplars as Pitt-Rivers, Petrie, and Worsaae. Yet archaeology has for the most part remained loyal to the notion of an integrative anthropology.

By the end of the nineteenth century, prehistoric archaeology possessed puzzles and problems, as well as methodologies for their solution, that were ample testimony to its right to stand as a coherent discipline. This does not mean there was anything like general agreement about the causes of social and cultural change and variation in the prehistoric past—far from it. Yet, as I shall discuss in the last essay, this set of puzzles, particularly the link between archaeology and the geographical readings of culture area theory, were to exercise archaeologists for much of the next century. The activities of the Fenland Research Committee, J. G. D. Clark's ecological archaeology, and Childean notions of culture history were all developments of this set of puzzles. They were also seen by practitioners to be taking place within the cognitive boundaries of history (the use of source criticism in ethnographic analogy, the perceived need to specify causal relations between historically linked events), physical anthropology (the link between the mental and the physical), and sociocultural anthropology, which had by the beginning of the twentieth century become much more concerned with describing and understanding specific cultural states.

Above all, during the last half of the nineteenth century we see the maturing links between the practice of archaeology and the communities that were most interested in its discoveries. The history of archaeology before the nineteenth century has many examples of antiquarians and archaeologists using their studies to support contemporary political agendas (or having those studies used by others in that way). Leland, Camden, and the early members of the Society of Antiquaries of London, for example, clearly understood this. In the nineteenth century the forces of revolution (in 1789 as well as 1848), independence movements (such as in Greece), the creation of new nations (such as Belgium, Germany, and Italy), and the creation of empires provided significant challenges to antiquarians and archaeologists. Some practitioners (such as Worsaae) were ardent nationalists who sought to enhance popular understanding and acceptance of the nation through a demonstration of (in the case of Denmark) its long history. Others were more exercised by a search for the "essence" of particular nations—a kind of bedrock cultural foundation that made the nation eternal rather than the product of contemporary politics. Archaeology, along with ethnology, played a highly significant role in all of these "nationalist" manifestations in the nineteenth century. More importantly, it was to continue doing this in the twentieth century in ways that were to pose serious moral and ethical challenges to practitioners.

Further Reading

Böhner, K. 1981. Ludwig Lindenschmidt and the Three Age System. In *Towards a history of archaeology,* ed. G. Daniel, 120–126. London: Thames and Hudson.

Boule, M., and H. V. Vallois. 1946. *Les hommes fossiles.* Paris: Masson et Cie.

Boyd Dawkins, W. 1880. *Early man in Britain and his place in the tertiary period.* London: Macmillan.

Burchfield, J. D. 1975. *Lord Kelvin and the age of the earth.* London: Macmillan.

Burrow, J. W. 1966. *Evolution and society.* Cambridge: Cambridge University Press.

Campbell, G. D. 1869. *Primeval man, an examination of some recent speculations.* London: Strahan.

Clarke, D. L. 1968. *Analytical archaeology.* London: Methuen.

Daniel, G. E. 1943. *The Three Ages: an essay on archaeological method.* Cambridge: Cambridge University Press.

Daniel, G. E. 1959. The idea of man's antiquity. *Scientific American* 201: 167–176.

Daniel, G. E. 1971. From Worsaae to Childe: the models of prehistory. *Proceedings of the Prehistoric Society* 37: 140–153.

Daniel, G. E. 1975. *One hundred and fifty years of archaeology.* 2nd ed. London: Duckworth.

Daniel, G. E. 1976. Stone, bronze and iron. In *To illustrate the monuments: essays on archaeology presented to Stuart Piggott on the occasion of his sixty-fifth birthday,* ed. J. V. S. Megaw, 35–42. London: Thames and Hudson.

Daniel, G. E. 1981. *A short history of archaeology.* London: Thames and Hudson.

Evans, J. D. 1981. Introduction: on the prehistory of archaeology. In *Antiquity and man,* eds. J. D. Evans, B. Cunliffe, and C. Renfrew, 12–18. London: Thames and Hudson.

Fowler, D. 1975. Notes on inquiries in anthropology: A bibliographic essay. In *Toward a science of man: Essays in the history of anthropology,* ed. T. H. H. Thoresen, 15–32. The Hague: Mouton.

Gillespie, N. C. 1977. The Duke of Argyll, evolutionary anthropology, and the art of scientific controversy. *Isis* 68: 40–54.

Gräslund, B. 1981. The background to C. J. Thomsen's Three Age System. In *Towards a history of archaeology,* ed. G. Daniel, 45–50. London: Thames and Hudson.

Grayson, D. 1983. *The establishment of human antiquity.* New York: Academic Press.

Gruber, J. W. 1965. Brixham Cave and the antiquity of man. In *Context and meaning in cultural anthropology,* ed. M. E. Spiro, 373–402. New York: Free Press.

Hammond, M. 1982. The expulsion of the Neanderthals from human ancestry: Marcellin Boule and the social context of scientific research. *Social Studies of Science* 12: 1–36.

Harris, M. 1968. *The rise of anthropological theory.* New York: Crowell.

Heizer, R. F., ed. 1962. *Man's discovery of his past: Literary landmarks in archaeology.* Englewood Cliffs, NJ: Prentice-Hall.

Horsman, R. 1976. Origins of racial Anglo-Saxonism in Great Britain before 1850. *Journal of the History of Ideas* 37: 387–410.

Klindt-Jensen, O. 1975. A history of Scandinavian archaeology. London: Thames and Hudson.

Kristiansen, K. 1981. A social history of Danish archaeology (1805–1975). In *Towards a history of archaeology,* ed. G. Daniel, 20–44. London: Thames and Hudson.

Leopold, J. 1980. *Culture in comparative and evolutionary perspective: E. B. Tylor and the making of primitive culture.* Berlin: Dietrich Reimer Verlag.

Lubbock, Sir J. 1865. *Pre-historic times.* Freeport, NY: Books for Libraries Press, 1971.

Lubbock, Sir J. 1882. *The origin of civilization and the primitive condition of man.* 4th ed. London: Longman, Green.

Montelius, O. 1888. *The civilization of Sweden in heathen times.* London: Longman.

Morgan, L. H. 1871. *Systems of consanguinity and affinity of the human family.* Washington, DC: Smithsonian Institution.

Morgan, L. H. 1877. *Ancient society.* London: Macmillan.

Nilsson, S. 1868. *The primitive inhabitants of Scandinavia.* London: Longman.

Pouchet, G. 1864. *The plurality of the human race.* London: Longman, Green, Longman and Roberts for the Anthropological Society of London.

Prichard, J. C. 1847. On the various methods of research which contribute to the advancement of ethnology and the relations of that science to other branches of knowledge. *British Association Reports* 16: 230–253.

Quatrefages De Breau, J. L. A. 1875. *Natural history of man,* trans. E. A. Youmanns. New York: Popular Science Library.

Quatrefages De Breau, J. L. A. 1879. *The human species.* London: Kegan Paul.

Rodden, J. 1981. The development of the Three Age System: Archaeology's first paradigm. In *Towards a history of archaeology,* ed. G. Daniel, 51–68. London: Thames and Hudson.

Rowe, J. H. 1962. Worsaae's Law and the use of grave lots for archaeological dating. *American Antiquity* 28: 129–137.

Rowley-Conwy, P. In press. *From genesis to prehistory. The archaeological Three Age System and its contested reception in Denmark, Britain and Ireland.* London: Oxford University Press.

Sackett, J. R. 1981. From de Mortillet to Bordes: A century of French palaeolithic research. In *Towards a history of archaeology,* ed. G. Daniel, 85–99. London: Thames and Hudson.

Schnapp, A. 1996. *The discovery of the past.* London: British Museum Press.

Sklenář, K. 1983. *Archaeology in Central Europe: The first 500 years.* Leicester, UK: Leicester University Press.

Stocking, G. W., Jr. 1968. Race, culture, and evolution. New York: Free Press.

Stocking, G. W., Jr. 1973. From chronology to ethnology: James Cowles Prichard and British anthropology, 1800–1850. In *Researches into the physical history of man,* by J. C. Prichard, ix–cx. Reprint ed. Chicago: University of Chicago Press.

Stocking, G. W., Jr. 1983a. History of anthropology. Whence/whither. In *Observers observed. Essays on ethnographic fieldwork,* ed. G. W. Stocking, Jr., 3–12. Madison: University of Wisconsin Press.

Stocking, G. W., Jr. 1983b. The ethnographer's magic. Fieldwork in British Anthropology from Tylor to Malinowski. In *Observers observed. Essays on ethnographic fieldwork,* ed. G. W. Stocking, Jr., 70–120. Madison: University of Wisconsin Press.

Stocking, G. W., Jr. 1984. Functionalism historicized. In *Functionalism historicized. Essays on British social anthropology,* ed. G. W. Stocking, Jr., 3–9. Madison: University of Wisconsin Press.

Stocking, G. W., Jr. 1987. *Victorian anthropology.* New York: Free Press.

Thompson, M. W. 1977. *General Pitt Rivers: evolution and archaeology in the nineteenth century.* Bradford-on-Avon, UK: Moonraker Press.

Trigger, B. G. 1978. *Time and traditions: Essays in archaeological interpretation.* Edinburgh: Edinburgh University Press.

Trigger, B. G. 1989. *A history of archaeological thought.* Cambridge: Cambridge University Press.

Tylor, E. B. 1865. *Researches into the early history of man.* London: John Murray.

Tylor, E. B. 1870. *Primitive culture.* London: John Murray.

Van Riper, E. B. 1993. *Men among the mammoths: Victorian science and the discovery of human prehistory.* Chicago: University of Chicago Press.

Vogt, K. 1864. In *Lectures on man,* ed. J. Hunt. London: Longman.

Waitz, T. 1863. *Introduction to anthropology.* London: Longman, Green, Longman and Roberts.

Weber, G. 1974. Science and society in nineteenth century anthropology. *History of Science* 15: 260–283.

Wilson, D. 1851. *The archaeology and prehistoric annals of Scotland.* London: Macmillan.

Worsaae, J. J. A. 1849. *The primeval antiquities of Denmark.* London: John Henry Parker.

MILESTONES IN THE NINETEENTH CENTURY

Establishment of the National Museum of Denmark (1807)

During the seventeenth century, Danish antiquarian Ole Worm had surveyed, recorded, and then published about many of the rune stones, burial sites, or other historic remains and monuments of Denmark. While this was ahead of its time, it was not until the early nineteenth century that concern about the destruction of ancient monuments and archaeological sites in the joint kingdom of Denmark and Norway resulted in protective legislation. While Sweden had already passed legislation to protect its monuments and artifacts in the seventeenth century, the rest of Europe was just beginning to protect, conserve, and collect artifacts of national heritage. Organizations in Denmark and Norway became interested in similar legislation. However, the English defeat of the Danish in 1801 and 1807 had also stimulated Danish national enthusiasm for its past greatness, now perceived to be under threat by contemporary politics.

A royal collection, or kunstkammer, comprising Ole Worm's collections and other artifacts, had been established in a royal palace, but it was disordered, overflowing with material, and inaccessible through lack of interpretation and display space to the public. In 1806 the Danish king Frederik VI set up a royal commission for the preservation of antiquities to advise him about legislation and collection. The antiquities commission appointed Professor Rasmus Nyerup (1759–1829) to research antiquities collections and site protection, and he traveled throughout Europe to study the best solutions. In 1806 Nyerup published his recommendations for legislation and for a central and national museum in the *Survey of the National Monuments of Antiquity Such as May Be Displayed in a Future National Museum.*

In 1807 legislation was passed to protect monuments and archaeological finds, and a commission was established to advise on founding a central and national museum. Nyerup became secretary and member of this commission and began to receive the first contributions of archaeological material for the future national museum, which joined the extant collections now moved and stored in the loft of the Trinitas Church in Copenhagen.

However, by 1816 the job had become too big for Nyerup, and a young numismatist who had a passion for Nordic antiquities, the right connections, and a talent for classification, Christian Jurgensen Thomsen (1788–1865), replaced him as commission secretary. Although it was Thomsen who brought chronological order and classification to the Danish national collection of antiquities, it was Nyerup's extensive research and determination that laid the foundations for one of the greatest and richest prehistoric collections in Europe.

In 1832 the Museum of Antiquities was moved to the Christiansborg Palace and displayed and explained according to Thomsens's Three-Age System—in Stone, Bronze, and Iron ages.

See also Worm Issues His Circular (1626); *Guide to Northern Archaeology* Published in English (1848); Publication of *Primeval Antiquities of Denmark* in English (1849).

Further Reading

Jensen, Jorgen. 1998. *Guides to the National Museum. Prehistory of Denmark.* Copenhagen: National Museum.

Klindt-Jensen, Ole. 1975. *A history of Scandinavian archaeology.* London: Thames and Hudson.

Kristiansen, Kristian. 2001. Denmark. In *Encyclopedia of archaeology, history and discoveries,* ed. T. Murray, vol. 1, 414–423. Santa Barbara, CA: ABC-CLIO.

Murray, T. 2001. Rasmus Nyerup. In *Encyclopedia of archaeology: history and discoveries,* ed. T. Murray, vol. 3, 964. Santa Barbara, CA: ABC-CLIO.

Napoleon I Funds the Excavation of Roman Sites and Antiquities (1808–1814)

Napoleon Bonaparte concluded a peace with the papal states in 1797, and the French army occupied the city of Rome in 1798, deposing and imprisoning Pope Pius VI. A Roman republic, supported by the French, lasted from 1798 until 1799, but the French stayed on the Italian Peninsula, and Rome was reoccupied by French troops in 1800 and again in 1808.

In 1809 the French prefect Camille de Tournon arrived in Rome to help manage its antiquities. Archaeological work in the city had continued during the past decade, despite the occupations and withdrawals of armies, presided over by a new commissioner of antiquities, Carlo Fea. Appointed by the new

Il Colosseo, *a painting of the Coliseum by Antonio Canaletto. (Corel)*

pope, Pius VII, Fea's task was to replace the ancient sculptures taken by the French army to Paris with new and even better examples of classical art.

In 1809 the occupation government or "consulta" established a commission to inspect and preserve Roman monuments. Commission members were de Tournon; Fea; the sculptor Canova, who was president of the Academy of St Luke; and two architects, Giuseppe Valadier and Giuseppe Camporese. The commission passed new laws preventing the illegal excavation and export of antiquities. In 1810 the commission was enlarged to fourteen, adding artists and antiquarians to its expert membership.

At the same time the commission designated six sites to be excavated by the architects Valadier and Camporese: the Forum Boarium, part of the Forum Romanum, the Temple of Antoninus and Faustina, the Colosseum, the Domus Aurea, and the Arch of Janus. The diggers comprised 800 unemployed and poor men, women, and children of Rome, who were paid one franc per cubic meter of earth and were fed once a day.

This investment in the archaeology of Rome was partly political, providing employment for the Roman poor, who had become even more disadvantaged because of the lack of church charities. All of the French generals and their armies who had occupied Rome, despite looting, had respected Rome's monuments and past, and French republicanism was supported by many Romans. But French respect for Roman antiquity was also part of the French Empire's identification with the ancient Roman Empire, an ideology that managed to survive the ancient regime and the revolution. De Tournon, nicknamed "Camillo Capitolino," was appointed to Rome because he was passionately interested in Roman antiquity. However, all of these factors had an impact on the kind of archaeological and conservation and restoration work that the French funded in Rome.

For example, in 1810, the Academia St. Luke was given the inadequate sum of 75,000 francs to repair all of its unearthed classical monuments. At the same time, Martial Daru received 200,000 francs to excavate works of art for French museums. And as they were in Paris, Roman antiquities were used as political symbols by the French, but this time they were used for that end in Rome itself. For example, in 1811, the newly cleared sites of the Forum, the Colosseum, and the area around the Capitol were illuminated to celebrate the birth of Napoleon's son.

As the result of an interview between De Tournon and Napoleon I in Paris later that year, the Roman excavations received a further one million francs per year, and work was extended to include the Capitol Garden, Trajan's Forum, and the Pantheon. However, this work was hampered by financial crises caused by the cost of demolitions and Parisian maladministration.

There is little doubt that the monuments of Rome benefited hugely from French funding. The Basilica of Maxentius and the Colosseum were cleared, exposed, and conserved, as were the Domus Aurea and the temples of Vesta and Fortune in the Forum Boarium. In the Forum Romanum substantial clearances uncovered Trajan's Column. The portico of the Temple of Antoninus and Faustina was exposed, as were the temples of the Dioscuri and Saturn. The Temple of Venus and Rome was discovered, the remaining columns of Vespasian rebuilt, and the hill below the Capitol cleared. For the first time in almost 2,000 years almost all of the monuments of ancient Rome could be seen, and modern Roman archaeology was born.

See also Foundation of the French Academy in Rome (1666); Foundation of the Louvre (1779–1793); Napoleon Loots Rome (1797).

Further Reading

Grummond, N. de, ed. 1996. *An encyclopedia of the history of classical archaeology*. Westport, CT: Greenwood Press.

Ridley, R. 1992. *The eagle and the spade: Archaeology in Rome during the Napoleonic era.* Cambridge: Cambridge University Press.

Publication of The Ancient History of North and South Wiltshire *(1812)*

Born into an aristocratic banking family, Richard Colt Hoare was financially independent and thus able to pursue a career in well-spent leisure. The premature death of his wife caused him to assuage his grief by traveling in Europe for two years, a journey that stimulated his interest (as it had for so many others who had taken the "Grand Tour") in monuments and antiquities. He returned to Britain and became Baron Hoare in 1787, and then he resumed traveling around Europe for the next three years, visiting and drawing archaeological sites, before the French Revolution made it impossible to continue.

It was this impasse that caused Colt Hoare to travel through Wales, England, and Ireland, visiting, drawing, and publishing accounts of the monuments of his own country. Between 1812 and 1821, he illustrated and published the two-volume *Ancient History of North and South Wiltshire* and the *History of Ancient Wiltshire.* These contained accounts of Stonehenge and Avebury, Roman roads and sites, and hundreds of barrows that he had explored with his protégé, William Cunnington. These books can be seen as the first attempts at recording the archaeology of a particular region.

Colt Hoare was a fellow of the Royal Society and the Society of Antiquaries, and he wrote numerous books, printed for private circulation, on history, architecture, and the archaeological sites, artifacts, and monuments of Europe, England, Wales, and Ireland. He financed his own archaeology team—comprising William Cunnington, draftsman Philip Crocker, and special workmen—and he believed excavations should be able to answer questions about the past. Unfortunately, the answers to the big questions—such as who had built the monuments, and why and when they were built—remained elusive.

Colt Hoare saw himself as a historian, and his arguments were based on facts, not on wild theories such as those of William Stukeley. He was one of the first of the new generation of romantic aristocratic gentlemen who were travelers, adventurers, artists, and journalist-writer-historians who also liked opening graves. Such antiquaries featured strongly in the pursuit of the understanding of the past during the last years of the eighteenth and the early nineteenth centuries. Their position, both chronologically and ideologically, was somewhere between the antiquarians of the Enlightenment and the professional archaeologists of the mid-nineteenth century.

See also Publication of *Britannia* (1586); Publication of *The Antiquities of Warwickshire* (1656); Publication of *Itinerarium Curiosum* (1724); Publication of *Nenia Britannica* (1793).

Further Reading

Cunnington, R. H. 1975. *From antiquary to archaeologist: a biography of William Cunnington 1754–1810.* Princes Risborough, UK: Shire Publications.

Sweet, R. 2004. *Antiquaries: the discovery of the past in 18th century Britain.* London: Hambledon and London.

Woodbridge, K. 1970. *Landscape and antiquity.* Oxford: Clarendon.

Foundation of Great Egyptian Collections in England and France (1815–1835)

The occupation of Egypt by Napoleon Bonaparte and the French army (1798–1805) was part of a strategy to attack British trade and threaten British interests in India, so as to have some bargaining power when negotiating for the planned French domination of Europe. Napoleon also believed Egypt would benefit from its occupation by the army of the most civilized contemporary nation, while the French scholars who accompanied his expedition would describe, interpret, and open up this oldest of civilizations to the rest of the world.

While Egypt was hardly unknown to nineteenth-century Europeans after almost 2,000 years of domination by Mamluks and Ottomans, the country and the physical remnants of its long history were still mysterious and unexplored. The occupation of Egypt by France, and then by England, was not only another stage in the destabilization of Ottoman rule, but also another incident in the worldwide phenomenon of Anglo-French animosity and competition. France and England had already carved out empires in North America, Africa, the Pacific, and the Far East, and Egypt was next. Indeed, the relationship between England and France was to dominate Egyptian politics for the rest of the nineteenth century, as either one or the other fell in or out of favor and influence with the Egyptian government, who were happy to use the rivalry to their own advantage.

Anglo-French political, strategic, and colonial competition created cultural competition—both had assembled classical collections and established large national museums in which to store and display them, and now they began to assemble Egyptian collections. The British captured the Rosetta stone and the collections of Napoleon's scholars and took them back to London, where they created great scholarly and popular interest. However, this did not prevent the encyclopedic publication by the French of their *Description de l'Egypte* between 1809 and 1827, which also increased wider awareness of, and admiration for, the monuments of ancient Egypt. The rediscovery of this old civilization, Europe's passion for collecting, the enormous quantity of sites and finds in Egypt, the easy access to sites along the Nile, the lack of difficulty in digging sand, the lack of value assigned to these finds by the Egyptian population and government, together with long-standing local traditions of grave robbing and antiquities trading, created a veritable river of antiquities flowing from Egypt into Europe.

In 1815 Muhammad Ali Pasha seized power in Egypt. To repay both France and England for not interfering with his coup, Ali Pasha began to open up the country to European investment and tourism. Together with the English he conquered the Sudan, and later, in 1833, while the Turks were defending their possessions in other parts of the Mediterranean, in Greece and Crete, Ali Pasha (briefly) invaded Syria.

In 1815, Henry Salt, after a lot of petitioning and string pulling in London, was appointed British consul-general in Egypt. Salt (1780–1827) trained as a portrait painter in London, and began his long love affair with Eastern antiquities in 1802 when he became secretary/draftsman to the aristocratic travel writer Lord Valentia, accompanying him through India, Ceylon, Abyssinia, and Egypt. The resulting book, published in 1802, was illustrated by Salt. Then Salt himself traveled to Abyssinia for the British government between 1808 and 1811, publishing his account of the journey in 1814.

While Salt was appointed British consul-general in Egypt to lobby on behalf of, and report on threats to, British interests in Egypt, the trustees of the British Museum also encouraged him to collect antiquities. He was also there to further his own interests in collecting, investing in, and selling antiquities, in the tradition of that other great consular collector in southern Italy, Sir William Hamilton. However, in Egypt Salt was directly competing with the interests of the French consul Drovetti, who deployed agents all over Egypt to find and bring him antiquities, and who was much favored by Ali Pasha.

It was the Swiss explorer Jean Louis Burckhardt who became a friend of Salt's in Cairo and introduced him to the former unemployed circus strongman and amateur engineer, Giovanni Belzoni. With Burckhardt's knowledge of Egypt, Belzoni, and other agents, such as Caviglia at the Pyramids and D'Athanasi at Thebes, Salt began to challenge Drovetti's antiquities monopoly. Both groups of consular agents roamed up and down the Nile collecting as much as they could transport, bribing local officials and workers to be uncooperative with or obstructive to the other group, beating each other to sites and loot, and then disputing who had the best pieces.

Drovetti's agents had been unable to move the colossal bust of Ramses II, and Salt, Burckhardt, and Belzoni saw it not only as a challenge to transport it and then donate it to the British Museum, but also as another defeat of the French in the great Anglo-French competition. While there is no doubt that Salt and Burckhardt wanted to use the display of Ramses II and other artifacts in London to raise the awareness of the glory of ancient Egypt, Salt also wanted to create a market for Egyptian antiquities there—one that would benefit the sale of his own collections. For a while Belzoni believed he was collecting directly for the British Museum, but eventually he came to some financial arrangement with Salt over the pieces he collected that were not forwarded to the museum, but were kept by Salt himself. Belzoni was more interested in the fame and the acclaim that went with the discovery of the antiquities than with amassing a fortune. In 1817 Belzoni accompanied the Ramses II statue and other pieces to London and set up their display, creating a local sensation. As their discoverer, Belzoni became famous in London, and his stories of hostile Turks in the desert and crypts full of mummies kept London society mesmerized and enthusiastic for more. Meanwhile Salt stayed in Cairo and almost died of typhus.

In 1818 Salt tried to sell his large collection of Egyptian antiquities to the British Museum, which was somewhat reluctant, having recently negotiated, at great expense, to purchase the Parthenon marbles from Lord Elgin. With the intervention of Salt's mentors, eventually they paid Salt almost half of what he had anticipated—enough to cover his costs. But they rejected the best piece in this collection—the alabaster sarcophagus of Seti I, Ramses II's father, which Salt eventually sold to a private collector, the architect John Soane, for 2,000 pounds.

Salt's young wife and second child died of typhus in Cairo in 1824, and he became embittered by Belzoni's fame, as he had financed and made possible Belzoni's discoveries. He continued collecting, hoping to earn enough to retire to England, but he was disillusioned with the British Museum. His second collection of some 4,000 artifacts, assembled between 1819 and 1824, was sold (on the advice of Champollion) to the king of France in 1825 for 10,000 pounds.

Salt never enjoyed his fortune or any retirement. He died in 1827 and was buried in Alexandria. In 1835 his third collection, assembled between 1824 and 1827, was sold at Sotheby's in London. It took seven days to clear it, and it was mostly acquired by the British Museum, on the recommendation of its newly appointed Egyptologist and keeper Wallis Budge.

See also British Museum purchases the Parthenon Marbles (1816); Publication of the *Description de l'Egypte* (1826); Publication of *The Manners and Customs of the Ancient Egyptians* (1847).

Further Reading

Athanasi, G. d'. 1836. *A brief account of the researches and discoveries in Upper Egypt, made under the direction of Henry Salt, Esq. to which is added a detailed catalogue of Mr. Salt's collection of Egyptian antiquities, illustrated with twelve engravings of some of the most interesting objects, and an enumeration of those articles purchased for the British Museum.* London: J. Hearne.

Fagan, B. 1975. *The rape of the Nile. Tomb robbers, tourists and archaeologists in Egypt.* Aylesbury, UK: Macdonald and Jane's.

Manley, D., and P. Rees. 2001. *Henry Salt: artist, traveller, diplomat, Egyptologist.* London: Libri Publications.

British Museum Purchases the Parthenon Marbles (1816)

Thomas Bruce, Lord Elgin (1766–1841), served in the army, married a Scottish heiress, and then became a diplomat. As an enlightened member of the British aristocracy of the eighteenth century he used his career and position in society to improve the knowledge of the arts and civilization of the classical world in England, and his wealthy wife shared his interests and was happy to support them with her considerable family fortune. In 1799 he became ambassador to the Ottoman court in Constantinople and requested government funds to finance his plans to document the monuments of classical Greek civilization in Athens. When this was refused he and his wife personally financed a team led by the Italian painter Lusieri, who began to draw the monuments and make casts of the sculptures on the Acropolis, while Elgin lobbied the Ottoman court in Constantinople to ensure official permission and to gain access to the monuments. It soon became apparent that the buildings and decorations on the Acropolis were under threat and were being constantly vandalized; smashed up for local lime making or rebuilding; acquired by collectors and their agents, including the Frenchman Fauvel; or used as target practice by members of the Ottoman army stationed in Athens.

Thomas Bruce, seventh Earl of Elgin. (Hulton Archive/Getty Images)

Elgin only visited Athens once during his time at Constantinople, but he was convinced by other expatriate residents in Athens that the only way to save the sculptures and inscriptions for posterity was not just to record and copy them but to remove them completely. He began to negotiate with the Ottoman authorities to this end. Meanwhile, the British had incurred the gratitude of the Ottoman court for their defeat of Napoleon and his army in Egypt, so Elgin was given permission to remove anything from the Acropolis that did not compromise its fortification against the local Greek population. Over three years Lusieri collected sculptures from the Parthenon and unearthed others from the rubble surrounding it, which included 247 feet of the Parthenon frieze, fourteen sculptures of metopes, seventeen figures from the pediment, four slabs from the Temple of Athena Nike, a caryatid from the Erechtheion, and bits and pieces of architectural details from the Propylaia and the Parthenon. Between 1804 and 1812 many of these were crated up and sent by ship to London, others were on the docks waiting to go when war between Britain and Turkey broke out and never left, and some went down at sea and (at great cost to Elgin) were salvaged. From 1803 until 1806 Elgin and his family, on their way home to England, were imprisoned in France. In 1807 the marbles that had arrived in London were unpacked and displayed to artists and the interested public. They created a sensation. They were acclaimed by international scholars, such as Visconti and Winckelmann, and eulogized by poets, such as Keats and Goethe.

In 1814, in need of funds after divorcing Lady Elgin, Lord Elgin began to lobby the British government to purchase his collection of marbles for the British Museum. The head of the Society of Dilettanti, art historian and collector Richard Payne Knight, was appointed by the board of the British Museum to negotiate with Elgin, and a Select Committee of the House of Commons was set up to debate the ownership of the marbles, their real worth and value, issues such as whether they should be restored or only conserved, and whether Elgin had acquired them legally. These questions were also widely debated in newspapers and within society, and some are still being debated almost two centuries later. As an expert witness Payne Knight testified before parliament that the sculptures were not Greek but late Roman (he was eventually proved wrong), which helped bring Elgin's price down to 35,000 pounds. The Select Committee eventually found that Elgin had acquired the marbles legally, and therefore they could be purchased from him by the British Museum. The committee also determined that they were unique, not copies and not Roman, and were made in the fifth century BC.

The marbles from the Parthenon have been on display in the British Museum since 1817, and they continue to have the impact Elgin believed they would, influencing and convincing thousands of artists, scholars, and tourists of the artistic greatness of classical civilization. However, their ownership continues to be controversial, perhaps even more so now, than during the nineteenth century. The marbles have become one of the most discussed examples of the crucial and ongoing debate about who owns the great monuments and artifacts and landscapes of the past—the world, their country of origin, or the country that displays them? What are they worth? And if they are unique, they are therefore irreplaceable and priceless. Do proof of ownership, exchanges of contracts, and bills of sale mean anything if something is part of a nation's patrimony, even if these legalities existed before the nation did? How do you stop the trade in antiquities? Because if there is a market for antiquities there will always be a way to supply it, and not only to wealthy individuals but also to wealthy government institutions such as museums.

The Parthenon marbles (also known as the Elgin marbles) were also one of the last, and dwindling in number, great collections assembled for and purchased by discerning and wealthy individuals. During the nineteenth century, publicly funded institutions, such as museums, universities, or the trustees of specialist societies, began to fund archaeological excavations and the acquisition of collections. Their justification, like Elgin's own, would be preservation, education, and display to a wider audience, and unlike Elgin, at least superficially, it was easier for them to claim and defend and justify their ownership of the past.

See also Foundation of Great Egyptian Collections in England and France (1815–1835); French Expédition Scientifique de Morée (1829–1831).

Further Reading

British Museum. 1975. *An historical guide to the sculptures of the Parthenon.* London: British Museum Publications.

Hitchens, C., ed. 1987. *The Elgin Marbles: Should they be returned to Greece?* London: Chatto & Windus.

St. Clair, W. 1997. *Lord Elgin and the Marbles.* 2nd ed. Oxford: Oxford University Press.

Publication of Descriptions of the Antiquities Discovered in the State of Ohio and Other Western States *(1820)*

Caleb Atwater (1778–1867) was an early North American antiquary and amateur archaeologist. Born in Massachussets, Atwater received a B.A. from Williams College and became a Presbyterian minister. He later studied and practiced law in New York City. After moving his legal practice to Circleville, Ohio, in 1815, he used his spare time to study and record local earthworks and antiquities. The American Antiquarian Society, established in 1812, published his work, finds, and conclusions as *Descriptions of the Antiquities Discovered in the State of Ohio and Other Western States* in the first volume of their transactions in 1820.

The earth mounds discovered west of the Appalachian Mountains that Atwater excavated and recorded contained artifacts made of pottery, shell, and native copper, and they challenged the widespread belief that Native American people were too primitive and inferior to have created anything like them, let alone designed and completed the extensive earthworks containing them. Indeed, at that time the bulk of observers would not even accept that the ancestors of the Native Americans were capable of such building feats.

Aerial view of Moundville Park, Alabama. (iStockphoto)

The origins of the earth mounds became the focus of ongoing debate. Some antiquarians and members of the public argued that they were built by Vikings or other Europeans, or by the ancestors of the Mexican Aztecs who later moved south. Other scholars proposed that indigenous Americans had destroyed the civilization that built the mounds and used this as part of a justification to in turn destroy them.

Atwater had his own theory about their origins. He believed the mounds had been constructed by Hindus who had migrated from India, via Ohio, to Mexico. Notwithstanding these now discredited hypotheses, Atwater's study contained valuable descriptions of the earth mounds, which were later destroyed.

See also Excavation of a Burial Mound in Virginia (1787); Establishment of Major U.S. Archaeological Institutions (1846–1866); Publication of *Ancient Monuments of the Mississippi Valley* (1847).

Further Reading

Atwater, C. 1820. *Descriptions of the Antiquities Discovered in the State of Ohio and Other Western States.* Archeological Americana: Transactions and Collections of the American Antiquarian Society I: 105-267.

Dunnell, R. 2001. United States of America, Prehistoric Archaeology. In *Encyclopedia of archaeology: History and discoveries,* ed. T. Murray, 1292–1294. Santa Barbara, CA: ABC-CLIO.

Murray, T. 2001. Caleb Atwater (1778-1867). In *Encyclopedia of archaeology: History and discoveries,* ed. T. Murray, 111–112. Santa Barbara, CA: ABC-CLIO.

Willey, G. R., and J. A. Sabloff. 1980. *A history of American archaeology.* 2nd ed. San Francisco: Freeman and Company.

Publication of Reliquiae diluvianae *(1823)*

English geologist, Anglican priest, and professor of mineralogy at Oxford University, William Buckland (1784–1856) was a "catastrophist," that is, he believed universal catastrophes had wiped out species and God had created new ones to take their place. Buckland studied the chronology and stratigraphy of caves and, along with the great French geologist Georges Cuvier, explored the association between fossil humans and the remains of extinct animals. As more and more evidence of the increasing complexity of plant and animal life in successive geological strata was found, Buckland argued that this was the result of separate and individual acts of creation and was not evidence of developmental sequence. He believed God, and not the natural world, was responsible for evolution.

In 1823, Buckland's *Reliquiae Diluvianae* listed all the then-known finds of fossil humans and faunal remains. He concluded that human bones were not as old as the animal bones with which they were found because they were intrusions, the result of geological processes, faults, or tectonic movements. For more than twenty years his views dominated the scientific establishment, until those of his student, geologist Charles Lyell (1797–1875), and archaeologists such as Sir Hugh Falconer, William Pengelly, Sir Joseph Prestwich, and Sir John Evans provided evidence of high human antiquity and superseded them.

See also Publication of *De l'origine et des usages de la pierre de foudre* (1723); John Frere Writes to the Society of Antiquaries of London (1797); High Human Antiquity in the Somme Valley (1841–1864); Excavation at Brixham Cave (1858–1859).

Further Reading

Murray, T., 2001. William Buckland (1784-1856) In *Encyclopedia of archaeology: History and discoveries,* ed. T. Murray, 225. Santa Barbara, CA: ABC-CLIO.

Murray, T., 2001. Sir Charles Lyell (1797-1875). In *Encyclopedia of archaeology: History and discoveries,* ed. T. Murray, 832. Santa Barbara, CA: ABC-CLIO.

Rupke, Nicolas A. 1983. *The great chain of history: William Buckland and the English school of geology (1814–1849)*. Oxford: Oxford University Press.

Decipherment of Egyptian Hieroglyphics (1824)

It is generally agreed that the last hieroglyphic inscription was carved in Egypt about 1,600 years ago, after the emperor Theodosius issued an edict against pagan cults. Before long, a script that had been in use since the beginning of the third millennium BC, for almost 5,000 years, became indecipherable to all Egyptians.

Travelers to Egypt have always been intrigued by hieroglyphic writing. Greek and Roman historians—both before and after the fifth century AD—believed that Egyptian hieroglyphics represented a form of sacred writing, and that the individual symbols represented whole words or ideas. This assumption was reinforced by the demise, in the third century AD, of the spoken language of Egyptian and its script (known as demotic), and their replacement by Coptic (from Qubti, the Arabic word for the Greek term "Aiguptios"). The separation of contemporary Egypt from its past was compounded by the fact that Coptic was written in Greek letters with a few demotic signs. The conceptual distance between the living and dead languages of Egypt was further increased after around 1000 AD, when Arabic replaced Coptic as the language of Egypt. From then on, Coptic was used only in Christian liturgy.

Nevertheless, during the six centuries following the triumph of Arabic in Egypt, European scholars and philosophers maintained an intense interest in both the Egyptian religion and the Egyptian obelisks and other monuments that had been brought to Italy during the Roman Empire. This interest gathered serious strength during the Italian Renaissance, inspiring travelers, such as Pietro della Valle in 1626, to bring back what proved to be Coptic grammars and dictionaries from the Middle East. These documents became the source of the first serious attempt to decipher ancient Egyptian, by the German Jesuit Athanasius Kircher, who was based in Rome. His *Lingua Aegyptiaca Restitua*, published in 1644, became the foundation of Coptic studies, and his assumption that the Coptic language derived from the ancient language of Egypt was a major step forward.

During the eighteenth century, as the scale of European archaeological surveys in Egypt expanded and the numbers of monuments and sites recorded by scholars increased, the cutting edge of decipherment moved to

France, where three important developments occurred. First, in 1761 the Abbe Barthélemy suggested that the cartouches or oval-shaped framed sections of the inscriptions contained the names of gods and kings. Second, in 1785, Charles Joseph de Guignes suggested that the three known Egyptian scripts (hieroglyphic, the early cursive script hieratic, and demotic) were connected. The final step was taken in 1797, by the Dane Jörgen Zoëga, when he suggested that the system of hieroglyphics included phonetic elements.

Two years later, during Napoleon's Egyptian campaign, French soldiers at Borg Rashid (meaning "the tower of Rosetta") unearthed a block of stone weighing 720 kilograms that was inscribed in three different scripts. One of the officers present, Lieutenant Bouchard, who had trained in archaeology, identified the three bands of scripts as hieroglyphic, demotic, and ancient Greek. Fortunately, engineers were on hand who could read the latter. That it was a decree of Ptolemy V dated 27 March 196 BC was interesting enough, but what fired up their imaginations (and that of the French scientists accompanying Napoleon) was the last sentence, which declared: "This decree shall be inscribed on stelae of hard rock, in sacred characters, both native and Greek . . ." Thus, they knew immediately that the top and middle bands of the scripts on the stela repeated the Greek inscription.

The subsequent history of the Rosetta stone (especially its removal to London) is more dramatic but very much less significant than the apparently mundane business of producing copies (by the English as well as the French) that allowed researchers all over Europe, not just in London, to work on decipherment. Although never free from personal and professional jealousies, the task of decipherment was to see great international cooperation, especially between English and French scholars, such as Sir Joseph Banks, Edme François Jomard (who was responsible for producing the great *Description de l'Egypte*) and Taylor Combe of the British Museum, even when their countries were officially at war. But it became obvious that the task of decipherment would require much more than the stone. The collections of inscriptions acquired over the previous century, but especially those acquired by French scientists who were part of Napoleon's expedition to Egypt, would be crucial.

Translators working on the ancient Greek quickly identified the significance of the inscription for Hellenists. Dating from a period barely 100 years after Alexander's conquest of Egypt in 332 BC, Ptolemy's decree provided much primary information about contemporary society and politics, particularly the extent to which Greek and Egyptian cultures were becoming integrated. Much more challenging was the task of deciphering the top and middle bands of the stone scripts. The fact that both script bands carried the same message as the Greek gave those linguists who felt up to the challenge some kind of starting point, but even getting this far required a phenomenal grounding in languages. Take the case of Silvestre de Sacy who knew Hebrew, Syriac, Chaldean, Arabic, Persian, and Turkish and was to hold significant teaching and administrative positions within the French education system. His approach was to start from the middle band, the demotic, a late form of the Egyptian language that was spoken and referred to mainly secular matters.

Beginning with Greek words such as *god* or *king* he sought their equivalents in the demotic, trying to identify the same words alphabetically. By doing this he was able to find the demotic equivalents of *Alexander, Alexandria, Ptolemy,* and a few others. He was also able to conclude that the demotic inscription was not a literal translation of the Greek. De Sacy gave up the challenge in 1802 to be replaced for a brief time by an amateur Swedish linguist, Johan David Åkerblad. While pursuing the same strategy of decipherment, Åkerblad managed to correct a few of de Sacy's readings and add some new ones of his own.

This early work, and that of many other would-be translators (some wildly eccentric) was to be completely overshadowed by the contributions of two geniuses, Sir Thomas Young and Jean-François Champollion (1790–1832). While both men displayed prodigious learning in all the relevant ancient and modern languages, it is clear that Champollion was largely responsible for deciphering the hieroglyphics.

Considered a dullard and a troublemaker by his teacher, Champollion was taken out of school in 1799, at the age of nine, to be privately educated until he moved to Grenoble to join his brother (and protector) Jacques-Joseph. In 1807, at the age of seventeen, Champollion finished an extraordinarily eclectic secondary school education and, shortly after, announced to Grenoble's Academy of Sciences and Arts that he would decipher Egyptian and reconstruct the religion, history, and geography of the country.

Champollion's future lay in Paris at the Collège de France with Silvestre de Sacy. There he studied Arabic, Persian, and especially Coptic, believing (as did others) that a valid decipherment would be based on that language. Over the next few years Champollion pursued a conventional academic career, returning from Paris to a job at the University of Grenoble in 1810. He also had to learn the ground rules of academic politics, losing the support of de Sacy to others and coping with constant fears that someone would beat him to the task of deciphering hieroglyphics. The greatest challenge to his priority was to come in 1814 from an extraordinary English polymath, Thomas Young, who followed de Sacy's basic method to increase the number of matches between Egyptian and Greek words. But as Champollion (and de Sacy himself) observed, this did not constitute the decipherment of a hieroglyphic alphabet or an understanding of ancient Egyptian grammar. Nonetheless it is commonly agreed that Young had identified a few symbols that represented sounds, and this gave support to the notion that the hieroglyphics had phonetic value.

Champollion's political and academic fortunes took a further battering with the defeat of Napoleon, a situation he was unable to reverse until 1822. Nevertheless, this was the most creative period of his short life, for he made three crucial discoveries that directly led to the decipherment. First, he was able to show that the "hieratic" script used in day-to-day ancient Egyptian documents was a cursive, simplified version of the hieroglyphic script and that the two functioned in accord with the same system. Then he established that demotic was a still more abridged cursive form of the hieroglyphics and was generally governed by the same rules. Finally, after he had returned to

Egyptian hieroglyphics. (Corel)

Paris from Grenoble in 1821, Champollion worked out that the hieroglyphics were phonetic. These great advances he was able to publish in 1822 in his famous *Letter to M. Dacier,* the permanent secretary of the Academié des inscriptions et belles-lettres, the key Parisian institution in his field. The task of decipherment had been completed; the new task of defining the grammar of ancient Egyptian could begin.

Here Champollion's unrivalled knowledge of inscriptions from all over Egypt and from all different periods came to the fore. By 1824 he reached the conclusion that the hieroglyphics sometimes express ideas, sometimes sound. It was, Champollion argued, a complex system simultaneously figurative, symbolic, and phonetic, in one and the same text, same sentence, and, almost, in one and the same word.

Appointed curator of the Louvre's Egyptian collection in 1826, Champollion traveled to Egypt. Over the next sixteen months, his alphabet was tested in hundreds of contexts, from the mouth of the River Nile to the second cataract, and over all relevant time periods. It passed with flying colors. In 1831 he became professor of archaeology at the Collège de France, only to die the following year—from a combination of diabetes, liver disease, and consumption—leaving his Egyptian grammar incomplete.

The scholar Alexander von Humboldt neatly summarized Champollion's achievement:

> I have arrived, after long study of Champollion's works, at the profound conviction that it is to him alone that this splendid discovery is due. No one can refuse him the merit of having been the first to affirm and prove that most of the hieroglyphic script is alphabetic, and while others have found a few phonetic signs, it is nonetheless clear that they would never even have succeeded in deciphering a significant number of proper names. Having taken the wrong path from the outset, they apparently did not devote themselves with sufficient patience to the study of the hieroglyphs, limiting themselves far too exclusively to the Rosetta inscription. (Hartleben 1990, 266–227)

See also Publication of *Oedipus Aegypticus* (1652–1655); Foundation of Great Egyptian Collections in England and France (1815–1835); Publication of *Description de l'-Egypte* (1826).

Further Reading

Adkins, L., and R. Adkins. 2000. *The keys of Egypt: the race to read the hieroglyphs.* London: HarperCollins.

Hartleben, H. 1990. *Jean-Francois Champollion: sa vie et son oeuvre, 1790–1832.* Paris: Pygmalion.

Pope, M. 1999. *The story of decipherment: from Egyptian hieroglyphics to Maya script.* Rev. ed. London: Thames and Hudson.

Solé, R., and D. Valbelle. 2001. *The Rosetta Stone.* London: Profile Books.

Publication of Description de l'Egypte *(1826)*

Description de l'Egypte is the direct outcome of a decision taken by the French general, Napoleon Bonaparte, to take a party of scholars with his army during the invasion and occupation of Egypt. Although the occupation eventually failed at the hands of Lord Nelson and the British navy and army, the same cannot be said for the work of the French scholars. Indeed, while the loss of the Rosetta stone to the British was a cruel blow to French prestige, it would transpire that the decipherment of Egyptian hieroglyphic writing would still be accomplished by a Frenchman—on the basis of excellent reproductions made by Napoleon's scholars before it was lost.

The compilation and publication of the French scholars' work, the *Description de l'Egypte,* took twenty-four years to complete, but when you consider its great size (some twenty volumes) and the, literally, cast of thousands who were involved in the whole process, there can be no accusation of dilatory behavior on the part of its editor, Jomard. Indeed the *Description de l'Egypte* is an encyclopedia of Egypt (both ancient and modern), at once a compilation of what was known and what had been discovered about Egypt during the time of the French occupation. In fact, the *Description* is about much more than the monuments of ancient Egypt (although this is, of course, the basis of much its fame). Expedition members, of whom there were 167 who were organized into the *Commission des Sciences et des Arts* of the *Armée d'Orient,* collected information about everything from animals and plants to domestic housing and material culture. Many of these "discoveries" were meticulously illustrated, thereby enhancing the impact of the book that was, in essence, a "total snapshot" of Egypt. Ranging far and wide and pursuing both practical and occasionally somewhat esoteric quests, Napoleon's scholars collected such a mountain of material that it is scarcely a surprise that it took Jomard twenty-four years to get it into print.

The *Description* had a resounding impact on the world of scholarship and in European society more broadly. When allied with Champollion's decipherment of Egyptian hieroglyphs it advanced European knowledge of this ancient civilization by a quantum leap. The great and popular passion for Egyptology had begun.

See also Decipherment of Egyptian Hieroglyphics (1824); Foundation of Great Egyptian Collections in England and France (1815–1835); French Expédition Scientifique de Morée (1829–1831); Publication of *The Manners and Customs of the Ancient Egyptians* (1847).

Further Reading

Bierman, J., ed. 1997. *Napoleon in Egypt.* Reading, UK: Ithaca Press: Los Angeles: Gustave E. von Grunebaum Center for Near Eastern Studies, 2003.

Denon, D. V. 1802. *Travels in upper and lower Egypt during the campaigns of General Bonaparte.* London: Longman.

Fagan, B. 1975. *The rape of the Nile: Tomb robbers, tourists and archaeologists in Egypt.* Aylesbury, Bucks, UK: Macdonalds and Jane's Publishers Ltd.

French Expédition Scientifique de Morée (1829–1831)

Probably as a consequence of the success of the scientific expedition to Egypt with Napoleon I, and the publication and acclaim of the resulting *Description de l'Egypte,* the French government founded and dispatched the Expédition Scientifique de Morée (the scientific expedition to Morea) in 1828 "to render homage to the glorious country that the armed might of France has set free" (Grummond 1996, 421). The naturalist Bory de Saint Vincent was appointed expedition leader, and was responsible for maintaining its scientific content and supervising topographers, entomologists, zoologists, geologists, and botanists. The antiquarian and architect Guillaume Abel Blouet (1795–1853) was appointed to record and explore the ancient monuments, along with a team of artists, draftsmen, and epigraphers.

Blouet had studied architecture in Paris between 1814 and 1820. In 1821 he won the Prix de Rome and traveled to live and study in Rome for the next five years, during which time he excavated and restored the Baths of Caracalla. In 1826 he was appointed to the Morea expedition by the Institut de France. Blouet presided over a six-week campaign to clear the Temple of Zeus at Olympia, during which three large fragments of the temple's metopes were unearthed and eventually taken back to the Louvre Museum in Paris. Blouet was convinced they were from a frieze about the labors of Herakles.

The resulting three volumes were published in Paris between 1831 and 1838 as the *Expédition Scientifique de Morée, ordonée par le gouvernment français:*

Architecture, sculptures, inscriptions et vues du Péloponnèse des Cyclades et de l'Attique. It is still used as a reference.

Blouet worked on the Arc de Triomphe de l'Etoile (in 1836) and the restoration of the chateau of Fontainbleau (from 1848 onward). He was professor of the theory of architecture at the Academie des Beaux-Arts, a member of the Institut de France, and president of the Societe Centrale des Architects.

See also Foundation of the Louvre (1779–1793); Napoleon I funds the Excavation of Roman Sites and Antiquities (1808–1814); Foundation of Great Egyptian Collections in England and France (1815–1835); Publication of *Description de l'Egypte* (1826).

Further Reading

Blouet, G. A. 1831–1838. *Expédition Scientifique de Morée, ordonée par le gouvernment français: Architecture, sculptures, inscriptions et vues du Péloponnèse des Cyclades et de l'Attique.* 3 vols. Paris.

Grummond, N. de, ed. 1996. *An encyclopedia of the history of classical archaeology.* Westport, CT: Green Press.

Discovery of the Neanderthals (1833–1900)

In 1830 Dutch paleontologist Phillip-Charles Schmerling (1790–1836) began to explore the caves around the Belgian city of Liege, after local quarrymen gave him fossils as a gift. Schmerling eventually searched some forty caves and published his finds in *Recherchés Sur les Ossements Fossiles Découverts dans les cavernes de la Province de Liège* (1833–1834). In this book he outlined his finds, which included sixty extinct fossil animal species, and from the caves at Engis and Engihoul, Chokier and Fond de Foret, from under a layer of breccia (a rock comprising small rock fragments cemented together) uncovered some human fossil remains in association with the bones of extinct fossil animals, and with stone and bone tools, and part of the skull of a human infant.

Schmerling was convinced that he had found evidence to prove high human antiquity. There was much interest in his book and in his discoveries by scholars in the rest of Europe, and English geologist Sir Charles Lyell visited him to inspect the evidence. Unfortunately, Lyell and others remained unconvinced of its validity, certain that caves were such geologically complex places that Schmerling's evidence was probably compromised. Lyell remained unconvinced until after Brixham Cave had been excavated in 1858, and its evidence compared with Boucher de Perthes' evidence from open sites found between 1841 and 1864. Too late for Schmerling, who became professor of geology in Liege in 1835, and died the following year.

In 1856 quarrymen unearthed human skeletal remains, buried 60 centimeters under the surface of a large cave located in the cliffs on the southern bank of the Dussel River in the Neander Valley in northern Germany. The remains were eventually examined by the anthropologist Hermann Schaffhausen (1816–1877) from Bonn University and deposited in the museum there. Between 1858 and 1859 the news and details of this skeleton were published. Schaffhausen found the skeleton to be different from those of contemporary humans. He believed the remains were part of the skeleton of a more primitive race, apelike in its morphology, contemporary with extinct fossil animals, and therefore very old. He did not recognize it as a human fossil or as an extinct human species because of its large brain size. In fact, at this stage, the Neander skeleton was regarded as an example of a lower and completely different race of humans and, for some time, was not even considered to be a missing link between apes and humans.

In 1864 British anatomist William King (1809–1886) proposed that the Neander skeleton be recognized as evidence of an extinct human species and gave it the designated name of *Homo neanderthalensis*. Few scientists supported him. Schmerling's child's skull from the cave of Engis became a more credible piece of evidence of high human antiquity after the discovery of the other Neanderthal remains, but it was not thought to be Neanderthal, just as his fossil and flint finds became more credible after evidence from Brixham Cave and Abbeville were accepted as valid. German archaeologist Rudolf Virchow believed that the morphology of the remains of the Neanderthal skeleton was attributable to diseases such as rickets and arthritis and that it was really a distorted modern human.

More Neanderthal-type skeletons kept turning up over the next fifty years, in 1848 in Gibraltar, in 1866 in Belgium, and in 1880 in Moravia; the latter two were clearly associated with stone tools and extinct fauna. In 1886 two almost complete Neanderthal skeletons were excavated, along with fossil faunal remains and stone tools, from the Spy Cave in Belgium. The same year Belgian anatomist J. Faiport (1857–1910) and Belgian archaeologist M. Lohest (1857–1926) published a report that confirmed all the other finds—the Spy Neanderthal skeletons were indeed an extinct human species.

In 1891 Dutch archaeologist Eugene Dubois excavated the remains of a *Homo erectus* (originally *Pithecanthropus erectus*) on the Indonesian island of Java. Dubois believed he had found the "missing link" between apes and humans. The remains of "Java man" were the first hominid remains to be accepted as material proof of a chain of connection between humans and their primitive ancestors. The debate about their significance led to the development of an evolutionary interpretation of extant European Neanderthal remains, led by German anatomists Hermann Klaatsch (1863–1916) and Gustav Schwalbe (1844–1916).

See also High Human Antiquity in the Somme Valley (1841–1864); Excavation at Brixham Cave (1858–1859); First *Homo Erectus* (1888–1895).

Further Reading

Smith, F. 1997. Neanderthals. In ed. F. Spencer, *History of physical anthropology.* 711–722. New York and London: Garland Publishing.

Stringer, C., and C. Gamble. 1993. *In search of the Neanderthals: Solving the puzzle of human origins.* London: Thames and Hudson.

Trinkaus, E., and P. Shipman. 1994. *The Neanderthals: changing the image of mankind.* London: Pimlico.

Decipherment of Cuneiform (1836–1857)

Henry Creswicke Rawlinson (1810–1895) joined the East India Company as an officer cadet in 1827, where his excellent language abilities (he spoke five) and leadership skills were recognized by the army. In 1833 he and other officers were sent to reorganize the shah of Persia's army. In 1836 he was posted to Kurdistan as an adviser to its governor, the shah's brother.

On an exploratory trip to Susiana (now southwestern Iran) Rawlinson became interested in cuneiform when he traveled past the huge trilingual inscription of King Darius I (548–486 BC) on the Great Rock of Bisitun. The language scripts on the rock were in Old Persian, Elamite, and Babylonian and were visible in detail through a telescope. Rawlinson's determination to translate them necessitated taking casts, made by working at the rock face 500 feet above the ground on ropes and pulleys. The risk proved to be worth the danger, and Darius's inscription became the "Rosetta stone" of Assyriology, although their decipherment proved to be as arduous as it had been to get a copy of them. By 1837 Rawlinson had deciphered the first two paragraphs of the Old Persian inscription, using his knowledge of modern Persian, an Indo-European language, and had identified proper names and titles. These two paragraphs were the basis of two papers sent to the Royal Asiatic Society in 1837 and 1839.

Rawlinson's military career began to interfere with his language studies. In 1838 he explored Persian Kurdistan for the Royal Geographic Society, for which he was awarded the Society's gold medal. In 1839 he was again posted to Iran to reinforce the Persian army by raising regiments from frontier tribes. In 1840, as part of an attempt to prevent the spread of Russian influence toward India, Rawlinson fought in the First Afghan War and became the East India Company's political agent in Kandahar in western Afghanistan. Throughout all of these years of travel and action he collected and copied inscriptions in the field and worked at deciphering cuneiform.

In 1842 Rawlinson returned to India, and the following year was appointed British consul to Baghdad and political agent for the East India Company in Turkish Arabia. His new diplomatic career would better suit his interests in epigraphy and field research. He was the successor of the remarkable Claudius Rich (1787–1821), who was appointed resident in Baghdad for the East India

Sir Henry Creswicke Rawlinson. (Hulton Archive/Getty Images)

Company when he was only 21 and died there of cholera at the age of 34. During his term Rich made one of the first collections of Mesopotamian artifacts in Europe, which his wife bequeathed to the British Museum. Rich's *Memoir on the Ruins of Babylon,* published in 1815, inspired both Layard and Rawlinson, and aroused great interest in Mesopotamia throughout Europe.

Rawlinson arrived in Baghdad in 1843 and later encountered Austen Henry Layard on a visit to French archaeologist Paul Botta's excavation at Khorsabad. It was an auspicious meeting, the beginning of a lifelong friendship and a lifelong working relationship in Mesopotamian archaeology. By 1846, almost a decade after he had copied it, Rawlinson had finally found enough time to complete the decipherment of Darius's inscriptions, which were published by the *Journal of the Royal Asiatic Society* as "The Persian Cuneiform Inscription at Behistun." It was as great an epigraphic achievement as Champollion's decipherment of Egyptian hieroglyphics, and it earned Rawlinson the joint titles of first successful "decipherer, and father, of cuneiform."

However, in the long term, cuneiform's decipherment was recognized as a joint effort. The Irish scholar Edward Hincks recognized that cuneiform was invented for a non-Semitic language. The French scholar Jules Oppert identified the Sumerian civilization of southern Mesopotamia. Edwin Norris, secretary, and later librarian, of the Royal Asiatic Society, eventually published the first Assyrian dictionary. And Rawlinson proved that Babylonian was a polyphonic language. All of these scholars contributed to the eventual decipherment.

The three scripts, Old Persian, Elamite, and Babylonian had all been in spoken and written use during Darius's reign, and were inscribed on the rock because of their widespread recognition throughout his kingdom. The latter two languages had been in use for almost 2,000 years before that. It took another decade before Babylonian was officially declared deciphered. In 1857 the Royal Asiatic Society sent the same cuneiform texts to Rawlinson, Hincks, and Oppert to translate and then compared their three translations to that by another independent scholar. All four had enough in common to declare, officially and finally, that Babylonian was readable.

The decipherment of Babylonian and Elamite cuneiform meant that the potentially long history of southern Mesopotamia, some 2,000 years of written history "before Christ" and even before the written history of the Bible, was accessible to scholars. Babylonian is today called Akkadian, a term that covers a number of Semitic languages used in Mesopotamia, and used by Akkadians, as ethnically and linguistically distinct from the earlier inhabitants, the Sumerians, and whose two principal dialects were Babylonian and Assyrian. This linguistic milestone was almost immediately put to use.

In 1850 Rawlinson published *Inscriptions of Assyria and Babylonia.* In 1851 the British Museum requested his help with revising the second half of the early cuneiform texts Layard brought from Nimrud, which resulted in the publication of the *Outline of the History of Assyria as Collected from the Inscriptions by Layard.* In between these publications Rawlinson went back to Baghdad for his second term of office, where he was able to help Layard with the next phase of his excavations.

In 1849 the British Museum commissioned Rawlinson to excavate in Babylonia, and in 1853 he finally found the time to do so. He unearthed the remains of a ziggurat at Borsippa, near Babylon in southern Mesopotamia, and some inscribed cylinders that commemorated the sixth century BC King Nebuchadrezzar of Babylon. It was to be his only experience of field archaeology and his last year in Baghdad—he resigned from the East India Company to work full time on the Asshurbanipal archives in the British Museum. He oversaw the publication of six volumes of inscriptions from Layard's excavations between 1861 and 1880.

In 1856 Rawlinson became a member of Parliament, and in 1876 a trustee of the British Museum. He continued to be involved in the Royal Asiatic Society and was its president from 1878 to 1888. He was also president of the Royal Geographic Society from 1871 to 1872 and from 1874 to 1875. He helped to organize the state visits of the shah of Persia to England in 1873 and 1889. Rawlinson was a royal commissioner for the Paris Exposition of 1878 and for the India and Colonial Exhibition of 1886.

See also Foundation of the Asiatic Society of Bengal (1784); Decipherment of Egyptian Hieroglyphics (1824); Publication of *Nineveh and Its Remains* (1849); Discovering the Riches of Central Asia—The Journeys of Sir Aurel Stein (1906–1930); Excavation of Ur (1922–1934).

Further Reading

Adkins, L. 2003. *Empires of the plain. Henry Rawlinson and the lost languages of Babylon.* London: HarperCollins.

Booth, A. J. 1902. *The discovery and decipherment of the trilingual cuneiform inscriptions.* London: Longmans, Green.

Dalley, S., ed. 1998. *The legacy of Mesopotamia.* Oxford: Oxford University Press.

Lawson, P. 1993. *The East India Company: a history.* London: Longman.

Lloyd, S. 1980. *Foundations in the dust: The story of Mesopotamia.* London: Thames and Hudson.

Rediscovering Maya Civilization (1839–1843)

Both American lawyer John Lloyd Stephens and English architect and draftsman Frederick Catherwood had traveled extensively through the Near East and Egypt, visiting all the ancient monuments and tourist sites before they embarked on their journey in search of the mythical ruined civilizations of Central America in 1839. Both had collaborated on popular and illustrated accounts of these travels. Consequently, both of them were well equipped to locate, assess, record, and excavate ruins and to profit from their experiences.

On their first trip to Mesoamerica they cut the remains of the Mayan city of Copan out of the rain forest, where they made detailed drawings of the site and copied the glyphs on its stelae, which they recognized as being a script of some kind. They traveled on to the great Mayan sites of Palenque and Uxmal, in difficult and dangerous circumstances, and it was only their poor health that caused them to go back to New York City. The resulting book—*Incidents of Travel in Central America, Chiapas and Yucatan*—in two volumes, written by Stephens and illustrated by Catherwood, was published in 1841. Stephens's excitement about the finds, and his knowledge of their significance, and Catherwood's technical expertise in drawing, ensured that the book was a huge success and a best seller. Stephens also recognized that he had seen the remains of what was a completely new and wholly indigenous civilization on the doorstep of the United States of America and within its sphere of influence.

In 1841, having made enough money from the sales of their books, Stephens and Catherwood returned to Mesoamerica to study and document Uxmal and then on to the sites of Chichen Itza, Cozumel, and Tulum. In 1843 they published *Incidents of Travel in Yucatan,* which proved to be as popular as their first books.

Both of them retired from archaeology, their health compromised after these arduous trips, although they both pursued business interests in Mesoamerica until their early deaths, Stephens in 1852 from the complications of long-term tropical illness, and Catherwood in 1854, one of three hundred passengers to go down with the SS *Arctic* in the middle of the Atlantic Ocean. Their books had an enormous impact on the development of history and archaeology in the United States. The Harvard historian of Mesoamerica, William Prescott, used them to help write his *History of the Conquest of Mexico* (1843), in which he recognized the long chronology of Central American civilization and its influence on other people in the North and South Americas and the Caribbean. During the 1840s and 1850s the United States was

Tourists view a section of the Mayan ruins of Uxmal. (Danny Lehman/Corbis)

busy with the politics of the region (the Mexican War) and within its own borders—and then during the 1860s with its own civil war. It would take another twenty years for American archaeologists to begin to explore Mesoamerica in greater detail and for American institutions such as Harvard University and the Peabody and Metropolitan museums to support and fund them and establish their collections.

See also Investigation of Palenque Begins (1787); Excavation of a Burial Mound in Virginia (1787); Publication of *Ancient Monuments of the Mississippi Valley* (1847); Establishment of Major U.S. Archaeological Institutions (1846–1866).

Further Reading

Bernal, I. 1980. *History of Mexican archaeology.* London: Thames and Hudson.

Schele, L., and P. Mathews. 1998. *The code of kings.* New York: Scribner.

Stephens, J. L. 1841. *Incidents of travel in Central America, Chiapas and Yucatan.* 2 vols. New York: Harper and Brothers.

Stephens, J. L. 1843. *Incidents of travel in Yucatan.* 2 vols. New York: Harper and Brothers.

High Human Antiquity in the Somme Valley (1841–1864)

Jacques Boucher de Perthes (1788–1868) was a local customs official who became involved in archaeology because of his membership in a local group of prominent citizens interested in current issues in politics and science, and his friendship with one of its members, a young doctor, Casimir Picard. An amateur archaeologist, Picard had discovered a number of archaeological sites in the Somme Valley that convinced him, and eventually Boucher de Perthes, of the high antiquity of humankind. After Picard's early death, Boucher de Perthes kept on working at various sites.

In 1837, below the walls of the town of Abbeville, in the same level and at a depth of more than seven meters, he found quantities of animal remains, pottery, and stone tools. While these finds were acquisitioned by the Natural History Museum, Boucher de Perthes published accounts of his and Picard's work in five volumes, entitled *De la création* (1838–1841) but was ridiculed by the Parisian scientific establishment.

In 1841, Boucher de Perthes found a site at the Menchecourt quarry located on the outskirts of Abbeville. Remains of Pleistocene mammals (elephants and hippopotamuses) had already been found here and studied by the great geologist Georges Cuvier. Boucher de Perthes unearthed what he called "antediluvian" (as in pre-flood) stone tools and polished axes, which he insisted on extracting in situ. He also retrieved an example of what would later become known as a Paleolithic bifaced ax. This discovery of artifacts and the bones of extinct animals in the same stratigraphic contexts were to play a vital role in establishing high human antiquity.

Over the next three years Boucher de Perthes explored other sites, and in 1844 he found a series of Paleolithic artifacts in a gravel quarry, in clearer association with animal bones than those he had found at Menchecourt. He brought them to the attention of the experts in Paris, who were, once again, highly skeptical.

In 1846, in an effort to have his work recognized, Boucher wrote a detailed summary (printed and bound) of his finds over the past ten years entitled *Antiquités celtiques et antédiluviennes,* had it printed and bound, and sent it to the Académie des Sciences in Paris—requesting their approval of his evidence before publishing it. The committee appointed to review the manuscript remained unconvinced of his evidence that human beings had lived at the same time as extinct mammals in antediluvian times and that human beings had been on the earth for much longer than the 4,000 years specified by the Bible. They refused to endorse it.

In 1849, Boucher de Perthes published his *Antiquités* anyway—he may not have had the support of the scientific establishment, but he did have some support. His general conclusions were backed by the president of the local society of antiquaries of Picardy and by Paris paleontologists Edouard Lartet and Geoffrey Saint Hilaire. At the core of his approach was the recognition of the importance of stratigraphy as a source of information about the age of finds and their associations. For Boucher de Perthes, the age of the artifact was based on its geology—on the position, contents, and context of the finds as well as the nature of the strata in which they were found. He also argued that all of the data—botanical, geological, stratigraphic—should be studied as a whole as the basis for the development of a new science of archaeology.

It would be another decade before Boucher de Perthes' contributions were recognized by the Académie, and this was largely because they were first recognized in England by the English scientific establishment. As he studied the *Antiquités celtiques et antédiluviennes,* Scottish researcher Hugh Falconer recognized the similarities between the Frenchman's illustrated artifacts and artifacts recently excavated in Brixham Cave in Devon. In 1858 he visited Boucher de Perthes in Abbeville where he examined the finds, which further convinced him of the veracity of human artifacts coexisting with extinct mammalian fauna. Falconer encouraged geologist Joseph Prestwich and archaeologist John Evans (an expert on stone tools) to visit Abbeville, where they too were convinced of the authenticity of the finds and were able to observe an Acheulean hand ax in situ at the Saint Acheul quarry in Amiens. Evans excavated an ax from the same gravel layer as the bones of an elephant. Then the entire committee of the Geological Society of London, including Sir Charles Lyell, all traveled to Abbeville to see the proof.

In 1859 geologist Joseph Prestwich supported the French discoveries with similar observations made at sites in Suffolk in a paper delivered to the Royal Society. He argued that "flint implements were the product of the conception and work of man" and that they were associated with numerous extinct animals. The consequence of this was that these finds proved, once and for all, that humans had lived on earth for much longer than the 4,000 years of Ussher's Biblical chronology. It was this paper, delivered in England, and the international recognition of Boucher de Perthes' work, that finally galvanized the French Académie des Sciences, who sent Albert Gaudry to Boucher de Perthes' excavations at Saint Acheul. Gaudry, who all along had believed Boucher was right, examined the evidence and reported back to the Académie. In the early 1860s Boucher de Perthes was finally given the recognition he had long deserved, and in 1864 he received the Legion d' Honneur, ironically not for his discoveries at Abbeville, but for his participation in the contentious "Moulin Quignon Affair."

See also Publication of *Annals of the World Deduced from the Origin of Time* (1658); Publication *De l'origine et des usages de la pierre de foudre* (1723); John Frere Writes to the Society of Antiquaries of London (1797); Discovery of the Neanderthals (1833–1900); Excavation at Brixham Cave (1858–1859).

Further Reading

Cohen, C., and J-J. Hublin. 1989. *Boucher de Perthes: 1788–1868: les origines romantiques de la préhistoire.* Paris: Belin.

Boucher de Perthes, J. 1847. *Antiquitées celtiques et antédiluviennes.* Treuttel et Wurtz, Libraires.

Van Riper, A. B. 1995. *Men among the mammoths: Victorian science and the discovery of human prehistory.* Chicago: University of Chicago Press.

Paul Botta Excavates "Nineveh" (1843–1845)

Paul Emile Botta (1802–1870) was the son of the distinguished Italian historian Carlo Botta, who began his career in the Middle East as physician to Egypt's Pasha Muhammad Ali. In 1833, Botta was appointed French consul in Alexandria, and then in 1840, he was transferred to Mosul, in what is now northern Iraq, with instructions to find and excavate the Biblical city of Nineveh.

Botta began excavating for the remains of Nineveh at the large mound of Kuyunjik (or Quyunjik), but in 1843 he abandoned this site for another more promising one, some 30 kilometers north, known as Khorsabad. This site had been recommended to him by locals as having "sculptured stones," and Botta began to find them almost as soon as he started his first trench. Eventually, he unearthed a large palace complex, comprising more than 100 rooms and connecting hallways, all of them lined with detailed sculpted bas-reliefs of gods, kings, warfare, and religious ceremonies. These were interspersed with walls covered in cuneiform script. The doorways were flanked by monolithic, carved, human-headed winged bulls. Botta wrote to Paris about his finds, believing them to be the remains of Nineveh. He requested financial assistance to employ workmen and pay for transportation and technical support in the form of an artist-draftsman to record the material in situ. Officials in Paris were delighted by his news, and they dispatched both money and the artist, Eugene Flandin, who arrived in Mosul more than a year after Botta's original request was made.

Botta and 300 workmen spent two years excavating the site. Flandin spent two years painstakingly recording every sculptured slab they uncovered and making detailed drawings of other aspects and artifacts at the site. Some of the slabs were shattered when they were removed, some broke later as a result of attempts to secure them for transportation to Paris, and some went to the bottom of the river as they were sent down to the port to be carried back to Paris by the French warship sent to help. Locals pilfered the site, and local Turkish officials hampered the excavations and even closed them down on a number of occasions.

The material that arrived in Paris in 1846—magnificent bas-reliefs, four-meter-high winged bulls with human heads, and many cuneiform tablets—caused huge interest and acclaim. Here, for the first time, were details of the everyday life of the ancient Assyrians, enemies of the Jews in the Bible—what they looked like and how they worshipped their gods, fought their enemies, treated their hostages, celebrated their achievements, and recorded their history. This recognition and excitement must have made all the difficulties Botta experienced worthwhile.

Botta had befriended the Englishman Austen Henry Layard (1817–1894) while the Englishman was traveling though Mosul to Istanbul in 1842. They had a lot in common. Both were well-educated and erudite young men, and both were interested in mounds and their possibilities, although Layard strongly disapproved of Botta's opium addiction. At this stage Botta was sinking test pits into the Kuyunjik mound. Layard heard about Botta's finds at Khorsabad, where he was working for Sir Stratford Canning, the English consul in Istanbul. Throughout this time Botta had kept Layard informed about his finds and magnanimously recommended that Layard try his hand at excavating at what they both thought could be the site of another Assyrian city—Nimrud.

In 1845, Layard, financed and supported by Canning, began to excavate at Nimrud. He discovered several Assyrian palaces, one of which had similar bas-reliefs to those discovered by Botta at Khorsabad. Unlike Botta, Layard lacked both finance and technical support at the site, but this was his chance to prove he had been right about the mounds and what they contained, and his chance to get future support and finance from the British Museum for more work if he could come up with some interesting finds. But at this stage archaeology was far from being a painstaking science. Tunneling and trenching around the largest and most spectacular finds of statuary and architectural remains destroyed many other artifacts and much archaeological information.

Removing them intact was risky, as was transporting them. And Layard had no Flandin to provide at least some record of artifacts before some were lost.

Botta and Layard met again in Paris in 1847, while Layard was on his way back to Britain, where the material from Nimrud was to be displayed at the British Museum. Botta and Flandin were beginning to work on the four-volume publication about their site, the *Monument du Nineveh* (1846–1850).

Returning to Mesopotamia in 1849, Layard began to excavate the huge mound of Kuyunjik. He soon realized why Botta had found little of interest: the Assyrian material was located under twenty feet of accumulated habitation debris. And so it was Layard found the ancient city of Nineveh at Kuyunjik, a spectacular site from which he unearthed (and destroyed) the most fabulous evidence of Assyrian culture.

During the 1850s the sites and their identities were eventually sorted out. What Botta had excavated at Khorsabad was the remains of the new palace of the Assyrian king Sargon II (ca. eighth century BC), which he had built as part of his new personally designed capital city. After the death of his father, Sargon II, on the battlefield, the new Assyrian king Sennacherib (704–681 BC) moved the administrative capital of his empire from his father's new city of Khorsabad to Nineveh (Kuyunjik), one of the oldest and richest cities of ancient Assyria. There he built a new palace—the largest in Assyria—and kept a large royal library and archive comprising thousands of clay tablets, all of which Layard had found. Layard's Nimrud was the second capital of ancient Assyria, succeeding the city of Ashur and predating Nineveh and Khorsabad.

There is little doubt that Botta's achievements at Khorsabad were well and truly eclipsed by Layard's at Nineveh. However, Botta and Flandin did a better job of excavating and recording the material and the site of Khorsabad than Layard did, at either Nimrud or Nineveh. Furthermore, the support of the French government for the excavation and publication of the remains was exemplary, especially compared with the lack of support Layard received from the British Museum or the British government.

Both Layard and Botta gave up archaeology. In 1848, with the establishment of the French Second Republic and the beginning of the eclipse of his work by Layard, Botta fell out of favor in Paris. He was sent as consul to the small and insignificant city of Tripoli, in what is now Lebanon, where he eventually died. By 1855 Layard had left archaeology and had taken up politics and diplomacy, becoming a member of Parliament and ambassador to Madrid and Constantinople, where among other things, he helped Heinrich Schliemann get permission to excavate Troy.

See also Decipherment of Egyptian Hieroglyphics (1824); Publication of *Description de l'Egypte* (1826); Decipherment of Cuneiform (1836–1857); Publication of *Nineveh and Its Remains* (1849); Schliemann Excavates Troy, Mycenae, Ilios, Orchomenos, and Tiryns (1870–1891).

Further Reading

Lloyd, Seton. 1980. *Foundations in the dust: the story of Mesopotamian exploration.* London: Thames and Hudson.

Murray, T. 2001. Sir Austen Henry Layard (1817–1894). In *Encyclopedia of archaeology: History and discoveries,* ed. T. Murray, 807–808. Santa Barbara, CA: ABC-CLIO.

Murray, T. 2001. Nimrud and Nineveh. In *Encyclopedia of archaeology: History and discoveries,* ed. T. Murray, 951–952. Santa Barbara, CA: ABC-CLIO.

Establishment of Major U.S. Archaeological Institutions (1846–1866)

During the nineteenth century, scientific and public interest in archaeology in the United States proceeded more slowly than in Europe. The indigenous people of the Americas were not the direct ancestors of the new immigrant settlers, nor were they participants in the new state, so there was no emotional interest, or financial investment, in their history. Indeed, it was expedient to regard them as both primitive and unchanging as a justification for displacing them and taking their land. However, as settlement expanded and the great ruins of the American Southwest were discovered, and American adventurers Stephens and Catherwood revisited the remains of the lost civilizations of the Aztecs and the Maya in Mexico and Guatemala, attitudes toward archaeology in the Americas began to change. At the same time the institutions that could begin to support and develop the new discipline of archaeology were established.

The Smithsonian Institution

Founded in 1846 as the result of a bequest by a wealthy Englishman James Smithson, the Smithsonian, from its very beginning, was interested in archaeology and ethnology. Its first publication in 1848 was *Ancient Monuments of the Mississippi Valley* by Davis and Squier. Based in Washington, D.C., the Smithsonian soon became an important adviser to the government of the United States as a source of scientific knowledge. In 1861 the Smithsonian Institution published an ethnological guidebook/questionnaire "Instructions for Research Relative to the Ethnology and Philology of America,"

The Smithsonian Institution, Washington D.C. (PhotoDisc, Inc.)

which was used by many missionaries, explorers, surveyors, and government agents as well as by Smithsonian staff as a basic means of record keeping for when they came into contact with indigenous Americans.

During the 1860s, as a result of U.S. government direction, the Smithsonian became the repository for the immense geographic and ethnographic collections and information gathered by all U.S. government departments. The Smithsonian initially funded John Wesley Powell's exploration of the Colorado River in 1868, and the pioneers of the archaeology of the American Southwest, such as the ethnologists Frank Cushing and William H. Holmes, became associated with the Smithsonian via Powell.

In 1879 the Smithsonian's Bureau of Ethnology, with John Wesley Powell (1834–1902) as its founder and leader, was created to preserve and publish all of the primary documents pertinent to Native Americans that had been deposited at the Smithsonian and to study the ethnography and linguistics of those peoples, in order to foster their better administration. The American National Museum was also founded to assist the bureau to attain these goals.

In that same year, Frank Cushing (1857–1900) joined the bureau. Both Powell and Cushing believed there was little difference between contemporary Native Americans and their prehistoric ancestors. Both believed that archaeologists could understand the past by working with ethnologists and modern "survivors," and that archaeology was a branch of anthropology. This attitude was described as "the direct historical approach."

In 1881 Powell recruited Cyrus Thomas to participate in an "Ethnology and Mound Survey." The results of this survey, published by Thomas in 1894, would finally demolish the popular and century-old mound builder theory and lead to the acceptance that the mounds had been built by the ancestors of Native Americans and not by a lost Hindu tribe. In 1891 Powell supported the preparation of the "Linguistic Map of North American Peoples" and the collection of vocabularies. In 1894 he changed the name of the bureau to the Bureau of American Ethnology to emphasize the geographic limit of its interests. Powell retired from the bureau in 1902 after twenty years as director, and archaeologist William Henry Holmes (1846–1933) succeeded him.

Holmes had joined the Smithsonian as an illustrator as early as 1871 and had participated in fieldwork in the Southwest in the mid 1870s. He had been involved with analyzing material for Thomas's survey and had pioneered material culture studies through his meticulous analysis of collections at the Smithsonian during the 1880s. From 1882 through 1894, Holmes was head curator of anthropology at the Smithsonian Museum, and then he moved to Chicago to become curator of anthropology at the Field Museum and professor of archaeology at the University of Chicago.

In 1903 Holmes appointed Ales Hrdlicka to the Smithsonian's new division of physical anthropology in the National Museum of Natural History. Over the next 40 years Hrdlicka built this department into one of the best in the world based on its extensive human osteological collection. Hrdlicka founded the *American Journal of Physical Anthropology* in 1918, and the American Association of Physical Anthropologists in 1930. The creation of the osteological collection has been the subject of much criticism in recent years as Native Americans have sought the repatriation of human remains collected by Hrdlicka and others, frequently without the consent of community members.

Holmes's work was based on his background in geology and his commitment to empirical observation, evolutionism, and archaeological uniformitarianism. He organized the archaeological record along geographical lines and into cultural areas, firmly rejected the possibility of an American Paleolithic, and still championed the direct historic approach. Toward the end of his career these tenets became impossible to sustain. Holmes's beliefs were supported by Hrdlicka, whose studies of the origins and antiquity of Native Americans through their skeletal material concluded that there was no early human settlement of the Americas.

The Folsom discovery in 1927 eventually showed that human antiquity on the North American continent reached back to the late Pleistocene period and that there had been enormous changes among Native Americans between then and the coming of the Europeans. American archaeologists would begin to fill in the details of those changes, and it would be the universities and their students and graduates who would lead the way.

The Peabody Museum

The Peabody Museum of American Archaeology and Ethnology was founded in 1866 in Boston by a large endowment from a wealthy local businessman who specifically wanted it used to research "the early races of the American continent," and to focus on doing so in the southwest and southeast United States and lower Central America. However, until 1887 the museum was only loosely connected to Harvard University, and its impact remained minimal. In 1874 Frederic Ward Putnam was appointed its curator and because of his force of character and interest in archaeology, he managed to convince Harvard to take both the museum and the discipline of archaeology on, becoming the first Peabody Professor of American Archaeology and Ethnology in 1887. With this formal relationship Putnam could now teach archaeology and supervise graduate students, and he led the first academic department to grant a Ph.D. in archaeology in North America, with the support of the Peabody's resources. Harvard and the Peabody Museum became the institutional base for the development of archaeology, and their graduates were employed by other new universities and museums. Encouraged by Putnam, financial support for the museum grew, including an especially large endowment by wealthy businessman Charles Bowditch, who was particularly interested in sponsoring research in Central America.

The organizational abilities of Frederic Ward Putnam (1839–1915), his influence on and support of students, and his popularization of archaeology established him as a major institution builder in the United States. Putnam initially worked on disproving the mound builder theory and establishing a prehistory of the country by finding evidence for the peopling of the Americas. He was also intent on setting standards for the new generation of archaeologists through his approaches to field excavation and documentation of sites.

Bowditch's support of the Peabody enabled the development of a research program in Central America and the integration of student training and research in this area. Between 1892 and 1915, the Peabody Museum funded and organized 12 archaeological expeditions to Guatemala. However, Bowditch specifically wanted his endowment to be used to research the writing and calendar systems of the ancient Maya, and so sites with inscribed monuments became the Peabody's priorities. After 1905 Bowditch's hopes for the archaeology of the Maya were realized by Putnam's graduate students Alfred M. Tozzer, Sylvanus Morley, and Herbert Spinden.

Other endowments to the Peabody included one for researching the living cultures and archaeological sites of the southwest United States. The resulting collections of pottery established the museum's interest and expertise in that area—and Alfred V. Kidder supervised the first Peabody field research on the Pueblos from 1908 to 1914.

In 1892 Putnam was placed in charge of the anthropology exhibition at the World's Fair in Chicago. Here, for the first time in the United States, the general public confronted anthropological subjects and saw evidence of Mayan architecture. Putnam's exhibition was so successful that between 1894 and 1895 he stayed on in Chicago to help found the Field Museum of Natural History. In 1894, while keeping his position as Peabody professor, Putnam joined the American Museum of Natural History in New York City to found their anthropology department. His field assistants there included Ales Hrdlicka, Alfred Kroeber, and Adolph Bandelier, and his codirector was the great anthropologist Franz Boas. Putnam and Boas jointly dispatched the Jessup Expedition to the North Pacific Coast in 1897. In 1904 Putnam left New York, and (still keeping his Peabody professorship) founded the Department of Anthropology at the University of California in Berkeley. He employed Alfred Kroeber as head of the department and the museum complex and director of the Ethnological and Archaeological Survey of California.

Putnam retired in 1909 after twenty-five years as secretary of the American Association for the Advancement of Science and twenty-five years of establishing museums and university departments for archaeology and anthropology all over the country. In 1917, on its 50th anniversary, the Peabody Museum and the Harvard Department of American Archaeology and Ethnology dominated archaeology in the United States; they had trained almost every specialist and had racked up extensive fieldwork experience.

From 1914 to 1929 the Peabody Museum maintained its research interest in the American Southwest. During the 1930s and 1940s Phillip Philips continued the museum's Southwestern research, establishing the Lower Mississippi Survey in 1933, the first of a number of systematic regional approaches to site location and the construction of culture histories. Walter Taylor's Ph.D. fieldwork in northern Mexico in 1938 and 1939 was sponsored by the Peabody. More students became involved in elucidating the human occupation of the Americas, inspired by the dating of the Folsom tradition in 1926 and by the Peabody's prehistoric field research in Europe, the Middle East, and India between 1929 and 1939.

In 1914 Sylvanus Morley left it to join the Carnegie Institution in Washington, D.C., where he established a Maya research program. From then on, the Peabody Museum explored south to non-Maya Honduras, Costa Rica, Mexico, and Guatemala—and then on into Panama and South America. In 1934 Dorothy Stone published field reports on her work in Honduras and became associated with the Peabody Museum—which began its interest in the prehistory of the Caribbean. During all of this time the Peabody's collections of artifacts, photographs, and archives of research expeditions massively expanded.

See also Rediscovering Maya civilization (1839–1843); Publication of *Ancient Monuments of the Mississippi Valley* (1847); Uhle Begins Scientific Archaeology in Peru (1895–1940); Machu Picchu Found (1911); Stratigraphic Excavation in the Americas (1911–1913); Publication of *Introduction to Southwestern Archaeology* (1924).

Further Reading

Brew, J. O. 1966. *People and projects of the Peabody Museum, 1866–1966.* Cambridge, MA: Peabody Museum.

Hinsley, C. 1994 *The Smithsonian and the American Indian: Making a moral anthropology in Victorian America.* Washington, DC: Smithsonian Institution Press.

Willey, G. R., and J. A. Sabloff. 1980. *A history of American archaeology.* 2nd ed. London: Thames and Hudson.

Publication of Ancient Monuments of the Mississippi Valley *(1847)*

As European settlers moved west to take up new land, contact with the indigenous owners and inhabitants increased. There was an ongoing frontier war between settlers and Native Americans, who were either exterminated or forced to leave their traditional lands. This dispossession and murder of Native Americans was justified by the new Americans as the consequence of their primitive state. At the same time that new land went under the plow so the evidence of the past of these original inhabitants began to be discovered and destroyed as well.

Caleb Atwater had studied and recorded earthworks in Ohio, publishing his work in 1820 in the first volume of the *Transactions of the American Antiquarian Society*. The earth mounds discovered west of the Appalachian Mountains contained artifacts made of pottery, shell, and native copper, and many new Americans believed they could not have been created by the ancestors of contemporary indigenous people, who were too primitive to have any worthwhile ancestors. Some antiquarians and members of the public believed the mounds to have been built by ancestors of the Mexicans or the Vikings, and then destroyed by the ancestors of contemporary indigenes. Atwater, despite similarities between some artifacts made by contemporary native peoples and those found in the mounds, postulated that the mounds were built by Hindus from India, who were on their way to found Mexican civilization.

Edwin Hamilton Davis (1811–1888) was a local Ohio doctor who shared Atwater's fascination for earth mounds and for elucidating their builders and their origins. He financed the surveying and stratigraphic excavation and recording of over a hundred of these mounds by local newspaperman turned archaeologist Ephraim G. Squier (1821–1888). Consolidating their research with the data of other researchers on prehistoric earthworks from the eastern part of North America, Davis and Squier wrote *Ancient Monuments of the Mississippi Valley*. This was the first publication of the newly founded Smithsonian Institution, in a series known as *Contributions to Knowledge,* edited by Joseph Henry, the renowned scientist and secretary to the Smithsonian, and supported by the American Ethnological Society. It was an auspicious beginning for archaeological research in North America, comprising contributions from passionate individuals, the careful recording of excavations, a consolidation of known data, the publication of finds, and the support of a government institution and a professional organization. In all, it was a blueprint for the possibilities of collaborative archaeological research, notwithstanding their adoption of Atwater's overall explanation for the mounds.

While they did not challenge Atwater's Hindu mound building theory, Davis and Squier did speculate on what function the mounds had—proposing a form of basic classification of mounds and hypotheses to investigate and verify it. They also realized, as Squier wrote, the significance of what they did, that "if these monuments were capable of reflecting any certain light upon the grand archaeological questions connected with the primitive history of the American continent, the origin, migration and early state of the American race . . . then they should be carefully and minutely and above all systematically investigated" (Squier and Davis 1848, 134). It is just such detail that ensures that their publication is still an important source of information for archaeologists today.

Davis moved to New York City to teach medicine, but he continued to guest lecture on his archaeological interests. In 1849, before he took up a diplomatic post in Nicaragua, Squier visited the mounds of western New York because he thought they might contribute to an understanding of the origins of the Ohio mounds and builders. Many scholars had begun to think Atwater's theory was nonsense, and that the ancestors of modern Indians had built the mounds. Among them were Samuel Haven, librarian of the American Antiquarian Society, and Henry Schoolcraft, who was the first excavator of the mounds to note the cultural continuities between the remains in the mounds and contemporary Native American artifacts. Daniel Wilson, the great Scottish antiquarian, newly arrived in Canada, also recorded his dissatisfaction with Atwater's mound builder theory in his second volume of *Prehistoric Man: Researches into the Origin of Civilization in the Old and New World* (1862).

In 1856 the Smithsonian Institution commissioned Samuel Haven to review the state of archaeological knowledge in the United States. The resulting publication, *The Archaeology of the United States, or Sketches Historical and Biographical, of the Progress of Information and Opinion Respecting Vestiges of Antiquity in the United States,* had as one of its conclusions the complete lack of evidence for the mound builder theory. However, Atwater's mound builder myth persisted in popular accounts of archaeology in North America until the end of the nineteenth century, primarily because it was closely bound up with the prevalence of negative views of the capacities of indigenous peoples. In an attempt to eliminate this myth from the popular imagination, Cyrus Thomas wrote his *Report on the Mound Explorations of the Bureau of Ethnology* in 1894, which finally put Atwater's theory to rest. And by this time the discoveries of substantial Native American ruins in the Southwest by archaeologists Frank Cushing and John Wesley Powell finally proved that the ancestors of contemporary Native Americans had indeed been possessed of a remarkable culture and civilization.

See also Excavation of a Burial Mound in Virginia (1787); Publication of *Descriptions of the Antiquities Discovered in the State of Ohio and Other Western States* (1820); Establishment of Major U.S. Archaeological Institutions (1846–1866); Stratigraphic Excavation in the Americas (1911–1913); Publication of *Introduction to Southwestern Archaeology* (1924).

Further Reading

Barnhart, T. A. 2005. *Ephraim George Squier and the development of American anthropology*. Lincoln: University of Nebraska Press.

Squier, E. G., and E. H. Davis. 1848. *Ancient monuments of the Mississippi Valley*, ed. D. J. Meltzer. Washington, DC: Smithsonian Institution Press, 1998.

Willey, G. R., and J. A. Sabloff. 1980. *A history of American archaeology*. 2nd ed. San Francisco: Freeman and Company.

Publication of The Manners and Customs of the Ancient Egyptians *(1847)*

John Gardner Wilkinson (1797–1875) was introduced to hieroglyphic study as a schoolboy at Harrow, where the principal was a friend of the Egyptian scholar Thomas Young. Wilkinson left Oxford University and traveled to Italy for the sake of his health. In Italy he met the antiquarian and classical archaeologist Sir William Gell, who encouraged his interests in hieroglyphics and Egyptian archaeology. In 1821, using his small personal income, Wilkinson traveled to Egypt, where he was to live for the next twelve years. During this time he visited every known and significant archaeological site in Egypt and Nubia, kept detailed records of those sites, and studied Arabic, Coptic, and hieroglyphics.

Wilkinson's first publication in 1828 on Egyptian hieroglyphics included the translation of the first reliable chronology of ancient Egyptian kings and dynasties. He spent four years in Thebes where he excavated and uncovered many tombs, which resulted in the publication of *Topographical Survey of Thebes* by the Royal Geographical Society in 1830. In 1833, on his return to England, Wilkinson was elected a Fellow of the Royal Society and published an account of his discoveries in *The Topography of Thebes and General Survey of Egypt*. His first popular book, it was described as the most significant work on ancient Egypt since the publication of the *Description de l'Egypte* by his chief competitors in the field, French Egyptologists.

However, Wilkinson's interests were significantly different from most of those who were working in Egypt at the same time—English, Prussian, Italian, or French. He was not solely interested in religious and funerary architecture or the history of art. He was more fascinated by the artifacts and details of everyday life. Wilkinson studied and drew plans of ancient cities and sites, among the most significant, and for the first time, El Amarna and Thebes. He also copied numerous tomb paintings and low relief sculptures, and studied, recorded, and translated inscriptions and papyri to increase his understanding of the social history of ancient Egypt.

Encouraged by the positive reception of his last book, in 1847 Wilkinson published three volumes on *The Manners and Customs of the Ancient Egyptians. Including their Private Life, Government Laws, Arts, Manufactures, Religion, Agriculture, and Early History, derived from a comparison of the early paintings, sculptures, and monuments still existing with the accounts of ancient authors.* Across 3,000 pages the volumes covered more than fifty different subjects—from everyday life to crafts, literature, astronomy, botany, and chronology—and contained illustrations and plans. Much of the information in the books was new and detailed knowledge, and all of Wilkinson's work and research was undertaken without any kind of government or institutional assistance—an extraordinary achievement for one man.

Wilkinson was elected a Fellow of the Geographical Society and was knighted in 1839, as much in recognition of his scholarship in his books as for his achievement in popularizing the discipline of Egyptology in general. He later wrote two more volumes on religion and mythology to add to the original three. Wilkinson returned to Egypt in 1842 and then again from 1848 to 1849. In 1843 he published a book on *Moslem Egypt and Thebes,* which was later incorporated into *Modern Egypt.* The latter was an encyclopedic guidebook for tourists in Egypt; it covered routes, hotels, how to hire donkeys and boats, the history of every site worth visiting, and hints on the wages, tipping, and management of servants.

Between 1849 and 1850 Wilkinson studied the Turin Royal Canon, publishing a complete facsimile of this important list of dynasties. He visited Egypt for the last time in 1855. He married and settled in England in 1856, but continued studying and publishing on Egyptology until his death. His contributions to Egyptology were recognized in his day as being as significant as those made by his contemporary, Sir Henry Rawlinson, to Assyriology. Some of his work, including maps, plans, and drawings of sites, were lost or destroyed, and much of what was left to the Bodleian Library, Griffith Institute, and the British Museum remains unpublished.

See also Foundation of Great Egyptian Collections in England and France (1815–1835); Decipherment of Egyptian Hieroglyphics (1824); Publication of *Description de l'Egypte* (1826); Decipherment of Cuneiform (1836–1857); Publication of *Nineveh and Its Remains* (1849); Mariette, Antiquities Law, and the Egyptian Museum (1858); Publication of *Denkmaler aus Aegypten und Aethiopien* (1859).

Further Reading

Fagan, Brian M. 1975. *The rape of the Nile: Tomb robbers, tourists, and archaeologists in Egypt.* Aylesbury, Bucks, UK: Macdonald and Jane's.

France, P. 1991. *The rape of Egypt.* London: Barrie and Jenkin

Wilkinson, J. G. 1847. *The manners and customs of the ancient Egyptians: including their private life, government, laws, arts, manufactures, religion, agriculture, and early history.* London: John Murray.

Guide to Northern Archaeology
Published in English (1848)

The son of a wealthy Copenhagen businessman, Christian Jurgensen Thomsen (1788–1865) began collecting coins and antiquities as a hobby that eventually grew into an unrivalled expertise. He succeeded Rasmus Nyerup when, in 1816, he was appointed Denmark's national antiquary and secretary of the antiquities commission. Part of Thomsen's task was to expand and rearrange the collections of the Museum of National Antiquities in Copenhagen and make them accessible to the public. This involved Thomsen in devising a chronology or method of explaining displays of archaeological artifacts and material, and he used the Three-Age System of Stone, Bronze, and Iron as the basis of his reorganization.

Rightly regarded as being one of the most significant conceptual advances in prehistoric archaeology, the Three-Age System had a long gestation that drew on the writings of classical historians and geographers and Enlightenment philosophers as well as the knowledge of Scandinavian antiquarians and their large collections of archaeological material. Historians of archaeology are fond of demonstrating that the idea of producing a sequence of human history tied to a gradual evolution in the complexity of technology and material culture (from Stone Age to Bronze Age and then to an Iron Age) is as old as the ancient Greeks. Certainly the discovery of contemporary peoples in the Americas and the Arctic who used stone tools and lived in a comparatively uncivilized state provided strong support for such ideas. It is also true, as Swedish archaeologist Bo Gräslund (1987) has argued, that other antiquarians, such as the German Friedrich Lisch (1801–1883), were persuaded that the writings of the ancients, the philosophers, and the explorers might unlock the secrets of European prehistory. However, it was Thomsen who did the most to develop and promote the Three-Age System—and between 1818 and 1825 he was the first archaeologist to formulate, define, and illustrate it with archaeological materials in the Danish National Museum.

Thomsen was also the first to publish the Three-Age System in 1836 as "Ledetraad til Nordisk Oldkyndighed"—in the form of the museum's guidebook more than a decade after he had used it as the chronological sequence for displaying the museum's collections. Thomsen defined the metal ages on the basis of types of weapons and tools and, as importantly, on find contexts. His numismatic background was of great benefit when investigating and compiling typologies of other materials. The guidebook provided an explanation of the objects in the collection within the context of a broader exposition of how archaeologists create information and how artifacts can be dated. This more complex understanding of how archaeologists could define chronology, in a way directly confirmed by field discoveries, was a significant reason for the early and widespread acceptance of the Three-Age System in Scandinavia and northern Germany.

Owing to Thomsen's extensive connections in scientific circles within Scandinavia and the similarities of archaeological material across the region, the Three-Age System was used by archaeologists and museums in Sweden and Norway before Thomsen's book appeared in 1836. Consequently, Scandinavian archaeological collections were the first in Europe to be organized both regionally and culturally, and they were homogenous, large, and coherent enough to make the next stage in the development of archaeology—that of scientific analysis, periodization, and more detailed chronology—possible.

In 1848 Thomsen's guidebook was published in English as *A Guide to Northern Archaeology* to a mixed reception. While generations of systematic fieldwork and not so systematic barrow and tumuli excavation had greatly increased the collections of pre-Roman archaeological material in Britain, British antiquarians and field archaeologists had been unable to establish any reliable and local chronology to explain it. Some British scholars, such as Sir John Lubbock, had kept up with Thomsen's Three-Age System and supported its publication in English, and its use in Britain, while others, such as the antiquarian Thomas Wright and the staff at the British Museum, dismissed it.

In 1849, a book by Thomsen's successor in Denmark, field archaeologist Jens Jacob Worsaae (1821–1886), was also published in English. In *The Primeval Antiquities of Denmark* Worsaae used the statigraphic context of excavated artifacts—that is, where and with what other materials they were found—to further illustrate the use of Thomsen's Three-Age System. And to add more weight to the arguments, Worsaae was a field worker, not just a museum reorganizer, and he had tested Thomsen's system in the field and on recently excavated material. In Britain, throughout the rest of the nineteenth century, differences of opinion about the value of the Three-Age System, along with the discovery of high human antiquity (ironically both were about the verification of the proof offered by "closed finds"), were aired in a wide variety of scientific and antiquarian associations.

See also Worm Issues His Circular (1626); Swedish Archaeological Service Founded (1666); Establishment of the National Museum of Denmark (1807); Publication of *Primeval Antiquities of Denmark* in English (1849); Typology Makes History (1850–1900); Publication of *Pre-historic Times* (1865); De Mortillet Classifies the Stone Age (1869–1872).

Further Reading

Gräslund, B. 1987. *The birth of prehistoric chronology: dating methods and dating systems in nineteenth-century Scandinavian archaeology.* Cambridge: Cambridge University Press.

Thomsen, C. J. 1848. Kongelige Nordiske Oldskriftselskab: *Guide to Northern Archaeology. By the Royal Society of Northern Antiquaries of Copenhagen. Edited for the use of English readers by the Right Honorable the Earl of Ellesmere.* London: James Bain.

Publication of Nineveh and Its Remains *(1849)*

Sir Austen Henry Layard (1817–1894) formed an interest in the civilizations of ancient Mesopotamia as a result of reading Claudius Rich's books *Memoir on the Ruins of Babylon* (1815) and the expanded *Second Memoir on Babylon* (1818). Rich had been the East India Company's political agent in Baghdad and was one of the first serious European collectors of Mesopotamian artifacts, which were later to be displayed at the British Museum.

However, it was the Frenchman Paul Emile Botta who was first to follow up the archaeological possibilities exposed by Rich. In 1843, with funding from the French government and the hard labor of 300 workmen, Botta excavated the site of Khorsabad believing it was the ancient city of Nineveh mentioned in the Bible. He unearthed the Palace of Sargon II (721–705 BC) and sent magnificent bas-reliefs and artifacts and many cuneiform tablets back to France for display in the Louvre Museum. Between 1846 and 1850, again with the help of the French government, Botta and the artist Eugene Flandin published *Monument de Nineve* in five illustrated volumes.

The success of Botta's excavations spurred Layard into action. He was able to convince his employer, the British ambassador to Turkey, to provide him with enough funds to begin to excavate. In 1845 he unearthed two palaces, one of which belonged to Ashurnasirpal II, an eighth century BC Assyrian king, in which he found late Assyrian reliefs, statuary, and other artifacts. He located another eight palaces, excavating from one of them the "Black Obelisk of Shalmaneser III," which shows the Biblical king Jehu submitting to the Assyrian king. These finds convinced the British Museum to take over funding Layard's excavations so that they could expand their Mesopotamian collections. However, the museum was not particularly generous, so Layard certainly did not have the luxury of being able to excavate slowly or carefully. He had minimal field support, and because he had no field artists was forced to do his own site drawings. Notwithstanding these difficulties Layard was particularly fortunate to have the support of Henry Rawlinson, who had replaced Rich as

The arrival of a colossal Assyrian statue of a winged bull at the British Museum in 1852. (Illustrated London News, *February 28, 1852)*

the East India Company's agent in Baghdad and who was later to become famous as one of the contributors to the decipherment of cuneiform.

In 1847 Layard's Mesopotamian finds were displayed in the British Museum and caused a sensation. Here was proof that the Bible was the truth, and its veracity was the subject of continual debate during the mid-Victorian age. Layard had brought home evidence that the Old Testament was based on real people, places, and events. The details provided by the artifacts were extraordinary; the clothing, jewelry, and hair and beard styles depicted were soon joined by other details of everyday life almost 2,000 years ago as recorded on clay tablets that Rawlinson began to translate and publish. The Assyrian display at the museum, accompanied by Layard's account of the excavations in *Nineveh and its Remains,* inspired not only an Assyrian style in fashions in jewelry, theater, architecture, hairstyles, and clothing, but also poetry about ancient Assyria from Tennyson and Byron.

Layard became a celebrity in England. He had also included in his book an account of his travels in northern Mesopotamia, a remote and exotic part of the Ottoman Empire, about which very little had been known, and so became almost as well known as an explorer as he was as an archaeologist. In 1851 a popular edition of *Nineveh and its Remains* was published and proved to be the greatest archaeological best seller in England during the nineteenth century (it was reprinted six times). However, as it proved, the site and the book were mistitled; Layard had not excavated Nineveh. What Layard had in fact found was the city of Nimrud, the Biblical city of Calah in the book of Genesis.

The huge popularity of the artifacts displayed and Layard's books caused the British Museum to give Layard more funding to return to Mesopotamia to excavate and to provide him with the support of artists in the field. However, their generosity did not extend to helping him publish his drawings of the first excavation, unlike the French government who had helped Botta to publish his. In 1849 the first large folio volume of drawings—*The Monuments of Nineveh*—was published by John Murray through private subscription. A second folio volume was published the same way in 1853.

In 1849 Layard returned to Mesopotamia and began to excavate the mound of Kuyunjik—which was in fact the city of Nineveh. He unearthed Sennacherib's palace (dating from the seventh century BC) and from it recovered superb examples of Neo-Assyrian art, including the famous winged bulls. The bas-reliefs showed kings hunting lions from chariots, the army and its weapons, court ceremonies, and Assyrian enemies being impaled and having their heads cut off. As important, Layard also unearthed a library and archive of thousands of clay tablets, all of which were sent back to the British Museum. He went on to excavate the palace of Assurbanipal (also dating from the seventh century BC) and then moved into southern Mesopotamia, testing the sites of Babylon and Nippur. In 1851 he returned to London and was acclaimed once again, with his new finds causing another popular sensation.

The British Museum and the Assyrian Excavation Fund continued excavation in Mesopotamia from 1853 to 1855 with Rawlinson's help. In 1854 Hormuz Rassam, Layard's former assistant, found the archives of Sennacherib's grandson Assurbanipal—and another 24,000 clay tablets and 30,000 fragments of clay tablets, covered in cuneiform, were sent back to London. Rawlinson retired from his diplomatic position to work full time at the museum translating and publishing the vast and unique information of the cuneiform collection, which he did for the next thirty years. The tablets contained unparalleled insights into the everyday life and extraordinary culture of one of the oldest civilizations on earth. Here were business letters and contracts; medicinal and mathematical treatises; copies of earlier Babylonian literary works, such as the myth of creation and the epic of Gilgamesh; and lists of kings.

Layard retired from archaeology but continued to be a celebrity in Victorian society. He worked with Rawlinson on the cuneiform collection and continued to write about and respond to the unfailing popular interest in Nimrud and Nineveh. In 1853 he published *Discoveries in the Ruins of Nineveh and Babylon,* the second folio volume of *The Monuments of Nineveh,* which contained some reconstructions of the Assyrian throne room and the city of Nimrud, and *Nineveh and Babylon: a Popular Narrative of a Second Expedition to Assyria, 1849–51.* In 1858 Layard published *Nineveh,* an abridged edition of *Nineveh and its Remains* in one volume. It was part of the series "Murray's Reading for the Rail," the Victorian equivalent of a modern paperback sold on a station bookstall. It was hugely successful as both a travel story and as a popularization of archaeology. In 1867 he published *Nineveh and its Remains: A Narrative of an Expedition to Assyria During the Years 1845, 1846 and 1847.*

Layard became a member of Parliament and between 1861 and 1866 was undersecretary for foreign affairs. He was British consul in both Spain and Constantinople (Istanbul), and in the latter position supported Schliemann's excavation of Troy. In 1869, at the age of fifty-two, he married his twenty-five-year-old second cousin and retired to live in Venice.

See also Decipherment of Cuneiform (1836–1857); Paul Botta Excavates "Nineveh" (1843–1845).

Further Reading

Layard, A. H. 1847. *Nineveh and its remains.* London: John Murray.

Layard, A. H. 1874. *Nineveh and Babylon: a narrative of a second expedition to Assyria, during the years 1849, 1850, & 1851.* London: Murray.

Lloyd, S. 1980. *Foundations in the dust: The story of Mesopotamian exploration.* Rev. and enlarged ed. London: Thames and Hudson.

Waterfield, G. 1963. *Layard of Nineveh.* London: J. Murray.

Publication of Primeval Antiquities of Denmark *in English (1849)*

Jens Jacob Worsaae (1821–1886) excavated and published his first archaeological paper at the age of seventeen, and became Christian Thomsen's assistant at the Danish National Museum of Antiquities in Copenhagen. In 1843 Worsaae wrote and published *The Primeval Antiquities of Denmark,* the result of his work with Thomsen, in which he observed that the Three-Age System was particularly dependent on the find associations of artifacts (that is, the stratigraphic contexts of the artifacts—where and with what other materials they were found). Unlike Thomsen, however, Worsaae did not just work in museums—his great strength was that he also worked in the field and was an excavator. In 1844 Worsaae gave up studying law and became a full-time antiquarian, and in 1847 he became the inspector of ancient monument preservation in Denmark.

Between 1846 and 1847, Worsaae traveled extensively in Europe and to England and Ireland. He was the first archaeologist to undertake a survey of German archaeological material—which was scattered among dozens of provincial museums, reflecting the political fragmentation of Germany. He observed that the preoccupation of English and French archaeologists with their Roman monuments had led them to neglect their prehistory and that Thomsen's Three-Age System could be applied to archaeological material across Europe. He understood that as a result of Thomsen's reorganization of archaeological material and their regional characteristics, Scandinavian archaeological collections were well ahead of any others in Europe and were well set up to begin to develop a more "scientific" archaeology—that is, one that involved a more detailed analysis of material and a more detailed chronology or periodization.

In 1848 the Danish Academy of Sciences established a multidisciplinary commission that included the zoologist Japhetus Steenstrup, the geologist Jorgen Forchammer, and Worsaae to study shell middens and geological and sea-level changes. In 1850 they discovered the enormous shell bank at Melgaard in Denmark and excavated numerous implements and bones from it. By the time they had finished the commission, they had studied and recorded more than fifty more shell-bank habitation sites in Jutland and Zealand in Denmark and Scania in Sweden. It was Worsaae who suggested that the enormous piles of shells represented the remains of meals eaten by Stone Age peoples over a very long period of time and were not the result of the action of the sea. In the early 1850s the three commissioners published six volumes of reports on these "kitchen middens," demonstrating their human origin and mapping patterns in accumulation. They also proved that the middens were occupied seasonally, and this fact, along with the distribution of hearths and artifacts, provided evidence of human behavior and activities at these sites.

In 1854 Worsaae became a professor, and in 1865, he became the director of both the Museum of Nordic Antiquities and the Ethnographic Museum in Copenhagen. There is no doubt that without Thomsen's and Swedish antiquarian Bror Hildebrand's pioneering reorganization of their national collections according to the Three-Age System and the "Kitchen midden" research, Worsaae would not have been able to take the next step in the development of archaeology—a more detailed prehistoric chronology. Worsaae divided the Stone and Bronze ages into two periods and the Iron Age into three, based on the typologies of material within their find contexts. On the basis of the Scandinavian collections and his great knowledge of European archaeological material, Worsaae became the first archaeologist to place prehistoric monuments in a wider and comparative context, both socially and historically, and he became known as the "founder of comparative archaeology."

In his lectures in 1857, Worsaae argued for a chronological division of the Stone Age into two periods, believing the shell-bank kitchen middens were from the earlier period and the Megalithic tomb period from the later. He published his observations in greater detail in *A New Division of the Stone and Bronze Ages* (1860) in which the find circumstances were the chronological starting point for observations about differences in types of materials. He argued that the early Stone Age comprised middens and rough flint and bone implements, and the later Stone Age comprised large stone monuments, stone chamber tombs and passage graves, and stone, bone, amber, and clay artifacts.

In the meantime, the discovery of cultural materials in the same strata (or find context) as extinct animal fossils in English and French caves supported Worsaae's hypotheses. He had met French archaeologist Jacques Boucher de Perthes on his travels in 1847, and no doubt Worsaae kept up with developments in the debate about "closed finds" as archaeological evidence of high human antiquity in France and England. In 1861 Worsaae drew up another chronology for the Stone Age across Europe—with cave finds first and earliest, followed by kitchen middens, and then by stone chamber tombs, which later became the accepted designations for the Paleolithic, Mesolithic, and Neolithic periods.

At the same time Worsaae's examination of numerous archaeological finds in barrows prompted him to argue that the Bronze Age could be divided into two periods on the basis of burial customs. In a paper published in 1860, he hypothesized that cremation was used at the end of the Bronze Age because most cremated finds were found at the top of barrows, while earlier and uncremated finds or inhumations were always at the bottom of the barrow. Worsaae was not the first to suggest this division in the Bronze Age, but his detailed accounts of find contexts gave the idea scientific credibility. Based on comparisons in stratigraphy, and although purely descriptive in nature, Worsaae's divisions nevertheless demonstrated the possibilities of relative chronology and dating according to the analysis of types of material, which was realized in greater detail by the next generation of archaeologists. In 1865, in writing about the antiquities of Schleswig and southern Jutland, Worsaae went on to suggest the division of the Iron Age into three periods on the basis of coins (Byzantine and native) found in closed finds (undisturbed archaeological sites).

From 1874 to 1877, Worsaae was minister for Danish cultural affairs. He was president of the International Archaeological Congresses at Copenhagen in 1869, Bologna in 1871, and Stockholm in 1874.

See also Worm Issues His Circular (1626); Swedish Archaeological Service Founded (1666); Establishment of the National Museum of Denmark (1807); *Guide to Northern Archaeology* Published in English (1848); Typology Makes History (1850–1900); Publication of *Pre-historic Times* (1865); De Mortillet Classifies the Stone Age (1869–1872).

Further Reading

Gräslund, B. 1987. *The birth of prehistoric chronology: dating methods and dating systems in nineteenth-century Scandinavian archaeology*. Cambridge: Cambridge University Press.

Worsaae, J. J. A. 1849. *The primeval antiquities of Denmark translated, and applied to the illustration of similar remains in England,* trans. W. J. Thoms, London: J. H. Parker.

Typology Makes History (1850–1900)

Because Scandinavia did not have the Roman monuments and remains that absorbed the archaeological efforts of much of the rest of Europe, interest in and protection of prehistoric material in Sweden, Norway, Denmark, and Finland meant that these countries were ahead of many others in their appreciation, conservation, and interpretation of this material. In the 1840s and 1850s the chief custodian of National Antiquities in Stockholm, Sweden, Bror Emil Hildebrand (1806–1884), began to assemble a national archaeological collection through careful excavation and the application of scientific approaches to classification of the artifacts. By 1850 Bror Hildebrand had reorganized the archaeological collections in Lund and Stockholm based on Christian Thomsen's Three-Age System.

By the 1860s the Stockholm archaeological collection was remarkable for the quality and breadth of its collections—which influenced the direction of archaeological research in Sweden for the rest of the nineteenth century. The homogeneity of prehistoric cultures in Sweden meant that its collections provided an overall picture of source material and evidence of local variations. So both general and typical artifact features were easily traced and were more accessible than ever before—as larger proportions of collections of artifacts were exhibited during the nineteenth century. Other European countries, such as England, France, and later Germany, did not have such national collections, so this ensured that Sweden dominated and led the development of prehistoric archaeology during this period.

Bror Hildebrand's achievements in museology were more than well matched by his abilities as an outstanding numismatist. In fact, he may not have been as effective in his museum role had he not had a numismatic background—a study based on types, details, and chronologies of coins. In this area Bror Hildebrand was once again influenced by Thomsen, a numismatist by training and who supervised his doctoral work on Anglo-Saxon coins. Bror Hildebrand recognized the value of coins for dating Scandinavian Iron Age sites and the artifacts and remains found with them. His classifications of the different flows of imported coins into Scandinavia during the Iron Age became an important starting point for determining Iron Age chronology.

From 1861 to 1862, Bror Hildebrand and his son Hans, accompanied by Swedish anthropologist Gustaf Retzius, visited Boucher de Perthes in France, and then Henry Christy in London, to examine the rapidly accumulating evidence for high human antiquity. While Bror Hildebrand had assembled a national database or collection of archaeological information and had begun to explore different methods to interpret it, it was his son Hans (1842–1913) who would continue his father's work and take the next step—breaking down long periods of time into discernable eras and writing history using the attributes of artifacts found with datable coins. A university graduate in the natural sciences, with interests in paleontology and geology, Hans Hildebrand combined experience in field archaeology with a detailed knowledge of numismatics and museum collections. From 1864 to 1865 Oscar Montelius and Hans Hildebrand helped Bror Hildebrand reorganize the Iron Age exhibition in the National Antiquities Museum in Stockholm.

In his essay "The Early Iron Age in Norrland" (1869), Hans Hildebrand dated types of artifacts via their find contexts. These were especially useful if they were "closed finds," that is, in sealed contexts of material, such as undisturbed burials. He compared these finds and sites with artifacts from sites in other parts of Scandinavia—and in noting similarities and differences created classifications of different types of material—and of the cultures who made, used, traded, changed it, and were buried with it. In *Towards a History of the Fibula* (1871) he argued on the basis of his descriptive typology that the Hallstatt and La Tène complexes (groupings of similar artifacts) were two successive horizons (or culture periods) at the end of the Bronze Age and the beginning of the Iron Age in central and in northern Europe.

In 1873, in his book *Scientific Archaeology, Its Task, Requirement and Rights,* written on his return from his second grand tour of European prehistoric evidence, Hans used the term "archaeological typology" to describe his research. Hildebrand illustrated the use of typologies of material in find contexts to describe cultures—and to compare them to other similar material without find contexts. He also emphasized the importance of central museums to the development of scientific archaeology and the development of a typological method.

In 1874, as general secretary of the International Archaeological Congress in Stockholm, Hans suggested that both the Hallstatt and La Tène complexes were cultural and chronological concepts—that is, archaeological constructs useful to fill in the gaps in prehistory. Between 1873 and 1880 he wrote and published *The Prehistoric Peoples of Europe,* a synthesis of archaeology, paleontology, geology, and Paleolithic prehistory—one of the first examples of a modern European prehistory. He succeeded his father as King's Custodian of Antiquities and Director of the National Museum in Sweden.

See also Discovery of the Neanderthals (1833–1900); High Human Antiquity in the Somme Valley (1841–1864); *Guide to Northern Archaeology* Published in English (1848); Publication of *Primeval Antiquities of Denmark* in English (1849); Excavation at Brixham Cave (1858–1859); Publication of *Pre-historic Times* (1865); De Mortillet Classifies the Stone Age (1869–1872).

Further Reading

Gräslund, Bo. 1987. *The birth of prehistoric chronology: dating methods and dating systems in nineteenth-century Scandinavian archaeology.* Cambridge: Cambridge University Press.

Klindt-Jensen, O. 1975. *A history of Scandinavian archaeology.* London: Thames and Hudson.

Publication of Wilson's Archaeology and Prehistoric Annals of Scotland *(1851)*

Born and raised in Edinburgh, Daniel Wilson (1816–1892) combined his knowledge of history and natural science with his skills as an artist and engraver to record and publish accounts of the monuments and collections of Scotland. Wilson's *Memorials of Edinburgh in Olden Times* (1848) established his reputation as a leading Scottish antiquarian, and he became an honorary secretary of the Society of Antiquaries of Scotland.

Between 1847 and 1851 Wilson began to reorganize the collections of the Society into a modern national archaeological museum for Scotland, based on the Three-Age System Christian Thomsen had devised for the National Museum of Antiquities in Copenhagen, Denmark. Like Thomsen, Wilson began by studying the collections and visiting sites throughout Scotland. The opening of the new display of Scottish antiquities was accompanied by a comprehensive catalog written by Wilson, *The Archaeology and Prehistoric Annals of Scotland,* the first study of prehistoric archaeology published in English.

There were many similarities between the archaeology of Scotland and that of Scandinavia, one of these being the absence of Roman occupation in much of the country. Consequently, Thomsen's chronology greatly aided Wilson's interpretation of prehistoric Scottish data. Wilson's application of the Three-Age System was subtle in that he achieved more than a basic chronological ordering by using it comparatively to delineate major stylistic differences between Danish and Scottish antiquities. Wilson also included material from the more recent Christian era in his display and catalog, and noted its differences to other evidence of the past.

As a historian Wilson understood that a historical discipline without written documents was a discipline in search of evidence. He believed that there was more to prehistory than the classification of archaeological assemblages and that these assemblages were evidence of their users' and makers' technology, social organization, religion, migrations, habits, thoughts, economies—in other words, evidence of cultural change in the history of humanity before written records. In *The Archaeology and Prehistoric Annals of Scotland* Wilson defined the long-term goals of the new discipline of prehistory. However, while the book was widely read and published in a second edition in 1863, it had little impact on the development of archaeology in Great Britain.

In 1853 Wilson migrated to Canada where he became a leading figure in higher education, and his interest in prehistory dwindled to collecting artifacts and visiting sites. Instead, he became passionately interested in anthropology and ethnology. He regarded North America as a kind of laboratory for studying the "essential characteristics of human beings," believing developments in the New World would help him understand those of the old. He visited Native American settlements and interviewed travelers, Indian agents, and missionaries who had been to the western part of Canada, recording the impact of the clash of cultures on the frontier, and he visited the libraries and collections of the eastern United States. In 1862 Wilson published *Prehistoric Man: Researches into the Origin of Civilization in the Old and New World.* While this sold well and was read widely in North America, Wilson's anthropological work was soon regarded as irrelevant.

See also High Human Antiquity in the Somme Valley (1841–1864); Establishment of Major U.S. Archaeological Institutions (1846–1866); Publication of *Ancient Monuments of the Mississippi Valley* (1847); *Guide to Northern Archaeology* Published in English (1848); Publication of *Primeval Antiquities of Denmark* in English (1849); Typology Makes History (1850–1900); Excavation at Brixham Cave (1858–1859).

Further Reading

Hulse, E., ed. 1999. *Thinking with both hands: Sir Daniel Wilson in the old world and the new.* Toronto: University of Toronto Press.

Trigger, B. 1999. Daniel Wilson. In *Encyclopedia of archaeology: The great archaeologists,* ed. T. Murray, 79–92. Santa Barbara, CA: ABC-CLIO.

Trigger, B. 2001. Canada. In *Encyclopedia of archaeology: History and discoveries,* ed. T. Murray, 249–259. Santa Barbara, CA: ABC-CLIO.

Wilson, D. 1851 *The archaeology and prehistoric annals of Scotland.* Edinburgh: Sutherland and Knox.

Romano-Germanic Central Museum Established in Mainz by Ludwig Lindenschmidt (1852)

During the first few decades of the nineteenth century, the many independent states of what would become modern Germany were full of enthusiastic antiquarians eagerly excavating, collecting, and founding museums. They were also equally eager to establish significant and ancient pasts. However, the archaeological collections and scholars of Germany reflected the country's political fragmentation, unlike those of her politically powerful neighbors Denmark and Sweden, where Thomsen and the Hildebrands were able to organize and study large, national, and homogenous archaeological collections and consequently develop theories about the development of northern European prehistory, such as the Three-Age System.

More systematic excavations, such as those at Hallstatt beginning in 1846, and interest in theories about whether Indo-Europeans, Celts, Germani, or Samartians were the ancestors of modern Germans, were all part of burgeoning German romantic nationalism, which culminated in the unsuccessful German revolutions of 1848. It was not surprising that as a result of this premature political failure, in the 1850s a number of museums with more national perspectives on German prehistory were founded. These included the Germanic National Museum at Nuremberg and the Romisch-Germanische Zentralmuseum (Roman-Germanic National Museum) at Mainz.

Many German prehistorians, such as Ludwig Lindenschmidt (1808–1893), were interested in "archaeo-geography," or the use of archaeological evidence to elucidate the ethnic histories of central Europe. However, many went further, using archaeological data for political ends, for resolving and justifying who was more entitled to what bit of central Europe because of the length and quality of their occupation of it. It was an obsession that was to continue throughout the rest of the century in the work of many German archaeologists such as Rudolf Virchow, and into the twentieth century with Gustav Kossinna.

Lindenschmidt's ideas about the development of German prehistory were threatened by the work of Thomsen and the Hildebrands. Lindenschmidt believed the major cultures of southern Europe and the Mediterranean had been the greatest influences on the development of prehistoric metallurgy in central Europe. His views were determined partly by the varied and difficult nature of archaeological evidence in Germany, unlike that in Scandinavia, but they were also determined by contemporary politics. German prehistorians opposed the Scandinavian or Nordic systems of classification on principle, in the same way as their politicians had justified the annexation of Denmark's Schleswig-Holstein by Prussia. Until the 1880s Lindenschmidt refused to accept the idea of separate Bronze and Iron ages—almost sixty years after most western European archaeologists.

For this reason Lindenschmidt was the driving force behind the foundation of the Romisch-Germanische Zentralmuseum in the Rhineland city of Mainz. The museum aimed at presenting the broad spectrum of Roman civilization, in addition to prehistoric and Mediterranean cultures other than Roman. Besides local finds, the collections included casts and copies of Roman antiquities from other parts of Germany and neighboring countries. It was defined by Lindenschmidt's ideas, but nevertheless it was an important attempt to create a central and national collection in order to come to grips with German prehistory. There is little doubt that it also reflected the political desire for German unification and nationhood.

Mainz had originally been the Celtic city of Mogonius, which was dedicated to the Celtic god of light Mogon. The Romans named it Mogontiacum when they established a legionary fortress there ca. 38 BC at the strategic point on the banks of the Rhine River, opposite the mouth of the Mainz River. It developed as a base and a river port for the Roman offensive against Germany. As the Roman frontier moved farther east, Mogoniacum changed from a frontier to a central garrison with a large and rich civilian settlement. It was destroyed by Germanic tribes, and then reconquered by the Roman emperor Vespasian (69–79 AD). In 83 AD the Roman emperor Domitian rebuilt its fortress in stone and built a wooden bridge across the Rhine River. After the fourth century AD, continuing invasions and Roman withdrawals led to its restoration as a garrison defending the Rhine.

In 1866 Lindenschmidt became one of the founding editors of the periodical *Archiv fur Anthropologie,* which became the forum for German anthropologists and archaeologists who lacked any national organizations. In 1870, the same year as German political unification, the German Society for Anthropology, Ethnology, and Prehistory was founded. The *Archiv* became its journal and continued to be published until World War II.

See also Sweden Passes Law to Protect National Antiquities (1630); Swedish Archaeological Service Founded (1666); Publication of *Recueil d'antiquités egyptiennes, etrusques, romaines, et gauloises* (1752–1767); Establishment of the National Museum of Denmark (1807); Publication of *The Ancient History of North and South Wiltshire* (1812); *Guide to Northern Archaeology* Published in English (1848); Publication of *Primeval Antiquities of Denmark* in English (1849); Typology Makes History (1850–1900); Iron Age Site of La Tène Discovered (1857); Publication of *Les vases céramiques ornés de la Gaule romaine* (1904).

Further Reading

Murray, T., 2001. Ludwig Lindenschmidt (1809-1893). In *Encyclopedia of archaeology: History and discoveries,* ed. T. Murray, 816. Santa Barbara, CA: ABC-CLIO.

Sklenar, K. 1983. *Archaeology in central Europe: the first 500 years.* New York: St Martin's Press.

Von Elbe, J. 1975. *Roman Germany: a guide to sites and museums.* Mainz: Von Zabern.

Iron Age Site of La Tène Discovered (1857)

The discovery of palafitic (built on poles) lake dwellings in Lake Zurich in 1854 heightened enthusiasm for national archaeology in Switzerland, especially after its cantons had recently fought a civil war and achieved political unification (1847). Swiss antiquarian Ferdinand Keller (1800–1881) found potsherds and stone, wood, and antler tools associated with the piles, which he believed to be the remains of the support structures for house platforms. Keller went on to examine all of the remains of palafitic lake dwellings across Switzerland, noting that they spanned both Neolithic and Iron ages; he attributed them to a homogenous Celtic population.

Keller's interpretation of the Swiss lake dwellings remains as being of "Celtic" provenance created great interest, not only in Switzerland but also all over Europe. Here was protohistoric archaeological evidence of the everyday lives of some of the "original" Swiss people, before their conquest by the Romans—people like the Iron Age Gauls and the Germanic tribes under investigation by archaeologists in France and Germany.

Interest in the Celts was soon further enhanced by the discovery of the site of La Tène, located on the shore of Lake Neuchâtel, in western Switzerland. It comprised the remains of two timber bridges across an inactive arm of the Thielle River and the remains of settlement on its southern bank. The La Tène site is strategic, located where the Thielle River links Lake Neuchâtel to Lake Bienne, and was discovered in 1857 by the collector Hansli Kopp, who was looking for lake dwelling sites and artifacts. In fact, the La Tène site was first thought to be a lake dwelling similar to others found on other Swiss lakes.

Excavation of the site and the observation of any stratigraphy was difficult, given that most of it was under water. Artifacts were pulled out of it by dragging and fishing and then by excavating in the water. Over a hundred swords, with decorated scabbards and fibulae, spearheads, and other bronze and iron weapons were found. During the years following its discovery, looting of the site was more common than archaeological research. From 1869 until 1883 the waters of the Swiss lakes were lowered by canal work, which exposed the surface of the site. By this stage most archaeologists believed the site was so disturbed and damaged that it was not worth excavating, so finds from it made their way via treasure hunters into private collections, and eventually into museums all over the world. In 1885 Swiss archaeologist Emile Vouga began the first professional excavation of the site, and from 1906 until 1917, his son, archaeologist Paul Vouga, continued it.

As early as 1865 Edouard Desor began to compare artifacts from the La Tène site with those found earlier at Tiefanu (Bern, Switzerland) and Alesia in France and to compare material from burial mounds around Neuchâtel with material from the Hallstatt burials in Austria. In 1868, from comparisons with material from Alesia and Tiefanu, he deduced that the La Tène material could be dated typologically to the period immediately before the Romano-Gallic wars ca. 60 BC. He also proposed that, based on the comparison between the different types and styles of burials and accompanying burial materials, the Iron Age could be divided into two distinct chronological and typological periods: the earlier Hallstatt period (ca. 1200–600 BC) and the later La Tène period (500–0 BC).

In 1872 Hans Hildebrand suggested giving the name La Tène to a specific culture of the Iron Age, and his definition was ratified at the international congress held in Stockholm in 1874. However, Hildebrand attributed the differences between the two cultures, Hallstatt, early Iron Age, and La Tène, later Iron Age, to geographical variation, but he was only partly right. Desor was eventually proved right about the chronological and typological differences.

In the end the La Tène site proved to be more famous and more archaeologically significant than the lake dwelling sites. The term La Tène is interchangeable with "Celtic" and refers to the later protohistoric Iron Age culture found in central and western Europe discovered and defeated by the Romans. These were the ancestors modern nineteenth-century nation-states wanted to find and romanticize.

See also Publication of the *Recueil d'antiquites Egyptiennes, etrusques, Romaines, et gauloises* (1752–1767); Establishment of the National Museum of Denmark (1807); Publication of *The Ancient History of North and South Wiltshire* (1812); Publication of the *Guide to Northern Archaeology* Published in English (1848); Publication of *Primeval Antiquities of Denmark* Published in English (1849); Typology Makes History (1850–1900); Romano-Germanic Central Museum Established in Mainz by Ludwig Lindenschmidt (1852); International Congress of Prehistory Established (1865); Publication of *Les vases céramiques ornés de la Gaule romaine* (1904).

Further Reading

Kaeser, M-A. 2004. *Les lacustres: Archéologie et mythe national.* Lausanne, Switzerland: Presse Polytechniques et Universiaries Romandes.

Kaeser, M-A. 2001. Ferdinand Keller (1800–1881). In *Encyclopedia of archaeology: History and discoveries,* ed. T. Murray, 760–761. Santa Barbara, CA: ABC-CLIO.

Kaeser, M-A. 2001. Edouard Desor (1811–1882). In *Encyclopedia of archaeology: History and discoveries,* ed. T. Murray, 423–424. Santa Barbara, CA: ABC-CLIO.

Kaeser, M-A. 2001. Switzerland. In *Encyclopedia of archaeology: History and discoveries,* ed. T. Murray, 1236–1244. Santa Barbara, CA: ABC-CLIO.

Megaw, V., and R. Megaw. 2001. Celts. In *Encyclopedia of archaeology: History and discoveries,* ed. T. Murray, 285–295. Santa Barbara, CA: ABC-CLIO.

Urban, O. H. Austria. 2001. In *Encyclopedia of archaeology: History and discoveries,* ed. T. Murray, 127–134. Santa Barbara, CA: ABC-CLIO.

Excavation at Brixham Cave (1858–1859)

Two members of the Royal Society and one self-educated schoolteacher with a passion for geology were involved in providing convincing proof that human beings had been on the earth for longer than the 4,000 years derived by Archbishop Ussher from the Bible. A crucial element of this proof was the demonstration that fossil finds from closed (such as cave) contexts were reliable sources of information.

William Pengelly (1812–1894) was the primary excavator of Brixham Cave, the site that provided the evidence for high human antiquity in Britain. A teacher and a philanthropist, Pengelly helped to found a Mechanics Institute and Natural History Society in the town of Torquay in southern England. He was interested in geology, early human history, and the antiquity of humanity, and he had published articles on these subjects in the journals of the Royal Society, the Geological Society of London, and the British Association for the Advancement of Science. In 1846 Pengelly began to reexplore the local prehistoric cave site at Kent's Cavern, which had been excavated between 1825 and 1829 by amateur archaeologist Father MacEnery, who had found tools and the remains of extinct animals underneath an undisturbed limestone floor. Pengelly carefully and systematically re-excavated the floor underneath the limestone and found numbers of stone and bone tools. While this confirmed Pengelly's growing belief that human beings had a longer history on the earth than the Bible estimated, the scientific evidence to support such a belief, and that would be accepted by the scientific community, was difficult to establish. There had been many instances of artifacts found with fossil animal remains at other sites, but the unsophisticated excavation techniques of the mid-nineteenth century could not be used to prove that the human material in the deposit had not made its way there as a result of more recent human or geological activities. The problem was proving that the sites were essentially pristine—that they had been virtually sealed after their last use—and that they could therefore be regarded as "closed finds." In this instance prehistoric archaeology needed the science of geology to help validate its evidence.

In 1858 Brixham Cave was discovered at a quarry on the southern Devon coast of England. The probability that it had not been accessible since the Ice Age attracted Pengelly's attention, and fortuitously, the interest of the geologist Hugh Falconer (1808–1865). A graduate of Aberdeen University and a Fellow of the Royal Society, Falconer joined the East India Company and worked for them as a botanist in northern India, where he had excavated mammal fossils and established his reputation as a paleontologist and paleobotanist. Ill heath caused his early retirement from service in India, but he continued to work on fossil collections in the British Museum in London and to research other European fossil assemblages.

Pengelly and Falconer met at the site, recognized its potential and their mutual interest in it, and agreed to become partners in its excavation. Falconer used his influence to acquire financial support for the excavation from the Royal Society, which formed a committee to supervise the work. This committee comprised the eminent geologists Godwin-Austen, Joseph Prestwich, and Sir Charles Lyell, the paleontologists William Buckland and Richard Owen, and representatives from the British Museum and the Geological Society.

Pengelly, Falconer, and Prestwich understood that stratigraphic control of the excavation was crucial to establishing any finds as scientific evidence, and all three brought their expertise to the task. While they expected to find animal fossils, they probably only hoped they might find artifacts as well. Work began in July 1858 and, with few interruptions, finished the following year. The first week of excavations entailed digging through the 7.5-centimeter thick travertine floor of the cave, which had sealed the deposit underneath. After this a trench was slowly dug through the different sections of strata full of the fossil bones of rhinoceros, hyenas, and other extinct mammals. At the end of the first month the first flint knife was discovered—followed by another six—some of which were undeniably in situ and therefore clearly associated with the mammal fossil remains.

Pengelly and Falconer were convinced that here at last was irrefutable evidence of high human antiquity, but Prestwich, Owen, and Lyell remained cautious, using the unstable geology of cave deposits to argue that this evidence alone was not enough to establish, without doubt, the case for longer human antiquity.

However, when the Brixham Cave evidence was compared to Boucher de Perthes' evidence from open sites, and their similarities noted, this cautious position became more difficult to sustain. Falconer traveled through France on his way to Italy for the summer, and visited Boucher de Perthes in the Somme Valley, and examined the French archaeologist's artifacts and sites. He wrote to Prestwich urging him to visit Boucher de Perthes and to examine the French finds. In April 1859 Prestwich and the stone tool expert John Evans (later Sir) traveled to the Somme Valley. They were impressed by what they saw and even witnessed the excavation of a flint hand ax from a gravel pit while they were there. Eventually, the whole committee, including Charles Lyell, traveled to France to see for themselves. In the meantime Falconer had excavated a cave site, the Grotta di Maccagnone, near Palermo, Sicily, and found similar evidence to that in Brixham Cave.

In 1859, after visiting Boucher de Perthes in France, Lyell startled a meeting of the British Association for the Advancement of Science by announcing that there was now undeniable evidence that human beings had lived at the same time as extinct animals. Prestwich and Evans published the finds, and confirmed their belief in the veracity of the evidence. In 1859 the Royal Society upheld that "flint implements were the product of the conception and work of man" and that they were associated with numerous extinct animals. In 1859, after recognition by the English scientific establishment, the French Académie des Sciences finally recognized Boucher de Perthes' evidence for the increased antiquity of mankind. Lyell reiterated his support for the evidence of high human antiquity in his book *Geological Evidence of the Antiquity of Man* (1863).

And finally in 1859, after many years' work, originally inspired by Lyell's uniformitarian geology, Charles Darwin's *On the Origin of Species* was published. Evolutionary biology and the human paleontological record would take the next step together—who and where were humanity's ancestors? Did they descend from apes? Archaeology had proven high human antiquity and, along with geology and paleontology, was to participate in and contribute to the huge public debate about the history of mankind.

See also Publication of *De l'origine et des usages de la pierre de foudre* (1723); John Frere Writes to the Society of Antiquaries of London (1797); Publication of *Reliquiae Diluvianae* (1823); Discovery of the Neanderthals (1833–1900); High Human Antiquity in the Somme Valley (1841–1864).

Further Reading

Gruber, J. W. 1965. Brixham Cave and the antiquity of man. In *Context and meaning in cultural anthropology*, ed. M.E. Spiro, 373–402. New York: Free Press.

Van Riper, A. B. 1995. *Men among the mammoths: Victorian science and the discovery of human prehistory*. Chicago: University of Chicago Press.

Mariette, Antiquities Law, and the Egyptian Museum (1858)

Auguste Mariette (1821–1881) was an artist and a teacher in both England and France who became interested in Egyptology through the work of his cousin, painter Nestor L'Hote, a member of Champollion's expedition to Egypt. Mariette learned Coptic and taught himself the fundamentals of Egyptology by studying museum collections and hieroglyphics from Champollion's grammar and dictionary. In 1849 he so impressed the professor of Egyptian archaeology in Paris that he was employed in a minor position at the Louvre Museum, completing an inventory of all of the Egyptian inscriptions and papyri in its collection.

Threatened by the recent collection of Coptic manuscripts stolen from monasteries in Egypt by the English, the Louvre sent Mariette to Egypt to acquire some for them. He also managed to get permission to undertake some excavation to enrich the museum at the same time. In 1850 Mariette arrived in Egypt only to find that all Coptic manuscripts had been sent to the patriarch in Cairo for safekeeping. With the unspent budget, and encouraged by the French consular and collecting community in Cairo, he began to excavate at Saqqara near the Great Pyramid, where he unearthed an avenue of sphinxes leading to a Greek and Roman temple. This success and his careful recording of the site so impressed the Louvre that they decided to fund more excavations with the proviso that Mariette get official permission to do so. The Egyptian government was lenient but acted to enforce the antiquities laws of 1835. Mariette could take back to France what he had excavated before his application for a permit—but anything that he found after the permit was issued would be the property of the Egyptian government. Guards were placed at the site.

All of this caused a quandary because by the time the Louvre had made its decision and the Egyptian government had issued its permit, Mariette had raised and borrowed funds to keep excavating and had found a superb site—the Serapeum of the Bulls of Apis. This massive underground mausoleum full of the stone sarcophagi of sacred and mummified bulls was also crammed with artifacts. The quandary was resolved by smuggling material from the Serapeum out at night and into the storehouse of the first site and claiming that it was all part of what had been excavated previously. Once the Serapeum was empty the Egyptian antiquities inspectors were allowed to inspect it; they found little of value.

The Louvre got a magnificent collection of more than 7,000 antiquities, and a grateful nation made Mariette a Chevalier de la Legion d'Honneur in 1852. In 1853 he uncovered the Valley Temple of Chephren at Saqqara, but ran out of funds to complete its excavation. In 1855 Mariette returned to Paris and to work at the Louvre as an assistant conservator in the Department of Egyptian Antiquities. He was acclaimed and feted in Prussia, London, and Turin, but was hardly noticed in Paris. His small salary from the Louvre and lack of a career path there embittered him, and he missed his life in Egypt and the excitement of archaeological discoveries and a supportive French expatriate community. He began to think of setting up an antiquities service in Egypt to protect their monuments and a museum to protect their artifacts—all for science. Was this the result of guilt at what he had done? Or was it because of the lack of recognition and income he had received from it? Was it the desire for power over other Egyptologists who had taken the material he had worked hard to acquire, and who had dismissed him because he was self-taught and from outside the academic circles of Paris? Or was it the realization that the competition for artifacts was ridiculous—that the knowledge of Egypt would benefit by collections that were accessible to many and were outside European institutions or private collections? Certainly there could be no better person than Mariette to ensure that Egypt would not be cheated out of its heritage yet again—he had done it so well himself and knew all of the ploys that could be used.

In 1857 Mariette returned to Egypt, seconded from the Louvre to prepare for a tour of the sites by Prince Napoleon, Emperor Napoleon III's cousin. Said Pasha was in power and very much under the influence of his childhood friend, the French diplomat Ferdinand de Lesseps. In preparation for the tour of the French prince Mariette was given an armed boat and was permitted to tour Egypt to prevent the removal of antiquities and to collect artifacts he thought the prince would like. Unfortunately, the prince's tour was cancelled at the last minute, and Mariette, determined to stay in Egypt and escape Paris and the Louvre, offered to stay and keep collecting for the prince in Egypt, if the prince would encourage the pasha to establish a museum in Cairo for Egyptian antiquities with Mariette as its head. In 1858, on the prince's recommendation, and with the backing of de Lesseps, Said Pasha appointed Mariette the director of antiquities in Egypt. He was allowed an armed steamboat and was given a labor force for excavations, now regarded as public works, and the funding and staff for a national antiquities service.

Since 1835 there had been an Egyptian national collection and an antiquities service. The former was stored first in the Ezbakiah Gardens, and later in the Cairo Citadel, and was regarded as a source of gifts for visiting foreign dignitaries. In 1855 Khedive Abbas I, then ruler of Egypt, presented what was left of the collection in its entirety to the visiting Austrian archduke Maximilian, who wanted to take some souvenirs home. Mariette's control over and organization of the antiquities service gave it some teeth for the first time in its history. He was also instructed to begin collecting for a proposed new museum in Cairo, acquiring a warehouse at the port of Bulaq to store artifacts, where tourists could view them.

Although the French were pleased by Mariette's appointment, other Egyptologists and collectors saw it as a threat to their business and livelihoods. Mariette applied himself to his new task with enthusiasm. At one stage his task force was involved with thirty-seven excavations, and almost 300 tombs were emptied at Giza and Saqqara. He then began to organize the clearance of all of the known great sites, such as Edfu, Karnak, and the temple of Hatshepsut at Deir el Bahri. This involved bailing out all of the sand and rubbish of the centuries or demolishing the houses and villages that had been built more recently on top of the sites.

To keep Said Pasha on his side Mariette gave him his share of the spoils in jewelry and gold. To speed up the process of clearance and excavation he often resorted to using dynamite, destroying valuable archaeological information in the process. And he proved to be ruthless. In 1859 Mariette and his men boarded a boat at gunpoint to take the contents of a ransacked rich tomb from a local provincial governor, who was on his way to give it to the pasha. He shot a member of the entourage who tried to stop him, and others were punched or sent overboard. Mariette then presented the magnificent jewelry of Queen Ah-Hotep to the pasha himself. In gratitude the pasha finally agreed to build a new museum.

In 1862 Mariette accompanied Said Pasha on his tour of France and England. After his death, the new ruler, Ishmail Pasha, continued to support Mariette's efforts and agreed to keep building the new museum, primarily to maintain good relations with Europe. Mariette supervised its building, and it opened in 1863. In 1867 Mariette managed the acclaimed Egyptian display in the Paris International Exhibition. His refusal to give the original jewelry that formed part of the exhibition to the French empress Eugénie created difficulties back in Egypt, but by 1869 he was in favor again as new excavations were required as part of the development of the Suez Canal. Unusually, he was also commissioned to write the libretto for Verdi's great opera *Aida*, first performed in Cairo in 1871!

Mariette refused all offers of appointments to the Louvre and the College de France and remained in Egypt, believing the museum and the antiquities service would disappear without him. He spent the last decade of his life writing up his finds. In 1875 he published *Abydos*, then he prepared his five volumes on *Dendera* (1870–1875), and in 1877 his book on *Deir el-Bahari*. In 1881, before his death that year, he helped to found the French Archaeological Commission in Cairo to ensure that French influence in Egypt continued.

Mariette was given a state funeral and was buried in the garden of the Egyptian Museum. High Nile floods in 1878 and 1890 caused the collections to be moved temporarily to Ishmail Pasha's palace. When the museum was relocated to a site at Qasr el-Nil in 1902 Mariette's remains were moved with it and reburied there. The architect Ludwig Borchardt installed the collection at the Cairo Museum in 1904.

The existence of the Egyptian National Museum in Cairo, the first national museum in the Middle East, the first museum of its kind in the world, with the largest and most comprehensive collection of ancient Egyptian civilization in the world, is due entirely to Auguste Mariette. And so was the beginning of the recognition of worldwide responsibility for the proper care and conservation of antiquities and for their preservation and survival in their country of origin.

See also Foundation of Great Egyptian Collections in England and France (1815–1835); Decipherment of Egyptian Hieroglyphics (1824); Publication of *Description de l'Egypte* (1826); Publication of *The Manners and Customs of the Ancient Egyptians* (1847); Publication of *Denkmaler aus Aegypten und Aethiopien* (1859); Publication of *A Thousand Miles up the Nile* (1877); Discovery of the Amarna Tablets (1887); Seriation and History in the Archaeology of Predynastic Egypt (1891–1904).

Further Reading

Fagan, B. M. 1975. *The rape of the Nile: Tomb robbers, tourists, and archaeologists in Egypt.* Aylesbury, Bucks, UK: Macdonald and Jane's.

France, P. 1991. *The rape of Egypt.* London: Barrie and Jenkins.

Lambert, G. 1997. *Auguste Mariette, ou, L'Egypte ancienne sauvée des sables.* Paris: JC Lattès.

Publication of Denkmaler aus Aegypten und Aethiopien *(1859)*

Karl Richard Lepsius (1810–1884) was educated at Leipzig, Gottingen, and Berlin universities and studied Egyptology under the influence of the Prussian scholars von Bunsen and Humboldt. Lepsius was studying in Paris when Champollion's hieroglyphic grammar was published. While learning hieroglyphics from it, he was able to verify Champollion's decipherment and expand and correct it. He then spent four years studying Egyptian collections in England, France, Italy, and the Netherlands.

The liberal and cultured King Frederick Wilhelm IV came to the throne of Prussia in 1840. He was a lifelong friend of the scholar/diplomat Christian von Bunsen, who as the Prussian king's representative in London reported to him about the Anglo-French rivalry, the new field of Egyptian discoveries, and the growth of the Egyptian collections in the British and the Louvre museums. Frederick Wilhelm wanted to increase the national prestige of Prussia and so decided to join the Anglo-French competition for antiquities in Egypt by funding the largest and best organized and equipped expedition to go there. He appointed Lepsius, who had become a lecturer in philology and comparative languages at the University of Berlin, as the expedition's leader.

After arriving in Alexandria in 1842, Lepsius managed to organize an audience with Muhammad Ali Pasha, who was so pleased by the Prussian king's gifts and letter to him, and wishing to annoy both English and French, gave the expedition unlimited permission to excavate wherever and to collect and keep whatever they wanted. Lepsius spent three years in Egypt surveying monuments and gathering objects. He excavated the site of the labyrinth in the Fayum and drew its stratigraphic sections; he traveled as far as Khartoum, Sinai, and Palestine; and he spent seven months in and around Thebes. Everywhere the expedition went there was careful and methodical documentation of sites, artifacts, and monuments; meticulous research; and comprehensive record keeping. The expense and expertise of the expedition changed the whole character of Egyptian exploration and brought it to a new level of rigor. Because they had the opportunity to excavate and record for the right reasons—that is, for the benefit of science and the inquiring public—and they could do it full time and in daylight, and because they were doing it legally, rather than at night and at random and illegally (as most excavations in Egypt were done), their efforts met with great success. Lepsius sent back to Prussia 15,000 antiquities and plaster casts, including three complete tombs found near the great Pyramid. The Prussian Expedition was a lesson in the benefits of amicable and scholarly cooperation, although it was the Prussians who gained the most by it. However, by the time the lesson had been learned and the potential of such cooperation glimpsed by Egyptologists, favor, power, and control over antiquities in Egypt had returned to the French under Auguste Mariette.

In 1846 Lepsius was promoted to professor at Berlin University, and in 1865 he became keeper of the Egyptian collections. In 1859 he published twelve illustrated volumes of *Denkmaler aus Aegypten and Aethiopien* (Monuments of Egypt and Ethiopia), the results of the Prussian expedition and the largest work on Egyptology ever published. His accompanying text to this was published after his death by Naville and others in five volumes between 1897 and 1913.

In 1866 Lepsius returned to Egypt to explore the Suez area and the east Delta, where he discovered the Canopus Decree at Tanis. The translation of this inscribed bilingual stone proved that the system of hieroglyphic translations pioneered by Champollion, and used by Lepsius and others, had been correct all along. Lepsius last visited Egypt in 1869 for the opening of the Suez Canal.

See also Foundation of Great Egyptian Collections in England and France (1815–1835); Decipherment of Egyptian Hieroglyphics (1824); Publication of *Description de l'Egypte* (1826); Publication of *The Manners and Customs of the Ancient Egyptians* (1847);

Mariette, Antiquities Law, and the Egyptian Museum (1858); Publication of *A Thousand Miles up the Nile* (1877); Discovery of the Amarna Tablets (1887); Seriation and history in the archaeology of Predynastic Egypt (1891–1904).

Further Reading

Fagan, B. M. 1977. *The rape of the Nile: Tomb robbers, tourists, and archaeologists in Egypt.* Aylesbury, Bucks, UK: Macdonald and Jane's.

France, P. 1991. *The rape of Egypt.* London: Barrie and Jenkins.

Lepsius, Karl Richard. 1849–1858. *Denkmaler aus Aegypten und Aethiopien,* 12 vols. Berlin.

Discovery of Angkor Wat and the Khmer Civilization (1860)

By the mid-nineteenth century the Indochinese peninsula had attracted French commercial and missionary interests. Cambodia, under a weak sovereign, and a long-term enemy of the Vietnamese and the Thais, was ceded to the French in 1864. Despite great resistance by the Vietnamese people, the French had conquered the rest of the region, except Thailand, by 1873.

There were several important exploratory expeditions though French Indochina during the mid- to late nineteenth century to chart the new territory, document its resources for future exploitation, and find potential trade routes to link the colony with markets in southern China. From 1858 until 1861 the French naturalist and explorer Henry Mouhot traveled through parts of Thailand, Laos, and Cambodia. In January 1860, while traveling in northwestern Cambodia he found the crumbling ruins of the imperial Khmer city and temple complex of Angkor Wat. Mouhot died of a fever in Laos in 1861, but in 1863, when his discovery of Angkor Wat was finally published in Paris in *Le Tour de Monde,* along with aerial drawings, it attracted great public interest. It was, as Mouhot described it at the time, "an architectural achievement which perhaps has not, and never will have, an equal in the world." Mouhot was right about the significance of Angkor Wat, but it was not until 1992 that the rest of the world caught up, and Angkor Wat was designated a World Heritage Site, and the most important archaeological site in Southeast Asia.

The temple complex of Angkor Wat was built between 1130 and1150 AD by the Khmer civilization, which dominated the region from around 600 until 1440 AD, the result of the long interaction between the two great civilizations of China and India. In the twelfth century and early thirteenth century Angkor reached its apogee.

Angkor Wat is a massive architectural complex in the ancient Khmer capital, surrounded by a large moat enclosing an area of two square kilometers. An elevated temple is enclosed within three walled galleries, each ornately sculpted. The outer enclosure is entered via a causeway to three towered gateways. Another walkway, lined by structures and basins, leads to the second gallery that rims the platform on which scenes from Hindu epics are sculpted. Only priests and kings could pass through the third gallery to the sanctuary surrounded by four towers.

The whole construct is the product of Hinduism—from its geometric forms (for example, the distances of the great causeway that correspond to the four great eras in the Hindu concept of time) to the layout of the structures that predicted lunar eclipses. It is the result of a number of builder-kings. The complex was reliant on the countryside for surpluses to maintain the court, army, and offices of state. The Khmer had no currency and so recompense came in the provision of merit for services to the deified ruler. Their dominance of the local countryside may have been undermined by the spread of Buddhism, and the growth of other local political powers such as the Thais and the Chams. The Thais, who had served as mercenaries in the Khmer army, attacked and destroyed Angkor in the fifteenth century AD.

In 1866 an expedition of the Mekong Exploration Commission traveled from Saigon up the Mekong River to southern China. Led by Francis Garnier and Captain Doudart de Lagree, its task was to find a navigable route from Cochin China to the Chinese province of Yunnan to get access to the profitable southern Chinese tea and silk markets. This expedition spent ten days surveying the Angkor region. Members copied ancient Khmer inscriptions and took some of its stone sculptures back to France.

One expedition member, Louis Delaporte, pursued his interest in Angkor by returning to it as the leader of the Mission d'Explorations des Monuments Khmers in 1873—to further document the site. He produced scale drawings of Khmer monuments and sculptures and wonderful illustrations of the Angkor ruins that captured the European imagination when they were displayed at the Paris Exhibition of 1878. Delaporte organized the Khmer Museum between 1873 and 1878 (which became the Museum of Indochina in 1882) and wrote a popular book on Khmer architecture. He became director of the Trocadero Museum (later the Musee de l'homme) in Paris.

In 1885 Auguste Pavie was appointed by the Cochin Chinese government to establish telegraph lines between southern Vietnam and northwestern Cambodia. Pavie's archaeological research at Angkor and his imaginative essays about this monument proclaimed its past glory, which he contrasted to the contemporary conditions of the Cambodians. We now know that the Cambodians had never entirely abandoned the crumbling ruins of Angkor and that the Cambodian state, in a diminished form, continued until, and throughout, the French colonial period. We also know that foreigners, both Asian and European, had visited the ruins for centuries before the French and yet it was the French expeditions that recaptured and popularized images in Europe of a glorious and vanished Cambodian past. And indeed it was just the beginning. Everywhere Europeans went in Southeast Asia they found evidence of great Asian civilizations—such as the monumental Buddhist temple of Borobudor (eighth–ninth centuries AD) and the Hindu temple of Prambanam (tenth century AD) on the Indonesian island of Java, the cities of Sukhothai (1287–1353) and Ayuthia (1347–1767) in Thailand, and the great Buddhist center of Pagan (1000–1287) in Burma.

Archaeology was a distinctly colonialist endeavor that was embedded in a broader civilizing mission. Archaeology, epigraphy, and art history were undertaken by a host of colonial officials and administrators who believed research on the cultures and history of this new French colony served as one means of gaining—and maintaining—colonial control over the region. In 1898 General Paul Doumer established a permanent archaeological mission in Indochina under the control of the Academie des Inscriptions et Belles Lettres, to coordinate all archaeology, epigraphy, art history, and history research in the region. From 1879 to 1885 Etienne Aymonier studied archaeological sites and Khmer inscriptions throughout Cambodia. He was also the founder of Cham studies, was the first professor of the Cambodian language, and laid the foundations of Khmer epigraphy in his book *Cambodge* (1901–1904). French archaeologists, such as Emile Carthailac, excavated the site of Samrong Sen and found bronze weapons and tools, evidence of an Indochinese Bronze Age. In 1901 Louis Finot was appointed first director of the permanent archaeological mission, which was then renamed the École Française d'Extreme Orient.

See also Foundation of the Archaeological Survey of India (1861); First *Homo erectus* (1888–1895); Uhle Begins Scientific Archaeology in Peru (1895–1940); Discovering the Riches of Central Asia—The Journeys of Sir Aurel Stein (1906–1930); Machu Picchu Found (1911); Discovery of the Indus Civilization (1920–Present).

Further Reading

Coe, M. D. 2003. *Angkor and the Khmer civilization.* London: Thames and Hudson.

Higham, C. 2001. *The civilization of Angkor.* London: Weidenfeld & Nicolson.

Mouhot, H. 1864. *Travels in the central parts of Indo-China, Cambodia, and Laos, during the years 1858, 1859, and 1860.* (Memoir of H. Mouhot [by J. J. Belinfante. Edited by C. Mouhot].) With illustrations. 2 vols. London.

Foundation of the Archaeological Survey of India (1861)

Field archaeology was first undertaken in India by James Prinsep (1799–1840), assay master of the British Mint in Calcutta, who became secretary of the Asiatic Society of Bengal in the 1830s. He encouraged the antiquarian interests of his European contemporaries in India by requesting that the East India Company's officers and other officials undertake and report on field investigations as they traveled around. He began the new and regular publication, *The Journal of the Asiatic Society of Bengal,* in 1832.

Prinsep's own interests encompassed coins and inscriptions. He was the first to study the Indo-Greek phase of history in India's northwest, inspired by his study of Greek coins in the Society's collection. He also realized that coins found in archaeological contexts could be used for dating sites. He deciphered both the ancient Brahmi script of the Asokan inscriptions of the third century BC in 1837 and the similarly dated Kharoshti script from the northwest of India.

The Archaeological Survey of India was established by the government of India in 1861, primarily because of Prinsep's protégé, Alexander Cunningham, who recommended that more systematic surveys and records of British India take place. The Asiatic Society of Bengal was concentrating on publishing rare examples of Indian literature and their own research. The government of India had grown from the trading East India Company supported by mercenaries to a colonial administration supported by the English army—and surveys of territories, even if they were archaeological, helped the security of provinces and frontiers. Cunningham became its first director on his retirement from military service. After four years the survey was disbanded and then reestablished in 1870–1871 with Cunningham again in charge. He retired in 1885.

Alexander Cunningham (1814–1893), army engineer, numismatist, and linguist, first worked for James Prinsep and the Asiatic Society of Bengal. He published in the Society's journal on scripts and coins, and later, on ancient

Indian architecture and dynastic issues. Cunningham also studied ancient Indian historical geography based on archaeological surveys and textual material. He followed the routes traveled by Alexander the Great (third century BC) and two famous Chinese Buddhist pilgrims to India in the fifth and seventh centuries AD—identifying famous sites along the way. Many of the most important ancient sites of India were found and identified by him. Cunningham was not an excavating archaeologist, but he made substantial contributions to the development of archaeology in India via mapmaking, surveying, and writing historical geographies. Twelve of the twenty-three volumes of the *Reports of Archaeological Survey of India* (published between 1862 and 1887), on archaeology between the northwestern hills and Bengal, were written by Cunningham.

In 1886 James Burgess succeeded Cunningham as director and served until 1889. He was an architectural surveyor, and his professional interest dominated the direction of the survey with the publication of many studies of ancient and medieval monuments. He appointed a government epigrapher and a curator of ancient monuments.

The Archaeological Survey of India, restructured and set up in 1900 by Viceroy Lord Curzon, was the result of Curzon's desire for a more integrated policy of site identification, protection, restoration, and conservation. John Marshall (1876–1958), director-general from 1902 to 1928, was hired by Curzon immediately after he finished his degree at Cambridge, on the basis of his archaeological experience in Greece and Turkey. In 1900, with support of Curzon and the Survey of India, Aurel Stein led his first expedition to Central Asia.

In 1903 the Archaeological Survey of India published a definitive conservation manual and began to publish detailed guidebooks to archaeological and historic sites on the Indian subcontinent. In 1904 an Ancient Monuments Preservation Act was passed by the Indian government to protect extant monuments and collect and conserve artifacts. In 1904 accounts of archaeological excavations were published in the annual reports of the Indian Archaeological Survey. Research scholarships for Sanskrit, Persian, and Arabic students were funded by the survey at Indian universities, and a publication for epigraphic research was established.

Marshall's survey became fully professionalized in 1906, responsible for all aspects of heritage management including conservation, excavation, epigraphy, museums, publishing—based on a regional structure.

See also Foundation of the Asiatic Society of Bengal (1784); Discovery of Angkor Wat and the Khmer Civilization (1860); Discovering the Riches of Central Asia—The Journeys of Sir Aurel Stein (1906–1930); Discovery of the Indus Civilization (1920–Present); Excavation of Ur (1922–1934).

Further Reading

Chakrabarti, D. K. 1988. *A history of Indian archaeology: From the beginning to 1947.* New Delhi, India: Munshiram Manoharlal.

Chakrabarti, D. K. 2001. South Asia. In *The Encyclopedia of Archaeology: history and discoveries,* ed. T. Murray, 1183–1194. Santa Barbara, CA: ABC-CLIO.

Imam, A. 1966. *Sir Alexander Cunningham and the beginnings of Indian archaeology.* Dhaka: Asiatic Society of Pakistan.

Sankalia, H. D. 1974. *Prehistory and protohistory in India and Pakistan.* Poona, India: Deccan College.

Research into Prehistoric Aquitaine (1862–1875)

The remarkable partnership between an English banker and a French paleontologist, both with an interest in human prehistory, resulted in the publication in 1875 of *Reliquiae Aquitanicae: being contributions to the archaeology and palaeontology of Perigord and the adjoining provinces,* the first book on European paleoanthropology to be published.

Wealthy English banker Henry Christy (1810–1865), collector and world traveler, became interested in human prehistory during a visit to the museums of Scandinavia. In 1856 while traveling in Mexico, Christy befriended and traveled with the young Edward Burnett Tylor (1832–1917), who became one of the founders of the new discipline of anthropology.

Edouard Lartet (1801–1871) was a French paleontologist who was the first to excavate the remains of the fossil apes *Pliopithecus* in 1837 and *Dryopithecus* in 1856. Lartet agreed with and supported Boucher de Perthes' and Joseph Prestwich's evidence for high human antiquity. In 1861 Lartet proposed a chronology for human skeletal and cultural remains, based on fossil animal bones found with them, in the stratigraphy of cave sites. His chronology comprised a series of epochs in the Paleolithic, named after the extinct mammoth, bear, and reindeer remains dominating each. It brought him to Christy's attention.

In 1862 they joined forces to unravel the mysteries of the developments of early European humans. Christy invested both money and time, and Lartet both time and expertise, and they systematically examined the caves situated along the Vezere River in southwestern France. By 1863 they had investigated the cave sites of Gorge d'Enfer, Laugerie Haute, la Madeleine, le Moustier, and les Eyzies. Based on the results of their explorations Lartet further refined his earlier classification of the Paleolithic period in France based on animal fossil finds. The cave of le Moustier provided material for the Mammoth and Great Cave Bear ages, which he concluded were contemporaneous. Material from la Madeleine provided insights into the Reindeer Age. This was the classificatory system that Gabriel de Mortillet reacted against, and he developed his own based on the stone tool types found at each site, rather than on the remains of extinct mammal species.

In 1864 Lartet and Christy published an account of the engraved and sculpted objects in antler, bone, and ivory that they had found at the cave sites. They did not regard these artifacts as primitive in any sense, suggesting they were evidence of the existence of a skilled and imaginative people capable of creating pieces of art. While many of these movable pieces were acquired by the Musée des Antiquités Nationales when it opened in 1867, their authenticity as examples of prehistoric imagination and skill were to be debated, with particular fierceness by de Mortillet, conservator at the museum, for the next forty years. The evidence for Paleolithic art was finally recognized as valid by Carthailac and Breuil after they visited the cave of Altamira in Spain in 1902. Both Christy and Lartet never doubted early humanity's abilities, and their work contributed greatly to a reappraisal of Paleolithic humans and to the contribution examples of Paleolithic art could make to understanding the social and cultural lives of early humans.

Christy began to write, compile, and edit the results of their collaborations, but he died before it could be finished. This now-classic text in European paleoanthropology *Reliquiae Aquitanicae: being contributions to the archaeology and palaeontology of Perigord and the adjoining provinces* (1875) was completed at the expense of Christy's estate by the geologist Thomas Rupert Jones (1811–1911) with chapters by Christy and Lartet, Lartet's son Louis, and other preeminent prehistorians such as Paul Broca, John Evans, Theodore Hamy, and Armand de Quatrefages.

Lartet went on to become professor of paleontology at the Museum of Natural History in Paris and president of the Société d'Anthropologie de Paris. He continued to publish on the evolution of mammals—providing evidence for his observation that the more ancient the species, the smaller the brain in comparison to the volume of the head and body.

All of the caves they had located and explored were re-excavated by other archaeologists in the twentieth century and provided a wealth of evidence of early European human development.

See also Discovery of the Neanderthals (1833–1900); High Human Antiquity in the Somme Valley (1841–1864); Excavation at Brixham Cave (1858–1859); Publication of *Pre-historic Times* (1865); De Mortillet Classifies the Stone Age (1869–1872); Recognition of Paleolithic Cave Art at Altamira (1879–1902); First *Homo Erectus* (1888–1895); Publication of *Les hommes fossiles, éléments de paleontologie humaine* (1921); Lascaux discovered (1940).

Further Reading

Lartet, E., and H. Christy. 1875. In *Reliquiae Aquitanicae; being contributions to the archaeology and palaeontology of Perigord and the adjoining provinces of Southern France.* London: Williams & Norgate.

Coudart, A. 2001. France. In *Encyclopedia of archaeology: Discoveries and history,* ed. T. Murray, 522–534. Santa Barbara, CA: ABC-CLIO.

International Congress of Prehistory Established (1865)

Notwithstanding the huge advances made in the methods of archaeology (and the startling discoveries that had been made), there was still very little institutional support for the discipline within the mainstream academy. There were no chairs specifically devoted to prehistoric archaeology at universities, and if it was taught there at all, it was taught by interested members of departments of history, geology, or anthropology. While some museums collected prehistoric material to help illustrate their national chronologies, others placed prehistoric artifacts in the natural history section beside exotic ethnographic displays of primitive peoples of the world. No museums specialized in prehistory. Worse still, mainstream and "hard" scientists and scholars considered it to be a scientifically dubious proposition, regarding prehistory as a cross between history and antiquarianism, with little scientific credibility.

As Marc-Antoine Kaeser has noted: "the first specifically prehistoric institution was in fact a journal: the *Materiaux pour l'histoire positive et philosophique de l'homme*" (Kaeser 2002, 173), which was launched in 1864 by French archaeologist Gabriel de Mortillet and was widely read throughout Europe. This landmark journal was followed by others, such as the German *Archiv fur Anthroplogie* and the Italian *Bulletino di Paletnologia Italiana* in 1866, for their archaeologists who, until 1871, had no unified nations, let alone national organizations.

An international congress of prehistory was the idea of Swiss archaeologist Edouard Desor (1811–1882). In its realization he was advised and helped by the French archaeologist Gabriel de Mortillet (1821–1898). Both became giants in the profession, but at this stage their archaeological careers were just beginning. Both were liberal, cosmopolitan polymaths, both had been exiled from their countries of origin for their liberal politics, and both were well connected and maintained scholarly networks that crossed national boundaries and institutions.

Edouard Desor was a Swiss citizen, born in Germany, who lived most of his life in the French-speaking part of Switzerland. Desor became a disciple of the naturalist Louis Agassiz, whom he met in Bern where Desor was living in exile from Germany. In 1848 Desor followed Agassiz to Harvard University and then undertook different geographical, geological, and zoological tasks and surveys for the U.S. government. In 1852 he returned to Neuchâtel in Switzerland to teach geology. Desor became interested in prehistory while traveling in Scandinavia in 1846, and one can only imagine that his interest was also stimulated by his experiences in North America. On his return to Europe this interest was consolidated by the work of his Swiss colleague, archaeologist Ferdinand Keller, who was excavating the remains of some prehistoric lake dwellings uncovered in Lake Zurich in 1854.

During this time Desor would have met Gabriel de Mortillet, who had also been forced into exile in Switzerland after 1848 because of his liberal political beliefs. Between 1852 and 1854 de Mortillet worked in Geneva, cataloging the museum's geological collections. Then he moved to Savoy to the museum in the town of Annecy, until he was forced to flee after Savoy was annexed by France. Between 1858 and 1863 de Mortillet worked in Italy for the Lombard-Venetian Railway Company and began his research into prehistory, prompted by the remarkable discoveries of prehistoric lake dwellings in Switzerland. In 1864 de Mortillet moved back to Paris and founded the prehistory journal *Materiaux pour l'histoire positive et philosophique de l'homme.*

In 1865 Desor wrote to de Mortillet suggesting they organize a large archaeological display at the International Exhibition that was due to be held in Paris in 1867. This would provide an excuse to initiate a meeting of international prehistorians who could participate in an international congress devoted to prehistory. De Mortillet supported the idea. However, they both had to protect it from being taken over by the conservative French scientific establishment, who, while skeptical about the bona fides of prehistory, saw it as an opportunity to make political capital for the French government. This is the reason why Desor and de Mortillet surreptitiously founded the congress in Italy and why they held its first session in Switzerland: the board of the Paris meeting was elected by the participants of the meeting of Neuchâtel instead of being appointed by the French imperial authorities (Kaesar 2002, 175).

In creating the congress both Desor and de Mortillet wanted to use it to finally differentiate prehistorians from antiquarians and historians. The organization of their congress, based around the methodology of prehistory, that is, on stratigraphy, technology, and typology, greatly limited the participation of antiquarians and historians. The fact that prehistorians aligned themselves with scientific evolutionism also had an impact on the nature and direction of the prehistory congress. This declared their profession to be involved with understanding the development of the whole of civilization and with the evolution of all of humanity—with universal themes outside geography, mythology, and nationalism.

And so it was that "the first specifically prehistoric association, the Congres international d'anthropologie et d'archaeologie prehistoriques was an international one" (Kaeser 2002, 174). The congress predated any national prehistory organization by forty years (most emerged at the beginning of the twentieth century) and it had an enormous influence of the direction and future development of the whole discipline.

After its foundation in la Spezia, Italy, in 1865 the congress met in Neuchâtel in 1866 (where it was chaired by Desor), Paris in 1867, Norwich and London in 1868, Copenhagen in 1869, Bologna in 1871, Brussels in 1872, Stockholm in 1874, Budapest in 1876, Lisbon in 1880, Paris in 1889, Moscow in 1892, Paris in 1900, Monaco in 1906, and Geneva in 1912. Its decline in frequency and popularity toward the end of the nineteenth century was due in part to its success, to the growing importance of new national associations of prehistorians, and to the growth of nationalism.

From the beginning the congress was a success. It facilitated the communication and discussion of recent archaeological finds and provided a forum for debates about issues, definitions, methodology, and evidence. As important, it provided international recognition of the existence of a specific scientific community involved in the study of prehistory, which was a distinctive and coherent discipline. The congress was regularly attended by leading prehistorians, by many other participants from the natural sciences, and by a range of specialists and amateur archaeologists. The existence of the congress also encouraged the growth of local institutional support of prehistory—as being a separate discipline from ethnology and natural history at universities and in museums. This in turn encouraged the confidence of the new community of prehistorians and led to their professionalization.

In Paris in 1867 the Musée des Antiquités Nationales at Saint Germain-en-Laye was founded to display Gaulish, Roman, Phoenician, and Greek antiquities. De Mortillet, who had set up a prehistory display at the Exposition Universal in 1867, was appointed to this new museum in 1868, where, under his influence, it began to collect, study, and display more prehistoric material.

De Mortillet later drew up the classification of stone-tool technology that remains the standard today; it had a worldwide impact on the study of Paleolithic archaeology and influenced the next generation of great French prehistorians. Desor went on to define the difference between Neolithic and Bronze Age sites, to familiarize many Swiss archaeologists with Nordic Mesolithic and French Paleolithic research, and to propose a chronological division of the European Iron Age based on typology.

See also *Guide to Northern Archaeology* Published in English (1848); Publication of *Primeval Antiquities of Denmark* in English (1849); Typology Makes History (1850–1900); Romano-Germanic Central Museum Established in Mainz by Ludwig Lindenschmidt (1852); Iron Age Site of La Tène Discovered (1857); Publication of *Les vases céramiques ornés de la Gaule romaine* (1904).

Further Reading

Kaeser, M-A. 2002. On the international roots of prehistory. Special Section: Ancestral Archives. *Antiquity* (76) 291: 170–176.

Kaeser, M-A. 2001. Edouard Desor (1811–1882). In *Encyclopedia of archaeology: History and discoveries,* ed. T. Murray, 423–424. Santa Barbara, CA: ABC-CLIO.

Nenquin, J. 2001. International Union of Prehistoric and Protohistoric Sciences. In *Encyclopedia of archaeology: History and discoveries,* ed. T. Murray, 671–674. Santa Barbara, CA: ABC-CLIO.

Publication of Pre-historic Times *(1865)*

One of the true giants of Victorian archaeology, Sir John Lubbock, first Baron Avebury (1834–1913), was a polymath. After Eton he went into the family banking business, but he was also a member of parliament, a university vice-chancellor, an office holder in most of the major scientific societies of his day, an entomologist of note, and an archaeologist. As an archaeologist he is notable for two different though clearly related reasons: first, as the author in

1865 of *Pre-historic Times, as Illustrated by Ancient Remains, and the Manners and Customs of Modern Savages,* to give its full title; and second, as the parliamentarian most responsible for the passage of Britain's first serious heritage protection measure, the Ancient Monuments Protection Act (1882).

Lubbock was a committed evolutionist and a close friend of Sir Charles Darwin who sought to demonstrate the reality of evolutionary theory through a quasi-universal history of humanity. In so doing he wrote what has been called "the most influential work dealing with archaeology published in the nineteenth century" (Trigger 1989, 114). Most famous as the text that introduced the terms Neolithic and Paleolithic into the archaeological lexicon, *Pre-historic Times* was a judicious mix of ethnography (of very doubtful quality) and archaeological discoveries, such as the Swiss lake villages, the Somme Gravels, and the Danish Kitchenmiddens (of very much higher quality). Lubbock does not conceal his desire to instruct the lay population about the meaning of human history—one of a single pathway to civilization that was by no means open to all races or even all classes. For Lubbock prehistoric archaeology provided eloquent testimony to the reality of that path, while contemporary ethnography and information gleaned from settlers in British possessions throughout the world bore testimony to the consequences of the spread of civilization. Yet Lubbock was deeply committed to a single origin of humanity and fought hard against what he considered to be the very dangerous falsehoods spread by supporters of the new discipline of anthropology who were often also believers in a multiple origin of humanity.

This mix of science and Victorian philosophy was extraordinarily successful. *Pre-historic Times* was indeed a book of its times, going through seven editions before Lubbock's death.

See also Discovery of the Neanderthals (1833–1900); High Human Antiquity in the Somme Valley (1841–1864); Publication of *Guide to Northern Archaeology* Published in English (1848); Iron Age Site of La Tène Discovered (1857); Excavation at Brixham Cave (1858–1859); Research into Prehistoric Aquitaine (1862–1875); De Mortillet Classifies the Stone Age (1869–1872); Recognition of Paleolithic Cave Art at Altamira (1879–1902); Publication of *Excavations in Cranborne Chase* (1887–1896).

Further Reading

Hutchinson, H. G. 1914. *Life of Sir John Lubbock, Lord Avebury.* London: Macmillan & Co.

Lubbock, J. 1865. *Pre-historic times, as illustrated by ancient remains, and the manners and customs of modern savages.* London: Williams and Norgate.

Murray, T. 1990. The history, philosophy and sociology of archaeology: The case of the Ancient Monuments Protection Act (1882). In *Critical directions in contemporary archaeology,* eds. V. Pinsky and A. Wylie, 55–67. Cambridge: Cambridge University Press.

Trigger, B. G. 1989. *A history of archaeological thought.* Cambridge: Cambridge University Press.

De Mortillet Classifies the Stone Age (1869–1872)

While the Hildebrands were defining Iron Age chronology in Sweden by using burial typology, in France prehistorians were trying to do the same for the Paleolithic period using stone tools. Gabriel de Mortillet (1821–1898) returned to Paris in 1864 after twenty years of political exile in Italy and Switzerland, where he had continued to research European prehistory while helping to build railways. He initially earned a living from the prehistory review he founded, *Les Materiaux pour l'histoire positive et philosophique de l'homme* until 1868, when he was employed as a conservator by the new Musée des Antiquités Nationales. De Mortillet was a socialist and a radical but also a democrat, an evolutionist, and a scientist. In 1884 he founded and began to edit the review *L'Homme,* as a vehicle to argue against Catholic and conservative science.

Between 1869 and 1872, de Mortillet developed a classification of stone tool technologies, initially because he disagreed with a scheme based on extinct mammal species put forward by paleontologist Edouard Lartet. De Mortillet's classification system was also the result of his reorganization of the Stone Age galleries of the Musée des Antiquités Nationales in 1868, which meant that he knew the material and its patterns and variations better than anyone else. De Mortillet's scheme was based on a technical progression of "the products of human industry," that is, the tools, and these were designated by the sites at which they were found. His classes of stone tools comprised Acheulean, Mousterian, Solutrean, and Magdalenian—and material from these eponymous sites, many of which had been explored by Henry Christy and Edouard Lartet, supported de Mortillet's idea of a linear chronological progression of greater refinement of stone and bone tool technology through the Paleolithic period.

However, material from the Aurignacian site did not fit into de Mortillet's evolutionary scheme. Originally, because of its bone tools, de Mortillet classified the Aurignacian period as occurring between the Solutrean and Magdalenian periods. However, the Aurignacian stone tool material was definitely pre-Solutrean period in type. Eventually, de Mortillet eliminated the Aurignacian completely because it did not fit into his classification scheme. Later he added the Chellean and Thenaisian classifications to the beginning of the scheme and Robenhausian to the end.

De Mortillet's scheme precluded any cross-cultural influences, evolutionary branching, or anything other than recognized types. Because it was "scientific," that is, based on biological and environmental changes that had an impact on human evolution and on tool-making abilities, de Mortillet argued that the Paleolithic period had developed along the same stages and in the same way everywhere else as it had developed in France—and that these tool types were universal. De Mortillet's scheme was debated by prehistorians during the later nineteenth century. However, it was not until 1907 that French prehistorian, Henri Breuil began to reinvestigate the Aurignacian period and established that de Mortillet's theory did not hold. Breuil argued that de Mortillet's scheme was too simplistic and too rigid. He asserted that evolution was not a uniform or smooth process—it was not linear; there were branches and dead ends in the evolution of other species and evidence of outside influences, such as the migrations of people into France during the Paleolithic era, that must have influenced cultural development and tool technologies. However, despite its obvious limits, de Mortillet's classification of tool types and sites remains useful and is used when talking about French sites and different kinds of stone tools.

De Mortillet also participated in the debate about human evolution and the development of the science of paleoanthropology. In 1868 several partial skeletons were found in the Cro-Magnon rock shelter near the site of Les Eyzies in France. They were believed to be from the late Aurignacian Paleolithic period—and while they provided evidence of strongly built individuals with brow ridges, large teeth, and big heads, these human fossils were different from Neanderthal skeletons in that they were long limbed. However, they were not modern humans—and the search for the direct modern human ancestor was still on. In his book *Le Prehistorique* (1883), de Mortillet, as a Darwinian evolutionist, deduced from Thenaisian stone tools that the ancestor of modern humans, which he called *Anthropopithecus,* must have originated in the tertiary period. Its stone tools, from the site of Thenay, were called eoliths, and the tertiary period designated Eolithic (as distinct from, and earlier than, the Paleolithic). He had no physical evidence to support his deductions, which were based on the logic and universality of his stone tool scheme—and the Thenaisian and Eolithic periods fitted snugly into it. De Mortillet's missing link, the *Anthropopithecus,* was imaginary—but using tools from three different tertiary sites, de Mortillet designated three different kinds of *Anthropopithecus* toolmakers without any skeletal material. His theory remained reasonably popular until the 1894 discovery by Dubois of "Java man" *Pithecanthropus,* which supplanted de Mortillet's *Anthropopithecus* as the missing link and a modern human ancestor.

For almost forty years de Mortillet refused to acknowledge the significance of evidence for Paleolithic art and religious practices. He maintained that Paleolithic people were too primitive in their biological and cultural development, and too low on the evolutionary ladder, to be more than "imititative of nature" in their art and were barbaric in their beliefs. The discoveries by Christy and Lartet of Paleolithic art in the 1860s, and then the discovery of the gallery of cave paintings in the cave of Altamira, were designated frauds by de Mortillet. However, growing evidence of thoughtful funerary practices and great skill in carving, engraving, and painting eventually proved the contrary for the Paleolithic period. De Mortillet died before Altamira was recognized as authentic and an extraordinary example of ancient art, and Paleolithic culture was regarded as being not so primitive as was first thought.

See also Discovery of the Neanderthals (1833–1900); High Human Antiquity in the Somme Valley (1841–1864); *Guide to Northern Archaeology* Published in English (1848); Excavation at Brixham Cave (1858–1859); Research into Prehistoric Aquitaine (1862–1875); Recognition of Paleolithic Cave Art at Altamira (1879–1902); First *Homo erectus* (1888–1895).

Further Reading

De Mortillet, G. 1869. Essai d'une classification des cavernes et des stations sous abri, fondée sur les produits de l'industrie humaine. *Comptes rendus hebdomadaires des séances de l'Académie des Sciences* 58: 553–555.

De Mortillet, G. 1872. Classification des diverses périodes de l'âge de la pierre. *Revue d'anthropologie* I: 432–437.

Gran-Aymerich, E. 1998. *Naissance de L'archéologie moderne 1798–1945.* Paris: Editions CNRS.

Kaeser, M-A. 2002. On the international roots of prehistory. *Antiquity* 76: 170–177.

Richard, N. 1991. L'Anthropopithèque de G. de Mortillet, le débat sur l'ancêtre de l'homme au XIXe siècle. *Les Nouvelles de l'archéologie* 44: 23–29.

Richard, N. 1999. Gabriel de Mortillet (1821–1898). In *Encyclopedia of archaeology: The great archaeologists,* ed. T. Murray, 93–107. Santa Barbara, CA: ABC-CLIO.

Richard, N. 2002. Archaeological arguments in national debates in late nineteenth century France: Gabriel de Mortillet's "La formation de la nation francaise" (1897). *Antiquity* 76: 177–184.

Schliemann Excavates Troy, Mycenae, Ilios, Orchomenos, and Tiryns (1870–1891)

Heinrich Schliemann, discoverer of Priam's hoard at Troy and the gold mask of Agamemnon at Mycenae, was more treasure hunter than model archaeologist. He did commit fraud, manipulate evidence for fame, jump to conclusions, and make absurd claims, and he did destroy valuable archaeological evidence. However, Schliemann's contributions to archaeology were enormous. His excavations created huge public awareness of and fascination for archaeology, and he raised the international profile of the discipline through publicity about his work.

Heinrich Schliemann (1822–1890) was born in northern Germany and was a sailor, shopkeeper, and merchant before becoming an archaeologist. Along with German he spoke French, Dutch, Greek, Russian, and English. A short visit to California during the gold rushes, and a longer period trading in Russia, consolidated his considerable personal fortune, and he began to travel extensively and write about his experiences. He became interested in history and archaeology, inspired by the successful careers and the fame of the great archaeologists Sir Austen Layard, Sir Henry Rawlinson, and Auguste Mariette.

In 1866 Schliemann began to study at the Sorbonne and became fascinated by the veracity of Homeric legends. In 1868 he visited the sites and places in Greece and Turkey written about by Homer. In 1869 he divorced his Russian wife, moved to Greece, and married a young Greek woman who was as passionate about Homer as he was, and who was well connected within Athenian society.

In 1870 Schliemann began to excavate at Hissarlik, the small Turkish village believed to be the site of Homer's Troy. Although he found many artifacts and architectural features, it took two years and a deep trench to get to the bottom of the site, to find what he considered to be a wall of the Trojan city of Homer. In 1871 Schliemann unearthed what he claimed to be "Priam's hoard" (a collection of artifacts supposedly belonging to the king of Troy during the Trojan War). Schliemann and his discoveries made newspaper headlines worldwide.

It is now clear that the material Schliemann claimed to be a Trojan hoard was assembled over time and from several different sites, which he smuggled out of Turkey and then used as proof that he had uncovered Homer's Troy. Schliemann had, in fact, found the remains of a city older than Homer's Troy but to reach them he had destroyed evidence of the very city described by Homer, which he was trying to find.

In 1876 Schliemann began to excavate within the citadel at Mycenae in central Greece, where he unearthed graves packed with golden artifacts: masks, diadems, goblets and other ornaments, gem-encrusted bronze swords, silver perfume bottles, and painted earthenware vessels. Schliemann believed he had found the graves of Agamemnon and his retinue, but the graves proved to be about three centuries older than the period during which the

Heinrich Schliemann. (Library of Congress)

Trojan War had occurred. Nevertheless, his discoveries made newspaper headlines worldwide once again.

In 1878, in response to widespread criticism of his work by journalists and archaeologists, Schliemann returned to Hissarlik to undertake more systematic excavations of the site. During this season the German archaeologist Rudolf Virchow visited and offered advice to Schliemann and lent credibility to the new series of excavations.

In 1880 Schliemann moved back to Greece to excavate Orchomenos, where the legendary king Minias and the Minoan people lived. He hired Wilhelm Dorpfeld, a young architect and secretary at the German Archaeological Institute in Athens whom he had met years earlier at Ernst Curtius' excavations at Olympia. It was the beginning of a collaboration that gave Schliemann the archaeological credibility he needed.

In 1882 Schliemann took Dorpfeld to Hissarlik for a third season of excavations. Dorpfeld quickly sorted out the stratigraphy of the walls, determined when they had been built, and rectified Schliemann's mistakes. Between 1884 and 1886 Schliemann began excavating in Greece again, at Tiryns, where he discovered more evidence of Mycenaean culture.

In 1889 Schliemann defended Dorpfeld and his new work at Hissarlik, appearing in person at the International Prehistory Congress in Paris. This resulted in a large number of archaeologists visiting the site in 1890 with Schliemann and Dorpfeld as their guides. Schliemann died in 1891 and all of Athenian society, including the king of Greece, were present at his burial in Athens.

See also Excavation of Olympia (1875-1881); Discovery of the Amarna Tablets (1887); Discovery of Minoan Civilization (1900-1935)

Further Reading

Allen, S. H. 1999. Finding the walls of Troy: Frank Calvert and Heinrich Schliemann at Hissarlik. Berkeley: University of California Press.

Klejn, L. 1999. Heinrich Schliemann (1822–1890). In *Encyclopedia of archaeology: The great archaeologists,* ed. T. Murray, 109–126. Santa Barbara, CA: ABC-CLIO.

Traill, D. A. 1995. Schliemann of Troy: treasure and deceit. New York: St Martin's Press.

Excavation of Olympia (1875–1881)

Heinrich Schliemann's success at unearthing the Homeric city of Troy inspired the government of a newly unified Germany to put its diplomatic weight behind a proposal by Ernst Curtius (1814–1896), the professor of classical archaeology at the University of Berlin, to excavate the great site of Olympia in Greece. Curtius had wanted to excavate the site for many years, but lack of funding and Greek cooperation had prevented it. Curtius was an exceptionally enlightened scholar who was passionately interested in classical Greek civilization, and who inspired many other scholars, one of whom was the German emperor Friedrich III. It was Friedrich's influence on the German government that guaranteed their support of Curtius's project.

In 1874 Curtius negotiated a unique archaeological contract with the Greek government, one that was eventually copied by other governments and by archaeologists working not only in Greece but also in other countries. The German government founded a branch of the Deutsches Archaologisches Institut (the German Archaeological Institute) in Athens, and agreed to fund all of the costs of the excavation (estimated at around $200,000 today). The German government also agreed that all of the excavated finds would stay in Greece, that they would be excavating for research purposes alone, and that German scholars would be allowed to publish the finds and their conclusions.

The Prussian expedition to Egypt in 1842, led by Karl Lepsius, had shown the archaeological world what could be accomplished with the support and cooperation of governments, particularly with regard to the achievement of high standards in recording and publishing accounts of excavations. So some parts of Curtius's contract with the Greek government were not without precedent. However, the fact that all of the finds remained in Greece was a radical departure from previous practices. This was also the first foreign government–funded archaeological expedition to take place in Greece, and it would soon become the model for future ones, as was the founding of foreign schools of archaeology in Athens and in other countries where archaeological work was being undertaken.

Olympia, the largest and most important shrine in ancient Greece, was painstakingly excavated by Curtius and his team between 1875 and 1881. Aware of all of the recent developments in European archaeology, Curtius kept careful records of the find contexts of artifacts. Model techniques of excavation and stratigraphic analysis were used, and the amount of valuable sculptural, numismatic, and epigraphic material found was enormous. Schliemann visited the site to learn from Curtius, after being criticized for his unscientific excavation of Troy. It was here that he met the architectural draftsman Wilhelm Dorpfeld (1853–1940), who was completing an architectural analysis of the site under Curtius. Dorpfeld was eventually employed by Schliemann at

Archway at the entrance to the original Olympic stadium in Olympia, Greece. (Corel)

Troy as part of his attempts to achieve scientific credibility. It was Dorpfeld who was to untangle the chronology and stratigraphy of Schliemann's site.

Excavations revealed the layout of Olympia and located the temple of Hera, the great altar of Zeus, and the Olympic stadium. The only major surviving sculpture by Praxitles, *Hermes Carrying the Infant Dionysius,* was unearthed at Olympia. The results were speedily published by Curtius in five volumes.

See also Publication of *Denkmaler aus Aegypten und Aethiopien* (1859); Schliemann Excavates Troy, Mycenae, Ilios, Orchomenos, and Tiryns (1870–1891).

Further Reading

Curtius, E. 1875. *Excavation of Olympia.* New York: A. S. Barnes & Co.

Chambers, M. 1990. Ernst Curtius. In *Classical scholarship: A biographical encyclopedia,* eds. W. Briggs and W. Calder, 37–42. New York: Garland Publishing.

Publication of A Thousand Miles up the Nile *(1877)*

Born in London, the daughter of an army officer, Amelia Edwards (1831–1892) developed an interest in Egyptian archaeology at an early age after reading Wilkinson's *Manners and Customs of the Ancient Egyptians.* She earned her living as a journalist, contributing articles and short stories to newspapers and magazines, writing eight novels between 1855 and 1880, and editing popular books on history and art. Edwards first visited Egypt and Syria in 1873–1874, and her interest in Egyptology was renewed. On her return to England she began lessons in reading hieroglyphics. However, it was the publication of the account of her trip *A Thousand Miles up the Nile* that enabled her to make a significant contribution to the understanding and preservation of the archaeological sites of the ancient Egyptians.

In *A Thousand Miles up the Nile* Edwards described the impact of tourism on Egypt and the great scramble for antiquities, the loss of information about the past as tombs were plundered and mummies unwrapped for their jewelry, the huge market in illicit antiquities, the wholesale destruction of buildings for their works of art by collectors, and the graffiti of tourists on walls and columns of great monuments. She also recorded her great admiration for the attempts of Auguste Mariette to preserve as much of Egypt's past as possible. *A Thousand Miles up the Nile* was a huge success, and two more editions were published in 1889 and 1891, raising awareness about the state of Egyptology and the desecration and pillage of Egypt's past.

At the same time the British Museum was keen to enhance its Egyptian collections. The Keeper of Coins and Medals, Reginald Stuart Poole, who was interested in Egyptian Biblical archaeology, was the only one of the museum's Egyptologists to support Edwards's attempts to establish a fund to continue to explore Egypt, while at the same time preserving its monuments in situ or in the museum in Cairo. In 1882 Edwards helped set up the Egypt Exploration Society "to cooperate with the Director of Museums and Excavations in Egypt, in his work of exploration . . . to conduct excavations especially on site of Biblical and classical interest, without infringing the Egyptian law, by which objects found are claimed by the Boolak Museum . . . (and to publish) results." It was the emphasis on Biblical sites that ensured wide support of the society by capturing the public's imagination and not interfering with the British Museum's interests. Contemporary and popular debate about the veracity of Biblical history ensured that even if the society did not bring home artifacts to enrich the British Museum, it could well bring home something even more interesting—archaeological evidence about events in the Old Testament.

The sponsors of the new Egyptian Exploration Society included the archbishop of Canterbury, the chief rabbi, the president of the Society of Antiquaries, the poet Robert Browning, Sir Austen Henry Layard, and Professor

Thomas Henry Huxley. The wealthy and well-known surgeon Sir Erasmus Wilson, who had recently paid more than 10,000 pounds to transport an Egyptian obelisk from Alexandria and erect it on the London embankment, also supported Edwards and the fund set up for Egyptian exploration. His donations enabled England to take its place at the forefront of European Egyptology.

In 1882, because of civil unrest, the British invaded Egypt, and Sir Evelyn Baring was appointed British agent and consul general. Baring refused to turn the British occupation of Egypt into an opportunity to divest the country of its antiquities by not helping the British Museum's aggressive agent in Cairo, Ernest Wallis Budge. Instead, Baring supported the new director of antiquities, Mariette's successor, Gaston Maspero, to develop the Antiquities Service so that it covered the entire Nile Valley with its staff of inspectors, ensuring its control over excavations and the preservation of ancient monuments. Baring and Maspero supported the Egyptian Exploration Society, especially because the society wanted to excavate for information and leave their discoveries in Egypt.

In the first instance the Egyptian Exploration Society raised funds to excavate on the Nile Delta where they expected to locate sites from Biblical history. They employed Swiss Egyptologist Edouard Naville, who was also Lepsius's literary executor, to manage their first expedition to find evidence of the exodus of the Israelites from Egypt. In 1883, at the site of Tell el-Maskhuta, Naville unearthed the remains of a city constructed by Ramses II, with a fortified military camp and several storehouses, which he claimed confirmed events in the Old Testament. The publication of Naville's finds on the front cover of the *Illustrated London News* increased the membership of and donations of funds to the society. Maspero was so pleased with the society's work that he allowed them to export some of the treasures they unearthed—which were later donated to the British Museum.

Amelia Edwards began to raise funds for the next expedition to excavate the eastern Nile Delta city of Tanis, and with Naville unable to participate, the young William Flinders Petrie was appointed expedition leader. Thus began Petrie's long and brilliant career in Egypt, and his on-and-off relationship with the Egypt Exploration Society. Petrie developed a strong working friendship with Edwards, who raised additional and separate funds to support his fieldwork when Naville returned as the society's chief excavator, and ensured continual support of Petrie up until, and then even after, her death. In an attempt to prevent the staff and agents of the British Museum from bringing more Egyptian artifacts back to London, she and Petrie founded the Society for the Preservation of the Monuments of Ancient Egypt. They persuaded the Egyptian Antiquities Service to tax every tourist in Egypt to specifically benefit the repair and maintenance of temples and tombs and for the museum in Cairo to charge fees and sell antiquities to the same end.

In 1891 new antiquities regulations were issued by Khedival decree in Egypt. They were that no excavations be permitted without being examined by a committee on Egyptology, and then only with the authority of the director of the Antiquities Service and Museum; that all objects excavated belonged by law to the state and should be deposited in the museum; and that in order to help fund excavations, the artifacts found would be divided into two portions, and the excavator and administrator would draw lots for them; and that the administrator could buy pieces at market prices from the excavator. Even Petrie thought these new regulations were a bit too strong—because it meant he would have to record every object on the site, because he would be deprived of half of them. These regulations were to have enormous consequences and benefits for Petrie's work on relative typology and for future Egyptologists because of the detailed recording of all material recovered at sites.

In 1891 Petrie began excavating at Tell el-Amarna, unearthing the remains of the heretic king Akhenaten's palace (ca. 1353–1337 BC)—the most important discovery since Mariette had unearthed the Old Kingdom statues (ca. 3000–2000 BC). The site became a new major tourist attraction. In 1892 Amelia Edwards died, raising funds for the exploration of Egypt's past up until the very end, and even founding an American branch of the Egypt Exploration Society. She willed money to establish a professorship of Egyptian archaeology at University College London and recorded her wish that Petrie be appointed to it.

See also Publication of *The Manners and Customs of the Ancient Egyptians* (1847); Mariette, Antiquities Law, and the Egyptian Museum (1858); Publication of *Denkmaler aus Aegypten und Aethiopien* (1859); Excavation of Olympia (1875–1881); Discovery of the Amarna Tablets (1887); Seriation and History in the Archaeology of Predynastic Egypt (1891–1904); World's First Archaeological Salvage Project? (1907–1932); Paleopathology in Nubia (1909–1911).

Further Reading

Edwards, A. B. 1877. *A Thousand Miles up the Nile.* London: Longmans. Paperback reprint, UK: Quentin Crew, 1982.

Fagan, B. M. 1975. *The rape of the Nile.* Aylesbury, Bucks, UK: Macdonald and Jane's.

James, T. G. H., ed. 1982. *Excavating in Egypt: the Egypt Exploration Society 1882–1982.* London: Published for the Trustees of the British Museum by British Museum.

Greenwell Publishes British Barrows *(1877)*

Historians of archaeology and antiquarianism in the late eighteenth and nineteenth centuries in England have rightly focused on the evolution of landscape and topographical studies as a major driving force in the development of method. Exemplified in the work of Richard Gough (particularly the *Anecdotes of British Topography,* an expanded edition of Camden's *Britannia* [1789], and *Sepulchral Monuments of Great Britain* [1799]), landscape and topographical studies taking place across the counties of England reached a large and expanding audience. Links between such studies and the writing of county histories and of course folkloric studies became more common fostered by, among others, Charles Roach Smith, whose "Antiquarian Notes" in *The Gentleman's Magazine* and *Retrospections Social and Archaeological* (1883) are rich sources of perspective, as are the editorials about the relevant archaeological and antiquarian societies that grew up at the time. Here the British Archaeological Association, founded by Charles Roach Smith and the truly indefatigable Thomas Wright, is an excellent example. Major works on Romano-British sites and antiquities (by Wright and others) were matched by those on the antiquities of earlier periods (by John Evans and others), but it was antiquaries such as Greenwell who greatly expanded the sheer mass of information on the sites and landscapes of pre-Roman times. These involved the acts of excavating, classifying, and comparing (the last of which was almost wholly dependent on timely and accurate publication, and the sharing of information at meetings and conferences) meaning that antiquarians were now much more aware of what others were doing. In this sense the institutional structures of archaeological antiquarianism acted precisely as they should, and the English scene expanded to the local to encompass regional, national, and international scales of comparison.

Greenwell had a strong sense of the importance of what he was doing. In the preface to *British Barrows* he spoke of the various causes for the destruction of barrows, observing:

> [S]till more have been destroyed under the influence of a curiosity almost as idle, by persons indeed of better education, but who thought that enough was gained if they found an urn to occupy a vacant place in the entrance hall, or a jet necklace or a flint arrow-point for the lady of the house to show, with other trifles, to her guests requiring amusement. (Preface b)

Clearly, responsible antiquaries should publish, but they should also have a proper appreciation of the history of their calling. The preface to *British Barrows* has a comprehensive and generous appreciation of the work of predecessors—particularly Colt Hoare (Wiltshire), Bateman (Derbyshire), Carrington (Staffordshire), and Ruddock (North Riding of Yorkshire)—but published works such as Warness' *Celtic Tumuli of Dorset,* Borlase's *Nenia Cornubiae,* and more famously, Douglas's great *Nenia Britannica* and the Reverend Bryan Fausett's *Inventorium Sepulchrale* were also acknowledged. These works covered much of England and allowed Greenwell (among others) to detect regional differences and similarities in site types and their contents (both skeletal and material cultural). However, it is the discussion of the crania (and the historical speculations of Greenwell and Rolleston about them) that are of greatest concern here.

Rolleston's discussion of the cranial series in *British Barrows* emulated Greenwell's preface in that it included a long discussion of the history of cranial analysis in Britain, focusing on data that had been retrieved from excavated tombs, as well as more modern observations taken in Europe and elsewhere. Rolleston's survey dwelt on the work of Wilde in Ireland, Daniel Wilson in Scotland, and of course Sven Nilsson in Scandinavia to make the point that crania were important historical data. Indeed, Davis and Thurnam's *Crania Britannica* (1865) was able to consider the issue of the aboriginal races of the British Isles because of the crania excavated by Bateman and others. Moreover, in Davis's subsequent *Thesaurus Craniorum* (1867), his sample of aboriginal crania had increased to 36, all sourced to barrows dug by Bateman, Ackerman, Mayer, and others. Thus, there was already a clear tradition of making history from what was then called "ethnological" or "anthropological" analysis.

For Rolleston (as for Greenwell) there was no doubt that the cranial series could be classified in traditional terms:

> A craniographer with Canon Greenwell's series before his eyes . . . would be impressed with the fact that out of the series, two sets, the one with its length typically illustrative of the dolichocephalic, the other by its breadth as typically illustrative of the brachycephalic form of skull, could at once be selected, even by a person devoid of any special anatomical knowledge. An antiquary similarly inspecting this series with a knowledge of archaeological history would, if he separated it into two groups, the one containing all the skulls of stone and bronze age, the other containing all the skulls of the bronze period, perceive that while the latter group comprised both dolichocephalic and brachycephalic crania and in very nearly equal proportions,

> none but the dolichocephalic skulls were to be found in any set of skulls from the barrows of the pre-metallic period. (Greenwell 1877, 627)

But what did this mean? Both Greenwell (and especially Rolleston) understood that the cranial series they were working on provided an exception to Thurnam's old rule that long heads went with long barrows (and were older) and broad heads went with round barrows (and were more recent). Yet neither the antiquarian nor the anatomist were prepared to argue, as Davis was to do in his *Thesaurus Craniorum,* that the skulls should be classified in one of the standard racial divisions (such as Gaelic) or one of the tribal divisions noted by the Romans (such as the Brigantes). The absence of secure absolute dates was obviously a problem here—both at the level of determining synchronicity or succession, as well as determining duration. But Greenwell had to account for the anomalous pattern, especially after he had accepted that Thurnam's rule generally held for the vast bulk of the data at hand and was strongly supported by the evidence drawn from material culture. It is worth quoting Greenwell's solution at length because of its focus on producing a racial history of subjection and eventual intermixture, one that seemed entirely reasonable having regard to history and contemporary circumstances:

> This condition may have been brought about, and probably was, by the fact that the intruding round-headed people, smaller as they may have been in number, were gradually absorbed by the earlier and more numerous race whom, by force of one advantage or another, they had overcome. This subdued long-headed people may very possibly, in the earlier times of the conquest, have been kept in a servile condition, and therefore were not interred in the barrows, the place of sepulture reserved for the ruling race by whom they were held in subjection, and hence the numerical superiority of brachycephalic heads in the barrows. But as time went on and intermixture between the two peoples became common, a change would have gradually taken place in the racial characteristics, until at length the features of the more numerous body, that is to say the dolichocephalic, would become the predominant type of the united people. (Greenwell 1877, 129)

So much for the past, but what about the present and the future? Much has been written by Stocking (1968, 1987), Burrow (1966, 1981), and others about the history of nineteenth-century anthropology and race theory, but there is still much to explore and understand. Significantly, both Rolleston and Greenwell were well aware of this larger dimension to their work, and Greenwell was absolutely right in his general methodological conclusion to *British Barrows*. By the end of the nineteenth century it was to become apparent that what English prehistoric archaeologists urgently needed to do was to write history and to make the classifications arrived at in England and on the continent relate in real historical terms to the patterns being noted in the field.

But prehistoric archaeology (as a part of anthropology) was far from alone in this concern with history and historicism. Although from the 1880s perceptions of human diversity made a forceful return to the ranks of anthropology, this diversity was clearly to be located in ethnic and cultural, rather than purely physical differences. Explanation for diversity and similarity was increasingly to be sought in cultural historical factors, rather than by appealing to the doctrine of independent inventions and the psychic unity of mankind. Real historical forces acting on real (different) groups of people, past and present, could explain the peculiar differences between human beings far more convincingly than generalized uniformitarian forces. Anthropology and prehistoric archaeology, previously focused on providing evidences of the evolution of human beings and their societies and cultures, now became more firmly linked to a less encompassing task—writing the ethnic histories of European nations. Greenwell's grappling with the patterns established in *British Barrows* is an excellent exemplar of what was to be transformed into culture historical archaeology.

See also Publication of *The Ancient History of North and South Wiltshire* (1812); Publication of *Primeval Antiquities of Denmark* in English (1849); Romano-Germanic Central Museum Established in Mainz by Ludwig Lindenschmidt (1852); Publication of *Excavations in Cranborne Chase* (1887–1896).

Further Reading

Burrow, J. W. 1966. *Evolution and society: a study in Victorian social theory.* London: Cambridge University Press.

Burrow, J. W. 1981. *A liberal descent: Victorian historians and the English past.* Cambridge: Cambridge University Press.

Greenwell, W. 1877. *British barrows, a record of the examination of sepulchral mounds in various parts of England, together with description of figures of skulls general remarks of prehistoric crania and an appendix by George Rolleston, M.D. Oxford.* Oxford: Clarendon Press.

Stocking, G. W., Jr. 1968. *Race, culture, and evolution. Essays in the history of anthropology.* New York: Free Press.

Stocking, G. W., Jr. 1987. *Victorian anthropology.* New York: Free Press.

William H. Jackson Visits Chaco Canyon (1877)

Chaco Canyon is a natural canyon located in the northwest of New Mexico that preserves the ruins of thirteen Native American settlements. The sites are the remains of large multistoried structures spread along the Chaco River. The canyon was probably occupied for 1,500 years and has been the focus of archaeological survey and excavation for more than a century. Pueblo Bonito, the largest site on the northern side of Chaco Canyon, covered more than three acres and comprised 800 rooms and many kivas (large ceremonial rooms). This D-shaped complex was home to more than a thousand people and is the largest stone-built site in the American Southwest. Field and irrigation systems have been found in the canyon, and water was channeled from the cliff tops to houses. Its abandonment by the western Anasazi people long before European contact remains one of the great mysteries of Southwestern prehistory.

Knowledge of Chaco Canyon and its ruins dates from Spanish expeditions against the Navajo in the seventeenth century. However, it was not until the middle of the eighteenth century that New Mexico was permanently settled, and even then the canyon became a kind of "no man's land" sandwiched between the semiarid plateau occupied by the Navajo and the growing irrigated agricultural lands of the southeast occupied by the newly arrived Spanish Americans. In 1774 conflict with the Navajo resulted in a new map of the area being produced and on it the name "Chaca" and its location appeared for the first time.

In 1823 a Spanish official, Jose Antonio Vizcarra, chased a party of Navajo into Chaco Canyon. He reported that the Chaco River was flowing and that it provided some good pastures and could be a source of irrigation for future dry farming. He also noted that there were the remains of several old pueblos (or villages). Vizcarra's trail through the canyon to the Navajo lands gradually became the main route taken by soldiers, missionaries, settlers, tramps, and traders in the area, until an easier and alternate road from Albuquerque became available in the 1860s.

The first official report on the ruins in Chaco Canyon was by Lt. James Simpson of the Army Topographical Engineers in 1849. Simpson found himself in the canyon surrounded by ruined buildings. He was excited enough to map, measure, and describe them, documenting seven major ruins and many smaller ones and giving them names provided by his indigenous and Mexican guides. Simpson reasoned that the Chaco River could have provided enough water to develop an agricultural oasis that could feed a large population. He had his own theories about who were the builders and occupiers of the settlements, rejecting the popular and contemporary "mound builders" theory of Aztec influence, for another based on the influence of the earlier Mesoamericans—the Toltecs.

The Corps of Topographical Engineers were the result of the frontier expansion of the United States, and they had been instructed that as part of their surveying they also had to report to the Smithsonian Institution on the details of the country they explored, such as its plants, animals, native people, geology, and ornithology. During the 1840s and 1850s these military expeditions explored, mapped, and reported on the ruins of the Pecos, the Pueblos of Acoma, and ruins of Canyon de Chelly and Casa Grande in Arizona. Simpson went on to report on the Casa Blanca ruin in Canyon de Chelly, while others drew many ruins and contemporary Indian villages, the most famous of which was the Pueblo of Zuni. In 1859 some cliff dwellings near Mesa Verde were reported, and the Grand Canyon, Yosemite, and Yellowstone regions were explored. All of the reports were published by the U.S. Congress and were widely circulated among the American public. The American West and the frontier became an important part of the American nation's identity. In 1869 that frontier moved even closer and became even more accessible with the opening of the transcontinental railway.

After the Civil War ended (1865) military expeditions to the west were replaced by expeditions led by scientists; under the auspices of the government, such as the U.S. Geological Survey of the Territories; from the Department of the Interior; and from other civilian institutions, such as the Smithsonian's Bureau of American Ethnology, led by scholars such as John Wesley Powell (1834–1902). Once again the results of these great surveys were published and achieved a wide and enthusiastic readership. As part of this national interest in the West the leader of the U.S. Geological Survey of the Territories, Ferdinand Vandiveer Haydon, hired famous landscape painter Sanford Gifford, and equally famous western photographer William Henry Jackson, to capture the romantic grandeur of the region and to generate propaganda for its appropriation. Jackson was already well known for his photographs of the Union Pacific Railroad, which he had taken from the cow catcher on the front of the locomotive.

In 1877 Jackson, as part of the geological survey's work, was guided into Chaco Canyon by one of Simpson's original indigenous guides. He began to explore, examine, and map the ruins described by Simpson, and in addition he visited Kin Kletso and Casa Chiquita on the bottom of the canyon as well

William Henry Jackson.
(Library of Congress)

as another new site to the north of Pueblo Bonito, which he named Pueblo Alto. He also discovered and described, for the first time, some of the stairways the ancient inhabitants of Chaco Canyon had carved out of the cliff faces of the canyon. He noted that vandalism and looting of the site had increased, as had its erosion.

As part of his survey work, prior to his visiting Chaco, Jackson had been to the contemporary Hopi villages and had seen other pueblo ruins in Mancos Canyon near Mesa Verde; so, fortunately, he was aware of ethnographic and anthropological studies about Native American people. He was the first explorer of Chaco to recognize and state that its remains were a much earlier manifestation of the extant indigenous cultures and peoples of the Southwest. Jackson had no need for "mound builders" or Aztecs and Toltecs to explain the origins of Chaco's sophisticated ruins.

Jackson wrote that the massive ruins comprised

> millions of pieces (that) had to be quarried, dressed roughly to fit their places and carefully adapted to it; the massive timbers had to be brought from a considerable distance, cut and fitted to their places in the wall and then covered with other courses; and then the other details of window and roof making, plastering, and construction of ladders, must have employed a large body of intelligent, well organized, patient and industrious people, under thorough discipline for a very long time. (Lister and Lister 1981, 14)

Jackson took more than 400 photographs of the ruins and the canyon to be published back East, but unfortunately he was using a new kind of film, and none of them could be developed. However, his work documenting the major ruins and other geographic features was detailed enough to be informative and to create great interest. His reconstruction of the largest structure, Pueblo Bonito, and his map of the site probably had more impact on those who saw them when they were published in 1877 in the *Tenth Annual Report of the United States Geological and Geographical Survey of the Territories* than any black and white photographs of ruins out of context.

In 1888, the same year the cliff palace at Mesa Verde was found by cowboys, Victor Mendeleff of the Bureau of American Ethnology spent six weeks photographing the Chaco Canyon sites, which were eventually published as an afterthought to his study of pueblo architecture. As a result of this publicity, and despite the difficulty of getting to it, Chaco Canyon received many visitors, many of whom looted it. In 1896 the Hyde expedition, commissioned by the American Museum of Natural History, and led by archaeologist Frederick Ward Putnam, arrived to excavate at Chaco. In 1906, to protect the site from further looting, Chaco Canyon was made a National Historical Park.

Jackson's report on and reconstuction of the ruins of the large pueblo settlement at Chaco Canyon was a significant contribution to the final demolition of the "mound builder" myth that had dominated the public perception of indigenous American people for most of the nineteenth century. Here was evidence that some indigenous groups had achieved a level of civilization that the hunter-gatherers and pastoralists of the East and Midwest had not.

See also Excavation of a Burial Mound in Virginia (1787); Publication of *Descriptions of the Antiquities Discovered in the State of Ohio and Other Western States* (1820); Establishment of Major U.S. Archaeological Institutions (1846–1866); Publication of *Ancient*

Monuments of the Mississippi Valley (1847); Stratigraphic Excavation in the Americas (1911–1913); Publication of *Introduction to Southwestern Archaeology* (1924).

Further Reading

Lister, R., and F. C. Lister. 1981. *Chaco Canyon: archaeology and archaeologists.* Albuquerque: University of New Mexico Press.

Greene, D. 2001. Chaco Canyon. In *Encyclopedia of archaeology: History and discoveries,* ed. T. Murray, 295–297. Santa Barbara, CA: ABC-CLIO,

Recognition of Paleolithic Cave Art at Altamira (1879–1902)

In the late nineteenth century, quantities of movable Paleolithic pieces of art, engravings, and sculptures of and on bone, ivory, and antler wood were exhumed from prehistoric sites along with animal and human bones and stone tools. Cave sites were sometimes decorated with engravings and paintings on their walls and ceilings, but the idea that early prehistoric humans could create art, as well as stone tools, was rejected by the French prehistorians Emile Carthailac and Gabriel de Mortillet, who argued that cave art was neither old nor authentic, and that primitive man was just that—too simple to have ideas about art or religion, let alone able to execute them in a recognizably artistic form. However, by the beginning of the twentieth century this notion was questioned, as more discoveries of movable and cave art were made at sites that were clearly from the Paleolithic period. There was now evidence of this kind of art, some of it contemporary, from all over the world.

The cave of Altamira, in the Santander Province in northern Spain, had been found by Don Marcelino Sanz de Sautuola, the local landowner in 1879. The ceiling of the huge cave was decorated with an array of polychrome bison figures. Unfortunately, Sautuola's claims for the high antiquity of the art were rejected by the archaeological establishment for twenty years. This was the outcome of several factors, among them: he was an unknown amateur, no Paleolithic art had ever been found outside France before, and the animal figures looked too fresh and sophisticated to be genuinely ancient.

Altamira contains a wealth of other paintings and engravings, including masks and quadrilateral signs like those of the cave of El Castillo in the same region. The two caves also contain identical multiple-line engravings of deer, both on the walls and on shoulder-blade bones of animal remains found in the cave. Some of these bones have been radiocarbon-dated to 13,550 BC. Altamira's art probably spans a period from about 20,000 to 14,000 years ago.

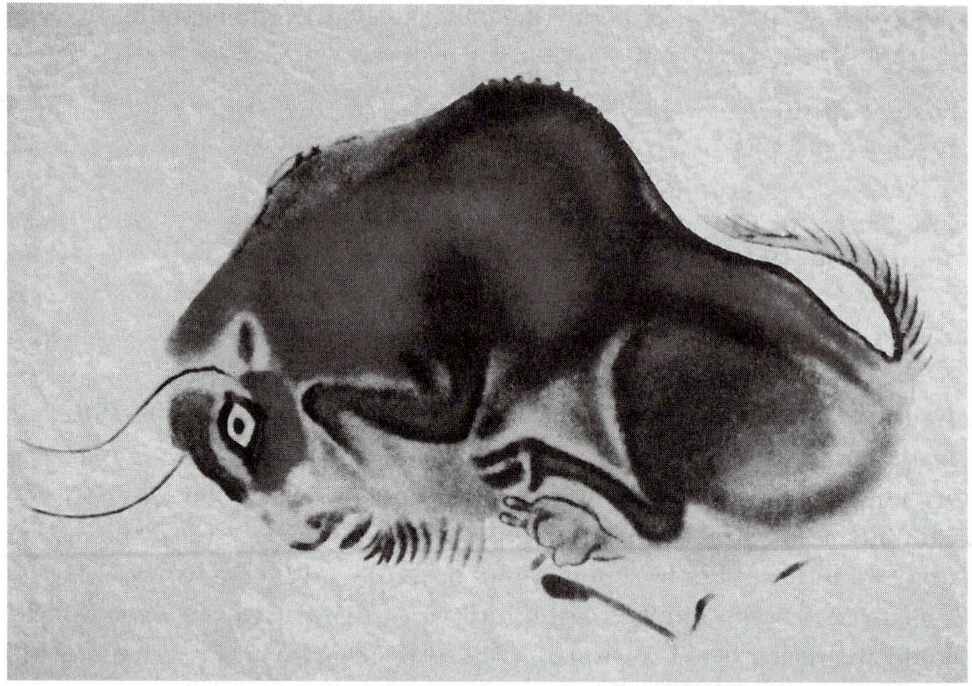

In 1902 Emile Carthailac and Henri Breuil, Parisian prehistorians, rediscovered and explored Altamira in Spain. (Corel)

Charcoal from black figures in different parts of the cave has produced direct dates from 16,480 to 14,650 years ago. But these radiocarbon dates of Altamira's material were only possible in the 1950s.

In 1902, Emile Carthailac and Henri Breuil, Parisian prehistorians, rediscovered and explored Altamira in Spain. Visiting the cave changed Carthailac's mind about its authenticity—was it the vastness and the fact it was so beautifully and extensively painted? Or that the animals portrayed on its walls were so identifiably extinct? For whatever reason, the visit to Altamira had such an impact on him that he wrote "Mea Culpa of a Skeptic," in which he apologized for his former stance and recognized the authenticity of Paleolithic cave art. Breuil and Carthailac explored the cave of Niaux in the Ariege in France, and much later, as the recognized expert on Paleolithic cave art, Breuil was the first to enter the cave of Lascaux after its discovery by schoolboys in 1940.

See also Discovery of the Neanderthals (1833–1900); High Human Antiquity in the Somme Valley (1841–1864); *Guide to Northern Archaeology* Published in English (1848);

Excavation at Brixham Cave (1858–1859); Research into Prehistoric Aquitaine (1862–1875); First *Homo Erectus* (1888–1895); Lascaux Discovered (1940); Discovery of Chauvet Cave (1994).

Further Reading

Bahn, P. 1998. *The Cambridge illustrated history of prehistoric art.* Cambridge: Cambridge University Press.

Bahn, P., and J. Vertut. 1988. *Images of the Ice Age.* New York: Facts on File.

Chippindale, C., and P. Tacon, eds. 1998. *The archaeology of rock-art.* Cambridge: Cambridge University Press.

Ramos, P. A. Saura. 1999. *Cave of Altamira.* New York: Abrams.

Discovery of the Amarna Tablets (1887)

The city of Amarna was established by the heretic, monotheist pharaoh Akhenaten as his capital for the worship of the god Aten during the eighteenth dynasty of Egypt (ca. fourteenth century BC). The Amarna tablets are named after the site of this city, Tell el-Amarna (in middle Egypt) where they were found, a place that had already been mapped and to some extent explored first by the French scientists who accompanied Napoleon I between 1798 and 1799. The site map was later published in the famous *Description de l'Egypte* between 1821 and 1830. In the meantime Sir John Gardiner Wilkinson made his own map of the site in 1824. However, intensive work on the site began in 1843 under the auspices of the Prussian expedition led by Richard Lepsius. During the course of two visits to the site (the last being in 1845) Lepsius recorded standing structures, paying particular attention to decoration and epigraphic remains. The results of this work were published between 1849 and 1913 in his *Denkmaler aus Aegypten und Aethiopien.*

In 1887 a local Egyptian woman dug up the first batch of clay tablets at the site of Amarna by accident. It seems that local scholars did not accept their provenance because they were in cuneiform, not hieroglyphics, and legend has it that many were either broken during the course of excavation or deliberately broken into pieces so that they could fetch more money on the antiquities market. Eventually, scholars recognized their significance. The Amarna tablets were part of what was probably some kind of record office in the pharoah's palace at the site. Some 379 tablets and fragments survive in different collections: 200 of them are now in Berlin, 82 in the British Museum, 50 in Cairo, and 22 in Oxford; a few are owned privately.

Akhenaten (1353–1337 BC) built the city El Amarna as a place to worship the god Aten. (Bettmann/Corbis)

The Amarna tablets were quickly deciphered, analyzed, and then published. Their importance as a major source of knowledge of the history and politics of the ancient Near East during the fourteenth century BC was immediately obvious. The bulk of the tablets are letters, interstate correspondence between the pharaohs Amenhotep III and Akhenaten (Amenhotep IV) and the governors of Amurru (northern Syria) and Canaan (Palestine), and the kings of Babylonia, Assyria, Hatti, and Mitanni. Written in Akkadian cuneiform script they detail diplomatic, trade, and marriage agreements; exchanges of gifts; and requests for help from the Egyptian pharaoh from the independent and dependent states of Babylonia, Assyria, Anatolia, Cyprus, Palestine, and Syria. The Amarna tablets are evidence of the widespread use of cuneiform, proof that Babylonian was the common diplomatic language, and evidence of the breadth of relations between states during the fourteenth century BC.

The discovery of the letters sparked intense interest, and a new round of excavation at Amarna began. Between 1891 and 1892, Sir Flinders Petrie's work continued to reveal much monumental architecture, as well as the remains of factories and houses, and also added to the number of tablets. This work was followed by a German team led by Ludwig Borchardt (1907–1914) whose excavations in the northern and southern suburbs of the city revealed the famous bust of Akhenaten's queen, Nefertiti, in the remains of a sculptor's workshop. Between 1921 and 1936 the Egypt Exploration Society sponsored excavations at the site by Leonard Woolley, Henri Frankfort, and others, and since 1977 they have sponsored excavation of the site by Barry Kemp.

See also Foundation of Great Egyptian Collections in England and France (1815–1835); Decipherment of Egyptian Hieroglyphics (1824); Publication of the *Description de l'Egypte* (1826); Publication of *The Manners and Customs of the Ancient Egyptians* (1847); Mariette, Antiquities Law, and the Egyptian Museum (1858); Publication of *Denkmaler aus Aegypten und Aethiopien* (1859); Publication of *A Thousand Miles up the Nile* (1877); Seriation and History in the Archaeology of Predynastic Egypt (1891–1904); Discovery of the Minoan Civilization (1900–1935); Discovering Tutankhamen's Tomb (1922–1932).

Further Reading

Baikie, J. 1926. *The Amarna age: a study of the crisis in the ancient world.* London: A. and C. Black.

Cohen, R. 1995. *On diplomacy in the ancient Near East: the Amarna letters.* Leicester, UK: Centre for the Study of Diplomacy, University of Leicester.

Kemp, B. 1989. *Ancient Egypt.* London: Routledge.

Publication of Excavations in Cranborne Chase *(1887–1896)*

The son-in-law of Sir John Lubbock, Lieutenant General Augustus Henry Pitt-Rivers (1827–1900) had led a full life as an army man before inheriting the large estate of Cranborne Chase in 1880. Pitt-Rivers had long held an interest in warfare, particularly weapons, and he had come to see the development in weapons of war as an excellent exemplar of the principles of evolution. This interest and the trend of his thinking expressed itself as a typology of weaponry that demonstrated the sequence of change over time. Pitt-Rivers's antiquarian interests developed further through exposure to the archaeological excavations of antiquaries such as Canon Greenwell, and from the early 1860s he was ready to branch out on his own.

The inheritance of Cranborne Chase afforded him the chance to indulge his antiquarian passions on the grand scale. As an army man, Pitt-Rivers inherently understood the virtues of order. He therefore chose to excavate stratigraphically. While this was itself no new thing in Britain or in other parts of Europe, his attention to detail (right down to the training of his workmen) achieved significant improvements in excavation and recording strategies. But there was more to it than just technical virtuosity. What reinforced Pitt-Rivers's commitment to careful and meticulous work was his firm belief that all information contained in the site (not just the bits that might be regarded as treasure) was vital in creating an archaeology based more on fact than fancy. As a result he is often called the "father" of British field methodology.

Important as his field methods were, what made Pitt-Rivers particularly influential was his strong commitment to communicating his work to other antiquaries and to members of the general public. The Cranborne Chase volumes are an especially handsome example of this commitment with detailed plans and measurements, excellent drawings of artifacts and features, and a text that was a model of clarity. Other excavators could read *Cranborne Chase* as an exemplar—a model of procedure—a goal that only the very few were rich enough to match. Nonetheless, the basis of aspiration was well and truly on public display. Pitt-Rivers took his public role (as an expounder of the principles of evolution) very seriously indeed. He was an avid member of the key scientific societies of his day; he was the first inspector appointed under the Ancient Monuments Protection Act (1882), a task he approached with particular relish; he regularly spoke in public; and he was a very strong supporter of museums, endowing several with his extensive collection of artifacts.

See also Excavation at Brixham Cave (1858–1859); Research into Prehistoric Aquitaine (1862–1875); Publication of *Pre-historic Times* (1865); De Mortillet Classifies the Stone Age (1869–1872); Excavation of Olympia (1875–1881); Seriation and History in the Archaeology of Predynastic Egypt (1891–1904); Stratigraphic Excavation in the Americas (1911–1913).

Further Reading

Barrett, J., R. Bradley, and M. Green. 1991. *Landscape, monuments and society: The prehistory of Cranborne Chase.* Cambridge: Cambridge University Press.

Bowden, M. 1991. *Pitt Rivers—The life and archaeological work of Lt. General Augustus Henry Lane Fox Pitt Rivers DCL FRS FSA.* Cambridge: Cambridge University Press.

First Homo Erectus *(1888–1895)*

Charles Darwin's *On the Origin of Species* (1859) did not discuss human evolution, but it was evident that his theories should help elucidate the ancestry of modern humans. While Darwin himself viewed evolution as an unpredictable branching process, most others, especially with regard to human evolution, saw it as an inevitable, sequential, and linear ascent from lower to higher human forms, or a hierarchy of human development with nineteenth-century humankind at its peak. In 1863 Thomas Henry Huxley published *Evidence as to Man's Place in Nature,* in which he argued for a simple human evolutionary sequence, from apes whose brains got larger, who then stood upright, to modern humans. However, Huxley agreed with other scientists that the original Neanderthal skull, found in 1856, with its apelike features, was the remains of another race—on the basis that its large brain precluded it from being a lower form of human. However, the discovery of more Neanderthal remains later in the nineteenth century led to their being widely and popularly regarded, despite contrary scientific arguments, as human ancestors and a missing link in the human evolutionary sequence.

Eugene Dubois (1858–1940) was a Dutch doctor and a specialist in human anatomy. Inspired by the work of Ernst Haeckel, who believed modern humans had descended from a group of apes in Asia, rather than from a group of apes in Africa, as Darwin suggested, Dubois traveled to the Dutch East Indies (now Indonesia) to search for proof. Haeckel's theory was based on the similarities between some anatomical features of the gibbons and orangutans of Southeast Asia and modern human beings, and he believed these apes were closest to the ancestors of early forms of men whose remains should be found in the same geographic area.

From 1888 until 1895 Dubois searched the Dutch East Indies for human ancestral remains, eventually finding the skullcap, thigh bone, and some molar teeth of a fossil hominid (designated by Dubois as *Pithecanthropus erectus*) along with other fossils, near the village of Trinil on the island of Java. Dubois believed these remains, known as "Java man," to be the missing link between apes and humans, and he returned to Europe with them, determined to have this recognized by the scientific community. But the skullcap, tooth, and femur could not be attributed to the one individual, and the evidence for an apelike ancestor was regarded as incomplete, and therefore unsustainable.

However, Dubois' fossil finds were the first to be accepted as material evidence for the process of human evolution, as proof of a chain of connection between humans and their primitive ancestors. For a while *Pithecanthropus* was regarded as being older than the Neanderthal skeletons, and as an earlier stage in the long process of evolution. The debate about the significance of Java man led to the reassessment of the extant European Neanderthal remains, which were now placed in the middle of the process of human evolution between Java man and modern humans. Out of these scientific debates the new science of paleoanthropology was born.

By the end of the nineteenth century the increasing amounts of Paleolithic and Neolithic human remains and examples of tools and art that were being excavated and discovered also had an impact on theories about human ancestors. Did the more highly evolved modern humans from central Asia who invaded Europe wipe out the less evolved primitive Neanderthals? Within the first twenty years of the twentieth century, *Pithecanthropus* and the Neanderthals were no longer seen as stages on the development ladder to modern humans. They were instead described as side branches, mistakes that had died out and were only distantly related to modern humans. This new theory would lead to the search for early non-Neanderthal human ancestors and to the forgery of evidence for this, in such cases as Piltdown man and the Moulin Quignon jaw. Eventually, the discovery of human fossils in Africa, China, and Australia led to the development of more theories about human ancestors. One hundred years and many similar fossil finds later, Dubois' missing link between apes and humans is now regarded as one of many examples of *Homo erectus*.

See also Discovery of the Neanderthals (1833–1900); Publication of *Les hommes fossiles, elémentes de paléontologie humaine* (1921); Discovery of *Australopithecus africanus* (1924); Excavation at Sterkfontein and Swartkrans (1948–Present); Discovery of *Zinjanthropus boisei* (1959); Excavations at Olorgesailie and Koobi Fora (1961–1983); Discovery of *Homo Habilis* (1964–1980); Discovery of Early Humans in Ethiopia (1966–1977); Discovery of the Footprints of Our Earliest Ancestors (1974–1981); Discovery of "Lucy" (1975); Announcement of the Toumai fossil (2002); Discovery of the "Hobbit" (2004).

Further Reading

Shipman, P. 2001. *The man who found the missing link: the extraordinary life of Eugene Dubois*. London: Weidenfeld & Nicolson.

Swisher, C., G. Curtis, and R. Lewin. 2000. *Java man: How two geologists' dramatic discoveries changed our understanding of the evolutionary path to modern humans*. New York: Scribner.

Theunissen, B. 1988. *Eugene Dubois and the ape-man from Java: The history of the first missing link and its discoverer.* Dordrecht and Boston: Kluwer Academic Publishers.

American Excavations in Mesopotamia at the Site of Nippur (1888–1900)

The first American excavation in Mesopotamia was the result of competition between a number of universities to dominate the study of the ancient Near East in the United States and the ambitions of Christian Americans to use Near Eastern archaeology and philology to prove the literal truth of the Bible. Along the way the University of Pennsylvania Museum of Archaeology and Anthropology was founded to conserve and display the finds from the Babylonian Exploration Fund's excavations of the site of Nippur in Mesopotamia. The Nippur expedition was the first to regard archaeology as subservient to Biblical studies, a significant element of the tradition of American "Biblical archaeology."

It was only a matter of time before the newest great power, the United States of America, became fascinated by the oldest civilizations in the Near East. In the 1850s, 1860s, and 1870s European scholars began to decipher the cuneiform texts (found by Sir Austen Henry Layard at Nineveh) that had been deposited in the British Museum under the stewardship of the great ancient linguist Sir Henry Rawlinson. During the same period American universities and cultural institutions were developing, and the growth of the study of ancient languages and comparative philology, originally included as part of Biblical studies, increased in popularity with the discoveries of ancient Near Eastern civilizations and their religious mythologies. To keep up with advances in these disciplines in Europe, as well as to explore their impact on the veracity of the Bible, a number of American scholars and universities began to compete to fund and support an American archaeological expedition to Mesopotamia.

As early as 1884, the prestigious American Oriental Society called for a Mesopotamian expedition, and prior to this the American Institute of Archaeology had sponsored a privately funded tour to the Near East. Individuals, such as Christian scholar John Punnett Peters, also became involved in the campaign for American participation in the archaeology of the region. As the son of an Episcopal priest, and a minister himself at a society church in New York City, member of an old New England family with connections to the wealthiest citizens of the American East Coast, graduate in Semitic studies at Yale University, and of further studies in Germany, Peters took it on himself to educate literate upper middle-class Americans about the importance of the ancient Near East. His message was straightforward—not only could they fill their museums with high-status trophies, similar to those found in European museums, but they could also use the work to defend the Bible and promulgate their faith. Peters began his campaign in New York City, but in 1884, when he moved to Philadelphia as a professor of Old Testament languages at a Bible college, he continued and was to achieve success there.

In Philadelphia Peters met, and greatly influenced, the brothers Edward and Clarence White Clark. With investments in coal, iron, steel, railroads, and the stock market, the Clarks were interested in Near Eastern archaeology. They were exceptionally wealthy, but they wanted more than just respect for their money. They wanted the enhanced social status that only participation in cultural institutions could confer. Peters introduced them to the provost of the University of Pennsylvania, William Pepper, who was master fund-raiser for his institution, and began to advise the Clarks on their cultural investments and returns.

In 1886 Pepper set up a Semitic languages program at the university to make the study of the ancient world more attractive to students, and he appointed Peters to teach in it, as well as German Assyriologist Hermann Hilprecht as its professor. By 1888 Pepper and Peters had established the Babylonian Exploration Fund (BEF) as a framework for channeling public and institutional support for their efforts. With Pepper as its chairman, Peters its scientific director, Edward Clark its treasurer, and other wealthy donors on its executive committee, the BEF had decided to use its funds on an expedition to Mesopotamia, and the task now was to decide what to do with any of the finds that were to be discovered. Pepper founded the University Museum to display and conserve the products of their labors.

The BEF expedition, comprising a professor, photographer, linguists, architect, director, and assistants, left for Mesopotamia in 1888 to excavate the site of Nippur. Located far from Turkish garrisons, towns, and roads in the southern Iraqi marshes, the site lay in a war zone between feuding nomadic Bedouin and local farmers. The BEF chose the site of Nippur on advice from Peters, who had learned of its importance as the oldest city from deciphered material from the Nineveh cuneiform tablets. The expedition braved negotiations with the Ottoman government and local Turkish officials; flies; heat; diseases; unfriendly armed locals; disputes between Hilprecht and Peters over how, where, and what they would excavate; and the management of 300 local diggers and their families, and they eventually began to excavate in 1889. There were three more expeditions to the site before 1900, with different directors and participants, but it was not until the last season that anything of significance was found, and the deep trenches cut into the site made the study of its architecture and any understanding of the site's development difficult. Because they had not found any large sculptures or monuments, Peters and Hilprecht purchased a number of both from other sites in Mesopotamia on their way home to the United States. These larger pieces appeased the BEF's donors and gave the interested public something to see in the museum.

The last expedition eventually unearthed 30,000 cuneiform tablets, comprising Sumerian myths and religious writings, and administrative and business records that spanned two millennia. Some of these were read, translated, and published by Hilprecht and his students, consolidating the University of Pennsylvania's position at the forefront of American Near Eastern studies over rival departments at Yale, Johns Hopkins, and Harvard, if only for a short period. Peters and Hilprecht both wrote popular accounts of their experiences, and other participants and scholars wrote about the excavation, Nippur's ancient architecture, and the significance of the material that had been unearthed.

However, the contents of the cuneiform tablets and their great significance for the study of Sumer and Akkad and the development of Near Eastern cultures were not completely understood until the middle of the twentieth century. The prime reasons for this delay lay in conflicts between Peters and Hilprecht, the university and the museum, and eventually between Hilprecht, the university, and most Near Eastern scholars in the United States over access to and publication of the contents of the cuneiform tablets.

Nonetheless, the BEF expedition to Nippur increased both scholarly and popular interest in archaeology of the ancient Near East. By 1900 the history, archaeology, and languages of the region were being taught across the United States, and there was a corresponding growth of specialist journals and academic organizations. In 1900 a corporation of American universities created the American School of Oriental Research in Jerusalem, and a similar school was later established in Baghdad. In the first decade of the twentieth century there were American archaeological expeditions in Palestine and Egypt. The expedition to Nippur had successfully harnessed Biblical scholarship and American Christianity to not only create but also to satisfy the fascination for the Biblical archaeology that would come into its own during the first half of the twentieth century, under the direction of William Foxwell Albright.

See also Decipherment of Cuneiform (1836–1857); Paul Botta Excavates "Nineveh" (1843–1845); Publication of *Nineveh and Its Remains* (1849); Discovery of the Amarna Tablets (1887); Seriation and History in the Archaeology of Predynastic Egypt (1891–1904).

Further Reading

Dever, W. 2001. Syro-Palestinian and Biblical archaeology. In *Encyclopedia of archaeology: History and discoveries,* ed. T. Murray, 1244–1253. Santa Barbara, CA: ABC-CLIO.

Hilprecht, H. V. 1903. *Explorations in Bible lands during the 19th century.* Philadelphia, PA: A. J. Holman.

Kuklick, D. 1996. *Puritans in Babylon: The Ancient Near East and American intellectual life, 1880–1930.* Princeton, NJ: Princeton University Press.

Murray, T. 2001. William Foxwell Albright (1891–1971). In *Encyclopedia of archaeology: History and discoveries,* ed. T. Murray, 78. Santa Barbara, CA: ABC-CLIO.

Potts, T. 2001. Mesopotamia. In *Encyclopedia of archaeology: History and discoveries,* ed. T. Murray, 871–878. Santa Barbara, CA: ABC-CLIO.

Sabloff, J. 2001. University of Pennsylvania Museum of Archaeology and Anthropology. In *Encyclopedia of archaeology: History and discoveries,* ed. T. Murray, 1307–1309. Santa Barbara, CA: ABC-CLIO.

Seriation and History in the Archaeology of Predynastic Egypt (1891–1904)

In 1886 Ernest Wallis Budge, of the Department of Oriental Antiquities at the British Museum in London, rejected a large amount of pottery and numerous small artifacts from an excavation in Egypt sent to the museum by the Egyptian archaeologist William Mathew Flinders Petrie (1853–1942). Budge regarded the material as not worth accessioning into the collection. This caused Petrie to break with the British Museum for the rest of his career. In response, he wrote to his patron, founder of the Egyptian Exploration Society Amelia Edwards, that the attitudes of the staff and trustees of the British Museum revealed their ignorance of scientific archaeology. While the British Museum was still acquiring the biggest and the best antiquities from ancient Egypt by any means, Petrie was interested in using scientific archaeology and analyzing the minutiae and details of a site to provide answers to questions about the development and history of this ancient civilization.

Petrie and Edwards were among a number of eminent "Egyptophiles" in England who supported the Egyptian Antiquities Service's task of keeping Egypt's monuments in Egypt for posterity and the rest of the world. They founded the Society for the Preservation of the Monuments of Ancient Egypt, which along with the Egypt Exploration Society, funded much of Petrie's scientific archaeological work in Egypt over the next forty years.

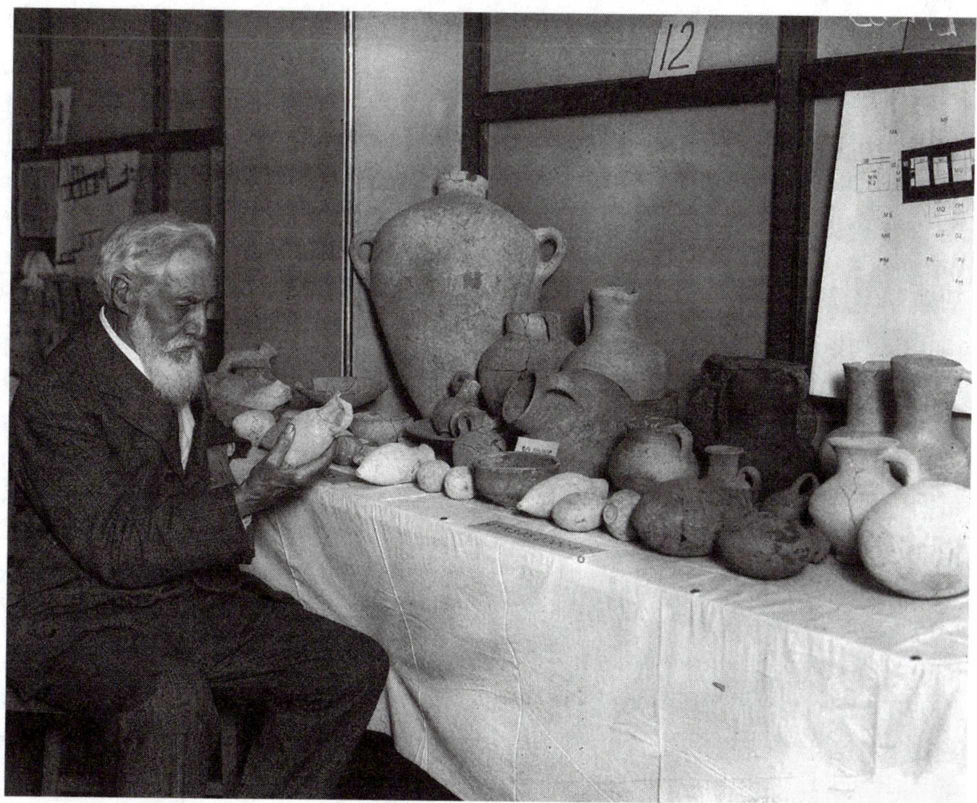

Sir William Matthew Flinders Petrie analyzing pottery. (Hulton-Deutsch Collection/Corbis)

Two interrelated archaeological milestones are attributable to Petrie—his great work on the seriation of archaeological remains and the fact that he was the first to work on the archaeology of the Predynastic cultures of southern Egypt. Without the puzzle of the prehistory of Predynastic Egypt, Petrie would not have made his breakthrough in sequence dating or seriation, which he used to provide a chronology based on successive changes in styles of pottery and artifacts. Without tight stratigraphic control, the close management of workmen, or the careful recording and detailing of his excavations and finds, Petrie would not have had clear control of his data, and he would have been unable to prove how seriation could work to help determine chronology. Petrie had perfected these field practices while excavating dynastic, Hellenistic, and Roman sites in Egypt—sites that themselves had independent chronologies (derived from written records) that he was able to deploy to validate his theories about using pottery seriation to determine chronology.

Between 1891 and 1892 Petrie dug the cemetery at the site of Nagada in southern Egypt. He excavated the remains of flint knives, mace heads, and sherds of handmade pottery—but no epigraphic evidence with which to date the site. While Petrie realized that he had found a more ancient culture than those of his other sites, such as Tanis or Amarna, how could he prove it? He took evidence from burials and compared similar groups of artifacts. He mapped their changes in manufacture, decoration, design, use, and popularity—and put them into a sequence of overlapping changes in details, which could be linked to the one before and after by at least one common feature, thereby creating a stylistic chronology. It did not matter that their dates were unknown. What was important was the evidence of changes over time. This was the core of "sequence dating" (or seriation), and it enabled him to order undatable Predynastic cultural remains into a relative chronology, enough to prove that this culture had evolved over a long time and was not the result of some external influence—such as invaders from another region, as was first thought. Here was evidence of the development of a Neolithic culture in Egypt.

Following Petrie's Predynastic sequence dating, terms to describe different phases of southern Egyptian Predynastic material culture and development were coined based on sites that typified the cultural remains of a different Predynastic phase or stage, that is, another 2,000 years (to ca. 4000 BC) of history prior to the Dynastic period of Egypt (ca. 2000 BC). The terms Amratian (adapted from the site of el-Amra), Gerzean (based on the site of Gerza), and Semainean (based on the site of el-Semaina) came into use, and are still used today. This is notwithstanding the more detailed chronological sequences based on further and more recent excavation of the Nagada cemetery in southern Egypt, and despite the use of radiocarbon dating.

In 1895 Petrie excavated at the site of Abydos, the earliest dynastic capital of Egypt. It was the royal burial site for the first two dynasties and a great religious shrine, as the location of the grave of the god Osiris. Everything of monumental and visual value at the site had been removed by Mariette and Maspero to the museum in Cairo, and all that was left were the remains of smashed pieces of pottery. By identifying the names of kings from pottery fragments and arranging them into a sequence of stylistic similarities and differences, Petrie was able to create a chronology for Abydos—with its tombs, shrines, and royal monuments—a site with evidence of the evolution of social complexity at the beginning of the Dynastic period, and a descendent of the Neolithic culture of Nagada. Once again Petrie used sequence dating or seriation to map changes in the Predynastic period and to identify different phases of predynastic pottery production.

Many of his contemporaries thought Petrie's detailed field methods, which required the careful recording of the exact position of each object, dreary and a waste of time. However, they provided the data with which to begin to discern patterns of archaeological information that could then be further extrapolated and interpreted. In 1904 Petrie wrote a manual—*Methods and Aims in Archaeology*. While it detailed the use of the serious stuff of archaeology, such as seriation and stratigraphy, Petrie's book also contained lots of useful advice for the field archaeologist about the choice and management of workmen and the necessity for archaeologists to get close to their data. Many of his field techniques are still in use—such as using chemistry to preserve delicate objects in the field and using photography for records. Petrie was a skilled photographer, and he developed his photographs on site to ensure that poor shots could be retaken. His own field records, preserved in the Petrie Museum at University College London, include registers, distribution lists, and tomb cards, which are still being studied and reinterpreted today.

See also Foundation of Great Egyptian Collections in England and France (1815–1835); Decipherment of Egyptian Hieroglyphics (1824); Publication of *Description de l'Egypte* (1826); Publication of *The Manners and Customs of the Ancient Egyptians* (1847); Mariette, Antiquities Law, and the Egyptian Museum (1858); Publication of *Denkmaler aus Aegypten und Aethiopien* (1859); Publication of *A Thousand Miles up the Nile* (1877); Discovery of the Amarna Tablets (1887); Discovering Tutankhamen's Tomb (1922–1932).

Further Reading

Drower, M. 1985. *Flinders Petrie: A life in archaeology*. London: Gollancz.

Drower, M. 1999. Sir William Matthews Flinders Petrie (1853–1942). In *Encyclopedia of Archaeology: The great archaeologists,* ed. T. Murray, 221–232. Santa Barbara, CA: ABC-CLIO.

Janssen, R. M. 1992. *The first hundred years: Egyptology at University College London, 1892–1992.* London: University College.

Uhle Begins Scientific Archaeology in Peru (1895–1940)

The four centuries of monument mining, ruin quarrying, and grave pillaging in Peru after the Spanish conquest led to a vast number of ceramic, textile, wood, and lithic artifacts collected by museums and individuals in Europe and the Americas. Very few of the vast numbers of gold artifacts ever made it to museums and were melted down locally. There was little information about the provenance of the remaining artifacts, and the first knowledge of Andean archaeology developed based on the analysis and comparison of the different types and styles of Peruvian artifacts in collections.

Knowledge of the history and development of civilization in Peru was, at first, determined by Inca propaganda. As an elite of 40,000 people, the Inca ruled over an empire of some 10 million other people, and at its peak, for a hundred years or so before the arrival of the Spanish, it dominated a vast geographic area of some 4,000 kilometers, from central Ecuador to central Chile. Inca history determined that there had been no other civilization before them, and that the Inca state had been founded at the religious capital of Cuzco—the navel of the civilized universe.

The great Prussian naturalist Alexander von Humboldt was the first scholar to bring Peruvian antiquities to the attention of Western scholars when he published an account of his travels through Latin America in 1814. As the collections of these artifacts grew in European museums, so did interest in understanding their origins and history. The German scholar Max Uhle (1856–1944) analyzed Inca artifacts from Cuzco and the older site of Tiwanaku at museums in Dresden, Berlin, and Leipzig before traveling to Peru in the 1890s. Uhle's first excavation was the site of Pachacamac (ca. 600 AD), the most important Inca settlement on the coast, near the modern Peruvian capital of Lima. Paying close attention to its stratigraphy, Uhle discerned that underneath the Inca burials there were at least three other levels of burials and styles of grave goods. He designated these stratigraphy by relating them to the identifiably Tiwanaku-style middle one, while the two on either side, both more local in style, were designated post-Tiwanaku and pre-Tiwanaku.

From 1900 on Uhle's research in Peru was funded by the University of California and other American institutions which purchased the artifacts from his excavations at the Huaca de La Luna site in the Moche Valley (ca. 700 AD), on the south coast at sites in the Ica (ca. 1000 AD) and Nazca (ca. 250 AD) valleys, and on the central coast near Ancon (ca. 600 BC). At all of these sites he found similar depths of stratigraphy to those he had found at Pachacamac. The majority of Uhle's collections of Peruvian archaeology were deposited at the museum at the University of California at Berkeley, where they attracted the interest of the anthropologist Alfred Kroeber, who interpreted them as evidence of his theories about the development of art and civilization.

Ruins of the ancient city of Pachacamac in present-day Peru. The Huari people built Pachacamac ca. AD 600–800. (Philip Baird/www.anthroarcheart.org)

The University of California at Berkeley continued its work in Peru in the 1930s and 1940s with excavations by Kroeber and his students, including William Duncan Strong. In the middle of the 1940s, with support from the new Institute for Andean Research, Strong, now professor at Columbia University in New York City, assembled a number of archaeologists and a multidisciplinary team to undertake the Viru Valley project in coastal Peru.

As part of the Viru Valley project American archaeologist Junius Bird excavated the site of Huaca Prieta on the Peruvian coast. Bird unearthed evidence of a preceramic, sedentary fishing and squash and bean farming community, who also grew the cotton they wove into superbly decorated twined textiles. It was dated to 2000 BC.

In the late 1940s American archaeologists Gordon Willey, Donald Collier, and John Rowe revisited the site of Huari, the capital of the Huari Empire in the Peruvian highlands. Because of the similarity in styles between Huari and Tiwanaco, Huari culture was first described wrongly as "Tiwanacoid." It is now understood that while Huari culture was contemporaneous with Tiwanaku, they were distinctly local cultures, products of their geography and environments—Huari in the central highlands, and Tiwanaku in the southern Altiplano and Titicaca region.

In the 1950s Bird's Peruvian preceramic site was further researched by Edward Lanning and Thomas Patterson. Excavating sites dated to 2300 BC, they established the significance of Peru's maritime economy to the development of Peruvian civilization. At the same time, archaeologists from Berkeley under John Rowe meticulously built on the ceramic research of Uhle and Kroeber to work out the pottery seriation and chronology of the south coast of Peru. In 1962 this resulted in the development of a six-period master sequence for Peruvian archaeology, which is still used today.

The Inca were the only culture to unite the whole of Peru—and that was only for a couple of hundred years before the Spanish arrived. They were an anomaly—as recognized by their own history. What is extraordinary about the last 4,000 years of Peruvian civilization and its archaeology is its complexity and its variations—the range of developments, the manifestations of groups and cultures across different regions and environments, and the complex relationships between them.

See also Establishment of Major U.S. Archaeological Institutions (1846–1866); Machu Picchu Found (1911); Stratigraphic Excavation in the Americas (1911–1913); Excavation of Fell's Cave (1936–1937); Publication of *Origin and Development of Andean Civilization* (1942); Publication of *Prehistoric Settlement Patterns in the Viru Valley* (1953); Excavation of Chavin de Huantar (1966–1980); Chan Chan Inscribed on the World Heritage List (1986); Discovering the "Lord of Sipan" (1987).

Further Reading

Menzel, D. 1977. *The archaeology of Ancient Peru and the work of Max Uhle.* Berkeley, CA: Lowie Museum.

Moseley, M. E. 2001. *The Incas and their ancestors: the archaeology of Peru.* London: Thames and Hudson.

Raymond, S. 2001. Peru. In *Encyclopedia of Archaeology. History and Discoveries,* ed. T. Murray, 1013–1018. Santa Barbara, CA: ABC-CLIO.

Section Three

Archaeology in the Twentieth Century and Beyond

WORLD ARCHAEOLOGY

In this essay I survey the history of archaeology in the twentieth century and seek to trace the broad boundaries of the archaeology of the first decade of the current century. As with the preceding essays my focus is on gaining an understanding of the development of archaeology as a discipline and the creation of what has been called "the archaeological perspective." By this I mean the notion that archaeological information, and the theories and methods that are used to both create it and analyze it, exist within a web of disciplines that help us comprehend the meanings of human history and the sense of what it is to be human.

In the earlier essays I sought to demonstrate that first antiquarian studies and subsequently archaeological research have been locked in a close and abiding relationship with the disciplines of history and anthropology. Indeed, for much of that period, and certainly for the nineteenth century, the theories archaeologists used to create plausible inferences about past human actions or the natures of past human societies were to all intents and purposes first ethnological and then subsequently anthropological theories. In this essay I demonstrate that this close relationship continued through the twentieth century and into contemporary practice.

However, continuity does not imply a lack of change in the context and content of that relationship. By the end of the nineteenth century it was generally agreed that archaeologists could contribute to our search for understanding by doing two things: first, by writing the ethnic prehistories of nations (through the mechanism of culture history), and second, by exploring the physical and cultural evolution of human beings. In the twentieth century archaeologists continued to do both (and to expand into other areas), but the context of archaeological studies was to change dramatically as developments in anthropological theory and the rise of a more self-consciously *archaeological* theory altered ideas of how archaeologists contribute to the study of human beings.

In this essay I review these continuities and discontinuities in the theory and practice of archaeology within the broader context of the creation of a global archaeology. During the twentieth century archaeology truly came of age and the 131 milestones I have included in Section Three give some idea of this massive expansion across all aspects of the discipline: areas being investigated; numbers of professional archaeologists; numbers of university departments, museums, government, and private agencies training or employing archaeologists; varieties of archaeology being practiced; time periods being investigated; and, of course, the social and cultural effects of the discipline. Indeed one of the great ironies for archaeology in the twentieth century is that these factors, which helped make archaeology a global enterprise, were the same factors that have tended to undermine the utility (or even the value) of a single overarching discipline that commands universal allegiance among practicing archaeologists.

As has been my practice in the earlier essays, I do not create a linked narrative history of archaeology in the period under review, focusing instead on major changes in our understanding of the "archaeological perspective." This means that I will not discuss in detail the history of any one aspect of archaeology, such as its highly significant relationships with paleoanthropology in the search for an understanding of human physical and cultural evolution, or its equally important links with archaeometry or archaeological science, which have been the source of so much important information about past climates, ecologies, and technologies and their intersections with human beings. More detailed discussion is found among the numerous milestones of Section Three.

Perhaps the most significant of all stories in the history of archaeology has been the rapid expansion in the range and variety of what archaeologists regard as information or data. Four centuries ago William Camden's data comprised ancient texts, landscapes, and material culture. In the twenty-first century archaeologists can use the discoveries of science and technology to wrest information from a near bewildering array of sources—everything from dating emissions of light from sands to recovering DNA from ancient tools. However, all of these great developments flowed, in part, from another somewhat more basic factor—the extraordinary increase in the amount of field survey and excavation that occurred during the twentieth century. Part of the reason for that great expansion has been the need to mitigate the impact of development on the archaeological record. In this sense the rapid growth in the world economy, particularly in Europe and North America, has had significant impacts across the globe, especially in major resource-development projects and development in the cores of major cities. In Section Three I mention the great importance of the Abu Simbel campaign as an exemplar of this process, but there are now many highly significant archaeology projects (such as Five Points in New York City) that are the result of the pressures of development.

I have mentioned that during the twentieth century the practice of archaeology moved from its birthplace and heartland of Europe, the Middle East, and North America into the rest of the world. Of course archaeology was practiced outside this heartland during the nineteenth century but generally only in small-scale and intermittent projects. The creation of a world archaeology, the greatest achievement of the discipline during the twentieth century, was the result of a wide range of factors, such as developments in method, theory, training, and education; changing attitudes to the importance of archaeological heritage; the growth of different interests in the past (especially among indigenous groups, the citizens of postcolonial nations, and of course diverse groups within societies); and the massive expansion in funding from both private and government sources. This last factor is a sure sign of the great significance of archaeology and archaeological heritage in the modern world.

The archaeology of the twenty-first century is dynamic and engaged with the societies who support it and consume its product. While the conceptual field is crowded and diverse, the resulting debates and disagreements are a sure testimony that archaeology has real consequence and that it retains its capacity to shed light on what it is to be human.

"Before the Deluge": Culture History Before the "New" Archaeology

In the last essay I discussed the rise of culture history in the nineteenth century, and in this section I will review some of its manifestations in the twentieth century. Although the overwhelming impression of archaeology in the past forty years has been of great upheavals in archaeological theory and broader perceptions of the purpose of the discipline, it is important to remember that for much of the twentieth century the program of culture history held undisputed sway. Indeed, it has often been observed that, notwithstanding all the overt disciplinary turbulence, the vast bulk of practitioners worldwide still adhere to many of its core principles.

Given the rich tradition of culture history archaeology in the twentieth century, there is a great deal that I simply do not have the space to discuss in detail. Chief among these is the absolutely crucial work of Gordon Childe, whose great contributions to archaeology have been extensively discussed elsewhere (see, for example, Harris 1994; Gathercole et al. 1995; Patterson and Orser 2004; Trigger 1980b). Childe's use of the concept of the archaeological culture, his proposition of the Neolithic and urban revolutions, and above all his sense of seeking answers to universal questions related to the process of civilization made him an archaeologist of enduring influence. Indeed, he is perhaps the archaeologist who did the most to make questions of social evolution mainstream within culture history, fifty years before the more avowedly "social" archaeologies of processual and postprocessual archaeology in the later decades of the twentieth century.

The tremendously important history of the use of culture historical archaeology by Nazi race scientists (which Gordon Childe was closely involved in; see Childe 1933, 1934) has been extensively explored by historians of archaeology (see, for example, Arnold 1990; McCann 1988; Veit 1989). Somewhat less contentious, but equally important, are the contributions made by Franz Boas (1858–1922) to the development of culture historicism, and that of the Scandinavian diffusionists such as Birkett-Smith, and the British varieties proposed by W. J. Perry, Grafton Elliot Smith, and W. H. R. Rivers. These have all been adequately discussed (see, for example, Daniel 1971, 1975, 1981b; Harris 1968; Langham 1981; Lyman et al. 1997; Lyman and O'Brien 2006; Trigger 1978, 1980b, 1989; Voget 1975). Clearly, Smith and Perry were to have a profound effect on the conduct of British archaeology during the period from 1900 to 1930, but as such their view of the historical process was really a development of the clash between Montelius and Reinach, which had occurred in the previous century.

I will briefly focus analysis on the *Kulturkreis* theoreticians of middle Europe and their links with Gustav Kossinna, who was accepted by Gordon Childe as a major influence on his conceptualization of the archaeological culture (Childe 1958; see also Trigger 1980b). However, one key assumption links all the varieties of culture historicism: culture was a special phenomenal domain; its actions interpretable in terms of its own laws, which were not reducible to psychological processes. Further, the operations of culture could not be explained by reductionist psychological processes. Here was a concept that was, in philosophical terms, essential. It was a thing-in-itself, a function of human nature, a special product with no natural referent. But how could it be described and then subjected to analysis?

The development of culture historicism was stimulated by an unlikely source. Adolf Bastian (1826–1905) had contended that there were elementary ideas common to all mankind and that they were a function of being human. These ideas only became historically significant in the minds of groups of people who inhabited particular geographical areas. The notion that distinct groups of people also had distinct territories had long been understood; after all, the natural world provided one justification, and the observation of human groups provided another. It was clear that different groups of people (no matter how difference was to be explained or measured) maintained their difference through a kind of isolation. Difference was also increased by the fact that different geographic conditions posed different adaptive problems; hence, they potentiated further differentiation in human ideas.

In Bastian's view human history could be interpreted as the results of a process whereby this isolation was broken down. In his view the great variety of human behavior was a product of isolation. However, the process could not be considered to be discontinuous. In the contemporary world, much of the cultural and social variety found among the "ethnographic other" was the product of such geographically regionalizing forces. Although Bastian was committed to the notion of essential psychic unity, his characterization of the process of isolation and unification was to provide a firm plank for the development of culture historicism.

In the second essay I briefly mentioned the work of Gustav Klemm as being central to the development of the culture history program. The author of a ten-volume culture history of mankind (1843), Klemm had sought the explanation of cultural difference in the mind and the products of mind. In Klemm's view there were active and passive races (the Germans, not surprisingly, were considered active) and these races proceeded throughout history on preordained paths of "upward" development. The active races proceeded faster than the passive, and the passive were really only capable of progress through the influence of active races. Once again, while there was no necessary geographical distinctiveness of races, the inhabitants of hotter, tropical climates were more likely to be passive than active. The crucial point here is that the distinctiveness of culture was an outgrowth of permanent, racially based, psychological difference.

With the growth of global exploration in the mid- to late nineteenth century, Klemm's classifications, which were derived from the older ethnographies and earlier explorations and which had directly influenced Tylor and Lubbock as well, could be placed on a sounder empirical footing. Klemm's central thesis, that there was a high correlation between technology, economy, environment, and race, was taken as the starting point for a new human geography. Just as Tylor had considered the history of contacts between peoples to be of great importance, contact that was measurable in terms of trade and exchange, the new geographers regarded the explanation of patterned distributions of items of technology and material culture as having high historical value.

Pitt-Rivers drew the same conclusion when discussing the explanations for similarities in material culture (see Pitt-Rivers 1906; Thompson 1977). He recognized the fact that Lubbock and Tylor had more frequently opted for independent invention as an explanation, in deference to the need to support the arguments of monogenism. However, in his view the monogenist/polygenist debate had been made entirely marginal by the work of Charles Darwin. Therefore, physical unity could not be assumed, and the job of the archaeologist—to explain cultural difference and similarity—could proceed unfettered by the demands of revealed religion:

> Amongst the questions which anthropology has to deal with, that of the descent of man has been so elaborately treated, and at the same time popularized by Mr Darwin, that it would be serving no useful purpose were I to allude to any of the arguments on which he has based his belief in the unbroken continuity of man's development from the lower forms of life. Nor is it necessary for one to discuss the question of the *monogenesis* or *polygenesis* of man. On this subject also Mr Darwin has shown how unlikely it is that races so closely resembling each other, both physically and mentally, and interbreeding as they invariably do, should on the theory of development have originated independently in different localities. Neither are we now, I think, in a position to doubt that civilization has been gradually and progressively developed, and that a very extended, though not by any means uniform, period of growth must have elapsed before we could arrive at the very high state of culture which we now enjoy. (Pitt-Rivers 1872, 158–159; original emphasis)

Although distinct differences of opinion would arise over whether human beings closely resembled each other mentally, and whether these "great" differences were in some way the result, or perhaps even the cause, of "lesser" physical differences, most antiquaries, ethnologists, or anthropologists would have agreed with Pitt-Rivers that similarities in material culture between different groups of people could only be explained in one, or perhaps both, of two ways, one by the notion of inheritance and

> the other by the view of the independent origin of culture in distant centers, assimilated in consequence of the similitude of the conditions under which it arose . . . It would be an error to apply either of these principles exclusively to the interpretation of the phenomena of civilization. In considering the origin of species we are under the necessity of allying ourselves either on the side of the *monogenists* or that of the *polygenists;* but in speaking of the origin of culture, both principles may be, and undoubtedly are, applicable. There is, in fact, no royal road to knowledge on this subject by the application of general principles: the history of each art, custom, or institution must be diligently worked out by itself, availing ourselves of the clue afforded by race as the only probable channel of communication and development. (Pitt-Rivers 1872, 160; original emphasis)

Notwithstanding Pitt-Rivers's appeal to strict inductions within the general sphere of racial theory and an opposition to the application of general principles, Friedrich Ratzel (1844–1904) presented European antiquaries and archaeologists with a framework that would indeed allow the application of general principles to the explanation of cultural variation. Ratzel's work (especially his *Anthropogeographie* [1882–1901]) spanned the entire globe, and his command over the information allowed the proposition of what he considered to be illuminating comparisons:

> The boundary between countries which do and do not use iron corresponds with those of other important regions of ethnographic distribution. Where there is no iron, cattle-breeding, the staple of which is oxen, buffaloes, sheep, goats, horses, camels, and elephants, is also unknown; pigs and poultry are seldom bred in lands without iron . . . In America, Oceania, and Australia [where iron is lacking] we have a much older stage of development; group marriage, exogamy, mother right, and clan division; in Europe, Africa, and Asia, the patriarchal system of the family, monogamy, states in the modern sense. Thus among mankind also east and west stand over against each other. America is the extreme east of the human race, and thus we may expect to

find there older stages of development than in Africa and Europe, the extreme west. (quoted in Voget 1975, 342–343)

While Ratzel might seem unconvincing today, in the heyday of culture history, when the drive was to produce historical explanations for difference and similarity in material culture, in fact all products of mind, both social and cultural, his natural classifications of geographical provinces and the chains of their connections were highly influential.

Further development of the *Kulturkreis* program occurred with the work of one of his students. Leo Frobenius (1873–1938) coined the term and defined it in the context of contacts between the Malayan archipelago and the East Coast of Africa— "a relatively bounded interactional region where similar culture features existed by virtue of historic contact" (Voget 1975, 350; see especially his *Weltgeschichte des Krieges* [1903]). However, the most complete methodological statement of *Kulturkreis* was to come from Fritz Graebner in *Methode der Ethnologie* (1911). Here the technique of recovering older cultural configurations through the analysis of the patterned distribution of cultural elements was demonstrated and defended (see Heine-Geldern 1964).

In Graebner's work the method was further developed to allow for the tentative establishment of the original homeland of a *kreis.* To enable these homelands to be identified, the entire range of sources of similarity and diversity were brought into play (physical, mental, and linguistic characters). Significantly, the fundamental process of cultural change for Graebner was migration—real, analyzable groups of people carrying real, analyzable cultural inventories. The archaeologists of the late nineteenth century had already arrived at that conclusion via a different route from Klemm, but they greeted Graebner's work with understandable enthusiasm as an independent confirmation of their own views.

The critical point of conjunction was at the level of culture process. Rather than holding the pluralist views of Pitt-Rivers, both the *Kulturkreis* and hyperdiffusionist anthropologists considered that all elements of material culture had only been invented once. Variability in material culture was not the outgrowth of multiple sequences of stages but of the effects of different environmental and mental conditions on the original invention.

The *Kulturkreis* school unashamedly opted for diffusion as the explanation of change, but to do so it had to remove the notion of psychic unity from ethnological theory. For Ratzel and his followers there were very few qualities of mind that were universal, and the presence of cultural similarities so widely spaced could only be explained by trade and migration from a *kreis*. Antiquaries and archaeologists, because of their close association with philologists, had long been used to the idea that such *kreise* or homelands had existed in the past, and that these should be real and archaeologically discoverable entities.

Once again, there was to be a coincidence of interest between the ethnologists, anthropologists, and archaeologists. If the integrative power of ethnology had been demonstrated by Nilsson back in the 1840s, a new framework of integration was required to establish racially or ethnically distinct groups of people within the classificatory chaos of late nineteenth and early twentieth century European prehistory. This new framework widened the basis of classification beyond the physical, to take account of the mental and all the products of mind. Important confirmation of the validity of this approach had been provided by the culture historians, but archaeologists were now to be called upon to deploy their classificatory skills to establish the material cultural correlates of distinct groups of peoples. The search for archaeological cultures was to be undertaken with renewed vigor and to reach its apogee in the archaeology of the great empires of the Near East, in Crete, and of course in Europe through Childe's work.

This change in approach for archaeology made possible, and was made possible by, developments in ethnological and anthropological theory. Clearly the concept of the archaeological culture could not be operationalized without the theoretical presuppositions of ethnological and geographical theory. Similarly, ethnological theory would have been impoverished without archaeological data. This circularity of arrangement, without the development of the empirical ramifications of culture historical theories, was to fuel archaeological research well into the twentieth century right across the globe.

By the end of the nineteenth century the connections and distinctions between archaeology and anthropology, as well as archaeology and history, had essentially been established. Archaeology, its conceptual field defined and secure within various traditions of anthropological and historical research, and its methodology developed to a stage where the discussion of temporal and cultural classifications could appeal to a widening store of empirical phenomena, was free to pursue problems of largely internal moment. Although in the United States the predominance of cultural rather than social anthropology meant that the boundaries between archaeology and "historical" anthropology were somewhat blurred, the same emphasis on writing prehistory and technical matters of classification and data retrieval was still present.

While it is clearly the case that changes in fashion and orientation in anthropology and history directly affected the interests and approaches of archaeologists working under the aegis of either anthropological tradition, practitioners could keep pace with such changes in meaning by changing the terms of their translations of material phenomena into first, archaeological, and then subsequently, anthropological, data. These changes were readily accomplished for four reasons.

First, archaeological data were considered to be impoverished testaments of human action compared with the richer data derived from sociocultural anthropology. Meaning and the power to convince thus lay with the disciplines that "managed" the latter data set.

Second, archaeological methodologies of description and classification were substantially relative rather than absolute. Given the anthropological and historical construction of archaeological data, there were few empirical grounds upon which those data, of themselves, could seriously disturb the intentions of their interpreters.

Third, despite the overt theorizing of practitioners such as Julian Steward (1902–1972) (see especially *Theory of Cultural Change: The Methodology of Multilinear Evolution* [1955]), Leslie White (1900–1975) (see especially *The Science of Culture: The Study of Man and Civilization* [1949]), and Gordon Childe, the bulk of archaeologists were largely implicit consumers of theory, devoting their energies to methodological and technical issues of data collection and classification.

Fourth, given the essentially empiricist orientation of archaeologists in the years before the 1960s, theoretical disputes were either settled on the authority of the archaeologists involved or were simply set aside for some future time when the data were in. Rarely were they explicitly discussed because they were considered to be speculative and lacking the possibility of an archaeological contribution to their solution. Thus, again with the exception of practitioners such as Childe, Steward, and Grahame Clark, few archaeologists recognized that existing differences of opinion about concepts and accounts of the nature of archaeological knowledge that lay within the source areas of archaeological theory could act as spurs to the development of such theory.

It would be going too far to argue that in the period prior to the proposition of the core epistemological insights of the "new" archaeology the discipline was untroubled by conflict and dispute. This patently is not the case, especially when we consider such issues as the proposition of diffusion or independent invention as alternative "motors" of culture change, the conflict between unilinear and multilinear views of the same process, and the celebrated disagreements between Clark (for example, 1939) and Childe over the merits of historical materialist analysis and the relations between archaeology and society. Differences of opinion were not confined to conceptual issues, however; they were present in the epistemological realms of the discipline as well. It is also true, as Fahenstock (1984) has noted, that after the 1930s archaeologists sought to understand aspects of the archaeological record through a variety of theoretical perspectives that now look to be quite "contemporary" in orientation and substance (see also Daniel 1975, 1981a; Leone 1982).

Notwithstanding these qualifications, however, the archaeology of the period up to the 1960s was far less troubled and divergent than that of the last forty-five years. Given the means of dispute settlement, and the overarching emphasis on empiricist epistemology with its links to a contained, essentially self-concerned archaeology, archaeologists dealt with perceived differences between the methodological rhetoric of archaeologists and what they actually *did* in three ways. First, these differences were considered to be part and parcel of an "impoverished" database with the inherent insecurities expressed by the notion of the "ladder of inference" (see Hawkes 1954; Smith 1955). Second, they were considered to be of no great significance given the greater meaning attached to sociocultural anthropological or historical researches. Third, they were considered to be resolvable by further technical sophistication in data gathering and analysis. All this was soon to change, and archaeology would never recover from the "loss of innocence" so clearly described by David Clarke (1973).

Theory Takes Center Stage: Debate About the Fundamentals of Archaeology

Beginning with a series of classic papers in the early 1960s and gaining notoriety with the landmark *New Perspectives in Archaeology* (Binford and Binford 1968), the program of processual archaeology sought to develop a different approach to achieving the tenets of anthropological archaeology—the idea of an archaeology that could make a significant contribution to anthropological theory. In this sense the goals of its major proponents (especially Binford 1962, 1964, 1972, 1978, 1981, 1983a, 1983b) were in part closely linked with the traditions of archaeology, and in part at least derived from the work of Willey and Phillips (1958), Leslie White (1949), and of course W. W. Taylor (1948).

However, processual archaeology was also self-consciously a major departure from the traditions of culture historical archaeology that had held sway for so long. Processual archaeology sought to move archaeology beyond classification and chronology to an understanding of human behavior in the prehistoric past (see especially Klejn 1977; Wylie 1982).

This last goal was to be achieved through a rigorous application of the scientific method to the archaeological process, to create hypotheses and test them via the development of technical processes and methodological theories. New sources of theory, derived from systems analysis and ecology, were linked with a long-standing focus on cultural evolution to create a framework where the archaeologists focused on what was generalizable or universal about human behavior. The specifics of local histories were considered to be capable of deduction from these more general principles and were further refined by the fine-scale analysis of local conditions. Archaeology's great contribution to anthropology was to be the characterization of these universals.

There was (and still is) considerable variation among self-declared processual archaeologists about their adherence to some, or all, of these fundamental principles, and there is considerable evidence to support an argument that the processual program evolved in the years between 1962 and 1985. Nonetheless, a commitment to functionalist and cultural evolutionist social theory, and to the notion that for archaeology to be a science it had to adopt the methodologies of sciences such as physics, lay at the heart of the program. These two "commitments" sparked considerable debate within archaeology, evoking strong support and equally strong rejection among the community of practitioners. An important area of debate was the "newness" of the "new" archaeology, and whether its break with traditional culture historical archaeology was really so sharp and transforming as that (for example) between classical Newtonian mechanics and the physics of relativity.

There were several camps in a debate that was clouded by the now well-recognized ambiguity of Thomas Kuhn's formulation of "paradigm" (1962) and the rhetorical advantage seized by both opponents and proponents of the "new" archaeology when they sought support from Kuhn's writings. The interests of the parties also varied widely. At one stage the core issue of the dispute appeared to rest on a link between "newness" and "archaeology as a science." In more recent times discussion centered on a putative link between the adoption of functionalist social theory and a positivist epistemology of science. Existing variation within the "culture" of archaeology, primarily located in differing interpretations of the links between archaeology, anthropology, and history that were held on either side of the Atlantic, also caused some variety in response. See, for example, the terms under which J. Hawkes (1968) and Hogarth (1972) took issue with McBurney and Clarke (1968).

One argument (J. Hawkes 1968) that was revived by the founder of post-processual archaeology, Ian Hodder, contended that archaeologists had long held the interpretative goals of the "new" archaeology, but that methodological attempts to circumvent the "ladder of inference" would replace the humanistic goals of archaeology with a mindless scientism. The new methodological aspects were thus a dangerous chimera, promising expanded understanding but delivering only a shell of determined human action. Another argument, most clearly associated with Martin (1971), was of the "mine eyes have been opened and now I can see" variety that made explicit appeal to the Kuhnian notions of gestalt shift and incommensurability. This view, ably supported by the work of Clarke (1972), Hill (1972), and Sterud (1973, 1978) (but see also the criticism of Cribb [1980]), deployed Kuhn to support a rhetoric of group identity and solidarity that even in the middle 1970s was questionable, to say the least (see, for example, Binford 1983a). Significantly, archaeologists were by no means alone in their appeal to the reality of a Kuhnian revolution within their discipline (see, for example, Scholte 1983).

Both views were explicitly attacked by Meltzer (1979; see also his 1981a response to Custer 1981), who attempted, by the risky tactic of using "what Kuhn really said/meant," to demolish the claim that there had been a substantial enough shift in the metaphysics of archaeology to qualify for the birth of a new paradigm. In Meltzer's view there had, instead, been a continuation of an "anthropological" metaphysics of archaeology, and the change from an idealist to a materialist ontology was merely part and parcel of the exploration of an existing ontological antinomy within anthropology itself. Meltzer concluded that there had been a change in methodology, not metaphysics. Hence the "new" archaeology had failed the test of a new paradigm. And the change was nowhere near equivalent to a major shift in scientific thinking. This assessment attracted trenchant criticism, especially from Wylie (1982, 374). For her, and for Binford, the move to functionalism and materialism was both the cause and effect of a genuinely new way of seeing the nature of archaeological records and the possibilities of archaeology as a discipline.

It is not my intention here to pronounce upon the subject myself, rather to indicate the fact that the rhetorical use by "new" archaeologists of the Kuhnian account of scientific change was especially powerful at a time when "new" archaeologists were attempting to illustrate the significance of their program as the best means of both resolving existing methodological problems in the discipline and expanding the nature of archaeological knowledge. Perhaps the real significance of the changes wrought by the "new" archaeologists can be gauged by the fact that since their proposal, debate among practitioners about such matters has intensified rather than lapsed.

The debate about the "newness" of the "new" archaeology was, and still is, a political one in the sense that it is a debate between rival readings of the authorities of archaeology. Even allowing for the inherent ambiguities of the Kuhnian account, it is preferable to conclude that claims of revolution or paradigm shift within archaeology, precisely because such changes are still very much in their infancy and are still the subject of intense debate, are much less interesting than the conflicting readings of the fundamentals about the archaeological perspective that they reveal.

Despite all the debate that has surrounded the "newness" of the "new" archaeology and the respective values of attempts made under its aegis to reestablish disciplinary objectives and practices within science, and bearing in mind that there was never wholesale agreement among "new" archaeologists about all conceptual and epistemological matters arising from that project, few practitioners and external observers have questioned that the conditions of archaeological practice have changed greatly since the 1960s. Even the most cautious observers will point to the substantial impact that developments in techniques of dating, excavation, and analysis and the growth of computer-aided systems of classification and ordination have had on the practice of archaeology (see, for example, Brothwell and Higgs 1969; Burghleigh 1981; Doran and Hodson 1975; Taylor 1985).

It is widely recognized that the application of radiometric dating systems to archaeology replaced, in most circumstances, the contentious and time-consuming practice of constructing relative chronologies in prehistoric archaeology, freeing practitioners from "floating" chronologies and allowing them sufficient time and energy to pursue issues of culture history and culture process. Archaeologists had been writing culture history since the days of Worsaae and Nilsson, a practice that increased in scale and scope with the work of practitioners such as Petrie and Montelius. Similarly, archaeologists and ethnologists such as Lubbock, Tylor, and Morgan had also considered more general issues of culture process within social-evolutionary frameworks.

These same issues had also been the subject of intense discussion in the period between the turn of the century and the advent of radiocarbon dating (see, for example, Childe 1925, 1935, 1956; Kluckhohn 1939, 1940; MacWhite

1956; Randall-MacIver 1932; Steward 1942, 1955; Steward and Setzler 1938; Tallgren 1937; Willey and Phillips 1958, but see also Fahenstock 1984; Meltzer 1979). Despite the fact that practitioners had been willing to advance dates for culture history, they did so on the understanding that dates established by inference from relative chronologies were inherently insecure.

Similarly, the insecurity of relative chronology flowed through to an insecurity about the values of generalizations that were habitually made about the causes of cultural change and variation and gained their most popular expression in the diffusion versus independent evolution debate (see, for example, Adams 1968; Daniel 1971; Haag 1957; Kroeber 1952; Perry 1924). The rivalry between unilinear and multilinear evolutionary trajectories as explanations for cultural change and variation was a further extension of that fundamental dispute. The degree to which radiometric systems of absolute dating were to make possible a review of culture histories and notions of culture process has been systematically discussed by Renfrew (1976). Critically, absolute chronology did not just require a realignment of existing chronologies, it also implied the need for a wholesale reassessment of what was to be explained.

The advent of absolute chronology was to have a greater impact on the practice of prehistoric archaeology than the initial nineteenth-century recognition of a high human antiquity, even though there have been consistent attempts to normalize its implications in much the same ways. On one level it made possible the development of a truly world prehistory (see Clark 1961). On another, subsequent developments such as potassium argon dating presented practitioners with a human timescale spanning some millions of years, which at the very least led to a revival of links between paleoanthropology and prehistoric archaeology (see, for example, Isaac 1972, 1981). While on still another level, practitioners were confronted with the need to understand the meaning of the archaeological record over shorter (10,000 year or 1,000 year) time spans. The quantification of both long and short time spans raised the critical issue of the highly complex and unique nature of archaeological records as records of human action and their implications for the constitution of general anthropological theory. In this sense absolute time was surely better than relative time, but how were archaeologists to interpret the meaning of archaeological records as records of human behavior, given the inherent imprecision of absolute archaeological time?

These were some of the direct implications of absolute dating. However, when we consider developments in techniques of excavation, analysis, and classification that have occurred since the 1960s, additional aspects of the significance of quantifiable time as requiring changes in the conditions of archaeological practice can be noted. Perhaps the most obvious of these has been the maintenance (indeed the development) of close relations between archaeology and the earth and physical sciences, especially through the multiplication of dating and sourcing systems that have flowed from activity in these areas. One outcome of this close relationship has been the development of specializations within archaeology itself, which are generally referred to under the rubric of archaeometry or "archaeological science." Another outcome has been an intensified sense of ontological and epistemological schizophrenia for archaeology. Practitioners live in two worlds, those of the natural and human sciences, and ideals and explanatory exemplars can (and frequently do) differ widely between those worlds.

A further aspect of that relationship has been the increasing impact of geomorphology on archaeology. Earth sciences in this situation have been productively linked with perspectives drawn from paleontology to form the basis of other specializations within archaeological practice, specifically of taphonomy (Behrensmeyer and Hill 1980; Gifford 1978, 1980, 1981). The links between archaeology and those fields of study that are currently grouped as the environmental sciences (particularly ecology) have been strong since Worsaae and the Danish Kitchenmidden Committee first sought to establish the environmental context of human action in prehistoric Denmark. These links were further strengthened in the period up to the 1960s through the articulation of palynological evidence and other perspectives drawn from geography, a practice clearly associated with the Fenland Committee and the work of J. G. D. Clark. Again, since the 1960s these areas of emphasis have also spawned specializations within archaeology that have either sought to integrate disciplinary goals under an ecological umbrella (for example, Butzer 1975, 1978, 1980, 1982) or to simply add texture to environmental reconstructions and to taphonomic issues (see, for example, Bryant and Holloway 1983).

On an entirely different level, practitioners sought (and found) in geography and economics both exemplars of changing directions in behavioral analysis (see especially Clarke 1968; but see also Chorley and Haggett 1967; Harvey 1969; Haggett 1965; Polanyi 1944; Zipf 1949) and models for the interpretation of settlement patterns (see e.g., Clarke 1977; Hodder and Orton 1976; Johnson 1977) and economic behavior (see e.g., J. G. D. Clark 1952; Godelier 1977; Hindess and Hurst 1975, 1977; Sahlins 1972).

The maintenance or strengthening of links between archaeology and the physical, earth, and life sciences and the parallel development of specializations within archaeology are examples of the influence of changes in analytical procedures. In the case of geography and economics there was an extension of links with the human sciences as well. Furthermore, the connection between temporal quantification and determination of rates of change has flowed on to an increasingly close association between archaeology and mathematical fields, such as topology, and the borrowing of physical and biological theories of change, such as quantum mechanics, punctuated equilibria, and even chaos theory (see especially Cooke 1979; Gould and Eldredge 1977; Prigogine 1978; Renfrew 1978, 1982b; Rosen 1979; van der Leeuw and McGlade 1997; Zeeman 1977).

The development of computer-aided systems of statistical analysis was widely recognized as a force for change in the conditions of archaeological practice. Clearly, the ability to mount complex multivariate analyses of human cultural change and variation greatly influenced the practice of archaeological typology and fostered the recognition of new patterns of association and divergence that became objects of investigation (see, for example, Clarke 1968; Gardin 1970, 1980). However, whether stimulated by changes in epistemology or by new views of what is to be explained, statistics also had an increasingly important role to play in the design of sampling and survey strategies in archaeology (see, for example, Schiffer and Gummerman 1977; Shennan 1988).

Developments in excavation techniques led to an increase in the amount of empirical data recovered. Clearly, those developments also reflected the influence of changing views of what is to be explained as well as ideas of what data are significant in explanation. The interpenetration of changes in the goals of archaeologists; technical and methodological borrowings from the physical, earth, and life sciences; and techniques of analysis and classification were clearly seen in the expansion of the archaeological database and in changes in excavation recording systems. On several notable occasions the association of these forces for change has even led to radical reinterpretations of sites, the most celebrated of which is Star Carr (Andresen et al. 1981; Mellars and Dark 1998).

In the preceding discussion I have sketched some of the generally accepted forces for change in the conditions of archaeological practice that occurred during the years when the "new" archaeology program attracted so much support and opposition. Other forces—such as the vast increase in the numbers of archaeologists, the expanding size and interdisciplinary nature of excavation and survey teams, the growing numbers of long-term and large-scale field projects, and the increased availability of research funds from grant-awarding bodies or as a result of the burgeoning field of cultural resources management (CRM)—should also be mentioned. Similarly, changes in the sociopolitical context of archaeology and the advent of subdisciplinary varieties such as historical archaeology and ethnoarchaeology were recognized as forces for change, although there is considerable dispute about the terms of their effects on archaeology since the 1960s. I shall have a bit more to say about them toward the end of this essay.

Notwithstanding the initial claim that most practitioners agreed that change has occurred, it is simply not the case that there is agreement about which of the forces for change has been the most influential. Nor is there agreement about whether it is possible to divorce the significance of changes in technique and relationship from other changes that have occurred in the structure of disciplinary concepts and epistemology and in the goals of archaeologists. Indeed, I have stressed that the significance of absolute dating for archaeology, precisely because it required the realignment of culture histories, and the reexamination of theories that had previously dominated the interpretation and explanation of cultural change and variation. Moreover, the advent of radiometric dating can be closely associated with other trends toward a developing understanding of the complexity of archaeological records and of their formation (see especially Schiffer 1976, 1987). How much the movement away from the empiricist restrictions of the "ladder of inference" was stimulated and given purpose by the discovery of quantifiable archaeological time is still difficult to gauge, but there can be no doubt that the increasing interest in goals other than the establishment of relative chronologies was directly related to it.

Thus far I have attempted to characterize the forces for change within post-1960s archaeology as being mutually supporting elements that sprang from a wide variety of sources. In so doing I have only mentioned in passing the tensions within the discipline that have resulted from those changes and, more importantly, from the wide variety of sources of change. The most significant of these came to form the core of an opposing program for archaeology, that of postprocessual archaeology, which came into being in the early 1980s and was most closely associated with the work of Ian Hodder (see especially 1982a, 1982b, 1982c, 1986, 1992), Daniel Miller (1985, 1987), Michael

Shanks and Christopher Tilley (see especially 1987a, 1987b). As with processual archaeology there was considerable variation in the views of those who identified as postprocessual archaeologists about details of epistemology, the importance of various types of social theories, and readings of the importance of sociopolitical context as a driver of knowledge. Again, postprocessual archaeology was (and is) a living program and consequently its conceptual "core" has changed and developed as archaeologists with new interests associate under its aegis.

Notwithstanding this, the original goals of the postprocessual program are clear enough. Born in opposition to the "new" archaeology focus on positivist science, and social theories of functionalism and cultural evolutionism, postprocessual archaeology sought to advance the cause of the particular, the individual, and the lived experience of human beings as knowledgeable actors in the past. A core proposal was that the "new" archaeology had restricted what archaeologists could explore and discuss, on the basis that no scientifically respectable answers were likely to come from the archaeological record for such matters as gender, identity, and ethnicity. These (and other issues) stressed by different social theories, such as structuralism, symbolism, structural Marxism, and feminism, were precisely what postprocessual archaeologists were interested in, as distinct from tracing out ancient cultural ecologies or culture histories. For Hodder and others the use by "new" archaeologists of science as the model epistemology for archaeology had produced a discipline that could not engage with contemporary research in the humanities and produced dehumanized pasts. Archaeologists needed to explore the rich contexts of past lives and the bankrupt epistemology of processualism should be swept away to allow this to happen.

In doing this postprocessual archaeologists embraced an epistemology of relativism, where knowledge was seen as being a product of societies and reflecting the views and interests of those societies. Thus, postprocessual archaeologists have been strongly supportive of the recognition of the importance of other agendas in archaeology, be they from other "marginalized voices" or from other interests, such as cultural heritage management.

In this brief and very general discussion of the debate between processual and postprocessual archaeology I indicated that the two major sources of disagreement were theoretical (in the sense of what social theories were appropriate to the discipline) and epistemological (in the sense of how archaeologists and others should judge archaeological knowledge claims). Another area of difficulty related to the existence of different opinions about the importance of the uniqueness of archaeological records as evidence of human action. The view that the character of those records might in some way constrain archaeological inference was contrasted with the postprocessual approach that this can be "controlled for" during the process of translation to archaeological data, and thence to "social" science data, by methodological strategies. Matters have stood unresolved since the 1980s, notwithstanding attempts by adherents of either view to demonstrate how much they do or do not have in common (see, for example, Dark 1995; Gibbon 1989; Johnson 1999; Jones 2002; O'Brien et al. 2005) or, alternatively, how the argument can only be resolved by dissolving archaeology into one or other of the very many varieties that have sprouted since the 1960s, such as ethnoarchaeology, material culture studies, or evolutionary archaeology. Indeed, as the decades have passed and new challenges from social theory or from history have come to the fore (such as gender archaeology, archaeological investigations of identity in all its myriad forms, and postcolonial archaeologies), debate about fundamental issues of purpose, ontology, and epistemology has become diffuse and unfocused, only to be replaced by a much greater concern with advancing the interests of one or other group. Nonetheless, debates about the epistemological and theoretical significance of archaeological records can still occur, although they are yet to return to the mainstream (see, for example, Lucas 2005; Murray 1999; van der Leeuw and McGlade 1997).

The Present and Near Future of Archaeology: Forces for Change and Divergence

In the closing sections of this essay I consider the nature and impact of two further sources of divergence and differentiation within contemporary archaeology that are likely to continue into the near future. Each source has a long history within archaeology, either as arguments about the nature of archaeological data or discussions about what constitutes the field of archaeological activity or the sociopolitical contexts of its practice. The first is the increasing importance of the sociopolitical context of the discipline vis-à-vis the goals and interests of practitioners, and the second is the multiplication of the varieties of archaeology that has occurred over the past quarter century. Both of these sources have acted, and will continue to act, in ways that might severely curtail or render irrelevant the notion of a world archaeology built on generally accepted methods and theories, pursuing generally agreed-upon questions and using generally accepted chronologies to foster global comparisons. Indeed, one important political context of practice (that of postcolonialism) finds considerable fault with such global discourses, seeing them instead as a form of cultural appropriation by the West of the patrimony of the marginalized or less economically developed (Gero 1999).

Whose Past Is it Anyway?

In the first essay I discussed the political implications of the demise of Geoffrey of Monmouth's *Historia regum Britanniae,* and elsewhere presented further examples of the political implications of the prehistoric past, especially in terms of the rise of romantic nationalism and imperialism (see Levine 1986), the implications of the monogenism/polygenism debate, and of course the links between archaeology and national politics (see, for example, Arnold 1990; Dietler 1994; Fowler 1987; Murray 1990; Pringle 2006; Slapsak 1993). If anything, the political implications of investigations of the prehistoric past grew in importance during the twentieth century. In Europe the work of apologists for pre–World War I German nationalism (for example, Kossinna 1911; Klejn 1999) sparked French, English, and Scandinavian responses. Two decades later Childe was actively opposing the claims of Nazi race historians (see, for example, Childe 1933, 1934).

Although the sociopolitical consequences of archaeology have long been appreciated, until recent years detailed investigations of those consequences have been few and far between, with the exception of the work of historians of archaeology, such as Daniel and Piggott (see also Crawford 1932). With the advent of the self-reflective turn promoted by the "new" archaeology, this situation changed dramatically. In the first essay I mentioned that developments in the history, philosophy, and sociology of science provided another spur to this change of attitude, but it would clearly be unwise to contend that archaeologists were merely reacting to changes that had happened within that field.

Moreover, while we might argue that some archaeologists saw in the "new" archaeology a need to understand the impact of archaeological knowledge on the general public (see especially Handsman 1980; Leone 1973, 1981a, 1981b; Meltzer 1981b; Willey 1980), other archaeologists have clearly responded to sociopolitical forces that occur outside archaeology but that directly condition the context of its practice (see, for example, Kane 2003; Kohl and Fawcett 1995; Meskell 1998; Pearson 1976). Here I refer to the rise during the 1980s and 1990s of movements for ethnic or racial self-determination, particularly the growth of political movements among the indigenous populations of former European colonies and the Americas (see, for example, Garlake 1982, 1984; Hall 1984; Langford 1983; Schrire et al. 1986; Trigger 1980a, 1984a, 1985; Ucko 1983a, 1983b, 1987).

Another important development during those years was a movement, particularly among Third World nations, to take control of the writing of their own histories by either placing restrictions on foreign scholars or restricting them altogether (see, for example, Healy 1984; Lorenzo 1981; Schmidt and Patterson 1996; Ucko 1995).

It is no surprise that these changes in the context of practice created strong tensions among the increasingly diverse group of practitioners. For some these movements for self-determination were viewed as providing a seedbed for an increasing diversity of goals and perspectives for the archaeologist, and an increasing likelihood of relativism. For them, particularly in circumstances such as those outlined by Garlake (1982), and perhaps by Langford (1983), the Western model of disinterested science was clearly at odds with other ways of knowing about the past or other ethical viewpoints. Indeed, it became clear that the case for the objectivity of Western science was not improved when historians of archaeology clearly established that in their relationships with other peoples archaeologists and anthropologists have sought (either consciously or unconsciously) to devalue their societies and cultures or to add support to the ideology of Western superiority and political domination (see, for example, Hodder 1984, 1985; Mulvaney 1981; Trigger 1980a, 1984a, 1985; Trigger and Glover 1981). Many of the resulting disagreements about whether archaeologists have the right to pursue their studies even though they might offend against local customs and beliefs have surfaced over the contentious issue of the excavation and analysis of human skeletal remains (see, for example, Bahn 1984; Rosen 1980), but during the 1980s they became much more encompassing (see, for example, Murray 1993, 2004). They have gained particular force in the fierce battles that have been waged over the repatriation of skeletal (and other) remains from museum collections (see, for example, Murray 1993, 1996a).

It is also understood that the great increase in the number of archaeologists being trained in Third and Second World countries during the last thirty years of the twentieth century became a powerful force for increasingly divergent readings of the meanings of the past and the role of the archaeologist. Significantly, these archaeologists, drawn from non-Western cultures, have been joined by some adherents of the postprocessual program, critical aspects of which were predicated on a relativistic reading of the meaning of the past. Conflict over skeletal remains does not exhaust the supply of current ethical difficulties (Vitelli 1996; but see also Dunnell 1984, 63).

In an important sense the foundation of the World Archaeological Congress (WAC), which arose in 1986 out of a conflict within the International Union of Prehistoric and Protohistoric Sciences (UISPP), became a litmus test of the extent to which the practice of archaeology was to be transformed by politics in the late twentieth century. Excellent analyses of the conflict exist (see especially Ucko 1987), and its broad bounds can be readily summarized. WAC is anticolonial in terms of its politics and the models of archaeological practice it supports and advocates. WAC came into being to make it possible for the "voices" of indigenous groups and marginalized peoples in the Second and Third Worlds to be heard and respected. In practice these have become many "voices" as people gain the space and the support to contest Western science and the universalizing and generalizing tendencies of archaeology practiced under its aegis. Of course, many practitioners who considered themselves to be postprocessual archaeologists were ardent supporters of these "alternative histories." However, it is by no means certain that its codes of practice could keep pace with the rapidly evolving (and diversifying) interests of this broad group by the late 1990s.

Archaeologists have also long been aware that there is a need to present the results of archaeological investigations to the public, if only to ensure public interest and support. In the past, efforts have spanned the exhibition of "finds" from excavations, the use of television and public lectures, and the publication of popular accounts of archaeology (see, for example, Ascher 1960; Beaudry and Elster 1979; Cunliffe 1981; Fagan 1977, 1984; Feldman 1977; Jordan 1981; Peters 1981). Equally important has been the maintenance of links between mainstream archaeology and interested laypeople through local archaeological and antiquarian societies (see, for example, Chapman 1985; Frison 1984; Hudson 1981; Mohrman 1985). By the late 1980s, archaeologists had developed a "public" discourse about the nature and aims of the discipline that frequently dispensed with a more authentic presentation of conceptual and epistemological differentiation within it.

During these years practitioners were also called upon to respond to strands of popular archaeology that ran counter to accepted professional standards of disciplinary practice or that advanced views of the past that ignore vital archaeological information. The recently revived debate about creationism is one example, but the works of Erich von Daniken, the nature of Atlantis, the precise locations of ley lines, the sightings of bigfeet of various kinds, and the peregrinations of Vikings or Welshmen are more persistent representatives of an "alternative" archaeology (see, for example, Cole 1980; Fagan 2006; Feder 1984). While contemporary practitioners could laugh at the expense of the lunatic fringe, historians of archaeology were also demonstrating that myth and reality can often be culturally contextual (Sabloff 1982; Silverberg 1968).

Another important area of change in the sociopolitical context of archaeology has been the consequent effects of changes within Western society generally, exemplified by the rise of the women's movement (see, for example, Gero 1985). From the 1980s the analysis of gender in archaeology and broader inquiries into the archaeology of sexuality and "queer" archaeology have generally become much closer to the mainstream of contemporary practice than ever before (see, for example, Gilchrist 1999; Nelson 2004; Schmidt and Voss 2000).

These are not the only aspects of sociopolitical context that are acting to diversify the interests of practitioners. Since the "new" archaeology there had been an upswing in critical self-reflection about the discipline. Wilk provided a clear statement of one aspect of this search for an understanding of the practice of archaeology:

> Archaeology has a dual nature; it simultaneously engages in a fairly rigorous pursuit of objective facts about the past and an informal and sometimes hidden dialogue on contemporary politics, philosophy, religion and other important subjects. It is this second dialogue, based on archaeologists' perception of the present and their experience of the world (including their experience of fieldwork), which brings innovation, passion, interest and relevance to the whole enterprise. This is what makes archaeology an essentially "reflexive" science, one which reflects back on the present as much light as it sheds on the past. (1985, 308)

Another aspect of this reflexive turn stems, characteristically, from the adherents of the postprocessual program. They, like Wilk, found the concepts and categories of archaeology to be a useful mirror of the means by which the experience of the present is comprehended by actors. Unlike Wilk, however, they were keen to attack the ontological and epistemological assumptions underpinning processual archaeology. Hodder (1984, 1985), Miller

(1985), and Miller and Tilley (1984) (but see also Trigger 1984a, 1984b, 1985) have all seen in processual archaeology a latent (capitalist?) ideology of dominance and control (see also Gadamer 1976; Habermas 1973, 1978 for a more developed account of this argument), in which systems theory and scientific epistemology have played their parts:

> In archaeology culture became equated with the control and capturing of nature not only in the sense that past material culture was labelled, categorized, controlled and administered, but also in the sense that a past was erected in which man gradually pulled himself out of the mists of irrational beliefs, achieved intelligent enlightenment, and obtained mastery over nature. (Hodder 1985, 19)

Miller and Tilley (1984, 2) also castigated the "new" archaeology for failing to consider the social production of archaeological knowledge and for emphasizing models of social action that stressed stability and equilibrium rather than conflict and contradiction. These failings were all held to be the products of the ideology that supported the plausibility of the "new" archaeology program.

Both aspects of this increasing interest in the sociopolitical context of archaeological knowledge during the last twenty years of the twentieth century were significant developments in our search for an understanding of the conditions of archaeological knowledge production. Practitioners were now clearly able to recognize that archaeological knowledge is not a morally or ethically neutral product, and that it exists as a representation of our views of ourselves and of our contemporary condition. Both processual and postprocessual archaeologists also stressed that for the past to be intelligible, it had to mirror the structures through which we seek meaning in the present.

Varieties of Archaeology

One of the characteristic features of contemporary archaeology is the large number of varieties of archaeology, from analytical to zoological archaeology. Indeed, many of the milestones included in Section Three refer to the rise of whole new fields, such as maritime archaeology or historical archaeology. This increase in variety expresses two important features of contemporary practice that have also acted as forces for divergence within the discipline, as the discipline has taken on ever-greater diversities of method, theories, perspectives, and (perhaps most important) agendas.

The first feature is that archaeological data are also anthropological, historical, architectural, sociological, and economic data. In other words the database of archaeology intersects with the databases of other disciplines. For example, in the burgeoning and increasingly influential field of historical archaeology (see, for example, Deetz 1977), practitioners readily use data from history, anthropology, economic history, and historical sociology when they pursue interpretation and explanation. Increasingly, the practitioners of those other disciplines "acquire" archaeological data to further their own ends.

Historical archaeology is also a useful example of the second feature, namely, that practitioners in these varieties of archaeology (such as classical archaeology) often experience difficulty in determining the distinctiveness of the archaeological perspective. In the past quarter century there has been an almost endless succession of integrative "paradigms," perspectives or approaches that have been promoted as the only sure guides to the "essence" of archaeology. During this period archaeology has been anthropology, human ecology, history, etc.

This "game of archaeological neologisms" expresses a fundamental feature of archaeology since the nineteenth century, simply that the nature of archaeological data seems to imply that meaning should be found elsewhere and that for archaeology to be a science it must ape the practices and procedures of physics, geology, or other disciplines with established dignity. Although the experience of practitioners clearly varies by country or culture (see e.g., Cleere and Fowler 1976 ; Renfrew 1982a; Trigger and Glover 1981) the same search for an integrative framework for archaeology crosses all boundaries. While it is beyond dispute that the practices and procedures of these other disciplines have aided archaeologists in the day-to-day business of the discipline by multiplying the sources of inference, and that a multistranded archaeology is more likely to expand the domain of archaeology itself, there is a darker side to variety when archaeology is dismembered by its constituent specialities (see Binford 1983b,16, for another interpretation of the problem).

During the course of the period under review perhaps the most significant source of variety has been the rise of cultural resources management archaeology (CRM) or Heritage Management archaeology. The nature, purpose, and limitations of CRM archaeology have been the subject of intense scrutiny, both by practitioners of the field and by interested and sometimes hostile observers (see, for example, Carman 2002; Cleere 1989; Fowler 1982;

Knudson 1982; Mulloy 1976; Schiffer 1979; Smith 2004; Tunbridge and Ashworth 1996; Wildesen 1982). This is not the place to survey the reasons for the rapid worldwide expansion of the field, but we should be clear that CRM exists to service legislation that has been supported (if not necessarily requested) by members of the public. CRM is not only the major employer of archaeology graduates, but it is also the area that has for some time now received the most funding. Consequently, in countries such as the United States and Australia by far the bulk of archaeological work is done by managers or by consulting or "public" archaeologists, and this has raised the issue of the scientific value of the work being done in this field of archaeology. CRM has also forged new links between archaeology and governments (see, for example, Flamm and Friedman 1981) and between archaeology and the general public. Some important implications of the rise of CRM were outlined by Green more than twenty years ago:

> The past fifteen years has seen a rapid expansion in archaeology, probably more than at any time in the history of the discipline. While this expansion has produced many benefits, it has also resulted in increasingly diverse values and conflicting ethics. Archaeology has moved out from academia into the worlds of business and government. Largely because of this, there has been an increase in the total amount of archaeological work being done annually, an increase in the total number of practicing archaeologists and, consequently, a greater diversity of personal goals and values. (1984, ix)

Significantly, practitioners of CRM have also become involved in aspects of archaeological practice, such as the pragmatics of earning a living or tendering for a contract, that have raised clear ethical issues. Indeed, the nature of conservation philosophies, significance decisions, and the establishment of a representative sample of the archaeological record to service both the future needs of practitioners and the general public, to say nothing of the ethical duty of the archaeologist to the database, have all been a major spur to the reflexive turn in archaeology (see, for example, Fowler 1984; Schiffer and Gummerman 1977; Smith 2004). Clearly, current disputes about fundamentals have begun to pose special problems for resource managers. How is significance to be established at a time when there are divergent views about the significance and relevance of archaeological problems? How can clients or governments be convinced by significance assessments when so many archaeological problems and perspectives appear to be long on rhetoric and short on realized potential? Wildesen saw the context of CRM archaeology as being preeminently a political one, and given the current state of dispute within general archaeology her view may well apply to the alarms in the groves of academe as well:

> Archaeology has climbed out of the pit and into the public eye, and archaeologists are enmeshed in issues of public policy that have a direct bearing on the profession and the future of their resource (and research) base. As with other disciplines, the addition of non-archaeological actors to the archaeological drama has led to increased emphasis on ethical codes, and to increased internecine struggle. (1984, 12)

Wildersen's observation also allows us to see the significance of an indigenous interest in archaeological heritage. Although the great battles over "ownership" of the past began in earnest nearly thirty years ago, matters related to the power that flows from control over access to the physical properties of heritage have now carried over into more explicit discussions of issues of interpretation (see, for example, Murray 1993, 1996b).

A Summary Discussion

During the course of the three essays I have sought to demonstrate that archaeological data have clear sociopolitical significance. In other words the discourse of archaeology has been appreciably shaped by its relevance to dominant political and social issues of any period. Although I did not pursue an investigation of pre–new archaeology in the same depth, I claimed that the authority structures of archaeology established during the nineteenth century have persisted to the present day.

Throughout this book I have also sought to establish that archaeologists responded to internal puzzles and problems generated by a database that was an almost constant source of surprise and revelation. The need to comprehend archaeological data has also reinforced a close association between archaeology and the "social," earth, life, and physical sciences. The discovery of high human antiquity, the perception of cultural variation within the Paleolithic, and the discovery of ancient civilizations all posed problems of geological, historical, and ethnological moment. Indeed, these discoveries became both the support of and testament to the effectiveness of an interactionist archaeological methodology. That methodology, although it began as a confection of antiquarian and geological approaches, clearly established that historical and anthropological knowledge of the prehistoric human past was possible, and that such knowledge was significant in our search for self-understanding. Yet for practitioners there was always a tension between what they desired to know of the prehistoric past and what they thought the empirical character of the record would allow them to plausibly know.

During the nineteenth century when ethnology (later anthropology) was believed by practitioners to constitute an effective framework for translating archaeological knowledge into anthropological knowledge, the "gaps" in the information content of the archaeological record could be plausibly filled by inference from anthropology. In the course of the twentieth century the integrative power of anthropology, hence its ability to unambiguously provide such a service to archaeology, has steadily declined as the practitioners of the constituent disciplines of anthropology became more concerned with internal problems and puzzles than with maintaining or extending the integrative project. Indeed, it has become increasingly apparent to social (if not cultural) anthropologists that what little of relevance archaeology has had to contribute could now be superseded by ethnohistory (see, for example, Geertz 1983, 1984; Sahlins 1976, 1983; Trigger 1982, 1985). Despite the serious attempts to integrate archaeology and cultural anthropology made by Harris (1994), Kroeber(1952), Steward (1955), and White (1949), American cultural anthropologists are by no means united about the value of such an integration.

In this essay I very briefly considered the impact of the "new" archaeology on the discipline. In a consideration of ontology I noted that "new" archaeologists (and later the "functionalists," processualists, or "behaviorists") tended to opt for the materialist side of the traditional ontological antinomy between materialism and idealism. Similarly, they adopted a contemporary version of the universal history project in the "human" sciences. Despite an earlier wrong-turning to positivism, the "new" archaeologists also sought escape from an empiricism that limited the security of archaeological knowledge claims to basic matters of subsistence and human-environment interactions and that decisively circumscribed an archaeological investigation of the meaning of cultural similarity and difference. I further observed that the overarching goal of the "new" archaeology was to increase the relevance of archaeology as a discipline by increasing its contribution to anthropology.

I then mentioned that there was never universal agreement about the nature of the project, the terms of archaeology's contribution to anthropology, or what constituted appropriate archaeological epistemology. In the course of discussion it became apparent that although there was (earlier) general agreement about a link between the status of science and the production of culturally meaningful statements about prehistoric human action, over the next two decades there was increasing dissatisfaction with a more pervasive link, that between a functionalist reading of materialist ontology and what was being promoted as appropriate archaeological epistemology. In this sense, although "new" archaeologists sought escape from the "ladder of inference" by adopting an antiempiricist epistemology so that archaeology could more effectively contribute to anthropology, there was increasing disputation about the "meaningfulness" of the anthropology that was to be the target of archaeological contributions. Indeed, postprocessual archaeologists fully supported such an agenda for archaeology.

The debate that has erupted around alternative "anthropologies" reveals two important conditions for archaeological knowledge production. First, the bulk of practitioners have accepted that the meanings of the archaeological record should be made manifest through the interaction of archaeology and anthropology and, second, that the significance of the empirical character of the archaeological record, as a determinant of the kind of anthropology archaeologists should adhere to, has become a matter of both epistemological and ontological dispute. Importantly, the rhetoric of both processual and postprocessual archaeologists includes statements to the effect that anthropology should not (or cannot) remain unchanged as a result of its encounter with archaeology. We might observe in passing that such changes have not yet become noticeable.

Concluding Remarks

In this essay (and throughout this book) my goal has been to describe and analyze the ways in which archaeologists have claimed knowledge of the past, and the means by which other members of society have come to accept this as being a legitimate thing to do. For much of its history archaeology has been unproblematically focused on discovery, be it of civilizations, sites, material culture, or knowledge about the human past derived from a wide range of sources. In the twenty-first century archaeologists continue to make discoveries that have the potential to dramatically affect the ways in which human beings see their histories. Nowhere has this been more clearly demonstrated than in the search for human ancestors and in continuing debates about the origins of modern humans.

I have also sought to stress the developing importance of explicit discussions about the theories archaeologists use to make sense of the past, and the fact that societies all over the globe now have a much greater stake in archaeological heritage. Since the nineteenth century the social and political context in which archaeologists have worked has been of great importance, but especially over the past thirty years, archaeologists and others have begun to explicitly acknowledge this and to openly explore its implications. Part and parcel of this new interest in the contexts of archaeological knowledge is a growing interest in the history of archaeology, because an understanding of the traditions of archaeological research, particularly the terms of archaeology's relationships with its cognate disciplines, can help practitioners (and others) to understand the grounds and significance of contemporary disputes within the discipline.

If all the ructions over relativism and objectivism that have taken place within philosophy over the past thirty years are to signify anything, it must be that sciences, whatever their stamp, require

> a more historically situated, nonalgorithmic, flexible understanding of human rationality, one which highlights the tacit dimension of human judgement and imagination and is sensitive to the unsuspected contingencies and genuine novelties encountered in particular situations. (Bernstein 1983, xi)

There was also a hidden agenda to the brief, selective, and highly generalized discussions of the history of archaeology that make up the essays in this book. If one accepts that the application of absolute dating systems to archaeology and the development of studies of archaeological site formation processes give good grounds for arguing that archaeological records are unique evidence of human action, then one is bound to accept that serious attempts to understand the meanings of uniqueness will profoundly disturb preexisting relationships between archaeology and its cognate disciplines as well as the nature of ontological and epistemological antinomies that have long provided the context of our search for the meaning of the prehistoric past. Archaeologists will not only require great intestinal fortitude as they contemplate the building of higher-level archaeological theory, but they will also need a strong sense of community to establish lines of demarcation between long- and short-span studies, between the goals of reconstruction and process, and between the now very wide varieties of archaeology from classical, to maritime, to historical. For it is clear that archaeology serves many other interests than those of its practitioners, who seek to understand the nature of human cultural and social behavior over a span of some millions of years.

An understanding of the history of archaeology is essential to both requirements. It is for this reason that I have emphasized the significance of archaeological data and archaeological problems and the notion that conflict with the "cultural norms" of archaeology has the benefit of making our options seem clearer. While the debates occurring within the contemporary human sciences are clearly important to archaeologists, the terms of these debates should not completely constrain the prosecution of archaeological goals and archaeological problems. Furthermore, it is also apparent that archaeologists have a great deal of work ahead of them "deconstructing" their own discipline, developing alternative approaches to the archaeological past, and "hammering out" theories and perspectives. Some time ago Tilley put the issues well:

> How are archaeologists to account for, understand and explain the changes that may be perceived in material culture patterning? A number of crucial questions arise for consideration: is an adequate conception of archaeological thinking inevitably radically pluralistic or should our explanatory and conceptual frameworks approximate to a single fundamental form? Do different conceptual frameworks involve any common suppositions? Are all kinds of conceptual frameworks equally ultimate or do some, more than others, depend upon the context of questioning? (1982, 363)

I think archaeologists can only answer these questions if they have a common "cultural" purpose, a basis for conversation that overarches divergent goals, interests, perspectives, or indeed the frameworks appropriate to understanding the different parts of archaeological records. In my view, this "cultural" purpose should be a search for the meaning and significance of archaeological records that does not proceed from a need or desire to guarantee the theoretical primacy of the present, but instead to foster an open exchange between pasts and presents. Postprocessual archaeologists have been particularly vocal about the possibility of archaeology acting as one focus for a critique of the ways in which we seek understanding of the present, but this cannot be achieved if practitioners substitute traditional sources of cognitive plausibility for the development of theories that more securely link theoretical abstraction and empirical data. Indeed, if the conversation of archaeology is to have one measure of success it will be a reexamination of the reasons why some assumptions about the nature of human action in the prehistoric and historic pasts are meaningful and others not. Above all, the reason for emphasizing a link between the uniqueness of archaeological records and the potential for reestablishing a sense of community in the discipline is to prepare the ground for a special kind of reasoning that is both a product of functioning communities and the spur to their formation:

> [*p*]*hronesis* is a form of reasoning that is concerned with choice and involves deliberation. It deals with that which is variable and about which there can be differing opinions (*doxai*). It is a type of reasoning in which there is a mediation between general principles and a concrete particular situation that requires choice and decision. In forming such a judgement there can be no determinate technical rules by which a particular can simply be subsumed under that which is general or universal. What is required is an interpretation and specification of universals that are appropriate to this particular situation. (Bernstein 1983, 54)

Further Reading

Adams, W. Y. 1968. Invasion, diffusion, evolution? *Antiquity* 62: 194–215.

Andresen, J. M., B. F. Byrd, M. D. Elson, R. H. McGuire, R. M. Mendoza, E. Staski, and J. P. White. 1981. The deer hunters: Star Carr reconsidered. *World Archaeology* 13: 31–46.

Arnold, B. 1990. The past as propaganda: Totalitarian archaeology in Nazi Germany. *Antiquity* 64: 464–478.

Ascher, R. 1960. Archaeology and the public image. *American Antiquity* 25: 402–403.

Bahn, P. 1984. Do not disturb? Archaeology and the rights of the dead. *Journal of Applied Philosophy* 1: 213–225.

Beaudry, M., and E. Elster. 1979. The Archaeology Film Festival: Making new friends for archaeology in the screening hall. *American Antiquity* 44: 791–794.

Behrensmeyer, A. K., and A. P. Hill., eds. 1980. *Fossils in the making. Vertebrate taphonomy and paleoecology*. Chicago: University of Chicago Press.

Bernstein, R. J. 1983. *Beyond objectivism and relativism.* Oxford: Blackwell.

Binford, L. 1962. Archaeology as anthropology. *American Antiquity* 28: 217–225.

Binford, L. 1964. A consideration of archaeological research design. *American Antiquity* 29: 425–441.

Binford, L. 1972. *An archaeological perspective.* New York: Academic Press.

Binford, L. 1978. *Nunamiut ethnoarchaeology.* New York: Academic Press.

Binford, L. 1981. Behavioral archaeology and the "Pompeii premise." *Journal of Anthropological Research* 37: 195–208.

Binford, L. 1983a. *Working at archaeology.* New York: Academic Press.

Binford, L. 1983b. *In pursuit of the past.* London: Thames and Hudson.

Binford, S., and L. Binford, eds. 1968. *New perspectives in archaeology.* Chicago: Aldine.

Brothwell, D., and E. S. Higgs. 1969. *Science in archaeology.* Rev. ed. London: Thames and Hudson.

Bryant, V. M., Jr., and R. G. Holloway. 1983. The role of palynology in archaeology. *Advances in Archaeological Method and Theory* 6: 191–224.

Burghleigh, R. 1981. W. F. Libby and the development of radiocarbon dating. *Antiquity* 55: 96–98.

Butzer, K. 1975. The "ecological" approach to prehistory: Are we really trying? *American Antiquity* 40: 106–111.

Butzer, K. 1978. Toward an integrated, contextual approach in archaeology. *Journal of Archaeological Science* 5: 191–193.

Butzer, K. 1980. Context in archaeology: An alternative perspective. *Journal of Field Archaeology* 7: 417–422.

Butzer, K. 1982. *Archaeology as human ecology.* Cambridge: Cambridge University Press.

Carman, J. 2002. *Archaeology and heritage: an introduction.* London: Continuum.

Chapman, C.H. 1985. The amateur archaeological society: A Missouri example. *American Antiquity* 50: 241–248.

Childe, V. G. 1925. *The dawn of European civilization.* London: Routledge and Kegan Paul.

Childe, V. G. 1933. Is prehistory practical? *Antiquity* 7: 410–418.

Childe, V. G. 1934. Anthropology and Herr Hitler. *Discovery* 15: 65–68.

Childe, V. G. 1935. Changing aims and methods in prehistory. *Proceedings of the Prehistoric Society* 1: 1–15.

Childe, V. G. 1956. *Society and knowledge.* London: Allen and Unwin.

Childe, V. G. 1958. Valediction. *Bulletin of the Institute of Archaeology* I: 1–9.

Chorley, R., and P. Haggett, eds. 1967. *Models in geography.* London: Methuen.

Clark, J. G. D. 1939. *Archaeology and society.* London: Methuen.

Clark, J. G. D. 1952. *Prehistoric Europe: The economic basis.* London: Methuen.

Clark, J. G. D. 1961. *World prehistory.* Cambridge: Cambridge University Press.

Clarke, D. L. 1968. *Analytical Archaeology.* London: Methuen.

Clarke, D. L. 1972. *Models in archaeology.* London: Methuen.

Clarke, D. L. 1973. Archaeology: the loss of innocence. *Antiquity* 47: 6–18.

Clarke, D. L., ed. 1977. *Settlement archaeology.* London: Academic Press.

Cleere, H., ed. 1989. *Archaeological heritage management in the modern world.* London: Unwin Hyman.

Cleere, H., and P. Fowler. 1976. US Archaeology through British eyes. *Antiquity* 50: 230–232.

Cole, J. R. 1980. Cult archaeology and unscientific method and theory. *Advances in Archaeological Method and Theory* 3: 1–33.

Cooke, K. L. 1979. Mathematical approaches to culture change. In *Transformations: Mathematical approaches to culture change,* eds. C. Renfrew and K. L. Cooke, 327–348. New York: Academic Press.

Crawford, O. G. S. 1932. The dialectical process in the history of science. *Sociological Review* 24: 165–173.

Cribb, R. 1980. A comment on Eugene L. Sterud's "Changing Aims in Americanist Archaeology: A Citation Analysis of American Antiquity—1946–1975." *American Antiquity* 45: 352–354.

Cunliffe, B. 1981. Introduction: The public face of the past. In *Antiquity and Man,* eds. J. D. Evans, B. Cunliffe, and C. Renfrew, 192–194. London: Thames and Hudson.

Daniel, G. 1971. From Worsaae to Childe: the models of prehistory. *Proceedings of the Prehistoric Society* XXXVII: 140–153.

Daniel, G. 1975. *One hundred and fifty years of archaeology.* 2nd ed. London: Duckworth.

Daniel, G. 1981a. Introduction: the necessity for an historical approach to Archaeology. In *Towards a History of Archaeology,* ed. G. Daniel, 9–13. London: Thames and Hudson.

Daniel, G. 1981b. *A short history of archaeology.* London: Thames and Hudson.

Dark, K. 1995. *Theoretical archaeology.* Ithaca, NY: Cornell University Press.

Deetz, J. 1977. *In small things forgotten: The archaeology of early American life.* Garden City, NY: Anchor.

Dietler, M. 1994. Our ancestors the Gauls: Archaeology, ethnic nationalism, and the manipulation of Celtic identity in modern Europe. *American Anthropologist* 96: 584–605.

Doran, J., and F. Hodson. 1975. *Mathematics and computers in archaeology.* Edinburgh: Edinburgh University Press.

Dunnell, R. 1984. The ethics of archaeological significance decisions. In *Ethics and values in archaeology,* ed. E. L. Green, 62–74. New York: Free Press.

Fagan, B. M. 1977. Genesis I.1; or, teaching archaeology to the great archaeology-loving public. *American Antiquity* 42: 119–125.

Fagan, B. M. 1984. Archaeology and the Wider Audience. In *Ethics and Values in Archaeology,* ed. E. L. Green, 175–183. New York: The Free Press.

Fagan, G., ed. 2006. *Archaeological fantasies; how pseudoarchaeology misrepresents the past and misleads the public.* New York: Routledge.

Fahenstock, P. 1984. History and theoretical development: The importance of a critical historiography of archaeology. *Archaeological Review from Cambridge* 3: 7–18.

Feder, K. L. 1984. Irrationality and popular archaeology. *American Antiquity* 49: 525–541.

Feldman, M. 1977. *Archaeology for everyone.* New York: Quadrangle.

Flamm, B., and J. L. Friedman. 1981. United States Department of Agriculture: Its role in the protection of our heritage and environment. *American Antiquity* 46: 188–191.

Fowler, D. 1982. Cultural Resources Management. *Advances in Archaeological Method and Theory* 5: 1–50.

Fowler, D. 1984. Ethics in contract archaeology. In *Ethics and values in archaeology,* ed. E. L. Green, 108–116. New York: Free Press.

Fowler, D. 1987. Uses of the past: Archaeology in the service of the state. *American Antiquity* 52: 229–248.

Frison, G. 1984. Avocational archaeology: its past, present, and future. In *Ethics and values in archaeology,* ed. E. L. Green, chapter 21. New York: Free Press.

Gadamer, H-G. 1976. *Philosophical hermeneutics.* Berkeley: University of California Press.

Gardin, J-C., ed. 1970. *Archeologie et calculateurs.* Paris: CNRS.

Gardin, J-C. 1980. *Archaeological constructs.* Cambridge: Cambridge University Press.

Garlake, P. S. 1982. Prehistory and ideology in Zimbabwe. *Africa* 52: 1–19.

Garlake, P. S. 1984. Ken Mufuka and Great Zimbabwe. *Antiquity* 58: 121–123.

Gathercole, P., T. H. Irving, and G. Melleuish, eds. 1995. *Childe and Australia: Archaeology, politics and ideas.* St. Lucia, Australia: University of Queensland Press.

Geertz, C. 1983. *Local knowledge: Further essays in interpretation.* New York: Basic Books.

Geertz, C. 1984. Distinguished Lecture: Anti anti-relativism. *American Anthropologist* 86: 263–278.

Gero, J. 1985. Socio-politics and the woman-at-home ideology. *American Antiquity* 50: 342–350.

Gero, J. 1999. The history of the World Archaeological Congress. http://ehlt.flinders.edu.au/wac/site/about_hist.php.

Gibbon, G. 1989. *Explanation in archaeology.* Oxford: Blackwell.

Gifford, D. 1978. Ethnoarchaeological observations of natural processes affecting cultural materials. In *Explorations in ethnoarchaeology,* ed. R. A. Gould, 77–101. Albuquerque: University of New Mexico Press.

Gifford, D. 1980. Ethnoarchaeological contributions to the taphonomy of human sites. In *Fossils in the Making: Vertebrate Taphonomy and Paleoecology,* eds. A. K. Behrensmeyer and A. P. Hill, 93–106. Chicago: University of Chicago Press.

Gifford, D. 1981. Taphonomy and paleoecology: A critical review of archaeology's sister disciplines. *Advances in Archaeological Method and Theory* 4: 365–438.

Gilchrist, R. 1999. *Gender and archaeology: Contesting the past.* London: Routledge.

Godelier, M. 1977. *Perspectives in Marxist anthropology.* Cambridge: Cambridge University Press.

Gould, S., and N. Eldredge. 1977. Punctuated equilibria: The tempo and mode of evolution reconsidered. *Paleobiology* 3: 115–151.

Green, E. L. 1984. Introduction. In *Ethics and values in archaeology,* ed. E. L. Green, ii–xii. New York: Free Press.

Haag, W. G. 1957. Recent work by British archaeologists. *Annals of the Association of American Geographers* 43: 298–303.

Habermas, J. 1973. *Theory and practice.* London: Heinemann.

Habermas, J. 1978. *Knowledge and human interests,* trans. J. J. Shapiro. 2nd ed. London: Heinemann.

Haggett P. 1965. *Locational analysis in human geography.* London: Edward Arnold.

Hall, M. 1984. The burden of tribalism: The social context of Southern African Iron Age studies. *American Antiquity* 49: 455–467.

Handsman, R. G. 1980. Studying myth and history in modern America: Perspective for the past from the continent. *Reviews in Anthropology* 7: 255–268.

Harris, D. 1994. *The archaeology of V. Gordon Childe: Contemporary perspectives.* Melbourne, Australia: Melbourne University Press.

Harris, M. 1968. *The rise of anthropological theory.* New York: Crowell.

Harvey, D. 1969. *Explanation in geography.* London: Edward Arnold.

Hawkes, C. 1954. Archaeological theory and method: Some suggestions from the Old World. *American Anthropologist* 56: 155–168.

Hawkes, J. 1968. The proper study of mankind. *Antiquity* 42: 255–262.

Healy, P. 1984. Archaeology abroad: Ethical considerations of fieldwork in foreign countries. In *Ethics and values in archaeology,* ed. E. Green, 123–132. New York: Free Press.

Heine-Geldern, R. 1964. One hundred years of ethnology theory in the German-speaking countries: Some milestones. *Current Anthropology* 5: 407–418.

Hill, J. N. 1972. The methodological debate in contemporary archaeology: A model. In *Models in archaeology,* ed. D. L. Clarke, 231–273. London: Methuen.

Hindess, B., and P. Q. Hurst. 1975. Pre-capitalist modes of production. London: Routledge and Kegan Paul.

Hindess, B., and P. Q. Hurst. 1977. *Mode of production and social formation.* London: Macmillan.

Hodder, I. 1982a. Preface. In *Symbolic and structural archaeology,* ed. I. Hodder, vii–viii. Cambridge: Cambridge University Press.

Hodder, I. 1982b. Theoretical archaeology: A reactionary view. In *Symbolic and structural archaeology,* ed. I. Hodder, 1–16. Cambridge: Cambridge University Press.

Hodder, I. 1982c. *The present past: An introduction to anthropology for archaeologists.* London: Batsford.

Hodder, I. 1984. Archaeology in 1984. *Antiquity* 58: 25–32.

Hodder, I. 1985. Postprocessual Archaeology. *Advances in Archaeological Method and Theory* 8: 1–26.

Hodder, I. 1986. *Reading the past.* Cambridge: Cambridge University Press.

Hodder, I. 1992. *Theory and practice in archaeology.* London: Routledge.

Hodder, I., and C. Orton. 1976. *Spatial analysis in archaeology.* Cambridge: Cambridge University Press.

Hogarth, A. R. 1972. Common sense in archaeology. *Antiquity* 46: 301–304.

Hudson, K. 1981. *A social history of archaeology: the British experience.* London: Macmillan.

Isaac, G. 1972. Chronology and the tempo of cultural change during the Pleistocene. In *Calibration of Hominoid evolution,* eds. W. W. Bishop and J. A. Miller, 281–430. Edinburgh: Scottish Academic Press.

Isaac, G. 1981. Archaeological tests of alternative models of early hominid behaviour: excavation and experiments. In *The emergence of man,* eds. J. Z. Young, E. M. Jope, and K. P. Oakley, 177–188. Philosophical Transactions of the Royal Society of London Series B 292. London: Royal Society.

Johnson, G. 1977. Aspects of regional analysis in archaeology. *Annual Review of Anthropology* 6: 479–508.

Johnson, M. 1999. *Archaeological theory.* Oxford: Blackwell.

Jones, A. 2002. *Archaeological theory and scientific practice.* Cambridge: Cambridge University Press.

Jordan, P. 1981. Archaeology and television. In *Antiquity and man,* eds. J. D. Evans, B. Cunliffe, and C. Renfrew, 207–213. London: Thames and Hudson.

Kane, S., ed. 2003. *The politics of archaeology and global identity in a global context.* Boston: Archaeological Institute of America.

Klejn, L. 1977. A panorama of theoretical archaeology. *Current Anthropology* 18: 1–42.

Klejn, L. 1999. Gustaf Kossina, (1858-1931). In *Encyclopedia of Archaeology The Great Archaeologists,* ed. T. Murray, 233–246. Santa Barbara, CA: ABC-CLIO.

Kluckhohn, C. 1939. The place of theory in anthropological studies. *Philosophy of Science* 6: 328–344.

Kluckhohn, C. 1940. The conceptual structure in Middle American studies. In *The Maya and their neighbours,* eds. C.L. Hay, R.L. Linton, S.K. Lothrop, A.L. Shapiro and G.C. Vaillant, 41–51. New York: Appleton-Century.

Knudson, R. 1982. Basic principles of archaeological resource management. *American Antiquity* 47: 163–166.

Kohl, P., and C. Fawcett. 1995. *Nationalism, politics, and the practice of archaeology.* New York: Cambridge University Press.

Kossinna, G. 1911. *Die Herkunft Germanen zur Methode der Siedslungs-archaologie.* Würzburg Kabitzsch, Germany: Mannus-Bibliothek.

Kroeber, A. L. 1952. *The nature of culture.* Chicago: University of Chicago Press.

Kuhn, T. 1962. *The structure of scientific revolutions.* 2nd ed. Chicago: University of Chicago Press, 1970.

Langford, M. 1983. Our heritage—your playground. *Australian Archaeology* 16: 1–6.

Langham, I. 1981. *The building of British social anthropology: W. H. R. Rivers and his Cambridge disciples in the development of kinship studies, 1898–1931.* Dordrecht, The Netherlands: Reidel.

Leone, M. 1973. Archaeology as the science of technology: Mormon town plans and fences. In *Research and theory in current archaeology,* ed. C. Redman, 125–150. New York: Wiley.

Leone, M. 1981a. Archaeology's relationship to the present and the past. In *Modern material culture. The archaeology of us,* eds. R. A. Gould and M. B. Schiffer, 5–14. New York: Academic Press.

Leone, M. 1981b. The relationship between artifacts and the public in outdoor history museums. *Annals of the New York Academy of Sciences* 376: 301–314.

Leone, M. 1982. Childe's offspring. In *Symbolic and structural archaeology,* ed. I. Hodder, 179–184. Cambridge: Cambridge University Press.

Levine P. 1986. *The amateur and the professional. Historians, antiquarians and archaeologists in 19th century England 1838–1886.* Cambridge: Cambridge University Press.

Lorenzo, J. L. 1981. Archaeology south of the Rio Grande, past and present. *World Archaeology* 13: 190–208.

Lucas, G. 2005. *The archaeology of time.* London: Routledge.

Lyman, R. L., and M. J. O'Brien. 2006. *Measuring time with artifacts: A history of methods in American archaeology.* Lincoln: University of Nebraska Press.

Lyman, R. L., M. J. O'Brien, and R.C. Dunnell, eds. 1997. *The rise and fall of culture history.* New York: Plenum Press.

McCann, B. 1988. The national socialist perversion of archaeology. *World Archaeological Bulletin* 2: 51–54.

MacWhite, E. 1956. On the interpretation of archaeological evidence in historical and sociological terms. *American Anthropologist* 58: 3–25.

Martin, P. S. 1971. The revolution in archaeology. *American Antiquity* 36: 1–8.

Mellars, P., and P. Dark. 1998. *Star Carr in context: New archaeological and palaeoecological investigations at the Early Mesolithic site of Star Carr, North Yorkshire.* Cambridge, UK: McDonald Institute for Archaeological Research.

Meltzer, D. J. 1979. Paradigms and the nature of change in archaeology. *American Antiquity* 44: 644–657.

Meltzer, D. J. 1981a. Paradigms lost—paradigms found? *American Antiquity* 46: 662–664.

Meltzer, D. J. 1981b. Ideology and material culture. In *Modern material culture: The archaeology of us,* eds. R. A. Gould and M. B. Schiffer, 113–125. New York: Academic Press.

Meskell, L., ed. 1998. *Archaeology under fire: Nationalism, politics and heritage in the Eastern Mediterranean and Middle East.* London: Routledge.

Miller, D. P. 1985. *Artifacts as categories.* Cambridge: Cambridge University Press.

Miller, D. P. 1987. *Material culture and mass consumption.* Oxford: Blackwell.

Miller, D. P., and C. Tilley. 1984. Ideology, power and prehistory: An introduction. In *Ideology, power and prehistory,* eds. D. P. Miller and C. Tilley, 1–15. Cambridge: Cambridge University Press.

Mohrman, H. 1985. Memoir of an avocational archaeologist. *American Antiquity* 50: 237–240.

Mulloy, E. D. 1976. *The history of the National Trust for Historic Preservation, 1963–1973.* Washington, DC: The Preservation Press.

Mulvaney, D. J. 1981. What future for our past? *Australian Archaeology* 13: 16–27.

Murray, T. 1990. The history, philosophy and sociology of archaeology: The case of the Ancient Monuments Protection Act (1882). In *Critical directions in contemporary archaeology,* eds. V. Pinsky and A. Wylie, 55–67. Cambridge: Cambridge University Press.

Murray, T. 1993. Communication and the importance of disciplinary communities: Who owns the past? In *Archaeological theory: Who sets the agenda?,* eds. N. Yoffee and A. Sherratt, 105–116. Cambridge: Cambridge University Press.

Murray, T. 1996a. On coming to terms with the living: Some aspects of repatriation for the archaeologist. *Antiquity* 266: 217–220.

Murray, T. 1996b. Towards a post-Mabo archaeology of Australia. In *In the Age of Mabo,* ed. B. Attwood, 73–87. Sydney: Allen and Unwin.

Murray, T., ed. 1999. *Time and Archaeology.* London: Routledge.

Murray, T. ed. 2004. *The archaeology of contact in settler societies.* Cambridge: Cambridge University Press.

Nelson, S. 2004. *Gender in archaeology: analyzing power and prestige.* Walnut Creek, CA: AltaMira.

O'Brien, M. J., R. L. Lyman, and M. B. Schiffer. 2005. *Archaeology as a process: Processualism and its progeny.* Salt Lake City: University of Utah Press.

Patterson, T., and C. Orser, Jr., eds. 2004. *Foundations of social archaeology: Selected writings of Vere Gordon Childe.* Walnut Creek, CA: AltaMira Press.

Pearson, R. J. 1976. The social aims of Chinese archaeology. *Antiquity* 50: 8–10.

Perry, W. J. 1924. *The growth of civilization.* London: Methuen.

Peters, E. 1981. Archaeology and publishing. In *Antiquity and man,* eds. J. D. Evans, B. Cunliffe, and C. Renfrew, 195–202. London: Thames and Hudson.

Pitt-Rivers, A. 1872. Address to the Department of Anthropology. *British Association Reports* 41: 157–174.

Pitt-Rivers, A. 1906. *The evolution of culture and other essays.* Oxford: Oxford University Press.

Polanyi, K. 1944. *The great transformation.* Boston: Beacon Press.

Prigogine, I. 1978. Time, structure and fluctuations. *Science* 201: 777–785.

Pringle, H. 2006. *The master plan: Himmler's scholars and the Holocaust.* New York: Hyperion.

Randall-MacIver, D. 1932. Archaeology as a science. *Antiquity* 7: 5–20.

Renfrew, C. 1976. *Before civilization: The radiocarbon revolution and prehistoric Europe.* Harmondsworth, UK: Penguin.

Renfrew, C. 1978. Trajectory discontinuity and morphogenesis, the implications of catastrophe theory for archaeology. *American Antiquity* 43: 203–222.

Renfrew, C. 1982a. Discussion: contrasting paradigms. In *Ranking, resource and exchange,* eds. C. Renfrew and S. Shennan, 141–143. Cambridge: Cambridge University Press.

Renfrew, C. 1982b. Comment: The emergence of structure. In *Theory and explanation in archaeology,* eds. C. Renfrew, M. J. Rowlands, and B. A. Seagraves, 459–464. New York: Academic Press.

Rosen, L. 1980. The excavation of American Indian burial sites: A problem in law and professional responsibility. *American Anthropologist* 82: 5–27.

Rosen, R. 1979. Morphogenesis in biological and social systems. In *Transformations: Mathematical Approaches to Culture Change,* eds. C. Renfrew and K.L. Cooke, 91–111. New York: Academic Press.

Sabloff, J. A. 1982. Introduction. In *Archaeology: Myth and Reality. Readings from Scientific American,* 1–26. San Francisco: Freeman.

Sahlins, M. 1972. *Stone Age economics.* Chicago: Aldine.

Sahlins, M. 1976. *Culture and practical reason.* Chicago: University of Chicago Press.

Sahlins, M. 1983. Distinguished Lecture: Other times, other customs: The anthropology of history. *American Anthropologist* 85: 517–544.

Schiffer, M. B. 1976. *Behavioral archaeology.* New York: Academic Press.

Schiffer, M. B. 1979. Some impacts of cultural resource management in American archaeology. In *Archaeological resource management in Australia and Oceania,* eds. J. McKinlay and K. Jones, 1–11. Auckland: New Zealand Historic Places Trust.

Schiffer, M. B. 1987. *Formation processes of the archaeological record.* Albuquerque: University of New Mexico Press.

Schiffer, M. B., and G. Gummerman, eds. 1977. *Conservation archaeology.* New York: Academic Press.

Schmidt, P., and T. Patterson, eds. 1996. *Making alternative histories: The practice of archaeology in non-Western settings.* Santa Fe, NM: SAR.

Schmidt, R., and B. Voss, eds. 2000. *Archaeologies of sexuality.* London: Routledge.

Scholte, B. 1983. Cultural anthropology and the paradigm-concept: A brief history of their recent convergence. In *Functions and uses of disciplinary histories,* eds. L. Graham, W. Lepenies, and P. Weingart, 229–278. Dordrecht, The Netherlands: Reidel.

Schrire, C., J. Deacon, M. Hall, and D. Lewis-Williams. 1986. Burkitt's milestone. *Antiquity* 60: 123–131.

Shanks, M., and C. Tilley. 1987a. *Re-constructing archaeology: Theory and practice.* Cambridge: Cambridge University Press.

Shanks, M., and C. Tilley. 1987b. *Social theory and archaeology.* Cambridge: Polity.

Shennan, S. 1988. *Quantifying archaeology.* Edinburgh: Edinburgh University Press.

Silverberg, R. 1968. *Mound builders of ancient America: The archaeology of a myth.* Greenwich, CT: New York Graphic Society.

Slapsak, B. 1993. Archaeology and contemporary myths of the past. *The Journal of European Archaeology* 1(2): 191–195.

Smith, L. 2004. *Archaeological theory and the politics of cultural heritage.* London: Routledge.

Smith, M. A. 1955. The limitations of inference in archaeology. *Archaeological News Letter* 6: 3–7.

Sterud, E. L. 1973. A paradigmatic view of prehistory. In *The Explanation of Culture Change: models in prehistory,* ed. C. Renfrew, 3–17. Pittsburgh, PA: University of Pittsburgh Press.

Sterud, E. L. 1978. Changing aims of Americanist archaeology: A citations analysis of American Antiquity—1946–1975. *American Antiquity* 43: 294–302.

Steward, J. H. 1942. The direct historical approach in archaeology. *American Antiquity* 7: 337–343.

Steward, J. H. 1955. *Theory of cultural change: The methodology of multilinear evolution.* Urbana: University of Illinois Press.

Steward, J. H., and F. M. Setzler. 1938. Function and configuration in archaeology. *American Antiquity* 4: 4–10.

Tallgren, A. M. 1937. The method of prehistoric archaeology. *Antiquity* 11: 152–161.

Taylor, R. E. 1985. The beginnings of radiocarbon dating in American Antiquity: Historical perspective. *American Antiquity* 50: 309–325.

Taylor, W. W. 1948. *A study of archaeology.* Memoir. Menasha, WI: American Athropological Association 69.

Thompson, M. W. 1977. *General Pitt-Rivers. Evolution and archaeology in the nineteenth century.* Bradford-on-Avon, UK: Moonraker Press.

Tilley, C. 1982. Social formation, social structures and social change. In *Symbolic and structural archaeology,* ed. I. Hodder, 26–38. Cambridge: Cambridge University Press.

Trigger, B. 1978. *Time and traditions: Essays in archaeological interpretation.* Edinburgh: Edinburgh University Press.

Trigger, B. 1980a. Archaeology and the image of the American Indian. *American Antiquity* 45: 662–676.

Trigger, B. 1980b. *Gordon Childe: Revolutions in Archaeology.* London: Thames and Hudson.

Trigger, B. 1982. Ethnohistory: Problems and prospects. *Ethnohistory* 29: 1–19.

Trigger, B. 1984a. Alternative archaeologies: Nationalist, colonialist, imperialist. *Man* (ns) 19: 355–370.

Trigger, B. 1984b. Archaeology at the crossroads: What's new? *Annual Reviews of Anthropology* 13: 275–300.

Trigger, B. 1985. The past as power. In *Who Owns the Past?*, ed. I. McBryde, 11–40. Melbourne, Australia: Oxford University Press.

Trigger, B. 1989. *A history of archaeological thought.* Cambridge: Cambridge University Press.

Trigger, B., and I. Glover. 1981. Introduction. *World Archaeology* 13: 133–137.

Tunbridge, J., and G. Ashworth. 1996. *Dissonant heritage: The management of the past as a resource in conflict.* Chichester, UK: J. Wiley.

Ucko, P. 1983a. Australian academic archaeology. Aboriginal transformation of its aims and practices. *Australian Archaeology* 16: 11–26.

Ucko, P. 1983b. The politics of the indigenous minority. *Journal of Biosocial Science* 8: 25–41.

Ucko, P. 1987. *Academic freedom and apartheid: The story of the World Archaeological Congress.* London: Duckworth.

Ucko, P. 1995. *Theory in archaeology: A world perspective.* London: Routledge.

Van der Leeuw, S., and J. McGlade, eds. 1997. *Time, process and structured transformation in archaeology.* London: Routledge.

Veit, U. 1989. Ethnic concepts in German prehistory: A case study on the relationship between cultural identity and archaeological objectivity. In *Archaeological Approaches to Cultural Identity,* ed. S. Shennan, 35–56. London: Unwin Hyman.

Vitelli, K. 1996. *Archaeological ethics.* Walnut Creek, CA: AltaMira.

Voget, F. W. 1975. *A history of ethnology.* New York: Holt, Rinehart and Winston.

White, L. 1949. *The science of culture: the study of man and civilization.* New York: Grove Press.

Wildesen, L. E. 1982. The study of impacts on archaeological sites. *Advances in Archaeological Method and Theory* 5: 51–96.

Wildesen, L. E. 1984. The search for an ethic in archaeology. In *Ethics and values in archaeology,* ed. E. Green, 3–12. New York: Free Press.

Wilk, R. 1985. The ancient Maya and the political present. *Journal of Anthropological Research* 43: 307–326.

Willey, G. R. 1980. *The social uses of archaeology.* Cambridge, MA: Harvard University Press.

Willey, G. R., and P. Phillips.1958. *Method and theory in American archaeology.* Chicago: University of Chicago Press.

Wylie, A. 1982. Positivism and the new archaeology. Ph.D. diss., SUNY Binghampton.

Zeeman, E. C. 1977. *Catastrophe theory: Selected papers 1972–1977.* New York: Addison-Wesley.

Zipf, G. K. 1949. *Human behavior and the principle of least effort.* Reading, MA: Addison-Wesley.

MILESTONES IN THE TWENTIETH CENTURY AND BEYOND

Discovery of Minoan Civilization (1900–1935)

Son of the famous antiquarian Sir John Evans, Arthur Evans grew up among some of the most notable archaeologists of the nineteenth century such as Lubbock, Falconer, Pitt-Rivers, and Montelius. His own great knowledge of material culture, ancient civilizations, and numismatics was surely influenced by his father. Arthur Evans graduated in history from Oxford University in 1874, and then pursued independent research on the history of the southern Slavic peoples of the Austro-Hungarian Empire, particularly the inhabitants of the modern states of Serbia, Croatia, Slovenia, Macedonia, Bosnia, and Albania.

In 1883 Evans and his wife took an extended tour of Greece, met Heinrich Schliemann in Athens, and visited his sites. It was this encounter that ignited his lifelong fascination with pre-classical Mycenean civilization. Over the next decade Schliemann's protégés in Greece excavated and studied numerous Bronze Age sites, cemeteries, and tombs and began to fill in the gaps in the prehistory of Greece. In 1897 this early work culminated in the publication by Christos Tsountas and J. Irving Manatt of *The Mycenaean Age,* the first great synthesis of Aegean prehistory.

During this time Evans was employed as keeper of the Ashmolean Museum in Oxford. In 1894, after the death of his wife, Arthur Evans visited Crete for the first time. His passionate interest in Cretan archaeology began shortly after. In 1895 he purchased part of Kephala Hill at Knossos from its Turkish owner, and he bought the rest of the site in 1899 after Crete gained independence from Turkey. Evans and Oxford colleague David Hogarth established the Cretan Exploration Fund, with links to the British School in Athens. Assisted by Evans's private income, they began to excavate the site in 1900.

English archaeologist Arthur Evans holds a Cretan sculpture of a bull's head at the exhibition of relics from Knossos, Crete, at the Royal Academy of London in 1936. (Hulton Archive/Getty Images)

During the first year of excavations, the plan of the Bronze Age palace of Knossos was uncovered, including the "throne room" and "magazines" or storerooms. Other finds included superb frescoes, traded items from Egypt and Babylon, and tablets covered with a linear script. Evans coined the term "Minoan" to describe the Bronze Age civilization of Crete, from the name of Minos, its legendary king. Knossos was the royal city of ancient Crete, and it had been occupied for almost 4,000 years. Evans dated the spread of Minoan civilization from around 3000–1000 BC. He also proved that it was older than that of the mainland Greek Mycenaean civilization and was able to use Minoan artifacts found in Egyptian sites, whose chronology was known, to cross-date similar artifacts at Knossos.

Evans's passion for Cretan archaeology was spurred by his interest in the nature and extent of oriental influences on the cultures of early Europe. He described Crete as "the halfway house between three continents . . . flanked by . . . Libya, linked by smaller island stepping stones to the Peloponnese and the mainland of Anatolia . . . it was called upon . . . to play a leading part in the development of . . . early Aegean culture" (John Evans in the "Monthly Review," 1901, quoted in B. Fagan, ed. 1996. *Eyewitness to Discovery,* Oxford: Oxford University Press, 188). Evans believed that Crete was the source of and center for Mycenean civilization and that the Minoans had conquered the Mycenaeans. He also believed that the decipherment of the Minoan Linear A and B scripts would prove him right. We now know that, in fact, the reverse was true. Instead, it was the Mycenaeans who conquered the Minoans and Knossos, and the last Cretan kings spoke Greek and not Minoan.

Nonetheless, Evans had found a brilliant and missing Bronze Age civilization, one that traded with the other great civilizations of the Aegean and Mediterranean. The Minoan civilization was the product of a remarkable mixture of influences, and it exerted great influence on others. The site of Knossos was excavated for the next eight years, after which, until 1931, Evans concentrated on restoring the palace, for which he was criticized. Between 1921 and 1936 Evans's most enduring legacy, the book *The Palace of Minos at Knossos,* was published.

See also Schliemann Excavates Troy, Mycenae, Ilios, Orchomenos, and Tiryns (1870–1891); Seriation and History in the Archaeology of Predynastic Egypt (1891–1904); Excavation of Gournia (1901–1908); Linear B Deciphered (1953).

Further Reading

Brown, A. C. 1983. *Arthur Evans and the Palace of Minos.* Oxford: Ashmolean Museum.

Casson, S., ed. 1972. *Essays in Aegean archaeology presented to Sir Arthur Evans in honour of his 75th birthday.* Freeport, NY: Books for Libraries Press.

Evans, A. 1909–1952. *Scripta Minoa, the written documents of Minoan Crete, with special reference to the archives of Knossos.* Oxford: Clarendon Press.

Evans, A. 1921–1936. *The Palace of Minos; a comparative account of the successive stages of the early Cretan civilization as illustrated by the discoveries at Knossos.* London: Macmillan and Co.

Horwitz, S. L. 2001. *The find of a lifetime: Sir Arthur Evans and the discovery of Knossos.* London: Phoenix Press.

Scarre, C., and R. Stefoff. 2003. *The Palace of Minos at Knossos.* New York: Oxford University Press.

Excavation of Gournia (1901–1908)

Harriet Hawes (1871–1945) was born into a wealthy manufacturing family in New England and graduated from Smith College in 1892. Four years later, inspired by recent excavations by Sir Arthur Evans on Crete, she joined the American School of Classical Studies in Athens. Discovering that female students were unable to participate in school excavations, and encouraged by Sir Arthur Evans and David Hogarth, Hawes decided to use her fellowship money to finance her own excavations. She chose a site at Kavousi in eastern Crete, where she directed more than 100 local workers to excavate early Iron Age houses and tombs, and kept meticulous records of her finds.

The results of her excavations, published in 1897 in *The American Journal of Archaeology,* were the basis of her master's thesis, which she completed at Smith College in 1901. That same year Hawes began to excavate Gournia, a Bronze Age town that is still the only well-preserved urban Minoan site on Crete. This time, however, she was sponsored by the American Exploration Society of Philadelphia for three seasons: 1901, 1903, and 1904. Her results were published in 1908.

The site of Gournia had been untouched for 3,500 years, and at the time of Hawes's excavation, was the oldest town to be discovered in Europe—older than both Knossos and Mycenae. While the magnificence of the Palace of Knossos was being unearthed, Hawes and her workforce discovered how the ordinary people of Minoan Crete lived: their houses and paved streets, workshops and tools, looms, fish hooks and sinkers, weapons and artists' paints, kitchen pestles and plates, children's toys, and religious practices. Hawes also unearthed sanctuaries and earth goddess statues.

Hawes was the first woman to direct an excavation, and she was also the first woman to publish her results. From 1900 until 1906 she taught archaeology, epigraphy, and modern Greek at Smith College. She married and had two children and continued to publish and teach, first at the University of Wisconsin and then at Dartmouth College (1910–1917). After World War I she became assistant director (1919–1924) and then associate director (1924–1934) of the Museum of Fine Arts in Boston. She taught at Wellesley College until 1936. In her later years she was more involved with the international peace movement and U.S. politics than she was with archaeology, becoming an active New Dealer in Boston in the 1930s.

See also Schliemann Excavates Troy, Mycenae, Ilios, Orchomenos, and Tiryns (1870–1891); Seriation and History in the Archaeology of Predynastic Egypt (1891–

1904); Discovery of Minoan Civilization (1900–1935); Linear B Deciphered (1953).

Further Reading

Fotou, V. 1993. *New Light on Gournia: unknown documents of the excavation at Gournia and other sites on the Isthmus of Ierapetra by Harriet Ann Boyd.* Austin: University of Texas at Austin, Program in Aegean Scripts and Prehistory.

Hawes, C. H., and H. B. Hawes. 1922. *Crete, the forerunner of Greece.* London, New York: Harper & Brothers.

Hawes, H. B., B. E. Williams, R. B. Seager, and E. H. Hall. 1908. *Gournia, Vasiliki and other prehistoric sites on the isthmus of Hierapetra, Crete; excavations of the Wells-Houston-Cramp Expeditions, 1901, 1903, 1904.* Philadelphia, PA: The American Exploration Society, Free Museum of Science and Art.

Publication of Die typologische Methode *(1903)*

Historian of archaeology Bo Gräslund's account of the career of Gustaf Oscar Augustin Montelius (1843–1921) raises important points about the reception of ideas. For Gräslund, what made Montelius famous was the publication of lesser, more derivative works, such as *Die typologische Methode* (1903), which was published in German, rather than his innovative work on Bronze Age chronology, which was only published in Swedish. Yet by 1885 the methods Montelius developed while working on the Bronze Age were instrumental in achieving larger syntheses that also specifically addressed more general theoretical issues such as the nature of change in prehistoric societies (generally, for Montelius, through the process of diffusion). A good example of such a synthesis is his *Der Orient und Europa* (1899), which was highly influential.

Montelius began his archaeological life in the Museum of National Antiquities in Stockholm. Like Thomsen and other museum archaeologists of the time, his primary interest was in creating chronologies using typologies of artifacts. These chronologies became the basis of European prehistory. His primary foci were first, the Bronze Age, and then later in his career, the Iron Age.

In his account of Scandinavian Bronze Age chronology (*Tidsbestämning inom Bronsåldern med Särskildt Afseende på Skandinavien* (*Dating in the Bronze Age with Special Reference to Scandinavia* 1885), Montelius provided absolute dates for his six periods of the Scandinavian Bronze Age. These were derived from the classic methodology of comparing closed finds from across Europe and into the Near East. This was a prodigious achievement, and Gräslund is right to stress its sheer intellectuality that set methodological standards and strongly influenced Gordon Childe.

Over the next twenty years, Montelius applied his method of cross-dating over a wider geographical area (both Europe and the Near East) and a longer timescale. His continental chronology was both the outcome and the justification of diffusionist thinking where civilization was brought into Europe from the Near East—*ex oriente lux* (out of the East, light)—that pervaded much of the thinking among European archaeologists until the introduction of radiometric dating during in the 1950s. Explicit methodological statements such as those found in *Die typologische Methode* enhanced the "rightness" of diffusionist thinking as it was argued to have been clearly based on objective scientific evidence.

Of perhaps equal importance was the sense that now that the chronology of later European prehistory was satisfactorily established, real historical questions of process and culture could be explored. Here Montelius's emphasis on the Near East as the primary source of cultural innovation did not find such widespread support, especially among adherents to the *Kulturkreise* school, or those with a belief in Germany as the source of cultural innovation (especially Kossinna and Schuchardt).

See also *Guide to Northern Archaeology* Published in English (1848); Publication of *Primeval Antiquities of Denmark* in English (1849); Typology Makes History (1850–1900); Romano-Germanic Central Museum Established in Mainz by Ludwig Lindenschmidt (1852); Iron Age Site of La Tène Discovered (1857); Publication of *Die Methode der Ethnologie* (1907); Publication of *Die Herkunft der Germanen* (1911); Publication of *The Dawn of European Civilization* (1925).

Further Reading

Gräslund, B. 1987. *The birth of prehistoric chronology*. Cambridge: Cambridge University Press.

Gräslund, B. 2001. Gustaf Oscar Augustin Montelius, 1843–1921. In *Encyclopedia of archaeology: The great archaeologists,* ed. T. Murray, 155–163. Santa Barbara, CA: ABC-CLIO.

Montelius, O. 1899. *Der Orient und Europa*. Stockholm: Konigl.

Montelius, O. 1903. *Die typologische Methode. Die älteren Kulturperioden im Orient und Europa, I, die methode*. Stockholm: Selbstverlag.

Trigger, B. 1989. *A history of archaeological thought*. Cambridge: Cambridge University Press.

Publication of Les vases céramiques ornés de la Gaule romaine *(1904)*

The archaeological career of Joseph Déchelette (1862–1914) was brief—fifteen years—between his retirement from his manufacturing business and his death during the first year of World War I. Dechelette was a self-taught scholar whose interest was in the period between prehistory and history, often called protohistory, the period of contact between Rome and Iron Age Europe.

Between 1895 and 1907, Dechelette took over the direction of the excavation of the site of Bibracte, located at Mont Beuvray. Bibracte was the fortified capital city of the Heduen tribe who were allies of the Romans and who defected to Julius Caesar at the beginning of the Gallic revolt of 52 BC; Vercingetorix had pleaded his case for a union of tribes against Casear there.

The site had been identified by Dechelette's uncle, Jean-Gabriel Bulliot, in the 1850s and its excavation begun by him in 1867. Excavations by Bulliot and Déchelette revealed that Bibracte was a sizable Gaulish town before it became a Roman one, a "civilized" place, ringed by walls and ramparts, constructed from wood and iron, and entered via monumental gateways. It was the home of artisans working in iron, bronze, and enameling. Bibracte had a large residential quarter, many wealthy houses, a marketplace, and religious sanctuaries.

The exploration of the site spanned a period of aggressive French nationalism. Beginning in the mid-nineteenth century with the emperor Napoleon III's support of Bulliot's claims that the medieval town of Autun was in fact the site of the Gallic oppidum of Bibracte, through to Déchelette's own death in 1914 on the western front of World War I, the place became a symbol for modern France—a symbol of its difference to, and independence from, the rest of Europe. Not only was Déchelette writing a new history for France, but he was also pioneering the new field techniques that enabled him to construct that history. His research at Bibracte contributed greatly to the development of Iron Age studies. "The Beuvraisian" was the name given to the last phase of the late La Tène period (140–30 BC).

Déchelette's first book, *Les vases céramiques ornés de la Gaule romaine,* published in 1904, demonstrated his encyclopedic knowledge and his interest in the structure of empirical archaeological information. It is a testimony to his great abilities as a synthesizer and pioneer of archaeological field techniques. His analysis of types of vases and their decorative techniques enabled him to identify their potters and the workshops that produced them. Through this he was able to trace the development of the ceramic industry in the Gallo-Roman era, which coincided with a shift in the centers of its production from northern Italy to the banks of the Rhine River. In this Dechelette moved from techno-chronological studies of archaeological material to economic history or historical anthropology. Between1908 and 1914 Dechelette wrote and published four volumes of *Manuel d'archéologie préhistorique, celtique et galloromaine*—a manual of national archaeology for France and a tribute to its long history.

See also Typology Makes History (1850–1900); Romano-Germanic Central Museum Established in Mainz by Ludwig Lindenschmidt (1852); Iron Age Site of La Tène Discovered (1857); Publication of *Pre-historic Times* (1865); Publication of *Die typologische Methode* (1903).

Further Reading

Buchesnschutz, O. 2001. Bibracte. In *Encyclopedia of archaeology: History and discoveries,* ed. T. Murray, 159–160. Santa Barbara, CA: ABC-CLIO.

Buchenschutz, O., I. B. Ralston, and J-P. Guillaument. 1999. *Le remparts de Bibracte.* Glux-en-Glenn, France: Centre Archeologique Europeen de Mont Beuvray.

Déchelette, F. 1962. *Livre d'or de Joseph Déchelette; centenaire, 1862–1962.* Roanne, France: Impr. Sully.

Déchelette, J. 1904. *Les vases céramiques ornés de la Gaule romaine: narbonnaise, acquitaine et lyonnaise.* Paris: A. Picard.

Olivier, L. 1999. Joseph Déchelette, 1862–1914. In *Encyclopedia of archaeology: The Great archaeologists,* ed. T. Murray, 275–288. Santa Barbara, CA: ABC-CLIO.

Discovering the Riches of Central Asia—The Journeys of Sir Aurel Stein (1906–1930)

Born in Budapest, Mark Aurel Stein (1862–1943) studied Persian and Indian archaeology at universities in Austria and Germany. Between 1884 and 1887, Stein studied classical and oriental archaeology and languages at Oxford University, where he met, and was greatly influenced by, the greatest of the explorer-scholars of the nineteenth century, Sir Henry Rawlinson. Stein would be the last, while Rawlinson was among the first, of a group of remarkable adventurers, such as Layard, Stephens and Catherwood, Cunningham, Stanley, Speke, Burton, and Shackleton, who traveled in often extremely difficult circumstances, out of contact with home, sometimes for years, to explore and map the world's unknown geographic regions. And like Layard, Rawlinson, Cunningham, Stephens, and Catherwood, Stein also recovered evidence of ancient texts and languages and civilizations.

In 1888 Stein traveled to India to become the principal of the Oriental College at Lahore and registrar for the Punjab University. For the next ten years he spent his vacations undertaking antiquarian and geographical research in Kashmir and on the northwest frontier of India (now northern Pakistan and eastern Afghanistan) and his spare time learning and translating Sanskrit, the Indo-Aryan literary language of Hindu religious texts or vedas, which was first used around 500 BC. He became well connected with the civil and vice-regal establishment of British colonial India.

In 1900, with the support of the viceroy of India, Lord Curzon, and the survey of India, Stein led his first expedition into central Asia, where he was to lead three more expeditions in 1906–1908, 1913–1916, and 1930. He took different routes each time to and from Turkistan, surveying, exploring, mapping, and excavating as he went. He traveled huge distances and brought back to India, and then to Britain, thousands of artifacts (as well as intelligence for the British government about what was happening in those mysterious regions). The political tensions between Britain and Russia, and Britain and Germany, that were prevalent during the late nineteenth and early twentieth centuries, had an impact on the politics and policies of their colonies in the east and in central Asia particularly. Geographic exploration of these regions was used to provide strategic and political information as well. Stein became a naturalized British subject in 1904, and between 1910 and 1929 was directly employed by the Archaeological Survey of India. He was knighted in 1912.

Stein's achievements were substantial. He explored a whole area of the world that was historically little known. Archaeologically it was essentially a blank spot on the map. Each of his expeditions created new knowledge about the past and the present of this vast region. On his first expedition he explored the southern oases of the Taklimakan Desert, and at settlements in the Khotan region he discovered numerous documents in ancient Tibetan, Chinese, and Kharoshti (a script used in the northwest of India around the third century BC).

On his second expedition he explored the dried-up Lop Sea bed and traced the centuries-old caravan route between China and the West by following the trail of Neolithic implements, metal objects, beads, and ancient Han coins. He visited the watchtowers of the ancient Chinese frontier, and at the site of Miran, in what is now Chinese central Asia, he found wall paintings of classical design. In perhaps his greatest find, Stein explored the "Cave of the Thousand Buddhas," where he unearthed a large number of documents and temple paintings not seen since the eleventh century AD. His success in this area inspired a number of expeditions by German and French archaeologists, who also carried off antiquities, and led to an increase in the Chinese government's animosity toward Western interference and rapacity.

Stein's third expedition completed his circuit of the Taklimakan Desert via Russian territory and traced the "Silk Route" to Samarkand, returning south through eastern Persia (now Iran) to Baluchistan (now part of modern Pakistan). Political difficulties in 1930 prevented the completion of Stein's fourth trip, but he did manage to travel 2,000 miles around the Taklimakan Desert anyway. Between 1927 and 1936, continuing political difficulties caused Stein to begin to explore the connections between the Indus civilization, unearthed by Sir John Marshall in the 1920s (now in modern Pakistan) and the civilizations of Mesopotamia in the Near East. To this end he discovered and mapped extensive Chalcolithic and Neolithic remains in northwestern India and southeastern and western Iran. In 1929 Stein carried out an aerial survey of the Roman frontier or "limes" in Iraq and the Jezira, and he investigated these finds on the ground and in detail between 1938 and 1939.

As a consequence of his travels throughout the Near East and central Asia, Stein became interested in searching for traces of Alexander the Great's eastern campaigns between 331 and 323 BC. He had found evidence of Alexander in southwestern Iran near Persepolis and in the Greco-Buddhist remains in the Swat Valley of northern Pakistan. In 1931 Stein traveled from Taxila, east of the Indus River, to the Jhelum River, where he located the site of the defeat of Poros and explained Alexander's tactics. His last expedition, undertaken in 1943 when he was at a really advanced age, traced the retreat of Alexander's army through Baluchistan. Stein died at age ninety-one, on a visit to Kabul, Afghanistan.

In many ways Stein was the last of the great explorers: physically tough, fearless, independent, possessed of a brilliant intellect, a superb linguist, and able to travel with only local colleagues and guides as companions. In other ways he was unique in the breadth of his achievements. Stein published scientific records and narrative accounts of all of his expeditions. He received honorary degrees from the universities of Oxford, Cambridge, and St. Andrews; the Founder's gold medal from the Royal Geographic Society; the Huxley Medallion; the Flinders Petrie Medal; and the gold medals of the Royal Asiatic Society and the Society of Antiquaries of London. He left his estate to create and support the Stein-Arnold Fund to be used for the geographic and antiquarian exploration of central and southwestern Asia.

See also Decipherment of Cuneiform (1836–1857); Foundation of the Archaeological Survey of India (1861); Schliemann Excavates Troy, Mycenae, Ilios, Orchomenos, and Tiryns (1870–1891); Discovery of the Indus Civilization (1920–Present); Discovering Tutankhamen's Tomb (1922–1932).

Further Reading

Mirsky, J. 1977. *Sir Aurel Stein: archaeological explorer.* Chicago: University of Chicago Press.

Walker, A. 1998. *Aurel Stein: pioneer of the Silk Road.* London: John Murray.

Wang, H., ed. 2004. *Sir Aurel Stein: proceedings of the British Museum study day, 23 March 2002.* London: British Museum.

Discovery of the Hittites (1906–1931)

The Hittites were known about for over two millennia, because they were mentioned in the books of Genesis and Joshua in the Bible, but the archaeological remains of their civilization, which had once threatened Egypt during the fourteenth century BC, remained elusive. It was not until the excavation of the Hittite capital of Hattussa (Boghazkoy in modern Turkey) from 1906 until the end of 1931, and excavations at other Hittite sites, that archaeologists were able to piece together evidence and describe this extraordinary civilization that had dominated Turkey and the Levant from ca. 3000–1000 BC. As the result of excavated material, by the 1940s the Hittite script and language dialects were deciphered. But the search for the Hittites began almost a century prior to this.

Many European explorers had roamed through the Turkish empire looking for classical and Biblical sites to loot during the late eighteenth and early nineteenth centuries. In 1834 the French antiquarian Charles Texier visited the town of Boghazkoy, 200 kilometers south of Ankara, in central Anatolia, in what is now the modern state of Turkey. He wrongly identified the ruins adjacent to Boghazkoy as being those of a city destroyed by the Persian king Cyrus the Great in the sixth century BC. However, he also noted that a nearby religious site was connected to a rock face decorated with strange hieroglyphics and carved figurative processions. More reports of similar hieroglyphics and low relief sculptures at sites all over Anatolia appeared over the next four decades.

In 1872, some examples of these strange Anatolian hieroglyphics were examined by Irish missionary William Wright, who attributed them to the Hittites. In the late 1870s, British Orientalist Archibald Sayce also attributed the new Anatolian script discovered by Wright to the Hittites, a group not only recorded in the Bible, but also mentioned in more recently translated Egyptian and Assyrian inscriptions. Sayce argued that the Hittites had an empire in the Near East, a suggestion that was discounted by scholars at the time. However, in the 1880s, Sayce's theory was vindicated through the excavation and translation of correspondence from a recently excavated diplomatic archive at the site of el-Amarna in Egypt. The archival material dated from the fourteenth century BC and mentioned a Hittite empire and its threat to Egyptian vassal states in Palestine and Syria. Other diplomatic letters between Egyptian and Hittite rulers were found in which the salutation of "brother" was used, an acknowledgment of great power, at least equal to that of Egypt, and marriage alliances between the royal families of both people were proposed.

Some Iron Age hieroglyphic texts and sculptures, dating from between the twelfth to eighth centuries BC, had been identified as belonging to the Hittites of the Bible. But the Hittites of the Amarna letters were older by more than 200 years, and their empire was at its peak during the late Bronze Age. It was evident that some of the monuments and inscriptions at the sites occupied by these later, Iron Age, and so-called neo-Hittites had been erected during the earlier Hittite empire that had threatened Egypt into a treaty. The search for evidence for the origins and the decline of this Bronze Age Hittite civilization was taken up by German, English, and French archaeologists.

In 1893–1894, Ernest Chantre found fragments of clay tablets in cuneiform script at Boghazkoy. In 1904 the English archaeologist John Garstang (1876–1956), who had become interested in the Hittites through fieldwork in Egypt with Flinders Petrie, requested permission from the Turkish government to excavate at Boghazkoy. This was at first granted, and then withdrawn through the intervention of the kaiser of Germany, who was a new and powerful Turkish ally. The site was given to German archaeologists to excavate. Garstang was allowed to excavate the late Hittite site of Skje-Geuzi in what is now Syria, and English archaeologist David Hogarth was permitted to work at the site of Carchemish, another Hittite site on the Euphrates River.

Excavations at Boghazkoy began in 1906, under the direction of Hugo Winckler for the Deutsche Orient-Gesellschaft (German Oriental Society) and Theodore Makridi Bey, second director of the Istanbul Museum. They found thousands of inscribed tablets that were from a palace and administrative complex. Some of the tablets had Akkadian script on them, and from this Winckler was able to translate the title "great king of the Hatti," and identify the Boghazkoy site as Hattussa, the capital of the Hittite empire. Excavations continued until the beginning of World War I, uncovering the palace complex, its storage rooms, and a large library. In the library excavators found wooden shelving around the walls to store the tablets, shelf labels, and subject catalog.

Most of the tablets were in fragments, but the larger pieces, numbering more than 10,000, were of great value to epigraphers for the details they eventually provided about life in Hattussa and the administration of the Hittite empire. By 1915 the Hittite language had been deciphered by the Czech scholar Bedrich Hrozny, and the huge amount of information on the Hattussa tablets was being deciphered and interpreted along with the archaeological evidence.

In 1907 a team of archaeologists and architects, directed by Otto Pushstein from the German Archaeological Institute, joined Winckler's team and surveyed and excavated the city walls. The three large gates within these walls, named for the distinctive sculptures associated with each—the sphinx, lion, and king's gates—and the upper walls were constructed during the last and most powerful phase of Hittite power. The style of the gates, in particular, revealed the extent of Egyptian influences on Hittite architecture during this period. The royal residence and palace administration were located on an acropolis linked to the upper city by a large bridge or viaduct. The palace storerooms contained large amounts of pottery, bronze weapons, and ceremonial artifacts, some of which were traded or looted objects. The upper city comprised more than thirty temples and their precincts, for some of the "thousand gods" of the Hittites. Impressive low-relief sculptures were found here, depicting major deities and kings.

The largest temple of Hattussa was located in the lower city, and it had twin precincts belonging to the two primary Hittite deities, the storm god Hatti and the sun goddess Arinna. Across from these temples, a complex of workshops for temple personnel—priests, musicians, weavers, potters, smiths, carpenters, and stonecutters—was found. Huge pottery storage jars containing grains and other commodities were also found. There was evidence that the Hittites traded not only with the Egyptians but also with the Mycenaeans and Assyrians and with "Mitanni," a city-state located in eastern Turkey.

Excavations resumed at Hattussa in 1931, jointly funded by the two German institutes and under the direction of archaeologist Kurt Bittel. Because Winckler had concentrated on locating tablets, and Pushstein on locating architectural monuments, Bittel concentrated on sorting out the site's stratigraphy to better understand the origins and fate of the Hittite empire. Excavation was again resumed after World War II, and by then other data from Hittite sites dug by English archaeologists and from Hittite sites from all over the Near East contributed to a much broader and long-term elucidation of Anatolian history and its connections with Syria, Palestine, Lebanon, Iraq, Egypt, and the Mediterranean. In the 1940s more information from inscriptions became possible through the discovery of Phoenician-Hittite inscriptions on the monumental gates at the site of Karatepe, an eighth century BC neo-Hittite fortified palace in southwestern Anatolia. These bilingual inscriptions led to the decipherment of the Luwian Hittite dialect.

See also Discovery of the Amarna Tablets (1887); Seriation and History in the Archaeology of Predynastic Egypt (1891–1904); Discovery of Minoan Civilization (1900–1935); Discovering the Riches of Central Asia—The Journeys of Sir Aurel Stein (1906–1930); Discovery of the Indus Civilization (1920–Present); Excavation of Ur (1922–1934); Excavation of Jarmo (1948–1954); Excavation of Jericho (1952–1958); First Excavation of Catal Hüyük (1961–1965).

Further Reading

Bittel, K. 1970. *Hattusha: the capital of the Hittites.* New York: Oxford University Press.

Garstang, J. 1910. *The land of the Hittites; an account of recent explorations and discoveries in Asia Minor, with descriptions of the Hittite monuments; with maps and plans, ninety-nine photographs and a bibliography.* London: Constable.

Hilprecht, H. V. 1903. *Explorations in Bible lands during the 19th century.* Philadelphia, PA: A. J. Holman.

Yener, K. A., and H. A. Hoffner, Jr., eds. 2002. *Recent developments in Hittite archaeology and history: Papers in memory of Hans G. Güterbock.* Winona Lake, IN: Eisenbrauns.

Publication of Die Methode der Ethnologie *(1907)*

Fritz Graebner (1877–1934) studied history at Berlin University and began working at Berlin's Royal Museum of Ethnography in 1899. He became fascinated by ethnographic problems, working with museum colleague Bernard Ankermann to found *Kulturkreislehre,* "the study of culture circles" or culture-historical ethnology, within the Berlin Society for Anthropology, Ethnology and Prehistory. Stimulated by the work of anthropologist Leo Frobenius and geographer Friedrich Ratzel, Graebner and Ankermann lectured on culture circles and culture strata in Oceania and Africa, rejecting the then dominant biological-evolutionary concepts of ethnography.

In 1907 Graebner moved to Cologne to work at the new Rautenstrauch-Joest-Museum and continued his theoretical research, the result of which was his book *Die Methode der Ethnologie (The Method of Ethnology)* (1907). Graebner's fieldwork area was the South Pacific, and in 1914 he was interned in Australia for the duration of World War I. He became professor at the University of Bonn in 1921, moved to University of Cologne in 1926, but retired because of ill health in 1928.

Graebner argued that it was possible to construct a universal history of humanity based on ethnographic interconnections; in other words, cultural mixing and borrowings could be traced back in time, via circles of influences and characteristics, to their "original" cultures. These were based on the distribution of material cultural traits—but there was little archaeological evidence to support them.

Graebner's pupil, Oswald Menghin (1888–1973), tried to extend the concepts of culture historians back into the Paleolithic period, and he wrote a world prehistory, compiling trait lists and diagnostic elements from archaeological evidence to designate three primary culture circles. Unfortunately, his theories were based on his preconceptions rather than on hard evidence, on patterns he looked for and found, ignoring any contrary information. Menghin argued that everything was interconnected, that all cultures had developed from a few original ones, and that history was hyperdiffusionist. But in fact, his theories were developed to accommodate his Roman Catholic fundamentalism, which rejected biological evolutionism. He was obsessed with the concept of "purity" in relation to all races and believed in autochtony, that people who lived thousands of years ago in a certain place were the direct physical and spiritual ancestors of the present inhabitants. This belief was also held by the German archaeologist Gustav Kossinna, whose settlement-area archaeology was concerned with locating racial homelands.

Menghin's political beliefs placed him to the right of German politics, and he supported the unification of Austria and Germany into one greater German state. During the 1920s and 1930s his cultural theories were also appreciated by Nazi ideologists, who placed their Aryan forebears in the center of any central European culture circles.

Menghin migrated to Argentina after World War II, where he taught enthnography and archaeology. He may have left the Old World behind, but his theories about the culture history of his New World home were still hyperdiffusionist. He argued that cultural advances in the Americas were directly linked to developments in the Old World and that the peopling of the continents and the development of complex civilizations in Mesoamerica and the Andes were not the result of the inventiveness of indigenous peoples or their independent responses to their environment or each other.

See also Romano-Germanic Central Museum Established in Mainz by Ludwig Lindenschmidt (1852); Publication of *Die typologische Methode* (1903); Paleopathology in Nubia (1909–1911); Publication of *Die Herkunft der Germanen* (1911); Publication of *The Dawn of European Civilization* (1925).

Further Reading

Graebner, F. 1911. *Methode der Ethnologie.* Heidelberg, Germany: C. Winter.

Kohl, P., and J. A. Perez Gollan. 2002. Religion, politics and prehistory. Reassessing the lingering legacy of Oswald Menghin. *Current Anthropology* 4: 561–586.

The World's First Archaeological Salvage Project? (1907–1932)

The great American archaeologist George Reisner (1867–1942) wrote his Ph.D. in Semitic languages at Harvard University, and then he became interested in Egyptian archaeology while studying in Germany. In 1897 he accompanied German Egyptologist Ludwig Borchardt (1863–1938) to Egypt, where he spent two years helping him to catalog the collections in the new Egyptian Museum of Antiquities. Reisner's first fieldwork was sponsored by the University of California, at a site in middle Egypt, and then in 1903 at the necropolis of Giza, beside the Great Pyramids. But in 1905 Reisner's work began to be funded jointly by Harvard University and the Boston Museum of Fine Arts, as the Harvard-Boston Expedition, which he would direct for the next forty years.

In 1907 construction of the first Aswan Dam began in southern Egypt; on completion it would flood more than 100 miles of a part of the Nile Valley, which had been part of the ancient kingdom of Nubia. The threatened destruction of the archaeological sites in the flood zone prompted the Egyptian government departments of antiquities and surveys to undertake the Archaeological Survey of Nubia—the world's first major archaeological salvage campaign. The survey continued until 1911, and Reisner was its director from 1907–1908.

Reisner's year with the survey was a crucial one, during which he developed the field methodology that was followed in all subsequent seasons (as well as by later expeditions to Nubia for almost the next fifty years). Reisner's methodology involved the use of standard recording forms, the systematic use of section drawings and stratigraphic records, and the deployment of multidisciplinary teams. Reisner's pioneering use of standardized recording procedures in the field, which allowed for the synthesis of large amounts of archaeological data, was to have a huge impact on fieldwork in the Americas for the next half century. After he pioneered its use in Nubia, it was adopted by a new generation of American archaeologists, such as Alfred Kidder and Sylvanus G. Morley, whom Reisner taught at Harvard. Both of these archaeologists would apply Reisner's methodology to North American and Mesoamerican sites with great success. In 1910 Reisner was appointed professor of Egyptology at Harvard and curator of Egyptian art at the Boston Museum of Fine Arts.

During this first season of fieldwork in Nubia, Reisner discovered the remains of several unknown Nubian cultures and devised a chronological sequence for them from grave and pottery typologies. In 1913 he returned with the Harvard-Boston expedition to southern Egypt and northern Sudan to elucidate this little-known culture. The earliest dynasties of ancient Egypt had traded with the black people of the kingdom of Nubia, better known as "the Land of Kush," beyond the first cataract of the Nile River at Aswan. Eventually, during the Egyptian Middle Kingdom, Nubia was occasionally garrisoned by the Egyptians to protect the safety of these important trade routes. The Nubians began to form their own independent states, one of which became the central kingdom of Kerma, which was at its most powerful around 2000 BC. The pharoahs of the New Kingdom subjugated Nubia, but in the eighth century BC, a dynasty of Nubian pharoahs conquered Egypt and held it until they in turn were defeated by the Assyrians.

For the next twenty years, until 1932, Reisner and his team excavated most of the monumental sites of Nubia, including the great early necropolis of Kerma, most of the huge brick fortresses built by the Egyptian pharaohs in Nubia, a complex of Kushite temples at Napata, and all of the royal tombs of the Kushite monarchs and their queens, both at Napata and at Meroe. Out of these exemplary excavations Reisner developed a chronological sequence for prehistoric Nubian culture and a detailed chronology for all of the rulers of the empire of Kush and their queens based mainly on the typological studies of their tombs.

Reisner excavated in the Sudan in the winter and Egypt in the summer. While Reisner's most famous work was in Nubia and the Sudan, he also made substantial contributions to Egyptian archaeology, and he excavated with his Harvard-Boston team at the great mastaba cemetery at Giza until his death. These excavations were models for their time. He died at his field camp in Giza.

See also Seriation and History in the Archaeology of Predynastic Egypt (1891–1904); Paleopathology in Nubia (1909–1911); Stratigraphic Excavation in the Americas (1911–1913); Saving Abu Simbel (1959–1980).

Further Reading

Adams, W. Y. 2001. George Reisner, 1867–1942. In *Encyclopedia of archaeology: History and discoveries,* ed. T. Murray, 1093–1095. Santa Barbara, CA: ABC-CLIO.

Adams, W. Y. 2001. Nubia. In *Encyclopedia of archaeology: History and discoveries,* ed. T. Murray, 954–963. Santa Barbara, CA: ABC-CLIO.

Reisner, G. A. 1923. *Excavations at Kerma.* Cambridge, MA: Peabody Museum of Harvard University.

Spencer, A. J. 1993. *Early Egypt: The rise of civilization in the Nile Valley.* London: British Museum Press.

Paleopathology in Nubia (1909–1911)

Born in Australia, Sir Grafton Elliot Smith (1871–1937) was a medical graduate who won a scholarship to travel to Cambridge University to further his anatomical research. In 1900 he became professor of anatomy in Cairo, Egypt, and returned to Britain in 1909 as an anatomy professor at Manchester University. In 1919 he became professor of anatomy at University College London.

During his time in Cairo, Smith became interested in paleopathology, the study of diseases in ancient populations through the examination of skeletal and biological remains. By the 1890s Flinders Petrie was using new X-ray technology on mummies to elucidate the causes of the deaths and the impact of their growth and development on their morphology. In his examination of mummies Smith began to record the development of splinting and other ancient medical treatments, mummification processes, and the impact of disease and diet on human skeletons. He was already an expert in this area when he became a major participant in planning and completing the first Archaeological Survey of Nubia, directed by American archaeologist George Reisner (1909–1911).

As part of preserving the sites and data to be submerged by the damming of the Nile River near Aswan, more than 10,000 burials were excavated and studied, the largest sample of burials ever excavated and analyzed from archaeological sites in one region. They revealed data about the prevalence and kinds of diseases in populations over time—evidence of gallstones, scrotal hernias, cancer, leprosy, tuberculosis, and smallpox were found, prompting some archaeologists at the time to remark that they knew more about the Egyptian and Nubian way of death than they did about their way of life. The methods Smith and his colleagues developed during these studies forever changed the nature and significance of paleopathology and its relationship with archaeology.

Smith's interests in and thoughts about ethnology and paleopathology, the results of his own research and his participation in the Archaeological Survey of Nubia, led him to theorize that all cultural development—especially agriculture, pottery, clothing, monumental architecture, and kingship—had originated in Egypt, which he believed to be "the cradle of civilization." These Egyptian innovations had then spread to the rest of the world via Egyptian merchants and their trade routes. His books, *The Migrations of Early Culture* (1915) and *The Ancient Egyptians and the Origin of Civilizations* (1923), elaborate these hyperdiffusionist ideas and were popular at the time of their publication, influencing the work of archaeologist Gordon Childe and anthropologists W. J. Perry and Herbert Fleure.

With his paleoanatomical expertise Smith also contributed to the debate about primate and hominid evolution, believing it was characterized by an increase in neurological sensory development in the areas of sight and hearing. He examined the Piltdown skull and declared it "the most primitive and most simian of human brains so far recorded," lending some credibility to this scientific hoax at the time of its perpetration.

See also World's First Archaeological Salvage Project? (1907–1932); Piltdown Unmasked (1955).

Further Reading

David, A., ed. 1979. *The Manchester Museum Mummy Project: Multidisciplinary research on ancient Egyptian mummified remains.* Manchester UK: Manchester Museum.

Davies, W. V., and R. Walker. 1993. *Biological anthropology and the study of ancient Egypt.* London: British Museum Press.

Elkin, A. P., and N. W. G. Macintosh. 1974. *Grafton Elliot Smith: The man and his work.* Sydney, Australia: Sydney University Press.

Smith, G. E. 1929. *Human history.* New York: W.W. Norton & Company.

Smith, G. E. 1931. *Early man: His origin, development and culture.* London: Benn.

Publication of **Die Herkunft der Germanen** *(1911)*

It has long been understood that the concept of an archaeological culture was derivative of the concept of culture itself. The concept of culture was one of the great achievements of nineteenth-century anthropology and geography, but it also owed much to new approaches to writing history that were pioneered in Germany and, shortly after, were seen in England. Again, throughout the second half of the nineteenth century antiquarians and archaeologists became more adept at the description and classification of material culture, the creation of typologies and regional sequences, and of course, at the vital business of mapping the locations of sites and their contents. These crucial developments had been the hallmark of Scandinavian archaeology, particularly through the work of those giants of archaeological method Thomsen, Worsaae, the Hildebrands, Sophus Muller, and Oscar Montelius.

Gustav Kossinna (1858–1931) was heir to this great tradition. Like them, his great goal was to effectively animate these typologies into history—to create interpretations of difference, similarity, change, variation, and stasis that would enable contemporary people to find meaning in the past. Unlike his predecessors, his chosen framework was the glorification of Germans and Germany at the expense of other European nations. Archaeology was racial and cultural politics for Kossinna, and its primary purpose was to support the ambitions of the German imperium.

The fundamental innovation in *Die Herkunft der Germanen* was the postulation of a methodology that equated patterned distributions in material culture with distinct ethnic groups. Defining regularly occurring assemblages of material culture, while not an easy or straightforward task, had been shown by the Scandinavians to be an achievable goal. The notion of interpreting this pattern as having been the outcome of knowable cultural processes allowed Kossinna to argue, by extension, that these archaeological phenomena were best understood as ancient manifestations of cultural processes that were operating in the contemporary world and that had been properly described by anthropologists and philologists. Thus, archaeological cultures (the *taxon* that was the fundamental unit of classification similar to the species in biology) were real entities made up of people who shared the same ethnicity and the same language. Mapping the distribution of these cultures over space and time would provide the basic evidence of racial history and allow the contemporary world to learn the lessons of the past that Kossinna believed were so important—the preeminence of the Nordic peoples, the existence of pure racial stock that had persisted for thousands of years as racial essences, and the search for the history of how German identity had manifested itself through the ages.

For Kossinna, the past and the present were intimately linked. Significantly, his method created the concept of an archaeological culture out of contemporary culture theory. He was also committed to creating prehistory in Germany and its border regions by beginning in the present and tracing back further and further into the past. Of course this ran the serious risk of creating a prehistory where the present is the inevitable outcome of the past, but Kossinna was hardly the first (or the last) archaeologist to accept the consequences of this inferential strategy.

For all of its unpleasantness, especially the assumption of Nordic racial superiority, Kossinna's methodology was a prodigious achievement that would play such a large part in the culture historical archaeology of Gordon Childe and others. With the wisdom of hindsight, especially after the horrors created by the German Nazi Party that were in part an outgrowth of the racism of Kossinna and others, we might ask why archaeologists did not look more closely at the assumptions that powered culture historical archaeology, but that would be to ask for a prescience that was entirely beyond many at the time.

See also Typology Makes History (1850–1900); Iron Age Site of La Tène discovered (1857); Romano-Germanic Central Museum Established in Maine by Ludwig Lindenschmidt (1852); Publication of *Die typologische Methode* (1903); Publication of *Die Methode der Ethnologie* (1907); Paleopathology in Nubia (1909–1911); Publication of *The Dawn of European Civilization* (1925).

Further Reading

Klejn, L. 1999. Gustav Kossinna, 1858–1931. In *Encyclopedia of archaeology: The great archaeologists,* ed. T. Murray, 233–246. Santa Barbara, CA: ABC-CLIO.

Kossinna, G. 1911. *Die Herkunft der Germanen; zur methode der Siedlungsarchäologie.* Würzburg, Germany: C. Kabitzsch.

Trigger, B. 1989. *A history of archaeological thought.* Cambridge: Cambridge University Press.

Machu Picchu Found (1911)

Hiram Bingham (1875–1956) was a lecturer in Latin American history at Yale University who married an heiress. In his researches Bingham found mentions of a secret capital of the Incas, from which they led a thirty-year campaign of resistance against the Spanish invasion and conquest. It is no surprise that Bingham became interested in locating it. In 1911 he led an expedition to Peru that rediscovered what he claimed was "the lost city of the Incas," the site of Machu Picchu, and captured the attention of a mass audience through his published descriptions.

Bingham was the last in a long line of American adventurers that had begun with Stephens and Catherwood. His account of finding Machu Picchu describes braving deadly vipers, bribing recalcitrant guides, struggling up difficult mountain trails in bad weather, crossing tenuously secured narrow bridges across deeply dangerous canyons, slashing through dense jungles, and holding on with his fingernails to cracks in rock faces in a hundred per cent humidity, until, finally:

> [H]ardly as we left the hut and rounded the promontory than we were confronted with an unexpected sight, a great flight of beautifully constructed stone-faced terraces, perhaps a hundred of them, each hundreds of feet long and ten feet high. They had been recently rescued from the jungle by the Indians. A veritable forest of large trees which had been growing on them had been chopped down and partly burned to make a clearing for agricultural purposes.
>
> . . . we patiently followed the little guide along one of the widest terraces and made our way into an untouched forest beyond. Suddenly I found myself confronted with the walls of ruined houses built of the finest quality of Inca stonework. It was hard to see them for they were partly covered with trees and moss, the growth of centuries . . . we scrambled along . . . suddenly without any warning under a huge overhanging ledge the boy showed me a cave beautifully lined with the finest cut stone. It had evidently been a Royal Mausoleum. On top of this particular ledge was a semi-circular building whose outer wall, gently sloping and slightly curved bore a striking resemblance to the famous Temple of the Sun in Cuzco. This might also be a Temple of the Sun . . . clearly it was the work of a master artist . . . this structure surpassed in attractiveness the best Inca walls in Cuzco . . . [then] . . . two of the finest and most interesting structures in ancient America made of a beautiful white granite, the walls contained blocks of Cyclopean size, higher than a man . . . the ruins of temples . . . unique among Inca ruins. Nothing just like them in design and execution has ever been found . . . [then] . . . a ceremonial edifice of peculiar significance—nowhere else in Peru is there a similar structure.
>
> It seemed like an unbelievable dream . . . It fairly took my breath away. What could this place be? . . . Would anyone believe what I had found? Fortunately

> in this land where accuracy in reporting what one has seen is not a prevailing characteristic of travellers, I had a good camera and the sun was shining . . . was this the capital of the last Incas (or) the birthplace of the first?" (Hiram Bingham 1948, in "Lost City of the Incas," quoted in B. Fagan, 1996. *Eyewitness to Discovery*. Oxford: Oxford University Press, 370–372)

It was the stuff of archaeological dreams. Between 1912 and 1915 the National Geographic Society funded Bingham's expeditions to map and excavate the site. Bingham was eventually expelled from Peru for violating his excavation permit and never returned. He gave up teaching and researching and became an aviator in World War I, and later, a successful politician.

Subsequent research has dispelled many of the mists of mystery, or the myths of history. Machu Picchu had never really been "lost"—there were local people living in it and farming its terraces when Bingham rediscovered it, and the site was known to the Spanish. However, nothing can detract from its spec-

The Inca ruins of Machu Picchu. (iStockPhoto.com)

tacular location on a 2,000-feet high mountain ridge in the Andes or from the significance of its ruins and their part in the extraordinary Inca civilization.

Located to the northwest of Cuzco, the site of Machu Picchu comprises temples, tombs, houses, and agricultural terracing made from local stone with the same high-quality techniques of building and engineering that were so common among the Inca. It was built during the reign of the Inca king Pachacuti (AD 1438–1471). At its peak, shortly before the arrival of the Spanish in 1532, the Inca Empire stretched 4,000 kilometers from Ecuador and Colombia to Chile, and encompassed more than a hundred societies, distributed across a diverse Andean environment of some eight million people.

While the world focused on Bingham's discovery of Machu Picchu, Peruvian archaeologist, Harvard graduate, and Inca descendent Julio Tello was excavating Chavin sites, from between 900 and 400 BC, in the northern Peruvian Highlands and beginning to elucidate the origins and development of Andean civilization.

See also Uhle Begins Scientific Archaeology in Peru (1895–1940); Publication of *Die Methode der Ethnologie* (1907); Stratigraphic Excavation in the Americas (1911–1913); Publication of *Origin and Development of Andean Civilization* (1942); Publication of *Prehistoric Settlement Patterns in the Viru Valley, Peru* (1953); Excavation of Chavin de Huantar (1966–1980); Chan Chan Inscribed on the World Heritage List (1986); Discovering the "Lord of Sipan" (1987).

Further Reading

Bingham, H. 1913. *The Discovery of Machu Picchu.* New York: Harper & Brothers.

Bingham, H. 1999. *The Ancient Incas: Chronicles from National Geographic.* Ed. A. M. Schlesinger, Jr. Philadelphia, PA: Chelsea House Publishers.

Bingham, H. 1977. *Lost city of the Incas: The story of Machu Picchu and its builders.* New York: Atheneum, first published 1948.

Moseley, M. 1992. *The Incas and their ancestors.* London: Thames and Hudson.

Stratigraphic Excavation in the Americas (1911–1913)

European geologists had developed the stratigraphic method, and European antiquarians and archaeologists had adapted it for archaeological use. The method was known in American archaeological circles in the 1860s (and even before, when we consider Jefferson's excavation of a burial mound near his home in Virginia in 1787). However, notwithstanding its proven usefulness in

Europe, it was not then widely employed in the Americas, except as a method of recording sites and excavations during the late nineteenth century.

There were several reasons for this. Many American archaeological sites, especially in the northeast, lacked deep stratigraphy. They were too thin for the stratigraphy to be seen, let alone to benefit from its use. Burial mounds and earthworks, which were deeper sites, comprised redeposited material, and understanding them required a level of interpretative sophistication that was not yet available. Paleo-Indian sites discovered prior to the 1920s were sparse and homogeneous, with few obvious changes in their composition over time.

The use of stratigraphic excavation began in the Americas as the direct result of the discovery of sites with deep stratigraphy and long periods of settlement in Mexico and in the Southwest and the employment of the first generation of graduate archaeologists. Both Manuel Gamio and Nels Nelson (the archaeologists concerned) were educated in anthropology and archaeology and had been taught by substantial figures in the discipline, Gamio by Franz Boas at Columbia University, and Nelson by Alfred Kroeber at Berkeley.

In 1913, Boas, as director of the International School of American Ethnology in Mexico City, encouraged his student Manuel Gamio (1883–1960) to use stratigraphic excavations on sites in the Valley of Mexico to help elucidate a sequence for pre-Columbian cultures. It has been suggested that a European geologist, Jorge Engerrand, on staff at the international school, may have suggested its deployment to both Boas and Gamio.

Gamio's excavation of the mound at San Miguel Amantla (Azcapotzalco) was the first use of stratigraphic excavation in the Americas. Using metric stratigraphy, that is, excavating by measurements of feet and not by the European natural stratigraphic method, Gamio traced the gradual transition of an older and archaic form of pottery than that of the Teotihuacán culture. Gradual cultural change was evidenced by a mixture of both pottery styles in the intermediate levels and by the transitional nature of different pottery forms. Gamio's exactions established the basic archaeological and culture sequence of Achaic/Teotihuacán/Aztec in central Mexico.

In 1913 archaeologist Nels Nelson (1875–1964) traveled to Europe and visited French and Spanish caves where Breuil and Obermeier were excavating stratigraphically. Nelson had previously used metric stratigraphic excavation on shell midden sites, such as Emeryville and Ellis Landing in California, but his professor at Berkeley, Alfred Kroeber, had disputed the validity of the cultural changes he had interpreted from the changes in the sequence of strata. On his return to America Nelson began to use stratigraphic excavation techniques on sites in the Southwest, but with generally poor results. In 1916 he found the right site at Pueblo San Cristobal in New Mexico.

The site was ten feet deep and cut by a stream. Nelson excavated by metric stratigraphic units of one foot, and pottery pieces from each unit were classified and counted by level. These collections revealed a succession of black and white styles of pottery in the earliest level, followed by glazed wares and paint-glazed types. Biscuit-ware style pottery remained the same throughout the site. Nelson had excavated the entire sequence of Galisteo Basin pottery styles in one site, providing evidence of a succession of stylistic and cultural transformations. Examples of these styles of pottery were excavated by Bandelier and Hewett at other sites. It was therefore possible to undertake comparative studies using pottery styles, and from these regional chronologies could be created. Nelson's excavation provided Southwestern archaeology with a proven field technique and a set of hypotheses about cultural change. Alfred Kidder was to benefit from them and to use them on a larger scale during his excavations at Pecos Pueblo.

Both Gamio and Nelson pioneered innovative field methods and both made quantum leaps in deciphering and interpreting archaeological material to provide the chronologies and cultural sequences for their regions. Both published their results in specialist journals, but to virtually no contemporary fanfare or recognition, and neither claimed great credit or great fame because of it.

See also Excavation of a Burial Mound in Virginia (1787); Publication of *The Population of the Valley of Teotihuacán* (1922); Publication of *Introduction to Southwestern Archaeology* (1924); The Pecos Conference (1927).

Further Reading

Adams, R. E. 1960. Manuel Gamio and Stratigraphic Excavation. *American Antiquity* 26: 99.

Bernal, I. 1980. *History of Mexican Archaeology.* London: Thames and Hudson.

Browman, D. 2003. Origins of Americanist stratigraphic excavation methods. In *Picking the lock of time. Developing chronology in American archaeology,* ed. J. Truncer, 22–39. Gainesville: University Press of Florida.

Cobean, R., and A. G. Mastache Flores. 1999. Manuel Gamio (1883–1960). In *Encyclopedia of archaeology: The great archaeologists,* ed. T. Murray, 325–333. Santa Barbara, CA: ABC-CLIO.

Nelson, N. 1916. Chronology of the Tano Ruins, New Mexico. *American Anthropologist* 18: 159–180.

O'Brien, M. J. 2003. Nels Nelson and the measure of time. In *Picking the lock of time. Developing chronology in American archaeology*, ed. J. Truncer, 64–87. Gainesville: University Press of Florida.

Willey, G. R., and J. A. Sabloff. 1993. *A history of American archaeology*. 3rd ed. New York: W. H. Freeman.

Discovery of the Indus Civilization (1920–Present)

Among the many tasks addressed by the new British viceroy, Lord Curzon, when he arrived in India in 1900, was the formulation and implementation of a preservation, conservation, and archaeological policy for managing and regulating India's historic sites and antiquities. He appointed John Marshall (1876–1951) to this task, which resulted in the passing of an Ancient Monuments Preservation Act in 1904 and the establishment of the Archaeological Survey of India in 1906.

The sites of Harappa and Mohenjo Daro had been noted in the early nineteenth century, and artifacts from them had been in circulation on the antiquities market for some time. However, it took archaeological excavation for their significance to be recognized. Harappa is located in the Upper Indus Valley, in the Punjab, and Mohenjo Daro is in the lower Indus Valley in the province of Sind. Both are now in modern Pakistan, but until 1949 they were part of British India. In 1920 Rai Bahadur Sahni of the Archaeological Survey of India began a small excavation at Harappa, while at the same time preliminary excavations at Mohenjo Daro were undertaken by his colleague, Rakal Das Banerji. Their discoveries led to more extensive excavations at both sites between 1923 and 1931, and to Marshall's direction of excavations at Mohenjo Daro, the better-preserved and more extensive site of the two.

Marshall, announcing its discovery in *The Illustrated London News* in 1924, described the Indus civilization as the contemporary of civilizations in Mesopotamia and Egypt, ca. 2300 BC, and equally unique. Indus civilization was pre-Vedic, that is, dating from before the period of the compilation of ancient Indian Vedic texts (ca. 1000 BC), the hitherto accepted beginning of Indian civilization. However, Marshall also described the Indus civilization as distinctively Indian, emphasizing that elements of and motifs from its crafts, sculpture, and art were the precursors of many of the features of traditional Hindu arts and crafts. The Indus civilization was literate, and it used weights and measures. There was evidence that its burnt brick cities were planned; they were constructed with citadels, residential sections, and a grid system of

Seal from Mohenjo Daro, part of the Indus civilization (2500–1700 BC). (Harappa Archaeological Research Project, Department of Archaeology and Museums, Government of Pakistan)

wide roads. There was also evidence that civic works, such as granaries, baths, temple precincts, drainage, and sanitation were built by its residents. Marshall also claimed there was evidence that some of the religious elements of the Indus civilization, such as male and female deities and animist cults, could also be found in Hinduism.

Based on evidence from Mohenjo Daro, Marshall delineated three developmental periods for Indus civilization—early, intermediate, and late; the last was determined by evidence of a massive decline in civic standards and depopulation of the site. He conjectured that this decline was probably caused by the so-called "Aryan invasions" of the subcontinent, believed to characterize the beginning of classical Indian Vedic civilization. During the 1930s smaller sites belonging to the Indus civilization, but over a wider area from the Indian coast to the Himalayan foothills, were identified, and some were excavated. They proved that Indus civilization was more extensive than had first been thought and it was not only a large urban phenomenon. Meanwhile, material from the excavations of these two cities was being analyzed and published.

In 1924, the same year Marshall announced the discovery of the Indus civilization, Leonard Woolley announced the discovery of the ancient Sumerian civilization at the site of Ur in Mesopotamia. And the relationship between these two "new civilizations" proved to be more than serendipitous. During the analysis of material from the Ur site, archaeologists noted that in occupation levels dating between about 2500 and 2000 BC, diagnostic artifacts from Harappa, such as stamp seals and incised carnelian beads, were found, as were other artifacts with citations about people from ancient India who were residing in Mesopotamia. Texts from the same period at Ur mention a trading partner "Meluhha," now identified as the Mesopotamian name for the Indus civilization. It became evident that four millennia ago, the Indus and Mesopotamian civilizations had traded extensively with each other, by sea from the Indian coast and through the Persian Gulf, and overland through what is now modern Afghanistan and Iran.

In 1944 Sir Mortimer Wheeler succeeded John Marshall as director of the Archaeological Survey of India. Britain was withdrawing from the subcontinent, preparing for the political independence of Pakistan and India, and Wheeler's task was to organize its archaeological survey and educate a number of Indian archaeologists to take over the management of their own heritage, under their own national government. Wheeler returned after independence and partition, as an archaeological adviser to the new government of Pakistan. During both of these appointments, during the 1940s and early 1950s, he directed the excavations of a number of sites from different periods, among them Harappa and Mohenjo Daro. At the former site, Wheeler excavated the city's large defensive walls. At Mohenjo Daro Wheeler excavated the citadel, discovering that important structures, comprising a granary, a large and deep ritual pool, and a suite of rooms probably used by priests, had been built on top of a 6-meter high, 8-hectare brick platform. Wheeler also excavated part of the residential area of the city, uncovering double-storied houses built around central courtyards; workshops of potters, jewelers, metalworkers, and other craftspeople; and networks of wide roads and smaller laneways.

As a result of these excavations Wheeler published *The Indus Civilization* in 1953. He described the phase of Indus civilization that built and occupied Harappa and Mohenjo Daro at their peak as "mature Indus civilization," and placed it between earlier and later occupations of the site. Based on evidence from the excavations of fortifications and the citadel, Wheeler argued that the Indus civilization was ruled by "priest-kings." He also extended the chronology devised by Marshall, dating Indus civilization from ca. 2500 to

1500 BC, based on evidence that its contact with Mesopotamia could be traced back to the Sargonic period (ca. 2300 BC). He agreed with Marshall that Indus civilization had probably been overthrown by the Aryan invasions, which he dated to ca. 1500 BC, based on evidence from the excavation of an unusual type of funerary ware. And lastly and most contentiously, Wheeler also argued that Indus civilization was not autochthonic, that is, it had not developed independently or indigenously within India, but it had derived from Mesopotamia itself, the result of the diffusion of culture from the west.

While they may have seemed reasonable at the time, and were taken seriously by some, Wheeler's theories about the origins and collapse of Indus civilization are now regarded as incorrect, the product of lack of data, the limitations of diffusionist theories, and the colonial mindset of his times. To say that Indus civilization was unique, and to extend the antecedents of Indian civilization back by 2,000 years, and then to say it was derivative and from the west, and not ancestral to the modern culture of India, was interpreted by some as a slap in the face to the new modern Indian state. India's struggle for independence from Britain had used pride in past cultural achievements to unite its different ethnic groups in its modern political struggle. While we now have much more evidence of and knowledge about Indus civilization, and the development of early civilizations in general, than Wheeler had during the 1950s, we are also more aware of the politics of the recent past.

There are currently two schools of thought about the origins, significance, and fate of the Indus civilization. One, popular with Pakistani archaeologists, views it as a mere episode in the history of south Asia, short lived and very much the product of its strong relationship and trade with, and influences from, western and central Asia. The other, popular with Indian archaeologists, argues for an autochthonic or indigenous approach. This involves finding evidence of a much longer period of development and decline and evidence that the Indus civilization's external trade patterns were not anomalous. Indian archaeologists argue that regional trade patterns were consistent over a long period—even up until the nineteenth century. This position also argues that evidence of the antecedents of traditional Indian culture can be found in the culture of the Indus civilization, and that it is an essential part of the long development of Indian history and culture.

We still do not know about the Indus civilization's system of government or social organization, its style and methods of, or reasons for, warfare, or the place of writing in its culture. Their script remains undeciphered. But we know a lot more about it because of more excavations and research. Many smaller sites belonging to the Indus civilization have been excavated by Indian and Pakistani archaeologists, and some have been found as far east as Rajasthan and around New Delhi in Uttar Pradesh. The prehistoric relationships between India and the Gulf and India and Afghanistan and Iran are better understood. We can also trace long-term changes in the climate and ecology of southern Asia—and what impact these had on human populations and settlement. We now know that the Indus civilization, like many other early civilizations based on city-states, grew out of, and then was imposed on, a still primarily hunting-and-gathering economy that also farmed and herded.

Excavations at Mohenjo Daro date its depopulation and decline to around 2000 BC. There is similar evidence of depopulation at Harappa and other settlements. However, evidence suggests that while this occurred at many settlements, it did not occur uniformly, or even at the same time. No evidence of a massive migration or a change in settlement patterns is evident in the archaeological record to date. We do know from evidence and the study of early city-state sites in other parts of the world, such as in Mesopotamia, China, Southeast Asia, and Mesoamerica, that their domination of the supporting rural population and economy could be tenuous, and even small changes in the environment, politics, or economics could have drastic consequences.

There is no evidence of invasion or pillaging and destruction of the cities and settlements. The funerary artifacts, used by Wheeler as evidence of Aryan invasion, have been identified as evidence of smaller reoccupations by different people in parts of the city. There is no chronological agreement between the appearance of the Vedic texts, the Aryan invasion (if there ever was one at all) and the decline of Indus civilization. However, there is evidence of the increasing desertification of the southern region of the Indus civilization, and sites in this region are now located in deserts. There is also evidence that the Indus civilization's settlements moved farther to the east over time—farther away from the Indus Valley itself. We know that at around the beginning of the second millennium BC the Iron Age cultures of northern India began to develop in size and power, and some believe the interaction between, or absorption of, the eastern settlements of the Indus civilization and these Iron Age cultures produced Vedic Indian civilization.

See also Foundation of the Archaeological Survey of India (1861); Discovering the Riches of Central Asia—The Journeys of Sir Aurel Stein (1906–1930); Excavation of Ur (1922–1934); Publication of *The Dawn of European Civilization* (1925).

Further Reading

Allchin, B., and R. Allchin. 1997. *Origins of a civilization: the prehistory and early archaeology of south Asia.* New Delhi: Viking.

Chakrabarti, D. 1988. *A history of Indian archaeology from the beginning to 1947.* New Delhi: Munshiram Manoharlal Publishers.

Chakrabarti, D. 2001. South Asia. In *Encyclopedia of archaeology: History and discoveries,* ed. T. Murray, 1183–1194. Santa Barbara, CA: ABC-CLIO.

Chakrabarti, D. 2004. *Indus civilization sites in India: New discoveries.* Mumbai, India: Marg Publications.

Kenoyer, J. 1998. *Ancient cities of the Indus Valley civilization.* Oxford: Oxford University Press.

Marshall, J. H. 1973. *Mohenjo-daro and the Indus civilization; being an official account of archaeological excavations at Mohenjo-daro carried out by the Government of India between the years 1922 and 1927. Edited by Sir John Marshall. With plan and map in colours, and 164 plates in collotype.* Delhi: Indological Book House.

Parpola, A. 1994. *Deciphering the Indus script.* Cambridge: Cambridge University Press.

Possehl, G. L. 2002. *The Indus civilization: a contemporary perspective.* Walnut Creek, CA: AltaMira Press.

Possehl, G. L., and M. H. Raval. 1989. *Harappan civilization and Rojdi.* New Delhi: Oxford & IBH Publishing Co., American Institute of Indian Studies.

Publication of Les hommes fossiles, eléments de paléontologie humaine *(1921)*

French paleontologist Marcellin Boule (1861–1942) was a student of Emile Carthailac and Louis Lartet, who were prehistorians and Paleolithic cave art specialists. Boule worked at the Museum of Natural History in Paris, and became professor of paleontology in 1903. He was one of the founders and an editor (1893–1930) of the distinguished journal *L'Anthropologie.* Boule's work dominated French paleontology during the first third of the twentieth century.

In 1908 Boule studied the first complete Neanderthal skeleton found at the French site of La Chapelle-aux-Saints. He concluded that Neanderthals were not the ancestors of modern humans, but a fossil hominid branch, with no contemporary descendents. In his reconstruction of the Neanderthal skeleton Boule created its classic and popular caricature—a slouching, hairy, simian-like hominid, with a low forehead, large suborbital arches, broad nose, and an animal face completely different from modern mankind. Boule's work on Neanderthals was definitive and became the theoretical and methodological standard.

Boule's expertise was also sought to evaluate the evidence of "Piltdown man," an English human ancestor or "missing link" that was, as was later proved, the product of a faked association of a modern human braincase with an apelike jaw. Ironically Boule rejected Piltdown man for the same reasons he had rejected the Neanderthals, and not because he recognized it as a forgery. Piltdown, he argued, could not be the missing link ancestral to modern humans. Like Neanderthals, Boule described the Piltdown material as evidence of another branch of the evolutionary development of non-Neanderthal and nonhuman lines. Boule used the same argument about *Homo erectus,* the first example of which was discovered by Dutch paleontologist Eugene Dubois on Java in 1888. He believed the hominid ancestor of modern human beings had yet to be found.

In 1914, Prince Albert I of Monaco, in recognition of Boule's work and the place of human paleontology at the cutting edge of the history of mankind, founded the Institut de paléontologie humaine in Paris, the first organization for specialized human paleontological research. Boule was its first director when the institute's new building opened in 1920. Boule's popular book *Les hommes fossiles, eléments de paléontologie humaine* summarized his thinking about the history of humankind for the general public, and it represents the apogee of his power over the scientific world and the popular imagination of the day. The first edition sold out within a year of its publication; a second edition was published in 1923, as was an English translation.

Boule believed his paleoanthropological work could revitalize prehistory by giving it the status of a "historical science." This status could be achieved through a combination of quaternary geology, zoology, paleontology, and archaeology, so that it became an alternative method of elucidating Paleolithic prehistory. Boule's methodology replaced that of the great nineteenth-century French archaeologist Gabriel de Mortillet, whose understanding of prehistory was based on the classification of artifacts and their typologies, linking technological change with biological evolution. Boule argued that stone tools and artifacts could be interpreted as chronological data only if they were part of geology and paleontology.

It was not until the 1950s that Boule's conclusions about Neanderthals were questioned and reexamined. Recent reanalysis of the La Chapelle skeleton has revealed that Boule made errors about the morphological differences between Neanderthals and modern humans. It is debatable whether differences were exaggerated because of the limited technology of the times in which Boule worked or whether it was a deliberate fabrication—

ensuring that there was no possibility that Neanderthals could ever be regarded as ancestral to modern humans.

See also Discovery of the Neanderthals (1833–1900); De Mortillet Classifies the Stone Age (1869–1872); First *Homo Erectus* (1888–1895) Discoveries at Zhoukoudian Cave (1921–Present); Discovery of *Australopithecus africanus* (1924); Piltdown Unmasked (1955).

Further Reading

Boule, M. 1921. *Les hommes fossiles, eléments de paléontologie humaine.* Paris: Masson.

Boule, M. 1923. *Fossil men.* English translation. Edinburgh: Oliver & Boyd.

Richard, N. 1999. Marcellin Boule, 1861–1942. In *Encyclopedia of archaeology: The great archaeologists,* ed. T. Murray, 263–273. Santa Barbara, CA: ABC-CLIO.

Van Reybrouck, D. 2002. Boule's error: On the social context of scientific knowledge. In *Ancestral Archives: explorations in the history of archaeology,* ed. N. Schlanger, 158–164. *Antiquity* 76: 291.

Discoveries at Zhoukoudian Cave (1921–Present)

Archaeological fieldwork in China during the first few decades of the twentieth century was conducted by Western archaeologists and paleontologists attached to the Geological Survey of China, who identified many Paleolithic and Neolithic sites. In 1921, as a member of the survey team, the Swedish geologist, Johann Gunnar Andersson (1874–1960) excavated one of the most significant Paleolithic sites in Asia—Zhoukoudian Cave in Hebei Province, forty-eight kilometers south of Beijing.

Among the material Andersson excavated were two anthropoid teeth and what he believed to be stone artifacts. On the basis of the teeth Canadian anatomist Davidson Black (1884–1934) identified a new early hominid form, which he called *Sinanthropus pekinensus,* or "Peking man" (now known as another example of *Homo erectus*). This find, and its potential importance for understanding the development of early humans in Asia, enabled Black to raise funds in America and Europe to conduct more detailed excavations at the site between 1927 and 1934.

The first major discovery of hominid remains at Zhoukoudian was made by the Chinese archaeologist Pei Wenzhong (1904–1982). In 1929 Pei excavated an almost complete *Homo erectus* skullcap. In 1930, with the help of French paleontologist Pierre Teilhard de Chardin (1881–1955), Pei found more *Homo erectus* fossils and began to study the artifacts found with them, at that time the largest example of such material in the world. He also extended excavations into a second or upper cave site, where the remains of seven anatomically modern *Homo sapiens* individuals were discovered in association with bone artifacts and with evidence of the use of fire. In 1931 Henri Breuil (1877–1961) examined the finds from the first site and confirmed the presence of stone artifacts. In 1935 Pei traveled to Paris to study for his doctorate with Breuil.

In 1934 Black died and was succeeded by the German anatomist and physical anthropologist Franz Weidenreich (1873–1948). By 1936 Weidenreich's meticulous studies of the dental and cranial Zhoukoudian *Homo erectus* material established its global significance. Weidenreich also identified three of the *Homo sapiens* remains from the upper cave as examples of Mongolian, Eskimo, and Melanesian racial groups, arguing they were the modern descendents of *Homo erectus* or Peking man, in support of his evolutionary theory of "regional continuity."

In 1937 excavations at Zhoukoudian closed down because of the Sino-Japanese War, and unfortunately all of the human fossil remains were lost during the early stages of World War II. Fortunately, Weidenreich's casts of the remains of more than 40 hominids and his detailed research notes and studies survived; they remain the primary sources for the study of the largest *Homo erectus* population in the world.

The Zhoukoudian finds had an enormous impact on the search for human origins in Asia. During the same period, fossil human remains from the island of Java, in Southeast Asia, were assembled by Weidenreich's colleague and collaborator G. Von Koenigswald (1902–1982), proving that Eugene Dubois's *Pithecanthropus* "Java man," found at the end of the nineteenth century, was neither a pathological specimen nor an anomaly. Zhoukoudian and Javanese finds were compared and both paleoanatomists argued for their synchroneity, and believed they were the early hominid ancestors of modern humans. Weidenreich eventually argued that all Asian fossil hominids were descended from the *Giganthopithecus* or giant extinct ape, but Von Koenigswald rejected this.

With the founding of the People's Republic of China in 1949 Pei Wenzhong became one of its foremost prehistoric archaeologists. Excavations at Zhoukoudian began again and new finds were made. In fact, Zhoukoudian and sites nearby continue to be excavated to the present day by Chinese archaeologists. During the 1950s discussions about the significance of the Zhoukoudian finds reignited. Pei Wenzhong argued that they were the oldest in the world, probably for political reasons, in support of communist Chinese nationalism and in response to early hominid finds in Africa. For a while it was even argued that the *Australopithecines*—fossil hominid human ancestors—had originated in Asia. Pei went on to excavate numerous Paleolithic and Neolithic sites all over China and to direct important paleontological research to elucidate paleoenvironmental changes in Asia.

In 1987, the Zhoukoudian caves were inscribed on the World Heritage List.

See also First *Homo Erectus* (1888–1895); Publication of *Les hommes fossiles, eléments de paléontologie humaine* (1921); Discovery of *Australopithecus africanus* (1924); Publication of *Formation of the Chinese People* (1928).

Further Reading

Boaz, N. T., and R. L. Ciochon. 2004. *Dragon Bone Hill: An Ice-Age saga of* Homo erectus. Oxford: Oxford University Press.

Jia, L., and W. Huang. 1990. *The story of Peking Man: From archaeology to mystery*. Oxford: Oxford University Press.

Publication of The Population of the Valley of Teotihuacán *(1922)*

In 1917 Manuel Gamio founded, and was the first director of, a federal department of anthropology in Mexico, where he received funding for the first multidisciplinary, long-term anthropological study in the Americas, "The Population of the Teotihuacán Valley." It was a unique project for its time, encyclopedic in its focus, taking five years; involving twenty scholars; and combining ethnography, archaeology, anthropology, geography, history, and demography. It focused on a whole region, and not just on one site.

Located forty kilometers from Mexico City, Teotihuacán was the largest and most powerful city (or city-state) in Mesoamerica between 100 BC and AD 750. It has been estimated that in AD 300 its population was approximately 200,000 people, making it one of the largest cities in the world at that time, and it covered over twenty square kilometers. Two of the largest temple pyramids in Mesoamerica, dedicated to the sun and the moon, are found at Teotihuacán, and there were at least one hundred other smaller pyramids at the site. The city's wealth depended on craft production and trade with and tribute from subject communities. However, by AD 950 Teotihuacán was in decline. The only city to match it in power, size, and wealth was the Aztec city of

Tenochtitlán (later Mexico City), whose heyday was in the fourteenth century AD, just before the Spanish arrived in Mesoamerica.

For five years Gamio directed the excavations, concentrating on the central Ciuadela plaza where the royal families of Teotihuacán had lived. He restored the sculptured facade of the Pyramid of Quetzalcoatl, the feathered serpent god, and determined chronology on the basis of stratigraphic excavation. Gamio explored the central axis of the city, known as the Avenue of the Dead, and the largest of the pyramids—the Pyramid of the Sun. Archaeologist Herman Beyer undertook the iconographic analysis of the art of Teotihuacán, and architectural drawings of reconstructions were by archaeologist Ignacio Marquina.

The project's report was published in five volumes in 1922, with a title matching the breadth of the work—*The Population of the Valley of Teotihuácan, the Environment in Which it Has Developed, its Ethnic and Social Evolution, and Efforts to Achieve its Betterment.* The first two volumes detailed the archaeological excavations, and other volumes contained reproductions of murals, pottery, figurines, tools, lithics, and luxury objects found in religious offerings. Studies of the valley's geology described the pre-Hispanic obsidian mines, which were a significant element in the economy of Teotihuacán.

The report also discussed the valley's physical environment, the physical anthropology of the pre-Hispanic population, Teotihuacán architecture, sculpture and ceramics, the geographic extension of the Teotihuacán culture, comparisons between Teotihuacán and Aztec civilizations, an ethnohistory of the Aztec culture, Aztec antiquities, colonial geography, demography, ideas and customs, political and religious history, economic organization, noble genealogies of Teotihuacán, indigenous codices and documents in Nahuatl, sixteenth-century churches, colonial religious painting, and the nineteenth-century population of the region.

Gamio's book also contained a detailed contemporary description of the valley comprising a census and its physical anthropology, as well as diet and diseases, ethnography, folklore, schools and education, economics, agrarian problems, irrigation systems, agriculture and forests, geology, road systems, contemporary plants, modern architecture, and the linguistics of contemporary Nahuatl speakers. Consequently, the report remains an indispensable reference source for central Mexican anthropology and history. Gamio's doctoral dissertion from Columbia University derived from it.

Gamio mistakenly identified Teotihuacán as the Toltec city of Tollan, mentioned in surviving ethnic chronicles. Although he had studied the ruins of the site of Tula, some seventy kilometers north of Mexico City, and correctly interpreted them as being constructed after Teotihuacán, he did not identify them as Tollan. This was proven later by archaeologist Jorge R. Acosta. Tollan was the Toltec city-state that succeeded Teotihuacán as the most powerful in the region, between AD 800 and AD 1200, prior to the Aztecs' rise to power at Tenochtitlán during the thirteenth century AD.

What Gamio had excavated and recorded was the second great sequence in Mexican civilization. The Teotihuacán report went beyond the boundaries of archaeology to become the first major anthropological study carried out in Mexico.

See also Stratigraphic Excavation in the Americas (1911–1913); Discovery of Olmec Civilization (1926–1942); Jorge R. Acosta Finishes Work at Tula (1961).

Further Reading

Bernal, I. 1980. *A history of Mexican archaeology.* London: Thames and Hudson.

Cobean, R., and A. Mastache Flores. 1999. Manuel Gamio, 1883–1960. In *Encyclopedia of archaeology: The great archaeologists,* ed. T. Murray, 325–333. Santa Barbara, CA: ABC-CLIO.

Gamio, M. 1922. *Introduction, synthesis and conclusions of the work The Population of the Valley of Teotihuacán.* Mexico: Tall. Gráf. de la Nación.

Discovering Tutankhamen's Tomb (1922–1932)

Beginning his career in Egyptian archaeology as an illustrator and draftsman, Englishman Howard Carter (1874–1939) received on-site training from the great archaeologist Sir William Flinders Petrie, and spent fifteen years excavating before he found the tomb of Tutankhamen in the already thoroughly excavated Valley of the Kings.

In 1909, Carter was hired by Lord Carnarvon, a wealthy English aristocrat with an interest in Egyptian archaeology, to search for a promising site to excavate. World War I put this search on hold, and during the years between 1918 and 1921, with no promising site found, Carnarvon became disenchanted with the whole idea. He and Carter agreed that 1922 would be their last year to search for a site, and Carter tenaciously kept on looking. In November he famously cabled Carnarvon: "At last have made wonderful discovery . . . a magnificent tomb with seals intact . . . recovered same for your arrival" (Murray 1999, 295). It was a discovery that would change their lives, and place their names and that of the minor Egyptian boy pharaoh on the front pages of newspapers across the world.

However, the opening of the tomb was a staged media event. There is little doubt that both Carter and Carnarvon had both entered the tomb the night before and, indeed, had taken artifacts from it before they invited the media to be present while they apparently broke the door seals and used a torch to first see "the wonderful things" inside. In the long term, fame and media attention would become a double-edged sword.

Carter's long training in the practical business of excavating tombs, as well as his skill in recording their contents, made him an ideal person to undertake the task of clearing and documenting Tutankhamen's tomb. However, almost overnight he was transformed from an unknown minor excavator and archaeological technician into a great archaeological discoverer. The media attention; the number of royal, grand, and ordinary visitors to the site; and the politics of Egyptian antiquities legislation and access soon made Carter's task of doing the right thing by his discovery fraught with difficul-

Howard Carter unwrapping the mummy of King Tutankhamen. (Library of Congress)

ties. Added to this, Carter's lack of formal education, his uneasiness about his social position, his obstinacy, and his past acrimonious relationships with the Egyptian Antiquities Service further complicated matters.

To the rest of the world Carter's discovery was about finding treasure and looting it—albeit for the best possible reasons. For Carnarvon the discovery was about enhancing his notoriety and his private collection. For Carter and his team of archaeologists, conservators, photographers, and illustrators, the tomb represented an unparalleled opportunity to record and preserve the contents of an undisturbed burial from a crucial period (1336–1327 BC) of Egyptian history. There is no better demonstration of just how far Egyptian archaeology had come from its tomb-robbing origins in the nineteenth century, and Amelia Edwards's grief for their loss and subsequent activism for their preservation. For the archaeological community the real value of the tomb's contents was the information it contained, the exceptional detailed evidence of Egyptian civilization.

Although the media attention never really died down, from 1925 until 1932 Carter and his team were able to concentrate on their real task—clearing, cataloging and conserving the artifacts. Carter's greatest gift to Egyptology and posterity was his successful completion of this monumental task—not a great scholarly work, and no new insights into the nature of ancient Egyptian life, but eight years of painstaking teamwork.

There is no doubt that Carter did well from his discovery of Tutankhamen's tomb through lectures in America and from his antiquities business. Unlike Sir Leonard Woolley, the discoverer of Ur in Mesopotamia, and Sir Arthur Evans, the discoverer of Knossos on Crete, Howard Carter received few academic and public honors, and most of these were from the United States. Sir Flinders Petrie wrote that Tutankhamen was indeed fortunate to have been found by Carter, but perhaps Carter was not so fortunate to have been made famous by Tutankhamen.

See also Publication of *A Thousand Miles up the Nile* (1877); Discovery of Minoan Civilization (1900–1935); Excavation of Ur (1922–1934).

Further Reading

Carter, H., and A. C. Mace. 1923–1933. *The tomb of Tutankhamun.* 3 vols. London: Cassell.

Desroches-Noblecourt, C. 1963. *Tutankhamun: Life and death of a pharaoh.* New York: New York Graphic Society.

Hoving, T. 1978. *Tutankhamun, the untold story.* New York: Simon and Schuster.

Murray, T. 1999. Howard Carter, 1874–1939. In *Encyclopedia of archaeology: The great archaeologists,* ed. T. Murray, 289–299. Santa Barbara, CA: ABC-CLIO.

Reeves, N. 1990. *The Complete Tutankhamun.* New York: Thames and Hudson.

Reeves, N., and J. H. Taylor. 1992. *Howard Carter before Tutankhamun.* London: British Museum Press.

Reeves, N., and R. Wilkinson. 1996. *The complete Valley of the Kings.* New York: Thames and Hudson.

Winstone, H. V. F. 1991. *Howard Carter and the discovery of the tomb of Tutankhamun.* London: Constable.

Excavation of Ur (1922–1934)

Leonard Woolley (1880–1960) was appointed assistant to Sir Arthur Evans, keeper of the Ashmolean Museum in Oxford, after taking his degree from that university. He and T. E. Lawrence (later known as Lawrence of Arabia) worked on the British Museum excavation at Carchemish in 1912, after which they both conducted an archaeological survey of northern Palestine. Woolley was an intelligence officer during the first few years of World War I and spent the last two years in a Turkish prisoner of war camp.

In 1922, after field seasons back at Carchemish and then in Egypt, Woolley was commissioned by the British and the University of Pennsylvania Museums to begin to excavate the mound of Ur, in what is now modern Iraq. The site had been identified as early as the 1850s, when cuneiform cylinders from it were brought back to Britain and translated by Sir Henry Rawlinson. There had been some excavation of the mound, the most recent just after World War I, but the earliest periods at the site, as was usual with the large tell mounds of the Middle East that were the result of thousands of years of occupation, were the most difficult to get to.

Woolley knew that the history of such a huge and complex site would be difficult to establish, and so he kept detailed records of pottery types and stratigraphy to aid in building comparative chronologies for the whole site. He first found the so-called "royal" cemetery at Ur in 1922, but apparently held off excavating it for four years, because, he said, he wanted his men to have greater excavation experience, and because he wanted to run a trial of the chronology he was working on and adjust it before tackling what he knew would be such an important part of the site.

But Woolley also wanted the finds to be given the kind of international publicity that Howard Carter was receiving for excavating Tutankhamen's tomb in 1922, so he determined not to compete with it. In 1926, Woolley's talent for publicity, his popular style of communication, the spectacular finds from the Ur cemetery, and the connections between Ur and the Bible meant that Ur and Woolley monopolized world newspaper headlines in the way he had planned they would. Tutankhamen was old news.

Woolley sank deep test pits to find the earliest levels. Under a layer at the site dated to ca. 4000 BC, a culturally sterile layer, perhaps deposited by a large flood, was found. This was quickly interpreted as the Biblical flood, but in fact flooding was common in ancient Mesopotamia. The layer could have been deposited by the movement of sand dunes. However, below this layer was evidence of the earliest occupation of the site, during the late Neolithic or Ubaid period (ca. 5000 BC). Evidence included the remains of mud brick and reed and mud buildings; domestic refuse, such as pieces of pottery with simple painted designs; stone tools for food preparation—for pounding, grinding, and cutting; sickles made of fired clay; and spindle worls. A number of Ubaid graves were also excavated—the dead were buried on their backs with pots, clay figures, beads, and animal bones, in different combinations, depending on the age and sex of the grave's occupant.

Woolley excavated other levels dated to the Uruk or Jemdat Nasr periods (ca. 3900–2900 BC). At this time Ur had grown to cover fifteen hectares and was an important regional center, with cone-shaped temples in its center. Excavations around a later ziggurat structure revealed an Uruk-period brick temple platform and a floor covered with clay cones used to decorate the façade. Pottery kilns and pottery were found, and a part of a cemetery from this period was also excavated. The bodies in these graves were laid on their sides in crouched positions, with clay and stone vessels, beads, and some metal (either copper or lead) vessels.

By 2900 BC, because of its position as a harbor at the head of the Persian Gulf, Ur was one of the wealthiest city-states of southern Mesopotamia. It was also an important regional and religious center. Ur's temple platform was rebuilt at least twice, and on it Woolley found kitchens, storerooms, and shrine rooms. These were underneath the massive ziggurat constructed by the Ur III period king Ur-Nammu. Close to this platform was a rubbish dump from the same period, known as "the seal impression strata" because of the large amount of clay seals found in it, covered in protocuneiform script, as well as large quantities of burnt mud brick debris, pottery, and clay tablets. Dug into this rubbish dump was a cemetery of some 2,000 graves, sixteen of which were designated the "royal tombs" of Ur.

View of the ziggurat and other ruins of the ancient city of Ur, an important Sumerian city in ancient Mesopotamia. (Nik Wheeler/Corbis)

The cemetery was used from the Early Dynastic III period until the Post-Akkadian period (ca. 2600–2100 BC), but its royal tombs were built during the earliest years of its use. Unlike the other graves of the cemetery, the royal tombs were specially built brick and stone chambers into which many dead were placed. All of the royal tombs contained the remains of a principal individual, as well as other burials of servants or followers, perhaps sacrificed to accompany them. The number of secondary burials ranged from six to eighty people.

Unlooted tombs contained wonderful grave goods: gold, silver, lapis, carnelian, and other semiprecious stone jewelry, and the most spectacular of which went on to define the art of Sumerian civilization—inlaid string instruments, golden helmets and headdresses, two lapis and gold rams in thickets, golden daggers with lapis-studded hilts, silver and gold vessels, and other weapons, musical instruments, seals, and furniture. Some royal burials contained horse carts, and many were for women. One particularly rich royal burial containing many of the finest artifacts, was of a woman in her forties. She had been buried with twenty-three retainers, surrounded by her possessions—

a lyre adorned with a golden bull's head, gold and silver vessels, jewelry, and a diadem of golden leaves and flowers.

Even the simpler burials in wooden coffins often contained vessels and weapons in gold or copper and gold and lapis jewelry—while one in particular contained a golden helmet in the form of a wig with a seal in the name of a king. While there were other graves with similar quality and quantity of riches, the royal tombs were the only ones to have been specially constructed and to have evidence of human sacrifice. The treatment of the principal burials, and the discovery of inscribed artifacts that name a person king or queen in some of these, led Woolley to argue for the "royal" designation. It also made for better headlines. But the inscribed artifacts were not directly associated with the principal deceased, and they could have been gifts to the dead rather than their own possessions.

The cemetery continued to be used during the following Akkadian period, when Ur was still an important city, even though it was ruled by the northern Mesopotamian city-state of Akkad. Woolley found an alabaster disk from this period that recorded a ritual libation and was dedicated by Enheduanna, high priestess of the patron god of Ur, Nanna, and the daughter of Sargon, the founder of the Akkadian dynasty. The installation of Sargon's daughter at Ur as high priestess was described by Woolley as one way in which Sargon made his conquest and rule of their city-state acceptable to the Sumerians.

For a hundred years (ca. 2100–2000 BC), Ur was the capital and ceremonial center of empire known as Ur III, and the city grew to cover fifty hectares. Ur III controlled most of Mesopotamia and the adjacent Zagros Mountains, and it was an important part of the trade between Mesopotamia and Iran, Afghanistan, the Arabian Peninsula, and India. The administration and finances of the empire were revealed by the large number of accounting tablets found from this period. The first king of the dynasty of Ur III was Ur-Nammu, who began the building program in the center of Ur that included a large ziggurat, other temples, a large sunken court in front of the ziggurat, a palace, storage buildings, and accommodation and tombs for the priestesses. This was enclosed by a wall and surrounded on three sides by river canals. Many of these buildings were finished by Ur-Nammu's son and successor, Shulgi, and it was Shulgi who also extended the Ur III empire to include Assyria and Iran. We know these details because Woolley excavated pieces of the carved monument known as the Stela of Ur-Nammu, which showed scenes from the history of Ur—of Ur-Nammu being inspired to build the new precinct, sacrificing animals, and providing music and musicians on its completion, and listing the canals he had built.

The ziggurat, dedicated to the god Nanna, and built by Ur-Nammu, had a huge base, 63 by 43 meters, and comprised three superimposed pyramid style brick platforms. Its antecedents could be traced to the platform temple form of Ubaid times, and its style was used in the subsequent construction of ziggurat temples at the sites of Eridu and Babylon. The main temple was built on the top platform and was accessible via a central steep staircase. The ziggurat was probably the highest point in the city, dominating it physically and culturally. Its high priestess continued to be the king's daughter or sister.

Woolley also excavated in two areas of the residential district of Ur from the same period. In one area he found numerous clay tablets, indicating that they were probably inhabited by temple officials. In the other area the excavated finds were more diverse. Both areas comprised densely packed buildings separated by narrow winding lanes. The houses were built around a central courtyard onto which most of the rooms opened. Many houses had shrine rooms, but less than 10 percent of them had identifiable kitchens, so there must have been central and communal food preparation and cooking areas. There were burials of all ages underneath floors of the houses, some in pits, others in clay coffins, pots, or brick tombs; many of the burials were accompanied by pottery and jewelry, some more wealthy than others.

Much of the religious center and parts of the city were destroyed ca. 2000 BC by Elamite and Amorite invasions. Ur was rebuilt by the kings of the nearby city of Isin, who claimed to be the heirs of Ur III, and it continued to be an important religious and commercial center during the Isin-Larsa period from ca. 2000–1760 BC. With the rise of Babylonian power (ca. 800 BC), and the continuing environmental degradation of southern Mesopotamia, Ur's population and power declined. The city walls and other public building were again destroyed around 1740 BC. In 1400 BC the occupying Kassite rulers restored many of its religious buildings.

The Biblical city, "Ur of the Chaldees," was another reason for the great public interest in the site. This was the period of Ur's history that coincided with rule of Ur by the Babylonians. The Chaldeans were a seminomadic ethnic people who settled in southern Babylonia, and along with the Aramaeans destabilized Assyria and Babylonia ca. 1000 BC. Later the Chaldeans resisted Assyrian occupation. The neo-Babylonian kings were erroneously described as a "Chaldean" dynasty. It is King Nebuchadrezzar who is mentioned in the Bible for his campaigns in Judea and Samaria, his conquest of Jerusalem, and his deportation of its inhabitants to Babylon. The kings, Nebuchadrezzar (ca.

700 BC) and Narbonidus (ca. 500 BC), rebuilt Ur's ziggurat and walls, but by ca. 400 BC the city was abandoned, primarily because of a change in the course of the Euphrates River and the conquest of southern Mesopotamia by the Persians under Cyrus.

While Woolley's excavations and analysis of material from the site of Ur provided wonderful details of Sumerian life, religion, politics, art, architecture, literature, ceremonies, clothes, food, weapons, and jewelry, there were still many important questions about Sumeria and the Sumerians that remain unanswered. Woolley's finds inaugurated a revival of interest in the archaeology and history of Mesopotamia. Excavations began at Kish and Warka (or Uruk), so that by 1931 the chronology of Mesopotamia prehistory was widely accepted: Ubaid, 4000–3500 BC, Uruk 3500–3200 BC, and Jamdat Nasr (Kish) 3200–2800 BC. Much of the popular appeal of Woolley's work at Ur flowed from the publication of two significant and popular books written by him, with the general public in mind: *Ur of the Chaldees* (1929) and *The Sumerians* (1930).

See also American Excavations in Mesopotamia at the Site of Nippur (1888–1900); Discovery of the Indus Civilization (1920–Present); Discovering Tutankhamen's Tomb (1922–1932); National Museum of Iraq Established (1923); Excavation of Jarmo (1948–1954); Excavation of Jericho (1952–1958).

Further Reading

Moorey, P. R. S., ed. 1982. *Ur "of the Chaldees": a revised and updated edition of Sir Leonard Woolley's Excavations at Ur.* Ithaca, NY: Cornell University Press.

Woolley, L. 1953. *Spadework: Adventures in archaeology.* London: Lutterworth Press.

Woolley, L. 1954. *Excavations at Ur; a record of twelve years' work.* London: E. Benn.

Winstone, H. V. 1990. *Woolley of Ur: The life of Sir Leonard Woolley.* London: E. Benn.

National Museum of Iraq Established (1923)

Gertrude Margaret Lothian Bell (1868–1926) was the daughter of a wealthy northern English industrialist, and one of the first female students at Oxford University, at Lady Margaret Hall. She graduated in 1888 at the age of twenty with first-class honors in history, the first woman to attain this distinction at the university.

In the 1890s Bell became interested in the history of the Near East after visiting her diplomatic relatives in Teheran. She learned Persian and then studied Arabic in Jerusalem. Over the next decade she traveled to Petra and Palmyra, through Syria and Cilicia (now eastern Turkey). She became a self-taught and competent field archaeologist and in 1907, with Sir W. M. Ramsay, she explored the Hittite and Byzantine sites of Bin-Bir-Kilisse. In 1909 she traveled down the Euphrates River from Aleppo and returned by way of Baghdad and Mosul in Iraq. In 1911 Bell explored Ukhaidir, a huge Abbasid palace. All of these travels resulted in popular publications. Bell then set out to explore central Arabia, where only one other European woman had been. Starting from Damascus she got as far as Hail, where she was kept as an honored prisoner to prevent her traveling farther, until she returned to Baghdad.

In 1914 with the outbreak of World War I, Gertrude Bell joined the Red Cross and worked in France. In 1915 she was sent back to London to reorganize Red Cross headquarters. When the Arabs rebelled against Turkish rule Bell was drafted into the War Office's Arab Intelligence Bureau and moved to Cairo. Her task was to collect and summarize information about the Bedouin tribes and sheikhs of northern Arabia whose rebellion against Turkey was supported by the British. She was later attached to the military intelligence staff of the Mesopotamian Expeditionary Force and became political officer and oriental secretary to Sir Percy Cox. Her special knowledge of Arab politics, her prewar friendships with Arab leaders, and her linguistic abilities were a valuable part of successful liaisons between the British and the rebelling desert tribes.

Bell moved to Baghdad in 1917, and she continued to act as an adviser in a civil capacity, as chief political officer, completing an administrative review of Mesopotamia in 1920. She and Sir Percy Cox, then high commissioner in Mesopotamia, strongly supported the election of Saud Emir Faisal and the creation of a new Arab government in Iraq.

While she continued her political work, Bell was made Iraq's first director of antiquities, responsible for all archaeological excavations and for establishing an antiquities service and a national museum in Baghdad. It was an auspicious appointment for one of the world's newest nations—which was the home of some of the world's oldest civilizations. Over the previous twenty years, before World War I, many of the Mesopotamian sites of the Biblical and classical world had been excavated. Between 1888 and 1900 French archaeologists unearthed evidence of Sumerian civilization at Telloh (Girsu in Lagash) ca. 3000 BC. In 1912 German archaeologists excavating at Uruk (Biblical Erech) found temple complexes and examples of pre-Sumerian script—the earliest examples of writing ever found (ca. 3400 BC). Other German excavations at Babylon, Borsippa, Fara, and Ashur, the first Assyrian capital, took place before the war.

In 1922 the British-American expedition under English archaeologist Leonard Woolley began to excavate the Sumerian city of Ur, uncovering important neo-Babylonian remains. Of equal importance, Woolley began to establish 5,000 years of history for Ur, and while excavating the nearby site of El-Ubaid (ca. 6000 BC) discovered the earliest Mesopotamian settlement of all.

The museum and the antiquities service were established in recognition of the significance and wealth of evidence of Mesopotamia's past. No doubt Bell had in mind as a model the successful museum and antiquities service Auguste Mariette had established in Egypt during the late 1850s, which ensured that the country of origin had some control over and share of excavated material, which could then be kept safely. Bell had the access to the decision makers of the British colonial government, and the will and interest to ensure that the museum and the antiquities service were put into place as part of the new government's administration. It was her greatest achievement.

The museum was inaugurated in 1923 and moved into its new building in 1926. Bell was looking for a permanent director of antiquities so that she could return to England after her years of service in Iraq when she died in Baghdad. She was buried in the English cemetery. In 1927, at the suggestion of King Feisal, a wing of the new museum was named for her.

Tragically, notwithstanding strong representations by archaeologists and others to the governments of the invading forces, the museum was extensively looted during the 2003 invasion of Iraq.

See also Marriette, Antiquities Law, and the Egyptian Museum (1858); American Excavations in Mesopotamia at the Site of Nippur (1888–1900); Excavation of Ur (1922–1934).

Further Reading

O'Brien, R. 2000. *Gertrude Bell: the Arabian diaries, 1913–1914.* Syracuse, NY: Syracuse University Press.

Wallach, J. 1997. *Desert queen: the extraordinary life of Gertrude Bell, adventurer, adviser to kings, ally of Lawrence of Arabia.* London: Phoenix Giant.

Winstone, H. V. F. 1993 *Gertrude Bell.* Rev. ed. London: Constable.

Publication of Air Survey and Archaeology *(1924)*

O. G. S. Crawford (1886–1957) combined his degree in geography with his experience as an observer in the Royal Flying Corps during World War I to pioneer the use of aerial surveying in archaeology.

In 1920 Crawford was appointed the British Ordnance Survey's first archaeological officer. Since the early nineteenth century when the survey had begun mapping Britain, it had recorded all of the monuments and earthworks that were visible from the ground. Crawford provided a different perspective. He began by locating archaeological features on military aerial photos, then he consulted the records of other institutions, and finally he undertook new field surveys mapping the traces of earthworks in the English landscape that were only visible from the air and recorded on photographs. In this way archaeological evidence—prehistoric, such as Celtic field systems; historic, such as Roman military camps; and even medieval and more recent disturbances to the earth—could be located, researched, and recorded. These traces of the past were sometimes in great danger of disappearing because up until this point they were "invisible." Crawford's aerial surveys and mapping ensured that they would survive and be recorded and protected.

Crawford's first book, *Man and His Past* (1921), described as a "topographical landscape history," established the new subfield of landscape archaeology. In the book Crawford classified human settlements according to their function and position in a structured landscape and provided them with a chronological framework. Crawford went on to demonstrate how effective the relationship was between aerial photography and archaeology, publishing *Air Survey and Archaeology* in 1924 and *Photography for Archaeologists* in 1929. He also surveyed for and drew up a remarkable series of period maps such as *Roman Britain* (1924) and *Britain in the Dark Ages* (1935).

Thanks to Crawford, mapping a site from the air became a standard tool of archaeological survey, and over the next few decades it was used to great effect all over the world. Aurel Stein flew over Iran with the Royal Air Force to map the Roman limes, and Sylvanus Morley hired a plane and a pilot in Guatemala to enable him to find Mayan ruins in the jungle. In the late twentieth century, computer and satellite-generated geographic information systems (GIS) mapping provided archaeologists with an even more accurate tool in locating and describing features in cultural and natural landscapes.

See also Application of GIS Technology to Archaeology (1980–Present).

Further Reading

Chippindale, C. 2001. O.G.S. Crawford, 1886–1957. In *Encyclopedia of archaeology: History and discoveries,* ed. T. Murray, 384–386. Santa Barbara, CA: ABC-CLIO.

Crawford, O. G. S. 1924. *Air Survey and Archaeology*. Southampton: Printed for H.M. Stationery Office at the Ordnance Survey.

Crawford, O. G. S. 1955. *Said and done: The autobiography of an archaeologist.* London: Phoenix House.

Discovery of Australopithecus africanus *(1924)*

Raymond Dart (1883–1988) worked with Sir Grafton Eliot Smith in London before teaching at universities in the United States. In 1922 he was appointed professor of anatomy at the University of Witwatersrand in South Africa. In 1924 Dart discovered a fossilized child's skull in a limestone deposit at Buxton Limeworks near Taung in Northern Cape Province, South Africa. In an article in *Nature* in 1925 Dart argued that the Taung skull was evidence of the presence of an anthropoid ape in Africa, and, based on elements of its morphology, it had become more human. He called it *Australopithecus africanus,* and while it could not be classified as a member of the ape family, Dart could not (at first) classify it as a member of the family Hominidae (or human family) either, because of its small brain size.

For the next twenty-five years the place of *Australopithecus* and its significance was disputed and Dart's expertise attacked. Dart argued that the size of the Taung skull's brain was not as important as its form, and that other early humans had shown that the principle of mosaic evolution was possible. This meant that some parts of the body hominized (that is, became more human) before others, and not just the brain (as argued by Eliot Smith and Sir Arthur Keith based on the Piltdown evidence). In the case of the Taung skull, dental and postural hominization (the ability to stand upright) were evident, even if an increase in the hominization of the brain was not.

By the late 1950s Dart was vindicated by further discoveries of other examples of *Australopithecus* in South Africa, by Robert Broom at Sterkfontein, and by Louis Leakey in Kenya. During the same period Piltdown was proven to be a fraud. However, given the difficulty of dating really ancient fossils, the question of whether *Australopithecus* was ancestral to modern humans could not be resolved at this stage.

In 1955 Dart proposed that before the Stone Age there had been a Bone Age or "osteodonokeratic culture"—when *Australopithecus* had used the bones, teeth, and horns of their animal prey as tools and implements. He based this argument on his extensive study of thousands of fossilized and broken bones from the *Australopithecus*-bearing cave of Makapansgat in the northern Transvaal. While this idea of a bone culture is no longer credible, the new discipline of taphonomy (the study of the transformation of materials into the archaeological record) was effectively born out of attempts to disprove Dart's hypothesis.

Dart's discovery of *Australopithecus africanus* and his interpretation of the significance of the Taung skull were radical for their time when modern paleoanthropology was still very much in its infancy. His was the first in a series of archaeological finds that would prove that Africa was the long-sought-for "cradle of mankind." During the 1930s Richard and Mary Leakey began to work at Olduvai Gorge in Kenya, in east Africa, where as early as 1911 the paleontologist Hans Reck had found fossils and stone tools. The evidence of early human fossil forms in southern Africa continued to increase.

By the end of the twentieth century *Australopithecus* was dated to ca. 3.32 to 1.6 million years ago, and was finally classified and accepted by physical anthropologists as ancestral to humans.

See also Discovery of the Neanderthals (1833–1900); First *Homo Erectus* (1888–1895); Publication of *Les hommes Fossiles, elémentes de paléontologie humaine* (1921); Discoveries at Zhoukoudian Cave (1921–Present); Excavations at Sterkfontein and Swartkrans (1948–Present); Piltdown Unmasked (1955); Discovery of *Zinjanthropus boisei* (1959); Excavations at Olorgesailie and Koobi Fora (1961–1983); Discovery of *Homo Habilis* (1964–1980); Discovery of Early Humans in Ethiopia (1966–1977); Announcement of Toumai Fossil (2002); Earliest Stone Tools Found at Gona (2003); Discovery of the "Hobbit" announced (2004).

Further Reading

Dart, R. 1959. *Adventures with the missing link.* With Dennis Craig. London: H. Hamilton.

Gundling, T. 2005. *First in line: Tracing our ape ancestry.* New Haven, CT: Yale University Press.

Johanson, D. C. 1996. *From Lucy to language.* New York: Simon & Schuster.

Publication of Introduction to Southwestern Archaeology *(1924)*

During the first three decades of the twentieth century, the archaeological exploration of the American Southwest contributed greatly to the development of discipline as a whole. Here was a large and underexplored area of North America, with indigenous people still occupying large parts of it and it also comprised substantial and well-preserved sites. The whole region was influenced by Mesoamerica, before the 400 years of recorded history following the arrival of the Spanish. The arid and sparsely populated Southwest had always been a frontier, a meeting place for different groups, and a place of migrations and movements of people across long distances in search of resources and trade. A homogeneous history and culture, a unique landscape that demanded unique adaptations to its difficult environment, and an indigenous population with strong ethnographic links to its past—America's Southwest provided rare and rich archaeological opportunities.

The discovery of the large pueblo settlement in Chaco Canyon in New Mexico, and many other similar ruins across the Southwest, helped to extinguish the persistent "mound builder" myth that had dominated the public perception of indigenous North Americans during the nineteenth century. The Southwestern pueblos constituted clear evidence that some Native American groups had achieved a level of social complexity that was unique in North America.

Alfred Vincent Kidder's doctorate at Harvard University was supervised by archaeologist George Reisner and anthropologist Franz Boas, and in Kidder they had a student worthy of both. In 1907 Kidder (1885–1963) and fellow student Sylvanus Morley had participated in Edgar Lee Hewett's Field School of American Archaeology in Santa Fe, New Mexico. In 1914 Kidder wrote his thesis on the style and decorative motifs of pueblo pottery, using ceramic materials to trace the cultural development of the Southwest. Kidder was analyzing Southwestern material in the same ways that other archaeologists had done with ceramic typologies and chronology in Egypt and southern Europe.

Between 1915 and 1924 Kidder excavated the massive site of Pecos Pueblo in New Mexico, which had been occupied in both prehistoric and historic times, providing American archaeology with several disciplinary milestones. Kidder used stratigraphic excavation at the site as a method of relative dating, at once establishing its value and potential to American archaeology. The use of stratigraphy had been the subject of much debate in North America until the Pecos excavation, where Kidder used it to map the site and its area of influence.

In 1917, as part of his research for the Pecos project, Kidder spent some time with the Hopi at their settlement at First Mesa, and then visited other nearby sites to compare pottery remains. In comparing his field finds to written accounts of Native American traditions, he was one of the first archaeologists to use ethnographic data from cultural anthropology in combination with archaeological data, raising both to a new interpretive level described as ethnoarchaeology.

In 1920 Kidder resolved some of the archaeological problems with burials at the Pecos excavation by employing physical anthropologists at the site. Reisner had used Grafton Elliot Smith's expertise in the Nubian survey in 1911 for the same reasons, but Kidder was the first to do this in the field in North America, and it resulted in a similarly fruitful outcome. The physical anthropological study of remains from Pecos provided valuable data about the epidemiology of its population, such as what their average life span and health were, what diseases and causes of death they experienced, and what their diet would have been.

Kidder's multidisciplinary approach to solving archaeological problems and puzzles at Pecos, and writing its history, also involved pottery analysts, chemists, engineers, and agronomists, along with ethnographers and physical anthropologists—all studying aspects of the material and the site and helping to analyze and explain what was going on there. They all made substantial contributions and proved their value to what became the first long-term and multidisciplinary project in North American archaeology.

The results of the Pecos Pueblo project were published in *An Introduction to Southwestern Archaeology,* the first popular archaeological synthesis about the Southwest and a pioneering culture history. Kidder placed the Pecos Pueblo archaeological material into four successive stages or different periods of cultural development, proving that the combination of stratigraphic excavation, along with detailed ceramic analysis, could map cultural growth over periods of time and across a landscape.

See also Publication of *Ancient Monuments of the Mississippi Valley* (1847); William H. Jackson Visits Chaco Canyon (1877); Seriation and History in the Archaeology of Predynastic Egypt (1891–1904); World's First Archaeological Salvage Project? (1907–1932); Paleopathology in Nubia (1909–1911); Stratigraphic excavation in the Americas (1911–1913); The Pecos Conference (1927); Establishing Dendrochronology (1929).

Further Reading

Givens, D. R. 1992. *Alfred Vincent Kidder and the development of Americanist archaeology.* Albuquerque: University of New Mexico Press.

Givens, D. R. 1999. Alfred Vincent Kidder, 1885–1963. In *Encyclopedia of archaeology: The great archaeologists,* ed. T. Murray, 357–369. Santa Barbara, CA: ABC-CLIO.

Kidder, A. V. 2000. *An introduction to the study of Southwestern archaeology.* With a new essay by D. W. Schwartz. London: Yale University Press.

Willey, G. R., and J. A. Sabloff. 1993. *A history of American archaeology.* 3rd ed. New York: W. H. Freeman.

Woodbury, R. B. 1973. *Alfred V. Kidder.* New York: Columbia University Press.

Publication of The Dawn of European Civilization *(1925)*

Vere Gordon Childe (1892–1957), archaeologist, prehistorian, and social theorist, was born in Sydney, Australia, on 14 April 1892 and died in the Blue Mountains of New South Wales on 19 October 1957. Although Childe became the most influential archaeologist of the twentieth century, he also published books on Labor politics, the sociology of knowledge, and social theory.

Childe was the son of a Church of England clergyman and was educated at the Sydney Church of England Grammar School. In 1913, he graduated from Sydney University with first-class honors in Latin, Greek, and philosophy. While at university he became a militant socialist. In 1914 he went to Queen's College, Oxford, to undertake research for a B.Litt. (1916) under the supervision of Sir John Beazley and in 1917 he was awarded first-class honors. One of Childe's closest friends at Oxford was Rajani Palme Dutt, later to be a leading figure in the British Communist Party.

Childe returned to Australia in 1916 and quickly became embroiled in radical politics, particularly in the anticonscription movement. For a time he was employed at Maryborough Grammar School in Queensland but, because of his radical politics, was not confirmed in a position in St. Andrew's College at Sydney University. Between 1919 and 1921, he was private secretary to John Storey, the premier of New South Wales. In 1921, he was appointed research and publicity officer in the Office of the Agent-General of New South Wales in London but was dismissed before the end of the year after the collapse of the Storey government.

Childe had traveled extensively in Greece, the Balkans, and central Europe and turned this to his advantage by earning at least part of his income in London from translating archaeological texts into English. Although he had some private funds Childe's finances were precarious until his appointment as librarian for the Royal Anthropological Institute (1925), where he was to remain until he became the first Abercromby Professor of Archaeology at Edinburgh University (1927). While working in the institute, Childe continued to travel extensively, visiting museums and archaeological sites and gaining the detailed firsthand knowledge that formed the foundation of his first great series of books: *The Dawn of European Civilization* (1925), *The Aryans* (1926), and *The Danube in Prehistory* (1929), which formed the basis of a new synthetic understanding of Neolithic and Bronze Age Europe.

At Oxford Childe had been influenced by Arthur Evans and John Myres, both ardent advocates of a search for the Indo-Europeans in ancient Greece. For Childe the Indo-Europeans were a tangible link between Europe and the Near East, and explaining the similarities and differences in their histories was to be his major intellectual challenge. In this there was a central issue—how could the Near East, that fount of innovation in agriculture, technology, and indeed civilization that had diffused to Europe—now be so far behind Europe? What was it about Europe (or more particularly the civilization it represented) that had allowed it to become the exemplar of human achievement?

This broader question, which was very much within the traditions of universal history so much associated with the Enlightenment, required Childe to be able to do two things: first, to be able to write the social and cultural prehistory of Europe, and second, to be able to identify the forces for change (diffusion, invasion, independent invention) and match these to the histories of real cultural groups. In other words, for Childe to achieve his great task he would have to be able to convincingly identify groups such as the Aryans. It was a challenge he was to fail.

The Dawn of European Civilization was the beginning of that great task, and it was written with verve and an attention to detail that ensured it would be an instant success. Revised and republished five times (1927, 1939, 1947, 1950, and 1957) *The Dawn* replaced the work of Montelius as the standard text on the later prehistory of Europe, and it was to maintain this position into the 1950s. Childe's use of the concept of culture (already found in the works of Kossinna) was to give him a theoretical framework within which to recreate and interpret his cultural groups. The archaeological culture was a tangible thing—an assemblage of remains that regularly recurred together—pottery types, implements, ornaments, cemeteries (or ways of disposing of the dead), and house forms were the primary material elements that made up an archaeological culture. What allowed for the extrapolation from material culture to people was a related assumption, that for people to share a common material culture they would need to share a common language.

In *The Dawn* Childe applied the concept of archaeological culture systematically, defining each culture chronologically and geographically through stratigraphy, seriation, and artifacts—so that the whole of Europe at any time in prehistory could be described as a complex mosaic of archaeological cultures. A special feature of *The Dawn* was the complex set of tables allowing readers to visualize the correlations between cultures in various places and at various times. In so doing prehistory was transformed into history and anthropology, as the task remained to explain the particulars of both history and society. How did the prehistoric societies function? What were the reasons for change and variation in the past?

These were tremendous challenges to archaeologists (ones, it might be argued, that we are still unable to satisfactorily meet), but they underwrote a prehistory that captured the popular imagination and very much framed the public perception of what archaeologists should attempt to achieve.

See also Typology Makes History (1850–1900); Romano-Germanic Central Museum Established in Mainz by Ludwig Lindenschmidt (1852); Iron Age Site of La Tène Discovered (1857); Publication of *Die typologische Methode* (1903); Publication of *Die Methode der Ethnologie* (1907); Publication of *Die Herkunft der Germanen* (1911); Excavation of Skara Brae (1928–1930); Publication of *The Mesolithic Age* and *The Mesolithic Settlement of Northern Europe* (1932 and 1936); Publication of *Man Makes Himself* (1936).

Further Reading

Allen, J. 1967. Aspects of Vere Gordon Childe. *Labour History* 12: 52–59.

Childe, V. G. 1925. *The dawn of European civilization.* London: Kegan Paul.

Gathercole, P. 1980. Childe's early Marxism. In *Critical Traditions in Contemporary Archaeology,* eds. V. Pinsky and A. Wylie. Cambridge; Cambridge University Press.

Trigger, B. 1980. *Gordon Childe: Revolutions in archaeology.* New York: Cambridge University Press.

Trigger, B. 1989. *A history of archaeological thought.* Cambridge: Cambridge University Press.

Trigger, B. 1999. Vere Gordon Childe (1892–1957). In *Encyclopedia of archaeology: The great archaeologists,* ed. T. Murray, 385–399. Santa Barbara, CA: ABC-CLIO.

Discovery of Olmec Civilization (1926–1942)

During the sixteenth century, Spanish missionaries and historians recorded information about the historic Olmec, whose name means "people of the land of rubber." This was the name the Aztecs gave to the people living on the southern edge of the Gulf of Mexico, where rubber trees are native. The application of "Olmec," in relation to evidence of a specific archaeological culture, began in the mid-nineteenth century, when it was used to describe the style of the huge sculptured stone heads found in the southern (modern) Mexican states of Tabasco and Veracruz. In 1892 the term "Olmec type" was also used to describe some terracotta figurines found in the southern Mexican states of Morelos and Guerrero.

In 1926–1927, archaeologists Frans Blom and Oliver La Farge reported finding more huge sculptured heads at the sites of Tres Zapotes and La Venta, and a large pyramid was found at the latter site. In 1929, while reviewing the publication of these sites, archaeologist Herman Beyer referred to them as "Olmec." In the same year, the scholar Marshall H. Saville used the term "Olmec" to describe the particular characteristics or style of stone sculptures—human heads with tiger-like faces and feline characteristics, such as slanted eyes, prominent canine teeth, and small nostrils.

Between 1928 and 1932 archaeologist George C. Vaillant excavated pieces of jade and pottery in the Valley of Mexico that had features in common with artifacts from the Gulf Coast, which he described as "typical Olmec style." He also noted that these artifacts were not related to the classic Mesoamerican styles of the Aztec, Toltec, or Maya, and that the monumental head sculptures were also found in the same horizon as a type of baby-faced figure that had been found in the south of Mexico. From then on Olmec began to be used to denote a culture, or an archaeological horizon, rather than just a style.

Between 1938 and 1945, the Smithsonian Institution's Matthew Stirling excavated the Olmec sites of Tres Zapotes, Cerro de las Mesas, La Venta, and San Lorenzo, uncovering an impressive array of Olmec artifacts, sculptures, stelae, altars, architecture, and sarcophagi as well as evidence of long occupations of these sites. In 1942–1943 Mexican anthropologist and collector Miguel Covarrubias found Olmec material at the site of Tlatilco on the outskirts of Mexico City.

Evidence of the Olmec culture had now been found as far north as the state of Michoacan, and as far south as Costa Rica. In 1943 Paul Kirchoff defined this region "Mesoamerica," that is, the area that had in common the following cultural elements: agriculture based on maize, beans, and squash; cities with ceremonial precincts and pyramid temples; a game played with a

Olmec sculpture at La Venta. (Philip Baird [http://www.anthoarcheart.org])

solid rubber ball; a similar cosmology and pantheon of gods; the practice of human sacrifice; and a ritual calendar of 260 days.

In 1942 the Mexican Society of Anthropology organized its second Mesa Redonda (round table) inviting scholars such as Alfonso Caso, Miguel Covarrubias, Wigberto Jimenez Moreno, Paul Kirchoff, Matthew Stirling, Eric Thompson, and others to discuss recent finds pertaining to Olmec culture, namely, the characteristics, locations, extensions, relationships, and the historic Olmec people.

To avoid confusion between the surviving Olmec people and the archaeological Olmec, it was proposed that the latter should be called the "La Venta culture"—as this was the best-known and biggest Olmec site. Other suggestions included Paleo-Olmec and Proto-Olmec. Eventually, the name of Olmec for a culture, style, and archaeological horizon won.

Discussions about the chronology of the Olmec also occurred. Some scholars, Thompson among them, believed the Olmec to be a recent culture, even contemporary with the Maya. However, Stirling and many Mexican archaeologists believed the Olmec style was pre-Maya, and was probably an archaic culture which influenced later ones.

At the round table evidence for and against both sides of the argument about the Olmec proceeded. Caso argued that Olmec culture was not primitive, but was refined, was well developed, and had influenced later cultures. He described the Olmec as "the mother" of other classic Mesoamerican cultures. Kirchoff argued that some of the cultural features of the Olmec, such as nose pendants, tattooing, and beards, were indeed very old—and were found in other older Mesoamerican cultures. Covarrubias provided evidence of Olmec styles on small stone sculptures, in semiprecious stones, and on altar carvings and sarcophagi, and he argued that it was connected to the archaic Totonac and to the oldest Maya and Zapotec styles. He too called it the "mother" of these cultures and of all Mesoamerican civilization.

The conclusions of the Mesa Redonda were incentives to further investigate the Olmec. In the 1950s archaeological projects in southern Mexico unearthed Olmec pottery and architecture. Stratigraphic excavations located Olmec materials at about 1000 BC, predating the classic period. Olmec artifacts were found in El Salvador, Guatemala, and Costa Rica. Other details about Olmec culture were discovered—they had played the Mesoamerican ball game, esteemed jade, practiced cranial deformation and head shaving, and used masks and pyrite mirrors.

It was not until the use of radiocarbon dating that the Olmec were indeed proved to be that "mother" culture, the earliest civilization of the Americas. They were at the peak of their power between 1200 and 400 BC—dates that make Olmec civilization contemporary with the ancient Old World civilizations of Egypt and the Near East. The number and volume of imported objects at Olmec sites, and the range of their settlements from the Valley of Mexico to Costa Rica, testify to their political, strategic, trade, and economic power.

It now seems likely that the Olmec devised Mesoamerican cosmology and cosmic geometry, the ordered division of space horizontally by the four cardinal points and vertically into two levels, high and low, a division they expressed in the construction of their ceremonial centers and cities. Olmec cities had religious, ceremonial, administrative, and social centers characteristic of all later Mesoamerican cultures. The Olmec also played their part in developing hieroglyphic-ideographic writing in Mesoamerica. Traces of the first stages in the development of a script can be seen at La Venta, and is known as Epi-Olmec, although a fully fledged writing system was not used for another 400 years or so, at around the beginning of the Christian era. The Olmec originated the concept of the Mesoamerican calendar based on a combination of the solar calendar of 365 days and the ritual calendar of 260 days.

See also Rediscovering Maya Civilization (1839–1843); Establishment of Major U.S. Archaeological Institutions (1846–1866); Stratigraphic Excavation in the Americas (1911–1913); Publication of *The Population of the Valley of Teotihuacán* (1922); Deciperhing the Dynastic Sequence at Piedras Negras (1960).

Further Reading

Benson, E., ed. 1981. *The Olmec and their neighbors: Essays in memory of Matthew W. Stirling.* Washington, DC: Dumbarton Oaks.

Coe, M., and R. Diehl. 1980. *In the land of the Olmec.* Austin: University of Texas Press.

The Pecos Conference (1927)

In 1927 A. V. Kidder organized the first Pecos Conference for archaeologists working in the American Southwest. Its purpose was to provide a forum in which common issues and problems could be discussed and resolved and to formulate a general classificatory scheme for Southwestern cultures that could be used across the region. The scheme was a continuation of the concepts outlined in his book, *Introduction to Southwestern Archaeology* (1924), but would be applied on a broader regional basis. The Pecos classification scheme divided the Southwestern Native American Anasazi culture into seven developmental periods, each characterized by distinctive pottery, house types, and settlement patterns. The classification scheme has stood the test of time and has been validated by Douglass's dendrochronology, or tree-ring dating system, which was developed using timber from Southwestern sites.

Participants in the Pecos Conference included the archaeologists Harold and Winifred Gladwin, who had excavated the impressive Hohokam site of Casa Grande in northern Arizona. The Gladwins used types of pottery to delineate the two occupations of Casa Grande. In 1934 they published their local refinement of the original Pecos classification system in *Method for the Designation of Cultures and Their Variations.* In 1936, building on the Gladwins' work, Southwestern archaeologist Florence Hawley published her encyclopedic *Field Manual of Prehistoric Southwestern Pottery Types.*

The development of ceramic classification in the Southwest was copied and spread to the rest of the United States, and systematic cultural classification systems were developed over the next two decades. Notable among these were the midwestern taxonomic method or the McKern system, published in 1936, which proved more useful for organizing museum collections than those in the field. Institutional recognition of the importance of these systems was evident in the appointment, between 1936 and 1941, of James B. Griffin as curator of the ceramic repository at the University of Michigan. Further local and regional classification details were filled in, with the founding in 1937, by Griffin and James Ford, of the Southeastern Archaeological Conference.

In 1941 Griffin and Ford, with colleague Phillip Phillips, began a survey of the Lower Mississippi Valley. Their report of this survey in 1951 realized the potential of stratigraphic excavation and pottery typology as outlined by Kidder in 1924, and at Pecos in 1927, and took it to the next level, into mapping cultural processes through spatial expanses and interareal interaction.

Ironically, when W. W. Taylor published his monograph *A Study of Archaeology* in 1948, Kidder and Griffin and their preoccupation with classification and typologies were among those he criticized. And yet without their fieldwork, their classificatory schemes, and their ability to manage and interpret data, the next phase of archaeology, the one Taylor complained was completely lacking, would not have been possible. Reliable chronology aside, classification, though not as an end in itself, would contribute substantially to the development and implementation of the "new" archaeology of the 1960s.

See also William H. Jackson Visits Chaco Canyon (1877); Stratigraphic Excavation in the Americas (1911–1913); Publication of *Introduction to Southwestern Archaeology* (1924); Establishing Dendrochronology (1929); Publication of *A Study of Archaeology* (1948).

Further Reading

Givens, D. R. 1992. *Alfred Vincent Kidder and the development of Americanist archaeology.* Albuquerque: University of New Mexico Press.

Givens, D. R. 1999. Alfred Vincent Kidder, 1885–1963. In *Encyclopedia of archaeology: The great archaeologists,* ed. T. Murray, 357–369. Santa Barbara, CA: ABC-CLIO.

Griffin, J. B. 1999. James Alfred Ford, 1911–1968. In *Encyclopedia of archaeology: The great archaeologists,* ed. T. Murray, 635–651. Santa Barbara, CA: ABC-CLIO.

Kidder, A. V. 2000. *Introduction to the study of Southwestern archaeology.* With a new essay by D. W. Schwartz. London: Yale University Press.

Willey, G. R., and J. A. Sabloff. 1993. *A history of American archaeology.* 3rd ed. New York: W. H. Freeman.

Williams, S. 1999. James Bennett Griffin, 1905–1997. In *Encyclopedia of archaeology: The great archaeologists,* ed. T. Murray, 451–459. Santa Barbara, CA: ABC-CLIO.

Excavation of the Athenian Agora (1927–Present)

The site of the original Athenian Agora, the focus of civil life in classical Athens, and the political and commercial center of the city for a thousand years, from ca. 500 BC until ca. AD 500, is probably the best understood classical site in the world. This detailed knowledge is the result of more than 150 years of excavation. The Greek Archaeological Society began to excavate the site in 1859, and they continued on and off during 1871, 1907–1908, 1910, and 1912. Between 1890 and 1891, the building of the railway from Athens to the port of Piraeus required salvage archaeology to be undertaken on the northern part of the site, and between 1891 and 1898 excavations were conducted by the German Archaeological Institute under the direction of Schliemann's protégé, Wilhelm Dorpfeld.

In 1922 the decision was made to excavate the area rather than to redevelop it for housing, but unfortunately, because of the influx of Anatolian, Ionian, and Pontic Greek populations from the modern state of Turkey, neither the Greek government nor the Greek Archaeological Society were able to keep funding the excavations. At this point the American millionaire John D. Rockefeller donated funds, and the American School of Classical Studies at Athens became responsible for the excavation.

The American School of Classical Studies at Athens is the largest foreign research center in Greece. It was established in 1882 by the Archaeological Institute of America to enable American scholars to study classical Greek monuments firsthand. The United States was following in the footsteps of European nations such as Germany, England, and France—all of which established schools in Athens at this time and for similar ends. It is a privately funded organization, dependent on university support and donations from individuals and foundations and it has continued to direct the Athenian Agora excavations with funds from the J. D. Rockefeller, Ford, Mellon Rockefeller, and Packard foundations—testimony to the significance of the site and the importance of classical Athens to modern Western civilization. The American School reconstructed the Stoa of Attalos (1953–1956), which was originally given to the city of Athens by the king of Pergamon ca. second century BC, and they landscaped the Agora Park in 1954.

The site of the Athenian Agora is located on the sloping ground northwest of the Athenian Acropolis, and its history is as long as it is complicated, unravelled and pieced together by the decades of excavations and matching the data derived from them to historical accounts. It was first used as a cemetery and a residential area during the Bronze Age, and its dedication to public use began in the sixth century BC. Its earliest buildings were a fountain house, law court, altar and sanctuary, and administrative buildings, set around a square, but these were damaged or destroyed by the Persians in 480 BC.

By the end of the fifth century BC a new Senate building had been constructed, along with a Senate dining chamber, a stoa (a colonnaded multipurpose building) for the use of the king archon, and another stoa for use by the lesser archons. The old Senate building became an archive, while the original fountain-house and law court survived on the south side of the square. The Doric marble temple, or Hephaisteion, occupied the west side of the square, and a state prison was located on its southwest. In the fourth century BC a new temple to Apollo and a monument for "Eponymous Heroes" were constructed on the west side, and a new fountain-house was built in the southwestern corner. In the third century BC, with Athens under Macedonian control, the only new building to be constructed was the arsenal, to the north of the Hephaisteion.

In the second century BC, under the Hellenistic kings, the old square was radically altered by being enclosed with monumental colonnades. A huge stoa was built across the square, dividing it into two. Along the east side, the Stoa of Attalos, a new large, two-story market building, and a new archives were constructed. The Roman attack on Athens in 86 BC damaged many of the Agora's buildings, but during Augustan times, a new marketplace, known as the "Roman Agora," was built. The old Greek square was filled in with a Roman odeon (or covered theater), and a number of reassembled sections of salvaged classical temples from other sites. Under the Roman emperor Hadrian in the second century AD, Athens once again flourished and new library, nymphaion (a semicircular fountain-house, decorated with sculpture-filled niches), and basilica were added to the Agora.

Midway through the third century AD the city was destroyed, and then refortified by constructing a large and long city wall of pieces of ruined Agora buildings. During the early fifth century AD a large gymnasium complex was built on the site of the old square, but by AD 582 the Slavs had invaded, and the Dark Ages descended on the Athenian Agora for the next three centuries, until houses began to be constructed on it ca. AD 1000.

See also World's First Archaeological Salvage Project? (1907–1932).

Further Reading

Camp, J. M. 1998. *The Athenian Agora: excavations in the heart of classical Athens.* Updated ed. London: Thames and Hudson.

Dyson, S. L. 1998. *Ancient marbles to American shores: Classical archaeology in the United States.* Philadelphia: University of Pennsylvania Press.

Hoff. M. 1996. American School of Classical Studies at Athens. In *An encyclopedia of the history of classical archaeology,* ed. N. T. de Grummond, 44–45. Westport, CT: Greenwood Press.

Thompson, H. A., and R. E. Wycherley. 1972. *The Agora of Athens: the history, shape, and uses of an ancient city center.* Princeton, NJ: American School of Classical Studies at Athens.

Publication of The Formation of the Chinese People *(1928)*

Chinese archaeology began during the first half of the twentieth century, primarily because of the emergence of a modern, centralized, self-governing Chinese nation. The search for scientific evidence to reconstruct Chinese history and prehistory was an important focus for the new Chinese state—keen to establish a new national identity and illuminate the cultural origins of the new nation. However, Chinese archaeology by Chinese archaeologists and for Chinese purposes was not realized until the late 1920s. Prior to this, during the early part of the twentieth century, even after the fall of the Manchu dynasty and the revolution of 1911, which established a national Chinese state, all archaeological fieldwork was undertaken by Western scientists attached to the Geological Survey of China.

The Swedish geologist Johann Gunnar Andersson, who first excavated the site of Zhoukoudian, was most famous in China for his discovery and excavation of the village of Yangshao in western Henan Province in 1921. This late Neolithic village gave its name to the culture that produced the type of coarse, painted pottery found at the site. Evidence of the Yangshao culture (ca. 500–2700 BC), in the form of its distinctive pottery, was found elsewhere in China.

Andersson believed that Yangshao was the "ancestor" or "mother" culture of the modern Han Chinese people and that its pottery style, because of its similarity to styles from the Near East, had been transmitted or brought to China from the West. For a new Chinese nation struggling to throw off Western political and economic domination, Andersson's ideas represented a kind of archaeological imperialism. His diffusion-based hypothesis about the origins of Chinese civilization and culture was debated over the next few decades, and disproving it became the major objective of Chinese archaeology. Chinese archaeologists were determined to find evidence for the indigenous origins of Chinese civilization.

The first Chinese scholar to undertake modern archaeological fieldwork was Li Chi (1885–1979), who excavated a Neolithic Yangshao culture site in southern Shanxi Province between 1925 and 1926. Li Chi was born in Hubei Province into a wealthy family. In 1918 he went to the United States where he earned a Ph.D. in anthropology from Harvard University in 1923, after which he returned to China and taught at Nankai University. In 1928 Li Chi published *The Formation of the Chinese People: An Anthropological Inquiry.* In the same year he was appointed the first director of the department of archaeology at the Institute of History and Philology at the Academia Sinica, which was established to excavate the capital city of the late Shang dynasty at Anyang, in the province of Henan. This was the first state-sponsored archaeological project in China, and fifteen seasons of excavation took place between 1928 and 1937, when the Sino-Japanese War broke out.

A vast number of artifacts were excavated from the site, including hundreds of bronze objects, nearly 25,000 pieces of inscribed oracle bone, and the remains of bronze and jade workshops, palace and temple foundations, and large royal tombs. These proved that the site was the capital city of the late Shang dynasty (ca. 1300 BC) and provided archaeological evidence confirming the existence of an ancient and indigenous Chinese culture.

These excavations shaped modern archaeology in China through their recruitment and training of young Chinese archaeologists (including Xia Nai, later director of the Institute of Archaeology) and their use of modern field archaeology techniques in combination with traditional Chinese historiography and antiquarianism. The ceramic and bronze vessel typology used by Li Chi at Anyang is still used in China. In 1949, with the communist takeover of mainland China becoming inevitable, Li Chi traveled to Chinese nationalist Taiwan to found a department of archaeology at the major university there.

Filling in the gap in the archaeological record between the late Shang dynasty, as evidenced by Anyang, and the Neolithic Yangshao culture, now became the focus of Chinese archaeological research. In 1930 Chinese archaeologists, conducting preliminary excavations in search of evidence of the progenitors of the Shang dynasty in eastern China, found the site of Chengziyai at the Longshan town, in the province of Shandong.

The same black pottery that had been found beneath Shang cultural remains at Anyang was found at the late Neolithic Longshan site (ca. 3000 BC). Its discovery provided the strong link between the earlier Longshan and later Shang cultures. However, eastern Longshan black pottery was evidence of indigenous Chinese cultural development, and it was proved to be independent of the Yangshao culture of painted pottery in the west of China. It was clearly not the result of diffusion from the West. This excavation identified a homeland for Shang culture and contributed to knowledge about the origins of Chinese civilization.

Between 1934 and 1937 the National Beijing Academy excavated at Doujitai in Shaanxi Province, investigating the prehistoric origins of the Bronze Age Zhou dynasty (ca. 1000 BC). This was the first major fieldwork for Su Bingqi (1909–1997), a major archaeological theoretician in China. Born in Hebei Province, Su attended Beijing University and worked with historians on China's early dynasties. In 1950, after the communist takeover, Su was appointed to the newly founded Institute of Archaeology at the Chinese Academy of Sciences. In 1952 he became a professor in the history department of Beijing University, founding mainland China's first academic archaeology program.

After fieldwork at Anyang, Xia Nai (1910–1985) had gone to Britain to study with Flinders Petrie at the University of London, from which he was awarded his Ph.D. in 1946. Between 1945 and 1949 Xia joined the Academia Sinica's expedition to the Chinese northwest to investigate Yangshao culture and to find evidence that would disprove Andersson's sequence of prehistoric cultures and diffusionist theory about the Western origins of Yangshao culture. In 1950 Xia Nai became deputy director of the newly founded Institute of Archaeology at the Chinese Academy of Sciences in Beijing and then director in 1962.

See also Discoveries at Zhoukoudian Cave (1921–Present); Publication of *The Dawn of European Civilization* (1925); Publication of *The Archaeology of Ancient China* (1963); Controversial Interpretation of Banpo Published (1963); Discovery of the Terracotta Warriors (1974).

Further Reading

Chang, K-C. 1986. *The Archaeology of Ancient China,* 4th ed. rev. and enlarged. New Haven, CT: Yale University Press.

Li, Chi. 1928. *The Formation of the Chinese people: an anthropological inquiry.* Cambridge, MA: Harvard University Press.

Liu, L., and X. Chen. 2001. China. In *The Encyclopedia of archaeology. History and discoveries,* ed. T. Murray, 315–333. Santa Barbara, CA: ABC-CLIO.

Olsen, J. 1999. Pei Wenzhong, 1904–1982. In *The encyclopedia of archaeology: The great archaeologists,* ed. T. Murray, 441–450. Santa Barbara, CA: ABC-CLIO.

Von Falkenhausen, L. 1999. Su Bingqi, 1909–1997. In *The encyclopedia of archaeology: The great archaeologists,* ed. T. Murray, 591–600. Santa Barbara, CA: ABC-CLIO.

Von Falkenhausen, L. 1999. Xia Nai, 1910–1985. In *The encyclopedia of archaeology: The great archaeologists,* ed. T. Murray, 601–614. Santa Barbara, CA: ABC-CLIO.

Excavation of Skara Brae (1928–1930)

Skara Brae is one of the most notable Neolithic village sites in the British Isles. Located in a sand dune on Orkney, an island off the north coast of Scotland, the site was inhabited between 3200 and 2200 BC and comprises eight houses with stone "furniture" of beds and storage areas. The houses were connected by covered passageways. Archaeological evidence testifies to the inhabitants keeping sheep and cattle, fishing, and growing cereal crops. The site was exposed during a violent storm in 1850 and was excavated by Gordon Childe between 1928 and 1930.

Childe sought to interpret the daily lives of the inhabitants by drawing an analogy between the society of crofters in the remoter parts of Scotland in the nineteenth century (about which quite a deal was known) and that of the residents of Skara Brae thousands of years before. While it cannot be considered to be entirely persuasive, what was significant was the attempt to secure a sense of the social world of a small remote site in the Neolithic period.

See also Publication of *The Dawn of European Civilization* (1925); Publication of *Man Makes Himself* (1936).

Further Reading

Childe, V. G. 1931. *Skara Brae. A Pictish village in Orkney.* London: Kegan Paul.

Trigger, B. 1980. *Gordon Childe: Revolutions in archaeology.* London: Thames and Hudson.

Historical Archaeology at Colonial Williamsburg (1928–Present)

In 1928 American billionaire philanthropist John D. Rockefeller began funding the excavation and restoration of colonial Williamsburg to turn it into a living museum in an ongoing archaeological, architectural, and curatorial process that has continued into the twenty-first century.

Initially, the architects were more interested in exposing the foundations of buildings than in excavating and analyzing recovered artifacts, but in 1957, with the appointment of English medieval archaeologist Ivor Noël Hume (1927–) this all changed, and archaeology and not architecture would play the greatest role in interpreting the site. Noël Hume introduced tightly controlled stratigraphic excavations, which when linked to the method of "artifact cross-mending," greatly improved the excavator's ability to interpret the sequential interrelationships between structures and other on-site features via potsherds and other artifacts.

Site reports were published, and as important, articles reflecting the accumulated knowledge of recovered archaeological assemblages began to rewrite not only local history, but also to have an impact on global colonial history and its archaeology. Noël Hume's archaeological expertise was matched by his abilities as a historian, particularly by his appreciation of the importance of primary archival resources to his archaeological work. He could thus do justice to both disciplines together, producing a fully *historical* archaeology. In 1966 he wrote *1775: Another Part of the Field,* which proved that he while could excavate and research history, he could also write it.

See also Excavation of Jamestown (1934–1957); Rebirth of Industrial Archaeology (1955); Excavation of Verulamium (1955–1961); Historical Archaeology First Taught

The reconstructed governor's palace in Williamsburg, Virginia. (National Archives)

at University (1960); Publication of *A Guide to Artifacts of Colonial America* (1970); The Garbage Project (1973–Present); Publication of *In Small Things Forgotten* (1977).

Further Reading

Greenspan, A. 2002. *Creating Colonial Williamsburg.* Washington, DC: Smithsonian Institution Press.

Handler, R., and E. Gable. 1997. *The new history in an old museum: Creating the past at Colonial Williamsburg.* Durham, NC: Duke University Press.

Noël Hume, I. 1966. *1775: Another part of the field.* New York: Knopf.

Schuyler, R. L. 2001. Historical archaeology. In *Encyclopedia of archaeology: History and discoveries,* ed. T. Murray, 623–630. Santa Barbara, CA: ABC-CLIO.

Establishing Dendrochronology (1929)

Andrew Ellicott Douglass (1867–1962) had a long and eminent career in astronomy, helping to establish and operate three major astronomical observatories—the Harvard College Observatory at Arequipa, Peru; the Lowell Observatory in Flagstaff, Arizona; and the Steward Observatory at the University of Arizona in Tucson—before he became involved in archaeology. And who would have thought that such an esoteric subject as astronomy could provide the dirt discipline of archaeology, at the other end of the scientific spectrum, with a scientific dating system that would change the writing of prehistory and history itself?

In the 1920s Douglass's interest in the effect of sunspots on the earth's weather led him to investigate the annual growth layers of Arizona pine trees to ascertain if there were any variations in tree-ring width. He discovered a relationship between rainfall and tree growth, and between cyclical variations in tree growth and sunspot cycles. Looking for extensive tree-ring records to help to substantiate his theories, Douglass asked archaeologists in Tucson for pieces of wood from the ruins of a Southwestern pueblo. Within a decade Douglass was able to date some of these wooden remains back to AD 100 and others to AD 700.

For the first time in the development of archaeology, here was a scientific way of determining the date of wooden material from sites, and therefore of the sites themselves. In achieving this, Douglass created a chronology that was independent of other chronologies devised from ceramics, stratigraphy, and of course, the written record.

Douglass went on to develop the study of tree rings into the science of dendrochronology or tree-ring dating. This type of dating made substantial contributions to archaeology in the Arctic, Britain, central Europe, and the Mediterranean Basin. Douglass also provided dendroclimatic and dendroenvironmental reconstructions for archaeology. He retired from astronomy to found and direct the Laboratory of Tree-Ring Research at the University of Arizona, which he helped to establish as the preeminent center for dendrochronological research.

See also Discovery of Radiocarbon Dating (1950); Archaeometry Defined (1958); Thermoluminescence in Archaeology (1960–Present).

Further Reading

Douglass, A. E. 1946. *Precision of ring dating in tree-ring chronologies.* Tucson: University of Arizona.

McGraw, D. J. 2001. *Andrew Ellicott Douglass and the role of the giant sequoia in the development of dendrochronology.* Lewiston, NY: Edwin Mellen Press.

Nash, S. E. 1999. *Time, trees, and prehistory: Tree-ring dating and the development of North American archaeology, 1914–1950.* Salt Lake City: University of Utah Press.

Foundation of the Indo-Pacific Prehistory Association (1929–1932)

In 1929, at a meeting for the preliminary organization of the Batavia Pacific Science Congress, the founder of the Pacific Science Association, Herbert E. Gregory, decided to include a prehistory section in the congress and delegated Dutch East Indies archaeologist P. V. Van Stein Callenfels to organize it. Participants included Callenfels, Davidson Black, Sir Grafton Elliot Smith, Henry Otley Beyer, Sir Richard Winstedt, and Victor Goloubew. They decided to form an organization to promote the prehistory of the Far East, called it the Indo-pacific Prehistory Association, and chose Hanoi for its first congress in 1932. This congress was followed by others: Manila in 1935; Singapore, 1938; but the fourth, proposed for Hong Kong in 1941, was canceled because of political problems caused by the outbreak of war. However, by 1938 participant numbers had doubled to twenty seven, and original delegates from the Dutch East Indies, Singapore, the Malay States, Thailand, Hong Kong, Japan, Cambodia, the Philippines, and Indochina were joined by others from China, Australia, and New Zealand.

The postponed fourth congress was jointly held, along with the Eighth Pacific Science Congress, in Manila in 1953. Delegates included representatives from many Pacific islands as well as those from nations who had attended previously. Eighteen countries were represented by 63 members and 17 associates and observers. The Far-Eastern Prehistory Association was formed and organized at the final business meeting of this congress.

Eleven council members were elected. These included such notables as Fred McCarthy from Australia, Li Chi from China, Roger Duff from New Zealand, Alexander Spoehr from the United States, Bernard Groslier from Indochina, and H. R. Van Heekeren from Indonesia, and Ichiro Yawata from Japan. Henry Otley Beyer from the Philippines was elected honorary chairman, and William Solheim was elected president and wrote the constitution.

The Indo-Pacific Prehistory Association has undergone several name changes since. At first it was known only through the names of its congresses, for example, the 1932 Hanoi congress was known as the First Congress of Far-Eastern Prehistorians, but after World War II its name was changed to the Far-Eastern Prehistory Association. This name continued until 1975 when it was changed to its final and present name—the Indo-Pacific Prehistory Association. This final name change occurred as the result of meetings at a major congress as part of the International Union of Prehistoric and Protohistoric Sciences.

Some of the proceedings of the early congresses were published, but in 1972 Solheim began editing *The Far Eastern Prehistory Association Newsletter* and continued until 1975 when Ron Lampert from Australia replaced him. The newsletter was replaced by the *Bulletin of the Indo-Pacific Prehistory Association* in 1980, and it has been edited by Australian Peter Bellwood since then.

See also International Congress of Prehistory Established (1865).

Further Reading

Bellwood, P., and W. G. Solheim II. 1984–1985. Introduction. *Asian Perspectives* 26 (1): 15–17.

Solheim, W. G. II. 2001. Indo-Pacific Prehistory Association. In *Encyclopedia of archaeology: History and discoveries,* ed. T. Murray, 646–647. Santa Barbara, CA: ABC-CLIO.

Publication of The Zimbabwe Culture *(1931)*

The site of Great Zimbabwe is located on top of a granite hill, in what is now the modern southeast African nation of Zimbabwe. During the first half of the twentieth century this was the British protectorate of Rhodesia. The site comprises an 11-meter-high stone-walled settlement with enclosure, towers, portals, and staircases on the hilltop; a huge enclosure located in the valley below includes a 178-meter-long outer wall and an interior conical tower. There are also ruins between the hill and the enclosure that comprise smaller individual enclosures with parallel passages connecting them. The name of the site means "houses of stone" in the local Shona dialect.

The existence of such a grand and substantial site was first mentioned in Portuguese texts in the sixteenth century. Portuguese traders were the first European explorers of this part of southern Africa, and the site of Zimbabwe—its origins, fate, and significance—were the subjects of contention from that time. It remained the stuff of mythology, buried gold, and lost civilizations, until 1890 when the German prospector and geologist, Carl Mauch, explored it. Even then Mauch believed he had found the palace of the Bibilical Queen of Sheba.

In 1890 the powerful southern African colonialist Cecil Rhodes, for whom Rhodesia was named, sent a team to the site in the hope they would confirm its Mediterranean provenance, rather than an African one, and provide him with further support for his colonization of the region. The investigators duly obliged, arguing that Great Zimbabwe had been built and occupied by Phoenicians. Denial of the African authenticity of Great Zimbabwe, in favor of a non-African provenance, was still being used as political justification for European colonialism as late as the 1960s in Rhodesia.

The ruins of Great Zimbabwe were looted during the late nineteenth century by prospectors searching for the legendary gold of King Solomon rumored to have been buried at the site. Pieces of ornamental stonework and artifacts were also taken for private collections. In 1902–1904 a large, but unfortunately unscientific, excavation destroyed most of the archaeological deposit in the stone enclosure, in order to clean it up for tourism.

In 1929 Gertrude Caton-Thompson (1888–1985) was invited by the British Association for the Advancement of Science to investigate the ruins of Great Zimbabwe in an effort to put to rest, once and for all, the debate about their origins and significance. Caton-Thompson was extremely well qualified for the job, having worked in Egypt with Flinders Petrie and Guy Brunton and then having led the Archaeological and Geological Survey of the Northern Fayum. Her resulting publications on the Predynastic and Neolithic cultures of ancient Egypt were milestones in their own right.

The Great Enclosure at Great Zimbabwe. (Corel)

During her excavations of Great Zimbabwe Caton-Thompson found artifacts in stratigraphic contexts that proved the site to be the result of an indigenous African culture, ca. eighth or ninth centuries AD. She also found evidence of trading links with other centers around the Indian Ocean. In her book *The Zimbabwe Culture* she argued that this site was African in every detail, and that it demonstrated originality and maturity and was the result of skill and civil cooperation. Despite scientific data to support all of these arguments, Caton-Thompson's finds were criticized and disregarded by many. She refused to work in southern Africa again.

From more recent work by African and European archaeologists, not only in eastern and southern Africa, but also at the site of Great Zimbabwe itself, we know that from ca. AD 900–1450 Great Zimbabwe was an important trading hub controlling local ivory and gold production and transportation between the Zimbabwean inland and the coast. These products were exchanged with Arab and Swahili traders, by the ancestors of the Shona, for woven cloth, glass beads, and porcelain. Great Zimbabwe also had contact with the inhabitants of the modern-day countries of Botswana, Mozambique, and South Africa. Its ruler lived in the hilltop complex surrounded by extended family groups. Its inhabitants herded cattle, farmed sorghum and millet, and depended on food tributes from surrounding farming communities, which are estimated to have had around 3,000 to 6,000 people. To extract this tribute members of the ruling family would be installed as local leaders.

It is argued that the decline of Great Zimbabwe was the result of environmental degradation, caused by deforestation and depletion of soil fertility because of the demands of its urban population, at its peak numbering between 12,000 and 15,000 people. The site was abandoned ca. AD 1500, its inhabitants moving on to the more fertile high plains of Zimbabwe, from which they were excluded during European colonization.

See also Publication of *The Desert Fayum* (1934); Southeastern and Southern Africa during the Iron Age: the Chifumbaze Complex (1960–1980).

Further Reading

Caton-Thompson, G. 1931. *The Zimbabwe culture: ruins and reactions.* Oxford: Clarendon Press.

Caton-Thompson, G. 1931. *The Zimbabwe culture: ruins and reactions.* 2nd ed. With a new introduction. London: Cass, 1971.

Caton-Thompson, G. 1983. *Mixed memoirs.* Gateshead, UK: Paradigm Press.

Publication of Greek Sculpture and Painting to the End of the Hellenistic Period *(1932)*

Sir John Davidson Beazley (1885–1970) was a graduate of and later the Lincoln Professor of Archaeology at Oxford University. He was an excellent classical scholar but his primary interest was in Greek art and Attic vase painting. Vase painting, because of its quality and the fact it had survived when all other forms of painting in ancient Greece did not, made it particularly important to the history of art.

By the early twentieth century the collections of Greek pottery formed by Sir William Hamilton and other aristocratic antiquarians during the late eighteenth and early nineteenth centuries had found their way into museums across Europe. German scholars such as Hartwig, Hauser, and Furtwangler had noted that some pots carried short inscriptions, including what appeared to be "signatures" or short texts giving the name of an artist, followed by a verb, as in "made by" or "painted by," which allowed a typology based on signed works to be created. German scholars applied this typology only to those pots that were signed and were diagnostic of a particular style or technique.

Beazley broadened this method to include the whole corpus of Attic pottery. By identifying the unconscious details of individual artists—such as painted features and elements—he was able to add unsigned pieces to the rest of the corpus of signed ones, and so tens of thousands of Attic red-figure and black-figure pottery could be grouped as the works of individual artists. Beazley's methods have been described as identifying the "hand" of the painters and potters of Athens, and these additional identifications supplemented the names of craftsmen that appeared on the pottery.

Thus, Beazley transformed the hitherto chaotic study of vase painting into an organized field, similar to other documented schools of painting. He went on to successfully apply his method to Etruscan, Corinthian, eastern Greek, and south Italian pottery.

See also Sir William Hamilton's Collections (1764–1798); Publication of *Geschichte de Kunst der Altertums* (1764).

Further Reading

Beazley, J. 1932. *Greek sculpture and painting to the end of the Hellenistic Period.* Cambridge: Cambridge University Press.

Beazley, J. 1956. *Attic Black-Figure Vase Painters.* Oxford: Clarendon.

Beazley, J. 1963. *Attic Red-Figure Vase Painters.* 2nd ed. Oxford: Clarendon.

Publication of The Mesolithic Age in Britain *(1932) and* The Mesolithic Settlement of Northern Europe *(1936)*

The last prehistoric period to be named and understood in any detail was that between the Paleolithic and Neolithic periods. In the early twentieth century it was designated the Mesolithic, literally "the middle Stone Age." Some of the reasons for this late identification and designation lie in the fact that its study fell between disciplines as well. At that time the Paleolithic period, from 30,000–10,000 BC, characterized by big-game hunters with large tools and cave paintings, was the province of geologists. The Neolithic period, from about 5000–2000 BC was the province of archaeologists. The 3,000 years of the Mesolithic were therefore a puzzle.

This time, ca. 9000–6000 BC, was thought to be a period of cultural regression because people had used simpler and smaller stone tools, or microliths, as distinct from the larger stone tools used during both the Paleolithic and Neolithic periods. So what was the Mesolithic? No great leaps forward in human culture seemed to be evident, and it was so insignificant that there was a debate about whether it was a period in its own right, or whether it should be called the epi-Paleolithic or the proto-Neolithic. During the late nineteenth century the great French archaeologist Gabriel de Mortillet claimed that Europe was unoccupied during the period between the cave painters and the crop planters—for him there was no Mesolithic. In the 1920s Gordon Childe dismissed it as making a negligible contribution to European culture.

In 1932, less than ten years after Childe's dismissive comments, English archaeologist Grahame Clark revolutionized our understanding of this period. The Mesolithic, Clark argued, was a time of major transformation in European prehistory. At its beginning humans were living as they had for the last 30,000 years, and at its conclusion they had adopted agricultural economies, had ranked societies, and had altered the natural environment to suit themselves. Clark believed the microliths they used were the basis of a versatile tool kit—a set of tools that could be adapted in a number of ways on a variety of resources—for arrows, spears, fish barbs, or as sickles for hunting and gathering. Instead of being evidence of forgetting how to make big tools, they were proof that big tools were no longer needed. Life in the Mesolithic required a whole range of smaller and composite tools, because people had diversified their food resources.

In his two books, *The Mesolithic Age in Britain* (1932) and *The Mesolithic Settlement of Northern Europe: A Study of the Food-Gathering Peoples of Northern Europe during the Early Post-glacial Period* (1936), Clark proved that the great changes in climate that had occurred during the Mesolithic period had an enormous impact on the environment in northern Europe and on the lives of the people who lived there. The effects of climate change included rising sea levels, which resulted in flooding of low coastal areas and the creation of new high coastlines, and global warming, which resulted in significant changes to vegetation and animal communities. Paleobotanic research and pollen analysis documented a radical change from open tundra to widespread forests by 8000 BC. The retreating Arctic ice cap caused the extinction of larger animals such as mammoths. Larger herbivores such as reindeer followed the ice cap north, while the smaller red deer adapted to the forest by living in smaller herds, and others, such as roe deer and wild boar, adapted by extending their ranges. There were a greater variety of smaller animals available for food, such as wildfowl, and there were more coastal resources, such as fish and shellfish. The humans who inhabited this warmer landscape made social, economic, and technological adaptations to survive.

Clark demonstrated that the archaeology of the Mesolithic provides evidence of a more intense exploitation of this new environment by hunter-gatherers. Smaller-scale resources, such as shellfish, nuts, and small birds, became important parts of the human diet, and they developed new hunting and harvesting strategies to maximize seasonal forest and marine resources and broadened the basis of their subsistence to include more species. Domesticated dogs appeared at around this time, probably as an aid to hunting and killing animals. These economic and technological developments during the Mesolithic period made a greater degree of sedentism possible. Humans reoccupied seasonal sites on lakeshores and seashores and in forests and at rock shelters in expectation of seasonal resources. At some point they may have stayed year-round in expectation of these resources and the need to defend them and their territory. Abundant and reliable food sources also meant a growth in population, economic success and wealth, and the development of trade networks. Clark was convinced that some of the characteristics of the Neolithic period originated during the Mesolithic.

See also Publication of *Pre-historic Times* (1865); De Mortillet Classifies the Stone Age (1869–1872); Publication of *The Dawn of European Civilization* (1925); Godwin and the Fenland Research Committee (1932–1948); Publication of *Man Makes Himself* (1936); Excavation of Star Carr (1949–1953).

Further Reading

Clark, J. G. D. 1932. *The Mesolithic Age in Britain.* Cambridge: Cambridge University Press.

Clark, J. G. D. 1936. *The Mesolithic settlement of Northern Europe: A study of the food-gathering peoples of northern Europe during the early post-glacial period.* Cambridge: Cambridge University Press.

Fagan, B. 2001. *Grahame Clark: An intellectual life of an archaeologist.* Oxford: Westview.

Rowley-Conwy, P. 1999. Sir Grahame Clark, 1907–1995. In *Encyclopedia of archaeology: The great archaeologists,* ed. T. Murray, 507–529. Santa Barbara, CA: ABC-CLIO.

Rowley-Conwy, P. 2001. European Mesolithic. In *Encyclopedia of archaeology: History and discoveries,* ed. T. Murray, 478–491. Santa Barbara, CA: ABC-CLIO.

Godwin and the Fenland Research Committee (1932–1948)

The first successful use of pollen analysis to explore vegetation history was by the geologist Lennart von Post, in Sweden in the 1920s. By identifying the relative abundance of pollen grains of different trees and plants in different strata, the ecology of an area during prehistoric times, that is, its climate, forest composition, and agricultural practices, and any changes to these over time, could be elucidated. This new scientific technique spread rapidly throughout Europe, so that by 1927 more than 150 papers about its use and the mapping of prehistoric ecologies had been published. In 1923 Harry Godwin began to employ pollen analysis for archaeological ends in England. Godwin (1901–1985) studied botany and geology at Cambridge University where he worked for the whole of his career.

During the 1920s and 1930s researchers began working together using pollen analysis to discover and map the impact of climate and human acitivity on the history of woodland (tree and shrub) vegetation. Refinements in technique led to the identification of many different kinds of pollen, such as the pollen of herbs and weeds and cereals, many of which were important indicators of past human activity. These refinements permitted the interpretation of certain features seen in pollen diagrams from natural deposits as the faint traces of the activities of the first farmers of the Neolithic period. One such feature is elm decline, which appeared in pollen diagrams as a noticeable and widespread reduction in elm pollen at a particular point, and was used to divide the Atlantic pollen zone from the succeeding sub-boreal one. Was this elm decline the result of human activity or climatic change or both? Many pollen diagrams revealed changes just above or after the decline horizon, which probably represented prehistoric episodes of woodland clearance, farming, and abandonment.

As pollen analysis developed across Europe, and its results were compared and tabulated, so could diagrams of different pollen compositions be mapped and divided into zones representing different phases of time, thus providing a means of dating suitable sediments. Precise correlations could be made within climatic, geographic, faunal, botanical, and archaeological pollen and sediment sequences. This chronology was used for the next twenty years until the advent of radiocarbon dating in 1950.

In September 1931, a fishing trawler dredged up a harpoon from the Lenan and Ower Bank in the North Sea. Godwin analyzed a sample taken from the North Sea bed and found it was boreal in age (that is, from before the sea-level changes after the last Ice Age). The harpoon was examined by members of the Prehistoric Society of East Anglia in 1932 and identified as an example of a finely barbed antler point, similar to those found at many Mesolithic Magelmosian sites across northern Europe and as far east as Estonia. What was even more interesting was that the sediment surrounding the harpoon was from fresh water. So this harpoon from under the sea was originally from a freshwater site, on hilly land that had been covered by the melting ice sheets at the end of the last Ice Age, when the Baltic and North seas had joined. What this proved was that the prehistory of Britain, prior to the end of the last Ice Age, was similar to that of northern Germany and Scandinavia, whereas its postglacial prehistory was unique. To further elucidate these thousand or so years of ecological changes and their impact on human populations and settlements, British archaeologists, following the example of their Scandinavian colleagues, began to work closely with paleobotanists, geologists, geographers, and biologists.

Godwin began to study the fens (or swamps) of East Anglia and Cambridgeshire with archaeologist Grahame Clark. The Fenland Basin of East Anglia was an ideal place to begin to study and map the history of British vegetation since the last Ice Age and to correlate this with geographic and demographic settlement changes at the same time. The area had been flooded by the North Sea and then covered by postglacial waterlogged deposits. During the sixteenth century AD the fens had been drained for agriculture, and by the twentieth century their upper peat beds had worn away in some places, so that banks of marine silt could be found. Air photographs (with O. G. S. Crawford) and ground surveys mapped the original fen waterways and the flat and built-up areas used for agriculture and settlements. In 1932, inspired by Godwin's expertise in pollen sampling and paleobotany and Clark's interest in using both for archaeological ends, the Fenland Research Committee (FRC) was established to conduct foundational research into the reconstruction of ancient British landscapes and environments. The FRC has been described as "the first truly modern prehistoric project, because of its interdisciplinary scope." At its peak, as Pamela Smith noted, it comprised foty-two specialists, including faunal, mollusk, and charcoal experts.

Godwin established the relationship between pollen zones and the stratigraphy of the peat by identifying the relative abundance of the pollen grains of different trees and plants in different strata. These analyses delineated the ecology of the area during prehistoric times, specifically its climate, forest composition, and agricultural practices. Godwin's pollen analyses of the peat deposits of these swamplands (or fens) elucidated the history of changes to their vegetation, and from these data Clark could interpret their impact on human occupants and geographic development. The FRC worked throughout the 1930s until 1948, when it became part of the subdepartment of Quaternary Studies at Cambridge University.

Clark and members of the FRC excavated and analyzed material from a number of different types of sites. At the site at Peacock's Farm Clark excavated flints from a Bronze Age level, and underneath that pottery from a Neolithic level, and below that a typical Tardenoisian core with other stone tool flakes and pieces from the Mesolithic period were found, the first time such a culture sequence had been demonstrated on a British site. The final report set the cultural remains in an environmental context. Other sites, such as Mildenhall Fen and a Bronze Age foundry, were explored for different reasons but in every case there was a conscious attempt to integrate archaeological and ecological information.

Other archaeologists at Cambridge, such as O. G. S. Crawford, Christopher Hawkes, and Stuart Piggott, all participated in the FRC's working committee. During the 1930s many undergraduates and postgraduates, such as Glyn Daniel, Thurstan Shaw, Charles McBurney, and J. Desmond Clark, had their first experience of fieldwork on FRC surveys and excavations. The FRC published five reports on archaeological excavations and thirteen studies of post-glacial history by Godwin, in preparation for his classic *History of British Flora.*

Godwin became a global leader in ecological thought and practice. His work in the fenlands with Clark and other scientists, along with their data and interpretation, was finally published in 1950 in *The History of British Flora.* In 1948 he became the founding director of the subdepartment of Quaternary Studies. In this position and later, as professor of botany, he contributed to the uses of radiocarbon dating, to the geological history of changes in land sea levels, and to the archaeological implications of this work. Palynology and paleobotany have long since become essential to the reconstruction of past climates and ecologies and central to the business of archaeology. Godwin was knighted in 1970. Clark was to become Disney Professor of Archaeology in Cambridge and was knighted as well.

See also Publication of *The Mesolithic Age* and *The Mesolithic Settlement of Northern Europe* (1932 and 1936); Excavation of Star Carr (1949–1953).

Further Reading

Clark, J. G. D. 1989. *Prehistory at Cambridge and beyond.* Cambridge: Cambridge University Press.

Fagan, B. 2001. *Grahame Clark. An intellectual biography of an archaeologist.* Boulder, CO: Westview.

Smith, P. 1997. Grahame Clark's new archaeology: the Fenland Research Committee and Cambridge prehistory in the 1930s. *Antiquity* 71: 11–30.

Publication of The Desert Fayum *(1934)*

The wealthy and financially independent Gertrude Caton-Thompson (1888–1985) began to study archaeology after a career in the civil service during World War I. She joined Flinders Petrie's excavations at Abydos in 1921 and later studied at University College London with Margaret Murray, and then spent a year at Newnham College, Cambridge, attending lectures on prehistory, geology, and anthropology.

Between 1922 and 1925 Caton-Thompson returned to Egypt to work with Flinders Petrie and Guy Brunton at the Predynastic site at Qau. While Brunton concentrated on the cemetery, Caton-Thompson excavated the settlement site at Hemamieh, and both found evidence of the Badarian civilization (ca. 5000–4500 BC). Named for the Badari site at which they were first found, Badarian artifacts were the earliest evidence of the reliance on domesticated crops and animals, that is, of a Neolithic period, in the Nile Valley. While there was plenty of Badarian pottery at the settlement site, Caton-Thompson also analyzed the lithic material to further understand some of the site's trade links. She then combined the sequences of both types of material, producing a wider understanding of Predynastic cultural development in ancient Egypt. She and Brunton published their work in *The Badarian Civilization* (1928).

The first work on the Predynastic, or prehistoric, sites of ancient Egypt had been accomplished by Flinders Petrie at the end of the nineteenth century. Predynastic Egypt refers to the period between ca. 5000 and 3000 BC, from the appearance of a Neolithic food-producing economy until the political unification of Egypt and the beginning of written Egyptian dynastic history. Petrie had already devised a chronology for Egyptian Predynastic cultures through the sequencing of different kinds of pottery, groups of artifacts, and tomb types, with each sequence described by type sites—such as the Badarian, which was known to be succeeded by the Nagada, Amratian, and Gerzean cultures. However, there were still many gaps in understanding the period, for example, just how much of the dynastic culture of ancient Egypt was the result of its Predynastic cultures? It was this question and others related to it that captured Caton-Thompson's interest.

In 1925, accompanied by the Oxford geologist Elinor Gardner, Caton-Thompson returned to Egypt to undertake an archaeological and geological survey of the northern Fayum. The Fayum was a fertile depression in the Egyptian Sahara, watered by an arm of the Nile River in flood and surrounded by arid land. Ten thousand years ago, as the floods receded in summer, the lake's shores could be used to grow crops; its shallows were rich with animal life, and its depths were full of crocodiles and fish. Surrounding groundwater supported swamps and forests, which had their own bird and animal life. It was a lush oasis for early Egyptian hunter-gatherers. At ca. 1990 BC the lake's water flow was restricted to reclaim farming land, and by the early twentieth century AD, the lake was greatly reduced in size and becoming more saline.

One of the first interdisciplinary surveys on settlement patterns and sequences in Egypt, the survey kept Caton-Thompson and Gardner working in northwestern Egypt on the desert margins until 1928. They found a variety of sites with a range of different characteristics that would radically alter knowledge of Predynastic Egypt.

Numerous small chert blades and other tools (called Qarunian), and the bones of fish, gazelle, hartebeest, hippopotamus, and other animals, provided evidence of earliest human occupation around the lake shore ca. 8000 BC. These people hunted, fished, and foraged. Plant remains included reeds and other marsh and swamp species. There is no evidence of agriculture, and all animal remains are from wild species. The rich resources of their environment allowed them to continue hunting and gathering, when at the same time, farther south in Egypt, other people were becoming sedentary, planting crops, and herding animals.

However, the Predynastic settlement sites that Caton-Thompson found on the edge of the Fayum, ca. 5500–4500 BC, were evidence of a later "Neolithic transition." During this period not only did people living around the Fayum continue fishing and gathering (from evidence of gazelle and fish bones), but also they began to plant wheat and barley and keep sheep, goats, and cattle. There were smaller sites that were seasonal fishing camps. Caton-Thompson also found silos full of wheat and barley that contained sickles and other tools. She did not find any evidence of permanent settlement or housing, and it was probable that the Neolithic Fayum people lived in reed huts and still moved seasonally. This was reinforced by evidence at these sites of large numbers of hearths and quantities of stone tools, pottery pieces, and animal remains, but little evidence of superimposed domestic debris. It seemed, from the evidence from Fayum settlement sites, that hunting and gathering had been an important part of Egyptian Predynastic life for a much longer time span than had been first thought. The Fayum people would have shifted their fields and settlements to exploit the rich soils left by the Nile River's flood fluctuations. The Fayum Neolithic became the earliest phase of Egyptian prehistory.

After around a thousand years of intensive occupation, the Fayum was abandoned ca. 4500 BC; only a few sites can be dated to ca. 4000 BC, and these appear to be seasonal fishing and hunting camps. It seems likely that once a way of life based on farming and raising herds of animals became well established, especially along the main valley of the Nile River, which was a larger area of reliable and fertile land, the Fayum became agriculturally marginal. By 4000 BC the Egyptian economy was becoming more urbanized, with the Nile River an efficient highway for trade and communications.

Notwithstanding the great increase in knowledge flowing from Caton-Thompson's work in the Fayum, many questions about the origins of the Neolithic period in Egypt remained unanswered. Egypt had the oldest known agricultural economy in the world—but wheat and barley are natives of southwestern Asia and were domesticated there more than a thousand years before they were planted at the Fayum. Were cereal and farming techniques introduced to Egypt from southwestern Asia? Did the Fayum people originate in the Jordan Valley, in the Near East? Or did they originate in the Sudan and the Sahara in northwestern Africa? Their styles of stone tools are similar to those found in Upper Egypt and in the Sahara, and they are different from the styles of stone tools from Syro-Palestine.

Caton-Thompson's and Gardner's epic work was published as *The Desert Fayum* in 1934. In 1929 Caton-Thompson was invited by the British Association for the Advancement of Science to investigate the great monumental ruins at Zimbabwe in southern Africa.

See also Seriation and History in the Archaeology of Predynastic Egypt (1891–1904); Publication of *The Zimbabwe Culture* (1931).

Further Reading

Caton-Thompson, G. 1983. *Mixed memoirs.* Gateshead, Tyne and Wear, UK: Paradigm Press.

Caton-Thompson, G., and E. W. Gardner. 1934. *The desert fayum.* London: The Royal Anthropological Institute of Great Britain and Ireland.

Murray, T. 2001. Gertrude Caton-Thompson, 1888–1985. In *Encyclopedia of archaeology: History and discoveries,* ed. T. Murray, 283–284. Santa Barbara, CA: ABC-CLIO.

Spencer, A. J. 1993. *Early Egypt: the rise of civilization in the Nile Valley.* London: British Museum Press.

Excavation of Jamestown (1934–1957)

Jamestown, the first permanent English settlement in North America, was established on Jamestown Island, Virginia, in 1607. In 1934 archaeological investigation at the site began under the auspices of the new National Survey of Historic Sites and Buildings, its objective being historic reconstruction. Differences between the architects and archaeologists involved led to Jean C. Harrington (1901–1998) being appointed as project director in 1936. He became one of the great contributors to the development of historical archaeology in the United States.

Harrington was both an experienced field archaeologist and an architectural engineer, which helped to resolve the impasse. At Jamestown he developed field techniques, analyses, and research frameworks for this new study of Euro-American sites, while supervising the work of his contingent of Civilian Conservation Corps labor until World War II, which terminated all relief-supported archaeology. However, at this stage a considerable amount of work by researchers, archaeologists, curators, and conservators had been accomplished, and a comprehensive record of all of their work made.

After the war Harrington excavated other historic sites, such as Sir Walter Raleigh's sixteenth-century fort in North Carolina, the eighteenth-century Fort Necessity in western Pennsylvania, and the Appomattox courthouse. In 1949, he returned to Jamestown to excavate the glasshouse site.

Work began at Jamestown again in 1954, funded by National Park funds and directed by John L. Cotter (1911–1999). Cotter was an experienced prehistoric and North American Indian sites field archaeologist, but his greatest contribution was to the development of historical archaeology in North America. He and his team undertook three seasons of extensive fieldwork at Jamestown between 1954 and 1956.

The 350th anniversary of Jamestown's founding in 1957 was the deadline for the site to be published in *Archaeological Excavations at Jamestown, Virginia* (1958). Both Harrington and Cotter and their work at Jamestown did much to establish the bona fides of the new discipline of historical archaeology.

See also Historical Archaeology at Colonial Williamsburg (1928–Present); Historical Archaeology First Taught at University (1960); Publication of *A Guide to Artifacts of Colonial America* (1970); Publication of *In Small Things Forgotten* (1977); Discovery of the African Burial Ground (1991); Excavation of New York City's "Five Points" (1991).

Further Reading

Cotter, J. L. 1959. *Archeological excavations at Jamestown Colonial National Historical Park and Jamestown National Historic Site.* Washington, DC: National Park Service, U.S. Department of the Interior.

Horning, A. J., and A. C. Edwards. 2000. *Archaeology in New Towne, 1993–1995.* Williamsburg, VA: Colonial Williamsburg Foundation.

Schuyler, R. 2001. Jean Carl Harrington (1901–1998). In *Encyclopedia of archaeology: History and discoveries,* ed. T. Murray, 612–614. Santa Barbara, CA: ABC-CLIO.

Schuyler, R. 2001. Historical Archaeology. In *Encyclopedia of archaeology: History and discoveries,* ed. T. Murray, 623–630. Santa Barbara, CA: ABC-CLIO.

Excavation of Maiden Castle (1934–1937)

Sir Robert Eric Mortimer Wheeler (1890–1976) was educated in the classics at University College London and in fine arts at the Slade Art School. He was one of the few young archaeologists to survive World War I. In 1920, after becoming keeper of archaeology at the newly founded National Museum of

Wales, Wheeler began to excavate the Roman forts of Segontium (1921–1922), Brecon Gaer (1924–1925), and Caerleon (1926).

At these sites Wheeler began to develop and test the excavation techniques for which he later became famous. The last great advances in this area were made by General Augustus Pitt-Rivers in the 1880s, and Wheeler built on these, clarifying site stratigraphy by keeping simple, graphic, and sectional records of surfaces and sections. In 1926 Wheeler declined the Abercrombie Chair of Archaeology in Edinburgh and moved to work at the London Museum, where he wrote a series of classic and popular catalogs based on his research on Roman, Viking, and Saxon London. He continued to be fascinated by the relationship between Iron Age and Roman society in Britain, excavat-

An archaelogist cleans a skeleton with a brush. Dr. Wheeler supervised the excavations at Maiden Castle, near Dorchester which have brought to light a number of skeletons. The excavations reveal the scene of a battle of AD 40. Photographed August 31, 1937. (Hulton-Deutsch Collection/Corbis)

ing at the Sanctuary of Nodens at Lydney in Gloucestershire (1928–1929), and at the late Iron Age and Roman city of Verulamium, near the town of St. Albans in southern England (1930–1933). At all of them Wheeler continued to develop his expertise in stratigraphic excavation and dating.

Between 1934 and 1937 Wheeler excavated the massive Iron Age hill-fort of Maiden Castle in Dorset in southern England. Many Iron Age hill-forts had been identified and excavated prior to this, but work had been hampered by the fact that they had either been excavated on too small a scale or without knowledge of pottery typology. *The Maiden Castle Report,* published in 1943, was a triumph, a book written in a highly direct and engaging style but full of important information.

Since his first excavations in Wales in 1921 until the last year at Maiden Castle in 1937, Wheeler had been refining his approach to excavation focusing on those elements such as excavation strategy and techniques, recording, and personnel management, which were also Pitt-Rivers's concerns. The fact that both men had distinguished military careers has not gone unnoticed. At Maiden Castle Wheeler excavated in a checkerboard of grid squares that achieved two significant goals. First it allowed him to open up large areas without losing stratigraphic control. Second, the squares could be effectively linked up to create a sense of near-continuous stratigraphy across a large site. The approach, called the "Wheeler method," set the benchmark in field excavation for the next forty years, achieving a goal that Pitt-Rivers never attained—to radically influence the process of field archaeology and through it to focus on the link between method and the reliability of interpretation. He was to use it to great effect in India during the 1940s and 1950s during excavation of Indus civilization sites.

See also Publication of *Excavations in Cranborne Chase* (1887–1896); Discovery of the Indus Civilization (1920–Present); Excavation of Verulamium (1955–1961).

Further Reading

Cunliffe, B. 1999. Sir Mortimer Wheeler, 1890–1976. In *Encyclopedia of archaeology: History and discoveries,* ed. T. Murray, 371–384. Santa Barbara, CA: ABC-CLIO.

Hawkes, J. 1982. *Mortimer Wheeler: Adventurer in archaeology.* London: Weidenfeld and Nicholson.

Sharples, N. M. 1991. *English Heritage book of Maiden Castle.* London: Batsford/English Heritage.

Wheeler, R. E. M. 1943. *Maiden Castle, Dorset.* Oxford: printed at the University Press by J. Johnson for the Society of Antiquaries.

Foundation of the Society for American Archaeology (1934)

The largest population of archaeologists in the world is located in North America, and English is the international language of archaeology. The Society for American Archaeology was founded by a new generation of professional archaeologists, and changes in membership and publications reflect social, political, and professional changes in archaeology in the United States.

During the 1930s the founding institutional work of Putnam and Holmes came to fruition. The first generation of graduate archaeologists in the United States was employed in universities, museums, research institutes, and government archaeology and heritage sectors at federal and state levels. One of the consequences of this increase in the number of archaeologists was the recognition, by both academic and general communities, of the significant contribution that archaeologists could make to understanding the past, which in turn led to further employment opportunities. There were also enough professional archaeologists to form organizations to communicate with each other and to promote and protect their mutual interests.

In 1934 the Society for American Archaeology (SAA) was founded to promote communication within the professional archaeological community and between professional and avocational archaeologists through various means, including a journal—*American Antiquity*. The 1930s were a period of tremendous growth in American archaeology—many state archaeological societies were founded, and new regional conferences provided forums for local archaeological communication. The Great Depression actually led to a vast increase in archaeological fieldwork as a way to relieve unemployment, and the increased work led to new organizations, new journals, and a perceived need for greater communication among archaeologists on the national level.

Membership in the society has always been open to anyone interested in furthering its objectives, and as a result, the SAA has a significant membership drawn from outside the United States.

See also International Congress of Prehistory Established (1865); Foundation of the Indo-Pacific Prehistory Association (1929–1931); First Meeting of the Pan-African Congress on Prehistory and Quaternary Studies (1947).

Further Reading

Christenson, A. L. 2001. Society for American Archaeology. In *Encyclopedia of archaeology: History and discoveries,* ed. T. Murray, 1172–1177. Santa Barbara, CA: ABC-CLIO.

The Trials of the Royal Savage *(1934–Present)*

Notwithstanding the very high public profile of underwater archaeology, the battle to preserve significant wrecks has been long and difficult and is far from over. The fate of a fifteen-ship American squadron that fought an action against the British in October 1776 (since called the Battle of Valcour Bay) is a case in point.

In the action the *Royal Savage* was captured and burned by the British. Other ships were lost, particularly the gunboats *Congress* and *Philadelphia.* After the battle the British attempted to salvage usable gear from the wrecks, and during the nineteenth century attempts were made to raise the other gunboats. Colonel Lorenzo F. Hagglund raised the American flagship *Royal Savage* (in 1934) and the gunboat *Philadelphia* (1935), using innovative salvage technology. Unfortunately, only the *Philadelphia* survived the process because it was acquired by the Smithsonian Institution. The *Royal Savage* had a sadder fate. The victim of inadequate conservation, it literally rotted away.

The rapidly increasing popularity of underwater archaeology that followed the invention of SCUBA technology also massively increased the risk to the integrity of the remaining wrecks in Valcour Bay. A measure of protection was secured when the site became a National Historic Landmark. Nonetheless the pressure continues, making it necessary to fully document what remains, and for the divers and the local heritage authorities to attempt to negotiate an outcome that does not further threaten the integrity of the site.

See also Excavation of a Bronze Age Ship at Cape Gelidonya (1960); Raising the *Vasa* (1961); Raising the *Mary Rose* (1967–1982); Finding the *Titanic* (1985–Present).

Further Reading

Bass, G. 2001. Nautical archaeology. In *Encyclopedia of archaeology: History and discoveries,* ed. T. Murray, 910–918. Santa Barbara, CA: ABC-CLIO.

Cohn, A., A. Kane, C. Sabick, and E. Scollon. 2002. *Valcour Bay research project: 1999–2001 survey results.* Vergennes, VT: Lake Champlain Maritime Museum.

Publication of Man Makes Himself *(1936)*

Man Makes Himself (1936) and *What Happened in History* (1942) are generally regarded as the two books where Gordon Childe most clearly and accessibly expounded the core themes of his work in archaeology. *Man Makes Himself* is a quintessentially popular book and it was (and continues to be) very widely read. One of the reasons for its popularity has to do with the clarity and directness of Childe's language, but a more important reason is its comprehensiveness and its simple but arresting universal message. This (and *What Happened in History*) are paeans to the reality of progress in human history.

Childe takes the human story from its very origins where people live as hunter-gatherers, then as farmers, then as city dwellers, and finally as members of complex states. In essence Childe's story is one of social evolution, of progress in technology, society, and economy as all three major elements of humanity become more complex. There are clear echoes of a similar universal goal pursued by Sir John Lubbock in his *Pre-historic Times,* first published about seventy years before. In *Man Makes Himself* we read primarily about the history of Europe in relation to its long association with the civilizations of the Near East (especially those of Egypt and Mesopotamia). We hear little, or nothing, of other parts of Asia, or the Americas. For Childe the essence of civilization, of progress, is manifest in the story of Europe.

But in his discussion of progress Childe carefully distinguishes between rational scientific knowledge (the engine of civilization and progress) and religion, which he regards as a negative retarding force. Thus *Man Makes Himself* is also at root a demonstration of the power of rational observation and objective knowledge, be it through his discussion of the development of metallurgical knowledge, the invention of the wheel or of sea craft, or indeed the development of agriculture.

See also Discovery of the Amarna Tablets (1887); Seriation and History in the Archaeology of Predynastic Egypt (1891–1940); Publication of *Die typologische Methode* (1903); Publication of *Die Methode de Ethnologie* (1907); Publication of *Die Herkunft der Germanen* (1911); Paleo-pathology in Nubia (1909–1911); Discovery of Indus Civilization (1920–Present); Excavation of Ur (1922–1934); Publication of *The Dawn of European Civilization* (1925); Publication of *The Desert Fayum* (1934); Publication of *World Prehistory: an outline* (1961); Publication of *The Evolution of Urban Society* (1966); Publication of *New Perspectives in Archaeology* (1968); Publication of *Analytical Archaeology* (1968).

Further Reading

Childe, V. G. 1936. *Man Makes Himself.* London: Watts.

Trigger, B. 1980. *Gordon Childe: Revolutions in Archaeology.* London: Thames and Hudson.

Trigger, B. 1999. Vere Gordon Childe, 1892–1957. In *Encyclopedia of Archaeology: the Great Archaeologists,* ed. T. Murray, 385–400. Santa Barbara, CA: ABC-CLIO.

Excavation of Fell's Cave (1936–1937)

Speculation about the human history of the Americas was constant after the Spanish invasions that followed the discoveries of Christopher Columbus. By the eighteenth century it was popularly believed that human history in North America was of no great antiquity, perhaps just a few thousand years at the most, and that the first settlers of the Americas had come from the Old World. However, by the mid-nineteenth century new excavations at Brixham Cave in Britain and the Somme Valley in France had radically extended the antiquity of mankind in Europe.

In the last two decades of the nineteenth century the debate about the origins and antiquity of Native American people continued between the founders of archaeology in the United States, Frederick Ward Putnam of Harvard's Peabody Museum, and William Henry Holmes of the Smithsonian Institution. The major bone of contention was the veracity of the evidence. Putnam believed the types of stone tools being found in great numbers were evidence of an extremely early human occupation, while Holmes believed the tools could have been unfinished or discarded and were not Paleolithic types of tools.

In 1902 the Paris-educated physical anthropologist Ales Hrdlicka (1869–1943) began to work as a field anthropologist for the American Museum of Natural History in New York City, and a year later, because of the interest in his work, he joined the new division of physical anthropology at the National Museum of Natural History at the Smithsonian Institution in Washington, D.C. Hrdlicka conducted anthropometric surveys in the American Southwest and northern Mexico and then went on to examine all of the skeletal remains attributed to "early man" in North America. His conclusions were that all of this material was from modern humans. None was from ancient human forms, and consequently, the occupation of the Americas was recent.

During the nineteenth century a number of sites with human skeletal remains and artifacts in the same strata as the remains of extinct mammals had been found in Argentina. In 1908 Argentinian scientist Florentin Ameghino proposed that, based on this evidence, humanity had evolved there and then spread to the rest of the world. In 1910 Hrdlicka and other North American scientists traveled to Argentina to evaluate these claims by examining the geology and the human remains, which they rejected.

In 1925 human artifacts, in direct association with extinct mammal remains, were discovered at Lone Wolf Creek in Texas. In 1926 chipped stone projectile points and extinct bison remains were found in an undisputed

Pleistocene context at Folsom in New Mexico. The deep clay site had been a water hole where bison had come to drink and been killed by hunters. Invitations were sent to eminent scientists to examine the remains in situ. In 1927 stone points of a similar shape were found under closed Pleistocene conditions and with extinct fauna in the Clovis-Portales region of New Mexico and at Lindemeier, Colorado.

The discovery of these Pleistocene sites proved that human beings had been in North America for approximately 12,000 years, at least 10,000 years longer than had been previously thought. Folsom and Clovis also provided the basis of a chronology that had at least the potential to be used across the Americas.

The assemblage found at the Clovis site comprised the oldest Paleo-Indian material to be found in North America, and its date was confirmed by the extinct animals found with it. Clovis sites were defined by the tools found in them: choppers, cutting tools, a variety of bone tools, and occasionally milling stones, in addition to the particular "Clovis" fluted stone tool points. The Clovis tool kit was nothing like the tools used by Native Americans at the time of contact with Europeans. By 1939 *Ancient Man in North America,* a synthesis of all of the evidence for Pleistocene and early Holocene occupations in North America, was published. The author, Marie Wormington, was one of the first North American female prehistorians; her book went through four editions and is still regarded as a classic in Paleo-Indian studies.

Paleo-Indian sites in South America have a similar tool kit to that of Clovis, except the diagnostic point is a fish-tail-shaped projectile rather than a fluted point. This assemblage could be found from the northern Andes to the plains of Argentina and south into Chile and Patagonia. While the Paleo-Indians of North America hunted mammoths and bison with their Clovis points, in Venezuela they used their fish-tail-shaped points to hunt mastodons, and in Patagonia they hunted horses and ground sloths. In 1936 Junius Bird (1907–1982), an archaeologist working for the American Museum of Natural History in New York City, began to excavate Fell's Cave, a cave site in Chilean Patagonia, which had been continuously occupied from Paleo-Indian times until the recent past. In the oldest deposit he found the distinctive fish-tailed-shaped projectile and ground-stone disks, along with the remains of extinct horses and guanaco. The site demonstrated that humans had occupied the most southern tip of the Americas between 11,000 and 10,000 years ago, much earlier than had been thought possible. Furthermore Bird's subsequent excavation of Cerro Sota Cave uncovered a complete Paleo-Indian cranium. It was small and had modest brow-ridges and little facial projection, all evidence of a fully modern human.

By 1940 Hrdlicka's conclusion that Paleo-Indians had come to the Americas relatively late had been proved wrong. As a consequence of Bird's finds, speculation in the anthropological and archaeological communities now moved on to just how long ago that occupation had been. If Paleo-Indians were in Patagonia by 11,000 years ago, and if they had come across the Asian land bridge before the last Ice Age and then moved through North America, there must have been people at the top of South America by at least 20,000 years ago, in order for them to be at the bottom by 11,000 years ago. And if that was the case—then they would have been in North America even earlier—say 35,000 years ago.

The discovery of radiocarbon dating has helped further develop Paleo-Indian chronology. Hearths associated with pebble and flake tools in southern Chile and northeastern Brazil suggest that people entered South America sometime before 35,000 years ago. Finds at sites in Mexico and Peru have been dated between 20,000 and 22,000 years ago. In North America, in southwestern Pennsylvania, and at the Meadowcroft Rockshelter, excavated in 1973, material has been dated between 21,000 and 16,000 years ago—much older than Clovis material. However, conclusions about Meadowcroft evidence remain controversial.

There is still a debate as to when human beings actually reached North America. Many argue that it must have been between 40,000 and 35,000 years ago. The diversity in stone projectiles and the variety of ecological adaptations in the archaeological record by 12,000 years ago can be used both to support this premise and to undermine it. More recently, the debate has focused on the possibility of a number of migrations from Asia, and even from Europe, into North America. Biological and genetic evidence from Aleuts, Eskimos, and Native American people suggest there were at least two, and even more, migrations of different but modern human groups. Linguistic differences between these groups also support this theory, and the debate continues.

See also High Human Antiquity in the Somme Valley (1841–1864); Excavation at Brixham Cave (1858–1859); Stratigraphic Excavation in the Americas (1911–1913); Excavation of Meadowcroft (1973–1978); Fate of "Kennewick Man" (1996–Present).

Further Reading

Adovasio, J. M. 2002. *The first Americans: In pursuit of archaeology's greatest mystery.* New York: Random House.

Bird, J. B. 1988. *Travels and archaeology in South Chile* (with journal segments by Margaret Bird; edited by John Hyslop; biographical essay by Gordon R. Willey). Iowa City: University of Iowa Press.

Dillehay, T. D. 2000. *The settlement of the Americas: A new prehistory.* New York: Basic Books.

Dillehay, T. D., and D. J. Meltzer, eds. 1991. *The first Americans: Search and research.* Boca Raton, FL: CRC Press.

Meltzer, D. J. 1993. *Search for the first Americans.* Washington, DC: Smithsonian Books.

Willey, G. R., and J. A. Sabloff. 1993. *A history of American archaeology.* 3rd ed. New York: W. H. Freeman.

Lascaux Discovered (1940)

In 1940 the cave of Lascaux in the Dordogne region of France was found by four schoolboys—it had the most spectacular collection of Paleolithic wall art yet seen. French archaeologist Henri Breuil was the first specialist to visit the cave and to verify its Paleolithic provenance. In 1902 Breuil and colleague Carthailac rediscovered and explored the cave of Altamira in Spain—and had put to rest all skepticism about the site and the authenticity of prehistoric cave art by announcing that the art on the walls of Altamira was Paleolithic and not fake. Since then the two had explored the cave of Naiux in France, and Breuil had become the world's expert on cave art.

Lascaux has never been completely excavated, so detailed information about chronology and occupation is lacking. Nonetheless it is believed to be a site that people visited occasionally and specially for ritual purposes. It is believed the art was not all created at the same time and was the result of a number of different episodes of decoration. Charcoal fragments have been dated to around 17,000 years ago. It is best known for its magnificent paintings—some 600, and for its engravings—some 1,500. These are all the more remarkable in that they appear in different sections of the cave.

The first space in the cave is the great "hall of bulls," about 20 by 5 meters, where the walls are covered in painted figures—the main group 5 meters long and dominated by four enormous black auroch bulls, along with smaller horses and deer and what appears to be an animal with two straight horns known as a unicorn. This space joins a gallery 20 by 1.5 meters by 3.5 meters wide that is decorated with paintings of cattle, deer, and horses. An adjoining shaft is decorated with the only human figure—a bird-headed

Painting of stag and reindeer at Lascaux Cave. (Corel)

man spearing a bison. A third space, 5 meters by 5 meters, is decorated with black deer heads and male bison. Another narrow shaft is decorated with engravings of felines. The Paleolithic entrance to the cave has never been found.

Ladders and scaffolds must have been used by the artists to get close to the higher surfaces, and there are pieces of wood in the caves that are probably the remains of these. In the highest space sockets are cut into the rock faces, some 20 meters above the floor. These were packed with clay and evidence of branches used to span the space has been pressed into the filler. At Lascaux there is abundant evidence of the techniques used to create Paleolithic cave art—stone tools for engraving, lamps, mineral fragments, basic mortars and pestles stained with pigments, and hollowed stones containing pigment powders. Sources for the ochre used in the cave have been identified.

Lascaux was opened for public visitation in 1948, but unfortunately because of modern algae and pollens and the heating of the atmosphere due to the large number of visitors, the surfaces of the cave complex began to deteriorate. In 1963 it was closed, but in 1983 a facsimile Lascaux was opened nearby.

See also Research into Prehistoric Aquitaine (1862–1875); Recognition of Paleolithic Cave Art at Altamira (1879–1902); Understanding the Mousterian (1953–1965); Discovery of Chauvet Cave (1994).

Further Reading

Bahn, P. 1998. *The Cambridge illustrated history of prehistoric art.* Cambridge: Cambridge University Press.

Bahn, P., and J. Vertut. 1988. *Images of the Ice Age.* New York: Facts on File.

Boule, M. 1921. *Les hommes fossiles, eléments de paléontologie humaine.* Paris: Masson.

Boule, M. 1923. *Fossil men.* English translation. Edinburgh: Oliver & Boyd.

Chippindale, C., and P. Tacon, eds. 1998. *The archaeology of rock-art.* Cambridge: Cambridge University Press.

Ramos, P. A. Saura. 1999. *Cave of Altamira.* New York: Abrams.

Ruspoli, M. 1987. *Cave of Lascaux.* London: Thames and Hudson.

Excavation of Sainte-Marie among the Hurons (1941–1951)

The archaeology, or the historical archaeology, of the European settlement of Canada began in the 1890s, when two seventeenth-century Jesuit mission sites were identified in southern Ontario. The first scientific excavation of a historic site in Canada was undertaken by Kenneth Kidd (1906–1994) from the Royal Ontario Museum, at the larger and earlier of the two sites—the mission of Sainte-Marie Among the Hurons. Kidd's excavations lasted from 1941 until 1943. After World War II, Wilfred Jury finished the excavations between 1947 and 1951. The mission was reconstructed as a tourist attraction.

Kidd was an ethnologist and a prehistoric archaeologist—and his two-year project at the mission founded historical archaeology in Canada. His book, *The Excavation of Ste. Marie I* (1949) was one of first books on historical archaeology to be published in North America. Kidd maintained his interest in the archaeology of the contact period between Europeans and Native American people, and in 1951 he published the popular book *Canadians of Long Ago: The Story of the Canadian Indian.* He also established the field of contact archaeology, researching and publishing the first important guide to an artifact category of European trade good (that of glass beads) found in historic sites on every continent. Since that time contact archaeology has grown into a globally significant field in archaeology.

See also Historical Archaeology at Colonial Williamsburg (1928–Present); Excavation of Jamestown (1934–1957); Historical Archaeology First Taught at University (1960); Publication of *A Guide to Artifacts of Colonial America* (1970); Publication of *In Small Things Forgotten* (1977); Publication of *Columbian Consequences* (1989–1991); Discovery of the African Burial Ground (1991); Excavation of New York City's "Five Points" (1991).

Further Reading

Clermont, N. 2001. Quebec. In *Encyclopedia of archaeology: History and discoveries,* ed. T. Murray, 1079–1083. Santa Barbara, CA: ABC-CLIO.

Kidd, K. E. 1949. *The excavation of Ste. Marie I.* Toronto, Canada: Toronto University Press.

Murray, T., ed. 2004. *Archaeology of contact in settler societies.* Cambridge: Cambridge University Press.

Schuyler, R. 2001. Kenneth E. Kidd, 1906–1994. In *Encyclopedia of archaeology: History and discoveries,* ed. T. Murray, 764–765. Santa Barbara, CA: ABC-CLIO.

Trigger, B. 2001. Canada. In *Encyclopedia of archaeology: History and discoveries,* ed. T. Murray, 249–259. Santa Barbara, CA: ABC-CLIO.

Publication of Origin and Development of Andean Civilization *(1942)*

While Max Uhle's contributions to the development of Peruvian archaeology were substantial, it was the local archaeologist Julio Cesar Tello (1880–1947) who was regarded as its "founding father" by Peruvians themselves. Tello was of Inca background and was studying medicine and working in a museum when he was awarded a scholarship to study anthropology at Harvard University, where he was taught by Frederick Ward Putnam, Ales Hrdlicka, and Franz Boas. He returned to Peru in 1913 after studying museology in Europe.

Tello was appointed director of the archaeological department of the Museum of Anthropology and Archaeology (the former Museum of Natural History) in Lima and accompanied American archaeologists, such as Kroeber and Hrdlicka, into the field.

In 1924 Tello became director of the National Archaeological Museum, a position he held until 1930. He also became professor of general archaeology in 1923, and later, from 1928 until his death, he was professor of American and Peruvian archaeology at the University of San Marco. Tello was involved in local politics and was a member of the Peruvian National Congress from 1917 until 1928. He wrote newspaper articles about archaeology, helping to popularize the subject and interest the people of Peru in it.

However, Tello's greatest contribution was to Peruvian prehistory. He excavated a number of important sites, such as the seaside necropolis of Paracas (ca. 500 BC), the coastal mound of Sechin Alto, and nearby sites in the Casma Valley. In the 1930s, during his fieldwork in the northern Peruvian highlands, Tello excavated the site of Chavin de Huantar, a town and temple complex built between 900 and 200 BC, whose monumental masonry and carved stonework was evidence of a previously unknown culture, and whose Chavin-style artifacts were found across northern, coastal, and central Peru.

In 1942 Tello published *Origen y desarrollo de al civilization andina* (*Origin and Development of Andean Civilization*) in which he argued that highland Chavin culture was the "mother culture" of Peruvian civilization, and that the origins of Chavin culture were in the Amazon Basin. He traced elements of Chavin iconography and styles of art in historic and contemporary indigenous beliefs and art. These he interpreted as evidence of continuity in Andean culture.

However, in the 1960s, evidence that Chavin art styles (particularly textiles) and larger-scale urban sites had developed elsewhere, and earlier than at Chavin de Huantar, proved Tello's theories about Chavin culture wrong. But he was right about some of the elements of its continuity and influence. We now know that the highland Chavin culture (ca. 500 BC) influenced the development of the coastal Moche culture (ca. AD 300), which in turn influenced aspects of the culture of the historic Chimu, who were subdued by the Inca. There is now greater evidence that coastal cultures were more influential in the development of Peruvian civilization than those in the highlands.

See also Uhle Begins Scientific Archaeology in Peru (1895–1940); Machu Picchu found (1911); Stratigraphic Excavation in the Americas (1911–1913); Excavation of Chavin de Huantar (1966–1980).

Further Reading

Moseley, M. E. 2001. *The Incas and their ancestors.* Rev. ed. London: Thames and Hudson.

Raymond, S. 2001. Peru. In *Encyclopedia of archaeology. History and discoveries,* ed. T. Murray, 1013–1018. Santa Barbara, CA: ABC-CLIO.

Tello, J. C. 1967. *Paginas escogidas.* Lima, Peru: Universidad Nacional de San Marcos.

Discovery of the Dead Sea Scrolls (1946–1970)

The term "Dead Sea Scrolls" refers to two groups of texts. The first group comprises Hebrew, Aramaic, and Greek Biblical and literary texts found in eleven caves near the site of Qumran in Jordan between 1946 and 1956. The second group, found at sites along the Dead Sea, between Qumran and Masada, and in the lower Jordan Valley during the 1950s and 1960s, and some more recently, comprises Biblical and non-Biblical, documentary and literary texts from the late Second Temple period in Judea, when the area was part of the Roman Empire. Both groups of texts had significant effects on Biblical scholarship and knowledge of the history of Judea and the Jewish population in the last century BC and the first two centuries AD.

The first fragments of the Dead Sea Scrolls, comprising excerpts from the Old Testament Book of Isaiah, were sold by Bedouin to dealers in Bethlehem. They had been found in jars in a cave by a Bedouin goat herder. As their significance became known, the caves near the site of Khirbet Qumran were identified as their source and excavations were undertaken. Text fragments discovered there belonged to the original fragments the Bedouins had sold—proving that the original site had been located. Bedouin began to compete with archaeologists to find more manuscripts. Four more similar deposits were found in adjacent natural caves over the next few years, the last with the most complete and important scrolls. Six manmade artificial caves

Qumran Caves (site of Dead Sea Scrolls). (Corel)

were also found containing manuscripts, and the richest of the finds came from one of these hollowed-out cave sites. Of more than 800 separate manuscripts found near Qumran, only nine are near complete.

The scrolls were purchased by Hebrew scholars and became revered and sacred relics, displayed in the "Shrine of the Book" in Jerusalem. For the new state of Israel and many of its citizens they took on even greater value as political symbols. Just like Israel itself, the Qumran Dead Seas Scrolls had been reclaimed and returned to where they had originated.

In 1947 the news of the discovery and the significance of the Dead Sea Scrolls was published in *The Bulletin of the American Schools of Oriental Research* by the great American Biblical archaeologist William Albright (1891–1971). However, initial excitement about the Qumran Dead Sea Scrolls fizzled out as they came under the control of officials and politicians, and then of scholars, some of whom were more interested in paleography, textual analysis, and their own intellectual preserves, rather than in sharing the texts. The study and publication of the Dead Sea Scrolls was slow because of the politics of the region and the Israeli takeover of the Palestine Archaeological Museum. Eventually in 1991, after almost thirty years of lobbying by a community of international scholars, the scrolls' texts were made more widely available. Their meaning and significance are the subjects of ongoing and contentious debates. The provenance of the texts remains an interesting issue. Who placed the manuscripts in the jars in the caves, and why?

Meanwhile the location of the eleven manuscript caves in the cliff face to the north and south of the settlement site of Khirbet Qumran, Jordan, led to their excavation between 1951 and 1956. Four occupation levels were found, one from the seventh century BC, and three others from around 100 BC to just after the fall of Jerusalem in AD 70. Excavation of the Khirbet Qumran site indicated that it was founded in 125 BC on the ruins of an Iron Age fort. This had been constructed during the expansion of the Hasmonean kingdom into areas around the Dead Sea. As the kingdom's trade and agriculture grew, so did the need for frontier defense. There was a gap in its occupation toward the end of the first century BC, and then the site was occupied by the religious community who are believed to have deposited the manuscripts in the caves. Their settlement was destroyed at the time of the first Jewish revolt against Rome as part of Vespasian's campaign in AD 68. It was reoccupied by Jewish rebels during another revolt in AD 132–135 and then finally abandoned.

See also Decipherment of Cuneiform (1836–1857); Paul Botta Excavates "Nineveh" (1843–1845); Publication of *Nineveh and Its Remains* (1849); American Excavations in Mesopotamia at the Site of Nippur (1888–1900); Discovery of the Hittites (1906–1931); Excavation of Ur (1922–1934); Excavation of Jericho (1952–1958).

Further Reading

Eisenman, R. H., and J. M. Robinson, eds. 1991. *A facsimile edition of the Dead Sea Scrolls.* Washington, DC: Biblical Archaeology Society.

Hodge, S. 2000. *The Dead Sea Scrolls rediscovered: An updated look at one of archaeology's greatest mysteries.* Berkeley, CA: Seastone.

Magness, J. 2002. *The archaeology of Qumran and the Dead Sea Scrolls.* Cambridge, MA: William B. Eerdmans.

First Meeting of the Pan-African Congress on Prehistory and Quaternary Studies (1947)

The first Pan-African Congress on Prehistory and Quaternary Studies was organized by Louis Leakey, who had been working in Africa since the 1930s. Before 1947 African prehistory fieldworkers met on rare occasions, if at all, and were separated by vast distances and into specialized areas determined by colonial history and politics. Unfortunately, their fragmented archaeological efforts reflected this isolation. Leakey and others not only recognized the need to improve communications between archaeologists, but also understood that at this stage in its development, African archaeology required a cooperative action and some understanding of the bigger or continental picture if it was to change from an archaeological backwater and live up to its great potential.

The 1947 meeting was the first opportunity since the end of World War II, and the first time many Africanist prehistorians, quaternary geologists, and human and animal paleontologists were able to discuss their work as a group. Out of it came agreements about terminology and typology; collaborative research programs; opportunities to share and compare data, visit sites, and examine collections of artifacts representing different regional sequences; and plans to keep meeting.

The next three congresses in the 1950s were the most crucial to the development of archaeology in Africa and witnessed the presentation of quantum leaps in the knowledge of African prehistory. In recognition of this, at the end of the 1960s, the congress became exclusively for prehistorians. It has been held every five years since.

Until the 1950s prehistoric data about the whole of Africa was scarce. During the 1950s this changed dramatically as professional archaeologists were appointed to African museums and universities and began to undertake fieldwork and to educate indigenous archaeologists. The nature of the archaeological data being collected and analyzed also changed because of developments in archaeological practice in Europe. Cambridge University archaeologist Grahame Clark taught a number of student archaeologists who began working in Africa in the 1930s, 1940s, and 1950s. Clark's interests in paleoenvironments, through his work with the Fenland Research Committee, and in changes to hunter-gatherer behavior during the European Mesolithic, had an enormous influence on his students, among them J. Desmond Clark and Thurstan Shaw. They began to correlate prehistoric environmental changes in Africa with their impact on animal behavior. At the same time Louis and Mary Leakey began to take a similar direction in their work, pioneering the "living floor" concept of excavation at Olorgesailie in Kenya.

Radiocarbon dating also had a huge impact on the development of African archaeology during the 1950s. It provided an absolute chronology for archaeological sites that formerly had to rely on stratigraphic geological chronology. With the problem of verification of chronology resolved, archaeologists could begin to concentrate on interpreting the data and answering questions about changing environments and their impact on the development of modern human beings.

At the second Pan-African Congress, held in 1952 in Algiers, the young Cambridge graduate J. Desmond Clark proposed to unite African prehistory through the correlation of its prehistoric cultures north and south of the Sahara. Against this background, in 1953 Clark began working at the site of Kalambo Falls in northern Rhodesia (modern Zambia), where he assembled a multidisciplinary team to reconstruct its paleoenvironments from the middle Pleistocene to the late Iron Age periods, some 200,000 years of archaeological deposit. A number of students and young graduates who were to become major figures in African prehistory participated in the excavation and its analysis and report writing.

At the third Pan-African Congress in 1955, at Livingstone, the famous South African paleontologist, Raymond Dart gave a paper on an "osteodontokeratic" culture based on examples of *Australopithecines* and the first complete analysis of an African faunal assemblage from the site of Makapansgat. At the same congress, Louis Leakey presented evidence that *Homo erectus* drove animals into swamps and subsequently butchered them at Olduvai, in Kenya, which he dated to around 1.1 million years ago.

In 1959, at the congress in Leopoldville, Leakey announced the discovery, and produced the remains, of the first early hominid to be found at Olduvai—Leakey's "missing link" *Zinjanthropus boisei.* This was the first archaeological excavation of a hominid to be broadcast on the new medium of television. Leakey's work secured ongoing financing from the National Geographic Society and the world's attention on African prehistoric archaeology. This find, together with other earlier fossil hominid finds at Kromdraai, Makapansgat, and Sterkfontein in South Africa, finally proved Africa to be "*the* cradle of mankind"—and a major focus of research into the Paleolithic period.

See also Discovery of *Australopithecus africanus* (1924); Publication of *The Mesolithic Age* (1932) and *The Mesolithic Settlement of Northern Europe* (1936); Godwin and the Fenland Research Committee (1932–1948); Excavations at Sterkfontein and Swartkrans (1948–Present); Discovery of Radiocarbon Dating (1950); Discovery of *Zinjanthropus boisei* (1959).

Further Reading

Gowlett, J. A. 1993. *Ascent to civilization: The archaeology of early humans.* New York: McGraw-Hill.

Phillipson, D. W. 1985. *African archaeology.* Cambridge: Cambridge University Press.

Robertshaw, P., ed. 1990. *A history of African archaeology.* London: Currey.

Publication of A Study of Archaeology *(1948)*

Walter Willard Taylor (1913–1997) received his Ph.D. from Harvard University in 1943. In 1948 he revised his doctoral dissertation and published it as the monograph *A Study of Archaeology,* a stinging critique of American archaeology before World War II and an attempt to reformulate the discipline of archaeology. Taylor argued that archaeology was a set of specialized techniques to gather cultural information, and that archaeologists were technicians and not writers of history. He criticized notable and contemporary American archaeologists such as Alfred Kidder and James Griffin, and in return was criticized for his style of argument. In the resulting furor the value of his theoretical and methodological insights were lost.

As a result Taylor was unable to find an academic position in the United States for a decade after the monograph was published. Although he did receive several research fellowships and taught at several universities in Mexico, he never held any notable archaeological or anthropological positions.

In the 1960s he helped found the department of anthropology at Southern Illinois University in Carbondale where he developed an excellent Ph.D. program. His publications after the monograph were minimal, and he failed to complete and publish his major fieldwork project in which he could have demonstrated the value of his arguments from the monograph and proved their validity.

Almost forty years later it is easier to be more objective about his monograph. Taylor was ahead of his time in advocating new approaches to archaeology, in his assessment of the importance of interdisciplinary research for archaeology, and in his arguments for the significance of an archaeological contribution to anthropological theory. In all of these he anticipated not only the new archaeology but also postprocessual archaeology. Although an inspiring teacher, Taylor was not successful as an archaeological mentor, and he had few students to carry on his ideas. His influence on developments in archaeology in the 1950s and 1960s was far less than it might have been.

See also Publication of *New Perspectives in Archaeology* (1968); Publication of *Analytical Archaeology* (1968).

Further Reading

Reyman, J. E. 1999. Walter W. Taylor, 1913–1997. In *Encyclopedia of archaeology: The great archaeologists*, ed. T. Murray, 681–700. Santa Barbara, CA: ABC-CLIO.

Taylor, W. W. 1948. *A study of archaeology*. American Anthropological Association Memoir 69. Menasha, WI: American Anthropological Association.

Excavation of Jarmo (1948–1954)

From the beginning of his career Robert Braidwood (1907–2003) was interested in the theories of Gordon Childe and others about the origins of civilizations. After World War II he began to search for a Near Eastern site that would provide evidence of the "Neolithic revolution." Following the theories of Childe, this was widely believed to have been the transition from hunting and gathering to farming and herding communities. As such this transition would represent the first rung on the ladder to the later development of early urban or city-state–based civilization, one likely triggered by environmental and population pressures.

Jarmo was a small village site in northwestern Iraqi Kurdistan, on the "hilly flanks" of the Zagros Mountains. Braidwood deliberately chose a site in a topographic zone where wild resources overlapped with domesticated ones, and where farming without irrigation would have been possible. The data from such a site would be different from what would have been obtained at sites in the "the fertile crescent" closer to the Euphrates and Tigris rivers. Braidwood and his team discovered that this small village had been occupied by a community between 100 and 150 people for several centuries during the seventh millennium BC. The deployment of a multidisciplinary team comprised of paleobotanists, zoologists and geologists, radiocarbon and ceramic experts, anthropologists, and archaeologists made it possible to recover and analyze plant and animal evidence at the site, along with the more traditional architectural and artifactual evidence.

The people of Jarmo had lived in rectilinear household complexes made from mud bricks. Their economy was based on growing and harvesting domestic emmer and eikorn wheat, barley, and lentils. They also harvested wild plants, such as field peas, pistachio nuts, acorns, and wild wheat and barley, and kept dogs, domestic goats, sheep, and later, pigs. However, they also hunted wild animals, such as cattle, onager, and other small mammals. The bones of lions, leopards, small wildcats, foxes, and lynxes were also found at the site, killed either for their pelts or to protect the occupants and their flocks.

The inhabitants of Jarmo made a variety of flint and obsidian tools ranging from large to very small sizes. Many milling and grinding stones were found as well as small celts and chisel-like implements and some stone beads, pendants, and bracelets. A small amount of obsidian was imported from Anatolia, and then worked at the site. Other imports included turquoise and marine shells. Stone bowls were made from local limestone, and a small amount of pottery was produced (an innovation that seems to have originated elsewhere) there. Many small clay figurines (human, animal, and geometric) were found, along with many bone tools (such as awls or perforators), bone spoons, and beads.

Our understanding of and interest in the transformation from hunter-gathering to food production has changed since the 1950s, when research focused on the environmental and population pressures that contributed to its occurrence. Prehistorians now focus on understanding the social reasons for the transformation, and the social and cultural consequences of such a major change in lifestyle. However, the importance of Braidwood's work at Jarmo has not changed. It provided the empirical evidence that such great cultural and economic changes had occurred, evidence as to how these early communities had changed from wild to domesticated resources, and evidence that this evolution had taken place over a longer period than had been thought. For many years Jarmo was the oldest agricultural and pastoral community in the world.

The interdisciplinary fieldwork Braidwood pioneered became the model for fieldwork investigations of important regional cultural and economic transitions, not only in western Asia, but also all over the world. The archaeological techniques and methodology Braidwood pioneered at Jarmo became central to mainstream archaeological research design.

See also Publication of *The Dawn of European Civilization* (1925); Publication of *Man Makes Himself* (1936); Publication of *The Evolution of Urban Society* (1966).

Further Reading

Braidwood, R. J., and L. S. Braidwood. 1950. Jarmo: a village of early farmers in Iraq. *Antiquity* 24: 189–195.

Braidwood, R. J., and G. R. Willey, eds. 1962. *Courses towards urban life.* Chicago: Aldine.

Watson, P. J. 1999. Robert John Braidwood, 1907-. In *Encyclopedia of archaeology: The great archaeologists,* ed. T. Murray, 495–506. Santa Barbara, CA: ABC-CLIO.

Willey, G. R., ed. 1982. *Archaeological researches in retrospect.* Washington, DC: University Press of America.

Excavations at Sterkfontein and Swartkrans (1948–Present)

The South African sites of Sterkfrontein and Swartkrans are located near the town of Krugersdorp in the Transvaal Province of modern South Africa. During the 1930s lime miners had uncovered fossilized bones at Swartkrans, but it was not until 1948 that Robert Broom and John T. Robinson found the first hominid fossils, which they identified as a new species of *Australopithecus.* Robinson's training as a zoologist greatly assisted the establishment of these fossils as early ancestral forms of human evolutionary lineage.

Broom and Robinson searched for more hominid fossils at the site during the 1950s and 1960s, and C. K. Brain took over from them in 1965 (and until the present). By 1965 more than 100 individual examples of the new species, known as *Australopithecus robustus,* had been excavated from the site, as well as the remains of six individual early *Homo* species—from the same strata as the *Australopithecus robustus* remains. Here was the first conclusive evidence that species of *Homo* and *Australopithecus* had existed side by side and at the same time during the Pleistocene—evidence confirming, and being confirmed by, similar evidence found at Lake Turkana in East Africa.

Meanwhile, excavations were undertaken at the nearby site of Sterkfontein. This site had been mined for lime since the 1890s, but the first hominid fossil was found, once again by Richard Broom, in 1936. Broom and Robinson worked at Sterkfontein during the 1940s, Robinson and Brain during the 1950s, P. V. Tobias until the 1990s, and A. R. Hughes until 1966.

More than 550 hominid fossils were found, along with the 100 excavated by Broom and Robinson. The majority of these were the remains of *Australopithecus africanus,* vindicating Raymond Dart's Taung discovery thirty-five years earlier. Faunal remains at this site were compared with similar securely dated faunal evidence from East Africa, which enabled the finds to be dated from ca. 2 to 1.8 million years ago. Stone tools in association with the remains of *Homo habilis* were also found in later strata. This find was the first example of *Homo habilis* to be found outside of Olduvai in northern Tanzania.

Evidence from the site of Swartkrans and Sterkfontein proved that there were two different species of *Australopithecus,* the younger of which, *Australopithecus robustus,* had lived in the same area a million years ago and at the same time as an ancestral human species, *Homo habilis.* These data radically changed research into the archaeology of Pleistocene hominids. Instead of having to focus on proving that the *Australopithecines* were ancestral forms of mankind, archaeologists could now begin to interpret their behavior from other paleobiological and paleoenivronmental data.

Swartkrans and Sterkfontein also provided evidence that the erect but smaller-brained *Australopithecus robustus* was a later form (ca. 1 million years ago) of *Australopithecus* than the erect but larger-brained *Australopithecus africanus* and *Australopithecus afarensis* (ca. 3–2 million years ago). Here was proof that erect bipedality had not only evolved prior to brain enlargement, but also that it was probably more important for the survival of a species, and thus human evolution, than brain size. The larger-brained *Australopithecus africanus and Australopithecus afarensis* had both died out before the smaller-brained *Australopithecus robustus,* who competed for the same resources as the early human ancestor *Homo habilis.* For the first half of the twentieth century paleoanatomists had believed it was the size and abilities of hominid brains, and not their means of locomotion, that had powered the human evolutionary process. Now it seemed to be the opposite.

By the 1960s, due in large part to both South and East African finds, it was generally accepted that the *Australopithecines* were part of the development of human kind, if not its direct ancestors. However, it was not generally accepted until the 1980s that there were two species of *Australopithecines*—the older, bipedal, smaller or "gracile," and omnivorous east African *Australopithecus afarensis* and *Australopithecus africanus,* and the younger, bipedal, robust, and herbivorous *Australopithecus robustus*—found at Swartkrans and Sterkfontein. It was Robinson who revised the *Australopithecine* taxonomy to this conclusion.

Continuing work at these sites has now enabled archaeologists, paleoanthropologists, and paleoanatomists to analyze more than 3,000 hominid specimens, the vast majority of which are *Australopithecus africanus.* These South African finds proved that two hominid species existed at the same time, that there were two species of *Australopithecines,* and that erect bipedalism had evolved prior to brain expansion, but that in the long run, it did not ensure that hominids, such as *Australopithecus robustus,* could escape extinction.

See also First *Homo Erectus* (1888–1895); Discoveries at Zhoukoudian Cave (1921–Present); Discovery of *Australopithecus africanus* (1924); Discovery of *Zinjanthropus boisei* (1959); Excavations at Olorgesailie and Koobi Fora (1961–1983); Discovery of *Homo Habilis* (1964–1980); Discovery of Early Humans in Ethiopia (1966–1977); Discovery of Footprints of Our Earliest Ancestors (1974–1981); Announcement of Toumai Fossil (2002); Discovery of the "Hobbit" (2004).

Further Reading

Golwett, J. A. 1993. *Ascent to civilization: The archaeology of early humans.* New York: McGraw-Hill.

Hilton-Barber, B., and L. R. Berger. 2002. *The official field guide to the cradle of humankind: Sterkfontein, Swartkrans, Kromdraai & Environs World Heritage Site.* Cape Town, South Africa: Struik Publisher.

Phillipson, D. W. 1985. *African archaeology.* Cambridge: Cambridge University Press.

Robertshaw, P., ed. 1990. *A history of African archaeology.* London: Currey.

Excavation of Star Carr (1949–1953)

Between 1949 and 1953, Grahame Clark directed the excavation of Star Carr, a lakeside, early Mesolithic site in northeastern Yorkshire, near the town of Scarborough.The waterlogged nature of the site meant that the preservation of the organic artifacts and remains was excellent. Pollen analysis and the remains of trees at the site were evidence of a lakeside, forested landscape, around two hundred years after the ice cap had retreated.

As the expert on the European Mesolithic, Clark was the ideal director of the excavation. Clark had based his revolutionary books on the Mesolithic period, written in the 1930s, on data produced by other people. Here was his opportunity to excavate and interpret new data and to compare it with previous data sets. Star Carr was an exemplary site.

The assemblage recovered from the site comprised simple microlithic (small) stone tools in the shape of barbs and arrows; flint scraps and burins used for working on antlers and bones; awls and axes; barbed spearheads made from red deer antler; elk antler mattocks for digging; scrapers made from wild ox bone; and a number of what appear to be masks made from red deer antlers, which may have been used as hunting camouflage or for ceremonial purposes. The remains of a wooden paddle were also found. Analysis of the animal remains revealed the subsistence patterns of the occupants and the nature of the social groups who used it. The animals they hunted included red deer, elk, roe deer, wild oxen, elk, wild pigs, and water fowl. There were no fish remains—perhaps they were not available in the lake this early, but the remains of two domestic dogs were found, among the earliest remains of this kind in Europe.

Based on the amount of animal bone found it was estimated that the site supported a group of around twenty-five people annually over a six-year period. However, if the occupation had been more intermittent, then the period of occupation was probably longer. The bone and antler technology, such as sickles and barbed points and arrows, was as distinctively Mesolithic as the lithic artifacts. Clark concluded that Star Carr was a specialized seasonal hunting and butchering site rather than a long-term occupation site, probably used by groups who moved on, depending on the season, to other camps on the coast or up onto the moors in the hills.

Excavations at Star Carr was published in 1954, and it reflected the careful analysis and resulting scope of interpretation by Clark and his colleagues. There were chapters on lake stratigraphy and pollen, animal bones, and the flint, bone, and antler tools.

Since 1954 other interpretations (and further excavations) have been made at Star Carr. It is perhaps the most eloquent testimony to the significance of the site, and the issues initially addressed by Clark, that it has continued to attract such attention and disagreement.

See also Publication of *The Mesolithic Age in Britain* (1932) and *The Mesolithic Settlement of Northern Europe* (1936); Godwin and the Fenland Research Committee (1932–1948).

Further Reading

Clark, J. G. D. 1932. *The Mesolithic Age in Britain.* Cambridge: Cambridge University Press.

Clark, J. G. D. 1952. *Prehistoric Europe: the economic basis.* London: Methuen.
Clark, J. G. D. 1954. *Excavations at Star Carr.* Cambridge: Cambridge University Press.
Fagan, B. 2001. *Grahame Clark: An intellectual biography of an archaeologist.* Boulder, CO: Westview.
Legge, A., and P. Rowley-Conwy. 1988. *Star Carr revisited.* London: Birkbeck College.
Mellars, P., and P. Dark. 1998. *Star Carr in context.* Cambridge: McDonald Institute for Archaeological Research.

Discovery of Radiocarbon Dating (1950)

During the twentieth century archaeologists were presented with a constant flow of techniques for dating archaeological objects, archaeological contexts, or both. The first of these, dendrochronology or tree-ring dating, was pioneered by A. E. Douglass in the first two decades of the twentieth century. Although it was originally developed in the southwest United States, the technique was used in other parts of the world with varying degrees of success. The story of dendrochronology mirrors that of other science-based dating technologies in the twentieth and twenty-first centuries in that the techniques themselves have become the subject of continuing research and development. While the great proliferation in absolute dating technologies that occurred in the twentieth century has often been explained as stemming from a desire to encompass more time with greater precision, it is also true that the archaeological scientists who create and use such techniques also need to devote considerable research time to understand their nature, prospects, and limitations.

This is perhaps most apparent in the development and application of radiocarbon dating. Given the fact that this was the first dating technology that depended on the establishment of regular, time-dependent processes (in this case radioactive decay), archaeologists and archaeological scientists have been researching this dating technique since its development by Willard Libby in 1949.

Radiocarbon dating has become the most widely used absolute-dating technology all over the world. Indeed, one of its very great strengths has been its capacity to create a "world prehistory" framework within which archaeologists could compare what was happening in parts of the world that had little or no shared history at that time. However, virtually from the time of its first application to archaeological contexts practitioners have recognized and worked to correct limitations in the technology, work that has led to the development of a thriving industry in dating research and the education of archaeologists in the business of collecting samples and interpreting dates. After fifty years of research we now have enhancements of Libby's original technique that can deliver more accurate absolute dates over longer time periods.

Some limitations in radiocarbon dating have been overcome by the development of new technologies, such as luminescence dating, which themselves have become the subjects of ongoing research. Given the fact that dating is so central to the business of doing archaeology in the early twenty-first century, any reputable undergraduate archaeology textbook contains exhaustive descriptions of techniques for dating materials as diverse as the enamel on teeth or the products of volcanic eruptions in the very remote human past. The identification of regular decay processes occurring in nature is an ongoing task designed to help archaeologists obtain absolute dates from seemingly intractable materials and improve our confidence in the reliability and precision of such dates. Notwithstanding the very great success achieved by dating specialists in the twentieth century, we should never forget that while the development and application of the technologies is important, the task of making sense of them remains firmly in the province of the archaeologist.

Willard Frank Libby (1908–1980) received is his Ph.D. in chemistry from the University of California at Berkeley in 1933, where he taught until 1941. He joined the Manhattan Project, to develop a nuclear weapon, at Columbia University, where he worked for the duration of World War II on gas-diffusion techniques for separating uranium isotopes into fissionable material.

In 1945 he became a professor of chemistry at the University of Chicago and began working at the Institute of Nuclear Studies, where he proved that the amount of radiocarbon in all living plants and animals begins to decay at death at a known rate. This meant that it would be possible to measure the amount of time since an organism had died by measuring the amount of radiocarbon remaining in it.

The consequences for archaeology were profound. The accuracy of this technique was tested by comparison with proven other dating techniques such as dendrochronology and on Egyptian mummies whose names were on known and dated king lists. The first actual radiocarbon or C-14 dates appeared in 1949.

Radiocarbon dating revolutionized the discipline of archaeology. There had not been a quantum leap of such size since proofs of antiquity of mankind deriving from sites such as Brixham Cave demolished the Biblical chronology of Archbishop Ussher in the mid-nineteenth century. No longer did archaeologists have to spend so much time developing and testing chronologies for their material. Here was an accurate method for dating any organic material from the last 40,000 years of human history.

During the 1950s, as more radiocarbon dates became available, many of them revealed problems with accepted typological dating techniques, while others were confirmed as correct. As a consequence, whole histories based on incorrect archaeological typologies and new radiocarbon recalibrations were rewritten, most notably in the prehistory of Europe. It took almost a decade for the consequences of radiocarbon dating to change the focus and direction of archaeology from the age and position of the piece of data in the puzzle—toward the meaning and significance and the details of the development of human history and civilization.

Since the 1950s there has been a massive expansion in research into different types of radiometric dating that have allowed archaeologists to date inorganic evidence (such as sands and volcanic rock) as well as organic remains (such as teeth, bones, and botanical remains). Potassium-argon dating was a crucial development in improving our understanding of the archaeology of Africa; it was applied in the early 1960s to date the rocks in which the fossilized bones of *Australopithecines* were found. The massive expansion in the chronology of human ancestors (the early dates added at least another million years to human history) profoundly changed the terms under which the human story could now be told.

See also Typology Makes History (1850–1900); Excavation at Brixham Cave (1858–1859); De Mortillet Classifies the Stone Age (1869–1872); Publication of *Die typologische Methode* (1903); Establishing Dendrochronology (1929); Archaeometry Defined (1958); Thermoluminescence in Archaeology (1960–Present); Publication of *World Prehistory: An Outline* (1961).

Further Reading

Aitken, M. J. 1990. *Science-based dating in archaeology.* London: Longman.

Libby, W. F. 1955. *Radiocarbon Dating.* 2nd ed. Chicago: University of Chicago Press.

Renfrew, C. 1973. *Before civilization: The radiocarbon revolution and prehistoric Europe.* London: Cape.

Taylor, R. E. 1987. *Radiocarbon dating: An archaeological perspective.* Orlando, FL: Academic Press.

Archaeology and Television (1952–Present)

Archaeologists have long understood the very great value of publicity, if only as a basis for persuading governments, institutions, or private individuals to invest in costly excavations. A significant part of this process of reaching the wider community is to communicate the significance of discoveries in a way that can enlighten the general public without getting too bogged down in detail or esoterica. Magazines such as the *Illustrated London News* in the early twentieth century and *National Geographic* have been extremely successful in this regard, developing an approach to archaeological research that is scientifically respectable as well as popular. Indeed, the fact that the National Geographic Society itself invests heavily in the research process is a major reason why it commands such respect.

Some archaeologists have been particularly adept at using the medium of television to communicate the significance of archaeology. Of course, television is a medium made for archaeology, and there are scores of examples of the close relationship that has built up since the 1950s. Archaeologists all over the world have used the medium, but the experience of British archaeology provides the richest and most sustained examples.

Beginning in 1952, with the host Glyn Daniel and the flamboyant Sir Mortimer Wheeler, the BBC created *Animal, Vegetable, Mineral?* in which, until the show ended in 1960, the BBC asked various panelists to identify a range of objects drawn from British museums. This afforded the opportunity for much jocularity, and the engaging personalities of many of the participants soon made it a top-rated show. Following this success (which came as a surprise to some given that there was not much color and movement) the BBC got the archaeologists out of the studio and into the field in a series of archaeological documentaries titled *Buried Treasure* (1954–1959). Major sites such as Skara Brae were visited, allowing viewers to more fully experience the power of television as a medium for communicating archaeology.

There was a gap in archaeology on TV until 1966, when the BBC established an Archaeological and Historical Unit. By the end of 1989 the unit had made in excess of 250 programs in the phenomenally successful *Chronicle* series, where audiences of up to 5 million were achieved.

After *Chronicle* there was something of a hiatus until the development of a new series created in radically different formats such as *Time Team* (1995–Present) and *Meet the Ancestors* (1998–2004). Although the bulk of media outlets continued to screen or commission series or one-off programs where archaeological discoveries played a part or were the particular focus, newer formats proved to be much more interactive or more clearly focused on the technology of archaeology—whether it be forensic archaeology, geographic information systems, or the application of archaeometry or archaeological science to solving archaeological puzzles and problems. The success of these formats spawned numerous programs dealing with everything from battlefield archaeology to "extreme archaeology" that have continued to deliver significant audiences. British archaeology has found a way to successfully communicate with a range of audiences for more than fifty years, and there can be little surprise that there is strong public support for the discipline there.

See also Publication of *Nineveh and its Remains* (1849); Schliemann Excavates Troy, Mycenae, Ilios, Orchomenos, and Tiryns (1870–1891); Publication of *A Thousand Miles up the Nile* (1877); Machu Picchu Found (1911); Discovering Tutankhamen's Tomb (1922–1932); Excavation of Ur (1922–1934); Excavation of Skara Brae (1928–1930).

Further Reading

Aston, M. 2000. *Mick's archaeology*. Stroud, UK: Tempus.

Jordan, P. 1981. Archaeology and television. In *Antiquity and Man,* eds. J. D. Evans, B. Cunliffe, and C. Renfrew, 207–213. London: Thames and Hudson.

Sutcliffe, R. 1978. *Chronicle: Essays from ten years of television archaeology*. London: British Broadcasting Commission.

Taylor, T. 2001. *Digging the dirt with Time Team*. London: Channel 4.

Excavation of Jericho (1952–1958)

Between 1952 and 1958, English archaeologist Kathleen Kenyon excavated the site of Jericho, in Palestine. While it could not be positively identified as the Biblical city of Jericho that fell to the Israelites, the site did provide important information about the development of a Neolithic period in the Near East. Kenyon found evidence that the early settlements at Jericho had practiced agriculture and animal domestication, dating them to around 4000 BC. However, with the use of the new radiocarbon dating technique, remains from Jericho, processed at Willard Libby's radiocarbon laboratory at the University of Chicago, were dated to between 10,000–9,000 years ago—twice the age of the original dating estimate, and twice the accepted age for the Neolithic period in the Near East.

Kathleen Kenyon (1906–1978) was the daughter of Sir Frederic Kenyon, keeper of manuscripts at the British Museum, and a history graduate of Somerville College, Oxford University. Her first excavation was with Gertrude Caton-Thompson at the site of Great Zimbabwe in southern Africa. Between 1930 and 1935 Kenyon worked with Sir Mortimer Wheeler at the

Roman town of Verulamium, near St. Albans in England, where she excavated the Roman theater. She also worked in Palestine at the site of Samaria, introducing Wheeler's methods of stratigraphic excavation at this site, and at the Roman city of Sabratha in Libya. In 1935 Kenyon helped Wheeler establish the Institute of Archaeology at London University, where she worked until 1962.

British archaeologist John Garstang had excavated the site of Jericho in Palestine between 1930 and 1936, uncovering Bronze Age levels and even Paleolithic evidence, but the political situation in Palestine prevented him from continuing. Kenyon began to re-excavate the site between 1952 and 1958, to clarify both its Biblical history and very early Neolithic evidence Garstang had uncovered. She dug trenches on the slopes of the tell to understand the history of the fortifications and excavated within the town walls for evidence of Mesolithic and Neolithic occupations.

Kenyon uncovered an uninterrupted sequence from the Natufian period (ca. 14,000 years ago) until the late Bronze Age (ca. 3,550 years ago). During the earliest period at the site, hunters camped around its natural spring, leaving flint and bone tools. From the next, or Neolithic 1, period (ca 10,300 years ago) there was evidence of built shelters and the use of obsidian tools—traded from the material's source in eastern Turkey, as part of an extensive trading network. During the subsequent period, a permanent town of domed, round, mud brick houses was built at Jericho, surrounded by a large stone wall with a tower, either for defense or protection. This community practiced weaving and skin-working, as evidenced by the excavation of bone awls, pins, and a shuttle. At around 7,000 years ago house shapes at Jericho became rectangular and with more rooms, and they were constructed around central courtyards with fireplaces. Skin-working and weaving continued, and the excavation of a group of human skulls, plastered and painted to represent human faces, indicates the possibility of some form of ancestor worship.

The site was abandoned and then reoccupied by two different groups of pottery-making people. The first group, designated Pottery Neolithic A, lived in pit houses dug into the debris of the previous occupation. The second, Pottery Neolithic B, constructed houses with stone foundations and mud brick walls. The analysis of plant remains from this period indicates that these people were herdsmen and hunters.

The site was again abandoned and then reoccupied at around 6,500 years ago by successive groups, as evidenced from different pottery styles excavated at the site. During the early Bronze Age (ca. 5,500 years ago) Jericho

Archaeologists clear the top of a tower believed to date back to 7000 BC during the excavation of Jericho. (Bettmann/Corbis)

was surrounded by two parallel mud brick walls and by an external ditch. There is evidence that irrigation was employed to produce food, and that enough wheat was grown to be stored in silos. International trade was thriving—as evidenced by the pottery and other objects imported from eastern Turkey, Syria, and Egypt. Then there is evidence that this town was violently destroyed, perhaps by a more general economic and environmental collapse, which in turn would have made it vulnerable to invasion. Jericho remained unoccupied for about 200 years—and then during Middle Bronze

Age (ca. 4,200 years ago) it was settled by the seminomadic Amorites, who heavily fortified the town via a series of three ramparts down the slopes of what had become a mound. This occupation also ended violently—either by an earthquake or by a possible Egyptian invasion.

The Late Bronze Age period (ca. 3,550 years ago) at Jericho was most likely the Biblical period, when the town was described in the Book of Kings as being occupied by the Israelites when they entered Canaan. Kenyon found little evidence from this period and no archaeological data to support the thesis that the town had been surround by a wall that was demolished by the Israelites under Joshua. The radiocarbon date for the Neolithic period from Jericho was confirmed by similar dates for the Neolithic farming village of Jarmo, in Iraq, which was excavated by American archaeologist Robert Braidwood during the late 1950s.

See also Excavation of Ur (1922–1934); Publication of *The Zimbabwe Culture* (1931); Excavation of Jarmo (1948–1954); First Excavation of Catal Hüyük (1961–1965); Publication of *The Evolution of Urban Society* (1966).

Further Reading

Holland, T. 1999. Kathleen Mary Kenyon, 1906–1978. In *Encyclopedia of archaeology: The great archaeologists,* ed. T. Murray, 481–493. Santa Barbara, CA: ABC-CLIO.

Kenyon, K. M. 1960–1983. *Excavations at Jericho.* London: British School of Archaeology in Jerusalem.

Moorey, P. R. S. 1979. Kenyon and Palestinian archaeology. *Palestine Exploration Quarterly* (Jan–June): 3–10.

Publication of Prehistoric Settlement Patterns in the Viru Valley, Peru *(1953)*

The Viru Valley Project was a product of the newly founded Institute for Andean Research and North American archaeologist Duncan Strong's interest in the prehistory of Peru. Strong had worked on archaeological material excavated by Max Uhle, under the supervision of Alfred Kroeber, as a postgraduate at the University of California at Berkeley. He later became a professor of archaeology at Columbia University. Strong devised the Viru Valley Project to further understand the chronology of prehistoric coastal Peru by surveying and studying settlement patterns. From the beginning the project was cooperative, involving a number of archaeologists with expertise in different areas, such as Wendell Bennet, James Ford, Clifford Evans, Donald Collier,

Junius Bird, and Gordon Willey. It was also multidisciplinary in that they collaborated with human geographers and anthropologists.

Settlement studies in archaeology were not new, and under the influence of the Columbia University anthropologist Julian Steward, some had already made significant contributions to understanding cultural development in the Americas. But Steward's focus on "cultural ecology," on the relationship between human beings and their environment, was considered simplistic. Many of the project team saw ecological settlement studies as only a preliminary step. They wanted to take the survey and the data to a new level of interpretation.

Willey regarded ecological factors as significant influences on settlement patterns, but he believed they were not the only factors evident in the archaeological record. For him settlement patterns were the result of human behavior—they provided evidence about human activities, such as the economic, social, and political organization of the societies who built and occupied them. Willey grouped sites, buildings, irrigation works, and temples that had been in use at the same time and began to reconstruct the patterns and changes in the valley over several thousands of years through surface and subsurface surveys. Sites were regarded as parts of networks with complementary roles within a culture or a region. There were a number of levels of interactions within and between sites—each shaped by different factors. Data from around, inside, and between structures and sites reflected family settlement and community organization, and the spatial distribution of sites and structures reflected the impact of trade, defense, and administration. The combined study of different levels of societies at different periods provided a great depth of information about changes in demography and the social, political, and religious institutions of these prehistoric societies.

Along with changes there were also continuities and discontinuities in social organization. This was another breakthrough, not only in the interpretation of data but also because it was possible to map internal transformations in social organization within the valley. These transformations, not those caused by diffusion or migration, took place over long periods of time.

Willey's *Prehistoric Settlement Patterns in the Viru Valley, Peru* inspired many other intensive surveys of changing settlement patterns in various parts of the world over the next few decades, such as Robert Adams in Iraq and K. C. Chang in northern China in the 1960s and Karl Butzer in Egypt and Richard Blanton in Oaxaca, Mexico, in the 1970s. All of these settlement studies revealed that the causes of the development of complex societies and cultural change are invariably complex, not the result of a few factors. Further,

Willey made a case for slow and gradual change coming from within societies rather than faster rates of change resulting from the application of external forces such as invasion, migration, or diffusion.

See also Uhle Begins Scientific Archaeology in Peru (1895–1940); Stratigraphic Excavation in the Americas (1911–1913); Publication of *The Population of the Valley of Teotihuacán* (1922); Publication of *Introduction to Southwestern Archaeology* (1924); Publication of *The Origin and Development of Andean Civilization* (1942); Publication of *Method and Theory in American Archaeology* (1958); Publication of the *Archaeology of Ancient China* (1963); Publication of *The Evolution of Urban Society* (1966).

Further Reading

Preucel, R. 1999. Gordon Randolph Willey (1913–). In *Encyclopedia of archaeology: The great archaeologists,* ed. T. Murray, 701–712. Santa Barbara, CA: ABC-CLIO.

Vogt, E. Z., and R. M. Leventhal, eds. 1983. *Prehistoric settlement patterns: Essays in honor of Gordon R. Willey.* Albuquerque: University of New Mexico Press.

Willey, G. R. 1953. *Prehistoric settlement patterns in the Viru Valley, Peru.* Washington, DC: U.S. Government Printing Office.

Willey, G. R., and J. A. Sabloff. 1993. *A history of American archaeology.* 3rd ed. London: Thames and Hudson.

Linear B Deciphered (1953)

During the first year of excavations at Knossos, the royal city of Crete, Sir Arthur Evans discovered many small clay tablets covered with a linear script. He began publishing some of the tablets in 1909 in *Scripta Minoa I,* but only a small fraction of the tablets found were published by the time the fourth and final volume of *The Palace of Minos* was finished after his death in 1935. Some historians of archaeology have blamed Evans's slow and incomplete publication of examples of the script for the length of time it took to decipher Linear B. Others have argued that Carl Blegen's excavation of the Mycenaean archive at the Palace of Nestor at Pylos in 1939 provided the vital clues for its eventual decipherment, and on that basis it only took seventeen years, and not fifty.

Sir John Linton Myres (1869–1954) had worked with Sir Arthur Evans on Crete in 1892 and had made substantial contributions to understanding the trade links between the ancient civilizations of Crete and Egypt by comparing Cretan vases with vase fragments found by Sir Flinders Petrie in Egypt. He became a professor of ancient history at Oxford in 1910. In 1927, on the death of Sir Arthur Evans, Myres took on the task of completing the editing and publishing of the Linear B tablets from Knossos. In 1930 Myres wrote his best-known and most popular book, *Who Were the Greeks?,* which was a combination of ancient history, archaeology, geography, and anthropology that went to the heart of a problem that was preoccupying archaeologists.

Carl William Blegen (1887–1971), professor of classical archaeology at the University of Cincinnati, and Alan Wace (1879–1957), director of the British School in Athens, were convinced that although Minoan in origin, Mycenaean civilization was not the result of the Minoan conquest of mainland Greece, as argued by Sir Arthur Evans, but was a combination of Minoan civilization with another civilization on the mainland. They based their doubts on the chronology devised by Blegen for mainland Greece for the Early, Middle, and Late Helladic periods, from the pottery sequence from their excavation of the prehistoric site of Korakou in Corinthia (1915–1916).

Wace began excavating Mycenae in 1921 (and finished with many interruptions in 1955) while Blegen investigated Troy, which he regarded as a key Aegean and Anatolian site. Between 1932 and 1938 Blegen tested sections of the mound of Troy that had been untouched by Schliemann and Dorpfeld and discovered that the previously identified nine cities of Troy only represented two or more phases of the Bronze Age out of a total of forty-six phases. Blegen attributed Homer's Troy to the major period VIIa (ca. 1250 BC) because there was strong evidence that the city was destroyed by war.

In 1939 Blegen returned to mainland Greece to find the Mycenaean capital of Messinia, which Homer described as belonging to King Nestor of Pylos. He excavated the hilltop of Espano Englianos and found a Mycenaean palace that was much better preserved and more carefully excavated, if not as large, than those at Mycenae and Tiryns. While its layout and decoration were similar to those of Minoan palaces, it was more fundamentally like Greek Mycenaean palaces. In this architectural analysis Blegen had accurately defined the extent of Minoan influence on Mycenaean Greece, which the decipherment of Linear B would confirm. Of equal importance were the hundreds of clay tablets inscribed with a script and dating from ca. 1250 BC that Blegen discovered at Pylos.

Building on work by A. E. Cowley, Alice Kober, and E. J. Bennett, Jr., the young English architect Michael Ventris (1922–1956) became interested in deciphering Minoan Linear B. Ventris was an accomplished cryptographer who published his first paper on the issue at the age of eighteen, but because of war service he had to wait until 1949 to resume work on its decipherment.

In 1952 Ventris announced that he had cracked the secrets of Linear B and had established that it was based on an archaic form of Greek. That same year Sir John Myres introduced Ventris to the Cambridge philologist John Chadwick, and together they collected further evidence that Ventris's approach was correct. The 1953 publication of "Evidence for Greek Dialect in the Mycenaean Archives" was a clear and effective statement of their work.

We now know that Linear B script was used in Minoan Crete and Mycenaean Greece between 1450 and 1200 BC. An earlier script, called Linear A, had been devised in Crete in the period between 1700 and 1450 BC. Linear B has been deciphered, but Linear A still provides a challenge. It is not without some irony that the first major test of the Ventris-Chadwick decipherment was provided by none other than Carl Blegen, who returned to Pylos in 1952 and discovered another 300 tablets covered in Linear B. The fact that these could be read, even though they (and other Linear B documents) are primarily invoices and "paperwork" involved in the administration of palace business, at once brought history closer to the Minoan and Mycenaean world.

All of this proved that the last kings of Crete were Greek speakers and led to a reevaluation of Evans's argument that the Minoans had conquered the Mycenaeans. It is now thought that the reverse was true, and that around 1450 BC, Knossos was conquered by the same people who ruled at Pylos and at Mycenae.

See also Schliemann Excavates Troy, Mycenae, Ilios, Ilios, Orchomenos, and Tiryns (1870–1891); Seriation and History in the Archaeology of Predynastic Egypt (1891–1904); Discovery of Minoan Civilization (1900–1935); Excavation of Gournia (1901–1908).

Further Reading

Chadwick, J. 1958. *The decipherment of Linear B.* Cambridge: Cambridge University Press.

Doblhofer, Ernst. 1971 *Voices in stone; The decipherment of ancient scripts and writings,* trans. M. Savill. New York: Collier.

Pope, M. 1975. *The story of archaeological decipherment: From Egyptian hieroglyphs to Linear B.* New York: Scribner.

Understanding the Mousterian (1953–1965)

Francois Bordes (1919–1981) began to study archaeology in Paris after World War II. Between 1948 and 1953 he excavated the Paleolithic cave site of Peche de L'Aze in the Dordogne, first discovered by French archaeologist Denis Peyrony in 1909. His work there, and later between 1953 and 1965, at the nearby cave site of Combe-Grenal, redefined knowledge of the European Middle Paleolithic. Bordes described it by its tool types as the "Mousterian" period, because the types of stone tools common to the Middle Paleolithic period were first unearthed at the French cave site of le Moustier.

To achieve this more detailed analysis of a period 80,000–35,000 years ago, Bordes combined stratigraphic techniques of excavation with statistical analysis. By mapping the position and distribution of artifacts across the "living floor" of a site, he identified the four different types of stone tool technology used during the Middle Paleolithic period—Acheulean hand axes, scrapers, and two different kinds of flaked tools. Bordes argued that because all of these kinds of tools were common to Middle Paleolithic sites, notwithstanding the fact that sometimes they were in different stratigraphic contexts and in different ratios, and found on sites located in different climate zones across Europe and the Near East, they were evidence of four different cultural traditions, that is of different ethnic or tribal groups.

Bordes' theories about the Mousterian were challenged in the middle 1960s by American archaeologists Lewis and Sally Binford, whose reanalysis of Mousterian sites led them to argue that these different stone tool types were part of a versatile and shared tool kit—evidence of different, but related and patterned, activities by one group or of different materials, rather than of different tools belonging to four different Mousterian "ethnic" groups. Variability for the Binfords had more to do with the process of adaptation than with "culture." There is no doubt that while Bordes proved the value of the use of statistical analysis to archaeology, his interpretation of the patterns that had been generated were highly debatable. Nonetheless, Bordes did prove that the Mousterian period was far more complex than was first thought, a fact that is well attested by the large literature that has followed the "Bordes-Binford Debate."

See also De Mortillet Classifies the Stone Age (1869–1872); Recognition of Paleolithic Cave Art at Altamira (1879–1902); Publication of *New Perspectives in Archaeology* (1968); Discovery of Chauvet Cave (1994).

Further Reading

Binford, L. 1999. François Bordes, 1919–1981. In *Encyclopedia of archaeology: The great archaeologists,* ed. T. Murray, 759–774. Santa Barbara, CA: ABC-CLIO.

Binford, L., and S. Binford. 1966. A preliminary analysis of functional variability in the Mousterian of Levallois Facies. *American Anthropologist* 68: 238–295.

Bordes, F. 1968. *The old Stone Age,* trans. J. E. Anderson. London: Weidenfeld & Nicolson.

Bordes, F. 1972. *A tale of two caves.* New York: Harper & Row.

Bordes, F. 1979. *Typologie du paléolithique ancien et moyen.* 3rd ed. Paris: Éditions du Centre National de la Recherche Scientifique.

Dibble, H. L. 1991. Mousterian assemblage variability on an interregional scale. *Journal of Anthropological Research* 47 (2): 239–257.

Sackett, J. R. 1981. From de Mortillet to Bordes: a century of French paleolithic research. In *Towards a history of archaeology,* ed. G. Daniel, 85–99. London: Thames and Hudson.

Rebirth of Industrial Archaeology (1955)

Portuguese scholar Francisco de Sousa Viterbo (1845–1910) first used the term "industrial archaeology" in 1896 to describe the study of the remains and processes of past industries. Museums of technology in Paris, London, and Vienna, founded in the late nineteenth century, collected technological artifacts, but in isolation from their contexts.

During the reconstruction of post–World War II Europe in the 1950s, Rene Evrard, the founder of the Museum of Iron and Coal in the Belgian city of Liege, used the term industrial archaeology as part of the goals of his institution. In England the term industrial archaeology seems to have been used by economic historians at the University of Manchester, before Michael Rix published an article about industrial archaeology in 1955.

In the 1960s and 1970s, important museums were established at Ironbridge in Shropshire, Coalbrookdale, Stoke-on-Trent, and Morwellham Quay to preserve industrial landscapes and their processes, transportation, and technologies. These were at risk of disappearing because of new economic developments and new technologies. During this period greater interest was paid to social, working, and regional history, probably in response to the recognition of huge changes taking place. There was similar attention to recording and conserving industrial landmarks in western Europe and North America.

Guidebooks such as *About Britain,* published for the Festival of Britain in 1951, Kenneth Hudson's book *Industrial Archaeology* (1963), and the series *The Industrial Archaeology of the British Isles* (published by David and Charles of Newton Abbot, England) encouraged popular appreciation and conservation of the monuments of British industry and their significance to the understanding of recent social, economic, and political changes.

Many of the early conservationists of industrial archaeology were amateurs who had particular interests—railways, canals, steam engines—and it was not until the 1970s that industrial archaeology began to be professionalized and began to be studied at the university level as part of historical or post-medieval archaeology. The first national organizations for industrial archaeology were established in the 1970s in England, North America, western Europe, and Australia.

See also Ironbridge Gorge Inscribed on the World Heritage List (1986).

Further Reading

Palmer, M., and P. Neaverson. 1998. *Industrial archaeology: principles and practice.* London: Routledge.

Trinder, B. 2001. Industrial archaeology. In *Encyclopedia of archaeology: History and discoveries,* ed. T. Murray, 661–669. Santa Barbara, CA: ABC-CLIO.

Piltdown Unmasked (1955)

In 1912, "Piltdown man," a skull and associated skeletal remains, stone tools, and fossil animal bones, was discovered in a gravel pit on Piltdown Common, in East Sussex, England, by Charles Dawson, an amateur geologist, and Arthur Smith Woodward, keeper of paleontology at the Natural History Museum in London. The skull, with its evidence of a large braincase and apelike jaw, but with modern teeth, was exactly what you would expect an early hominid ancestor to look like, and it was presented to the Geological Society of London, as just that. Woodward created a new genus and species for it—*Eonthropus dawsoni* (Dawson's Dawn Man). Coming at a time when skeletal evidence of the physical evolution of human beings was extremely rare, and most of it was found in Germany and France, the Piltdown discovery achieved great notoriety.

As Frank Spencer (1990) has noted, however, from the very first the Piltdown remains were regarded as problematic. Early reconstructions of the skull using the physical evidence available, by Woodward, the neuroanatomist Sir Grafton Elliot Smith, and the anatomist Sir Arthur Keith from the Royal College of Surgeons, differed. As early as 1914, the American paleontologist William King Gregory suggested that it could be a hoax, while another American specialist suggested that the site context was unreliable. Dawson and Woodward staunchly defended their find. In 1917, after Dawson's death, Woodward announced that in 1915 Dawson had found more cranial remains, called Piltdown II, close to the first site. The exact location of the find was never confirmed.

As time passed and other discoveries of fossil hominids were made in Asia and Africa that were dramatically different from Piltdown, the English remains came to be seen as anomalous, rather than of great interest. In 1953 the Oxford physical anthropologist J. S. Weiner reanalyzed them and concluded that the braincase and jaw were from separate animals, a suspicion confirmed by fluorine testing. Further analysis demonstrated that the jaw was that of an ape and that the teeth had been deliberately altered and stained to match the color of the braincase fragments. By 1955, the entire Piltdown collection was rejected as fraudulent.

Of course the revelation of fraud requires the identification of the forger, and solving this mystery has become one of the most enduring detective stories in the history of physical anthropology. The list of suspects has included most of the people who were in any way associated with Piltdown. As time has passed (and the debate continues) serious cases have been made (such as the Spencer/Langham argument that it was Sir Arthur Keith) but none have persuaded everyone. Most recently, a Natural History Museum staff member, Martin Hinton, was advanced as the forger, but this case was even less convincing. In the absence of a signed confession by the forger we are left with a range of probabilities and best of all, an unending "whodunnit."

There is every reason to believe that there was a greater purpose to the forgery than to simply hoax the scientific community. The passionate European nationalism that contributed to World War I probably had a role to play. Why else were all these British experts so eager to believe in the finds and to take them so seriously? Because they wanted evidence of early man to be found in Britain—like it had been found in France and Germany—because it was proof that their origins were as good, if not better, or were as early, if not earlier, than those of the others. The nationalism that helped to foster the origins of antiquarianism and scientific archaeology played itself out in the early years of Piltdown as well.

See also Discovery of the Neanderthals (1833–1900); Excavation at Brixham Cave (1858–1859); First *Homo erectus* (1888–1895); Discoveries at Zhoukoudian Cave (1921–Present); Discovery of *Australopithecus africanus* (1924); Discovery of *Zinjanthropus boisei* (1959); Excavations at Olorgesailie and Koobi Fora (1961–1983); Discovery of *Homo Habilis* (1964–1980); Discovery of Early Humans in Ethiopia (1966–1977); Discovery of Footprints of Our Earliest Ancestors (1974–1981); Announcement of Toumai Fossil (2002); Discovery of the "Hobbit" (2004).

Further Reading

Spencer, F. 1990. *Piltdown: A scientific forgery.* London: Oxford University Press.
Spencer, F., ed. 1990. *The Piltdown papers.* London: Oxford University Press.
Weiner, J. S. 1980. *The Piltdown Forgery.* London: Oxford University Press, 1955.

Excavation of Verulamium (1955–1961)

The Roman town of Verulamium, in Britain, was excavated for the second time between 1955 and 1961 by Sheppard Frere. The evolution of the development of this Romano-British center and the impact of Roman influences on the everyday lives of local people from ca. AD 50 to 350 were documented in the archaeological evidence. Frere and his team also uncovered some of the best-preserved wall paintings from Roman Britain. This work was complemented by another extensive excavation at a large cemetery south of Verulamium during the 1960s.

The Roman town of Verulamium was built on the site of an earlier Iron Age settlement. From the beginning it was a "municipium," that is, a settlement whose inhabitants had been allies of Rome during the invasion and conquest of Britain, and who, as a reward for this loyalty, were recognized as a self-governing community with legal privileges.

Verulamium was always an important center for the Romans and became one of the largest towns in Roman Britain; its status was reflected by the number and the scale of the public buildings built there. The early Roman town, founded ca. AD 50, was laid out and built in a grid pattern but was destroyed during the Boudiccan revolt of AD 60–61. It was rebuilt with a monumental forum and opened by Roman governor Agricola in AD 79. The town was a multifunctional hub, similar to those built by the Romans in Gaul, comprising a temple and altar and a market square, against which was a basilica. In the second century AD a theater was built, an initiative of the emperor Hadrian.

There was another fire in AD 155, which destroyed much of the timber-built town. The forum was repaired, two more temples were built, and the market hall was remodeled. New public baths were built outside the town walls. Later these walls were rebuilt as the city expanded, and two monumental arches were constructed to mark its original limits and record its status. At the same time there is evidence of Roman civil engineering—of sewers, drains, and works to supply clean water.

Excavations at Verulamium provided evidence of the slow conversion of local people to Roman town life. In addition to temples dedicated to Roman gods, buildings for worshipping native gods were found. Local building design and techniques of construction gradually became more Roman. However, there were no Roman-style town houses with dining rooms in Verulamium until the middle of the second century AD. It has been thought that this lag was because living in town was a seasonal occurrence for the local landed classes. The development of Roman-style villas on rural estates was also slow.

The first evidence of a conversion of local Britons to town life occurs ca. AD 155, after the second fire, when larger and more luxurious town houses were built on top of what had been small shops and workshops. It seems that by the middle of the second century AD not only had the wealthier people of Verulamium been converted to town life, but they had also developed a distinctly British style of town house, with an L-shaped courtyard plan of ten to thirty

The Roman town of Verulamium, in Britain, was excavated for the second time between 1955 and 1961 by Sheppard Frere. (Hulton-Deutsch Collection/Corbis)

rooms connected by a corridor. The discovery of mosaics and wall paintings at the site was more proof of the Romanization of the local population and the emigration of skilled artisans from Europe to undertake such fine work.

The economic crisis of the Roman Empire during the third century AD seemed to have minimal impact on Roman life in Verulamium. Large town houses continued being built between AD 215 and 240. As late as AD 220 a long porch was added to the basilica, the temple was surrounded by new colonnades, the theater was reconstructed and enlarged, the market hall was rebuilt, and a third monumental arch was erected. The population in the city increased (at its greatest it was estimated to be 15,000–20,000), and there were more artisans, more manufacturing and industry, and more migrants living within its boundaries. Two more monumental arches and several large shops were constructed in the city after AD 275.

In AD 273 a third gate was built in the city walls to facilitate access to the road to Silchester. Archaeological evidence revealed that it comprised a single carriageway and two foot passages, flanked by rectangular towers. Its date is proven by the coin hoard found in one of the towers. The building of this tower on the city walls, and another in AD 350, provides evidence for the viability and continuation of city life in Verulamium at least until the end of the fourth century AD. While the rest of the Roman Empire experienced great upheavals, Roman Britain continued as it had been—perhaps because it was so far away from the center of things.

All of this work at Verulamium proved that the Romano-British town was richer and larger than had been thought. In fact, it was probably as big as some of the larger towns in Gaul, such as Arles. And its public buildings were as good in their design as those in Gaul, and, in the case of the forum at Verulamium, and the theater at Canterbury, they were of an even larger scale than those in Paris.

See also Excavation of Maiden Castle (1934–1937); Excavation of Fishbourne Palace (1960–1970); Publication of *Britannia: a history of Roman Britain* (1967); Excavation of Vindolanda (1973–1994).

Further Reading

Niblett, R. 2001. *Verulamium: The Roman city of St. Albans.* Stroud, UK: Tempus.

Frere, S. S. 1983. *Verulamium excavations.* Vol 2. London: Society of Antiquaries of London.

Millet, M. 2001. Britain, Roman. In *Encyclopedia of archaeology: History and discoveries,* ed. T. Murray, 217–222. Santa Barbara, CA: ABC-CLIO.

Publication of **Prehistoric Technology** *(1957)*

As a result of the Russian Revolution of 1917 the practice of archaeology across the entirety of the Soviet state was centralized and its research outcomes determined by communist party ideology and political power brokering. In the 1930s archaeological artifacts were renamed "material culture," and archaeology became the Marxist history of material culture. Archaeologists were instructed to follow the examples of patriotic Soviet historians and base their work on empirical facts and historical materialism and fill in the gaps in the great Russian ethnogenesis. Archaeology was defined by one bureaucrat as "history armed with a spade."

In the 1950s, after Stalin's death, there was a shift in archaeological focus from Marxist history toward more mainstream interests in cultural change and pan-Slavic archaeology. Even in its isolation and with its focus limited by the state, the archaeology of the Soviet Union proved to have much to offer Western archaeology. From the start it concentrated on the material culture of everyday lives rather than on grand monuments and wealthy burials. So Soviet sites were mainly large-scale horizontal excavations of workshops, camps, and settlements—and in a few cases this resulted in the excavation of the first Paleolithic dwellings and Neolithic villages in the world. It also emphasized understanding the economic, social, and political nature of past societies and modes of production through their material culture, a much broader idea of the past, rather than one obsessed only by data and typologies. The state-enforced insistence on empiricism mean that scientific and technical developments in archaeology were "safe" and encouraged.

In the 1930s the archaeologist Sergei Semenov (1898–1978) pioneered the investigation of implement traces with a binocular microscope. He proposed a method of typology based on determining the function of an implement by its form. Semenov's microscopic work could determine the use of prehistoric stone and bone tools by identifying the processes that caused the use-wear patterns found on them. His approach followed the Soviet Union's Marxist interest in production methods and a historical view of the past.

In 1964 Semenov's book, *Prehistoric Technology* (published in the Soviet Union in 1957), was translated into English and had a great impact on Western archaeologists. His techniques became the basis of modern use-wear studies that unlocked much new information about the use of ancient technology.

See also Typology Makes History (1850–1900); De Mortillet Classifies the Stone Age (1869–1872); Archaeometry Defined (1958).

Further Reading

Klejn, L. 2001. Russia. In *Encyclopedia of archaeology: History and discoveries,* ed. T. Murray, 1127–1145. Santa Barbara, CA: ABC-CLIO.

Miller, M. O. 1956. *Archaeology in the USSR.* London and New York: Atlantic Press.

Semenov, S. A. 1964. *Prehistoric technology: An experimental study of the oldest tools and artefacts from traces of manufacture and wear,* trans. M. W. Thompson. London: Cory, Adams & Mackay.

Excavation of Shanidar Cave (1957–1961)

The huge cave of Shanidar is located on the Baradost Mountain, in the Zagros mountain range of Iraqi Kurdistan, 400 kilometers north of Baghdad, at 746 meters above sea level, close to the borders of modern Iran, Iraq, and Turkey. It was discovered by Ralph Solecki in 1951, who returned to excavate fourteen meters of deposit to the cave's bedrock in 1953, 1956–1957, and 1960. The material was analyzed in the museum in Baghdad in the 1960s and 1970s, reexamined again in the 1980s, and is still the subject of great debate.

The Shanidar Cave was an important base camp for hunters and gatherers, and later, a seasonal residence for herders before the Neolithic period. Goats were the main animal hunted during the Paleolithic period, while later there was a change in diet and more sedentary behavior, evidenced by the remains of domesticated sheep in the proto-Neolithic levels at the site. Modern Kurdish herders still used the cave at the time of Solecki's discovery. While the Neanderthal remains received the most attention during the 1950s, the Shanidar site was also significant for its evidence of technological evolution from the Mousterian period (60,000–40,000 years ago) to the late Paleolithic or Baradostian period (about 25,000 years ago), and through to the Mesolithic, proto-Neolithic, Neolithic, and modern periods.

The first Neanderthal fossils to be excavated at the site were those of a crushed, almost complete skeleton of a child of nine months, designated "Shanidar child" or Shanidar 7. Then three adult partial skeletons were excavated, Shanidar 1, 2, and 3; Shanidar 1 had the most complete postcranial skeleton and skull. More of Shanidar 3 was excavated, and then another partial skeleton (Shanidar 5), and then a multiple burial of three skeletons (Shanidar 4, 6, and 8), and finally, a child's skeleton (Shanidar 9). Of the nine individuals, four seemed to have been killed by a rock fall when the ceiling of the cave collapsed. Another four were buried separately in a kind of natural rock crypt, and the last, Shanidar 9, was found on the occupation floor. The skeleton of one mature male adult dating to ca. 46,000 BC had lost his right arm. Another male adult had been speared in his rib cage before being crushed by the rock fall. Another skeleton had been buried with local field flowers, evidenced from the high amount of pollen levels, and their type, in the surrounding soil.

In the 1950s this was the only site in southwestern Asia where Neanderthal remains had been found. These had been found in association with evidence of a Mousterian-type culture—a variety of stone flaked tools and cores. Shanidar also provided an excellent sample of Neanderthal remains because of the range of individuals of both sexes and various ages. But most of the attention was focused on the interpretation of the evidence provided about the Shanidar Neanderthal's burials and lifestyles. One of the male adults had suffered from a disabling disease for some time before his death. Solecki believed this was evidence that the man must have been cared for and helped by other members of the group in which he lived, otherwise he would not have survived for any length of time. Naturally, this raised the question of whether Neanderthals had a concept of social obligation similar to that of modern human beings. And did the flowers that had been placed with the skeleton of another Shanidar Neanderthal mean that Neanderthals grieved for and revered their dead? Were Neanderthals "human" in their behavior? In his popular book *Shanidar: The First Flower People* (1971), Ralph Solecki thought it possible. Debate continues.

See also Discovery of the Neanderthals (1833–1900); First *Homo Erectus* (1888–1895); Publication of *Les hommes fossiles, elémentes de paléontologie humaine* (1921); Discoveries at Zhoukoudian Cave (1921–Present); Understanding the Mousterian (1953–1965).

Further Reading

Corbey, R., and W. Roebroeks, eds. 2001. *Studying human origins: Disciplinary history and epistemology.* Amsterdam Archaeological Studies 6. Amsterdam: Amsterdam University Press.

Solecki, Ralph S. 1972. *Shanidar: The humanity of Neanderthal man.* London: Allen Lane.

Trinkaus, E. 1983. *The Shanidar Neandertals.* London: Academic.

Van Riper, A. 1993. *Men among the mammoths.* Chicago: University of Chicago Press.

Archaeometry Defined (1958)

In 1958, British archaeologist Christopher Hawkes coined the term "archaeometry" as the name of the journal of the Research Laboratory for Archaeology and the History of Art at Oxford University. Over the next few decades archaeometry would become a field of study in its own right.

The term archaeometry was coined to describe the use of "hard" or physical science to analyze and interpret archaeological data. This had often occurred in the nineteenth century, such as when geology was used to help prehistorians devise a chronology for Paleolithic artifacts, or to establish the veracity of archaeological evidence, as in the case of stone tools found in Brixham Cave and the Somme River gravels. Andrew Douglass's application of dendrochronological techniques to timber in archaeological sites in the 1920s was an early example of archaeometry in which astronomical dating techniques were adapted to archaeological ends.

In the 1920s and 1930s the techniques of pollen analysis of archaeological deposits, pioneered by geologists and botanists, were used at a number of archaeological sites across Europe to determine the botanical composition of ancient environments and changes in climate and land use.

The identification of the origins and routes of archaeological trade goods was not a new area in archaeology, but in the 1930s new techniques in microscopy and chemistry led to American archaeologist Anna Shepard analyzing minerals in pottery and identifying their sources. From these data she was able to map the trading of pottery across the southwest United States.

During the 1940s the scientific techniques used in geoarchaeology, zooarchaeology, and paleoethnobotany all made substantial contributions to archaeological knowledge, as excavation teams became more multidisciplinary in their focus, maximizing their data to interpret environmental exploitation and changes and to understand economic and cultural changes in prehistoric times.

In the 1950s techniques of nuclear research were applied to archaeology, resulting in the use of neutron activation analysis and spectrometry. These chemical analysis techniques were useful in determining the origins of pottery, and even different pottery factories within the same areas. The techniques were also successfully applied to other artifacts made of obsidian, marble, chert, volcanic rock, amber, and metals. Studies of the trade routes and economies of ancient societies were also greatly enhanced through the use of these techniques. The use of magnetometry to find archaeological sites was first used by Oxford University physicist Martin J. Aitken in the 1950s. This technique relied on measuring the strength of a local magnetic field and then detecting spatial anomalies within it. Resistivity, the technique of passing alternating current through the ground to determine the electrical resistence of different compositions of sediments, was also developed by Aitken, as a complementary technique to magnetometry.

These are just a few of many examples of the application of techniques from the physical, chemical, earth, and biological sciences to archaeology. Archaeological science, or archaeometry, is a major contributor to knowledge about the past, providing information about age, nature, and relationships that is crucial to archaeological interpretation and explanation.

See also Typology Makes History (1850–1900); Publication of *Die typologische Methode.* (1903); Publication of *The Population of the Valley of Teotihuacán* (1922); Publication of *Introduction to Southwestern Archaeology* (1924); Publication of *Air Survey and Archaeology* (1924); Establishing Dendrochronology (1929); Godwin and the Fenland Research Committee (1932–1948); Discovery of Radiocarbon Dating (1950); Publication of *Prehistoric Settlement Patterns in the Viru Valley, Peru* (1953); Publication of *Prehistoric Technology* (1957); Thermoluminescence in Archaeology (1960–Present); The application of GIS Technology to Archaeology (1980–Present).

Further Reading

Leute, U. 1987. *Archaeometry: An introduction to physical methods in archaeology and the history of art.* Weinheim, Federal Republic of Germany: VCH Verlagsgesellschaft mbH.

Ramenofsky, A. F., and A. Steffen, eds. 1998. *Unit issues in archaeology: Measuring time, space, and material.* Salt Lake City: University of Utah Press.

The journal *Archaeometry* (published by the Oxford University Research Laboratory for Archaeology and the History of Art) has reported work in this field since its foundation in 1958. Other major journals in the field include *Journal of Archaeological Science, Geoarchaeology,* and *Radiocarbon.*

Publication of Method and Theory in American Archaeology *(1958)*

The ideas in *Method and Theory in American Archaeology* were first outlined by Gordon Willey and Phillip Phillips in a paper in *American Anthropologist* in 1955. Willey had excavated throughout the Americas and had recently established the subfield of settlement pattern archaeology through its application to the Viru Valley project. He and Phillips turned their broad knowledge and synthetic abilities toward providing a classificatory scheme for the prehistory of the Americas. Both were anthropological archaeologists focused on doing archaeology to understand past human behavior and the cultural process. In some ways the book can be seen as an attempt to meet the challenge posed by W. W. Taylor in his controversial *A Study of Archaeology* (1948) with Willey and Phillips seeking to describe and explain patterns of cultural stasis and transformation on a broader, and over a longer, scale for the archaeology of the entire Americas.

Willey and Phillips described human behavior in the archaeological record via horizon and tradition. Horizon meant "the geographical distribution of cultural traits and assemblages" and tradition, "the temporal continuity in a particular group of traits or assemblages within a specific geographic locale" (from Preucel 1999, 6). Their classifications were based on the different technological and economic factors that characterized hunter-gatherers and agriculturalists, the most important distinction in prehistory, and within these classifications they designated two stages—Lithic and Archaic—for hunter-gatherers, and three stages—Formative, Classic, and Postclassic for agriculturalists. They were stages of increasing complexity. The Lithic phase denoted big-game hunting, and the Archaic, a phase of intensive collecting. The Formative phase represented developing village agriculture, Classic represented the rise of early civilizations, and Postclassic represented pre-Hispanic civilizations.

For Willey and Phillips, while the classification was sequential it was not deterministic; it remained firmly grounded in anthropologist Julian Steward's concept of multilineal evolution. While some cultures passed through several of these stages, not all of them did or had to. Stages were the result of many different factors, such as environment, ecology, economics, or demography. There was not one evolutionary map for all. Like the European Three-Age System, Willey and Phillips's classificatory scheme described rather than explained the reasons for changes and the methods of change in cultures. Explanation still relied on concepts of diffusion and migration, just like any other of the culture historical classification schemes that had developed since the nineteenth century.

Method and Theory in American Archaeology soon came under attack from the new or processual archaeologists of the 1960s, who defined their own methods and aims as contrary to the culture historical approach of Willey and Phillips. New archaeologists (such as Lewis Binford) were interested in the development of a new science of the archaeological record that would contribute to an understanding of global issues and global cultural change.

See also Stratigraphic Excavation in the Americas (1911–1913); Publication of *The Population of the Valley of Teotihuacán* (1922); Publication of *Introduction to Southwestern Archaeology* (1924); Publication of *A Study of Archaeology* (1948); Publication of *Prehistoric Settlement Patterns in the Viru Valley, Peru* (1953).

Further Reading

Preucel, R. 1999. Gordon Randolph Willey (1913–). In *Encyclopedia of archaeology: The great archaeologists,* ed. T. Murray, 701–712. Santa Barbara, CA: ABC-CLIO.

Vogt, E. Z., and R. M. Leventhal, eds. 1983. *Prehistoric settlement patterns: Essays in honor of Gordon R. Willey.* Albuquerque: University of New Mexico Press.

Willey, G. R., and P. Phillips. 1958. *Method and Theory in American Archaeology.* Chicago: University of Chicago Press.

Willey, G. R., and J. A. Sabloff. 1993. *A history of American Archaeology.* 3rd ed. London: Thames and Hudson.

Excavation of Igbo-Ukwu (1959)

The English archaeologist Charles Thurstan Shaw (1914–) played a significant role in the discovery of the African Iron Age. His career exemplifies the change from colonial rule to political independence in Black Africa, the establishment of archaeology departments at African universities and the education of local African archaeologists, and the need to know more about African society and culture before contact with Arabs and Europeans. His search for an understanding of the development of precolonial West Africa not only contributed to the emergence of an archaeology for the whole African continent, but also it helped Africa to rediscover itself.

A Cambridge graduate, Shaw began to teach archaeology at Achimota College in West Africa (now Ghana) in 1937, where he was also in charge of the Anthropology Museum. During the 1950s he returned to Ghana where he was involved with founding both the Ghana National Museum and the archaeology department at the University of Ghana. In 1959 Shaw was invited by the Nigerian government's antiquities department to excavate the site of Igbo-Ukwu in southeastern Nigeria.

Dating between the eight and eleventh centuries AD the Igbo-Ukwu site was the rich and elaborate burial complex of a person of great importance. It comprised two chambers, the lower one lined and roofed with wood and containing an ornately dressed male corpse sitting on a stool, surrounded by personal artifacts and three large elephant tusks. The upper chamber contained the remains of five other people, possibly attendants. Two large pits of artifacts were located nearby, one in which objects were laid out ceremonially as they would have been in a relic house, the other into which they were haphazardly placed. Bronze artifacts were found in all areas of the site—elaborate and delicately decorated vases, bowls in the shape of shells, body ornaments and ceremonial regalia, and the handles of personal artifacts. The iconography of these bronze items was the same as that used on locally made pottery found at the site—but the technological sophistication of the bronze work was unique and without any known local antecedents.

Shaw's work at Igbo-Ukwu proved that around the end of the first millennium AD, a complex society where great wealth and religious and political power was held by an elite had thrived in this southern corner of the Nigerian forest. The bronze vessels were manufactured locally by skilled craftspeople. The large number of glass beads found in the burial site indicated that this society engaged in long-distance trade with North Africa, despite its isolation from the Sudanic kingdoms and the Arab traders of the Sahara. It also proved that the wealth and craftsmanship of the later west African kingdoms of Ife and Benin had local stylistic and technological antecedents, and that Ibgo-Ukwu must have been developing its power and influence, as well as its technology, in this area for some time before the end of the first millennium AD.

See also First Meeting of the Pan-African Congress on Prehistory and Quaternary Studies (1947); Southeastern and Southern Africa during the Iron Age: The Chifumbzae Complex (1960–1980); Excavation of Jenne-Jeno (1974–1998).

Further Reading

Connah, G. 1999. Charles Thurstan Shaw (1914–). In *Encyclopedia of archaeology: The great archaeologists,* ed. T. Murray, 727–742. Santa Barbara, CA: ABC-CLIO.

Connah, G. 2004. *Forgotten Africa: An introduction to its archaeology.* London; New York: Routledge,

Phillipson, D. W. 1985. *African archaeology.* Cambridge: Cambridge University Press.

Robertshaw, P., ed. 1990. *A history of African archaeology.* London: Currey.

Discovery of **Zinjanthropus boisei** *(1959)*

Louis Leakey (1903–1972) was born in Kenya to missionary parents and grew up among the tribal Kikuyu. He studied archaeology and anthropology at the University of Cambridge. In 1926 he returned to East Africa and began to investigate the prehistory of the Rift Valley. In 1936 he married the artist and archaeological draftsperson Mary Douglas Nichol (1913–1996). They worked together in East Africa for more than thirty years.

Between 1936 and 1962 many examples of *Australopithecines* (small-brained, bipedal hominid fossils) were found in South Africa at the sites of Sterkfontein, Kromdraai, Makapansgat, and Swartkrans. These finds not only firmly established the study of the earliest archaeological records for the evolution of mankind, but also raised the strong probability that Africa was the "cradle of humanity," and not Europe or central Asia. Louis and Mary Leakey believed humankind had originated in Africa, and they began to look for more evidence to support this.

During the 1940s the Leakeys pioneered Paleolithic "living floor" archaeology at Olorgesailie, investigating fossil pollens and paleoenvironmental data in an attempt to more fully interpret stone tools found at the same levels. They also began looking for the makers of the Oldawan stone tools they had found in the ancient deposits of the Olduvai Gorge, an ancient lake basin in northern Tanzania in the East African Rift Valley. In 1959 the remains of *Zinjanthropus boisei* discovered by the Leakeys were described as not another ancestral form of the southern African *Australopithecines,* but *the* ancestor of modern humans.

Within five years *Zinjanthropus boisei* had been displaced as *the* fossil ancestor of modern humans, by Louis Leakey's new "directly connected" fossil human find *Homo habilis.* As the number of human fossil finds increased over the next few decades, so did the debates about the phylogenetic relationships among *Australopithecus* species and the evolutionary relationships between *Homo* and *Australopithecus. Zinjanthropus boisei* is now known as *Australopithecus boisei,* one of at least five other species of *Australopithecus.*

While Leakey's simplistic views on human evolution have now been generally rejected, his finds were significant contributions to the knowledge of fossil human evolution. The discovery of the remains of *Zinjanthropus boisei,* and the resulting publicity generated through media coverage, in combination with other fossil hominid finds in East Africa in the 1960s, shifted the search for human origins to Africa.

See also Discovery of *Australopithecus africanus* (1924); First Meeting of the Pan-African Congress on Prehistory and Quaternary Studies (1947); Excavations at Sterkfontein and Swartkrans (1948–Present); Excavations at Olorgesailie and Koobi Fora (1961–1983); Discovery of *Homo Habilis* (1964–1980); Discovery of Early Humans in Ethiopia (1966–1977); Discovery of Footprints of Our Earliest Human Ancestors (1974–1981); Announcement of Toumai Fossil (2002); Earliest Stone Tools Found at Gona (2003); Discovery of the "Hobbit" (2004).

Further Reading

Isaac, G. and E. R. McCown, eds. 1976. *Human origins: Louis Leakey and the East African evidence.* Menlo Park, CA: Benjamin.

Leakey, M. D. 1984. *Disclosing the past.* New York: Doubleday.

Morell, V. 1995. *Ancestral passions: The Leakey family and the quest for humankind's beginnings.* New York: Simon & Schuster.

Saving Abu Simbel (1959–1980)

The Nile River has long been the life force of Egypt, and the use and regulation of its water has been the most important factor in the survival and prosperity of its people. The first major damming of the Nile River, in the form of a huge 30-meter-high, 2-kilometer-long granite barrage, began in 1898, under the supervision of English engineers. Completed in 1902, the barrage was one of the largest dams in the world. The continuing need for more water to support both agricultural and population growth in Egypt caused the level of the barrage to be raised by 5 meters between 1902 and 1912, and then by 41.5 meters between 1924 and 1934. These additional engineering works provided the justification for the First and Second Archaeological Surveys of Nubia.

Nubia is the modern name for a region the ancient Egyptians called Kush, and the Greeks and Romans called Aethiopia. It comprises the most southern part of modern Egypt and the most northern part of the modern republic of Sudan. Nubia was politically part of Egypt, but its history, culture, ethnic, and linguistic profiles were far from wholly Egyptian. However, because of its location on the Nile River, on the major trade route between Africa and the Mediterranean, it was always affected by the history and politics of Egypt. The Nile Valley was the oldest, safest, and richest trade route in the ancient world. From Africa and via Nubia, Egypt received its gold, ivory, ebony, and other important raw materials as well as slaves. In return, Nubia imported wine and beer, copper tools, and weapons from Egypt.

The First Archaeological Survey of Nubia (1907–1911) was originally directed by the great American archaeologist George Reisner (1867–1942) and subsequently by C. M. Firth. The Second Archaeological Survey of Nubia (1929–1934) was undertaken in response to an increase in the size of the dam. More water was needed to support the estimated increase in Egypt's population to 16 million in 1934 (it was 6 million in the 1880s). The resulting increase in the size of the reservoir meant yet more sites, as far as the Sudanese border, would be inundated. The directors of the second survey were English archaeologists Walter. B. Emery and Leslie P. Kirwan. Although the excavation of tombs still predominated—there were some 2,000 tombs at seventy-six sites—two forts and some settlement and town sites were also excavated. The richest finds included the royal tombs at Ballana and Qustul near the Sudanese border, comprising the burial tumuli of the local Nubian rulers of the fifth century AD. These contained royal regalia, weapons, jewelry, and horses buried with silver harnesses.

Other salvage operations included the German expedition to the Pharaonic center of Aniba; a survey, by French historian Ugo Monneret de Villard, of the literary and archaeological documentation of Christian Nubia; and an exploration of the oldest remains of lower Nubia and Egypt from the Paleolithic period by American archaeologists, Sandford and Arkell, from Chicago's Oriental Institute of Archaeology. Consequently, Egyptian Nubia was well explored and recorded before it was submerged, but the surveys and excavations did not include sites and monuments located on the higher levels of the valley that would be immune from the flooding of this second reservoir.

In 1954 the Egyptian and Sudanese governments recognized that their national survival and development in the postwar modern world was at risk because of their heritage. The remaining historic and archaeological sites, stelae, and architectural monuments of Nubia, which had survived previous damming because of their locations on higher terrain, would be submerged by the waters of a higher and larger dam at Aswan, with a reservoir 500 kilometers long.

By the end of the 1950s Egypt's population was estimated to reach 27 million, almost double what it had been in 1934, and by the 1980s it would likely reach 40 million. Another larger dam for the Nile River was seen as a major priority if Egypt was to support this population increase and to provide additional hydroelectrical power necessary for industrial development. The new dam was to increase cultivated land by 4 million square meters. It could convert 7 million square meters of land in Upper Egypt to perennial irrigation, would ensure water during drought years and prevent flood during wet years, and would produce 10,000 million kilowatts of electricity.

In 1959 the Egyptian and Sudanese governments both realized that any attempt to save the monuments from submersion would be impossible without substantial international aid. They requested the assistance of UNESCO (the United Nations Education and Scientific Organization), which was responsible for conserving and protecting examples of world heritage. This was the first request of this nature the organization had received, and its response was also the first of its kind, but this was exactly what it had been created to do, even if the task was literally monumental. On 8 March 1960, UNESCO launched an appeal to governments, institutions, public and private foundations, and individuals for technical and financial contributions to save the Nubian monuments and sites from destruction.

The Third Archaeological Survey of Nubia was the twenty-year-long International Campaign to Save the Monuments of Nubia: twenty years of fundraising; cooperation between United Nations member states, Egypt, and Nubia; and painstaking and heavy work by many different experts and ordinary people. Forty archaeological expeditions were sent to Nubia from America, Asia, Europe, and Africa. The Nubian stelae and monuments were excavated and documented, dismantled, or carved up and moved to another site and reassembled in six groups, the first five in Egypt and the sixth in Sudan. The architectural monuments included the Greco-Roman temples of Philae Island near the earlier Aswan dam, which was the most famous complex and the first to be relocated. Philae's temples were sacred to the goddess Isis and were one of the most important shrines in Roman times. They had been submerged for most of the time since the second dam was built, and were only completely visible when the dam waters receded. Their relocation would overcome this problem.

The second group of relocations was made up of the temple of Beit el Wali, originally located 50 kilometers south of Aswan, and carved into the rock of the Nile Valley by Ramses II in the thirteenth century BC. Close by was the temple of Kalabsha, built by the Roman emperor Augustus and dedicated to the local god Manulis. The Kiosk of Qertassi, built during the same period as the Philae temples, was located 45 kilometers south of Aswan near the High Dam, and the rock temple of Ramses II at Gerf Hussein was originally located 87 kilometers south from Aswan.

The third group was made up of the temples of Dakka and Maharraqa, both from the Ptolemaic period, which were located 106 kilometers and 125 kilometers south of Aswan, and the temple at Wadi es Sebua, 160 kilometers south of Aswan, which was another temple erected by Ramses II.

The fourth group comprised the temple of Amada, located at Korosko, 205 kilometers south of Aswan, which was the oldest of the Nubian monuments to be moved. It was built during the reigns of Tutmosis II and Amenophis II in the fifteenth century BC. On the opposite bank of the Nile,

Ramses II had carved the rock temple of Derr. Pennut's Tomb was also located near the former site of Amada.

Finally, 280 kilometers south of Aswan, the most famous and imposing rock temples of Ramses II at Abu Simbel were located. These were reconstructed 60 kilometers above their original site. On the opposite bank of the Nile, at Abu Oda, the small rock-cut temple of King Horemheb was constructed at the end of the fourteenth century BC, and a fortified town from the later period built on the rock of Gebel Adda. The temples of Aksha, Buhen, Semna East, and Semna West were relocated in the garden of the Museum of Antiquities in Khartoum, the capital of Sudan.

In addition, as tokens of its appreciation, and in return for the help they received, the Egyptian government donated four temples: the temple of Debod, originally located 15 kilometers south of Aswan and built during the Greco-Roman period, was moved to Spain; the temple at Taffa, built during the Greco-Roman period, was donated to the Netherlands; Dendur, built 70 kilometers south of Aswan by the Roman emperor Augustus, went to the United States; and from Ellesiya, 228 kilometers south of Aswan, Tuthmosis III's rock-cut chapel was relocated in Italy.

The international campaign also inspired renewed worldwide interest in Egyptian and Nubian civilizations. The Sudanese government built a new Museum of Antiquities in Khartoum for its monuments, documents, and excavated material. The Egyptian government built a Nubia Museum in Aswan and a new National Museum of Egyptian Civilization in Cairo. Appeals to fund both of these institutions were launched in the 1980s, after the salvage campaign was completed.

This was the first example of using the power of international cooperation for cultural ends, and it is testimony to its success that it was not the last. The Indonesian Buddhist site of Borobudur, the city of Venice, the Acropolis of Athens, and the site of Mohenjo Daro in Pakistan have all received funding for conservation and protection through UNESCO's international appeals.

See also World's First Archaeological Salvage Project? (1907–1932); Paleopathology in Nubia (1909–1911).

Further Reading

Keating, R. 1975. *Nubian rescue.* London: R. Hale.

Säve-Söderbergh, T., ed. 1987. *Temples and tombs of ancient Nubia: the international rescue campaign at Abu Simbel, Philae and other sites.* London: Thames and Hudson; and Paris: UNESCO.

Historical Archaeology First Taught at University (1960)

American archaeologist John L. Cotter (1911–1999) directed the excavation of Jamestown, Virginia, between 1953 and 1956 where the first permanent English settlement in America was established in 1607.

After working at Jamestown, Cotter returned to Philadelphia and in 1959 completed his doctorate in anthropology at the University of Pennsylvania. He joined that university's staff in 1960, and until 1979 was adjunct associate professor of American civilization. In 1961 Cotter taught the first course in American historical archaeology ever offered at an American university, and at any university anywhere in the world. He continued to do so for almost twenty years. In 1967 he was among the founders of the Society for Historical Archaeology, becoming its first president and editor of its journal *Historical Archaeology.*

See also Historical Archaeology at Colonial Williamsburg (1928–Present); Excavation of Jamestown (1934–1957); Excavation of Saint-Marie Among the Hurons (1941–1951); Publication of *In Small Things Forgotten* (1977); Discovery of the African Burial Ground (1991); Excavation of New York City's "Five Points" (1991).

Further Reading

Cotter, J. L. 1959. *Archeological excavations at Jamestown Colonial National Historical Park and Jamestown National Historic Site.* Washington, DC: National Park Service, U.S. Dept. of the Interior.

Schuyler, R. L. 2001. Historical archaeology. In *Encyclopedia of archaeology: History and discoveries,* ed. T. Murray, 623–630. Santa Barbara, CA: ABC-CLIO.

Excavation of a Bronze Age Ship at Cape Gelidonya (1960)

The Bronze Age shipwreck at Cape Gelidonya off modern Turkey, which was first located in 1954 by a sponge diver, was relocated by Peter Throckmorton, who gained the agreement of the University Museum of the University of Pennsylvania to undertake an excavation.

The Cape Gelidonya wreck proved to be a major milestone in maritime archaeology. It was the first excavation to be entirely undertaken on the seabed under the supervision of a diving archaeologist. Perhaps as significant, it was also the first maritime excavation conducted to the standards of a terrestrial dig.

This more intensive excavation strategy paid off handsomely in that the wreck held significant information. First, radiocarbon dating indicated a provenance of 1200 BC (± 50 years). The cargo was mostly scrap bronze that was to be recycled and ingots of tin and copper that would go into the process. Much of the material was of Cypriot origin. For archaeologist George Bass, a close inspection of the cargo and what he has interpreted as being the personal possessions of the crew clearly indicated that the vessel came from the eastern Mediterranean (probably from Canaan) rather than from Mycenae, which was the common assumption for vessels of the Bronze Age.

See also Trials of the *Royal Savage* (1934–Present); Raising the *Vasa* (1961); Raising the *Mary Rose* (1967–1982); Excavation of the *Batavia* (1972–1976); Finding the *Titanic* (1985–Present).

Further Reading

Bass, G. F. 1970. *Archaeology under water.* Harmondworth, UK, and Baltimore, MD: Penguin.

Bass, G. F. 1972. *A history of seafaring based on underwater archaeology.* London and New York: Thames and Hudson and Walker.

Bass, G. F. 2001. Nautical archaeology. In *Encyclopedia of archaeology: History and discoveries,* ed. T. Murray, 910–918. Santa Barbara, CA: ABC-CLIO.

Throckmorton, P. 1964. *The lost ships: An adventure in underwater archaeology.* Boston: Little, Brown.

Deciphering the Dynastic Sequence at Piedras Negras (1960)

In 1960 Tatiana Proskouriakoff published "Historical implications of a pattern of dates at Piedras Negras, Guatemala" in the journal *American Antiquity,* in which she deciphered the dynastic sequence of the Maya site of Piedras Negras. This article is regarded by Maya epigraphers as perhaps the most important in all of Maya studies. In it Proskouriakoff showed that the carved stone monuments were grouped into "sets," each of which addressed the reign of an individual king. She identified birth and coronation glyphs, as well as years of successive kings and their birth and accession dates, and showed that the same pattern seemed to occur at other classic Maya sites. She also noted that many of the dates recorded seemed not to be associated with astronomical phenomena or events—which had previously been assumed. Proskouriakoff successfully tested this approach at the neighboring site of Yaxchilan.

Thus, an important step was taken in transforming our understanding of Maya writing from something sacred and esoteric to the veritable stuff of history.

See also Investigation of Palenque Begins (1787); Rediscovering Maya Civilization (1839–1943); Discovery of Olmec Civilization (1926–1942); Publication of *A Forest of Kings* (1990).

Further Reading

Coe, M. 1999. *Breaking the Maya code: The last great decipherment of an ancient script.* Rev. ed. London: Thames and Hudson.

Proskouriakoff, T. 1960. Historical implications of a pattern of dates at Piedras Negras, Guatemala. *American Antiquity* 25(4): 454–475.

Solomon, C. 2003. *Tatiana Proskouriakoff, interpreting the Ancient Maya.* Norman: University of Oklahoma Press.

Excavation of Fishbourne Palace (1960–1970)

The site of Fishbourne Palace, near Chichester in southern England, was excavated by the Sussex Archaeological Society with archaeologist Barry Cunliffe. The only example of a classical Roman luxury villa built in Britain, it is believed to have been the home of the client British king Cogidubnus, who ruled Sussex until ca. AD 69.

Originally an Iron Age Oppidum (or fort), the site of Fishbourne began its association with Rome when it became a military base and depot with granaries as part of the Roman invasion of Britain. This early settlement was later replaced by a larger residential structure, and then in AD 75 with the more substantial 4-hectare building identified as a "palace."

The few rural Romano-British villas that have been identified and excavated were usually remodeled and rebuilt Iron Age farmhouses, and none of them are as early and extensive, or as opulent, as that found at Fishbourne. Most of these villas were built toward the end of the fourth century AD, at the peak of Britain's Romanization, and were associated with existing rural settlements. While they were decorated in Roman style with mosaics and wall paintings, included bathhouses and under-floor heating, and were high-status Roman-style residences built for the native elite, they were still part of working farm estates. Fishbourne, on the other hand, was not connected with estate management, and it is the only example of a classical luxury villa, belonging to an exceptionally wealthy owner, who not only imported marbles, sculptures, and other art objects from Rome, but who also imported a skilled workforce of artisans to build and decorate his impressive nonprovincial residence.

The site was rediscovered in 1960 due to the construction of a water main at the village of Fishbourne on the main road north of the city of Chichester. First finds comprised a large stone building and its mosaic floors, which proved to be of surprising early provenance (ca. AD 75–80). Further trenching unearthed a building that was over 300 feet long and seven more mosaics, including one of a boy riding a dolphin. Eventually, the site was the subject of nine field seasons and ten years of work, and it continued to surprise everyone with its size and opulence.

In 1963 the north wings and west wings of the building were uncovered. By 1965 the remains of a large audience chamber in the west wing and a great impressive entrance hall opposite in the east wing were found, as well as a huge central courtyard and garden (250 by 320 feet). The garden was surrounded by colonnaded walks and had an extensive drainage system, and a formal design of paths and beds that would have displayed water features and statuary. In 1966 the bath suite was found, and in 1967 an extensive south wing or "owner's wing," 300 feet long and 70 feet wide, was found to enclose the courtyard on the southern side. Beyond this was another garden that extended 350 feet to where the original harbor would have been, but which is now silted up.

Most of the 900 archaeological workers at the site were volunteers. Funds were raised by the Chichester Civic Society, and a large part of the site was eventually purchased and presented to the Sussex Archaeological Trust, which then prepared the site for public presentation. Conservation, restoration, and protection of the site were ensured with the building of a modern roofed structure. A museum to display and store the finds was also built, and the Roman garden was laid out. Fishbourne Palace now receives more than 250,000 visitors a year.

As to whether it belonged to Cogidubnus, "Legate of the Emperor in Britain," it seems likely, but the jury is still out.

See also Excavation of Maiden Castle (1934–1937); Excavation of Verulamium (1955–1961); Publication of *Britannia: A History of Roman Britain* (1967); Excavation of Vindolanda (1973–1994).

Further Reading

Cunliffe, B. W. 1971. *Excavations at Fishbourne,1961–1969.* London: Society of Antiquaries.

Cunliffe, B. W. 1998. *Fishbourne Roman palace.* Rev. and updated ed. Stroud, UK: Tempus.

Millett, M. 2001. Britain, Roman. In *Encyclopedia of archaeology: History and discoveries,* ed. T. Murray, 217–223. Santa Barbara, CA: ABC-CLIO.

Southeastern and Southern Africa during the Iron Age: The Chifumbaze Complex (1960–1980)

During the 1960s and 1970s, while the protohistory of West Africa was being elucidated, archaeologists began to excavate at Iron Age sites across central, eastern, and southern Africa to fill in the great gaps of knowledge about the history of the other side of the continent. Iron smelting had occurred in North Africa in the eighth century BC, and in Egypt earlier than this. There was evidence of iron working and Iron Age pottery in West Africa ca. seventh century BC and in East Africa ca. 1000 BC. However, in southeastern Africa, iron working was not evident until AD 400, prompting questions: How this knowledge spread? Why did it take so long to get to the far south of the continent?

Early Iron Age archaeological evidence, comprising distinctive iron tools and pottery styles, was remarkably homogeneous over some 9 million square kilometers of southeastern and eastern Africa. It became known as the Chifumbaze complex, after the site in Mozambique where it had been first excavated.

Not only were Chifumbaze complex sites and their artifacts different from earlier sites because of their use of iron, many of them also constituted the first evidence of settled village life, herding domestic animals, and cultivating crops and, south of Tanzania, of the manufacture of pottery. The fact that so many simultaneous cultural changes had occurred together was interpreted as being evidence of the migration of large numbers of people who had brought these changes with them. Sites supporting this interpretation were found all over eastern and southern Africa, and pollen evidence from Lake Victoria revealed that there was a reduction in forest vegetation around 500 BC, either as the result of climate change or felling trees for the necessary charcoal manufacture used in iron smelting. There was no evidence that the tree felling was due to clearance for agriculture. The earliest site belonging to the Chifumbaze complex was found on the west side of Lake Victoria, and dated 2,500 years ago (ca. 500 BC), and one of its latest sites was located in Natal in southern Africa and dated to the third century AD, or 1,700 years ago. Thus, the dates were later in the south than the north, implying that the people who used the Chifumbaze complex had originated in northwestern and central Africa and had moved down through eastern Africa and into southern Africa.

Chifumbaze people used iron axes, hoes, arrow points, and spearheads. The presence of hoes and grindstones were interpreted as being evidence of agriculture, and the few plant remains found indicate that they planted and harvested millet, sorghum, cowpeas, squash, and beans. These plants had originated north of the equator. The remains of domesticated sheep or goats and cattle are also found in Chifumbaze complex sites; and cattle became more numerous in southeastern Africa between 1,300 and 1,200 years ago (seventh to eighth centuries AD). Chifumbaze people hunted using iron-tipped weapons, and wildebeest, buffalo, and antelope remains are found in their sites. There is evidence that these wild species decreased in dietary importance as domestic species increased. By 1,000 years ago (ca. tenth century AD) the Chifumbaze communities in the central and western savannas, and those in the southeast, could be differentiated on the basis of their wealth. For the former, wealth was based on metal, for the latter it derived from cattle ownership. These distinctions became more prominent over the next few centuries.

The similarity of the Chifumbaze complex to archaeological evidence found in Chad, western Zaire/Congo, northern Angola, and Cameroon around 2,300 years ago (second or third centuries BC), led to the theory that the Chifumbaze complex people originated from this part of Africa. Other excavations provide evidence of the migration of iron-using farmers, ca. 1,800 years ago (second century AD), some 3,000 kilometers throughout Mozambique, Malawi, eastern Zambia, and Zimbabwe, and south into the Transvaal, Swaziland, and Natal.

However, this did not mean that the local stone tool-making hunter-gatherers had been completely displaced by the migrating Chifumbaze complex people. There is evidence that they adapted to this migration by moving on and/or by trading with them. The African Rift Valley missed out on the migration completely, either because of its aridity or because of a more effective resistance by hostile hunter-gatherer populations. Nonetheless, evidence suggests that the denser the occupation of the Chifumbaze complex people, the greater the dislocation and displacement of local hunter-gatherer populations. The herding of domestic animals meant competition for local pasture resources, and by 500 years ago (ca. AD 1500) many of the hunter-gatherers were either absorbed into the growing population of the Chifumbaze complex or forced to keep moving on.

Notwithstanding problems arising from integrating archaeological and linguistic evidence, some archaeologists have used it to theorize and elucidate the history of the movement of the Iron Age Chifumbaze people. The geographical distribution of both is the same; Bantu languages are spoken by 200 million people, with a degree of intercomprehension, from the Cameroon and eastern Nigeria to Namibia in the south. Linguists believe the ancestral Bantu language was spoken by people some 3,000–4,000 years ago in what is now Cameroon and eastern Nigeria, and then these people dispersed in two waves into eastern and southern Africa, supported by the contemporary existence of two major Bantu language groups. The first or western Bantu language group is spoken from the eastern edge of the equatorial forest, through Gabon and into central Zaire, and finally through the southern savanna—where there was interaction between western and eastern Bantu-speaking groups.

However, the Chifumbaze complex correlates with the geographical coverage of the eastern Bantu group. Its sites are found in areas in which modern eastern Bantu dialects are spoken, from the area north of Lake Tanganyika, down through Malawi, southwestern Kenya, northwest Tanzania, Rwanda, eastern Zambia, eastern Congo, and south Uganda, and into Zimbabwe and Mozambique. Their expansion was limited by the northern edge of the southwest African zone of desert vegetation and the long grass plains of what became the Orange Free State, by the Drakensberg plateau, and in the south by the winter rainfall zone. The latter prevented agriculture and cereal production. The pastoralists of Bantu society around 500 years ago (ca. AD 1500) eventually expanded past these environmental barriers into parts of southern Africa and Namibia.

What caused the dispersal of the Bantu speaking/Chifumbaze complex people is still not understood, but it was probably due to population pressures in the original Bantu homeland in Cameroon and eastern Nigeria. Helped by their iron-making skills and by their practice of herding and agriculture, the Chifumbaze complex people spread across a sparsely inhabited landscape—at a pace estimated to be some 350 kilometers every twenty years.

See also Publication of *The Zimbabwe Culture* (1931); Excavation of Igbo-Ukwu (1959); Excavation of Jenne-Jeno (1974–1998).

Further Reading

Chami. F., G. Pwiti, and C. Radimilahy, eds. 2001. *People, contact, and the environment in the African past.* Dar es Salaam, Tanzania: DUP Ltd.

Connah, G. 2001. *African civilizations: an archaeological perspective.* 2nd ed. Cambridge: Cambridge University Press.
Fagan, B. M. 1965. *Southern Africa during the Iron Age.* London: Thames and Hudson.
van der Merwe, N., and T. N. Huffman, eds. 1979. *Iron Age studies in Southern Africa.* Claremont, South Africa: South African Archaeological Society.
Phillipson, D.1985. *African archaeology.* Cambridge: Cambridge University Press.

Thermoluminescence in Archaeology (1960–Present)

Like radiocarbon and potassium argon dating in the 1960s, thermoluminescence dating has revolutionized our understanding of prehistory, because it provides reliable and universally applicable techniques for dating artifacts made of mineral grains such as quartz and feldspar, which have been exposed to heating. Common artifacts that can be dated this way include flint stone tools, pottery, burned stones, and earth ovens.

Thermoluminescence (TL) is a property of insulating (generally crystalline material) that has been exposed to ionizing radiation (alpha and beta particles and gamma rays from naturally occurring uranium and thorium, and radioactive potassium in the environment, as well as cosmic rays). Long-term exposure to ionizing radiation is built up or trapped over time in the lattice of crystals. When heated above 500 degrees centigrade this store of energy is released in the form of emitted light called TL, and the TL clock is reset back to zero. In the case of ceramics, the measurement of TL emitted can indicate the time elapsed since the last firing.

TL was first observed in 1663 by the English chemist Sir Robert Boyle, who reported on the remarkable glowing properties of a large diamond to the Royal Society. In 1905 this phenomenon was recognized as being the result of radiation. After World War II, TL was used to monitor the radiation exposures of people who had been in contact with radioactive materials. In 1952, an American scientist, Farrington Daniels, a TL researcher at the University of Wisconsin, recommended the use of TL to date fired pottery. The firing of clay into pottery releases all previously accumulated TL, and TL builds up from zero. George Kennedy, from the University of California at Los Angeles, was the first to use it for dating pottery in 1959.

During the 1960s, major developments and refinements were achieved after dedicated laboratories were established, such as that at Oxford University by English scientist Michael Aitken. It was only in the 1970s that TL was applied routinely in archaeology with levels of precision of plus or minus 10 percent. The benchmark book on the process, *Thermoluminescence Techniques in Archaeology* by S. Fleming, was published in 1979.

During the 1980s, the major advance of using optical dating (OD) developed out of the use of TL. Rather than dating minerals that have been exposed to heat, OD measures exposure to light, that is, the stored energy released by an exposure to a beam of light, for instance, of blue/green light or infrared radiation. Optically stimulated luminescence (OSL) includes both types of stimulation as well as the use of other wavelengths and so is an umbrella term.

Since the 1980s TL, OD, and OSL have been used to date other materials, such as geological sediments, some of which were last exposed to sunlight a million years ago. The use of this technique for paleoclimatology and its impact on future long-term climate modeling have been significant.

See also Discovery of Radiocarbon Dating (1950); Archaeometry Defined (1958).

Further Reading

Aitken, M. J. 1985. *Thermoluminescence dating.* London: Academic Press.

Aitken, M. J. 1998. *An introduction to optical dating: The dating of quaternary sediments by the use of photon-stimulated luminescence.* Oxford: Oxford University Press.

Fleming, S. J. 1979. *Thermoluminescence techniques in archaeology.* Oxford: Clarendon Press.

Jorge R. Acosta Finishes Work at Tula (1961)

In 1961 Mexican archaeologist Jorge R. Acosta (1904–1975) finished his twentieth field season investigating the site of Tula, capital of the Toltec empire during the tenth and eleventh centuries AD. Acosta's work at Tula provided archaeologists with evidence that Toltec cultural, architectural, and artistic ideas directly influenced many successive Mesoamerican civilizations, especially the Aztecs.

In the 1940s there were many debates among Mesoamerican archaeologists about two poorly understood pre-Columbian cultures, the Olmec and the Toltec. The Toltecs were mentioned in many pre-Hispanic chronicles as the ancestors of the Aztecs and other peoples. The Aztecs considered the Toltec period to have been the "golden age" of Mesoamerican history. The name Toltec means "people of the place of reeds," and the Toltec capital city, Tollan, or "the place of reeds," figures in the origin myths of many Mesoamerican peoples from the Maya to the Aztecs. Because of the widespread origin

Close-up view of the Toltec stone figures at Tula, dating from ca. AD 900. (Corel)

myths involving Tollan, there were many places in Mexico that used or incorporated the name, which was corrupted by the Spanish to Tula.

Tollan was supposedly located somewhere in the central highlands of Mexico. Tollan was the Mesoamerican ideal of civilized life, and the Toltecs were lauded as master craftsmen and artists. Later peoples went to great lengths to claim Toltec heritage. For example, the ruling families of the cities in the Valley of Mexico all claimed descent from Toltec royal lines, and those groups that did not have Toltec blood sought to marry into lineages that did. Possessing a royal Toltec ancestry was a significant prerequisite of legitimacy. The Aztecs were one such group, claiming Toltec ancestry and then reinforcing their Toltec heritage by looting the site of Tollan and incorporating its sculpture and other relics into the buildings and ritual offerings at their own imperial capital.

As early as 1885, French archaeologist Désiré Charnay, among others, proposed that the site of Tula in the state of Hidalgo was the legendary Tollan. However, many twentieth-century scholars believed that it was Teotihuacán. During the 1930s the distinguished Mexican ethnohistorian Jimenez Moreno analyzed all of the place-names and geographical regions mentioned in the chronicles concerning the location of ancient Tollan, and concluded that most of them identified Tula as the Toltec Tollan. His conclusions were supported by archaeologists in Mexico's newly founded National Institute of Anthropology and History (INAH), and by its first director Alfonso Caso. In 1940 INAH appointed Jorge R. Acosta to begin excavating Tula. During his first field season Acosta sank numerous test pits and trenches all over the site, providing him with ceramic evidence that placed the Toltec empire after the decline of Teotihuacán and before the rise of the Aztecs. At the first roundtable conference of the Mexican Society of Anthropology in 1942, with Tula and the Toltecs as its themes, Moreno's and Acosta's work was considered and discussed by more than thirty archaeologists. They concluded that Tula, Hidalgo, was indeed the Tollan described in the chronicles of central Mexico. Acosta was to excavate the site for the next twenty years.

See also Investigation of Palenque begins (1787); Rediscovering Maya Civilization (1839–1843); Stratigraphic Excavation in the Americas (1911–1913); Publication of *The Population of the Valley of Teotihuacán* (1922); Discovery of Olmec Civilization (1926–1942); Publication of *Ceramics of Monte Alban* (1967).

Further Reading

Bernal, I. 1980. *A history of Mexican archaeology.* London: Thames and Hudson.

Cobean, R., and A. G. Mastache Flores. 1999. Jorge R. Acosta, 1904–1975. In *Encyclopedia of archaeology: The great archaeologists,* ed. T. Murray, 425–439. Santa Barbara, CA: ABC-CLIO.

Davies, N. 1977. *The Toltecs until the fall of Tula.* Norman: University of Oklahoma Press.

Raising the Vasa *(1961)*

In 1961, the hull of the seventeenth-century Swedish royal war galleon, the *Vasa,* rose to the surface of the Baltic Sea—333 years after she sank. The *Vasa* was on its way to be excavated, preserved, and restored, after six years of underwater conservation and engineering. The next stage, preserving the *Vasa*'s waterlogged timber hull, the largest wooden and organic artifact in the world, took another nineteen years and required the development of pioneering nautical conservation techniques.

The *Vasa* sank on her maiden voyage in 1628, because of listing that flooded her open gun ports. These were open because a cannon salute had just been fired, a similar fate to that of the English warship, the *Mary Rose,* which sank in 1545. The *Vasa* was the largest galleon of her day, with two gun decks and sixty-four bronze cannon. She was skeleton built, primarily from northern oak; her bow timbers were steam curved and then fixed onto ribs. Her triple-laminated oak walls were 46 centimeters thick, her main mast was 57 meters high, her rudder was more than 9 meters deep, and she took more than three years to construct. Her cannon weighed 100 tons, and her stone ballast 120 tons. She carried cannonballs, gunpowder, extra firearms, food, and supplies in 2,000 wooden casks. Added to this were her officers and crew of 133 sailors.

The cannon were salvaged in 1663, after other attempts to raise her had failed. Then her mast and some of the intricate wooden carvings that decorated her hull were grappled and pulled off her. After that the wreck of the *Vasa* became the stuff of legend for three centuries. In 1956 the *Vasa* was relocated by shipwreck enthusiast and amateur archaeologist Anders Franzen. However, the wreck was quickly claimed by the Swedish navy, whose chief diver reported her upright, up to her original waterline in mud, and with a remarkably intact hull.

The *Vasa*'s hull was intact primarily because Baltic Sea waters are brackish and free of oxygen. This prevented sea worm damage. Futhermore, water temperatures had been fairly constant for the past 300 years. Her location meant she had not been subjected to current or ice damage, and her oak timbers, with their high levels of iron, had survived in relatively good condition. The *Vasa*'s hull was an example of ship design about which little was known, as no records of nautical architecture from the period had survived, and the contents of her hull could provide archaeologists with a unique cross section of seventeenth-century life at sea. A *Vasa* committee was formed and the decision made to raise and salvage her, in order to preserve and restore the ship.

Right from the very beginning archaeologists and conservationists were breaking new ground in the solutions and techniques they had to come up with to solve the many problems associated with the *Vasa* project. Unlike other shipwrecks the *Vasa* would not be excavated first and then lifted out of the water, nor would her contents be excavated, and her hull left on the sea floor because it was rotten. Instead, because the preservation of her hull was unusually good, it was decided that the *Vasa* would be lifted and moved in several steps to shallower locations until she could be excavated in dry dock. Not that she could ever be dry—waterlogged organic artifacts need to be kept wet, otherwise they deteriorate rapidly—and the *Vasa* was the largest waterlogged organic artifact in the world.

All loose objects from on and around the *Vasa's* bow and stern in the mud were brought up, recorded, and then resubmerged in tanks of water. Navy divers began drilling tunnels beneath the *Vasa's* keel. Six tunnels, three on each side of the ship, took a year to complete, and then strong cables were fed through the tunnels and two specially designed and built salvage pontoons used the cables to lift the *Vasa* out of her clay bed, swing her around and move her slowly toward the shore, gradually into more shallow water, but at the same time, for conservation reasons, keeping her submerged fifty feet below the surface. Meanwhile, repairs to her hull, which involved plugging thousands of oak pegs into holes where iron nails had rusted out, covering gun ports, and supporting her planks, continued underwater. Eventually, six years later in 1961, after a great deal of underwater conservation work and planning, and with all the main leaks sealed, the *Vasa* floated once again, if only for a hundred yards, onto a special pontoon, where she could be seen inside a prestressed concrete framework. The entire pontoon, with the *Vasa* in its center, crossed the harbor six months later for excavation and conservation, on its way to a sheltered location near Skansen Park.

At the same time water had to be pumped onto the *Vasa*'s hull faster than it was leaking out of it. All work on the hull took place under the spray of water jets, while inside workers began to probe and sieve the mud for finds, and to wash and record them. More than 100 tons of cargo and 100 tons of finds were gradually removed from the ship. Loose finds were placed into vats containing rot-preventing liquid, and then cleaned, preserved, and recorded. They comprised pails, human bones, cannonballs, copper powder, ramrods, powder barrels, ropes, shovels, wooden pulleys and blocks, wooden boxes, firearms, food casks, general spares, gunpowder kegs, ropes, spare canvas, tools, bronze coils, copper articles, earthenware, fabric, felt gloves, hats, leather garments and shoes, wooden objects, metal boxes, musket shot molds, pewter tankards and plates, pottery, and twine.

The waterlogged timber hull of the *Vasa* was the largest of its kind ever recovered, and the largest wooden and organic find in the world to undergo preservation. Ninety percent of the *Vasa*'s hull is oak, and while the surface layer had changed composition over time in the water, the interior was in good condition. However, preserving the hull for posterity would pose a challenge. Little information was available about this kind of conservation, because it had never been done before on such a scale. At the same time solutions for the *Vasa* were being improvised in Sweden, Danish conservators were working with similar constraints on preserving some Viking ships, and the two groups began to collaborate on solving related conservation problems. A *Vasa* advisory preservation committee was set up to hold regular meetings and come up with advice and ideas.

It took a year to clean the hull before preservation could begin, and while it presented special conservation problems, preservation of the larger wooden items, such as the keel, frame, and planking, proved to be more of a problem. The answer to preserving waterlogged ship timbers and preventing rot, distortion, and shrinkage while doing so, eventually came in the form of polyethylene glycol (PEG), which could be sprayed or brushed onto wooden artifacts, and while the PEG was being absorbed by the wood, it was drying out, the PEG more or less replacing the water, but as a more stable material. PEG is not toxic, and it is cheap and readily available, but finding the right solution of PEG for the task took a great deal of time and research, and then maximizing PEG's properties took even longer. Eventually PEG solution was pumped from a 3,000-liter tank through a pipeline with outlets at three levels inside and outside the *Vasa* onto the entire hull—approximately four acres total surface, while larger wooden pieces were hand painted and sprayed with PEG as well. It took five men five hours to complete this task—and it was accomplished every day from April 1962 until February 1965, when times between spraying were gradually extended, until they finished in 1979. During this period the articles published describing detailed procedures with PEG were becoming the foundations of a new science of conservation for artifacts recovered by maritime archaeology.

From its inception in 1956, the aim of the *Vasa* project was to present the ship in its original condition for public display. By the 1980s parts of the ship that had been destroyed, such as the main deck, stern castle, and bow and fittings inside, had been rebuilt by shipwrights and other technicians using original timbers. Approximately 95 percent of the *Vasa* is original. In the 1990s one of the masts was replaced. The *Vasa* is permanently on show at Skansen in Sweden, and profits from admissions and associated retail go back into restoration. It has become a national treasure and a national monument in Sweden.

See also Trials of the *Royal Savage* (1934–Present); Excavation of a Bronze Age Ship at Cape Gelidonya (1960); Raising the *Mary Rose* (1967–1982); Excavation of the *Batavia* (1972–1976); Finding the *Titanic* (1985–Present).

Further Reading

Bass, G. 1972. *A history of seafaring based on underwater archaeology.* London and New York: Thames and Hudson and Walker.

Bass, G. 2001. Nautical archaeology. In *Encyclopedia of archaeology: History and discoveries,* ed. T. Murray, 910–918. Santa Barbara, CA: ABC-CLIO.

Franzén, A. 1974. *The warship* Vasa*: Deep diving and marine archaeology in Stockholm.* 6th ed. Stockholm, Sweden: Norstedt.

Saunders, R. 1962. *The raising of the* Vasa*: The rebirth of a Swedish galleon.* London: Oldbourne.

Publication of World Prehistory: An Outline *(1961)*

Grahame Clark's intention with the book *World Prehistory: An Outline* was to create a kind of "statement of the moment" for our understanding of global prehistory. Although there were acknowledged gaps and shortcomings in the data and its presentation, Clark sought to synthesize the work of half a century with new information derived from radiocarbon chronology. Inevitably, the book reported in greatest detail the archaeology of places where the most work had been done. In 1961 this was still in Europe and the Near East, but in succeeding editions (in 1969 and 1977) the archaeology of other parts of the world, particularly of Africa, East Asia, and Oceania, gained greater coverage.

Although it has been often stated that *World Prehistory* made no great theoretical statements (or indeed made much of a contribution to our understanding of the processes that underwrote the change and variation that was the stuff of global prehistory), the fact remains that here for the first time was a compilation of what was known. Certainly the notion of creating a global *chronology* (as distinct from history) was challenging enough in 1961 with radiocarbon dating still in its infancy. Creating a global *prehistory,* as distinct from a catalog of what was known was an even greater challenge.

In an important sense Clark's attempt to discern a thread that would link the human experience over some millions of years was very much within the tradition of evolutionary universal histories of the kind produced nearly a century before by such as Sir John Lubbock (particularly in his *Pre-historic Times*). *World Prehistory* told an evolutionary story as well, but one where the pace and direction of change was not universal, in some ways harking back to the view of Europe held by Gordon Childe in many of his works, but most famously in *The Dawn of European Civilization.* Such universal histories did not dwell on the particular histories of places or peoples and this (plus the general shortage of data available to Clark for the first edition) makes *World Prehistory* a somewhat abstract and disengaged text. But for all its shortcomings Clark gave prehistoric archaeology a gift of the first importance—a global conspectus (if not perspective) on their subject supported by new and old information.

See also Publication of *The Dawn of European Civilization* (1925); Publication of *The Mesolithic Age* (1932) and *The Mesolithic Settlement of Northern Europe* (1936); Publication of *Man Makes Himself* (1936).

Further Reading

Clark, J. G. D. 1961. *World prehistory: an outline.* Cambridge: Cambridge University Press.

Clark, J. G. D. 1969. *World Prehistory: a new outline.* Cambridge: Cambridge University Press.

Clark, J. G. D. 1977. *World prehistory: In new perspective.* Cambridge: Cambridge University Press.

Fagan, B. 2001. *Grahame Clark: an intellectual biography of an archaeologist.* Boulder, CO: Westview.

First Excavation of Catal Hüyük (1961–1965)

Between 1961 and 1965, archaeologist James Mellaart excavated the site of Catal Hüyük in Turkey, the largest Neolithic site to be located and explored at that time. Mellaart discovered a wealthy and sophisticated early farming settlement and trade center—and dramatically changed knowledge and understanding of Neolithic societies. Until the excavation of Catal Hüyük, many archaeologists believed that prehistoric Turkey never experienced a Neolithic period, and that the development of early farming and herding communities was restricted to southern Mesopotamia and Palestine, with the site of Jericho, excavated in the 1950s, being one of the best examples of this phenomenon.

Archaeologists knew that around 10,000 years ago the economy of people in the Middle East and Egypt changed from foraging—that is, hunting and gathering—to food production. Evidence for the early domestication of plants, such as different seed cultivars and tool types, now points to its having evolved on the margins of the fertile river valleys of the Tigris and Euphrates and the Nile. And it was not immediate. While some people began to intensively collect and cultivate grain crops, they probably also kept hunting such wild game as ibex, gazelle, boar, and birds, to support food derived from farming. At the same time people also began to tame some animals, such as goats and sheep, which eventually became pastoral flocks that could be exploited despite seasonal, environmental, and climatic changes.

Aerial view of the archaeological site at Catal Hüyük, a Neolithic farming settlement. (Yann Arthus-Bertrand/Corbis)

In 1935 Gordon Childe, in *New Light on the Most Ancient East,* described this transition as "the Neolithic revolution." Childe argued that by becoming food producers, independent of wild resources and their distribution, Neolithic societies could also become sedentary, developing specialized pastoral economies and social hierarchies, producing artifacts for trade and specialized crafts and craftspeople, and laying the foundations of the relationship between urban and rural economies that enabled the growth of the city-states of the early Bronze Age. The site of Catal Hüyük seemed to be the perfect illustration of Childe's theories, but what was more surprising was just how wealthy and sophisticated it was.

Located on the southern-central Anatolian plain, 50 kilometers south of the modern Turkish city of Konya, on what was a lake, Catal Hüyük grew to cover 21 hectares between 6250 and 5400 BC. Its residents were farmers who used irrigation. The settlement comprised a large cluster of mud brick and timber houses and courtyards, but there were no streets. Access to houses and traffic routes were from and across the rooftops. Most houses were one large 6 by 4-meter room, with smaller storage areas off this. Some had built-in mud brick benches, sleeping platforms, domed ovens, and wall niches. Some were decorated with murals and bulls' heads—and the ceremonial nature of many of the artifacts also found in these particular rooms led Mellaart to surmise they were shrine rooms.

The bones of the settlement's dead were first cleaned of flesh, either by burial or exposure elsewhere, and then wrapped and deposited, some with exotic grave goods, under the sleeping platforms in many of the houses. With each new burial the older bone bundles were moved and rearranged. Some burials were accompanied by high-status artifacts such as stone vessels, obsidian mirrors, shell jewelry, and food offerings, which were considered to be evidence of social differentiation.

However, the occupants of Catal Hüyük not only farmed, but they also mined, worked, traded, and controlled the trade in obsidian, or volcanic glass, throughout the region, and as far away as Jericho. This was another source of their wealth and contributed to the growth in and maintenance of the size of the settlement. In exchange for their obsidian the residents of Catal Hüyük imported luxury items, such as turquoise, shells, flint, and copper, from as far away as Iran, Syria, and Jordan—evidence of a substantial long-distance Neolithic exchange network.

More than fifty different types of stone tools were found at Catal Hüyük, manufactured from local obsidian or imported flint, and ranging in function from weapons to ceremonial uses. Stone tool manufacture declined around the middle of the sixth century BC, when the use of copper became widespread. Jewelry, awls, needles, hafts, hairpins, beads, and even fishhooks were made from animal bones. Wooden bowls and boxes, baskets, textiles, and leather artifacts were also found. The pottery used by Catal Hüyük's occupants was functional and monochrome. Clay and stone figurines of the mother goddess, a popular local deity, and animals, were also found.

English archaeologist Ian Hodder returned to the site in 1993 as head of a large international team. Work continues there.

See also Discovery of the Hittites (1906–1931); Excavation of Jericho (1952–1958); Publication of *The Evolution of Urban Society* (1966).

Further Reading

Hodder, I., ed. 1996. *On the surface: Çatalhöyük 1993–95*. Cambridge: McDonald Institute for Archaeological Research; London: British Institute of Archaeology at Ankara.

Mellaart, J. 1967. *Çatal Hüyük: A Neolithic town in Anatolia*. London: Thames and Hudson.

Yakar, J. 1991. *Prehistoric Anatolia: The Neolithic transition and the early Chalcolithic period.* Tel Aviv, Israel: Institute of Archaeology: Tel Aviv University, Supplement 1, 1994.

Excavations at Olorgesailie and Koobi Fora (1961–1983)

In the 1960s the "Old" Stone Age period in Africa, ca. 1.5 million to 100,000 years ago, was the least understood period in the human history of the continent. However, by the end of the 1970s, this trend had reversed, and significant headway had been made in exploring the links between the evolution of human beings and changes in material culture (especially with regard to lithic technology). This was particularly important in the development of our knowledge of the Acheulean industry.

For over a million years Acheulean stone tools were used in eastern Africa, between densely forested areas and the eastern savanna. They appear in sites along with the fossilized remains of early human ancestors *Homo erectus, Homo ergaster,* and *Homo sapiens.* Acheulean tools are also evidence that these hominids behaved differently than the *Australopithecines,* some of which, such as *Australopithecus robustus,* coexisted with the *Homo habilis,* who were known to be associated with the earlier Oldowan lithic industry. While Acheulean artifacts were commonly found all over East Africa, undisturbed sites containing them were not—and it was to the location and excavation of these pristine sites that archaeologists turned their attention.

In 1961, Cambridge-trained and African-born archaeologist Glyn Isaac began to work at the site of Olorgesailie, located in the Kenyan Rift Valley, fifty kilometers west of Nairobi. The site comprised large concentrations of stone tools in what used to be a sandy area bordering a small lake, dating to ca. 800,000 years ago. The patterns of Acheulean axes at the site suggested that they had been used by groups of hominids. In one area numbers of gelada baboon bones were found beside hand axes, which Isaac interpreted as evidence that the baboons were killed by the hominids, as no hominid bones were found there. The stone tools were manufactured from raw materials located some distance away from the site itself. Finally, there was no evidence of the collection of plants or harvesting at this site. This led to Olorgesailie being described as a butchering and seasonal camping site, where hominid groups came to hunt and cut up their prey before returning to other sites, which Isaac interpreted to be evidence of early hominid behavior.

From 1966 until the 1980s Richard Leakey and Glyn Isaac led an interdisciplinary research team that surveyed, mapped, and excavated sites with Acheulean artifacts near ancient water channels in the Koobi Fora region, in northeast Lake Turkana in northern Kenya. They and their multidisciplinary teams concentrated on recovering as much contextual data as possible from the sites in order to reconstruct the environments that would enable them to infer the possible behaviors of inhabitants. Fossil pollens contained information about the ancient flora of the region, and innovative taphonomic (site formation) studies were pioneered. The mammalian fossil record of suids (pigs), bovids (cattle), equids (horses), and proboscideans (elephants) helped to date and provided evidence of local paleoenvironmental conditions. Compared with other remains, this fossil record also helped to cross-date fossil sites in East Africa, where radiometric dating could not be used. Studies of mollusk (shellfish) remains provided evidence of rates of evolutionary change. Faunal studies at Koobi Fora eventually mapped 3 million years of change.

Hominid fossils at Koobi Fora sites ranged from 4 to 1.7 million years ago, with the best cranial evidence dating from 2 to 1.4 million years ago. Evidence of both *Australopithecus* (*Australopithecus afarensis* and *Australopithecus africanus*) and two *Homo* species were found. Sites with Acheulean artifacts were dated to ca. 1.3 million years ago.

Isaac and Leakey ran the East Turkana Research Project from 1971 until 1983. Both educated and encouraged a new generation of archaeologists from African nations. Isaac helped Desmond Clark establish the University of California at Berkeley as the center for the study of African prehistoric archaeology. In 1983 he became professor at Harvard University, but unfortunately, he died prematurely in 1985. Richard Leakey became director of the National Museum of Kenya and continued to work in Africa.

The contribution of work at Lake Turkana to the study and knowledge of *Australopithecus* has been substantial. The large number and great variety of hominid fossils found there, including *Australopithecus afarensis, Australopithecus africanus,* and two species of *Homo,* the earlier of which overlapped in time with the *Australopithecines,* helped to confirm similar evidence found elsewhere in East and South Africa.

See also Discovery of *Australopithecus africanus* (1924); First meeting of the Pan-African Congress on Prehistory and Quaternary Studies (1947); Excavations at Sterkfontein and Swartkrans (1948–Present); Discovery of *Zinjanthropus boisei* (1959); Discovery of *Homo Habilis* (1964–1980); Discovery of Early Humans in Ethiopia (1966–1977); Discovery of Footprints of Our Earliest Ancestors

(1974–1981); Announcement of Toumai fossil (2002); Earliest Stone Tools Found at Gona (2003); Discovery of the "Hobbit" (2004).

Further Reading

Harris, J. M., ed. 1983. *Koobi Fora research project, Vol. 2. Proboscidea, Perissodactyla, and Suidae: the fossil ungulates.* Oxford: Clarendon.

Harris, J. M. 1991. *Koobi Fora research project, Vol. 3. The Fossil Ungulates—geology, fossil artiodactyls, and palaeo-environments.* Oxford: Clarendon.

Isaac, G. 1977. *Olorgesailie: archeological studies of a Middle Pleistocene lake basin in Kenya.* Chicago: University of Chicago Press.

Isaac, G., ed. 1997. *Koobi Fora research project. Vol. 5. Plio-Pleistocene archaeology.* Oxford: Clarendon.

Leakey, M. G., and R. E. Leakey. 1978. *Koobi Fora research project. Vol.1. The Fossil Hominids and an introduction to their context, 1968–1974.* Oxford: Clarendon Press.

Wood, B. 1991. *Koobi Fora research project. Vol. 4. Hominid cranial remains.* Oxford: Clarendon Press.

Discovering the Pleistocene in Australia (1962)

The settlement of the continent of Australia in the late eighteenth century brought Europeans into contact with indigenous people whom the Europeans regarded as the most primitive people on earth. From 1788 and throughout the nineteenth century, detailed studies of aboriginal life and customs were undertaken for a variety of reasons. The aboriginal population was decimated by European diseases, social dislocation, and frontier violence, and many believed they would die out completely. The need to provide a record of these "savage" people and the details of their traditional societies motivated many studies, which used a combination of the disciplines of ethnography, anthropology, and archaeology.

European observers generally believed that either aboriginal society had remained fixed and unchanged since the initial colonization of Australia, or that it had experienced growth, stasis, and degeneration. In either case Australian Aborigines (particularly the Tasmanians) were believed to be the best examples of what Europeans had looked and behaved like long ago. Thus, an important early stimulus of anthropological inquiry was the sense that Europeans were documenting their own prehistory in their studies of Australian Aborigines. However, some complication arose when it became more widely appreciated that there were real social and cultural differences between aboriginal societies at contact and differences in the physical features of aboriginal populations. A further complication was the fact that this identifiable cultural variation included stone technologies that in Europe were both Paleolithic and Neolithic in age.

During the first century of settlement questions about the origin and antiquity of Aborigines dominated: Where had they come from? How long had they been there? Were the Aboriginal Tasmanians and mainland Aborigines the same people? By the end of the nineteenth century, largely as the result of work done by Australian geologists and paleontologists such as Edgeworth David, it was more widely appreciated that the physical geography of Australia had been far from static. Ice ages had carved glaciers, sea levels had fallen and risen, and the climate of the continent had changed dramatically. The aboriginal people of Australia had obviously responded to these changes, but for how long? And where had their history gone? And how could it be written?

Although there had been a long tradition of private inquiries into aboriginal culture—as manifested in collections of artifacts, in the proceedings of mainstream scientific societies such as the various state Royal Societies, and in more low-key gatherings of naturalists and antiquarians—the systematic investigation of the archaeology of Australia did not really begin until the 1920s, and until the 1950s it was dominated by museum personnel.

In 1917 the zoologist, anthropologist, and archaeologist Norman Tindale (1900–1993) joined the staff of the South Australian Museum in Adelaide. In 1929 he conducted the first scientific excavation in Australia at the site of Devon Downs, on the Murray River in South Australia. The site was a limestone shelter with six meters of archaeological deposit—or 6,000 years of aboriginal history. The excavation proved that types of stone tools and the remains of animals eaten by the occupants of the shelter had changed over time. Here was the first empirical evidence of cultural change in Australian prehistory, although Tindale believed it was the result of movements of distinct prehistoric populations or cultures, rather than of adaptation by stable population. The excavation was also the basis for Tindale's pioneering attempt to establish an Australian culture sequence. Tindale began anthropological work in the 1930s first in the Mann Ranges of South Australia, and then in the Warburton Ranges of Western Australia. Ironically, it was not for his excavation of Devon Downs, but rather for his tribal map of Australia that was based on his later ethnographic fieldwork and research, for which he is most famous. It is still widely used today.

Between 1935 and 1936, Fred McCarthy (1905–1997), from the Australian Museum in Sydney, excavated the Lapstone Creek rock shelter in the Blue Mountains outside Sydney, New South Wales. Here he recovered evidence of cultural change in the form of changes in stone tool technology and animal bones. In 1949 McCarthy, who was a stone tool typologist, with Elsie Barmell and H. V. V. Noone, wrote *The Stone Implements of Australia.* Their classifications of aboriginal stone tools remains important. McCarthy's (1905–1997) career extended beyond museum work to include foundational studies in Australia prehistoric archaeology, comparative archaeological fieldwork in Indonesia, ethnographic fieldwork in Arnhem Land and Cape York in northern Australia, and the key administrative role of first principal of the Australian Institute of Aboriginal Studies.

In 1940 the geomorphologist Edmund Gill, at the Museum of Victoria, dated an aboriginal cranium from a site at Keilor near Melbourne, Victoria, to around 15,000 years ago. In the 1950s Gill pioneered the use of radiocarbon dating and published the first radiocarbon date for an Australian site. In the 1950s the American anthropologist D. S. Davidson and the physical anthropologist N. G. MacIntosh excavated sites in northern Australia.

In 1953 John Mulvaney (1925–), an Australian archaeologist educated at Cambridge University, returned to teach at Melbourne University's history department. He taught the first university course in prehistory in Australia and began a program of field survey, excavation, and analysis of archaeological material and documentary research into aboriginal history. In 1956 Mulvaney excavated a limestone shelter site at Fromm's Landing in the Lower Murray Valley, which had occupational deposits spanning the last 5,000 years. The changes he found in stone tool technology and animal remains paralleled the sequences Tindale found at the nearby site of Devon Downs. Mulvaney's site also included one of the earliest securely dated finds of the dingo, or wild dog, in Australia.

In 1962 Mulvaney excavated Kenniff Cave in southern central Queensland. This large, open, sandstone shelter, decorated with stenciled art, had been used as a campsite by aboriginal people for 19,000 years and had three meters of occupational deposit. Mulvaney used radiocarbon dating on the Kenniff Cave material, which proved the Pleistocene occupation of Australia, ca. 19,000 years ago. This meant the aborigines had been in Australia before sea-level changes significantly increased distances between Australia and Island Southeast Asia. He also noted that there was conclusive evidence for cultural change in Australia. Mulvaney had demonstrated high human antiquity in Australia.

In 1965 John Mulvaney moved to Canberra to the Research School of Pacific Studies at the Australian National University (ANU). In 1969 he finished *The Prehistory of Australia,* and in 1970 was appointed foundation professor of prehistory at the ANU. Mulvaney continued to direct much of the agenda of Australian prehistoric archaeology over the next two decades.

The work of Tindale and McCarthy created a platform of data and interpretation that both identified and explained cultural changes in precontact Aboriginal society, even if it was limited by contemporary cultural values. In concert with researchers such as D. S. Davidson, McCarthy and Tindale went on to produce foundational analyses of aboriginal art and material culture that, although they had little impact on Australian society before the 1960s, made possible the phenomenal advances of professionally trained archaeologists since the early 1970s.

See also Lake Mungo Inscribed on the World Heritage List (1981); Ice Age Tasmania Clashes with the Political Present (1981).

Further Reading

Golson, J. 1986. Old guards and new waves: reflections on antipodean archaeology 1954–1975. *Archaeology in Oceania* 21: 2–12.

Griffiths, T. 1996. *Hunters and collectors: The antiquarian imagination in Australia.* Cambridge: Cambridge University Press.

Mulvaney, D. J. 1969. *The prehistory of Australia.* London: Thames and Hudson.

Mulvaney, D. J., and J. Kamminga. 1999. *Prehistory of Australia.* Sydney: Allen and Unwin.

Field Archaeology in Epirus (1962–1964)

In 1962 English archaeologist Eric Higgs began an intensive survey of Epirus in northwest Greece, in an attempt to locate Paleolithic sites. Over the next few seasons, and in collaboration with the local Greek ephor of archaeology, Higgs and his crew excavated the rock shelters of Asprochaliko and Kastritsa, which provided valuable data about the relationships between sites, the distribution of natural resources, animal domestication, and the prehistoric economies of the region. Higgs's primary interest was to chart the impact on and limitations of the landscape with respect to the passage of the seasons and the availability of resources for its prehistoric inhabitants.

Epirus was an excellent place to explore the operation of such variables, given that it was arid at lower altitudes and on the coast during the summer months, and snowbound at higher altitudes during the winter. The herds of red deer, which were the foundation of the prehistoric economy of the region, were completely dependent on the availability of good fodder. The sites of Kastritsa and Asprochaliko were complementary seasonal sites, used annually as the deer moved up to their summer, and then down to their winter, pastures.

Significantly, Higgs noted that the same routes used by Paleolithic deer hunters were still being used by contemporary Greek shepherds, who moved their sheep in search of good pastures. Higgs also suggested that the relationship between the Paleolithic hunters and their red deer may have started out as opportunistic, but over time probably became closer and more dependent. Was it merely animal instinct that took the deer up into the mountains during summer and back down to the littoral during the winter? Or were they encouraged, or even herded there, by their human hunters? If this were the case then it was perhaps not too great a leap to think of deer herders as being protopastoralists who, while not "domesticating" red deer, to all intents and purposes managed them in much the same way.

Higgs's work in Epirus was fundamental to his later development and enunciation of site catchment analysis, that is, the total area from which the contents of a site are derived and its economic potential, according to the principle of paleoeconomy, with its emphasis on long-term patterns in land use and the exploitation of plant and animal resources. Between 1967 and his death in 1976, Eric Higgs continued to develop his paleoeconomic theories through his direction of the British Academy Major Research Project on the Early History of Agriculture, based at the department of archaeology at Cambridge University.

See also Publication of *The Desert Fayum* (1934); Excavation of Jarmo (1948–1954); Excavation of Star Carr (1949–1953); Publication of *Prehistoric Settlement Patterns in the Viru Valley, Peru* (1953); Publication of *Analytical Archaeology* (1968).

Further Reading

Bailey, G. N. 1999. Eric Higgs, 1908–1976. In *Encyclopedia of archaeology: The great archaeologists,* ed. T. Murray, 531–565. Santa Barbara, CA: ABC-CLIO.

Higgs, E. S., ed. 1972. *Papers in economic prehistory.* Cambridge: Cambridge University Press.

Higgs, E. S. 1975. *Palaeoeconomy.* Cambridge: Cambridge University Press.

Publication of The Archaeology of Ancient China *(1963)*

The Archaeology of Ancient China, first published in 1963 (and reprinted three more times in 1968, 1977, and 1986) became the most comprehensive and authoritative account of Chinese archaeology available in English. Significantly it covered the geography and environment of China, along with a history of antiquarianism and archaeology in China, to provide the basis of a detailed understanding of the *why* as well as the *what* of Chinese archaeology.

Kwang-chi Chang's account of the evolution of complex societies in China was heavily influenced by his strong adherence to the anthropological perspective in archaeology, particularly through his innovative use of the principles of settlement archaeology.

Born in Beijing, Chang grew up on mainland China during the last years of the Chinese monarchy, the Japanese invasion, and World War II. He and his family migrated to Taiwan in 1946, where he was jailed for one year as a political prisoner at the age of eighteen. In 1955 Chang began graduate studies in anthropology at Harvard University, finishing his Ph.D. in 1960. He taught at Harvard and became a professor there in 1977. During the 1980s Chang built collaborative relationships with archaeologists in the People's Republic of China. In the 1990s he initiated the first Sino-American collaborative field project in China since World War II, at Shangqiu, Henan, investigating the origins of the Shang dynasty.

The Archaeology of Ancient China acted as a bridge between East and West, in terms of allowing Western archaeologists to perceive the truly great significance of the archaeology of ancient China and allowing Chinese archaeologists to begin to engage once again with other ways of seeing and doing archaeology.

See also Discovering the Archaeological Riches of Central Asia—The Journeys of Sir Aurel Stein (1906–1930); Discoveries at Zhoukoudian Cave (1921–Present); Publication of *The Formation of the Chinese People* (1928); Controversial Interpretation of Banpo Published (1963); Discovery of the Terracotta Warriors (1974).

Further Reading

Chang, K-C. 1963. *The archaeology of Ancient China.* New Haven, CT: Yale University Press.

Chang, K-C. 1986. *The archaeology of Ancient China.* Rev. 4th ed. New Haven, CT: Yale University Press.

Liu, L. 2001. Kwang-chi Chang (1931–2001). In *Encyclopedia of archaeology: History and discoveries,* ed. T. Murray, 298–299. Santa Barbara, CA: ABC-CLIO.

Liu, L., and X. Chen. 2001. China. In *Encyclopedia of archaeology: History and discoveries,* ed. T. Murray, 315–333. Santa Barbara, CA: ABC-CLIO.

Controversial Interpretation of Banpo Published (1963)

In 1963 results from the excavation of the remains of a Neolithic Yangshao village (ca. 5000–4000 BC) at the site of Banpo, near Xi'an, the capital of

Shaanxi Province in central China, were published. What distinguished this publication was the fact that archaeologists devised a Marxist interpretation of the finds that accorded well with Chinese communist ideology.

Excavated between 1954 and 1957, the Neolithic village of Banpo has a great significance in the history of Chinese archaeology for several reasons. First, the well-preserved remains of houses, ditches, and burials and the large number of artifacts that were found during excavation make this a "type site" (that is the site becomes the "ideal example" of a particular group of identifiable artifacts and the group of people who used them) for the Yangshao phase of the early Chinese Neolithic period. This period was considered to be the source of Chinese civilization in the central plains region.

Second, the site was interpreted as providing clear evidence of the existence of a matrilineal society during the Neolithic period, an interpretation that followed the analysis of precapitalist societies put forward by Friedrich Engels in his *Origins of the Family, Private Property and the State* (1884). The first attempt to interpret ancient Chinese history with a Marxist model of social evolution was by Guo Moruo in his *Study of Ancient Chinese Society* (1930). Under the communist regime, and influenced by Soviet archaeology, many Chinese archaeologists wanted to use the Marx-Engels theory of social evolution in archaeological practice. The Marxist interpretation of Chinese history was seen as a new mission for the discipline in addition to its primary task—to find the origins of Chinese culture. At Banpo the two could be combined. It was to become the most successful example of the application of this evolutionary scheme in Chinese archaeology.

The excavations led by Shi Xingbang revealed a large portion of a Yangshao settlement. Based on burials and residential patterns, the Banpo Neolithic village was described as a matrilineal society in which women enjoyed high social status and in which pairing marriage was practiced. This interpretation became standard at many Neolithic sites from the Yangshao period. The Marxist evolutionary model became commonly accepted by many Chinese archaeologists.

Third, the site was transformed into a major museum based around a building that completely enclosed a large portion of the site, including different types of houses and burials. This major museum, which recently had a tourist village constructed adjacent to it, continues to play a significant role in informing the Chinese people about life in Neolithic China.

See also Publication of *The Formation of the Chinese People* (1928); Publication of *The Archaeology of Ancient China* (1963).

Further Reading

Chang, K-C. 1986. *The Archaeology of Ancient China.* 4th ed., rev. and enlarged. New Haven, CT and London: Yale University Press.

Liu, L., and X. Chen. 2001. China. In *Encyclopedia of archaeology: History and discoveries,* ed. T. Murray, 315–333. Santa Barbara, CA: ABC-CLIO.

Wu Xi, ed. 1994. *Ruins of Banpo Village: A tourist's guide.* China Nationality Art Photograph Publishing House.

Discovery of Homo Habilis *(1964–1980)*

In 1964 the discovery of a new human ancestor, *Homo habilis,* was announced. Not since 1891, with Dubois' discovery of *Homo erectus* in Java, had there been any announcement of a new *Homo* species, and not since Dart's discovery of *Australopithecus africanus* in 1924 had there been such controversy. It took twenty years for *Homo habilis* to be accepted by the scientific community, the second great paradigm shift in the study of paleoanthropology in the twentieth century.

The first evidence of the stone tool making human ancestor *Homo habilis* was unearthed at the Leakeys' famous site of Olduvai, in northern Tanzania in 1959. However, its significance was eclipsed by the discovery of *Australopithecus (Zinjanthropus) boisei* at the same site a few weeks later.

Between 1960 and 1963 Jonathon Leakey unearthed evidence of a number of hominids distinctly different from *Australopithecus boisei,* but with similarities to the earlier and neglected find of 1959. In 1964 Louis Leakey, Phillip Tobias, and John Russell Napier, three of the foremost African paleoanthropologists of the time, announced in the journal *Nature* that, based on the analysis of dental, cranial, and hand and foot bone evidence, there was now a new human ancestor, a hominid species they called *Homo habilis.* It is ironic that in the long run, the famous *Australopithecus boisei,* which Louis Leakey claimed to be "the missing link" between apes and humans, amid great international fanfare and publicity, would eventually be eclipsed in scientific significance by something that he originally ignored. *Homo habilis* has proven to be more of the "link" Leakey was searching for, but not in the form he envisaged it.

This new species, dating between 1.9 and 1.6 million years ago, was morphologically different from the three *Australopithecines (africanus, robustus, boisei)* and endocranially different from either *Homo erectus* or *sapiens.*

Homo habilis was more advanced than *Australopithecus africanus* but not as "modern" as *Homo sapiens.* It was also a contemporary of *Australopithecus boisei,* which meant that it was possible that these two different species of hominids were living side by side at Olduvai during the Pleistocene, but evolving and using the landscape in different ways.

The debate about the bona fides of *Homo habilis* lasted for twenty years, and comprised discussions about phylogenic relationships between species based on degrees of morphology, differing cranial capacities of hominids as determining membership of either *Homo* or *Australopithecine* genuses (*Homo habilis* had a smaller brain than *Homo erectus*), and the validity of using stone tool evidence in defining and dating hominid taxa. *Homo habilis* was a serious challenge to prevailing paleoanthropological knowledge, in much the same way that *Australopithecus africanus* had been earlier, and it took *Australopithecus africanus* thirty-five years to be accepted as a new species (from Dart's first evidence in 1924 at Sterkfontein until Broom's discoveries in 1960).

By 1980 many of the objections to the creation of a separate species for *Homo habilis* had been addressed by research on and comparisons with more

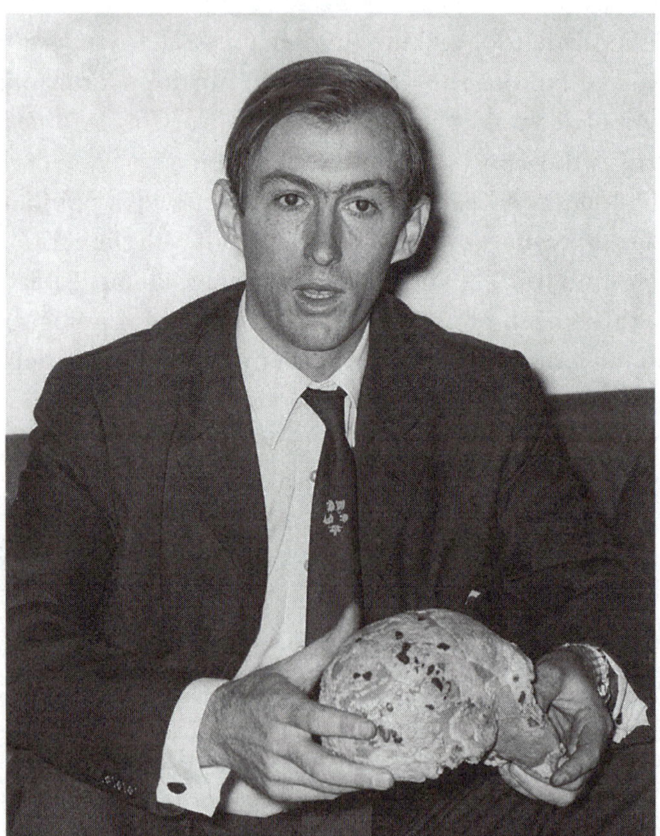

Richard Leakey with hominid skull. (Keystone/Getty Images)

of the examples of *Homo habilis* excavated at Omo in southern Ethiopia, at Sterkfontein in South Africa, and at other sites in Kenya and Uganda. More recent research has concluded that the endocranium of *Homo habilis* provides neurological evidence for its use of spoken language and articulate speech—believed by some to be the major diagnostic features of the genus *Homo.* In the late 1980s, at excavations at Olduvai by Donald C. Johanson, the partial skeleton of *Homo habilis* was excavated, igniting a debate once more. But this time it is not about the validity of the species of *Homo habilis,* but about the variability within it.

More recently, the discovery of still other species of *Homo,* such as *rudolfensis* and *ergaster,* has reignited earlier debates about species and led to more discussions about a revised taxonomy for human ancestors and human ancestral species.

See also Discovery of the Neanderthals (1833–1900); First *Homo Erectus* (1888–1895); Publication of *Les hommes fossiles, elémentes de paléontologie humaine* (1921); Discovery of *Australopithecus africanus* (1924); Excavations at Sterkfontein and Swartkrans (1948–Present); Discovery of *Zinjanthropus boisei* (1959); Excavations at Olorgesailie and Koobi Fora (1961–1983); Discovery of Early Humans in Ethiopia (1966–1977); Discovery of Footprints of Our Earliest Humans (1974–1981); Excavation of Jenne-Jeno (1974–1998); Discovery of "Lucy" (1975); Announcement of Toumai Fossil (2002); Earliest Stone Tools Found at Gona (2003); Discovery of the "Hobbit" (2004).

Further Reading

Facchini, F. 2003. *A day with* Homo habilis: *Life 2,000,000 years* ago. Brookfield, CT: Twenty-First Century Books.

Johanson, D. C., and J. Shreeve. 1990. *Lucy's child: The discovery of a human ancestor.* London: Viking.

Tobias, P. V. 1991. *Olduvai Gorge. Vol.4. The skulls, endocasts and teeth of* Homo habilis. Cambridge: Cambridge University Press.

Publication of The Evolution of Urban Society *(1966)*

Robert McCormick Adams (1926–) became interested in social evolution through his work with archaeologists Robert Braidwood and Gordon Willey in Iraq and South America, both of whom advocated multidisciplinary approaches to prehistoric archaeology and pioneered the use of settlement patterns and demography. Adams was also interested in comparative social theory and ethnographic analogy and Gordon Childe's theories about technology and social organization and social evolution.

Adams' book *The Evolution of Urban Society: Early Mesopotamia and Prehispanic Mexico* (1966) demonstrated how powerful archaeological data could be when combined with anthropological analysis. It became an instant classic in anthropology, providing detailed comparisons between the two best-known cases of the evolution of ancient states within a rigorous theoretical framework. *The Evolution of Urban Society* identified similarities in development among different states without masking evidence for difference and diversity among states.

Adams also made a singular contribution to social evolutionary theory with his argument against Karl Wittfogel's assertion that the requirements of large-scale irrigation caused the rise and determined the character of ancient states. His discussion of New and Old World data sets demonstrated that large-scale irrigation was the consequence, not the cause, of dynastic states.

Adams went on to publish other books fleshing out these themes and analyzing new data. In *Land Behind Baghdad: A History of the Settlement of the Diyala Plain* (1965) he surveyed 7,000 years of a crowded cultural landscape, with *The Uruk Countryside: the Natural Setting of Urban Societies* (1972) he focused on explaining the process of urbanization in Mesopotamia, and in *Heartland of Cities: Surveys of Ancient Settlement and Land Use on the Central Floodplain of the Euphrates* (1981) he sought to link changing agricultural productivity in the region with the history of climate change. All made their mark on our understanding of the rise of complex societies in Mesopotamia and, of course, on their eventual collapse.

Robert Adams was professor of anthropology at the Oriental Institute at the University of Chicago from 1962 to 1983, and in 1984 he became secretary of the Smithsonian Institution in Washington, D.C., a position he held until his retirement in 1994.

See also Publication of *The Population of the Valley of Teotihuacán* (1922); Excavation of Jarmo (1948–1954); Publication of *Prehistoric Settlement Patterns in the Viru Valley, Peru* (1953); Publication of *Method and Theory in American Archaeology* (1958).

Further Reading

Adams, R. M. 1966. *The Evolution of urban society: Early Mesopotamia and prehispanic Mexico.* London: Weidenfeld & Nicolson.

Yoffee, N. 1999. Robert McCormick Adams, 1926–. In *Encyclopedia of archaeology: The great archaeologists,* ed. T. Murray, 791–810. Santa Barbara, CA: ABC-CLIO.

Discovery of Early Humans in Ethiopia (1966–1977)

From 1966 until 1974, French, Kenyan, and American scientists participated in the multidisciplinary International Omo Research Expedition, named for the Omo River in Ethiopia, the main source of Lake Turkana. In the lower Omo Valley they located extensive Pliocene and Pleistocene sedimentary deposits. The fossil hominids in these deposits dated to ca. 3 million years ago, and while robust in form, proved to be *Australopithecus afarensis.* As it was with Koobi Fora, of almost greater long-term interest and impact was the mapping of the chronological sequences of faunal, sedimentary, and volcanic deposits, dating from ca. 4.2 to 1.4 million years at Omo. They are still the longest and most continuous sequence known.

In 1973 another multidisciplinary team, comprising Maurice Taieb, Donald Johanson, Yves Coppens, and Jon Kalb began the International Afar Research Expedition in Ethiopia. The Hadar area was chosen because of its potential to provide a range of information about the Pliocene period, when it was a freshwater lake surrounded by marshes and swamps, fed by rivers from the Ethiopian highlands.

During the first season the remains of fossil hominids and the remains of another eighty-seven animals were found. In 1974 more hominid remains were unearthed, and then the 3-million-year-old partial skeleton of a small hominid (*Australopithecus afarensis),* whom Johanson called "Lucy," was excavated. In 1975 a single site, perhaps the result of a catastrophe, with the remains of thirteen fossil hominids of different ages, were excavated. These dated from 3.6 until 2.9 million years ago, and were first thought to be from three different species. In 1978 paleoanthropologists Johanson, Coppens, and Tim White agreed that they were all sexually dimorphic examples of *Australopithecus afarensis,* as was Lucy. Skeletal research on their pelvises and knee joints revealed that they were fully bipedal (a conclusion confirmed by the hominid footprints at Laetoli) but had a range of morphological differences from modern humans. They were more robust all over, and the phalanges of their hands and feet were longer and more curved, leading to speculation that this could have been the result of a semiarboreal existence. In 1976–1977 Oldowan-style stone tools were excavated at a site east of Hadar, but from younger strata. However, these were dated to ca. 2.6 million years ago—and remain the oldest to be found until 2003.

Paleoenvironmental reconstruction based on microfaunal and pollen studies demonstrated that the area was wetter and more humid than it is today. Fossil remains included crocodile and hippopotamus megafauna—a very different faunal assemblage from that found in sites of similar age at Laetoli, Tanzania. The combination of early hominid material from Hadar, Laetoli, and Koobi Fora finally clinched the bona fides of a new hominid species, *Australopithecus afarensis,* dating to ca. 4–3 million years ago. The excavation of more examples of this earlier and more primitive *Australopithecine* intensified debates about its relationship to *Australopithecus robustus* and to the genus *Homo* for most of the 1980s, until more work in South Africa on *Australopithecus robustus* led to a resolution.

See also Discovery of the Neanderthals (1833–1900); First *Homo Erectus* (1888–1895); Publication of *Les hommes fossiles, elémentes de paléontologie humaine* (1921); Discovery of *Australopithecus africanus* (1924); Excavations at Sterkfontein and Swartkrans (1948–Present); Discovery of *Zinjanthropus boisei* (1959); Excavations at Olorgesailie and Koobi Fora (1961–1983); Discovery of *Homo Habilis* (1964–1980); Discovery of Footprints of Our Earliest Ancestors (1974–1981); Discovery of "Lucy" (1975); Announcement of Toumai fossil (2002); Earliest Stone Tools Found at Gona (2003); Discovery of the "Hobbit" (2004).

Further Reading

Coppens, Y. 2002. *Lucy's knee: The story of man and the story of his story.* Trans. N. Strike. Pretoria, South Africa: Protea Book House.

Fattovich, R. 2001. Africa, Horn of. In *Encyclopedia of archaeology: History and discoveries,* ed. T. Murray, 35–43. Santa Barbara, CA: ABC-CLIO.

Johanson, D. C., and M. A. Edey. 1982. *Lucy, the beginnings of humankind.* New York: Warner Books.

Johanson, D. C., and J. Shreeve. 1989. *Lucy's child: The discovery of a human ancestor.* New York: Morrow.

Picq, P. G., and N. Verrechia. 1996. *Lucy and her times.* New York: H. Holt.

Excavation of Chavin de Huantar (1966–1980)

During the 1960s and 1970s excavations at the site of Chavin de Huantar in Peru by Louis Lumbreras and Richard Burger drastically changed our understanding of this site and its occupants, the Chavin people. It is now thought that Chavin de Huantar was the main temple center of a religious cult that at its peak dominated the Peruvian northern highlands between 400 and 200 BC, and greatly influenced the development of the textiles, pottery, sculpture, and architecture of later Andean civilizations.

The site of Chavin de Huantar was found in the late nineteenth century and first excavated by the Peruvian archaeologist Julio Tello (1880–1947) between 1919 and 1941. It is located 3,185 meters above sea level in the modern Peruvian province of Huari, and the site has been looted, mined, weathered, and threatened by mudslides and more recent agricultural reclamation. Tello gave part of the name of the site, Chavin, to its builders and occupants, and to their distinctive iconography and textile and pottery styles. The previously unknown Chavin culture developed in this high valley of the Andes Mountains between 1500 and 300 BC.

Tello discovered a rectangular platform complex and an enormous stone building, which was locally known as a castillo, decorated with stone stelae and carvings of felines, raptorial birds, and serpents. At the peak of its power and population the city covered 40 hectares, and 3 hectares of that was dedicated to the castillo complex. Tello discovered that there were in fact two mounds, which he described as the "old" and "new" temples, although there is no evidence that they were constructed at different times, and they jointly formed the castillo. Tello's work at Chavin de Huantar proved that it had been the capital and center of a culture whose influence extended throughout the central Andes Mountains and onto the northern coast of Peru during

Main portal and complex at Chavin, built ca. 800 BC (Philip Baird (http://www.anthroarcheart.org))

the first millennium BC. In 1942, in his book *Origen y Desarrollo de la Civilización Andina* (Origin and Development of Andean Civilization), Tello argued that Chavin culture was the first, autochthonous and progenitor civilization of ancient Peru, and that it had probably originated in the Amazon Basin.

By the 1960s many of Tello's claims for the Chavin had been discounted by subsequent archaeological investigations. Evidence for the development of Chavin-style settlements, similar pyramid forms, and the use of Chavin art styles, was found at sites older than the foundation of Chavin de Huantar, proving it was neither first nor autochthonous. As a result of this work, dates for the period of Chavin dominance were revised to around 2,900–2,200 years ago (ca. 900–200 BC) with the Chavin apogy ca. 2,400–2,200 years ago (ca. 400–200 BC). But Tello had been right about Chavin de Huantar's significance to and central role in the development other Andean cultures.

At the same time other scholars began to decipher the Chavin religious pantheon and its iconography, both of which were illustrated in the architecture and decoration of the castillo at Chavin de Huantar. The Chavin's gods formed a cosmic hegemony represented by composite eagle, serpent/caiman, and feline forms associated with air, water, and earth, the habitats of each animal.

The earliest and predominant deity, depicted on the Lanzon Stela and located in the main gallery of the old temple at the center of the castillo temple complex, was a dualistic human and animal god. The god depicted on the later Raimondi Stela, once again centrally located in the complex, was a staff god of supernatural synthesis. There were also other forms, such as that represented on the Tello Obelisk discovered outside the castillo, of a caiman (South American crocodile) with gourds, chili peppers, and manioc, suggesting that it may have been the donor of these jungle plants.

Analysis of other sites and Chavin iconography led archaeologists to describe the site of Chavin de Huantar as the central oracle center of a religious cult that dominated the north-central area of Peru between 2,400–2,200 years ago (ca. 400–200 BC). The Lanzon god was the principal deity or oracle that was consulted by pilgrims from all over Peru. Because Chavin de Huantar was located between the coast and the Amazon jungle, it was also an important trade and communication center, and both of these geographic areas in turn influenced the layout, construction, and decoration of the castillo. Jungle iconography, in the form of animals and plants, was used on sculptures such as the Tello Obelisk, and coastal contacts influenced the construction and design of the U-shaped mounds that make up the castillo, the forms of the sunken circular and rectangular plazas, and the feline sculptures—all of which can be found at coastal archaeological sites before 3,000 years ago (ca. 1000 BC).

The final pieces of the puzzle of Chavin de Huantar emerged as the result of archaeological work in the 1970s. Excavations at the castillo by archaeologist Louis Lumbreras, between 1966 and 1972, unearthed the sunken circular plaza (mentioned above as being a coastal architectural form) and a large number of votive ceramics. He also discovered that the castillo's engineering and hydraulics were remarkably sophisticated. It seemed that different levels of chambers, galleries, and air and water conduits could be used to flush and vent the building with such force it would sound as though it was roaring. The exceptional masonry work and fabulous stone art were testimony to great craftspeople, and the whole castillo complex was the result of a substantial, well-organized, and cooperative labor force and the sophisticated management of resources needed to build it. Lambreras hypothesized that such a complex could not have been achieved by just the local population or through the export of locally produced crafts. However, it could be accomplished by the orders of the priest/interpreter/shamans of a powerful god who carried the dual staffs of social and cosmic unity; who was widely acknowledged and respected; and to whom tithes, taxes, and offerings were paid in different forms, such as labor, slaves, and raw materials.

In the mid-1970s American archaeologist Richard Burger excavated a number of domestic and residential sites away from the castillo complex at Chavin de Huantar that provided evidence of everyday Chavin economic and social life. Burger discovered that the site's peak in population, and the Chavin's period of greatest and widespread influence, coincided between 2,400 and 2,200 years ago (ca. 400–200 BC) with a period of drought. City residents living close to the castillo had a better diet, with more camelid protein, than those residents living on the margins of the settlement. Graves excavated at other Chavin sites from this period contain bodies wearing gold crowns, beads, earrings, pectoral decorations, and shells, which provide evidence for the beginnings of class formation. Burger hypothesized that because resources were more limited during a drought, they required some kind of allocation, based on abilities, roles, power, or wealth, and this probably contributed to the rise of Chavin secular leadership and social differentiation.

Archaeologist Michael Moseley argued that the spread of Chavin trade and ideological influence 2,400–2,200 years ago was also related to the drought. Evidence from Chavin de Huantar demonstrates that obsidian use increased by 500 percent during this period. Its source, in the south of Peru, meant it was traded over very long distances.

But it was in the area of textile production that the Chavin cult would have its greatest impact on Peru. Without paper, it was textiles, which are flexible, graphic, portable, and illustrative, that spread Chavin ideas and ideology throughout the Andes. The largest collection of undisputed Chavin-style art found outside the site of Chavin de Huantar is a collection of cotton fabric remains from a looted tomb almost 400 kilometers away on the Peruvian coast at a site near Paracas. The textile remains were not from garments; they were the remains of panels of cloth on which there were Chavin motifs and numerous depictions of the staff god. And they were not locally produced or regional in style or motif—they were completely Chavin. It seems that 2,400–2,200 years ago at Chavin de Huantar, the weaving of ornate, high-status cloth and the use of tapestry, different dying techniques, and dyed camelid wool with coastal cotton revolutionized Andean textile production and spread the Chavin cult as well.

While they may not have been the "Andean mother culture," as Tello claimed, there is no doubt that the Chavin hugely influenced the development of other successive Andean cultures, whose ceramics, religious pantheons, architecture, sculpture, textiles, masonry techniques, and metal work all have elements and echoes of Chavin style and iconography.

See also Uhle Begins Scientific Archaeology in Peru (1895–1940); Publication of *Origins and Development of Andean Civilization* (1942); Chan Chan Inscribed on the World Heritage List (1986); Discovering the "Lord of Sipan" (1987).

Further Reading

Burger, R. L. 1992. *Chavin and the origins of Andean civilization.* London: Thames and Hudson.

Moseley, M. E. 1992. *The Incas and their ancestors.* London: Thames and Hudson.

Raymond, J. S. 2001. Peru. In *Encyclopedia of archaeology: History and discoveries,* ed. T. Murray, 1013–1018. Santa Barbara, CA: ABC-CLIO.

Publication of Britannia: A History of Roman Britain *(1967)*

Sheppard Frere was professor of the archaeology of the Roman provinces at the University of London from 1961 until 1966, when he was appointed emeritus professor of the archaeology of the Roman Empire at Oxford University. Writing in the preface of the first edition of *Britannia* (there were another two, in 1974 and 1986), Frere stated that "advances made during the twenty-five years prior to the 1960s made R. L. G. Collingwood's great summary of the subject in *Roman Britain and the English Settlements* (1936) . . . out of date." Frere was both the catalyst and beneficiary of many of these advances, which included the use of aerial surveys to locate and identify Roman sites; the excavation of urban, religious, domestic, and rural Roman sites; and the professionalization of archaeology after World War II. His six years of excavation and analysis at the Roman site of Verulamium also greatly contributed to a new understanding of the process of the Romanization of Britain.

In 1970, Frere helped establish the journal *Britannia* in recognition of the growth in the importance and sophistication of Roman archaeology. Although the greatest achievements in Roman archaeology in Britain occurred during the 1970s, they are due in part to the inspiration, influence, and interest generated by Frere himself and the forum provided by *Britannia.*

See also Excavation of Verulamium (1955–1961): Excavation of Fishbourne Palace (1960–1970); Excavation of Vindolanda (1973–1994).

Further Reading

Millett, M. 1995. *English Heritage book of Roman Britain.* London: Batsford/English Heritage.

Millett, M. 2001. Britain, Roman. In *Encyclopedia of archaeology: History and discoveries,* ed. T. Murray, 217–223. Santa Barbara, CA: ABC-CLIO.

Frere, S. S. 1967. *Britannia: A History of Roman Britain.* London: Routledge and Kegan Paul.

Publication of Ceramics of Monte Alban *(1967)*

The appearance of *Ceramics of Monte Alban* completed the publication of the first major long-term excavation of the capital city of one of the earliest and most important Mesoamerican states. Jorge Acosta (1904–1975) with colleagues Alfonso Caso (1896–1971) and Ignacio Bernal (1910–1992), detailed the evidence of Monte Alban's growth and collapse, so that it could be compared with data from other Mesoamerican sites, all of which declined toward the end of the classic period (AD 300–700). These three Mexican archaeologists laid the foundations for later work at Monte Alban and for contemporary knowledge of Zapotec civilization.

In 1931, when Caso, Bernal, Acosta, and others began work at Monte Alban, little was known about the archaeology of the Valley of Oaxaca or about the differences between the Zapotec and the Mixtec. As it was, Monte Alban was such an extraordinary site that it took thirty-five years to achieve an understanding of it, not only to excavate it (the excavation of the Grand Plaza alone took eighteen seasons), but also to analyze and compile the data and reconstruct some of the buildings. Like the Olmec and the Toltec, here was a whole other unique Mesoamerican city-state that had been rediscovered.

The site of Monte Alban was the capital and center of the Zapotec civilization of southern Mexico, and it is located in the modern Mexican state of Oaxaca, overlooking the fertile Oaxaca Valley. The name Zapotec refers to a group of languages spoken by the inhabitants of Oaxaca, and it is now the name of the ethnic group that still lives in the area. Monte Alban was founded 2,500 years ago (ca. 500 BC) on top of a specially leveled hill, 400 meters high. The settlement grew in population and power, and its influence spread around and then outside the Oaxaca Valley, where its inhabitants subdued and enslaved those of other communities. The people of Monte Alban traded with the other significant power of ancient central Mexico, the city of Teotihuacán. At its peak (ca. AD 500), the city had a population of around 20,000 people who lived on terraces built on the sides of the hill, surround-

Zapotec architecture at Monte Alban. (Corel)

ing an impressive ceremonial center that featured temples and a palace complex in the classic Zapotec tablud-tablero architectural style.

The decline of Monte Alban during the eighth century AD was linked to the decline of Teotihuacán and the widespread disruption of trade routes across Mesoamerica. By AD 900 Monte Alban's population was only 4,000, and its temples were falling down. In the fourteenth century AD, when the Mixtec invaded central Mexico, they settled at the base of the Monte Alban hill and buried their own elite in the Zapotec tombs.

See also Publication of *The Population of the Valley of Teotihuacán* (1922); Discovery of Olmec Civilization (1926–1942); Deciphering the Dynastic Sequence at Piedras Negras (1960); Jorge R. Acosta Finishes Work at Tula (1961); Publication of *A Forest of Kings* (1990).

Further Reading

Blanton, R. 1978. *Monte Alban: Settlement patterns at the ancient Zapotec capital.* New York: Academic Press.

Caso, A. 1967. *La cerámica de Monte Albán.* Mexico City: Instituto Nacional de Antropología e Historia.

Cobean, R. H., and A. G. Mastache Flores. 1999. Jorge R. Acosta, 1904–1975. In *Encyclopedia of archaeology: The great archaeologists,* ed. T. Murray, 425–440. Santa Barbara, CA: ABC-CLIO.

Cobean, R. H., and A. G. Mastache Flores. 2001. Mexico. In *Encyclopedia of archaeology: History and discoveries,* ed. T. Murray, 878–896. Santa Barbara, CA: ABC-CLIO.

Excavation of Ozette (1967–1981)

The excavation of the Native American village of Ozette between 1967 and 1981 provided American archaeologists and the descendents of the site's original inhabitants with unparalleled details about Native American life before European contact. Excavations were undertaken with the full cooperation of the Makah Nation. Here was a prime example of the benefits of archaeologists and Native American people cooperating to preserve and document indigenous heritage.

Ozette is a coastal shell midden and village site on the Olympic Peninsula of Washington State on the northwest coast of the United States. It includes several locations on the mainland and nearby islands and is one of five Makah Indian tribal villages that were occupied for at least 2,000 years, until the beginning of the twentieth century.

The Ozette site was first test excavated by archaeologist Richard Daughtery in 1967. In 1970 tidal erosion uncovered the remains of a whaling village that had been covered by a mudslide 500 years ago. The mud had not only covered six wooden houses, but it had also "sealed" them and consequently preserved their entire contents. This meant that artifacts made from organic materials, which are rarely found at archaeological sites because of rapid deterioration, had survived. Here were artifacts, such as boxes, baskets, cloth, wooden structures, and carved and decorated items, that had never made it into museum collections before.

Ozette was a multiseason site where whales were processed. Excavation of the site provided archaeologists with a complete material record of daily and seasonal village life. Northwestern Native American coastal cultures subsisted on what the sea supplied them, hunting and catching whales, sea lions, seals, otters, ducks, geese, and shore birds and gathering shellfish.

Ozette presented a unique opportunity to study the Native American coastal village before European contact. In recognition of this, funding for a decade of excavation was provided by a number of sources. The 55,000 artifacts found made Ozette one of the most significant archaeological discoveries in North America.

The nature and success of the agreement between the contemporary Makah Indians and the archaeologists were also unique. In recognition of the Makah's direct ancestors who had lived at Ozette, all excavated material was kept on the tribal reservation in a museum managed by tribal members. Makah representatives participated in excavating and preserving finds. In this case both the Makah's pride in their past and their traditions and the research outcomes for the archaeologists were satisfied. The excavation became a model for other interactions between archaeologists and Native people in other parts of North America.

In 1979 the Makah Cultural and Research Center, located at Neah Bay, the center of the present day Makah Nation, was opened so that the public could see the legacy of Ozette. This nationally recognized museum features full-scale replicas of cedar longhouses as well as whaling, sealing, and fishing canoes. On display are about 1 percent of the 55,000 artifacts recovered from the site.

See also Vermillion Accord and NAGPRA (1989–1990); Fate of "Kennewick Man" (1996–Present).

Further Reading

Samuels, S. R., ed. 1991. *Ozette archaeological project research.* Pullman: Dept. of Anthropology, Washington State University.

Raising the Mary Rose *(1967–1982)*

In 1967 the remains of the great English Tudor warship, the *Mary Rose,* which had sunk in 1545, were located and identified using seabed sonar. In 1982, after fifteen years of study and underwater excavation, her hull was raised and moved to a purpose-built "wet" dock and museum, and the treasure trove of beautifully preserved Tudor artifacts it contained was put on display.

The *Mary Rose* was built in Portsmouth in 1511 and named for King Henry VIII's favorite sister who, for a short period before the death of her elderly royal husband, was the queen of France. During the first half of the sixteenth century the use of cannon on warships required changes in their construction. In essence, they had to become larger and stronger while maintaining a degree of maneuverability. The traditional "clinker" ships, which were built of overlapping planks fixed to an internal frame, began to be replaced by ships built with smooth planking, fitted edge to edge. To some extent this was because of the need to use lidded gun ports that could be opened and fastened, enabling large numbers of cannon to be deployed at the crucial time, but would effectively seal the hull against flooding when closed. The *Mary Rose* was refitted and rebuilt in 1536 with extensive modifications to her gun decks. While no original or refit plans survive, there are records of her carrying ninety-one cannon after 1536, and a number of these were placed on lower gun decks at gun ports cut through the main hull close to her waterline—these were most at risk of flooding if she went about with her gun ports open.

In July 1545 the *Mary Rose* was part of a naval force of sixty ships King Henry VIII assembled in Portsmouth against a threatened invasion by the French. With 60 more ships on their way from London and the west country to join this fleet, the English were still outnumbered by the French fleet of 225 ships. The original fleet was deployed to draw some of the French fleet into the Solent River and into the range of the English cannon. While hoisting sail and getting under way to help another warship, the *Henry Grace a Dieu,* which was coming under fire from the French, the *Mary Rose* suddenly listed while going about. With all of her gun ports opened and her cannon run forward ready for action, water began to flood her hull. The consequent loss of stability and added weight on one side from both cannon and water caused her to capsize. She sank quickly, drowning 200 of her crew, including her captain, Sir George Carew. There were only forty survivors. Years later Sir Walter Raleigh wrote that her demise was caused by a design fault: too little freeboard between the lower gun port sills and the water. Evidence indicates that the lower gun ports were indeed open and their lids lashed against the hull when she sank.

Some attempts were made to refloat her and, when these failed, to salvage her contents. During the former, her mainmast was torn out, and during the latter, many of her cannon were recovered. The weight of her cannon and contents had embedded the hull of the *Mary Rose* into the river sediments so that she rested on hard clay on her starboard side at a 60-degree angle, acting as silt trap. The starboard side and its contents rapidly filled up with silt, leaving the port side and structures out of the sediment and silt. They were eroded by marine organisms and currents, and eventually collapsed. During the sixteenth and seventeenth centuries the entire site was covered with a layer of hard, grey, shell-filled clay, which not only sealed it from further erosion, but also covered any traces of her location. The site was forgotten.

Because of the way she sank, and the quick envelopment by anaerobic silts of nearly the whole of her starboard side, one half of the warship, with its decks, cabins, companionways, the remains of her crew, and thousands of artifacts, was preserved.

In 1836 some of the timbers from the collapsed port side were found, and some artifacts were salvaged by divers, using primitive sealed helmets and air pumps. However, they did not penetrate the surviving half of the hull, and everything they found was from the collapsed port side.

In 1965, local diver Alexander McKee and members of his diving group began to use sonar to map known shipwrecks in the Solent River, and the remains of the *Mary Rose* first reappeared as "a sub-sea anomaly" on the sonar survey. McKee and others were sure they had found the remains of the *Mary Rose,* and they formed a committee to lease the area of the seabed on which she lay and to continue to explore the site. Between 1968 and 1971 volunteer divers, using probes, water jets, and a dredger to remove the top layer of grey clay, attempted to prove that this was indeed the site of the *Mary Rose.* Eventually, they began to find timber, and then an iron gun, and on 5 May 1971, three of her port frames were found—proof positive that they had found the ship.

At this stage the whole *Mary Rose* project became a professional concern, with full-time staff and fund-raisers. The scale of the excavation increased dramatically, and to support this, the Mary Rose Trust was formed in 1979, with HRH Prince Charles, as its first president. The same year the Portsmouth City Council purchased the salvage vessel *Sleipner* from Sweden, where it had been used during the recovery of the Swedish warship the *Vasa*. This earlier and famous underwater excavation and hull recovery would contribute to the *Mary Rose* project in many ways over many years—with advice, expertise, experience, resources, and techniques of recording, salvage, preservation, and conservation. With the *Sleipner* moored above the site, the Mary Rose Trust was able to deploy a full-scale diving program, with divers and finds staff working in shifts.

Over the next few years the remains of the *Mary Rose* were carefully excavated and recorded as she lay on the seabed. Divers used trowels, airlifts, and their hands to gently expose artifacts and structural timbers. The visibility at the site was less than half a meter, the river currents were strong, the water was icy, and the archaeological grid was a yellow gas pipe. Artifacts were surveyed and recorded before being taken to the surface and cleaned, where they were recorded again in greater detail, and then sent ashore to conservators. This process was followed for everything from arrowheads to unopened sea chests, leather shoes and clothes, and cannonballs—20,571 artifacts in all. Between 1979 and 1982, there were 27,831 dives to the site, and it was estimated that divers spent 11.8 person-years on the seabed.

Many new techniques of survey and recording were developed for the *Mary Rose* project. These included acoustic range meters and a new system of direct survey measurement using specially written computer software that allowed divers to measure and record artifacts at the site with a minimum of difficulty. Still and video photography were also used, and the notes of individual divers, more than 31,000 sketches and written descriptions, also provided valuable information for archaeological supervisors.

All of the ship's internal structure, except for the main and orlop deck beams, was removed before the hull shell could be raised. The problems associated with this phase of the project were worked on for a number of years, and in response to contingencies presented by continuing archaeological exploration. Eventually, the remaining hull was lifted a few centimeters off the seabed by a giant floating crane, which continually adjusted a suspended mooring system, one side of which was fastened onto the hull's timbers at sixty-seven points, and which spread the loading force and reinforced the structure

Mary Rose *raised at Portsmouth, England. (Corbis)*

at the same time. It was then transferred underwater into a lifting cradle, which supported the hull from below, while the mooring system kept it stable from above, and then the entire structure—lifting cradle, ship's hull, and mooring/structure system—was brought to the surface.

The *Mary Rose* was raised in 1982, more than 400 years after she sank, and fifteen years after she had been rediscovered. She was towed to the Portsmouth naval base wrapped in protective foam and polythene and then constantly sprayed with clean cold water to keep her wet, thereby preventing decay. She was moved into a specially constructed ship hall in 1983 and placed on display while being cleaned, recorded, conserved, and reassembled. The last timber from the excavation was put back into place in 1993. In 1994 the ship began to be "actively" conserved, that is, continuously sprayed with a solution of polyethylene glycol. The wax in this product will gradually replace the water content of the timbers, eventually allowing the spraying to be stopped in twenty years' time.

Meanwhile, the 20,571 artifacts from the *Mary Rose* were being conserved, cataloged, and studied. The wet and anaerobic conditions in which the artifacts had lain, enabled them to reemerge in an excellent state of preservation, especially those made of organic materials, which are usually the first to perish. However, all of these artifacts are unique sources of information about life on board the ship and life in Tudor times. While original inventories for the cargo of the *Mary Rose* have been found—it is the everyday artifacts and unlisted items that are of greater interest to historians. These include the captain's compass, navigational instruments, spare axles and wheels for guns, seamen's and officers chests and their contents, belt buckles, knives, purses, tankards, everyday ceramics, chess, backgammon and dice sets, beds, cabin furniture, coins, books, medicine, and unrecorded rigging and ordnance details. A museum for storing and displaying these artifacts occupies a building behind the ship hall.

See also Trials of the *Royal Savage* (1934–Present); Excavation of a Bronze Age ship at Cape Gelidonya (1960); Raising the *Vasa* (1961); Excavation of the *Batavia* (1972–1976); Finding the *Titanic* (1985–Present).

Further Reading

Marsden, P. 2003. *Sealed by time: The loss and recovery of the Mary Rose.* Portsmouth, UK: Mary Rose Trust.

McKee, A. 1982. *How we found the Mary Rose.* London: Souvenir Press.

Rule, M. 1982. *The Mary Rose: The excavation and raising of Henry VIII's flagship.* London: Conway Maritime Press.

Publication of Analytical Archaeology *(1968)*

In 1968, young Cambridge archaeologist David Clarke published *Analytical Archaeology,* in which he argued that archaeology must become a science by developing an explicitly archaeological theory based on more rigorous systems of classification of artifacts that mirror those used in biology. An important part of this process of rethinking archaeological phenomena was a concentration on understanding the ways in which theories or interpretations could effectively link empirical observations with an understanding of scale (both in space and time) as a determinant of what archaeologists could observe and discuss.

Clarke's call for a more scientifically engaged, more transparent, and less subjective archaeology resonated strongly with a new generation of archaeologists in the United Kingdom and North America. In Clarke's view archaeology had lost its innocence about theory and about its place in the human sciences. No longer could archaeology stay as an "undisciplined empirical discipline," effectively divorced from the outside world and pursuing narrow problems of typology and culture history. A new dawn beckoned.

See also Publication of *New Perspectives in Archaeology* (1968).

Further Reading

Clarke, D. L. 1968. *Analytical archaeology.* London: Methuen.

Clarke, D. L. 1970. *Analytical Archaeology:* An epilogue. *Norwegian Archaeological Review* 3: 25–33.

Fletcher, R. 1999. David Clarke, 1938–1976. In *Encyclopedia of archaeology: The great archaeologists,* ed. T. Murray, 836–855. Santa Barbara, CA: ABC-CLIO.

Shennan, S. 1989. Archaeology as archaeology or as anthropology? Clarke's *Analytical Archaeology* and the Binfords' *New Perspectives in Archaeology* 21 years on. *Antiquity* 63 (241): 831–835.

Trigger, B. 1989. *A history of archaeological thought.* Cambridge: Cambridge University Press.

Publication of New Perspectives in Archaeology *(1968)*

Following hard on the heels of important individual work, best expressed in classic early papers (1962, 1965, 1967), Lewis Binford and his then wife, Sally Binford, created one of the great conference volumes of all time when they and like-minded "new" archaeologists nailed their colors to the theoretical mast. This was the dawn of processual archaeology, a conscious departure from the culture history of Robert Braidwood and Gordon Childe and directly engaged with the previous work of Walter Taylor.

Binford and Binford's introductory essay (1968b) made it clear that no longer should archaeologists feel their capacity to contribute to the broader goals of anthropology should be limited by perceptions of the "limitations" of the archaeological record. For the Binfords such limitations were the result of poor methodology (itself an outcome of low aspirations on the part of archaeologists). Archaeologists should now seek to explore historical and cultural processes, such as domestication of plants and animals, urbanization, indeed civilization, as their primary goal. Through this the archaeologist's desire to know about the past would create challenges for the development of method and theory, and there would be no mute acceptance of a set of a priori limitations.

At the heart of the Binfords' approach was an expanding set of possibilities, in part supported by increasing amounts of information available to the archaeologists through developments in archaeological science, but in large measure deriving from a strong belief that archaeological theory was for archaeologists to build and that to do this practitioners would have to embrace the logic of science. In many ways the focus on systems theory and lawlike generalizations about the past, and the strong emphasis on methodology expressed in the introduction, represented one side of a classic dualism between the tenets of science and humanism that continue to exert such creative tension in archaeology. These debates have continued since *New Perspectives,* and in a sense the discipline has failed to retain a sense of the wonder and possibility that was expressed in this landmark book.

See also Stratigraphic Excavation in the Americas (1911–1913); Publication of *Introduction to Southwestern Archaeology* (1924); Publication of *A Study of Archaeology* (1948); Publication of *Prehistoric Settlement Patterns in the Viru Valley, Peru* (1953); Publication of *The Evolution of Urban Society* (1966); Publication of *Analytical Archaeology* (1968).

Further Reading

Binford, L. 1962. Archaeology as anthropology. *American Antiquity* 28: 217–225.

Binford, L. 1965. Archaeological systematics and the study of the culture process. *American Antiquity* 31: 203–210.

Binford, L. 1967. Smudge pits and hide smoking: The use of analogy in archaeological reasoning. *American Antiquity* 32: 1–12.

Binford, L., and S. Binford, eds. 1968a. *New perspectives in archaeology.* Chicago: Aldine.

Binford, L., and S. Binford. 1968b. Archaeological perspectives. In *New perspectives in archaeology,* eds. L. Binford and S. Binford, 5–32. Chicago: Aldine.

Shennan, S. 1989. Archaeology as archaeology or as anthropology? Clarke's *Analytical Archaeology* and the Binfords' *New Perspectives in Archaeology* 21 years on. *Antiquity* 63 (241): 831–835.

Trigger, B. 1989. *A history of archaeological thought.* Cambridge: Cambridge University Press.

Excavation of Port Essington (1969)

Historical archaeology in Australia began in the 1960s. The excavation of the site of Port Essington, a British military encampment in the Northern Territory by Jim Allen—then a doctoral student at the Australian National University—was one of its major early successes. Allen sought to understand the site within wider historical and archaeological contexts and argued that the Port Essington settlement was not just a failed attempt at colonization but also a successful, if short-term, display of British military presence in the region that achieved a number of strategic imperial goals.

In 1969 Jim Allen wrote the first doctoral dissertation on historical archaeology in Australia on the site of Port Essington in the Northern Territory. Within the next few years a number of other European settler sites had been excavated for doctorate studies, for student training purposes, or as salvage projects.

It was the beginning of a whole new kind of archaeology on the continent of Australia—one that dealt with the recent past, with European colonization and settlement, and with contact between the settlers and local indigenous people. As in North America, the archaeology of Australia's recent past provided alternative social and local histories to those written by mainstream historians, demonstrating the value of this perspective to younger nations whose European past may have been short, but whose need to come to terms with it and value it was just as strong as it was with older nations. Perhaps these factors also coincided with the graduation of the first generation of professional archaeologists from Australian universities and the growth in interest in recording and preserving evidence of the colonial past, which, as was the case with much of the natural environment, came under threat from urban and suburban development in the 1970s.

Although the Australian Society of Historical Archaeology was founded in 1971, it was not until 1983 that the field had grown to the point that the first issue of its journal was published, and it listed a bibliography of more than 450 entries on historical archeology in Australia.

See also Historical Archaeology at Colonial Williamsburg (1928–Present); Excavation of Jamestown (1934–1957); Excavation of Sainte-Marie Among the Hurons (1941–1951); Historical Archaeology First Taught at University (1960); Publication of *A Guide to Artifacts of Colonial America* (1970); Publication of *In Small Things Forgotten* (1977); Discovery of the African Burial Ground (1991); Excavation of New York City's "Five Points" (1991).

Further Reading

Allen, J. 1969. *Archaeology and history of Port Essington.* Ph.D. diss., Australian National University, Canberra.

Allen, J. 1973. The archaeology of nineteenth-century British imperialism: An Australian case study. *World Archaeology* 5: 44–60.

Lawrence, S. Australia, Historical. In *Encyclopedia of archaeology: History and discoveries,* ed. T. Murray, 114–121. Santa Barbara, CA: ABC-CLIO.

Publication of A Guide to Artifacts of Colonial America *(1970)*

In 1970 Ivor Noël Hume (1927–) revolutionized the understanding of seventeenth- and eighteenth-century archaeology in English North America, and by extension the world, with his book, *A Guide to Artifacts of Colonial America.* It remains the only general source for the field.

Noël Hume came to America in 1957 to begin work at Colonial Williamsburg in Virginia. Over the next thirteen years he excavated sites, explored archival sources, and accumulated knowledge about archaeological assemblages from colonial North America. *A Guide to Artifacts of Colonial America* was the culmination of this research, presenting detailed information about artifact types, common and uncommon, that made up colonial assemblages. It achieved its primary purpose, providing a tool for professionals that faciliatated consistent description and identification of colonial material culture, so successfully that it has been regarded as the fundamental resource in the field. Noël Hume organized the book alphabetically and listed forty-three categories of artifacts, including buttons, ceramics, glassware, and firearms. A fully revised edition was recently released, testifying to its enduring value.

See also Historical Archaeology at Colonial Williamsburg (1928–Present); Excavation of Jamestown (1934–1957); Excavation of Sainte-Marie Among the Hurons (1941–1951); Historical Archaeology First Taught at University (1960); Publication of *In Small Things Forgotten* (1977).

Further Reading

Noël Hume, I. 1970. *A guide to artifacts of Colonial America.* New York: Knopf.

Noël Hume, I. 2001. *A guide to artifacts of Colonial America.* Philadelphia: University of Pennsylvania Press.

Schuyler, R. L. 2001. Historical archaeology. In *Encyclopedia of archaeology: History and discoveries,* ed. T. Murray, 623–630. Santa Barbara, CA: ABC-CLIO.

Schuyler, R. L. 2001. Ivor Noël Hume (1927–). In *Encyclopedia of archaeology: History and discoveries,* ed. T. Murray, 643. Santa Barbara, CA: ABC-CLIO.

Early Agriculture at Kuk Swamp, New Guinea (1970–Present)

In 1966, archaeologist Jack Golson began to excavate the site of Kuk Swamp, located among extensive wetlands at the base of the Upper Wahgi Valley, one of the largest intermontane valleys in the highlands of New Guinea, 1,560 meters above sea level. Here Golson found evidence of the development and use of irrigation, drainage, and agriculture, which he dated to ca. 9,000 years ago. This was a remarkably early date for New Guinea, whose agricultural practices were believed to have originated or been "triggered" by developments in Southeast Asia ca. 3500 years ago.

Up until Golson's work at Kuk, New Guinea was regarded as a Stone Age anomaly. So this early date for agriculture in New Guinea, earlier than any agriculture sites found on the Asian mainland, not only challenged assumptions about the origins and spread of agriculture, but also challenged fundamental assumptions about the development of human civilization. Since the 1920s archaeologists theorized that plant domestication developed in a few central or "core" areas, such as the Near East, China, South America, Mesoamerica, and the eastern United States, and then spread to other parts of the world. In these core areas, plant domestication and agriculture were linked to the growth of social complexity and towns, to the rise of early states, and hence to the development of civilization. The Kuk finds prompted these questions: Why and how had plant domestication and agriculture occurred this early in the New Guinea highlands? What had prevented the development of a complex society and civilization like the others? Understanding the former was thought to provide a basis for answering the latter.

Golson's controversial finds required ongoing work by a multidisciplinary group of scientists. In recent times, work on Golson's discovery has intensified, and the new evidence, comprising calibrated radiocarbon dates as well as stratigraphic, archaeobotanical, and paleoecological analyses (including diatom, insect, phytolith, pollen, and starch grain analyses), was assembled and published in 2003. This recent work conclusively demonstrated that plants were exploited, and some were cultivated, on the wetland margins of Kuk Swamp ca. 10,000 years ago, and that agriculture developed independently in the highlands of New Guinea at least 7,000 years ago. It also proved that two of the world's most valuable crops, sugar cane and bananas, originated there ca. 7,000 years ago.

The transition from gathering and foraging to cultivation took several thousand years, and three phases of archaeological evidence at Kuk illustrate this shift.

The oldest evidence, ca. 10,000 years ago, comprises pits, stake holes and postholes, runnels, and a channel on slightly elevated and better-drained banks of soil. On one side is the edge of a wetland, and grassland is on the other. These finds are consistent with the sowing, digging in, and tethering of plants, and with improving their immediate drainage, and are probably the result of using dryland practices on the wetland margins during a drier period.

The archaeobotanical evidence of edible plants at Kuk expands and complements the archaeological finds. Edible plants such as bananas would have grown in the forests during the first and oldest phase of agriculture, ca. 10,000 years ago, and would have been gathered, transplanted, and tended in their wild forms on the wetland margins. There is evidence of forest disturbance, cultivation on the wetland margins, and microfossils from taro and bananas at Kuk during this early period.

There is also evidence that taro originated in the New Guinea lowlands and was deliberately taken to the highlands and cultivated. Taro starch grains were found on the worked edges of stone tools from this early phase, and from the next phase. Taro and bananas were the most important food staples in the New Guinea highlands until Europeans introduced sweet potatoes 300 years ago.

The second phase of archaeological evidence, ca. 7,000 years ago, comprises disturbed mounds, with stake holes, postholes, and charcoal to create better-drained and aerated soils along the wetland margins. This implies increasing reliance on the wetland for subsistence and efforts to increase the availability of edible and other useful plants by cultivating them. So between 7,000 and 6,300 years ago, using mounds, the planting and husbanding of wild species at the margins of the swamp became more intensive. There is also evidence at this time for the deliberate planting of bananas.

While banana phytoliths are present throughout Kuk, evidence for the deliberate planting, and consequent hybridization of bananas, occurs during the second and third phases of agricultural development, ca. 5,000–4,500 years ago. Kuk has the earliest date for the domestication of bananas, which prior to this, was believed to have taken place in Southeast Asia.

The third phase of archaeological evidence, ranging from 4,500 to 3,000 years ago, comprises networks of ditches and large drainage channels for deliberate, ongoing, and intensive cultivation of edible and useful plants. Some of these plants, such as bananas, yams, and sugar cane, were thought to have been brought to New Guinea as a consequence of the "Austronesian" expansion (migrations across Melanesia from Southeast Asia ca. 3,500 years ago). Evidence from Kuk proves that they were in fact cultivated in the New Guinea highlands for at least a thousand, if not several thousand, years before these migrations, and that they probably originated there. And archaeological evidence from sites in Island Melanesia corroborates that these plants were also cultivated there at similarly early dates, again before the Austronesian expansion.

Evidence from Kuk proves that the New Guinea highlands were a primary center of agricultural development and plant domestication ca. 6,500 years ago, rather than a secondary and passive recipient of these developments via Southeast Asia from mainland Asia. While growth in social complexity and towns, and the development of civilization, can all be linked to the early use of agriculture at other "core" areas, in New Guinea this did not occur, or it did not occur in a similar way. Perhaps highland New Guinea societies, although characterized by high-status "big men," are fundamentally persuasive, egalitarian, and consensual, rather than hierarchical, and have always been so. Kuk makes it clear that prehistoric human societies were not all uniform, and they did not all move along similar developmental trajectories despite similar characteristics, such as the early development of agriculture.

See also Lapita Homeland Project (1983–1990); Dating the Settlement of New Zealand (1991).

Further Reading

Denham, T. P., S. G. Haberle, C. Lentfer, R. Fullagher, J. Field, M. Therin, and N. Porch. 2003. Origins of agriculture at Kuk Swamp in the highlands of New Guinea. *Science* 301 (5630): 189–193.

Golson, J. 1977. No room at the top: agricultural intensification in the New Guinea highlands. In *Sunda and Sahul: Prehistoric studies in South East Asia, Melanesia and Australia,* ed. J. Allen, 601–638. London: Academic Press.

Excavation of the Batavia *(1972–1976)*

In 1963 a lobster fisherman discovered the wreck site of the Dutch East India Company ship *Batavia,* which had sunk in June 1626 off the Abrolhos Islands on the coast of Western Australia. In 1964 the Western Australian State Government enacted legislation (later revised to the Maritime Archaeology Act 1973) to protect this and other historic wrecks—the first legislation to protect maritime archaeological sites in Australia. At the same time a department of maritime archaeology was founded at the Western Australian Museum, resulting in the first professional maritime excavation in Australia, that of the *Batavia* by museum staff between 1972 and 1976.

The Dutch first visited the coast of Western Australia in 1606, blown off course on the way to their great trading post at Batavia (modern Jakarta) in what is now Indonesia. In 1616 the Dutch trader Dirk Hartog left a plate on what is now called Dirk Hartog Island, at Shark Bay, commemorating his landfall. This was taken back to Amsterdam by another Dutch visitor, Vlamingh, who saw it in 1697, and left in its place a commemoration of his visit.

The *Batavia* is Australia's second-oldest known shipwreck. The oldest is the English East India Company ship the *Trial,* which went down off the north coast of Western Australia in 1622. The Dutch pioneered a faster route across the Indian Ocean to Indonesia that took them close to the great and unknown southern continent. The *Trial* went down while taking this new route. After the *Batavia* disaster in 1629, other Dutch East Indies ships, such as the *Vergulde Draeck* in 1656, the *Zuytdorp* in 1712, and the *Zeewijk* in 1727, met with the same fate. The wrecks of all of these ships have since been found.

In 1972 the government of the Netherlands transferred their rights to the Dutch shipwrecks along Western Australia's coast, thus ensuring that the material remains excavated from the site of the *Batavia* between 1972 and 1976 could be conserved and kept in Australia. In 1976 the Commonwealth Government of Australia enacted national legislation (Historic Shipwrecks Act 1976) designed to protect all shipwreck sites for the Australian community.

Artifacts found at the site included evidence of ballast that could be sold when the ship reached its destination, such as a prefabricated portico, ornate silverware, ceramics, and bricks, and of the ship's main cargo—silver coins used by the Dutch East India Company to buy spices. Many of the chests of coins had been salvaged by the captain of the *Batavia* when he returned with help, and those left were old German and Dutch coins that would not have been in circulation but would have been collected as bullion. During the excavation, part of the *Batavia's* hull was found and recorded, and then raised and conserved. It was the stern quarter of the port side of the ship up to the top of the first gun deck, including the transom and stern post. Research on this find revealed that the *Batavia* had been built from the keel up, with a double layer of planks, and the ribs were added later. Modern Dutch interest in this find, and in their maritime heritage, led to a full-scale replica of the ship being built in Holland, which has since voyaged to Australia.

The story of the wreck of the *Batavia* also had an impact on the cultural imagination of Australia. As the first group of Europeans to spend any time on the continent, their experiences have been the subject not only of several histories, but also of novels, and most recently of an opera, commissioned as part of the celebrations for the centenary of the Federation of Australia.

Three hundred sixteen people survived the wreck on two waterless islands. The captain of the *Batavia,* Francisco Pelsaert, all of his senior officers, and some crew and passengers, forty-eight in total, took a small boat to search for fresh water on the mainland. They were unsuccessful, but after thirty-three days they made it to Batavia and raised the alarm. The governor of Batavia gave Pelsaert another boat, and he set out to rescue the survivors. However, it took sixty-three days to relocate the wreck and the survivors. During this time there had been a mutiny and 125 men, women, and children had been massacred. The mutineers were executed, bringing the total number of survivors to only 116.

Further Reading

Dash, M. 2002. *Batavia's graveyard.* New York: Crown Publishers.

Green, J. N. 1989. *The Loss of the Verenigde Oostindische Compagnie retourschip Batavia, Western Australia 1629: an excavation report and catalogue of artefacts.* Oxford, England: B.A.R.

Lawrence, S. 2001. Australia, Historical. In *Encyclopedia of archaeology: History and discoveries,* ed. T. Murray, 114–121. Santa Barbara, CA: ABC-CLIO.

Excavation of Meadowcroft (1973–1978)

Meadowcroft Rockshelter (in southwestern Pennsylvania) is the oldest Paleo-Indian occupation site in North America. It was continuously occupied for 16,000 years to around 600 years ago; the later occupation occurred up to the late eighteenth century AD. The site was discovered in 1955 but not excavated until the 1970s, when archaeologist James Adovasio carried out extensive work there. Features included fire pits, ash and charcoal, hearths, refuse, and storage pits. Seventy radiocarbon samples were dated in the 1970s, and because of controversy over claims for much earlier dates of occupation, a further forty have been dated since.

It is argued that Meadowcroft Rockshelter was a base from which Paleo-Indians hunted and collected and where they processed their food. Its occupation was probably seasonal (mostly in autumn) but continuous. Consequently, it is thought to provide some of the most reliable evidence of all of the major stages of the human history of North America, and it predates early Clovis sites. Stone tools and bone, shell, basket cords, and ceramic materials have been found at the site. The stone tools are evidence of craftsmanship and skill, and the earliest of those found at the site are the earliest securely dated stone tool assemblages in eastern North America, dating to the end of the last glacial period. Thus, they are thought to testify to the arrival of people in this part of the continent.

The site also provides the largest collection of plant and animal remains in a single site in North America. Faunal remains include the bones of deer, elk, bear, raccoon, mollusk shells, feathers, claws, insect carapaces, eggshells, and fish scales—the remains of more than a hundred different species. Plant remains include evidence of the earliest use of corn in eastern America, about 600 years ago, and the earliest use of squash and ceramics.

See also Stratigraphic Excavation in the Americas (1911–1913); Excavation of Fell's Cave (1936–1937); Excavation of Ozette (1967–1981); Vermillion Accord and NAGPRA (1989–1990); Fate of "Kennewick Man" (1996–Present).

Further Reading

Adovasio, J. M. 2002. *The first Americans: In pursuit of archaeology's greatest mystery.* New York: Random House.

Carr, K., and J. M. Adovasio, eds. 2002. *Ice Age peoples of Pennsylvania.* Harrisburg: Pennsylvania Historical and Museum Commission, in cooperation with the Pennsylvania Archaeological Council.

Dillehay, T. D. 2000. *The settlement of the Americas: A new prehistory.* New York: Basic Books.

Dillehay, T. D., and D. J. Meltzer, eds. 1991. *The first Americans: Search and research.* Boca Raton, FL: CRC Press.

Meltzer, D. J. 1993. *Search for the first Americans.* Washington, DC: Smithsonian Books.

Excavation of Vindolanda (1973–1994)

The site of the Roman fort at Vindolanda on Hadrian's Wall in northern England was excavated between 1970 and 1973 and provided insights into the life and organization of a unit of the Roman army on the frontier. The data came not only from the excavation of the seven successive forts erected on the site, but also from deciphering a well-preserved archive of handwritten texts on wooden writing tablets (ca. AD 100).

During the 1970s urban redevelopment in the British cities of London, York, Carlisle, Lincoln, and Colchester necessitated the creation of large rescue archaeology programs. Excavations at Fishbourne and Verulamium greatly increased the knowledge of Roman Britain in the areas of early urban and regional development, the economy, conditions of life, and the impact of Romanization on local populations. Religious sites at Bath, Uley, and

Hayling Island provided new data on Roman and British religious practices. At the same time large-scale aerial photographic work revealed thousands of new Roman sites—from villas to small villages and farms, roads, and forts.

Notwithstanding all of this work, there was still much to be learned about life on Hadrian's Wall, the best-known frontier of the Roman Empire, which was also the most important monument built by the Romans in Britain. The wall was manned by the Roman army for 300 years. After the conquest of northern Britain by Governor Agricola in AD 79 a fort was constructed at Vindolanda, at the site of Chesterholm, on the earlier frontier of the Stangate Road. It was a decisive location, on the major east-to-west road, midway between the modern cities of Carlisle and Newcastle, which became major Roman towns, and fifty kilometers south of the line of the later Hadrian's Wall. Seven successive forts were built at Vindolanda, and along with them, during the second and third centuries AD, a large civilian settlement with houses, shops, an inn or mansio, and military bathhouse developed.

Debris from the military bathhouse included hairpins and combs, evidence that women were also using it. The inn, mansio, or rest house was patronized by officials and the carriers of the imperial post traveling along Hadrian's Wall. Two tombs were also excavated. The garrison consumed large quantities of beef, lamb, pork, and deer, and some evidence of cabbage and hazelnuts was also found. During the third and fourth centuries AD, the fort was garrisoned by the fourth cohort of the Gauls, a mixed infantry and cavalry regiment from France.

The first five forts were timber constructions that rotted over time, requiring demolition and rebuilding every decade or so. As part of this process lay-

Roman towers at Vindolanda. (Chris McKenna)

ers of turf and clay were laid down on top of the demolition debris, and then the new fort was built on top of them. The sealing of the debris in wet anaerobic conditions ensured an excellent degree of preservation of many of the details of human activities. The construction of stone forts above the site also protected it.

Along with the excavation of the forts, between 1973 and 1994, 200 square meters of the adjacent stone settlement site was also excavated. Finds included leather, textile, and wooden objects; metal tools and utensils; a range of floral and faunal remains; and, most surprisingly and importantly, 2,000 Roman documents.

These comprised carbon-based ink scripts on wafer-thin sheets of wood about the size of modern postcards. They are letters, accounts, store lists, rosters, reports, and other military information. They are an especially valuable archive because they contain information about a period of Romano-British history that had few historical sources, and they provide information about the spoken Latin of the first century AD. More than half of the texts came from the residence of the prefect of the ninth cohort of Batavians, Flavius Cerialis, between AD 101 and 104. Some of the letters are between officers' wives, from ordinary soldiers, and even from slaves. Many are official correspondence between cohort officers. But what is also unique about them is that they are truly messages from the ordinary people of the time, something that is not usually preserved. The "vulgar" Latin used by the letter writers was also of great interest to Roman epigraphers and historians, and it has been useful in comparison with other evidence of Roman handwriting from Egypt and with classical sources.

See also Excavation of Verulamium (1955–1961); Excavation of Fishbourne Palace (1960–1970); Publication of *Britannia: A History of Roman Britain* (1967); Excavations in the City of York (1973–Present).

Further Reading

Birley, R. 1977. *Vindolanda: A Roman frontier post on Hadrian's Wall.* London: Thames and Hudson.

Bowman, A. K. 1994. *Life and letters on the Roman frontier: Vindolanda and its people.* London: British Museum Press.

Millett, M. 1995. *English Heritage Book of Roman Britain.* London: Batsford/English Heritage.

Millett, M. 2001. Britain, Roman. In *Encyclopedia of archaeology: History and discoveries,* ed. T. Murray, 217–223. Santa Barbara, CA: ABC-CLIO.

Excavations in the City of York (1973–Present)

As the subject of a remarkable and large-scale urban excavation project in England during the 1970s, the city of York became the benchmark for the whole practice of medieval archaeology in Europe. Its conservation, exhibitions, research, public education programs, publications, and museums all demonstrate the enormous value of European medieval archaeology, not only for local heritage and history, but also as a basis for attracting tourists.

The city of York is located in northeastern Britain. Founded by the Romans in AD 7, who named it Eboracum, it has been a major urban and regional center ever since. At the end of the twentieth century it became the showcase of a thousand years of medieval history and the importance of using medieval archaeology to retrieve it.

The York Archaeological Trust was founded in 1972, in response to increasing development in the city. Excavations began in 1973 and have continued to the present day. However, these first excavations focused on the period of Roman occupation, AD 71 to the fifth century. Roman headquarters, defenses, and a bathhouse were unearthed. Flooding during the late fourth century AD destroyed much of the buildings and features of the original Roman harbor facilities.

There was little archaeological evidence from the fifth and sixth centuries AD, the period immediately after Roman withdrawal. However, an excavation at the Fishergate site, near the Fosse River, provided archaeologists with evidence of an Anglo-Saxon trading settlement, called Eoforwic, which provisioned the royal and ecclesiastic populations of the city from the seventh to ninth centuries AD. Evidence of the remains of timber buildings, of craftspeople working metals, leather, furs, bones, antlers, and wood, and of weaving textiles was found there.

However, it was the excavations of the Viking city of Jorvik, buried deep beneath the present-day city, that were the most spectacularly successful. The Vikings invaded the north of England between the late eighth and the mid-ninth centuries AD, with only Alfred the Great, king of Wessex in the south, successfully resisting them. The country was partitioned, and the north and the east came under the Vikings or "Danelaw" and were colonized by Danes and Norwegians. These invaders brought their traditions and culture with them from Scandinavia, as well as their farming and administrative systems and practices, their "Old Norse" language, and their northern European styles of art, clothing, house design, crafts, and industries. Hundreds of villages in Yorkshire were either settled or founded by Vikings during this period, and many still have Viking names.

The Vikings were able to invade northern Britain because of their ships and their shipbuilding technology. Viking longships carried their armies and settlers, and they used large cargo boats to trade across Europe, as far as Byzantium and the Muslim Near East, establishing trading settlements and creating markets as they went.

The Vikings conquered and settled York ca. AD 866, and archaeological evidence shows that the city greatly expanded in population and wealth under their rule. By the tenth century they had rebuilt and renamed York "Jorvik," and made it one of the largest, richest, and most famous cities in the whole of Britain. It had a substantial population and was full of rich merchandise and skilled craftspeople. Traders from all over Europe, especially from Denmark, visited it regularly. Jorvik was the capital of northern England and one of Europe's great trading ports during the medieval period.

Excavations between 1976 and 1981 at the Pavement site and later at the Coppergate site, part of the main route through the city to the northern bridge, provided archaeologists with unique insights into everyday Viking life in Jorvik. Because of the wet conditions of these sites the remains of wooden and thatched and daubed houses, workshops, warehouses, and shops were preserved and rediscovered, along with the remains of imported goods; locally produced craft pieces; and precious organic artifacts made from wood, leather, textiles, and plants. Domestic artifacts from oak houses built in the tenth century AD comprised cooking utensils, bowls, gaming pieces, boots and shoes, pins, needles, and spindles. Local crafts included jewelry making (using gold, silver, copper, amber, and jet), metal working, antler comb and implement making, leather work, textile dyeing and weaving, and wood lathing. In 1984 the Jorvik Viking Centre was erected on the Coppergate site to display the Viking finds and some of the original site.

Jorvik was ruled by puppet kings appointed by Scandinavia and then by a succession of Scandinavian monarchs, the last of whom, Erik Bloodaxe, was expelled in AD 954. The Normans entered York in 1068 after resistance by its people. A fire demolished most of the Viking city, which was recorded as having smoldered for two days.

Archaeologists have also excavated two castles built by William the Conqueror (1028–1087), as well as St. Mary's Benedictine Abbey, parish churches, a leper colony, and the old Jewish burial ground.

See also Excavation of Verulamium (1955–1961); Excavation of Fishbourne Palace (1960–1970); Excavation of Vindolanda (1973–1994); Publication of *Novogrod in Focus* (1996).

Further Reading

Greene, D. 2001. York. In *Encyclopedia of archaeology: History and discoveries,* ed. T. Murray, 1335–1336. Santa Barbara, CA: ABC-CLIO.

Hall, R. A., and P. Ottaway. 1999. *2000 years of York: The archaeological story.* York, UK: York Archaeological Trust.

Mytum, H. 2001. Medieval archaeology in Europe. In *Encyclopedia of archaeology: History and discoveries,* ed. T. Murray, 861–869. Santa Barbara, CA: ABC-CLIO.

Smyth, A. P. 1975. *Scandinavian York and Dublin: The history and archaeology of two related Viking kingdoms.* Dublin, Ireland: Templekieran Press.

The Garbage Project (1973–Present)

In 1973, Mesoamerican archaeologist Bill Rathje founded "The Garbage Project" at the University of Arizona, using archaeological science to study contemporary urban refuse and develop better waste-management strategies. Garbology, or the archaeological study of contemporary urban refuse, became a subspeciality within archaeology and other behavioral sciences.

Understanding the genesis of the Tucson Garbage Project and Rathje's personal journey from Maya archaeologist to the founder of garbology is made much easier by Rathje's evocative writing on the subject. A gifted communicator and teacher, Rathje was one of the first of a new generation of archaeologists working in the early 1970s who comprehended the value of modern material culture studies for the development of archaeological method and theory. Rathje has stated that he started thinking about contemporary refuse from the perspective of a traditional archaeologist in the late 1960s. It was an extension of his long-standing interest in the Maya collapse, discussions with students and colleagues, and the assumption that if archaeologists gleaned important information about extinct societies from old garbage in sites, then they should also be able to discover important information about contemporary societies from more recent garbage. If stone tools, pieces of pottery, and the bones and seeds from ancient sites were the result of past lifestyles, so too the packaging, food debris, and other discards in modern refuse sites were details of everyday present lives. For Rathje the beauty of such contemporary studies is that they have the capacity to shape our understanding of the present while providing tools for enhancing our understanding of the past.

Over a period of fourteen years the Garbage Project established and refined its collection, recording, and analytical methodologies to the point where Rathje was able to reach an audience far outside archaeology. Indeed, the first reports produced by the project led to changes in recycling and the development of effective waste minimization strategies at a local level. Rathje has observed that the quality of the data produced by the project in the 1980s helped persuade authorities who were responsible for municipal waste management that they needed to know more about what was being dumped in landfills (and what was happening to the refuse after it was dumped) if they were to ensure efficacy and public safety. Since that time the Garbage Project has continued to refine its methodologies and undertake detailed studies across America, and Rathje has taken his message all over the world.

Garbology had been validated as a new kind of archaeology—one that could make an immediate public contribution to important contemporary issues about sustainability and waste management—and our future quality of life.

See also Rebirth of Industrial Archaeology (1955); Historical Archaeology First Taught at University (1960); Publication of *New Perspectives in Archaeology* (1968); Publication of *In Small Things Forgotten (1977).*

Further Reading

Rathje, W. L. 2001. Garbology: the archaeology of fresh garbage. In *Encyclopedia of archaeology: History and discoveries,* ed. T. Murray, 558–567. Santa Barbara, CA: ABC-CLIO.

Rathje, W. L., and C. Murphy. 2001. *Rubbish!: The archaeology of garbage.* Tucson: University of Arizona Press.

Discovery of the Terracotta Warriors (1974)

In 1974 one of the greatest archaeological discoveries of the twentieth century was made in Shaanxi Province, in the People's Republic of China, by farmers digging a well. Little did they know they had located only one part of the vast mortuary complex of China's first emperor. The well digging led to the excavation of the astounding subterranean chambers containing 7,000 life-sized terracotta warriors and their horses from the army of Qin Shihuang di (221–206 BC), part of an extensive mausoleum, which had survived for more than 2,000 years under twenty meters of soil.

China's first emperor, King Zheng, was born in 259 BC and became king of the Qin state at the age of thirteen. He ruled for 36 years, taking over government at twenty-one, conquering the Qin's six rival states, and forming China's first united territory. He pronounced himself the greatest of rulers and first emperor, hence his title Qin Shihuang di. He consolidated his empire, conscripting millions of laborers to build roads, canals, palaces, and links between existing defensive walls in the north to form the famous "Great Wall."

Qin Shihuang di spent a lot of time planning and constructing his mausoleum, beginning when he first took the throne, continuing for nearly forty years, and finishing four years after his death when the Qin empire was defeated (206 BC) and invaded. It has been estimated that 700,000 people worked on this project, which comprised a whole complex of palaces above ground, as well as hundreds of underground chambers containing artifacts, life-size figures of people and animals, and the tombs of the emperor's family, officials, and attendants. There are seventeen satellite tombs around the central one.

The emperor's burial chamber lay at the center of the complex, some 2 square kilometers, laid out like a replica of the imperial city—mimicking his real life so that it could continue after death. All above-ground structures were reputedly destroyed in antiquity. The underground army of terracotta warriors and horses replicated Qin military forces in real life. China's first emperor was also the first to incorporate a mound over the burial chamber—a feature that was to become more common in royal burials. Before this, royal burials were in vertical pits with no above-ground features. Originally estimated to be 500 meters on each side and 115 meters high—the burial mound is now 350 by 345 meters and half the original height. Twenty-three meters below the mound is a 4-meter-high and 460 by 392-meter brick burial chamber. To keep it secret, all of those who worked on the tomb were killed. Chinese archaeologists have found no evidence of disturbance and believe the tomb is still intact.

The pottery figures, bronze weapons, bricks, and tiles unearthed by the well diggers were recognized as being similar to other remains found near the tomb of Qin Shihuang di, a large burial mound some distance from the well, by staff from the Shaanxi Provincial Relics Bureau of the People's Republic of China. Excavations began soon afterward and continued for two years, when it became clear that the terracotta warriors and horses were replicas of the emperor's army, buried with him for his use in the afterlife. Three other subterranean chambers or pits were located, a total of four, representing a military unit—three armies and a command headquarters. Three of the chambers are filled with terracotta warriors and one is empty—perhaps never completed.

Part of a buried terracotta army related to the mausoleum of China's first emperor, Qin Shihuang di. (iStockphoto.com)

Pit 1 holds the main army of 6,000 terracotta soldiers and horses in battle array led by archers and chariots. Pit 2 contains 1,400 terracotta soldiers, cavalrymen, and horses and 90 wooden war chariots. Pit 3, the smallest, was the command headquarters, and it contains a chariot drawn by four terracotta horses, 68 elaborately dressed terracotta soldiers, and the skeletons of animals that would have been used for divination before battle. Altogether there are 7,000 terracotta warriors, 600 horses, and thousands of bronze spears, arrows, and swords.

Pits 1 and 2 are a series of parallel earthen-walled trenches supported by wooden columns and floors paved with bricks. They were originally roofed with wooden beams and straw and bamboo mats. There was evidence that the pits were looted by an invading army who then set fire to wooden structures, which collapsed onto the terracotta figures.

Archaeologists have not yet found the kilns and workshops involved in the manufacture of the terracotta army, but they have identified the names of 85 craftsmen stamped onto excavated figures. These people would have been the overseers—name stamping onto products was a means of quality control during the Qin dynasty—but there would have been many more workers involved on a production line.

All of the figures were made from local clay, sifted, washed, and then mixed with ground quartz. Bodies were manufactured separately, built up using clay coils, but many of the body parts were mass-produced in molds. Heads were roughcast and then features, such as noses, ears, faces, and hair were cemented on individually. Finally, the figures were slipped with clay, and details such as costume and armor were sculpted on. Horses were constructed by joining cast sections of body, neck, ears, forelocks, manes, and tails. Legs were tempered for extra strength to support the weight of head and body, and then after clay slipping individual details, such as saddles and harness, were sculpted onto the forms. They would have been fired at 1,000 degrees centrigrade, with small holes to allow for gas escape. They were then brightly painted with pigments suspended in lacquer.

There are no two identical faces in the terracotta army—hairstyles, facial characteristics, and individual personalities were all sculpted in detail, and they reflect the cultural diversity of the Qin empire and its army—made up of local Shaanxi people and recruits from central Asia and southern China. The average height of the warriors is 1.8 meters, which was probably more of an ideal and larger than they really were. The horses are more realistically sized.

In 1987 the terracotta warriors in the mausoleum of Qin Shihuang di in Lishang, Shaanxi Province, China, were inscribed on the World Heritage List. A major museum was built over Pit 2 to display the weapons and bronze horses and chariots as well as the statues in situ.

Since the terracotta army was found and uncovered, 120 underground chambers have been located and excavated as well. One chamber is an imperial stable with skeletons of hundreds of horses, some buried alive, along with terracotta figures of stablemen and containers filled with grain and straw. Thirty chambers contain clay coffins with the bones of animals and birds—representing the exotic animals of the imperial hunting park with kneeling terracotta figures of their keepers. A small chamber containing a terracotta replica acrobatic troupe, to amuse the emperor, was also found.

An underground armory for the terracotta army was also found. It was 13,000 square meters laid out in timber-covered trenches, containing life-sized suits of armor for men and horses as well as helmets, all made of finely polished limestone plates connected with copper wires, and with sets of reins. The stone armor imitates the leather armor of the Qin army. This pit was plundered and burned following the fall of the Qin empire. A pit contains hundreds of terracotta sacrificial animals—pigs, chickens, and dogs. There is also a chamber containing twelve life-sized civil officials wearing high-ranking headdresses as well as bronze weapons, wooden chariots, horse skeletons, and harnesses. Eight of the officials were scribes judging by their tools—knives for splitting and scraping wood or bamboo slips, and whetstones for sharpening knives. It was probably an administration department for the Qin government. Two burial sites contain the men, women, and children who died during forced labor at the mausoleum. One is a large mass grave filled with skeletons, and the other is a cemetery with 103 graves containing fourteen skeletons each. Among one hundred of the skeletons examined, three were adult females, two were children aged six to twelve years, and the rest were young male adults—the most sought-after laborers, although it seems that women and children were not spared forced labor. A few skeletons covered with tiles inscribed with their names, places of origin, and the reason for their sentence were obviously high-status individuals, but they came from the six rival states conquered by the Qin. Their common sentence was forced labor in lieu of fines. A stonemason's workshop was also found. The construction of the mausoleum necessitated a huge quantity of limestone, which was quarried in the mountains north of the Wei River and transported to an enormous stone masonry workshop covering 75 hectares. Excavations found stone slabs, iron tools, pottery utensils, and iron shackles and clamps worn by convicts.

Excavation continues.

See also Publication of *The Formation of the Chinese People* (1928); Publication of *The Archaeology of Ancient China* (1963); Controversial Interpretation of Banpo Published (1963).

Further Reading

Chang, K-C. 1986. *The archaeology of Ancient China.* Rev. 4th ed. New Haven, CT: Yale University Press.

Liu, L., and X. Chen. 2001. China. In *Encyclopedia of archaeology: History and discoveries,* ed. T. Murray, 315–333. Santa Barbara, CA: ABC-CLIO.

O'Connor, J. 2002. *The emperor's silent army: Terracotta warriors of ancient China.* New York: Viking.

Wu Xiaocong. 1998. *The subterranean army of Emperor Qin Shi Hwang.* Beijing: China Travel and Tourism Press.

Discovery of Footprints of Our Earliest Ancestors (1974–1981)

From 1974 until 1981 Mary Leakey worked at the site of Laetoli, in Tanzania, where she and her team discovered a new, and what proved to be the earliest, species of *Australopithecine, Australopithecus afarensis.* Formally recognized by the scientific community in 1978, *Australopithecus afarensis* was a small-brained, "gracile," and bipedal hominid whose footprints, 4 million years ago, were imprinted into the volcanic tuff, and discovered in 1976, also at Laetoli.

The Plio-Pleistocene fossil beds of Laetoli, discovered in 1911, are located south of the Olduvai Gorge in northern Tanzania. Both Louis and Mary Leakey visited the site in 1935 and in 1959, where they found many vertebrate fossils, but no stone tools. The German paleoanthropologists who worked at Laetoli until the beginning of World War II found hominid fossils, which they had identified as belonging to *Australopithecus africanus,* although as early as the 1940s, others thought they might be evidence of another species of *Australopithecus.*

Mary Leakey revisited Laetoli in 1974, locating a number of hominid fossils that could be dated from the surrounding lava formations to ca. 2.4 million years ago. On the basis of this promising start, Mary Leakey and a team funded by National Geographic Society worked at the site from 1975 until 1981. Hominid fossils were found in strata dated to 3.6 and 2.5 million years ago, and hominid fossils and stone tools were found in strata dating to 1.4 million years ago.

There was some discussion between Mary Leakey and physical anthropologist Tim White about the designation of the earliest fossils into *Homo* or *Australopithecine* genuses. This was later resolved during the 1980s through comparison with other fossil hominid evidence from Olduvai in Tanzania, Koobi Fora in Kenya, and Omo and Hadar in Ethiopia.

These earliest fossil hominids did not have the strong features of *Australopithecus robustus,* although they did have the smaller brains and the apelike characteristics of *Australopithecus africanus,* and yet they were not the same. In 1978 this new species was recognized and named *Australopithecus afarensis.* However, the comparatively short time it took for *Australopithecus afarensis* to be recognized as a new species was attributable to other remarkable evidence found at Laetoli.

In 1976, taphonomist Andrew Hill found a trail of fossil animal footprints imprinted into volcanic tuff near Laetoli. Excavations by Mary Leakey at the footprint site uncovered another five sets of tracks, which she described as belonging to a slow-moving, bipedal hominid. While this conclusion was disputed at the time, by 1978 more footprints had been discovered within a kilometer of the first set. These were more clearly diagnostically hominid, that is, they were similar to those made by modern humans, with a strong heel strike and an arched foot. Because *Australopithecus afarensis* fossil material was found in contexts immediately above and below that containing the footprints, it was inferred that these were the early hominids who had made them, an inference supported by the morphological (muscular-skeletal) evidence of *Australopithecus afarensis.*

There are now more examples of *Australopithecus afarensis* than of any other *Australopithecine,* and it is now regarded as the oldest, dating to ca. 4 –3 million years ago. Along with *Australopithecus africanus* (ca. 3–2 million years ago), examples of which were also found at Laetoli, *Australopithecus afarensis* is described as one of the "gracile" *Australopithecines,* as opposed to the more solidly built *Australopithecus robustus* of southern Africa.

See also Discovery of the Neanderthals (1833–1900); First *Homo Erectus* (1888–1895); Publication of *Les hommes fossiles, elémentes de paléontologie humaine* (1921); Discovery of *Australopithecus africanus* (1924); Excavations at Sterkfontein and Swartkrans (1948–Present); Discovery of *Zinjanthropus boisei* (1959); Excavations at Olorgesailie and Koobi Fora (1961–1983); Discovery of *Homo Habilis* (1964–1980); Discovery of Early Humans in Ethiopia (1966–1977); Discovery of "Lucy" (1975); Announcement of Toumai Fossil (2002); Earliest Stone Tools Found at Gona (2003); Discovery of the "Hobbit" (2004).

Further Reading

Hay, R. L., and M. D. Leakey. 1982. The fossil footprints of Laetoli. *Scientific American* 246: 50–57.

Leakey, M. D., and J. M. Harris, eds. 1987. *Laetoli, a Pliocene site in northern Tanzania.* Oxford: Clarendon Press.

Phillipson, D. 1985. *African Archaeology.* Cambridge: Cambridge University Press.

Excavation of Jenne-Jeno (1974–1998)

American archaeologists Rod and Susan McIntosh significantly advanced our understanding of the archaeology of Iron Age Africa through their excavation of the mound at Jenne-Jeno, located on the upper Niger River Delta, in the modern African state of Mali. During the 1970s and 1980s, the impact of African political independence on archaeology was demonstrated by the initiation of numerous regional studies, which focused on local origins and developments. The sites of Jenne-Jeno (ancient Jenne) and Jenne itself spanned 2,000 years of occupation and, because of the archaeological work at the site, were subsequently inscribed on the World Heritage List.

It was well known, and described in detail by Arab chroniclers, that between AD 800 and 1500 the wealthy and sophisticated Sudanese kingdoms of Ghana, Gao, Takrur, Tegdauost, and Mali dominated the western Sudan, between Lake Chad and the Atlantic Ocean, and the resources and trade routes farther south, and across central and west Africa. During the nineteenth century these Sudanic kingdoms became French colonies, and during the early twentieth century they were part of French West Sudan. Before the 1960s their historical significance was determined by their relationship with North Africa.

This "Arabist perspective" meant that the cultural and political achievements of these Sudanic people were seen to be the direct result of their contact and trade with North Africa. French archaeologists and historians who worked in the region were responsible for this colonial attitude, but this does not diminish their contributions to its history and archaeology. The French identified, surveyed, and protected many of the major sites and compiled a detailed history of the region and its long relationship with the Arab/Berber world. They also began the rediscovery of the protohistory of western Africa and the Sudanic kingdoms and began to educate local African archaeologists after World War II. During the 1970s French archaeologist Raymond Mauny excavated the Sudanic kingdom sites of Koumbi Saleh and Gao.

Nonetheless, until the 1970s the whole sub-Saharan nature of the Sudanic kingdoms was ignored. Instead, historians concentrated on its architecture, inscriptions, trans-Sahara trade, and imports, but rarely investigated the local context and content of these sites. Indeed, a rereading of Arab chronicles during this period reveals detailed descriptions of local pagan cults, fetishes, shrines, and sorcery, which were distinctly West African in provenance, but had neither been noticed nor investigated. It became obvious that if historical sources contained such different perspectives, then a scientific and thorough archaeological investigation and analysis of these sites was bound to come up with neglected evidence about the origins and development of complex societies in the Sudanic kingdoms before Arab contact. During the 1980s the consolidation of political independence in Africa impelled archaeological investigations to answer some important questions about the African past.

Jenne-Jeno (or Djenne) was an important staging post on one of the wealthiest and most famous trade routes that operated across Africa over the past 500 years. Gold, mined to the south of Jenne, was transported to this river town, and then shipped in canoes to Timbuktu. From there it was sent via camel trains to North Africa, and then on to Europe. Jenne-Jeno also supplied the arid inland town of Timbuktu with most of its food in the form of cereals and dried fish.

The excavation of the large, six-meter-deep occupation mound, and the analyis of data by the McIntoshes, revealed that the city of Jenne-Jeno was founded 2,250 years ago (ca. 250 BC) by iron-using people who herded stock; fished and hunted; grew rice, millet, and sorghum; and were also craftspeople and traders. The excavation of another two sites at Jenne-Jeno provided evidence that the city had grown rapidly throughout the first millennium AD until it covered, at its greatest extent, 76 acres in AD 850, when its population was estimated to be around 27,000 people. During this period Jenne-Jeno was surrounded by a 4-meter-high and 2-kilometer-long, mud brick defense wall. After AD 1200 Jenne-Jeno's population declined, and it was abandoned 200 years later.

The excavation of Jenne-Jeno proved that urban settlement and a complex society (based on the creation of enough food surplus to trade for raw materials, such as iron and copper, via long distance and east-west trade in West Africa) had developed long before the trans-Saharan trade with the North African Arabs, which was documented as beginning after the ninth century AD. The idea that the Sudanic kingdoms were the result of contact with northern Africa was disproved, as was the idea that Black Africa was incapable of "civilization" without northern influences. Here was an indigenous, wealthy, Iron Age culture of great social, cultural, and political sophistication, in contact with and influencing the rest of West Africa a long time before the arrival of Arabs or Europeans.

See also First Meeting of the Pan-African Congress on Prehistory and Quaternary Studies (1947); Excavation of Igbo-Ukwu (1959); Southeastern and Southern Africa during the Iron Age: the Chifumbaze Complex (1960–1980); Discovery of the African Burial Ground (1991).

Further Reading

Connah, G. 2004. *Forgotten Africa: an introduction to its archaeology.* London: Routledge.

MacIntosh, R. J. 2001. Africa, Francophone. In *Encyclopedia of archaeology: History and discoveries,* ed. T. Murray, 21–35. Santa Barbara, CA: ABC-CLIO.

MacIntosh, S. K. 2001. Africa, Sudanic Kingdoms. In *Encyclopedia of archaeology: History and discoveries,* ed. T. Murray, 71–78. Santa Barbara, CA: ABC-CLIO.

McIntosh, S. K., and R. J. McIntosh. 1980. *Prehistoric investigations in the region of Jenne, Mali: A study in the development of urbanism in the Sahel.* Oxford: BAR.

Muzzolini, A. 2001. Africa, Sahara. In *Encyclopedia of archaeology: History and discoveries,* ed. T. Murray, 71–78. Santa Barbara, CA: ABC-CLIO.

Discovery of "Lucy" (1975)

During the 1960s and 1970s, excavations of early hominid remains at sites in Omo and Hadar in Ethiopia, by the multidisciplinary International Omo and Afar Research Expeditions, demonstrated that some of the *Australopithecus* species occupied a greater area and more diverse environments for a much longer time than had been previously thought.

In 1975, the 3-million-year-old skeleton of an *Australopithecus afarensis,* called "Lucy" by paleoanthropologist Don Johanson, was found at Hadar. Lucy was the most complete and oldest-known hominid to be found. The analysis of Lucy and of other *Australopithecus afarensis* remains from other sites eventually led to its recognition as a different species of *Australopithecus,* and as the oldest *Australopithecus* to be found thus far. Analysis of the pelvises

Donald Johanson and the remains of "Lucy." (Bettmann/Corbis)

and knee joints of the hominids revealed they were fully bipedal (a conclusion confirmed by the hominid footprints at Laetoli) but had a range of morphological (muscular-skeletal) differences from modern humans. They were more robust all over, and the phalanges of their hands and feet were longer and more curved, leading to speculation that this could have been the result of a semiarboreal existence.

See also Discovery of the Neanderthals (1833–1900); First *Homo Erectus* (1888–1895); Publication of *Les hommes fossiles, elémentes de paléontologie humaine* (1921); Discovery of *Australopithecus africanus* (1924); Excavations at Sterkfontein and Swartkrans (1948–Present); Discovery of *Zinjanthropus boisei* (1959); Excavations at Olorgesailie and Koobi Fora (1961–1983); Discovery of *Homo Habilis* (1964–1980); Discovery of Early Humans in Ethiopia (1966–1977); Discovery of Footprints of Our Earliest Ancestors (1974–1981); Announcement of Toumai Fossil (2002); Earliest Stone Tools Found at Gona (2003); Discovery of the "Hobbit" (2004).

Further Reading

Coppens, Y. 2002. *Lucy's knee: The story of man and the story of his story.* Trans. N. Strike. Pretoria, South Africa: Protea Book House.

Johanson, D. C., and M. A. Edey. 1982. *Lucy, the beginnings of humankind.* New York: Warner Books.

Johanson, D. C., and J. Shreeve. 1989. *Lucy's child: The discovery of a human ancestor.* New York: Morrow.

Phillipson, D. 1985. *African archaeology.* Cambridge: Cambridge University Press.

Picq, P. G., and N. Verrechia. 1996. *Lucy and her times.* New York: H. Holt.

Excavation of Ban Chiang (1975)

In the 1970s the important site of Ban Chiang in northern Thailand was excavated by archaeologists from the University of Pennsylvania and staff from Thailand's Department of Fine Arts. Occupied for more than 3,000 years, from the Stone and Neolithic ages and through the Bronze and Iron ages, it not only provided a continuous chronology for the prehistory of Southeast Asia, but also provided evidence of early rice cultivation and the use of early bronze technology.

Even by the 1970s little archaeology had been undertaken in Southeast Asia. The 8-hectare site of Ban Chiang, located in the Songkram Valley in Thailand's Khorat Province, was occupied between 4,600 and 1,700 years ago (ca. 2600 BC and AD 300). Evidence of postholes, pits, and deep middens with fragmentary artifacts, indicates that its inhabitants lived in pile-built dwellings; fished; grew rice; raised pigs, cattle, water buffalo, and chickens; and made pottery, the earliest of clay tempered with rice chaff, using the paddle and anvil technique.

Ban Chiang's cemeteries were used for 2,000 years, and mortuary remains included diverse ceramics, distinctive styles of vessels, bronze and iron implements and ornaments, and animal sacrifices. Stone and shell ornaments and tools found in the graves were evidence of networks of extensive regional trade. Burial rituals at the site changed around 3,000 years ago (ca. 1000 BC) when numbers of large pots were smashed over interred bodies. Some graves from 3,200 to 2,800 years ago (ca. 1200–800 BC) contained bronze ornaments and tools, but there was little variation in grave goods that would have provided evidence of social hierarchies. This occurred later, 2,500 years ago (ca. 500 BC), when iron and bronze forged differentiating social groups—and when chiefdoms and early states emerged.

The excavation of the site of Ban Chiang helped to fill in the gaps in the prehistory of Southeast Asia. Small groups of hunter-gatherers were living on a larger Southeast Asian mainland, extending further into the sea, during the Ice Age. As sea levels rose because of global warming, the descendants of these people retreated to higher ground and into river valleys, like that of Ban Chiang. These seasonally flooded areas proved to be ideal for rice growing, and rice was the staple crop 7,000 years ago (ca. 5000 BC).

Around 5,000 years ago (ca. 3000 BC) the population and numbers of settlements of these Neolithic, sedentary rice-farming communities increased. At the same time, trade, using the networks of rivers between coastal and hinterland communities, increased. By 3,500 years ago (ca. 1500 BC), copper and tin ingots and finished artifacts were being traded by mining and smelting communities.

The majority of artifacts at Ban Chiang before 2,500 years ago (ca. 500 BC) comprised metal-based socketed axe heads, arrowheads, spears, and ear ornaments. A number of ceramic crucibles, stone and ceramic furnaces, and stone molds for melting metal before casting were found at Ban Chiang. Toward the end of the site's occupation iron weapons, glass ornaments, and elaborately painted pottery were found, and from children's graves only, clay rollers, used to print hemp textiles.

Ban Chiang provides evidence that the development of a Bronze Age culture does not necessarily result in the development of the state, complex social hierarchies, and urban civilization. At the same time the Bronze Age Shang civilization of China was experiencing all that is described here, the people of Ban Chiang, despite the sophisticated technology employed there, lived in villages, and their communities had little social hierarchy.

Ban Chiang was inscribed on the World Heritage List in 1992, because it is the most important prehistoric settlement so far discovered in Southeast Asia. It marks an important stage in human cultural, social, and technological evolution. The site presents the earliest evidence of farming in the region and the manufacture and use of metals.

See also Discovery of Angkor Wat and Khmer Civilization (1860); Foundation of the Indo-Pacific Prehistory Association (1929–1932).

Further Reading

Higham, C. 1989. *The archaeology of mainland Southeast Asia: From 10,000 BC to the fall of Angkor.* Cambridge: Cambridge University Press.

Higham, C., ed. 1984. *Prehistoric investigations in northeast Thailand: Excavations of Ban Na Di, Non Kao Noi, Ban Muang Phruk, Ban Chiang Hian, Non Noi, Ban Kho Noi and site surveys in the Upper Songkhram and Middle Chi Valleys.* Oxford: BAR.

Higham, C., and R. Thosarat. 1998. *Prehistoric Thailand: From early settlement to Sukhothai.* London: Thames and Hudson.

Pietrusewsky, M., and M. T. Douglas. 2002. *Ban Chiang, a prehistoric village site in northeast Thailand, I - The human skeletal remains.* Philadelphia: University of Pennsylvania Museum of Archaeology and Anthropology.

Publication of In Small Things Forgotten *(1977)*

In 1977 James Deetz's popular introduction to historical archaeology, *In Small Things Forgotten,* was published. Reprinted many times since, it exemplifies Deetz's extraordinary ability to communicate the significance and the excitement of undertaking historical archaeology. This book in particular, and others by James Deetz (1930–2001), influenced and inspired the next generations of historical archaeologists.

In Small Things Forgotten has been described as an American classic because of its clever and imaginative fusion of a wide diversity of material culture with written documents to explore the nature of ordinary lives in colonial America. Deetz's goal was to demonstrate that mainstream historical analysis focused only on the written document, which effectively hid from view the bulk of a population that was illiterate. What kinds of understanding could be achieved through such a silencing? For Deetz written documents also carried the possibility of authorial or institutional bias. Far better, for him, was for historians to engage with the material lives of their subjects—the small things of everyday life that are forgotten because their users left scant trace in the written record. These small things, when carefully collected and sensitively interpreted, contain a vast storehouse of insights into life in colonial America.

Notwithstanding the fact that the bulk of examples of the great value of integrating diverse and cross-cutting lines of evidence were primarily drawn from colonial New England, his message has resonated far from there to the borders of the former British Empire. Here the experience of colonists, and of the archaeologists who have sought to understand them, have much in common with New England.

See also Historical Archaeology at Colonial Williamsburg (1928–Present); Excavation of Jamestown (1934–1957); Excavation of Sainte-Marie Among the Hurons (1941–1951); Historical Archaeology First Taught at University (1960); Publication of *A Guide to Artifacts of Colonial America* (1970); Discovery of the African Burial Ground (1991); Excavation of New York City's "Five Points" (1991).

Further Reading

Deetz, J. 1977. *In small things forgotten: The archaeology of early American life.* Garden City, NY: Anchor Press/Doubleday.

Deetz, J. 1993. *Flowerdew Hundred: The archaeology of a Virginia Plantation, 1619–1864.* Charlottesville and London: University Press of Virginia.

Beaudry, M. C. 2001. James Deetz, 1930–2001. In *Encyclopedia of archaeology: History and discoveries,* ed. T. Murray, 412–413. Santa Barbara, CA: ABC-CLIO.

Schuyler, R. L. 2001. Historical archaeology. In *Encyclopedia of archaeology: History and discoveries,* ed. T. Murray, 623–630. Santa Barbara, CA: ABC-CLIO.

Yentsch, A. E., and M. Beaudry. 1992. *The art and mystery of historical archaeology: Essays in honor of James Deetz.* Boca Raton, FL: CRC Press.

Discovery of King Philip's Tomb (1977)

In 1977 Greek archaeologist Manolis Andronikos (1919–1992) discovered an undisturbed fourth century BC tomb in the royal cemetery of Macedonian kings at Aigai, in what is now the modern Greek city of Vergina. Evidence suggests that it belonged to Alexander the Great's father, King Philip II of Macedon, who was assassinated in 336 BC.

Philip II of Macedon ruled from 359 to 336 BC, gaining control of most of mainland Greece by 338 BC. Fortunately, his two-chambered tomb was undisturbed, and Andronikos was able to excavate it systematically, providing a wealth of data and details about early Hellenistic culture.

The outer smaller tomb contained a gold box embossed with a star burst, or "star of Vergina," a symbol of the Macedonian kings, in which lay cremated human remains wrapped in a purple cloth, with a small gold oak wreath. There was evidence of horse sacrifices and the remains of a small altar.

The inner tomb comprised marble doors and walls decorated with elaborate wall paintings of a hunting scene. Armor, such as a cuirass of iron scales covered with fabric; spearheads; butt spikes; the remains of furniture decorated with ivory and glass; and silver vessels were also found around a marble sarcophagus in which there was another gold ossuary box or larnax, again containing human remains. These, however, were wrapped in a gold and purple cloth, on top of which was a wreath of myrtle leaves made of gold.

The size of the tumulus covering the tomb, and the richness of the grave goods inside it, indicated that it must have belonged to Macedonian royalty. The styles and details of the grave goods, compared to other chronologically verified artifacts, dated their manufacture to ca. 350–325 BC. This led Andronikos to conclude that the tomb probably belonged to King Philip II of Macedon, the father of Alexander the Great, and that the remains inside the golden larnax in the marble sarcophagus were his. This was supported by the work of forensic scientists who identified the human remains in the main tomb as being male and mature. Reconstructions of the skull and face proved that this royal male had only one eye. Historians knew that Philip II reportedly lost an eye during battle, all of which seemed to add further weight to the possibility that this was indeed his tomb.

The excavation of this superb Hellenistic royal tomb, and its identification as being that of Philip II, increased the fame of Manolis Andronikos within Greece itself. Modern Greece has always derived pride and national identity from its glorious and unique past, and here was another direct link to that. Macedonia became *the* place to dig in Greece. Some forty excavations were undertaken over the next few years, and there was a consequent increase in academic and popular publications about the region.

In the 1980s Andronikos supported Melina Mercouri, the famous actress and then Greek minister for culture, in her demands for the repatriation of the Parthenon sculptures (the Elgin marbles) from the British Museum to Athens. In 1992 when Andronikos died, he was given a state funeral, like Heinrich Schliemann, and the honor of becoming the first Greek archaeologist to be depicted on a postage stamp.

In 1993 the star of Vergina became the national symbol of Greece, amid claims by the former Yugoslavian republic of Macedonia that the star of Vergina was their national symbol and not for Greece to take. Its status remains contentious.

See also Schliemann Excavates Troy, Mycenae, Ilios, Orchomenos, and Tiryns (1870–1891); Excavation of Olympia (1875–1881); Discovery of Minoan Civilization (1900–1935); Excavation of Gournia (1901–1908); Excavation of the Athenian Agora (1927–Present); Publication of *Greek sculpture and painting to the end of the Hellenistic Period* (1932); Linear B Deciphered(1953).

Further Reading

Andronikos, M. 1964. *Vergina: The prehistoric necropolis and the Hellenistic palace.* Lund, Sweden: C. Bloms Boktryckeri.

Andronikos, M. 1978. Regal treasures from a Macedonian tomb. *National Geographic* 154: 54–77.

Andronikos, M. 1978. The royal tomb of Philip II. An unlooted tomb at Vergina. *Archaeology* 31: 33–41.

Given, M. 2001. Greece. In *Encyclopedia of archaeology: History and discoveries,* ed. T. Murray, 593–602. Santa Barbara, CA: ABC-CLIO.

Excavation of the Hochdorf Tomb (1978–1979)

The excavation of the undisturbed rich tomb of a late Hallstatt (sixth century BC) prince at Eberdingen-Hochdorf, near the modern city of Stuttgart, Germany, was painstaking. This site provided a great deal of detailed information about the Iron Age of eastern-central Europe and evidence of its contact with the cultures of Etruria, Greece, and western Europe and their impact on its development.

The cultural traditions of the late Bronze Age and Early Iron Age of Europe, 3,200 to 2,500 years ago (ca. 1200 and 500 BC) were named "Hallstatt" by archaeologist Paul Reinecke (1872–1958), after an early designated "type" cemetery and salt-mining site on the western side of Lake Hallstatt in Austria. The Hallstatt period encompasses the early part of the Iron Age, just as the La Tène site in Switzerland is used to designate and differentiate the later Iron Age period, ca. the fifth century BC, until the expansion of the Roman Empire during the late second century BC. The Hallstatt Iron Age is regarded as the period in which European "Celtic" culture developed, while the La Tène period represents its efflorescence or apogee.

The term Hallstatt encompasses a number of sites of contemporary and regional cultural Iron Age variations, such as Biskupin in Poland, Sticna in Slovenia, and the Hueneburg and Hohanasperg of southern Germany. Some of these were centers of production and/or fortified settlements during the early Iron Age. All of them, however, have evidence of the development of a strong local social hierarchy, in which the control of trade with Mediterranean cultures was a significant factor in social differentiation and maintaining political power.

There are approximately one hundred "princely" wagon graves, all of which are located in eastern southwestern Germany, within ten kilometers of the mountain stronghold of Hohanasperg. The Hallstatt Iron Age is typified by these rare, rich tumuli burials, despite the fact they comprise only five percent of tumuli burials. La Tène, or later Iron Age burial practices, were distinctly different.

These rich, princely tumuli burials have a number of features in common, including central wooden funeral chambers under large earthen mounds, which were often surrounded by later multiple burials. Items placed in the funeral chamber included four-wheeled wagons, sheet-gold body ornaments, iron swords, furniture, and imported Greek and Etruscan metal drinking vessels. The graves were visible in most cases, being mounds over 10 meters high, and many of their funeral chambers were disturbed and robbed during the 2,000 years after they were built, sealed, and covered. A number were "scientifically" excavated during the nineteenth century, and as late as 1953 the grave of "the princess of Vix," from about 2,500 years ago (ca. 500 BC), was excavated in the Seine River valley in France. This grave contained the largest known Greek-made bronze crater or wine-mixing cauldron (1.64 meters high and weighing 208 kilograms).

In 1977 an amateur archaeologist reported the discovery of a hitherto unnoticed tumulus. It had eroded to field level and was at risk from further erosion and plowing. The tumulus was 60 meters in diameter, surrounded by a stone wall, and contained two wooden chambers, one within the other. The outer oak chamber was 7.5 meters square. The inner burial chamber was 4.7 meters square and 1 meter deep. The space between them was filled with stones, and there was almost fifty tons of earth mound above them. It dated to the late Hallstatt period, 2,525 years ago (ca. 525 BC).

The Hallstatt burial at Eberdingen-Hochdorf is not only the best-excavated Hallstatt princely grave because of the rigorous and modern standards of excavation, conservation, and analysis and the multidisciplinary support used at the site, but also because of the quality of the archaeological information it contained. Unusually, the Hochdorf burial had survived undisturbed. Its wood, leather, textile, bark, and other organic material artifacts were all in good condition, and its grave goods were in the positions in which they were placed when the chamber was originally sealed. The central wooden funeral chamber was divided into two halves. The western side of the chamber contained the remains of a male body, laid out with other items, and the chamber's eastern half was occupied by a long, iron-sheathed wooden wagon, with four massive, ten-spoked wheels and bronze vessels, tools, and horse harnesses laid out on its chassis.

The clothed male corpse was laid on its back on a badger-hair blanket, resting on a bronze couch that was elaborately decorated with scenes of dancing armed warriors and horse-drawn wagons, driven by people with goads or lances. The male corpse wore a textile garment and a large conical hat made of birch bark. On his feet were curly, pointed hide shoes covered with gold leaf, and around his neck were a torc of sheet gold and a necklace of amber beads. Two serpent-form gold fibulae, reminiscent of the "Situla" art of the eastern Alps area, were placed on his chest, and a sheet-gold bracelet was placed on his right forearm. A wide belt plaque with sheet-gold decoration encircled his waist. Beside the belt was a bronze dagger covered in gold leaf decoration. His head was placed on a mat made from woven plant fibres.

The floor underneath the body was strewn with flowers and branches. The couch was of Mediterranean style, similar in construction to Greco-Etruscan divans of northern Italy, which were used for banqueting. The person was between thirty and forty years old and was tall (1.8 meters high), the product of generations of privileged diet, which was probably the result of a hereditary or dynastic transmission of power.

The small cloth bag on his chest contained three large iron fishhooks, a piece of horse-mane fishing line, a nail clipper, and another toilet implement. Near his head were two wooden combs and an iron razor.

A quiver of fifteen arrows was placed over the left side of his chest. A large sheet-iron drinking horn, decorated with gold stripes, hung on the southern wall directly above his head. Eight smaller drinking horns of similar style, but made of auroch horns, hung on the adjacent wall. At the feet of the corpse was a large bronze cauldron of around 500 liters, on a wooden support. The cauldron, which had contained hydromel or mead, was covered with a cloth on which was a small sheet gold drinking cup. The cauldron was of Greek origin, and probably made with a northern barbarian customer in mind; it had been damaged and repaired, while its wooden stand was of local provenance. The inclusion of the large metal drinking horn, large cauldron, and small golden cup on this side of the chamber and in close proximity to the corpse emphasized their important role in his life, and the importance of his sharing food and drink with his community.

Carpets and wall hangings covered the floor and walls of the chamber. On the other side of the funeral chamber the four-wheeled wagon with iron fittings had many items deposited on its chassis, including a maple yoke, pieces of two richly decorated horse harnesses, a goad, a set of three bowls, nine bronze dishes and plates (either imported or copies of Mediterranean-style vessels), an ax, an iron knife, a branch of antlers, and an object with an iron point. The bowls, like the cauldron and couch, had been used and repaired. The bowls, dishes, and plates once again emphasized the importance of sharing food and drink, but these items on the wagon were of local provenance rather than the imported items on the other side of the chamber.

The Hochdorf grave contained a number of different elements that are evidence of the dynamic evolution of local Hallstatt culture at this point during the late sixth century BC and were the result of a number of different cultural influences. For "a closed find" this grave was hardly culturally static.

The most usual form of burial in this region was cremation. The erection of tumuli with central wooden funeral chambers was a more recent innovation, more commonly used for high-ranking males by Hallstatt groups east of the Rhine. However, the inclusion of bowls and a large knife or dagger reflects the traditions of local and early Iron Age male weapon graves, except that the bowls in those were, usually, local pottery, not metal and Mediterranean in style. The inclusion of toilet implements—razor and bracelet—and the placement of a metal drinking service at the feet of the deceased are also features of male weapon graves of this western region. However, the division of funeral goods, and their arrangement on and around the corpse, was more Mediterranean in style.

The couch was a luxurious and high-status piece of furniture. It was decorated with Hallstattian themes, but it was of Mediterranean provenance and style. Such a couch was associated with the Mediterranean rite of banqueting, with the sharing of food and drink. But was it used for the same purpose by the deceased? Or was it adapted and used as a throne or a bed by its owner, given that he was buried on it?

The eight drinking horns are of a type usually found in the graves of La Tène aristocrats, and they appear to be of eastern European origin, or local copies influenced by eastern European types. These were used for drinking beer, and the large iron drinking horn hung closer to the corpse would have been used for the same purpose. The Greek cauldron and golden cup would have been used to prepare and drink Greek-style products such as wine or hydromel, and the size of the cauldron indicates this would have been done for a large number of people.

We know from the excavation of the tumulus that all of the sheet-gold items on the body, the torc and perhaps even the small gold cup, were manufactured on site especially for the deceased. These were all made from the same gold, and evidence of the techniques of the gold-smelting process (such as traces of the metal) was found in the soil of the tumulus.

Other artifacts were placed on and around the body after it was installed in the burial chamber. The body would have been stored elsewhere while the funeral chamber was prepared. The items of greatest social status, such as the wagon, bronze cauldron, and horse harnesses, would have been placed in the burial chamber over a longer period, given that the wagon had to be dismantled and reerected, and the other valuables had to be gathered, stored, and guarded.

The amount of cooperation and management required to build the funeral chamber, manufacture the sheet-gold items, arrange and furnish the contents of the grave, and then build up the tumulus are evidence not only of the importance of the occupant, but also of the continuing dominance of the local social hierarchy by his successors. The inclusion and unusual placement of Mediterranean goods in the grave are evidence not only of the imitation and adaptation of Mediterranean-style banqueting and funerary practices, but also of the high status these goods and practices bestowed on their owners. The Hallstatt princes and their communities traded raw materials for luxury Mediterranean goods—and this access to, and evidence of, the Mediterranean world gave them great status and power within their communities.

The Hochdorf burial provided a unique insight into the life and death of an early Iron Age aristocrat, a dynamic Iron Age culture, and a multicultural Europe.

See also Iron Age Site of La Tène Discovered (1857).

Further Reading

Carr, G., and S. Stoddart, eds. 2002. *Celts from antiquity.* Cambridge: Antiquity Publications.

Cunliffe, B. 1997. *The ancient Celts.* Oxford: Oxford University Press.

Megaw, V., and R. Megaw. 2001. Celts. In *Encyclopedia of archaeology: History and discoveries,* ed. T. Murray, 284–295. Santa Barbara, CA: ABC-CLIO.

Olivier, L. 1999. The Hochdorf 'princely' grave and the question of the nature of archaeological funerary assemblages. In *Time and Archaeology,* ed. T. Murray, 109-138. London: Routledge.

Application of GIS Technology to Archaeology (1980–Present)

Archaeologists have always used geographical tools and methods, from map making and site-catchment analysis to landscape archaeology and aerial photography. Surveying, mapping, describing, and recording data are fundamental to interpreting archaeological landscapes, both surface and subsurface.

In the 1980s archaeologists began using computerized geographic information systems (GIS) to manipulate archaeological data. GIS helped to create whole new sets of archaeological information from preexisting data by reorganizing and reformatting it into new spatial patterns and models of interactivity.

GIS is a spatially referenced database that allows for the storage of a great deal of information derived from a diversity of sources. Its easy retrieval and mathematical manipulation and the visualization of the results within its spatial context make it highly applicable to archaeological contexts. The core of the analytic power of GIS lies in its ability to handle digital maps to create new information from preexisting data. It was originally developed for military use during the 1970s. In 1982 archaeologists applied the new technology to a study of the settlement patterns in relation to the seasonal availability of natural resources in western Arizona. Database management and cultural resource management applications began in the mid-1980s, and by the end of the 1980s GIS was being used in site prediction models.

With the advent of GIS, archaeologists were, for the first time, able to quickly and efficiently link the geographic position of mapped features with qualitative and quantitative information about sites, the spatial distribution of natural resources and human and plant populations, the placement and descriptions of artifacts and material, and the spatial relationship among all of them.

By enabling the management of extensive, spatially related databases, GIS has provided archaeologists with a powerful analytical tool, one that can lead to the discovery of the various levels of spatial patterns in the archaeological record. This in turn can lead to a more in-depth analysis of the underlying principles of those spatial patterns.

See also Publication of *Air Survey and Archaeology* (1924); Establishing Dendrochronology (1929); Godwin and the Fenland Research Committee (1932–1948); Discovery of Radiocarbon Dating (1950); Archaeometry Defined (1958); Thermoluminescence in Archaeology (1960–Present).

Further Reading

Allen, K., S. Green, and E. Zubrow. 1990. *Interpreting space: GIS and archaeology*. London: Taylor & Francis.

Lock, G., and Z. Stancic. 1995. *Archaeology and geographical information systems: A European perspective.* London: Taylor & Francis.

Wheatley, D. 2002. *Spatial technology and archaeology: The archaeological applications of GIS.* New York: Taylor & Francis.

Lake Mungo Inscribed on the World Heritage List (1981)

The Willandra Lakes region (of which Lake Mungo is a part) covers 240,000 hectares of a semiarid landscape in the southwest of New South Wales, Australia. The region has been inscribed on the World Heritage List for outstanding natural and cultural values. In an important sense the nature of the landscape, which has a complex history related to water levels in the lakes (itself a function of climatic fluctuations over the past 60,000 years), is closely related to the ancient human history of the region. It is this history that particularly concerns us here.

Beginning in 1968 excavations in the sand dunes that were formed on the banks of Lake Mungo have revealed that the area was first occupied between 50,000 and 40,000 years ago. The 1968 excavations uncovered a cremated female, and given its great antiquity (now thought to be about 40,000 years old) it has been claimed to be the oldest cremation site in the world.

In 1974 the remains of a male covered with ochre (also now thought to be of a similar date to the female remains found in 1968) were found in the same area. Both skeletons have been carefully examined, and consensus reached, that these are fully modern humans. Indeed, they are particularly early examples of that species. There is also consensus that they provide extremely early evidence of human ritual behavior. Much is now known about the lifestyle of the people who lived at Lake Mungo during the last Ice Age. Detailed reconstructions of the flora and fauna of the region have been undertaken, and the complex geomorphology of the region is better understood.

Given the extreme significance of the region and its human history, Lake Mungo has regularly been seen as a test case for the application of different dating systems to archaeological materials—be they sediments or human bone. In 1999, dates of 62,000 years ago, based on mitochondrial DNA extracted from the bones of Mungo Man, caused a furor. More recently, dates on the sedimentary envelopes containing the burials, derived from cutting-edge radiometric dating technology, have pegged the date for both individuals back to around 40,000 years ago.

Lake Mungo is also significant as a site where archaeologists and the local indigenous community have been able to collaborate in managing this unique chapter in human history. The human remains that have formed such a central part of the story have been returned to the control of the community.

See also Discovery of Radiocarbon Dating (1950); Thermoluminescence in Archaeology (1960–Present); Discovering the Pleistocene in Australia (1962); Ice Age Tasmania clashes with the Political Present (1981); Discovery of the "Hobbit" (2004).

Further Reading

Mulvaney, D. J., and J. Kamminga. 1999. *Prehistory of Australia.* Sydney: Allen and Unwin.

Murray, T., ed. 1998. *Archaeology of aboriginal Australia.* St. Leonards, Australia: Allen and Unwin.

Murray, T. 2001. Australia, Prehistory. In *Encyclopedia of archaeology: History and discoveries,* ed. T. Murray, 121–127. Santa Barbara, CA: ABC-CLIO.

Ice Age Tasmania Clashes with the Political Present (1981)

The southwest of the island state of Tasmania has always been an isolated area. The first Europeans to have any impact on it were timber cutters and miners. Fortunately, their impact was marginal, and its unique landscape of pristine, dense, southern nothofagus rain forests was technically still wilderness in the second half of the twentieth century, occasionally penetrated by hikers, adventurers, speleologists, and photographers, but in reality a great unknown.

By the 1960s the greatest threat to the area came from the Hydro Electric Commission, the state's largest employer, which had so far successfully dammed many rivers on the island. But its most recent project, the building of three dams on Lake Pedder between 1966 and 1973, had created a conservationist or "green" backlash. Although the campaign against the Lake Pedder dams was unsuccessful, the members of the Tasmanian Wilderness Society, the primary and most organized opposition to it, had learned many valuable lessons about campaigning, using the media, and Australian mainland conservation groups and politics, so they were groomed for the Hydro's next project. The great rivers of the Tasmanian southwest, the Gordon and Franklin, the last wild rivers on the island, were slated for damming in the 1970s.

The Tasmanian Wilderness Society, and groups like the Australian Conservation Foundation, believed the conservation of wild places was absolutely crucial for the future. Their values were also becoming mainstream, shared by much of the Australian voting public. During the 1970s, in recognition of this, the Australian Labor government established bureaucratic structures that allowed for the preservation and management of areas of natural and biological significance, such as the Great Barrier Reef and Kakadu, and areas of cultural significance, such as Lake Mungo. The conservation of southwest Tasmania, the last refuge of numerous endangered botanical and biological species, and one of the few significant examples of southern temperate rain forest left in the world, became a major political issue in Australia.

The archaeology of this area, almost a quarter of Tasmania, was unknown. During the 1960s and 1970s, archaeologists such as Rhys Jones and Jim Allen began to unravel the prehistory and colonial history of this small island, but the archaeology of the southwest, primarily because of its inaccessibility, was underexplored. With the threat of damming the archaeological exploration of this region became urgent.

In 1976 stone artifacts of Pleistocene age were found in the cemented limestone floor of Beginners Luck Cave, located at the edge of the Tasmanian southwest. Speleologists reported other caves along the limestone cliffs of the Gordon and Franklin rivers. In 1977, archaeologists Rhys Jones and Don Ranson excavated one of these, known as Kutikina, a site that was to figure prominently in arguments to save the region from flooding.

Kutikina contained artifacts and animal food remains that dated from 20,000 to 15,000 years ago. At that time this part of Tasmania was the southernmost tip of Sahul, and only a thousand kilometers from the Antarctic sea ice. Kutikina would have been only one hundred kilometers from the west coast, and surrounded by a very different landscape than it is today. The whole area was higher in altitude, and the source of the Franklin River was a twelve-kilometer-long glacier. The vegetation around the cave consisted of patches of grassland in valleys, low scrub on ridges, stunted trees and shrubs in gullies, rain forest in protected locations, and alpine moorlands at higher altitudes. It was a freezing, bleak, and difficult landscape for any animal, let alone for humans. Then, about 13,500 years ago with glaciers melting and warmer conditions, dense forest and scrub colonized most of the Tasmanian southwest, and the human occupation of its caves and rock shelters was thought to have stopped.

Today Kutikina is located a few meters from the Franklin River and hidden by dense rain forest. It has a large entrance chamber 18 meters long, and 200 meters of passages with many surface openings. The floor of the cave was sealed by calcium carbonate flowstone, and below this stone cap was the archaeological deposit, comprising 37,000 stone artifacts, some sharp-tipped bone points, and 35 kilograms of bone fragments, mostly from the local species, Bennett's wallaby. Tools included notched and roughly denticulated flakes, small core fragments with abruptly retouched edges, and in the upper levels 160 small thumbnail scrapers and a few flakes of glassy impactite from a meteorite crater, located twenty-six kilometers northwest of Kutikina, known as Darwin Crater. The crater site provided material for the finest cutting-edge stone tools made in Tasmania during the Pleistocene period, and the material was transported to other sites as far as one hundred kilometers away.

At around the same time as the archaeology of Kutikina was underway, senior Australian archaeologist John Mulvaney joined the campaign to save the Tasmanian southwest and prevent the damming of the Gordon and Franklin rivers. Mulvaney was the chief Australian delegate to the UNESCO meeting in Paris that framed the criteria for inscribing sites onto the World Heritage List. He was appalled by the actions of the Tasmanian government and the Hydro commission and by the lack of action to prevent the dams by the federal Australian government, led by Prime Minister Malcolm Fraser. He joined the protest campaign and not only worked to get the area nominated for listing as World Heritage, but also, along with other archaeologists, went public in his defense of it, describing the archaeology of Kutikina and the archaeological potential of the area as "a vital document of human cultural history," and of international significance for human colonization during the Pleistocene.

The discovery of Kutikina and its archaeological significance added even more weight to arguments for preserving the Tasmanian southwest. The depth and richness of its deposits paralleled those of the caves of France during the Upper Paleolithic Age. Here was a whole new Paleolithic frontier, about which scientists knew very little. Aboriginal people had been living successfully in the Tasmanian southwest, like the ancestors of western Europeans in the mountains of France, during the last glacial period ca. 24,000–13,500 years ago.

In 1983 the Australian Labor Party, led by Bob Hawke, won the federal election, and a large proportion of its majority of votes were gained by promising to stop the damming of the Gordon and Franklin rivers. Later that year the Tasmanian state government challenged the legislation the new federal government enacted to prevent the damming, and lost. Southwest Tasmania was saved.

The archaeological potential of the region is still being realized and unraveled. There are still numerous Pleistocene cave sites in its rugged landscape. In the 1980s and 1990s Professor Jim Allen and the Southern Forest Archaeological Project, based at La Trobe University in Victoria, received funding to search for and excavate sites in the region. Warreen Cave, eleven kilometers from Kutikina, was one of these, and it is now the oldest-known site in the southwest, dating from 35,000 to 16,000 years ago. Other sites explored, such as Bone Cave and Nunamira Cave, were also visited by aboriginal people ca. 30,000 years ago.

Archaeologists believe the small stone tools used by these tough foragers provided them with flexibility and mobility to survive in what was a difficult environment. Most of the sites reveal a dependence on the consumption of Bennett's wallaby, which grazed the grasslands and congregated in forest margins. Most of the bone remains are smashed to get at marrow, which contained fatty acids required to help more easily convert the wallaby meat into energy and to increase the blood flow of these prehistoric hunters to keep them warm. The cave deposits may be the result of hundreds of years of visits by people, rather than by sedentary occupation and regular seasonal activities. The presence of the remains of emu eggshell in the caves' deposits suggests that they were used in late winter or early spring.

Sites close to the Tasmanian southwest have also been excavated to enhance the understanding of how far and wide, and for how long, this glacial foraging took place. Did the prehistoric visitors to the southwest's caves spend part of the year on the coast collecting shellfish; harvesting sea birds, chicks, and eggs; and hunting seals? Did they also forage across the plains of what is now Bass Strait?

There were people occupying the rock shelter site of Parmerpar Meethaner near Cradle Mountain in central northern Tasmania, ca. 35,000 years ago. While the terrain and climate were similar to the southwest, the species they hunted and ate were more diverse, but they had similar stone tools. At the sandstone rockshelter of ORS 7 on Tasmania's central plateau, there is evidence that people occupied the site from ca. 30,000 until 10,000 years ago. There is evidence that stone tools were carried long distances to these and other cave sites further east.

See also Discovering the Pleistocene in Australia (1962); Lake Mungo Inscribed on the World Heritage List (1981); Discovery of the "Hobbit" (2004).

Further Reading

Allen, J., R. Cosgrove, and S. Brown, 1988. New archaeological data from the southern forests region, Tasmania: a preliminary statement. *Australian Archaeology* 27: 75–88.

Bonyhady, T., and T. Griffiths, eds. 1996. *Prehistory to politics. John Mulvaney, the humanities and the public intellectual.* Melbourne, Australia: Melbourne University Press.

Cosgrove, R. 1995. *The illusion of riches. Scale, resolution and explanation in Tasmanian Pleistocene human behaviour.* Oxford: BAR International Series No. 608.

The Lapita Homeland Project (1983–1990)

In the early 1980s it became apparent that while much work had been devoted to exploring the settlement of the remote Pacific, and considerable work had also been undertaken tracing the outer margins of the area in which the Lapita cultural complex was found, little was known about the area closest to the "mainland" of New Guinea—the Bismarck Archipelago. Archaeologists Jim Allen, Jim Specht, and others argued that it was impossible to truly understand the phenomenon of Lapita pottery, and the core of the Lapita cultural complex and its distribution, without closely examining the area that was most likely to have been its point of origin, the Bismarcks. No Lapita pottery had been found to the west of that archipelago.

The Bismarck Archipelago covers more than 400,000 square kilometers, and the task of conducting fundamental archaeological research over such a wide area was daunting. Although 80 percent of this area was sea, the goal of building on early studies of obsidian and pottery trade in the region to create a true regional sequence could only be met by a large-scale and multiteam project. At the Pacific Science Congress in 1983, Allen and his associates received sufficiently strong backing from the delegates to pursue such a plan. However, fieldwork on this scale was new to Oceania, and it took another year and a reconnaissance, locating sites on key islands in the Bismarcks, before the project became a reality.

Allen outlined six major questions for the fieldwork and research to answer:

- What was the nature of late Pleistocene/early Holocene human occupation in the Bismarck Archipelago?
- Was horticulture part of the subsistence strategy throughout the Holocene in the Bismarck Archipelago or was it a later introduction?
- What was the nature of ceramic development or introduction and its subsequent evolution in the region?
- To what degree is the distribution of Lapita sites in the region a reflection of cultural preferences, or a reflection of subsequent human and/or natural alterations to the landscape?
- How far might studies of contemporary trading systems in the region elucidate the nature of past long distance and local exchange patterns?
- What was the technological range of obsidian exploitation, and what measures of specialization and production can be determined from these data through time?

(Allen 1991, 3. From Allen, J. 1991 Introduction. In Allen, J., and C. Gosden, eds., 1991. *Report of the Lapita Homeland Project, 1-8.* Canberra, Australia. Department of Prehistory, Research School of Pacific Studies, Australian National University.)

All fieldwork was undertaken between May and September 1985 by 24 archaeologists working on 19 separate projects, some involving survey and others involving excavation. Logistics for the project were complex and difficult, but they were made possible by using a 65-foot yacht that transported and supplied the archaeological teams around the research area.

At the conclusion of fieldwork the organizers began a series of Lapita workshops that continue to this day as data are generated. Analysis revealed archaeological information of great significance. Here are just two highlights.

As a result of excavations in New Ireland, the antiquity of human settlement of the Pacific east of New Guinea was quadrupled, and the very high antiquity of trading systems (especially in obsidian, but also in terrestrial animals) has been established. Overall, it is now clearly understood that the history of the Lapita interaction sphere from around 3,500 years ago is very much more complex (and interesting) than was at first thought. The Lapita Homeland Project achieved many of the goals set by its proponents, but perhaps the most fundamental achievement has been the massive boost it gave to our search for understanding the human history of the Pacific, a search that continues unabated.

See also Foundation of the Indo-Pacific Prehistory Association (1929–1931); Discovery of Radiocarbon Dating (1950); Thermoluminescence in Archaeology (1960–Present); Discovering the Pleistocene in Australia (1962); Dating the Settlement of New Zealand (1991).

Further Reading

Allen, J. 2001. Papua New Guinea and Melanesia. In *Encyclopedia of archaeology: History and discoveries,* ed. T. Murray, 999–1006. Santa Barbara, CA: ABC-CLIO.

Allen, J., C. Gosden, and J. P. White, eds., 1989. Human Pleistocene adaptations in the tropical island Pacific: recent evidence from New Ireland, a Greater Australia outlier. *Antiquity* 63: 548–561.

Kirch, P. V. 2001. Polynesia. In *Encyclopedia of archaeology: History and discoveries,* ed. T. Murray, 1045–1056. Santa Barbara, CA: ABC-CLIO.

Kirch, P. V., and T. L. Hunt. 1988. The spatial and temporal boundaries of Lapita. In *Archaeology of the Lapita Cultural Complex: a critical view,* eds. P. V. Kirch and T. L. Hunt, 9–31. Seattle, WA: Thomas Burke Memorial Museum Research Report No. 5.

Discovery of Lindow Man (1984)

In 1984 the body of a man preserved in peat was discovered in Cheshire, England. Conserved in his entirety, the body of Lindow man provided archaeologists with a wide range of information about his life and death more than 2,000 years ago.

Approximately seven hundred hundred human bodies have been discovered in the peat bogs of northern Europe, but few survive intact, primarily because of the circumstances of their discovery, usually as the result of peat-cutting machinery. Peat bogs provide waterlogged, anaerobic, and antibacterial conditions that preserve human soft tissue. Bodies of men and women have been found, but no children's bodies have yet been found. Many have been dated to medieval times by their clothing and accompanying artifacts, but the most interesting and best-preserved bodies date between from 2,800 years ago (ca. 800 BC) to AD 200, from the period of the European Iron Age until the Roman Empire. The most famous of these intact bodies are the Tollund, Grauballe, and Lindow men, named after the peat bogs from which they were recovered. While some of the bog bodies were the result of accidental deaths, some are wetland burials, some are murder victims hidden in bogs, and some would have been suicide burials excluded from Christian graveyards. A few are thought to have been ritual burials and/or executions.

The conservation and analysis of these bog bodies was pioneered by Danish archaeologist Hans Helbaek, who worked on both the Tollund and Graubolle men, who were found in peat bogs in central Jutland in Denmark. Tollund man, discovered in 1950, died 2,100 years ago (ca. 100 BC). Based on the account of the Roman historian Tacitus, who wrote about the practices of the Germanic tribes of the north in his *Germania,* we know that "cowards, shirkers and sodomites are pressed down under a wicker hurdle into the slimy mud of a bog," while "traitors and deserters," he also noted, "are hanged on trees."

It is possible that Tollund man was a criminal or a victim of ritual sacrifice. He was naked except for a pointy leather cap, and he had been strangled by the noose around his neck before being thrown into the bog. His last meal was a gruel of barley, linseed, knotweed, dock, and camomile seeds. Graubolle man was discovered in 1952. His throat had been cut, and he had been hit on the head as well. His stomach contents comprised sixty-three varieties of seeds, such as rye, buttercup, nightshade, clover, and spelt, and he had died 2,070 years ago (ca. 70 BC).

Helbaek's analysis of food residues laid the foundations for their continued use and refinement by archaeologists. Unfortunately, techniques of preservation were not so successful in the 1950s, and only the heads of the Tollund and Graubolle men survive in museums today.

Lindow man was luckier to be unearthed later in the twentieth century—when techniques of freeze-drying had improved, and he survives as he was found, because of the work of the conservation staff of the British Museum. Lindow man, however, had one leg missing—probably because of peat-cutting machines, which destroyed another two to three bog bodies lying near his before they were turned off.

Lindow man was approximately twenty-five years old when he died from being struck on the back of the head twice, garroted, and his throat cut. Perhaps he too was a ritual sacrifice. He lived during the first and second centuries AD. He was found naked except for a fur armband. As with the other bog bodies, everything was analyzed, from the species of fur on the band and the leather of the garrotte down to his blood group, the insects and pollen in the peat surrounding his body, and the contents of his last meal. His stomach contents comprised the remains of cereals, such as emmer, wheat, barley, and oats.

The decline in wetland areas across northern Europe, and the wide use of peat-cutting machinery mean that there will be even fewer bog bodies to analyze in the future.

See also Discovery of "Otzi the Iceman" (1991).

Further Reading

Greig, J. 2001. Palynology in archaeological research. In *Encyclopedia of archaeology: History and discoveries,* ed. T. Murray, 988–991. Santa Barbara, CA: ABC-CLIO.

Stead, I., J. Bourke, and D. Brothwell, eds. 1986. *Lindow man, the body in the bog.* London: British Museum.

Turner, R., and R. G. Scaife. 1995. *Bog bodies: New discoveries and new perspectives.* London: Published for the Trustees of the British Museum by British Museum Press.

Finding the Titanic *(1985–Present)*

The *Titanic* struck an iceberg at 11:40 p.m. on 14 April 1912. At 46,328 gross tons, she was the largest ship afloat. On her maiden voyage from Southhampton to New York she carried 2,224 passengers. Two and a half hours after striking the iceberg the *Titanic* sank, and 1,522 people died. Locating the wreck of the *Titanic* proved to be a major challenge after she sank. Raising her, or simply retrieving relics from the wreck, sunk in 13,000 feet of water, was an even more daunting task.

The first challenge, locating the wreck, was accomplished in September 1985 when a joint U.S.-French expedition found her southeast of Newfoundland. The driving force behind the expedition was Robert D. Ballard (1942–), a long-time advocate of using remote sensing, instead of manned submersibles, to undertake research and exploration at great ocean depths. Ballard, who trained as a geologist, was involved in developing systems that would allow scientists to visit great depths via robots and fiber-optic imaging equipment. This system, developed in conjunction with the U.S. Navy, was called *Argo*.

Ballard and a team from Woods Hole took *Argo* aboard the U.S. Navy research ship *Knorr* and met with a French team from Research Institute for

The deep-sea camera sled Argo, *seen here being launched from the* Knorr *in 1985, was the first vessel to find the* Titanic. *(Ralph White/Corbis)*

Exploitation of the Sea (IFREMER). *Argo* was deployed, and soon after succeeded where so many others had failed. A second vehicle, *Angus,* took still photos of the wreck.

Finding the *Titanic* wreck was one task, albeit vitally important, but dealing with its consequences has proved to be quite another. Here the line between science and the incentives of commercial salvage became hard to hold as Ballard and many others voiced their opposition to the disturbance of what is, in effect, a mass grave. Nonetheless, his partners from IFREMER conducted a salvage campaign in 1987, thereby flouting the U.S. Congress, which had acted to preserve the wreck. The French argued that as the *Titanic* was in international waters it was outside U.S. jurisdiction. Using the three-man sub *Nautile,* the French retrieved artifacts that were later put up for sale. They argued that (unlike Woods Hole) theirs was a commercial operation and that some financial recompense for the scale of their investment of time and expertise was only right and proper.

Since then other parties have joined in the search for salvage, and the integrity of the *Titanic* is under increasing threat.

See also Trials of the *Royal Savage* (1934–Present); Excavation of a Bronze Age Ship at Cape Gelidonya (1960); Raising the *Vasa* (1961); Raising the *Mary Rose* (1967–1982).

Further Reading

Ballard, R. D. 1995. *The discovery of the Titanic.* Toronto, Canada: Madison Press Books.

Ballard, R. D. 2004. *Return to Titanic.* Washington, DC: National Geographic.

Bass, G. 2001. Nautical archaeology. In *Encyclopedia of archaeology: History and discoveries,* ed. T. Murray, 910–918. Santa Barbara, CA: ABC-CLIO.

Chan Chan Inscribed on the World Heritage List (1986)

In 1986 the site of Chan Chan in Peru, the world's largest mud brick city and the largest pre-Columbian city in South America, was inscribed on the World Heritage List. At the same time it was also placed on the World Heritage List in Danger, to protect it from looting and mining.

Archaeologists began to excavate the remains of this capital city of the Chimu civilization in the 1970s. Work has revealed 600 years of its history, and much information about its occupants, the last 30,000 of whom were conquered and enslaved by the Incas shortly before the Spanish arrived.

Chan Chan is located in the Moche Valley of Peru, on the northern Pacific coast near the modern city of Trujillo, 300 kilometers north of Lima. Excavation of the site by American archaeologists Michael Moseley and Carol J. Mackey began in 1969, and it continues under the Peruvian Instituto Nacional de Cultura. Established ca. AD 850, Chan Chan flourished until 1470, eventually covering more than 20 square kilometers, with a 6-square-kilometer civic center. At its peak the Chimu culture controlled 600 kilometers, or almost two thirds, of the coast of Peru.

The city of Chan Chan comprised different kinds of architecture and constuction material, according to its inhabitants' occupations and class. The rulers of Chan Chan were a minority of around 6,000 who occupied huge rectangular ciudalelas, or fortresses, in the city's center. These elite residences contained palaces, temples, tombs, gardens, wells, offices, servants' quarters, and storage areas. Archaeologists uncovered the remains of about a dozen ciudalelas built by slave labor. The slaves mixed clay, sand, and silt to make thousands of mud bricks, to construct walls, some 10 meters high.

Each ciudalela was finished with a coating of mud into which patterns were incised. Interior walls were decorated with friezes of all forms of sea life, land and forest animals, and geometric shapes.

Each successive ruler of the Chimu built his own ciudalela, and each new ruler built one during his reign while the rest of the family either remained in the old ruler's or joined the nobility or aristocracy. The largest part of these fortress-like compounds was a secluded, centrally located platform mausoleum of one or two stories, with multiple interior chambers and cells, including the main tomb, and a shrine complex for primary and secondary burials of members of the elite. Looters left enough evidence in these tombs for archaeologists to ascertain their contents, which comprised shells, llama bones, the bones of young women, and fine textiles, pottery, and other elite goods. We know from Spanish records that the mausolea also contained quantities of precious metals.

Some thirty similar but much smaller compounds with lower walls were built nearby for officials and the nobility. Other inhabitants, primarily craftspeople, lived in densely packed barrios around the ciudalelas. These had small patios and irregular rooms constructed from cane. It has been estimated that at its peak some 26,000 Chimu craftspeople produced fine textiles; jewelry; gold, silver, and copper objects; and pottery; and 3,000 of them directly serviced the ruling elite and resided beside the ciudalelas. Agricultural workers lived on their farms or in villages scattered across Chimu territory. Chan Chan was the center for craft production for the Chimu's empire, and it produced, stored, and displayed great wealth. After their conquest of Chan Chan, the Inca transferred many of these craftspeople to their capital at Cuzco.

The Chimu kingdom was the largest state to develop in Peru before that of the Incas, and its cultural antecedents were the local and earlier Moche and Huari cultures. The Chimu spoke a now extinct language called Yunca, but had no form of writing. Their economy was based on intensive agriculture, supported by intricate irrigation systems. Chan Chan's fortunes were linked to the availability of water, and the city had many large wells that tapped into the water table. As agriculture expanded and intensified, the water table was elevated—and the city grew toward higher ground and deeper and deeper wells had to be dug. A vast canal system was built above the city to bring water to it and to irrigate surrounding agricultural land. A flood in AD 1100, thought to have been the outcome of an El Niño event, damaged this system and much of Chan Chan itself. The subsequent drought caused a dramatic decline in population growth and in farming around the city.

Chimu territorial expansion seemed to have had an impact on the politics of its elite. Archaeological evidence from the excavation of the ciudalelas, in the form of differences in tomb construction, points to a power struggle between junior and senior sections of royal kin groups.

By the fifteenth century AD two dominant groups were competing with each other for the domination of Peru—the Chimu and the Inca. The protracted drought experienced by the Chimu people probably tipped the balance of power in favor of the Inca—who were in turn conquered by the Spanish.

See also Uhle Begins Scientific Archaeology in Peru (1895–1940); Machu Picchu Found (1911); Publication of *Origin and Development of Andean Civilization* (1942); Publication of *Prehistoric Settlement Patterns in the Viru Valley, Peru* (1953); Excavation of Chavin de Huantar (1966–1980); Discovering the "Lord of Sipan" (1987).

Further Reading

Hall, S. 1992. *Cattigara: Legend and history.* New York: Vantage Press.

Moseley, M. E. 1992. *The Incas and their ancestors.* London: Thames and Hudson.

Moseley, M. E., and K. C. Day, eds. 1982. *Chan Chan, Andean desert city.* Albuquerque: University of New Mexico Press.

Raymond, J. S. 2001. Peru. In *Encyclopedia of archaeology: History and discoveries,* ed. T. Murray, 1013–1018. Santa Barbara, CA: ABC-CLIO.

Full documentation of the nomination of Chan Chan to the World Heritage List can be found at the UNESCO Web site: http://whc.unesco.org/pg.cfm?cid=31&id_site=366.

Ironbridge Gorge Inscribed on the World Heritage List (1986)

In 1986, two miles of the Ironbridge Gorge in the Midlands of Britain was inscribed on the World Heritage List because of its value as a testament to the importance of the Industrial Revolution in human history.

The steep valley of Ironbridge Gorge is home to a sequence of historic sites and buildings involved in iron making and producing fine china, tiles, and clay tobacco pipes. It also contains the essential elements of the industrial revolution—canals, railways, inclined wharves, and an iron bridge over the Severn River. Nationally important collections of machines, fine china, tiles, and iron work, and examples of these first modern mass-produced articles, are stored and displayed in the preserved historic factories and houses at the site.

At the center of the Ironbridge Gorge Museum landscape is the site of Coalbrookdale, where in 1709 Abraham Darby I developed the process of smelting iron with coke instead of with charcoal. This process revolutionized iron making. The Darby family continued to smelt iron at the site during the next two centuries, and expanded production from cooking pots to wrought iron, cast iron steam engine cylinders, bridges (such as the one spanning the museum site, after which it is named), and by the nineteenth century, decorative and intricate metalwork that was exported all over the world.

Coalbrookdale has a number of restored historic buildings that were part of the Coalbrookdale Company. These include the Coalbrookdale Museum of Iron and the Darby Furnace, as well as the Darby houses, which evoke the lives of the industrial community at the site between 1715 and 1900.

Other sites at the gorge include the following:

- Blists Hill Victorian Town, one of the largest open-air museums in Britain, is a historical re-creation of the shops, back streets, gardens, offices, pubs, and factories of a nineteenth century industrial town. It even contains a working foundry and iron mill.
- The Coalport China Museum displays the national collections of Caughley and Coalport china in the restored building of the old Coalport china works and describes the work of the factory employees.
- The Tar Tunnel, the source of a natural bitumen that oozes from the walls, was discovered 200 years ago and is located close by, beside the Shropshire Canal.
- The Old Severn Warehouse, built in 1834, was the Coalbrookdale Company's warehouse and is now the Museum of the Gorge. An exhibition of its history is featured.
- The Iron Bridge, cast in 1779, and the symbol of the iron-led revolution that began in the gorge, still spans the river. An exhibition of its history is in the original tollhouse.
- The Jackfield Tile Museum displays collections of decorative tiles and ceramics.
- The Brosely Pipeworks, two miles from the Iron Bridge, was the site of one of the most prolific clay-tobacco-pipe-making factories in Britain, and its products were exported all over the world. Production finished in the 1950s, and the pipe works reopened as a museum in 1996.

See also Rebirth of Industrial Archaeology (1955).

Further Reading

Clark, C. M. 1993. *English Heritage book of Ironbridge Gorge.* London: Batsford.

Hayman, R., W. Horton, and S. White. 1999. *Archaeology and conservation in Ironbridge.* York, UK: Council for British Archaeology.

Trinder, B. 2001. Industrial archaeology. In *Encyclopedia of archaeology: History and discoveries,* ed. T. Murray, 661–669. Santa Barbara, CA: ABC-CLIO.

Discovering the "Lord of Sipan" (1987)

In 1987 grave robbers unearthed a spectacular burial near the village of Sipan in northern Peru. Archaeologist Walter Alva was called in to salvage what turned out to be the burial of a Moche lord—and the richest tomb so far found in Peru since Pizarro's conquest. Until the Sipan excavation, the little that was known about the Moche civilization (ca. first to seventh centuries AD) was the result of studying their pottery.

The name Moche derives from the Moche Valley on the Peruvian northern coast, where evidence of the architecture and pottery of this distinctive culture was first found in the early twentieth century. It was clear, even then, that the Moche were influenced by the earlier Chavin culture, and that they in turn influenced their successors, the Chimu. The large pyramids erected by the Moche, first at Huaca del Sol, and later, further inland at Galindo and Pampa Grande, map the spread of their territorial control before the end of their political power.

The Moche built irrigation systems to intensively farm the surrounding coastal river valleys, producing beans, maize, cotton, and other crops to feed their large population. They also fished using reed boats and nets, hunted deer, domesticated ducks, and used llamas as pack animals and for their wool. The reasons for the demise of the Moche are part of ongoing debates about the rise and fall of many other Andean civilizations from prehistory until the Spanish conquest: Was it because of a long drought caused by an El Niño event? Was it due to a rebellion against its small ruling elite? Or was it the consequence of the development of a rival state (in the case of the Moche or the Huari)? Or was it because of all of these reasons?

Until the site of Sipan was excavated, almost everything archaeologists knew about the Moche came from their wonderful sculpted ceramic vessels and painted pottery. These provided details of the Moche's everyday lives and provided evidence of their social structure in their depictions of Moche rulers and lords, religious ceremonies, weapons, and battles.

The excavation of Sipan began in 1987 as a rescue project as the site was under threat from extensive looting. A few months later Walter Alva and his Peruvian colleagues were rewarded with the sensational discovery of the tomb of the "Lord of Sipan." The discovery not only galvanized the world of American archaeology, but it also led to technical support from Germany and Spain for the conservation of large quantities of precious metals, jewels, ceramics, and carved wood found in the tomb. Conserved excavated material made significant additions to the Brüning Museum, in nearby Lambayeque.

The Lord of Sipan was buried in a wooden sarcophagus. At his head were found the skeletons of two young women, and at his sides the skeletons of a dog and two llamas. The skeleton of a young man carrying a shield was located nearby. The Lord of Sipan's corpse was covered with gold, silver, copper, and jewels. His decoration included gold necklaces, and his skull rested on a large plate made of gold.

Two years later, and close to this tomb, further excavation revealed the tombs of "El Sacerdote" (The Priest) and "El Viejo Señor de Sipan" (The Old Lord of Sipan), the excavation and analysis of which have continued to expand our understanding of Moche life more than 1,700 years ago.

See also Chan Chan Inscribed on the World Heritage List (1986)

Further Reading

Kirkpatrick, S. D. 1993. *Lords of Sipan: A tale of pre-Inca tombs, archaeology, and crime.* New York: H. Holt.

Longhena, M., and W. Alva. 1999. *Splendors of the ancient Andes.* London: Thames and Hudson.

Moseley, M. E. 1992. *The Incas and their ancestors.* London: Thames and Hudson.

Raymond, J. S. 2001. Peru. In *Encyclopedia of archaeology: History and discoveries,* ed. T. Murray, 1013–1018. Santa Barbara, CA: ABC-CLIO.

The Vermillion Accord and NAGPRA (1989–1990)

In 1989 the World Archaeological Congress staged an Inter-Congress in Vermillion, South Dakota. The key result of that meeting was the Vermillion Accord on Human Remains. The accord expressed the aspirations of indigenous groups from around the world with respect to the activities of archaeologists and physical anthropologists. These were contained in six principles:

1. Respect for the mortal remains of the dead shall be accorded to all, irrespective of origin, race, religion, nationality, custom, and tradition.

2. Respect for the wishes of the dead concerning disposition shall be accorded whenever possible, reasonable, and lawful, when they are known or can be reasonably inferred.
3. Respect for the wishes of the local community and of the relatives or guardians of the dead shall be accorded whenever possible, reasonable, and lawful.
4. Respect for the scientific research value of skeletal, mummified, and other human remains (including fossil hominids) shall be accorded when such value is demonstrated to exist.
5. Agreement on the disposition of fossil, skeletal, mummified, and other remains shall be reached by negotiation on the basis of mutual respect for the legitimate concerns of communities for the proper disposition of their ancestors, as well as the legitimate concerns of science and education.
6. The express recognition that the concerns of various ethnic groups, as well as those of science, are legitimate and to be respected will permit acceptable agreements to be reached and honored.

The Vermillion Accord also sought to introduce important changes to the relationships between indigenous peoples and the cultural institutions (such as the Smithsonian Institution) that had long been based on a lack of consideration of the aspirations and interests of indigenous communities, matched by a stronger focus on preserving human remains and artifacts for scientific study and popular edification.

The advances made at Vermillion were soon followed by one of the most significant pieces of federal legislation, the Native American Graves Protection and Repatriation Act (NAGPRA) of 1990. NAGPRA was a concrete statement about the need to find balance between the interests of indigenous peoples in the maintenance and revitalization of their cultures (and the assumption of control over culture and identity) and those of wider American society (including those of science and the major cultural institutions). Given the highly sensitive nature of human remains, NAGPRA focused on burial sites and funerary objects, but behind these clearly vital matters lay highly significant and contentious issues such as cultural affiliation, cultural patrimony, the structure of indigenous political formation, and rights to possession and tribal land.

NAGPRA provided guidelines concerning the excavation and removal of human remains and objects of indigenous North Americans on federal or tribal land and established process to help federal agencies and museums determine which indigenous group was the most appropriate to take responsibility for the disposition of human remains and associated material culture. Of equal importance, NAGPRA required that all museums inventory all relevant objects and document their provenance, making it possible for communities to seek repatriation.

Given the high hopes that were held for NAGPRA, it is not surprising that it has failed to live up to the expectations of many indigenous North Americans. Certainly, issues related to the determination of cultural affiliation and the time limits that have been claimed to exist with respect to proving such affiliations have meant that NAGPRA has been tested by many groups (not just indigenous ones) in the courts. Nonetheless, it represents a serious attempt to seek balance in a highly contentious but extremely important relationship lying at the core of settler societies.

See also Excavation of Ozette (1967–1981); Lake Mungo Inscribed on the World Heritage List (1981); Discovery of Lindow Man (1984); Fate of "Kennewick Man" (1996–Present).

Further Reading

Barkan E., and R. Bush, eds. 2002. *Claiming the stones/naming the bones: Cultural property and the negotiation of national and ethnic identity.* Los Angeles: Getty Research Institute.

Brown, M. 2003. *Who owns native culture?* Cambridge, MA: Harvard University Press.

Fine-Dare, K. 2002. *Grave injustice: The American Indian repatriation movement and NAGPRA.* Lincoln: University of Nebraska Press.

A Web site that deals with NAGPRA in a thorough and comprehensive fashion is maintained by the National Park Service, U.S. Department of the Interior, at http://www.cr.nps.gov/nagpra/.

A copy of the Vermillion Accord can be found at the World Archaeological Congress Web site at http://ehlt.flinders.edu.au/wac/site/about_ethi.php.

Publication of Columbian Consequences *(1989–1991)*

Although archaeologists from former European colonies in North America, South Africa, Australia, and New Zealand were interested in exploring the archaeology of colonization (see, for example, Allen 1969; Deagan 1983; Deetz 1963; Fitzhugh 1985), the celebration of the quincentenary of the voyage of Christopher Columbus to the Americas in 1992 fostered a major reassessment of research in this field and numerous assessments of its impact. No other publication demonstrates this better than the three volumes of the series *Columbian Consequences* (published in three volumes in 1989, 1990, 1991) edited by David Hirst Thomas, an archaeologist from New York City's Museum of Natural History, which documented the richness and diversity of contact research being undertaken in the United States and attempted to right what Thomas felt to be a major wrong.

Thomas believed the most significant reason for embarking on an archaeological exploration of the consequences of European colonization in the United States was that the role of the Spanish colonizers had been masked in narrative histories of colonization and life on the frontier. By focusing the three volumes on the consequences of the Spanish colonization, Thomas and the Society for American Archaeology, which backed the project, wanted to challenge, change, and replace the dominant Anglo- or Francocentric views of the European colonization of the United States. *Columbian Consequences* fulfilled these expectations—it was a signal achievement and remains so.

This editorial agendum reflects the scale and style of historical archaeology undertaken in North America since the field began to rapidly expand (both within and outside universities) in the 1960s. During this time archaeologists, historians, and ethnohistorians have charted the extraordinary variety and richness of indigenous American societies and the equally diverse histories of their experiences of contact. As has often been observed, the European invasion and settlement of the Americas is one of the most significant passages of human history, causing the fundamental reorganization of the ecology of two continents and the lives of their inhabitants (both indigenes and invaders). Documenting, understanding, and explaining these impacts in the Caribbean, the United States, and Canada was the primary focus of the archaeologists, ethnohistorians, and historians involved in the project, who trawled the past 500 years of colonial history to write exemplary studies of contact, slavery, frontiers, and nation-building that have become disciplinary landmarks of equal importance to *Columbian Consequences* (see for example Crosby 1986, 1994; Deagan 1991; Ferguson and Green 1983; Lightfoot 1995; Rogers 1990; Rogers and Wilson 1993; Trigger 1980).

North American research on historical archaeology in general, and contact archaeology in particular, is characterized by the scale of the enterprise (see, for example, Miller et al. 1996) and the diversity of histories produced, be they of diasporas or migrations or communities created from (among a host of alternatives) slave or free, Creole and Maroon populations. North

American historical archaeology also exhibits a strong theoretical focus where practitioners have sought to understand change and variation in historical societies (and the consequences of interactions across boundaries and frontiers—both temporal and spatial) through concepts such as acculturation, dominance, resistance, ethnogenesis, gender, and frameworks broadly described as evolutionary theory and world systems theory (Silliman 2005; and especially the papers in Cusick 1998 and Rogers and Wilson 1993).

Such diversities of problem, data, and theory have also required archaeologists, ethnohistorians, and historians to reflect on difficult issues arising from the integration of all this variety into coherent analysis. A focus on the methodology of history writing in contact contexts has also required archaeologists to think more clearly about the value of previously strongly drawn boundaries between history and prehistory and the structural relationships between diverse databases. Last, but certainly by no means least, has been a long-standing interest in modeling the consequences, for American indigenous populations, of diseases brought by invaders.

See also Excavation of Port Essington (1969); Publication of *A Guide to Artifacts of Colonial America* (1970); Publication of *In Small Things Forgotten* (1977); Discovery of the African Burial Ground (1991); Excavation of New York City's "Five Points" (1991).

Further Reading

Allen, F. J. 1969. Archaeology, and the history of Port Essington. Ph.D. diss., Australian National University, Canberra.

Crosby, A. W. 1986. *Ecological imperialism: The biological expansion of Europe, 900–1900.* Cambridge: Cambridge University Press.

Crosby, A. W. 1994. *Germs, seeds and animals: Studies in ecological history.* Armonk, NY: M. E. Sharpe.

Cusick, J., ed. 1998. *Studies in culture contact: Interaction, culture change, and archaeology.* Carbondale: Center for Archaeological Investigations, Southern Illinois University.

Deagan, K. 1983. *Spanish St. Augustine: The archaeology of a colonial Creole Community.* New York: Academic Press.

Deagan, K. 1991. Historical archaeology's contributions to our understanding of early America. In *Historical archaeology in global perspective,* ed. L. Falk, 97–112. Washington, DC: Smithsonian Institution Press.

Deetz, J. 1963. Archaeological investigations at la Purisima Mission. *Archaeological Survey Annual Report* 5: 161–241.

Ferguson, L., and S. Green. 1983. Recognizing the American Indian, African and European Record of Colonial South Carolina. In *Forgotten places and things: Ar-*

chaeological perspectives on American history, ed. A. Ward, 275–281. Albuquerque, NM: Center for Anthropological Studies.

Fitzhugh, W., ed. 1985. *Cultures in contact.* Washington, DC: Smithsonian Institution Press.

Lightfoot, K. G. 1995. Culture contact studies: Redefining the relationship between prehistoric and historical archaeology. *American Antiquity* 60 (2): 199–217.

Miller, H., D. Hamilton, H. Honerkamp, S. Pendery, P. Pope, and J. Tuck, eds. 1996. The archaeology of sixteenth and seventeenth-century British colonization in the Caribbean, United States and Canada, Guide to Historical Archaeology Literature 4. Bethlehem, PA: Society for Historical Archaeology.

Rogers, J. D. 1990. *Objects of change. The archaeology and history of Arikara contact with Europeans.* Washington, DC: Smithsonian Institution Press.

Rogers, J. D., and S. M. Wilson, eds. 1993. *Ethnohistory and archaeology. Approaches to postcontact change in the Americas.* New York: Plenum.

Silliman, S. 2005. Culture contact or colonialism? Challenges in the archaeology of Native North America. *American Antiquity* 70 (1): 55–74.

Thomas, D. H., ed. 1989. *Columbian consequences. Volume 1, Archaeological and historical perspectives on the Spanish borderlands west.* Washington, DC: Smithsonian Institution Press.

Thomas, D. H., ed. 1990. *Columbian consequences. Volume 2, Archaeological and historical Perspectives on the Spanish borderlands east.* Washington, DC: Smithsonian Institution Press.

Thomas, D. H., ed. 1991. *Columbian consequences. Volume 3, The Spanish Borderlands in Pan-American perspective.* Washington, DC: Smithsonian Institution Press.

Trigger, B. 1980. Archaeology and the image of the American Indian. *American Antiquity* 45 (4): 662–676.

Publication of A Forest of Kings *(1990)*

In 1990 Mayanists Linda Schele and David Freidel published *A Forest of Kings: The Untold Story of the Ancient Maya.* Combining archaeological evidence with history deciphered from Maya inscriptions and glyphs, this popular book made the mysterious Maya more accessible to twentieth-century readers.

Linda Schele (1942–1998) had been deeply involved in the decipherment of Maya hieroglyphic writing and, by the 1980s, had developed a way of interpreting the essence of Maya society through the integration of studies of its art, archaeology, and hieroglyphic writing. This approach was exemplified in *A Forest of Kings,* which she cowrote with Freidel. Their story was one of war, territorial expansion, and the very great impact of ritual—particularly ritual associated with the passage of time. *A Forest of Kings* was structured around detailed discussions of each of the Maya centers that allowed Schele and Freidel to weave inscriptions, art, architecture, and archaeology into a persuasive tapestry of life among the classic Maya. Significantly, Schele and Freidel sought to maximize the impact of the deciphered inscriptions in the sense that they could "go beyond" the translated text and empirical evidence to produce plausible interpretations of Maya life.

See also Investigation of Palenque begins (1787); Rediscovering Maya Civilization (1839–1843); Publication of *The Population of the Valley of Teotihuacán* (1922); Discovery of Olmec Civilization (1926–1942); Deciphering the Dynastic Sequence at Piedras Negras (1960); Jorge R. Acosta Finishes Work at Tula (1961); Publication of *Ceramics of Monte Alban* (1967).

Further Reading

Coe, M. 2000. *Breaking the Maya code: The last great decipherment of an ancient script.* Rev. ed. London: Penguin.

Proskouriakoff, T. 1960. Historical implications of a pattern of dates at Piedras Negras, Guatemala. *American Antiquity* 25 (4): 454–475.

Schele, L., and D. Freidel. 1990. *A forest of kings: The untold story of the ancient Maya.* New York: Morrow.

Solomon, C. 2003. *Tatiana Proskouriakoff, interpreting the Ancient Maya.* Norman: University of Oklahoma Press.

Discovery of the African Burial Ground (1991)

The only intact colonial African cemetery in North America so far discovered was revealed during construction of the U.S. General Services Commission building at 290 Broadway in New York City. It stretches for more than five city blocks, from Broadway to Lafayette Street (east) and from Chambers Street to Duane Street (north). On the discovery of the remains of more than 400 individuals, construction immediately stopped, and a program of salvage archaeology began. The site is massive (some six acres in extent) and has a long history of use during the seventeenth and eighteenth centuries.

Although there were numbers of slaves in New York City (then New Amsterdam) since 1626, the area became a cemetery when a local church (Trinity Church) refused to allow the burial of Africans in its grounds. At that point the site was over a mile from the outskirts of the city and was effectively wasteland. This was the only place that could be used for such a sacred purpose. The expansion of the city during the eighteenth century meant that the site was taken away from the local African population and backfilled with soil, rock, and trash from adjacent potteries and leather works. The sacred history of the place faded from the general memory of the city, although it is likely that African Americans would not have forgotten.

Since its rediscovery and the long-running program of research on the human remains and associated material culture (which took place at Howard University in Washington, D.C.) the site has become a National Historic Landmark. On 4 October 2003, the remains were returned to Lower Manhattan and a Rite of Ancestral Return commemorative ceremony was performed. Future construction has been banned from the site, and the remains can rest undisturbed. Apart from providing a strong reminder of the African history of New York City, the analysis of the remains and their associated artifacts has provided a unique window into colonial American history.

See also Historical Archaeology at Colonial Williamsburg (1928–Present); Excavation of Jamestown (1934–1957); Excavation of Sainte-Marie among the Hurons (1941–1951); Historical Archaeology First Taught at University (1960); Publication of *A Guide to Artifacts of Colonial America* (1970); Publication of *In Small Things Forgotten* (1977); Publication of *Columbian Consequences* (1989–1991); Excavation of New York City's "Five Points" (1991).

Further Reading

Hansen, J., and G. McGowan. 1998. *Breaking ground, breaking silence: The story of New York's African burial ground.* New York: Henry Holt.

A very useful online resource can be found at the Web site supported by the U.S. General Services Administration, where a complete list of relevant reports can be found and downloaded: http://www.africanburialground.com/ABG_FinalReports.htm.

Discovery of "Otzi the Iceman" (1991)

In 1991 two hikers discovered the frozen body of a Bronze Age man in glacier ice in the Similaun Pass in the Tyrol Alps between Austria and Italy. Modern archaeological and biological forensic techniques have provided a wealth of information about the life and death of this mummified 5,000-year-old person.

"Otzi the Iceman," "Similaun man," or just "Iceman" was discovered by chance. At first the hikers and authorities thought he was of very recent provenance, but this serendipitous find turned out to be the oldest complete human body ever found. Over the next few years, although now carefully preserved at the University of Innsbruck's Institute of Prehistory and Early History, the Iceman was examined by numerous international scientific experts, for twenty-minute intervals, each adding their expertise, building up as complete a picture of his life and death during the Bronze Age as evidence allowed.

The Iceman was discovered at an altitude of 3,200 meters, making him not only the oldest body to be found in Europe, but also the highest prehistoric find as well. His body had been air dried before being enveloped by the glacier about 5,300 years ago. He was between thirty and forty years old, based on dental evidence, and he was 156–160 centimeters (5 feet 2 inches) high. His brain, muscles, heart, liver, and digestive organs were in good condition, although his lungs were blackened—probably from smoke from open fires. Eight of his ribs had been fractured, some of these had healed and others were healing when he died. Tattoos were found on both sides of his lower spine and on his left calf and right ankle, comprising two-centimeter-long parallel vertical blue lines. On his inner knee there was a tattoo of a blue cross. Most of his fingernails, except one, had dropped off. Analysis of the remaining one indicated that he had used his hands to work, and that he had also been ill, based on reduced nail growth, at four-, three-, and two-month intervals before his death. DNA analysis of his tissue confirmed that he was of central or northern European origin.

The Iceman died with a variety of clothing and other possessions made from organic materials that usually do not survive. In this case, because they had been frozen, they had been preserved. These were the everyday belongings of a man from the late Stone Age, which, until now, had been the subject of speculation and ethnographic analogy. The Iceman's clothing, comprising pouch, loincloth, and leggings, were made from eight different species of animal, were carefully stitched together with sinew, and had been repaired. His coat was deerskin, his hat was bearskin, his calfskin shoes were filled with grass for warmth, and he had an outer cloak of woven grass or reeds. This latter garment was similar to those recorded as being worn by local people as late as the nineteenth century. His clothing did not belong to someone of high social status—evidence that the Iceman was probably a farmer and a shepherd.

The Iceman's equipment is the earliest of its kind to be found in Europe and comprised over 70 artifacts. He carried a small, 9.5-centimeter copper ax, with a yew wood haft and leather binding. He also had an unfinished yew

Otzi the Iceman. (Corbis)

bow, with 14 arrows in a deerskin quiver, only two of which were ready to use, with flint tips and feather fletching. Other artifacts found with the Iceman included a flint knife with a wooden handle and grass string sheath; a hazel and larch wood frame of what was probably a rucksack; a lime wood handle with a sharpened antler tip inserted into one end; a retouching tool for flint scraping; two birch bark containers; a small marble disc on a leather thong; a piece of net; two types of fungus—one a tinder fungus, and the other, on a leather thong, may have been medicinal; other flints, such as a scrapers and awls, and one for making fires; and small quantities of antlers and bones for sharpening into points. Iceman had used a surprisingly large variety of different plants to manufacture his kit. Food evidence included a sloe (a kind of plum) berry, fragments of meat bone from the vertebrae of an ibex, and some cereal grains.

Radiocarbon dates confirmed that Iceman died 5,200 years ago (ca. 3200 BC) at the beginning of the European Bronze Age. The wide variety of wood and animal species used by the Iceman in his tool kit and clothing is impressive. So too are his techniques for working wood, flint, leather, and grasses. In fact, the archaeological evidence revealed more about the Bronze Age world than just the body. However, all of this evidence, and the evidence from his body, particularly his age, diet, diseases, and genetics, greatly enhanced our understanding of the early Bronze Age in Europe. And all of this from a chance discovery that could have disappeared back into the snow again without ever being found.

See also Paleopathology in Nubia (1909–1911); Discovery of Lindow Man (1984).

Further Reading

Bortenschlager, S., and K. Oeggl, eds. 2000. *The Iceman and his natural environment: Palaeo-botanical results.* Vienna, Austria: Springer.

Dubowski, M. 1998. *Ice mummy: The discovery of a 5,000-year-old man.* New York: Random House.

Fowler, B. 2001. *Iceman: Uncovering the life and times of a prehistoric man found in an alpine glacier.* Chicago: University of Chicago Press.

Excavation of New York City's "Five Points" (1991)

Writing the histories of cities has been a focus for archaeology throughout the history of the discipline. Many of these "urban" excavations—of Pompeii, Rome, Nineveh, Athens, Troy, Ur, York, and Novgorod—are archaeological milestones in their own right. More recently, historical archaeology has made substantial contributions to unraveling the development of modern cities around the world. In particular, the excavation of a nineteenth-century site in New York City's "Five Points" helped rewrite the social history of the immigrant and working class people that lived in that city's most notorious slum.

Urban renewal and redevelopment in the centers of many modern cities has threatened the integrity of the archaeological remains to be found there. In 1991 the excavation of the Five Points site, before the erection of a new courthouse in Foley Square in Lower Manhattan, uncovered the remains of a nineteenth-century mixed, residential-commercial working-class neighborhood that was the home of many recently arrived immigrants, primarily from Ireland and eastern Europe.

Located northeast of New York's City Hall, on what is now the southern edge of Chinatown, Five Points got its name from the five corners created by the intersection of three streets, and it has been described as "the most chronicled neighborhood in the U.S.A." As early as the 1840s British author Charles Dickens was one of many writers and slum reformers who visited and wrote about Five Points, which became the source of many newspaper stories about its lurid goings on and squalid tenements, saloons, prostitutes, and dance halls. The demonization of Five Points was used primarily to prove the superiority of the observers—be they from other countries, other parts of the United States, or adherents of religions not strongly represented at Five Points.

Notwithstanding the fact that within this working-class community there were real tensions between "Nativists," that is, those born in America, and the large numbers of the Irish migrants, recent work by historians has argued that the bad reputations of slum districts were much exaggerated for political purposes. No one could deny that there was great poverty and desperation, unsanitary conditions, vice, and drunkenness at Five Points. However, there is also evidence, from housing, census, and taxation records, that many of the slum's inhabitants were hard-working people with strong family ties, who lived relatively "normal" lives, and who were trying to achieve something better for themselves or even to leave the slum.

Eventually, the Five Points district was pulled down, and the remains of its houses were covered by new buildings in the early twentieth century. In the 1990s these too were demolished. In the meantime federal legislation in the United States provided for the funding of archaeological excavation as part of the budgeted costs of construction projects. With this new redevelopment, almost a century after they had been covered, the remains of the district of Five Points reappeared, and the excavation and its analysis, directed by Dr. Rebecca Yamin for John Milner and Associates, provided a fascinating window on New York City's history.

Yamin and her team excavated twenty-two archaeological features on the site, dating from 1790 to 1890. During this one hundred-year period Five Points changed from an outlying industrial area to one of the most congested residential neighborhoods in New York City. The excavations recovered 850,000 artifacts from twenty-two abandoned privies and cisterns on fourteen historic properties, which included a brothel, a brewery, an eating house, an oyster house, a bakery, and a saloon, as well as from residences and an Irish tenement.

During the first quarter of the nineteenth century, the population and buildings of Five Points comprised workplaces that were also the homes of artisans and their families. By the 1840s these had been demolished and replaced by large tenements to cheaply house numerous newly arrived German and Irish migrants. Lot 6, 472 Pearl Street, the most intensively investigated of all the features uncovered, perfectly illustrates these changes. At the beginning of the nineteenth century it was the home of carpenters and their families. In the 1840s it was the home of a rabbi/tailor and his family, students, and apprentices. In 1848 it became a five-story tenement, owned and built by an Irish migrant made good to house refugees from the Irish potato famine.

Almost 100,000 artifacts associated with this tenement site were found, and most of this material relates directly to women, and provides evidence of their domestic lives. Many women cooked, cleaned, and laundered not only for their family members, but for paying boarders, particularly single men, as well. There is evidence that residents engaged in sewing, rug making, and clothing recycling. They cared about their surroundings, because the remains of ornaments and flowerpots have been found, and they placed Staffordshire figurines of shepherds and shepherdesses on their mantlepieces, set their dining tables with matching sets of dishes, and drank tea from teacups and saucers imported from England. The residents also ate large quantities of meat, primarily pork, and in the earlier years of the century, they also ate fish. These remains are also proof that some residents did not live in abject poverty.

Some of the people of Five Points had money for luxuries as well, testified by the large number of tobacco pipes found in the site. From the remains of medical items, some residents could also afford to buy treatments from pharmacies or drugstores, and from the remains of toys and slate pencils, some parents had enough money to spend some on their children. Women could afford to wear ornamental hair combs and buy mirrors.

Most Irish residents were laborers but there is evidence of cottage industries undertaken in their homes, such as jewelry and toothbrush making. Most of the residents from eastern Europe were Jewish and were tailors and dealers in secondhand clothing. These ethnic differences can also be seen in the remains of different diets and choices of consumer goods. Archaeological evidence in the form of large numbers of chamber pots, washbowls, and lice combs, along with census information taken at different times, reveals that living conditions in the tenement were overcrowded and unsanitary.

In addition to the assemblages derived from residential contexts, the artifacts from public buildings provide a more balanced picture of life in the slum. While numerous glass bottles were found from the saloon site, many small plates and master ink bottles were also found. The former were used to serve the free lunch that came with the alcohol purchased. The latter were used to decant ink into smaller bottles for use by residents.

The assemblages excavated from Five Points were stored in the basement of the World Trade Center. None of it could be salvaged after the destruction of the twin towers on September 11. Fortunately, much of it had been analyzed, researched, and published, so not all was lost. Five Points set many archaeological benchmarks—and the archaeology of the modern city is now a global phenomenon. Other urban sites that have been recently excavated and have provided a wealth of alternative information about the recently vanished past include Cape Town, South Africa; Sydney and Melbourne, Australia; Quebec, Canada; Lowell, Massachusetts; West Oakland, California; Washington D.C,; and London and Sheffield in the United Kingdom.

See also Historical Archaeology First Taught at University (1960); Publication of *A Guide to Artifacts of Colonial America* (1970); Publication of *In Small Things Forgotten* (1977); Discovery of the African Burial Ground (1991).

Further Reading

Mayne, A., and T. Murray, eds. 2001. *The archaeology of urban landscapes: Explorations in Slumland.* Cambridge: Cambridge University Press.

Yamin, R. 1997. New York's mythic slum: Digging lower Manhattan's infamous Five Points *Archaeology* 50 (2): 44–53.

Yamin, R. 1998. Lurid tales and homely stories of New York's notorious Five Points *Historical Archaeology* 32 (1): 74–85.

Yamin, R., ed. 2000. *Tales of Five Points: Working class life in nineteenth century New York.* 6 vols. New York: General Services Administration.

Dating the Settlement of New Zealand (1991)

The islands of New Zealand were among the last places in the world to be colonized by humans. In 1770 English explorer Captain James Cook and his scientific companion, botanist Joseph Banks, noted how similar the Maori inhabitants of New Zealand were to other people on the islands of the southern Pacific. But Cook, especially after his third and final visit to New Zealand, also noted their differences, such as fortified villages, carved canoes, weapons, and ornaments, and the fact the Maori did not erect the monumental stone pyramid temple complexes of other eastern Polynesian cultures.

European accounts from the early nineteenth century recognized the Polynesian origins of the Maori. Not only were they similar in appearance to tropical Polynesians, but they also spoke a Polynesian language. They noted that while the Maori shared a common language and social organization, they also demonstrated a range of economic and social differences and adaptations to the colder southern Pacific environment. The most obvious difference was the practice of sedentary horticulture on the warmer northern island and mobile and seasonal hunting and gathering on the colder southern island.

In 1839, the same year European settlers concluded a treaty with the Maori, geologist Richard Owen theorized that it was the Maori who had hunted the large megapode bird, the moa, to extinction. In the 1870s the first archaeological evidence from sites confirmed this, linking Maori weapons with moa bones, and estimating that the arrival of the Maori and the demise of the moa probably occurred ca. 1,300 years ago. There was never any doubt that the Maori had come to New Zealand from somewhere in Polynesia. In fact, their oral history described their large canoes arriving. However, writing the history of their colonization would prove a difficult and contentious task.

The origins and migration of the Maori remained central to the debate; only the details changed according to the different perspectives of the protagonists—enthusiastic amateurs, museum personnel, ethnographers, and the Maori themselves. Were the Maori different from other Polynesians because they were a combination of Melanesians and Polynesians? Were other people living in New Zealand before the Maori came, and were the Chatham Islanders all that was left of these people afterward? Did the Maori originate in India, Micronesia, or Hawaii? Were there two migrations, as Maori oral history described? What all of these questions had in common was that none were based on archaeological evidence.

After World War I, New Zealand's first professional anthropologist, H. D. Skinner from Cambridge University, began teaching at the Otago University and Museum on the south island. Based on his research into tanged adzes in New Zealand, Polynesia, and the Chatham Islands and the spread of Austronesian language groups, Skinner eventually discounted the two waves of Maori migration theories. He also argued that the Maori were culturally and linguistically closest to eastern Polynesians (e.g., those people living in Hawaii, the Marquesas, and Easter Island) and had probably originated there, rather than in western Polynesia (e.g., from Samoa, Tonga, and neighboring islands).

Skinner's student, Roger Duff (1912–1978), who became the director of the Dominion (later the National) Museum in Wellington, introduced modern archaeology to New Zealand during his excavation of Wairu Bar, on the south island, between 1939 and 1952. It was a rich site comprising thirty-six human burials with grave goods, moa skeletons, artifacts made from moa eggs, tanged adzes, fishhooks, and whale ivory jewelry, as well as evidence of housing, stone working, and cooking and midden remains. Duff divided New Zealand prehistory into two periods: the first and earliest, or "moa hunter," was defined by archaeological sites only, and the later, or "Maori," was defined by ethnographic accounts from initial European contact. Duff's analysis of evidence from excavations confirmed the two migrations theory, and the prevailing chronology for the discovery of New Zealand. This comprised initial discovery ca. AD 950, and then the arrival of the great canoe fleet, with Polynesian domesticated plants such as kumara and taro at AD 1350. Duff's analyses also confirmed the eastern Polynesian origins of the Maori. In 1955 the radiocarbon dating of Wairu Bar to AD 1150 did not change his conclusions.

In 1950 the new anthropology department at Auckland University employed Cambridge-educated archaeologist Jack Golson, who began a surveying, recording, and excavation program aimed at understanding differences between Duff's two Maori cultural phases. Golson argued that the differences between them were attributable to local adaptations and developments rather than to different episodes of migration. During the 1960s, as many of the Pacific Islands became politically independent, archaeological research refocused on their origins and the history of the relationships between them. New Zealand became a leader in this research because of its many resources: the Polynesian Society, which was founded as early as 1892 to conserve, record, and publish the customs, history, and languages of the Maori and other people of the Pacific; and the Alexander Turnbull Library in Wellington, which was the major repository of Maori and Pacific material. The United States of America's outstanding Bishop Museum in Hawaii also provided leadership and resources for this research.

In the late 1960s archaeologist Leslie Groube began to question the two Maori cultural /migration phase conclusions. He argued that the changes in adze forms and ornaments on which they were based were stylistic changes rather than functional ones, and there was little archaeological evidence of change from simple to complex settlements or of two migrations. The so-called later Maori phase was not only the direct result of post-European contact, but the ethnographic accounts of the nineteenth century had not discerned the immediate impact and extent of the changes to Maori society caused by early European contact.

Groube's argument sent everyone back to the field, but armed with the latest developments in modern archaeology—radiocarbon dating, archaeological science, paleobotany, and palynology. And archaeology itself had moved on from its preoccupation with periods and phases to tracking processes in the archaeological record, which required new techniques in data collection and different sources of information: distribution and types of settlement sites, house forms, agriculture, foraging patterns, shell-midden contents, regional studies, population studies, the impact of economic and social organization, and multidisciplinary cooperation. This same style of archaeology was also being applied to the prehistory of Melanesia and Polynesia. Over the next two decades, while the number of archaeologists working in New Zealand and the amount of archaeology undertaken expanded, the prehistory of New Zealand was finally unraveled.

During the 1980s archaeologist Janet Davidson concluded that all Maori material culture—stone tools, fishing gear, ornaments, adzes, house and settlement forms, burials, warfare, pa design, art styles, and types of agriculture—changed at different times and in different places to different stimulation, and that there was no evidence of two phases of development or migrations in New Zealand prehistory. At around the same time archaeologists Wilfred Shawcross and Athol Anderson, who had been excavating and analyzing shell-middens, arrived at similar conclusions. Leslie Groube and Geoffrey Irwin, working on the prehistoric demography and settlement patterns of the north island, concluded that for the two centuries before European contact this island was overpopulated and under social and environmental stress. The intense pressure on its natural and agricultural resources resulted in the increase of the construction and abandonment of fortified pa (or hill forts) to protect these resources, and for the movement of north island Maori groups onto the south island.

Athol Anderson also reexamined the moa extinction on the south island. He found that the extinction, which occurred 400–900 years ago (ca. 1200–1600 AD), had been rapid and coincided with a period of small or "base" settlements with access to local rich resources of seals and moas—until the latter disappeared. This was an unsustainable and consequently short-lived strategy. Subsequently, larger villages grew up, mainly in response to the increasing numbers of visits of people from the north island, which had a more organized economy based on stored foods, trade and exchanges, and the payment of tributes to chiefs, but who were beginning to experience overpopulation and increasing competition. Radiocarbon dating found little evidence for the settlement of New Zealand earlier than AD 1000.

By the 1990s archaeologists regarded the initial colonization of New Zealand as a forced, but planned, migration of hundreds of people from

Polynesia. Such migrations were a standard Polynesian response to overpopulation, which was probably occurring in Polynesia as a result of agricultural intensification and competition for resources, as indeed happened on the north island of New Zealand during the seventeenth and eighteenth centuries, resulting in the movement of some groups to the south island.

The use of computer simulations of extensive voyages across the Pacific; experimental voyages in replica canoes; the increase in knowledge of currents, climate patterns, and prevailing winds; and the increase in knowledge of Polynesian navigation, sailing techniques, and canoe technology led to the conclusion that it is entirely possible that the Polynesian migrations to New Zealand were planned, and that there were voyages back to Polynesia as well. This means that there were probably multiple episodes of discovery and colonization and that there was continuous interaction between the different islands of the Pacific. This is supported by the use of X-ray fluorescence to source basalt artifacts such as adzes, some of which were traded over 1,500 kilometers from Samoa to the Cook Islands and from the Marquesas to the Society Islands. Other research involving tracing mitochrondrial DNA variations in Pacific rats, which were used as food on long canoe voyages, also demonstrates long-term interisland contact.

On arrival in New Zealand ca. AD 1000 these small and mobile groups of Polynesian migrants would have lived by hunting the moas and seals and on other rich, pristine natural resources. The use of Polynesian-style swidden agriculture, which involved field preparation and the cutting down and burning of forests, would have occurred later on when these large natural resources began to decline. By AD 1500, within a few hundred years of their arrival, the eastern Polynesian styles of adze blades, fishhooks, and personal ornaments were superseded by the distinctive Maori styles of these and by new adaptations to the cooler climate of New Zealand—carved wooden canoes and houses, clothing, pas, and curvilinear art forms.

See also Lapita Homeland Project (1983–1990).

Further Reading

Anderson, A. 1989. *Prodigious birds: Moas and moa hunting in prehistoric New Zealand.* Cambridge: Cambridge University Press.

Anderson, A. 1991. The chronology of colonization in New Zealand. *Antiquity* 65: 767–795.

Irwin, G. 1992. *The prehistoric exploration and colonisation of the Pacific.* Cambridge: Cambridge University Press.

Discovery of Chauvet Cave (1994)

Three friends (one of whom gave his name to the cave) were caving on a winter's Sunday in the Ardèche Valley in southeastern France. They ventured into a well-known cavity and decided to explore an area of fallen rocks within the cave a little more closely than they had done before. They discovered a passage out of the cave and into a shaft, which they descended, to find a series of caverns containing extraordinarily rich cave paintings, and the bones of animals still lying on the floor. The cave system was over 400 meters long.

It was obvious that they had found one of the major cave art finds of the century. The site was quickly designated an historic monument, and the legal work required for the government to acquire the cave from its owners began and was completed in early 1997. Security was tight from the outset; 24-hour guards and doors and alarm systems were installed. Learning from the lessons of contamination at Lascaux Cave, officials developed strict protocols

Prehistoric image of a human hand, stenciled on the interior of a cave in Chauvet, France. (AFP/Getty Images)

for the few visitors who have been allowed into Chauvet for the purposes of study or photographic recording.

The images of the cave art that have been released by the authorities show just how spectacular the Chauvet paintings are, both in subject matter and treatment. There are scenes of lions hunting bison and of horses, mammoths, rhinoceros, reindeer, red deer, Megaceros deer, musk ox, panthers, and an owl in both black and red. There are also human hand and palm prints and stencils in red.

The faunal remains are equally important. Many cave bear skeletons were found on the floor of the cave, along with the remains of ibex and wolves. The bears left their footprints and scratches in the cave.

Thirty radiocarbon dates have been collected from Chauvet Cave, which scientists believe indicate that the cave was visited during two different periods. The bulk of the images seem to have been drawn between 30,000 and 32,000 years ago (ca, 30,000–28,000 BC) in radiocarbon years (which was the earliest occupation). The site was reoccupied from between 25,000 and 27,000 years ago (ca. 25,000–23,000 BC). Remarkably, the footprints of a child have been found in the cave, but it is believed that these date from the later period.

See also Research into Prehistoric Aquitaine (1862–1875); Recognition of Paleolithic Cave Art at Altamira (1879–1902); Lascaux Discovered (1940).

Further Reading

Clottes, J., ed. 2003. *Return to Chauvet cave.* London: Thames and Hudson.

Chauvet, J-M., E. B. Deschamps, and C. Hillaire. 2001. *Chauvet cave: The discovery of the world's oldest paintings.* London: Thames and Hudson.

Publication of Novgorod in Focus *(1996)*

For nearly 70 years the medieval site of Novgorod in the former Soviet Union has been excavated, the largest excavation ever undertaken in Russia. The scale of work undertaken at the site, and the quantity and quality of the finds, make Novgorod not only the most important archaeological site in Russia, but also the most important European medieval archaeological site. In 1996 papers about it were translated into English and published by Henrik Birnbaum as *Novgorod in Focus.* For the first time the details of this remarkable site, which elucidates the origins and development of the early Russian state, became widely available in the West.

The site of one of Russia's oldest towns, Novgorod is located 160 kilometers south of the modern city of St. Petersburg on the Volkov River. It can be reached from the Baltic Sea, or from the Gulf of Finland along the Neva River via Lake Ladoga, and then into the Volkov River.

Until the excavation of Novgorod, the archaeology of Russian history between the ninth and fourteenth centuries AD was virtually unknown, primarily because medieval Russians lived in wooden buildings that rarely survived the common hazard of fire. Few artifacts from the period survived as well. There were few documentary sources from the period, and any that remained were official, and therefore limited in the information they provided. Myths, legends, and stories about this early formative period of Russian history were concocted during the fifteenth to seventeenth centuries for nationalist reasons to help explain the evolution of the modern Russian state. Because of its importance, and the lack of evidence about it, Novgorod was always the subject of political interpretation. During the mid-nineteenth century Czar Nicholas I, and his historian Uvarov, regarded Novgorod as an example of the benefits of a strong but benign monarchy. During the mid-twentieth century the communists described Novgorod as the cradle of Russian democracy.

The systematic excavation of the remains of the medieval city began in 1932. Both historians and archaeologists believed the excavation would be an objective window onto the medieval past, but results were beyond their original expectations. The wet conditions prevailing at the site meant that there was good preservation of organic artifacts made from wood, bone, leather, textiles, and bark.

During the next sixty years, 21,000 square meters of the city were excavated, and a great deal of data were accumulated. Blocks of the medieval town, with its wooden roads and buildings, have been unearthed and dated using dendrochronology. There have been 150,000 individual finds, including tools, weapons, pottery, clothes, furniture, horse equipment, shoes, musical instruments, toys, food remains, icons, books, craftsmen's raw materials, and imported items.

Perhaps the most remarkable and valuable of all of the finds, however, has been the discovery of more than 800 written birch bark documents containing unique information about the community of Novgorod between the eleventh and fifteenth centuries. These valuable historical sources are letters, contracts, notes, complaints, bills, school exercises, and administrative details.

Furthermore, data from the site have begun to answer many questions about the history of Russian statehood during this period by providing details about the economics, social structure, and politics of Novgorod. Some of the larger issues to be elucidated include the better understanding of Novgorod's republican system of government, which was a complete anomaly in Russia. Was it the result of western European influence? And why did this powerful and wealthy city-state fall to the Muscovites in the fifteenth century, instead of conquering them?

We now know that the area around Novgorod was first settled by Varangian Vikings from the area of Pomerania in the western Baltic, who were forced to migrate east during the eighth and ninth centuries by the growing population and power of the Saxons. The Varangians traveled up Russia's network of rivers and were followed by German and Swedish merchants from the Hanseatic League ports at Lubeck, Visby, Riga, Dorpat (Tartu), Reval (Tallinn), and Gotland; by Danes and people from the area that became modern Poland; and then by eastern Baltic people, such as Estonians, Lithuanians, and Finns.

The Varangians founded a hill fort and trading post near what became Novgorod, as a base for their business of escorting and protecting merchants and their goods traveling to and from Scandinavia and Byzantium. The earliest rulers of Novgorod were Varangians, who were sometimes resented by local Slavic people for their special privileges in the town—as rulers, enforcers, and protectors.

The town was established AD 859 beside the original Varangian hillfort, its name literally meaning "new town." The fort continued to be used as the official residence of the princes of Novgorod, which was useful after they were eventually exiled from living inside the city walls, and the town itself was the combination of three other trading posts around it. A new fortified center, or kremlin, was constructed and this was where Santa Sophia Cathedral was first erected in AD 989, and then reerected between AD 1045–1050 after a fire destroyed the original building.

Novgorod was one of the great centers of Old Russian/ Byzantine culture, the northern-most outpost of Byzantium, east of the Balkans. It controlled land from the Arctic and White seas in the north to the Ural Mountains in the east. It was located at a major crossroads of eastern European waterways that connected the Baltic to the Black and Mediterranean seas, and eastern Europe and Scandinavia to Christian Byzantium and the Muslim Near East.

Novgorod also had strong ties to western Europe—in much the same way St. Petersburg did during the eighteenth, nineteenth, and twentieth centuries.

Originally administered by the archbishop of Kiev, Novgorod was part of the eastern Byzantine church. Its first bishop was Greek, but his successor in AD 1036 was a native Russian. Its official conversion date was AD 988 but archaeological evidence shows that local pagan and combinations of pagan-Christian rituals were still being used there in the twelfth and thirteenth centuries. In the late sixteenth century there were sermons recorded that criticized heathen and pagan customs—some 500 years after the conversion. In AD 1071 most of the population of Novogorod supported a pagan leader against the Christian bishop and the prince, and took to the streets and rioted.

By the fourteenth century the population of Novgorod was around 30,000 people. At this same time it has been estimated that Paris had a population of 80,000; London 35,000–40,000; while Milan, Venice, Florence, and Naples had 50,000 each. Lubeck, Valencia, and Lisbon were the same size as Novgorod. Kiev, the first capital city of Russia, had a population of 40,000 in the early thirteenth century. Moscow eventually outgrew both Novgorod and Kiev in size, but during this period it comprised only 20,000 people.

Novgorod survived the Mongol invasions of AD 1040–1238, unlike Kiev, by collaborating with them and becoming their tributary dependent. During its heyday, from the twelfth to the fifteenth centuries, Novgorod was known as the "Republic (or Realm) of St. Sophia"—a city-state led by its archbishop who presided over a council of lords and other governing groups. Before this Novgorod was governed by princes (who were related to the rulers of Kiev) through a town council, but after the destruction of Kiev and the retreat of the Mongols, Novgorod ruled itself via a town council or veche, open to all free men, although this was always dominated by the boyars (noble land owners) and merchants.

The prince of Novgorod was elected by the free men of the city, and his former military, judicial, and economic power was taken over by members of the veche, a unique arrangement in Russia. The veche chose the legislators, executives, and administrators, including the lord mayor of the city. Eventually, during the fifteenth century, the numerous subdivisions of power and factions created by the veche, and their support of and patronage by the emerging duchies of Poland, Lithuania, and the Muscovite state, led to the city's downfall and its incorporation into Muscovy.

The birch bark documents suggest widespread semiliteracy among the ordinary people. Despite the personal nature of these documents (love letters and complaints are among them) many would have been written by scribes or clerics on behalf of the sender. They also confirm that the language used by the inhabitants was a local form of the last phase of the ancestral language of the ancient Slavs, a blend of both eastern and western Slavic with some characteristics of southern Vlavic or Slovenian, and very different from common Russian or the Ukrainian language spoken in Kiev.

We also know a lot more about the social hierarchy in the town and its impact on politics from the residences that have been excavated. The feudal lords or boyars were at the top socially because they owned the land, even though they lived mostly in the city in mansion compounds, which also housed servants and artisans. Many of these lined the main streets of the city. Merchants controlled and made money from long-distance trade and bought land as well. Then there were the clergy—a whole other hierarchy politically allied to the boyars. Ordinary people, laborers, craftspeople, manual workers, shopkeepers, peddlers, peasant farmers, and slaves (who were mostly criminals) were at the bottom socially and were known as "black" folk.

The veche was an oligarchy of boyars and merchants, a predemocratic forms of government, and one that was completely different from any other forms of government in Russia at the time, which were usually autocratic and absolutist. Conquest by the Muscovite state in AD 1478 ended Novgorod's independence and dramatically weakened its ties with western Europe. These were restored two centuries later during the reigns of Peter the Great and the empresses Elizabeth and Catherine, and the foundation and development of the city of St. Petersburg.

The archaeological remains of craft industries in Novgorod were substantial, reflecting its strong trading and manufacturing economy and its sophisticated and skillful tradespeople. Many different wooden musical instruments have been excavated with strings, pipes, and rattles—and have greatly expanded knowledge about medieval music. Artifacts from churches include carved ivory staffs, ornamental metal book bindings, plates, cups, and censers. Embroidered shrouds and everyday textiles, as well as enameled items and jewelry of Byzantine origin, have also been found.

Evidence of the Novgorod scriptoria has been located. This church library produced manuscripts decorated with illuminations and miniatures that were traded throughout the monasteries of the Eastern Orthodox Church. Examples from Novgorod's own schools of icon and fresco painting and many architectural details have been recovered.

Novgorod was a wealthy and sophisticated city of learning, commerce, and craftsmanship, similar to the Renaissance city-states of western Europe, as well as being in touch with and a product of the eastern Byzantine world.

See also First Archaeological Collections in Russia (1715); Foundation of the Hermitage (1768); Russia Gets a Slice of Classical Antiquity (1782); Excavations in the City of York (1973–Present).

Further Reading

Birnbaum, H. 1996. *Novgorod in focus: Selected essays.* Columbus, OH: Slavica Publishers.

Rybina, E. 2000. Novgorod. In *Medieval archaeology: an encyclopedia,* ed. P. J. Crabtree, 239–241. New York: Garland Publishing.

Yanin, V. L. 1990. The archaeology of Novgorod. *Scientific American* 262 (2): 84–91.

Yanin, V. L., et al. 1992. *The archaeology of Novgorod, Russia.* Lincoln, UK: Society for Medieval Archaeology, Monograph Series 13.

Fate of "Kennewick Man" (1996–Present)

On 29 July 1996 two men found a skull on the shores of the Columbia River near Kennewick, Washington. While it was first assumed that the skull might be a police matter, it was quickly established by an attending anthropologist that more human remains were present. It was assumed that these were likely to be the remains of a white settler because the bones were in excellent condition and the skull exhibited features more akin to Caucasian shapes. This original determination was made problematic by the discovery of an arrow point (made of stone) stuck in the pelvis, but things got rapidly more complicated when the human remains were dated via radiocarbon to about 9,000 years ago. These two points, the form of the skull and the early date, were to form the basis of conflict for at least the next six years.

What makes this conflict particularly bitter and potentially divisive is the fact that the remains were found on land under the control of the U.S. Army Corps of Engineers (COE). As a government agency it is bound by the Native American Graves and Repatriation Act (NAGPRA 1990) to repatriate human remains to an "affiliated tribe for reburial." Notwithstanding the great age of the human remains, and some significant questions being raised by scientists about whether "Kennewick Man" could be legitimately considered to be an ancestor of contemporary Native North Americans, the Umatillas tribe made a formal claim to the bones, and the COE began the process of returning them.

This sparked legal action on a number of fronts, the most significant being by a group of scientists who sought to overturn the decision of the COE and to have the right to continue scientific analyses of the human remains. The basis of their objection to the repatriation was that cultural affiliation (as required by the act) had not been proven, and that there was real doubt about whether the remains were those of a Native American (as defined in the act). A coalition of tribes, supported by the U.S. federal government, opposed this action.

Arguments over the rights and wrongs of the case, particularly whether it was appropriate for archaeologists to oppose indigenous self-determination in this and other matters (frequently described as a conflict between "colonial" science and indigenous rights), were intense. Some archaeologists thought the case would permanently damage relationships between the profession and Native Americans (there were many indigenous groups arguing just this), and others (such as David Thomas) sought a more cooperative relationship that recognized the rights and interests of all stakeholders. In the end the key national body, the Society of American Archaeology, supported the thrust of the scientists' objections, although it declined to support the argument that the remains were not those of a Native American.

Since then two judgments have been reached, both supporting the case of the scientists, and accepting that no valid case of affiliation under the NAGPRA statute could possibly be made for an individual of such antiquity. In the second judgment (following the hearing of an appeal against the original decision) the federal court also raised doubts about whether the remains were those of a Native American.

On Monday, 19 April 2004, the U.S. Court of Appeals for the Ninth Circuit declined to reconsider its previous ruling that permitted scientific testing of Kennewick Man. The human remains continue to be stored at the Burke Museum in the University of Washington. Scientists sought a return of access from the U.S. government (which is opposing their request) and Native American organizations explored legal options (such as a further appeal to the Supreme Court) so that their interests in the fate of Kennewick Man were represented. It was not surprising that another of those options, to seek an amendment to NAGPRA that overcomes the decision of the court to apply stringent tests of affiliation, was explored. In July 2005 scientists regained access to the remains (which continue to be housed at the Burke Museum).

In February 2006, at the annual meeting of the American Academy of Forensic Scientists in Seattle, Washington, Douglas Owsley (Smithsonian Museum), lead scientist on the interdisciplinary Kennewick Man study, presented the most recent research findings. Detailed investigation of the skeletal material has concluded that Kennewick man was buried by other humans. He was laid out on his back with his arms at his sides, palms down, his legs straight, and placed with the river to his left and his feet in a downstream direction. His head was raised so that he was looking east toward the rising sun.

The stone spear or dart point found embedded in Kennewick Man's hip, and studied via CT scanning, did not seem to be a classic Cascade type, and entered the body from the front. Scientists concluded that the point had not been the cause of death, but was a well-healed fracture. In fact the cause of death is still unknown, and the skeleton had sustained many injuries.

Scientists also concluded that Kennewick Man's skull seems to be different from those of other Indian tribes living in the same area. Other details about the 9,300-year-old human, such as the origins of the stone point in his hip, and what he ate, and how he lived, are still the subject of research.

In August 2006 a new bill sponsored by U.S. Congressman Doc Hastings was introduced in the U.S. Senate. The bill comprised a revision to the Native American Graves Protection and Repatriation Act, advocating that ancient remains should be allowed to be studied by scientists and not automatically returned to Native American tribes. This bill also counters another introduced by the Senate Indian Affiars Committee, chaired by Senator John McCain (Republican, from Arizona), to amend NAGPRA so that the precedent caused by Kennewick Man be eliminated in the future: that is, that all ancient remains would be automatically turned over to Native American claimants even when a substantial relationship to present-day tribes is lacking.

Research on Kennewick Man continues, as does legal debate about who owns the past.

See also The Vermillion Accord and NAGPRA (1989–1990).

Further Reading

Chatters. J. 2001. *Ancient encounters: Kennewick Man and the first Americans.* New York: Simon and Schuster.

Thomas, D. H. 2000. *Skull wars: Kennewick Man, archaeology, and the battle for Native American identity.* New York: Basic Books.

Web site: http://www.kennewick-man.com (for "Tri-city Herald's Kennewick Man Virtual Interpretive Centre").

Meeting of the Eighth International Congress of Egyptologists (2000)

In 2000 the Eighth International Congress of Egyptologists took place at the Mena House Oberoi Hotel, beside the Giza pyramids. The congress was attended by 1,400 scholars, 500 of whom were Egyptian. Four hundred papers were given, and more than half of these were published in three volumes, the first on archaeology, the second on history and religion, and the third on language, literature, museology, and conservation.

Almost two hundred years had passed since Napoleon commissioned the first scientific expedition that brought ancient Egyptian civilization to the attention of the world.

Egypt is a country with a past that continues to fascinate both specialist scholars and ordinary people. Since Napoleon's expedition Egyptology has become a multidisciplinary giant, with data from archaeology, linguistics, literary criticism, art history, bioanthropology, philology, sociology, epigraphy, and geology all contributing to the modern understanding of ancient Egypt. Never before have the opportunities to understand an ancient culture been greater or more comprehensive.

At one of the millennium debates held as part of the congress, archaeologist David O'Connor outlined the achievements of Egyptology over the past fifty years and highlighted some of the problems it would face over the next fifty. He singled out the Nubian Salvage Campaign and the reconstruction of Abu Simbel as particularly striking examples of international collaboration, as well as international recognition of the significance of Egypt's World Heritage sites.

O'Connor also noted that since the 1970s, as a result of the intervention of Egyptian government agencies and research institutions, the pattern of research had changed. He identified the increase in regional studies (such as in the Delta) and work on urban sites as two cases in point. Perhaps as important is the claim that Egyptology (as with so many other aspects of archaeology) has suffered a downturn in real investment during a period when costs have escalated. An exception to this trend is the funding of long-term projects—some of which are still going after thirty years at sites such as Tell el Dab'a, Herakleopolis, Abydos, and Hierakonpolis, or those beginning in the 1990s at sites such as Buto, Qantir, Tanis, Tell Basta, Tell el Amarna, Elephantine, and a number of Coptic sites.

O'Connor and other congress attendees identified three crucial issues for Egyptian archaeology in the twenty-first century.

The first relates to the continuation of archaeology in Egypt: how will it survive and be practiced for the next fifty years?

This is dependent on the attitudes of the modern, contemporary Egyptian population to all of the material remains of the past of their country—be those remains prehistoric, ancient, Roman, medieval, Islamic, colonial Victorian, or postwar independence. For this archaeological heritage to survive and to be protected and conserved, let alone excavated, Egyptian citizens have to continue to value it and be proud of it. For this to occur, archaeology has to be of national and popular interest to the Egyptian people. And this is the responsibility not only of the Egyptian government and Egyptian archaeological institutions and professionals, but also of the foreign institutions and scholars who work in Egypt. Funding and resources to educate Egyptian colleagues and cadres and to ensure a future for archaeology in the country are regarded by O'Connor and others as being essential. The future of the past in Egypt should be bright considering the large number of Egyptian nationals who now practice as archaeologists.

The second issue for the practice of archaeology in Egypt in the twenty-first century is dependent on the resolution of the first. If the resources are forthcoming and the Egyptian people allow it, then the archaeology undertaken in Egypt must make the most of its resources.

In O'Connor's view, despite two hundred years of exploration and exploitation, the archaeological landscape of Egypt is still neither well known, nor systematically mapped. Discovery and knowledge are the result of visibility, the relationship of a site to known history, serendipitous or accidental, or as a result of salvage in the face of development. For this reason O'Connor and others identified the need for the complete exploration and documentation of the archaeological landscape, similar to the Nubian Salvage Campaign but on a bigger scale, with thorough surveys and mapping, then coring and the use of remote sensing technologies, such as ground-penetrating radar.

This approach would enable Egyptian agencies and scholars to focus on the areas of the archaeological record that are not only at risk but are also missing and need to be understood. Such a national survey and mapping program would provide a secure frame of reference for ongoing archaeological work, focusing research, targeting resources, and prioritizing archaeology. It would also help to plan salvage archaeology and help the government manage development more strategically. International funding and cooperation on a scale even greater than what was harnessed to complete the Nubian Salvage Campaign would be essential for the entire project. It would require, at the very least, pooling resources for the long term. And, as with other problems, the ongoing success of archaeology in Egypt will be dependent on international cooperation and collaboration.

The third issue, while dependent on the resolution of the other issues, could begin immediately. O'Connor and some of his colleagues argue for doing more with all of the data they have now, by employing more comprehensive and cooperative theoretical explorations to explore the data through building models and testing, debating, and reformulating them. Once again this requires collaboration and cooperation. It involves thinking outside the particular discipline and working with other disciplines. The millennium congress itself was an excellent example of the potential of this approach.

See also Publication of *Oedipus Aegypticus* (1652–1655); Publication of *Recueil d'antiquitiés égytpiennes, étrusques, romaines et gauloises* (1752–1767); Foundation of Great Egyptian Collections in England and France (1815–1835); Decipherment of Egyptian Hieroglyphics (1824); Publication of the *Description de l'Egypte* (1826); Publication of *The Manners and Customs of the Ancient Egyptians* (1847); Mariette, Antiquities Law, and the Egyptian Museum (1858); Publication of *Denkmaler aus Aegypten und Aethiopien* (1859); Publication of *A Thousand Miles up the Nile* (1877); Discovery of the Amarna Tablets (1887); Seriation and History in the Archaeology of Predynastic Egypt (1891–1904); World's First Archaeological Salvage Project? (1907–1932); Paleopathology in Nubia (1909–1911); Discovering Tutankhamen's Tomb (1922–1932); Saving Abu Simbel (1959–1980).

Further Reading

Hawass, Z., and L. P. Brock. 2003. *Egyptology at the dawn of the twenty-first century. Proceedings of the Eighth International Congress of Egyptologists, Cairo, 2000.* Cairo: The American University in Cairo Press.

Announcement of Toumai Fossil (2002)

In 1996 French and African paleoanthropologists discovered the skull of a seven-million-year-old human-like creature in the modern central African state of Chad, over a thousand kilometers west of the great east African hominid finds of the twentieth century. It took eight years of analysis, discussion, review, research, and comparison for the bona fides of a new hominid to be accepted by the scientific community, with the publication of the find in *Nature* in 2002. Significantly, there were nearly fifty authors on the paper, from Africa, Europe, and America, and representing all of the scientific disciplines required to authenticate the evidence. Named "Toumai" (meaning "hope of life" in the local African Goran language), the skull not only pushed the date of human ancestry back by 3 million years, but it also required a complete rethink of current knowledge about human evolution.

The nearly complete cranium (minus the lower jaw) of what is now called *Sahelanthropus tchadenis* is apelike but with a more human short face. Its remaining small teeth, especially the canines, resemble human teeth, and have the thicker tooth enamel of humans as well. It has the brow-ridges common to other members of the *Homo* genus and evidence, where the spinal column entered the head, that it was probably bipedal (that is, stood upright and walked on two legs). So the seven-million-year-old Toumai is more *Homo*-like than the oldest *Australopithecines* (the early species of *Homo,* so far found, date to ca. 1.8 million years ago).

Animal fossils found with Toumai Man included the remains of grassland species, such as rhinoceros, giraffe, and horse; woodland species, such as pig and elephant; and wetland species, such as fish and crocodile. Such diversity suggests that the Toumai individual exploited the resources of a range of habitats, which included lakes, forests, and grasslands.

The Toumai find challenges existing narratives of human evolution. Based on DNA, scientists believe humans and chimpanzees (our closest animal relative) shared a common ancestor. Toumai, dated to 7 million years ago, means that this common ancestor would have evolved much earlier than has hitherto been thought. Does this mean the genetic and molecular changes take a lot longer than we thought possible as well? Toumai has more "modern" human-like features than those of the fossil *Australopithecus* apemen found over the last seventy years, which occurred later (ca. 2–4 million years ago). Are modern humans more directly ascended from Toumai than from the eastern and southern African *Australopithecines*?

Toumai is the first fossil human of such a great age to have been found west of the Rift Valley. The oldest before Toumai, examples of *Australopithecus afarensis,* were found at Hadar in Ethiopia and at Laetoli in Tanzania. Before Toumai, and for most of the last century, paleoanthropologists believed the formation of the East African Rift Valley, ca. 5 to 7 million years ago, separated and cut off ape populations, and put those groups of apes living on open grasslands under pressure to leave the trees and forage more widely, and eventually to do so on two legs. However, this has always been too simple an explanation for human evolution, and now Toumai, from western Africa, has challenged existing views that the cradle of humanity was in East Africa. It now seems at least possible that human ancestors may have originated elsewhere in Africa, that their habitats were more diverse, and that they were more widely spread across Africa as well.

See also Discovery of the Neanderthals (1833–1900); First *Homo Erectus* (1888–1895); Publication of *Les hommes fossiles, elémentes de paléontologie humaine* (1921); Discovery of *Australopithecus africanus* (1924); Excavations at Sterkfontein and Swartkrans (1948–Present); Discovery of *Zinjanthropus boisei* (1959); Excavations at Olorgesailie and Koobi Fora (1961–1983); Discovery of *Homo Habilis* (1964–1980); Discovery of Early Humans in Ethiopia (1966–1977); Discovery of Footprints of Our Earliest Ancestors (1974–1981); Discovery of "Lucy" (1975); Earliest Stone Tools Found at Gona (2003); Discovery of the "Hobbit" (2004).

Further Reading

Brunet, M., F. Guy, D. Pilbeam, H. T. Mackay, Al Likius, A. Diimboumalbaye, A. Beauvilain, and C. Blondel. 2002. A new hominid from the Upper Miocene of Chad, Central Africa. *Nature* 418: 145–151.

Earliest Stone Tools Found at Gona (2003)

In 2003, at the site of Gona in Ethiopia, a team of archaeologists excavated a number of stone tools that were made and used between 2.5 and 2.6 million years ago—the oldest stone tools in the world. Gona is situated in the Awash Valley, an area adjacent to Hadar, where the famous example of *Australopithecus afarensis* known as "Lucy" was found in 1975.

This excavation was undertaken by the Gona Paleoanthropological Research Project, led by Ethiopian archaeologist Sileshi Semaw and funded by the Leakey Foundation. Semaw first participated in the international excavations in Ethiopia during the 1970s and 1980s and then went on to study for and complete his Ph.D. in the United States.

The site of Gona is located on what was the bank of an ancient river. Several hundred artifacts were found in the 4-meter-wide by 1-meter-deep excavation. The stone tools are directly associated with animal bones found in the same context. The tool types themselves are well-made examples from the Oldowan tradition, first found by the Leakeys at Olduvai Gorge. Their makers used the river as the source of a variety of different kinds of stone cobbles from which they were made into two types of tools. The first comprise "cores" made from stone cobbles with flakes knocked off sides by hitting them with another rock. This produced a jagged, chopping, or cleaver-like implement that could fit into a hand and be used for hammering, chopping, and digging. The other stone tools, made as a consequence of cobble striking, are known as "flakes," sharp-edged, thin pieces of stone from the sides of the cobble, used as knives for cutting and butchering. Both types of stone tools, because of their direct association with the animal bones in the same site, indicate they were used to butcher animals for food, evidence that their makers' diet included meat.

None of this stone tool material was much different from what had been already been found in Ethiopia, Kenya, and Tanzania. What makes it remarkable is not only the discovery of stone tools with animal bones, but also the fact they could be dated to 2.6 million years ago—the earliest example of stone tool making and use in the world to be found, 500,000 years older than anything similar and reliably dated.

So who made them? The stone tools were evidence of greater skill than archaeologists expected of any hominids that were around that long ago. Were they *Australopithecines,* or members of the genus *Homo?* Or were they made by other transitional human ancestors? There is evidence, ca. 2 million years ago, that *Homo* was using a more advanced tool kit—"Acheulean" in style, comprising bifaced axes and a variety of choppers, cleavers, hammers, and flakes as knives and scrapers.

However, other evidence from the site of Bouri, ninety kilometers from Gona, found in eroding sediments beside what was an ancient freshwater lake, may help to provide an answer. Here, between 1996 and 1999, Ethiopian anthropologist Berhane Asfaw, and colleagues from the United States and Japan, excavated fossils of what may be a direct human ancestor and an evolutionary link between *Australopithecus* and *Homo.* These fossils, dated by the argon-argon radioisotopic method to ca. 2.5 million years ago, comprise different parts of the skeletons of six individuals, including parts of thigh and arm bones, skullcap, jaws, and teeth.

This potential human ancestor has been called *Australopithecus garhi,* the word "garhi" meaning "surprise" in the local Afar language. The analysis of the remains of *Australopithecus garhi* has revealed that its thigh bone (femur) had elongated by 2.5 million years ago, a million years before the forearm had shortened, creating the proportions we recognize as being human. Its teeth are larger than those of "Lucy" and other members of *Australopithecus afarensis*. Its braincase, face, and palate are more primitive than *Homo*. It lacks the specialized cranial characters of the robust apemen of eastern and southern Africa. According to the paleoanthropologists, this unique combination of features makes it a new species.

What is even more interesting is that along with the initial discovery of some of the pieces of *Australopithecus garhi*, arm and leg bones, stone tools, and animal remains were also found. The animal bones are those of antelopes and horses. Some of the antelope bones were marked by stone tools. Scientists cannot prove that this species used stone tools, but the proximity of cut-marked antelope bones provides circumstantial support for this idea. However, they are sure that the stone tools were used to get meat and marrow from the mammals.

Is *Australopithecus garhi* a direct ancestor of other *Homo* species and of modern humans? More fieldwork, excavation, analysis, and research will be necessary to ascertain its bona fides. Identifying it as a new species is just the beginning. Debate about the number of branches of early hominids—and their arrangement on the family tree—is far from over. As with the Toumai fossil, the more we find out about the evolution of mankind, the less we seem to know.

However, when the finds from Bouri are compared to the finds at Gona, the puzzle gets even more interesting. Both sets of animal bones were contemporary, so both sites and their remains are similar in age, and both show evidence of stone tool cut-marks. Did *Australopithecus garhi* make the stone tools and butcher the animals found at Gona? Semaw's Gona artifacts and animal bones are evidence that their makers were carnivorous at this early stage. Of course, this does not necessarily mean they were hunting animals; these could be the remains of scavenged animals.

More recently, a partial skull and a hominid mandible were excavated at Gona in association with other examples of stone tools. Semaw believes the hominids that made and used the Gona stone tools were probably *Australopithecus garhi*. He and his team also know that they have only just begun—there is at least another two decades of research and analysis of the site before any questions, apart from dating, can be answered. The Gona material is kept at the National Museum of Ethiopia in Addis Ababa.

See also Discovery of the Neanderthals (1833–1900); First *Homo Erectus* (1888–1895); Publication of *Les hommes fossiles, elémentes de paléontologie humaine* (1921); Discovery of *Australopithecus africanus* (1924); Excavations at Sterkfontein and Swartkrans

(1948–Present); Discovery of *Zinjanthropus boisei* (1959); Excavations at Olorgesailie and Koobi Fora (1961–1983); Discovery of *Homo Habilis* (1964–1980); Discovery of Early Humans in Ethiopia (1966–1977); Discovery of Footprints of Our Earliest Ancestors (1974–1981); Discovery of "Lucy" (1975); Announcement of Toumai Fossil (2002); Discovery of the "Hobbit" (2004).

Further Reading

Asfaw, Berhane, Tim White, Owen Lovejoy, Bruce Latimer, Scott Sikmpson, and Gen Suwa. 1999. *Australopithecus garhi*: A New Species of Early Hominid from Ethiopia. *Science* 284: 629–635.

Semaw, S. 2000. The world's oldest stone artefacts from Gona, Ethiopia: Their implications for understanding stone technology and patterns of human evolution between 2.6–1.5 million years ago. *Journal of Archaeological Science* 27: 1197–1214.

Discovery of the "Hobbit" (2004)

In 2004 in a limestone cave known as "Liang Bu," on the Indonesian island of Flores, Indonesian and Australian archaeologists and paleoanthropologists discovered the skeleton of a new, small species of human that would have only been about one meter high, fully grown. The 18,000-year-old remains, popularly known as the "Hobbit" (after J. R. R. Tolkien's mythic creatures who were as small), was named *Homo floresiensis,* was female, had long arms, and walked upright. An examination of the teeth and cranium confirmed it was an adult. Stone tools found with the skeleton were surprisingly sophisticated given the brain size of the Hobbit, which is about that of a grapefruit, and comparable to that of chimpanzees. These tools also imply a certain degree of cooperation between Hobbits, especially when the size of the game they pursued is taken into account.

Located east of the Wallace Line, Flores was an isolated environment, a real "lost world," where archaic animals, extinct elsewhere, evolved into giant and dwarf forms through allopatric speciation. Other faunal remains from the site provide evidence that the small Hobbit shared the island with giant tortoises and huge lizards, including Komodo dragons, pony-sized elephants or Stegodons, and rats the size of Labrador dogs. With its long arms it was probable that the Hobbit may have spent a lot of its time in trees, away from carnivorous lizards, but it would have hunted the small elephants and large rats. It is thought that some 12,000 years ago a volcanic eruption made these unique species, including the Hobbit, extinct.

There has been, and continues to be, serious debate about the evolutionary history of *Homo floresiensis*; indeed, there are still questions about whether the Hobbits were a separate species. Some observers believe it probably evolved from the earlier *Homo erectus,* examples of which have been found elsewhere in Indonesia. It would have been isolated on the island of Flores about 100,000 years ago, by the Sunda Strait, evolving its tiny physique in isolation from any other hominids. But even this simple story contains puzzles. How did the ancestors of the Hobbits get to the island of Flores in the first place, as the journey would have involved crossing open water?

The remains of eight other Hobbits have since been found, but their identification as members of a new *Homo* species remains contentious. Some paleoanthropologists and archaeologists have argued that the Hobbit is not a new species but a modern *Homo sapiens* with microcephaly. The entire Hobbit skeletal material ranges in date from 94,000 to 13,000 years ago, with the latter date representing the most recent extinction of a hominid. It has been argued that the modern people of Flores may have seen the Hobbits. Local folk stories, from as late as the nineteenth century, describe them as timid, cave dwelling, small furry people who muttered, and who were known as "Ebu Gogo."

Much work remains to be done on the skeletal remains and the associated material culture. Further excavations have the clear potential to help resolve the most likely scenario for the life and death of the Hobbit.

See also Discovery of the Neanderthals (1833–1900); First *Homo Erectus* (1888–1895); Publication of *Les hommes fossiles, elémentes de paléontologie humaine* (1921); Discovery of *Australopithecus africanus* (1924); Excavations at Sterkfontein and Swartkrans (1948–Present); Discovery of *Zinjanthropus boisei* (1959); Excavations at Olorgesailie and Koobi Fora (1961–1983); Discovery of *Homo Habilis* (1964–1980); Discovery of Early Humans in Ethiopia (1966–1977); Discovery of Footprints of Our Earliest Ancestors (1974–1981); Discovery of "Lucy" (1975); Announcement of Toumai Fossil (2002); Earliest Stone Tools Found at Gona (2003).

Further Reading

Brown, P., T. Sutikina, M. J. Morwood, R. P. Sejona, E. Jatmiko, Wayhu Saptomo, Rokus Awe Due, et al. 2004. A new small-bodied hominin from the late Pleistocene of Flores, Indonesia. *Nature* 431: 1055–1061.

Morwood, M. J., R. P. Soejono, R. G. Roberts, L. S. Sutikana, K.E. Turney, W. J. Westaway, J. Rink, X. Zhao, G. D. Van den Berg, et al. 2004. Archaeology and age of a new hominin from Flores in eastern Indonesia. *Nature* 431: 1087–1091.

Wong, K. 2005. The littlest human. *Scientific American,* February: 40–49.

Index